Guide to Test Automation Architecture

A roadmap for building sustainable test automation frameworks for modern software

Craig Risi

bpb

www.bpbonline.com

First Edition 2025

Copyright © BPB Publications, India

ISBN: 978-93-65899-702

LIMITS OF LIABILITY AND DISCLAIMER OF WARRANTY

To View Complete
BPB Publications Catalogue
Scan the QR Code:

www.bpbonline.com

Dedicated to

*This book is dedicated to my wonderful wife, without whom
I would not have been able to pursue my passions*

About the Author

A man of many talents, but no sense of how to use them. **Craig** could be out changing the world but would prefer to make software instead. Probably the reason why Nick Fury refused to take his calls. He possesses a passion for software design, but more importantly software quality and designing systems that can achieve this in a technically diverse and constantly evolving tech world.

Craig has over 20 years' experience across the development, testing and management disciplines in a variety of software industries, but still feels he learns something new every day. It is that continued change and evolution of the software industry which motivates him to keep learning and finding ways to improve. More than just playing with tech though, it is the people that make a software come together – and so, Craig believes in developing people and empowering them to make a success out of the software they build.

When not playing with software, he can often be found spending time with family, writing, designing board games, or running long distances for no apparent reason. He is also a massive fan of comic books and Star Wars, so if you see him concentrating intensely, he is probably just trying to use the force.

Craig is also the writer of several books and writes regular articles on his blog sites and various other tech sites around the world. He is an international speaker on a wide range of different software development topics.

About the Reviewer

Aleksandr (Alex) Karavanin is a seasoned production network engineer at Meta, where he has been developing full-stack software products to automate Meta's largest AI data centers worldwide. His expertise extends beyond Meta, as he has also designed and implemented various software applications running on AWS and Azure. Alex is passionate about ML and AI, as well as performance programming using Rust and Go. As a recognized expert in his field, he has been participating as a presenter and judge at multiple industry conferences.

Acknowledgement

Writing this book has been both a professional milestone and a personal journey, and I am deeply grateful to those who have supported and inspired me along the way.

To my wife, thank you for your unwavering love, patience, and belief in me. Your encouragement gave me the strength to continue writing, learning, and growing.

To my mentors, colleagues, and peers in the software engineering and quality engineering communities, thank you for sharing your wisdom, challenging my thinking, and pushing me to grow. The insights and experiences I have gained from working alongside you have profoundly shaped the perspective I bring to this book.

I would also like to thank BPB Publications for their guidance, editing, and feedback in making this book a significantly better product than what it started out as.

And finally, to every individual who has crossed paths with me on this journey—whether through a conversation, a collaboration, or a moment of inspiration—know that your impact is deeply appreciated and has left a lasting mark on this work.

This book is as much yours as it is mine.

Preface

In today's fast-paced software development landscape, the ability to deliver high-quality applications rapidly and reliably is not just a competitive advantage—it is a necessity. Test automation has emerged as a cornerstone of modern development and DevOps practices, but the true value of automation lies not merely in writing scripts, but in building robust, scalable, and maintainable automation frameworks that can evolve alongside the systems they test.

This book was born out of years of hands-on experience, lessons learned, and conversations with practitioners across industries who have faced the complexities of testing modern software systems. It is written for software architects, engineers, SDETs, and quality engineers who are tasked with building automation frameworks that go beyond short-term fixes and instead provide long-term strategic value.

Rather than focusing solely on tools or technologies—which are ever-changing—this book emphasizes foundational principles, architectural strategies, and practical design patterns that can help you create tool-agnostic frameworks capable of adapting to new requirements, technologies, and team structures. It provides a holistic view of what makes a framework succeed, from coding standards and test data management to modular design, reporting, integration with CI/CD pipelines, and sustainability over time.

My goal with this book is not only to provide guidance, but also to encourage a mindset shift: to see framework development not as a one-time task, but as a continuously evolving effort that supports agility, reliability, and quality at every stage of software delivery.

Whether you are just beginning your journey in automation or looking to improve and modernize existing frameworks, I hope this book serves as both a practical guide and a source of inspiration.

Chapter 1: Introduction to Test Automation

Description: Test automation has become the backbone of software quality assurance in today's fast-paced development environments. This chapter examines its critical role in modern software development and its alignment with software architecture principles. The focus is on how automation minimizes time-to-market while ensuring quality, how well-designed frameworks reduce maintenance costs, and why tool-agnostic frameworks are essential for flexibility and scalability in multi-tool ecosystems.

Chapter 2: Understanding Test Automation Frameworks

Description: A solid foundation begins with understanding what test automation frameworks are and why they matter. This chapter delves into the core components of a framework and categorizes various types of automated testing, from unit and integration to performance and UI testing. It emphasizes how a well-designed framework provides consistent, repeatable, and reliable testing outcomes while enabling collaboration across engineering and QA teams.

Chapter 3: Designing with Architecture in Mind

Description: Software architecture principles like scalability, maintainability, and extensibility are as important for testing frameworks as they are for application development. This chapter discusses applying architectural design patterns—such as modularization, abstraction, and layering—to test frameworks. It also explores how architectural patterns like the Facade, Adapter, and Observer can enhance the framework's adaptability and reduce complexity.

Chapter 4: Designing Modular Test Frameworks

Description: Modularity is the key to building scalable and maintainable frameworks. This chapter outlines strategies for separating test logic, test data, and configurations into distinct, reusable components. It emphasizes the importance of creating modular frameworks that are easy to extend and adapt as requirements change, with practical examples of reusable components for reporting, data management, and test orchestration.

Chapter 5: Testability and Software Design

Description: Test automation is most effective when systems are designed with testability in mind. This chapter introduces best practices for integrating testability into software architecture, such as dependency injection, interfaces, and loose coupling. It also provides an overview of tools and techniques that make complex systems more testable, ensuring automation efforts remain efficient and reliable.

Chapter 6: Test Orchestration and Execution

Description: The heart of any test automation framework is its orchestration and execution capabilities. This chapter explains how to design a custom test runner that supports managing test suites, handling parallel execution, and generating detailed reports. It also discusses scheduling tests and coordinating execution across environments for maximum efficiency.

Chapter 7: Test Data Management

Description: Managing test data is one of the most challenging aspects of automation. This chapter explores strategies for test data generation, storage, and management, including techniques for maintaining consistency across test environments using mocks, stubs, and other state management tools. It also covers the principles of data-driven testing to ensure frameworks can handle diverse inputs and configurations seamlessly.

Chapter 8: CI/CD Integration and Quality Gates

Description: This chapter explains how to embed test automation frameworks into CI/CD pipelines to accelerate software delivery. It provides practical steps for automating test execution as part of the build process and implementing quality gates to enforce standards for build success. The chapter also highlights how to ensure smooth integration with popular CI tools like Jenkins, GitHub Actions, or Azure Pipelines.

Chapter 9: Handling Asynchronous and Distributed Systems

Description: Modern software systems are often asynchronous and distributed, posing unique challenges for test automation. This chapter examines strategies for testing microservices, event-driven architectures, and distributed systems. It explores techniques for managing dependencies, orchestrating complex workflows, and addressing common pitfalls in testing asynchronous components.

Chapter 10: Security, Performance, and Resilience Testing

Description: Test automation frameworks must extend beyond functional testing to cover critical cross-cutting concerns. This chapter demonstrates how to integrate security, performance, and resilience testing into the same tool-agnostic framework. It discusses embedding chaos testing practices to validate system robustness and using performance tools to measure and optimize system throughput and latency.

Chapter 11: Overview of Tools Used in Test Automation

Description: In this chapter we analyze the different types of popular test automation tools that are available on the market. We will start off by looking at criteria to evaluate and help teams identify the best approach to selecting the right tool for their use case, before diving into the pros and cons of many different tools - at both a functional and performance testing area.

Chapter 12: Case Study: Building a Scalable Framework From Scratch

Description: Through a practical example, this chapter walks readers through the step-by-step implementation of a test automation framework. From defining initial requirements to making architectural decisions and solving key challenges, this case study provides an in-depth look at what it takes to build a scalable, tool-agnostic framework from the ground up.

Chapter 13: Case Study: Migrating to a Tool-agnostic Framework

Description: Transitioning from a tool-specific to a tool-agnostic framework comes with its own challenges and lessons. This chapter shares a real-world case study of how a team successfully migrated their legacy framework, detailing their strategy, solutions to technical hurdles, and the approach taken to win team adoption and maintain seamless operations during the transition.

Chapter 14: Case Study: Framework Evolution and Continuous Improvement

Description: The journey of test automation frameworks does not end with their initial implementation. This chapter examines how frameworks can evolve over time to adapt to new requirements and technologies. It discusses strategies for managing technical debt, balancing incremental updates with long-term architectural improvements, and fostering continuous improvement through feedback loops and monitoring.

Chapter 15: Embracing AI and ML in Test Automation

Description: Artificial intelligence and machine learning are transforming test automation. This chapter explores how AI-driven tools can enhance test case generation, test selection, and execution. It also covers machine learning techniques for identifying flaky tests and using predictive models to improve test stability.

Chapter 16: Emerging Trends and Technologies

Description: The future of test automation frameworks lies in embracing emerging technologies. This chapter highlights trends such as serverless computing, containerized architectures, and cloud-native testing tools. It offers insights into how frameworks can adapt to modern architectures and stay relevant in a rapidly evolving technological landscape.

Chapter 17: Conclusion: The Path to Sustainable Test Automation Frameworks

Description: The book concludes with a reflection on the importance of designing test automation frameworks with scalability, flexibility, and sustainability in mind. It emphasizes the need for continuous learning, iterative improvements, and fostering collaboration between engineering, QA, and DevOps teams. By applying the principles and strategies outlined in this book, readers can create frameworks that not only meet current testing needs but also evolve to handle the challenges of the future.

Code Bundle and Coloured Images

Please follow the link to download the
Code Bundle and the *Coloured Images* of the book:

https://rebrand.ly/cce949

The code bundle for the book is also hosted on GitHub at
https://github.com/bpbpublications/Guide-to-Test-Automation-Architecture.
In case there's an update to the code, it will be updated on the existing GitHub repository.

We have code bundles from our rich catalogue of books and videos available at
https://github.com/bpbpublications. Check them out!

Errata

We take immense pride in our work at BPB Publications and follow best practices to ensure the accuracy of our content to provide with an indulging reading experience to our subscribers. Our readers are our mirrors, and we use their inputs to reflect and improve upon human errors, if any, that may have occurred during the publishing processes involved. To let us maintain the quality and help us reach out to any readers who might be having difficulties due to any unforeseen errors, please write to us at :

errata@bpbonline.com

Your support, suggestions and feedbacks are highly appreciated by the BPB Publications' Family.

Did you know that BPB offers eBook versions of every book published, with PDF and ePub files available? You can upgrade to the eBook version at www.bpbonline.com and as a print book customer, you are entitled to a discount on the eBook copy. Get in touch with us at :

business@bpbonline.com for more details.

At www.bpbonline.com, you can also read a collection of free technical articles, sign up for a range of free newsletters, and receive exclusive discounts and offers on BPB books and eBooks.

Piracy

If you come across any illegal copies of our works in any form on the internet, we would be grateful if you would provide us with the location address or website name. Please contact us at business@bpbonline.com with a link to the material.

If you are interested in becoming an author

If there is a topic that you have expertise in, and you are interested in either writing or contributing to a book, please visit www.bpbonline.com. We have worked with thousands of developers and tech professionals, just like you, to help them share their insights with the global tech community. You can make a general application, apply for a specific hot topic that we are recruiting an author for, or submit your own idea.

Reviews

Please leave a review. Once you have read and used this book, why not leave a review on the site that you purchased it from? Potential readers can then see and use your unbiased opinion to make purchase decisions. We at BPB can understand what you think about our products, and our authors can see your feedback on their book. Thank you!

For more information about BPB, please visit www.bpbonline.com.

Join our Discord space

Join our Discord workspace for latest updates, offers, tech happenings around the world, new releases, and sessions with the authors:

https://discord.bpbonline.com

Table of Contents

Prologue

Once upon a deployment...

A young, ambitious developer named Sam worked for a growing tech startup called QuickShip. The startup prided itself on building and shipping fast. Sam loved writing code, and racing against time to deliver features ahead of schedule.

"Why waste time testing?" Sam often argued. "We build it, we ship it. If there is a bug, we will fix it later. That is what hotfixes are for!"

Sam's manager, Carol, an old hand in the industry, gently warned him. "Fast does not always mean right, Sam. A strong foundation matters, or everything collapses." Sam dismissed the idea.

One Friday afternoon, QuickShip launched its flagship product—a slick e-commerce platform. Sam had added loads of new features: "Buy now," "Discount calculators," "One-click checkout." No one bothered with tests; after all, Sam was confident in his code.

At first, everything was perfect. Customers loved the speed and features. Sam was celebrated as a "code genius," and QuickShip was on cloud nine.

But that night, chaos erupted.

Orders were charging customers twice.

Discounts applied on the wrong products.

The "One-click checkout" would randomly empty carts.

Some customers could not buy anything at all.

Social media exploded with complaints. Refund requests poured in. "QuickShip" trended for all the wrong reasons.

Sam worked all weekend on frantic hotfixes, pulling all-nighters and drinking more coffee than water. But every "fix" broke something else because the code was tangled, untested, and brittle. Sam could not keep up.

On Monday, Carol sat down next to Sam and said, "This is the cost of skipping quality engineering and testing. We have built a castle with no foundation, and now it is crumbling."

Sam stared at his screen, overwhelmed. For the first time, he understood: code that is not tested is not done.

Over the next few weeks, Carol and Sam worked together to build something better. They designed a test automation framework, one that ran every time they made changes. It checked the checkout flow, verified discounts, and ensured no part of the platform broke unexpectedly.

Sam learned about unit tests, integration tests, and end-to-end automation. They abstracted away the tools so the tests could adapt as QuickShip grew. It took time, but with every release, the confidence in the code increased.

Soon, the panic of deployment days disappeared. QuickShip's customers noticed too, orders were smooth, refunds dropped, and trust was restored.

Sam proudly explained to new developers, "Testing is not a waste of time; it is how you deliver reliable, fast software without burning yourself out."

The moral of this story is that building software without testing may seem fast, but bugs have a way of catching up. A strong foundation of good-quality engineering and automation ensures your software stands the test of time—and stress. And this book is all about building on that strong foundation.

Software quality, testing, and, test automation are vital pillars of modern software delivery, and organizations increasingly recognize their significance. However, despite their importance, many companies hastily adopt automation approaches without investing the necessary time and effort to build a robust, scalable test automation framework, one that truly supports long-term delivery success.

This book aims to achieve the following outcomes:

- Emphasize that automation frameworks are foundational to software quality, not optional extras.
- Highlight the long-term cost savings of investing in maintainable and scalable frameworks.
- Encourage leadership to treat test architecture as part of core software engineering, not just **quality assurance (QA)** tooling.
- Demonstrate how a solid framework supports faster delivery, early bug detection, and reliable releases.
- Promote frameworks to enforce standards, ensure consistency, and reduce flaky tests.
- Provide practical patterns for modular and tool-agnostic framework design.
- Guide teams in separating concerns: test logic, execution engines, data management, and reporting.
- Teach testers and **quality engineers (QEs)** how to build reusable components that support multiple application layers (UI, API, DB).
- Show software engineers how to integrate test automation into CI/CD pipelines and deployment workflows.
- Equip teams to make decisions on when to refactor, extend, or rebuild parts of the framework.
- Offer strategies to evolve legacy test suites into modern, maintainable structures.
- Share best practices for collaboration between QA, developers, and DevOps to ensure framework alignment.
- Provide checklists, examples, and case studies to bridge theory and practice.

Unlike other books focusing on specific tools, this book takes a tool-agnostic approach to test automation framework design. By doing so, we remove dependency on particular tools—tools that are constantly evolving—and instead, shift the focus to principles and practices that enable organizations to establish their foundation for test automation success.

We will explore a variety of topics, beginning with the role of test automation in software architecture. From there, we will dive into the core aspects of building a tool-agnostic test automation framework, combining fundamental concepts with advanced design principles. This book is designed to appeal to a diverse audience, from those new to the field to technical experts, offering insights for anyone involved in the software delivery process.

To help readers understand the practicality of many of the book's points, we included three case studies to show that the different elements discussed can be applied to multiple use cases. Lastly, this book will conclude by looking at some of the future trends that software and test engineers need to be aware of.

We hope, at the end of this book, you will be fully prepared to design and build a test automation framework that can cater to any type of software application, architecture, and scenario.

CHAPTER 1
Introduction to Test Automation

Introduction

The software development landscape has changed dramatically over the last few decades, driven by technological advancements, growing user expectations, and the need for faster, more reliable delivery. Previously, software was developed primarily for standalone systems or basic client-server architectures, but today it spans cloud computing, microservices, mobile applications, AI, and IoT. The shift towards DevOps, agile methodologies, and **continuous integration/continuous delivery (CI/CD)** has redefined how software is developed, tested, and released, focusing on speed and collaboration.

With this shift, development cycles have become shorter, and the emphasis has moved toward delivering high-quality software more frequently. This demand has increased the reliance on automation, streamlined workflows, and tools that improve team collaboration and software stability.

In addition, modern software applications have grown exponentially in complexity due to multiple layers of dependencies, integration with third-party services, support for distributed systems, and a diverse range of user interfaces. Applications today may need to serve millions of users in real-time, requiring scalability in performance and architecture.

To address this complexity, teams must adopt practices and tools that ensure efficiency and scalability in the development and delivery processes. These practices include cloud-native architectures, containerization, microservices, and orchestration technologies such as Kubernetes, which allows efficient resource management and easy scaling. At the same time, there is a need for streamlined workflows to minimize bottlenecks and avoid disruptions during software delivery, which is where agile practices and automation come into play.

Structure

In this chapter, we will go over the following topics:

- Test automation as an enabler for agile development
- Importance of test automation
- Alignment with software architecture principles
- Importance of scalability in a framework

- Testability as a first-class citizen
- Architecture decisions
- Security and test automation
- Test-driven and behavior-driven development
- Tool-agnostic frameworks and their importance
- Future-proofing the framework

Objectives

By the end of this chapter, readers will gain a comprehensive understanding of the pivotal role that test automation frameworks play in modern software development. They will also learn how aligning with architectural principles and prioritizing testable design can help overcome various design challenges that hinder test automation goals, ultimately ensuring long-term success.

We will explore the critical role test automation plays in the broader software development process. We will also explore key architectural principles that should guide the framework development process. Finally, we will examine how the design of a system or application significantly impacts the success of software testing and automation. We will highlight the importance of involving software testing engineers in the design phase to ensure the system is crafted with testing in mind from the outset.

Test automation as an enabler for agile development

Test automation has become a cornerstone in modern software development. As a result, manual testing processes cannot keep up with the fast pace of agile development, and relying solely on manual testing often leads to delays and missed defects. Test automation provides a solution by enabling fast, consistent, and repeatable tests that can be integrated into CI/CD pipelines.

By automating key parts of the testing process, teams can ensure that new code does not introduce regressions or other issues, without slowing down development velocity. Automated tests can run continuously during development, from unit tests to functional and performance testing, ensuring that any issues are caught early.

Moreover, automation supports scalability by allowing tests to be executed in parallel across different environments and platforms, ensuring comprehensive coverage. This efficiency enables teams to maintain high software quality even as they scale their applications and adopt more complex architectures.

Importance of test automation

In this section, we will begin by showcasing key examples of the benefits that test automation offers to the software development process. We will highlight several important points here and delve into the details of how to implement them in subsequent chapters.

Accelerating delivery cycles

Automation reduces manual testing effort by enabling the execution of repetitive tests automatically, without human oversight. Automated tests, such as unit tests, integration tests, and end-to-end tests, can be scheduled to run continuously throughout the development lifecycle. This drastically reduces the time spent on regression testing and frees human testers to focus on more exploratory or high-value activities.

By reducing manual effort, automation:

- **Speeds up test execution:** Automated tests run faster and can be executed across multiple environments simultaneously.

- **Improves consistency:** Automated scripts perform the same steps each time, eliminating the possibility of human error.

- **Enables continuous feedback:** Automated tests can provide immediate feedback on the quality of the code, allowing developers to fix issues as soon as they arise.

- **Shortens release cycles:** With faster and more reliable testing, the overall development cycle shortens, leading to faster and more frequent releases.

Improving software quality

Software test automation is not simply about its contribution to reducing testing times, but it can also allow software testers themselves to focus on better testing. Automation frees testers from the burden of repetitive and mundane tasks, such as running regression tests, performing routine checks, and validating user interfaces. This liberation allows them to redirect their efforts toward more valuable activities, such as:

- **Exploratory testing:** Testers can engage in exploratory testing, where they actively explore the application to identify edge cases, usability issues, and other potential problems that automated tests may not cover. This creative approach leverages the testers' intuition and experience, leading to valuable insights and improvements.

- **High-value testing:** By focusing on high-value areas such as performance, security, and user experience, testers can contribute to aspects of the application that directly impact user satisfaction and business outcomes. This shift toward qualitative assessments enables teams to prioritize critical features and deliver better software.

- **Innovation and continuous improvement:** With more time available for exploratory and high-value testing, teams can also innovate and experiment with new testing methodologies or tools, further enhancing their testing capabilities and overall product quality.

- **Collaboration with development teams:** Testers can work more closely with developers to ensure that the software meets business requirements and user expectations. This collaborative approach fosters a culture of shared responsibility for quality across the entire development team.

All of these activities improve the quality of software with time spent focused on real measures to test new software, rather than time spent on rechecking previous testing efforts.

Early bug detection

Automated tests are typically run at multiple stages of the development process, including unit testing during development, integration testing after merging, and end-to-end testing in pre-production environments. This early and frequent testing ensures that defects are identified and addressed before they escalate into more significant issues.

Early detection of bugs reduces the cost and time associated with fixing them. The later a defect is discovered in the software lifecycle, the more expensive it becomes to resolve. Automating tests at every stage helps catch issues when they are cheaper to fix, ultimately reducing the overall development cost.

Consistent testing across environments

Automation ensures that tests are executed consistently across different environments (development, staging, production) and configurations (different browsers, devices, and operating systems). This consistency helps uncover environment-specific issues that might arise due to differences in setups.

By maintaining the same testing procedures across environments, teams can ensure that they are delivering a product that behaves as expected, regardless of where it is deployed. This consistency builds user confidence and reduces the likelihood of post-release issues.

Enhanced reliability

Regular automated testing contributes to the reliability of the software by ensuring that features work as intended and that existing functionality is not disrupted by new changes. This reliability is crucial for maintaining user trust and satisfaction.

Faster feedback loops

Automation allows for rapid feedback loops, thus enabling teams to quickly identify issues and make necessary adjustments. This speed enables a more agile development approach, allowing teams to swiftly adapt to evolving requirements and user feedback.

Automating repetitive testing tasks enhances software quality by allowing testers to concentrate on exploratory and high-value activities. It leads to early bug detection, promotes consistent testing across environments, and ultimately contributes to the development of robust and reliable software. Embracing automation as a fundamental part of the testing process enables teams to achieve greater efficiency and deliver higher-quality products that meet user expectations.

Reducing technical debt

Technical debt refers to shortcuts and compromises made during development that may lead to more significant problems later. It accumulates when teams prioritize speed over quality, often resulting in poorly written code, insufficient testing, and other issues that can complicate future development.

One way to manage technical debt is through proactive planning and continuous refactoring. Teams should allocate time in each development cycle to address accumulated debt, improve code quality, and test coverage. Implementing best practices, such as code reviews, automated testing, and adherence to coding standards, can help minimize the long-term impact. By treating technical debt as an ongoing concern rather than an afterthought, teams can maintain a balance between rapid development and sustainable software quality.

Promoting best practices

Automated testing encourages developers to adhere to coding standards and best practices, as automated tools can flag violations or deviations from established guidelines. This leads to cleaner, more maintainable code that is less prone to issues.

Regular code reviews, facilitated by automation tools, help identify potential technical debt before it accumulates, fostering a culture of quality and accountability within the development team.

In addition to automated testing and code reviews, integrating static code analysis and **continuous integration (CI)** pipelines can further reduce technical debt. Static analysis tools detect code smells, security vulnerabilities, and performance issues early in the development process, allowing teams to address them before they become critical. Meanwhile, CI pipelines ensure that every change is tested and validated, preventing regressions and maintaining a high level of software quality. By leveraging these practices, teams can create a more resilient and scalable codebase.

Cost savings by avoiding expensive late-stage bug fixes

Fixing bugs late in the development lifecycle can be significantly more expensive than addressing them early. As software progresses toward production, the complexity of issues tends to increase, often leading to higher costs associated with fixing them.

According to an industry study conducted by *IBM Systems Sciences Institute*[1], the cost to fix a defect increases exponentially the later it is discovered. For instance, a defect identified during the design phase might cost 1x to fix, while the same defect discovered during production can cost up to 10x or more.

Late-stage bug fixes often require extensive rework, which can delay project timelines, disrupt team productivity, and increase the risk of further issues arising from hurried changes.

Minimizing downtime and disruptions

Identifying and fixing issues early helps avoid costly downtime and disruptions in production environments. This is particularly critical for businesses that rely on software for core operations, as even minor disruptions can lead to significant revenue loss and damage to reputation.

Early detection ensures smoother deployment cycles and reduces the need for emergency patches or hotfixes that can interrupt normal business operations.

Predictable budgeting and resource allocation

With fewer late-stage fixes, teams can better predict budgets and resource allocations for projects. This predictability allows organizations to allocate resources more efficiently and focus on strategic initiatives rather than constantly fixing issues.

Improved customer satisfaction

By delivering high-quality software with fewer defects, organizations can enhance customer satisfaction and trust. Satisfied customers are more likely to remain loyal and recommend the software, leading to increased revenue and growth opportunities.

Reducing costs and risks in software development is achievable through early detection of issues and a commitment to minimizing technical debt. By leveraging automation and adopting a proactive approach to quality assurance, organizations can avoid expensive late-stage bug fixes and ensure a healthier, more maintainable codebase. The long-term savings and reduced risks associated with these practices not only contribute to improved project outcomes but also position organizations for sustained success in a rapidly evolving technological landscape.

Even when developing **minimum viable products** (**MVPs**) to quickly validate ideas and gain market feedback, prioritizing quality and customer satisfaction remains essential. Delivering an MVP with fewer defects enhances the user's initial experience, building trust and increasing the likelihood of early adoption and positive feedback. While speed is critical in MVP development, incorporating basic quality assurance measures and minimizing technical debt from the outset can reduce rework and accelerate future iterations. This balance between speed and quality not only improves customer perception but also lays a stronger foundation for scaling the product efficiently based on real-world insights.

Alignment with software architecture principles

Having explored the benefits of test automation, let us shift our focus to how aligning it with software architecture principles is crucial for its success. Traditionally, test automation was often treated as a separate process, executed hastily to minimize effort, with little emphasis on thoughtful design. However, with test automation frameworks now serving as the backbone of software delivery and being executed and maintained more frequently than ever, it has become essential to adhere to sound architectural principles when designing these frameworks.

A well-designed test automation framework plays a vital role in supporting these principles, ensuring that testing processes can adapt to the growing demands of modern software. A well-architected test automation framework aligns with core software architecture principles, such as modularity, separation of concerns, and reusability. Here is how it complements these principles:

- **Modularity:** A well-structured test automation framework is modular, meaning it is composed of independent components or modules that can be developed, tested, and maintained separately. This aligns with the architectural principle of modularity, allowing teams to work on different parts of the framework without affecting others.

    o   For example, the framework can separate test data management, test execution, and reporting functionalities into distinct modules. This separation facilitates easier updates and enhancements, as changes to one module do not impact the others.

- **Separation of concerns:** A test automation framework should encapsulate testing logic separate from application code, adhering to the principle of separation of concerns. This makes the framework easier to maintain and evolve, as changes in the application's implementation do not require extensive modifications to the tests.

    o   By employing design patterns such as the **Page Object Model (POM)**, where test scripts interact with abstracted page objects rather than the application directly, the framework can adapt to changes in the application interface without significant test rewrites.

- **Reusability:** A well-designed framework promotes the reuse of test scripts and components, which is essential for efficiency and maintainability. This reusability mirrors architectural principles that encourage using established patterns and components to reduce redundancy and improve productivity.

    o   For instance, common test utilities, assertion libraries, or data-driven testing components can be reused across multiple test cases, reducing duplication and simplifying maintenance.

- **Integration with CI/CD pipelines:** A robust test automation framework integrates seamlessly with CI/CD pipelines, enhancing the software development lifecycle. This integration aligns with architectural principles that emphasize continuous feedback and iterative development, enabling teams to deploy code with confidence.

Importance of scalability in a framework

As applications grow in size and complexity, the test automation framework must also scale accordingly. Here are some key considerations to keep in mind in the design of testing frameworks for ensuring scalability:

- **Support for distributed testing:** To handle the increased volume of tests as applications grow, the framework should support distributed testing capabilities. This allows tests to be run across multiple machines or environments simultaneously, reducing the time required for execution.

    o   Implementing solutions, such as Selenium Grid or cloud-based testing platforms, can facilitate parallel execution and ensure that the framework can accommodate increasing testing demands.

- **Dynamic test management:** The framework should incorporate dynamic test management features that allow teams to easily add, remove, or modify tests without disrupting the overall structure. This flexibility enables the framework to evolve alongside the application.

    o   Implementing tagging or categorization for tests can help manage large test suites efficiently, allowing teams to run specific subsets of tests based on the changes made to the application.

- **Performance and load testing:** As applications scale, performance and load testing become increasingly important. The test automation framework should include capabilities to simulate high user loads and assess application performance under stress, ensuring the application can handle increased traffic without degradation.

    o   Integrating performance testing tools (more on these in *Chapter 11, Overview of Tools Used in Test Automation*) into the automation framework can provide comprehensive performance testing capabilities, allowing teams to identify bottlenecks and optimize application performance.

- **Continuous monitoring and feedback:** Implementing monitoring and reporting tools within the framework helps teams receive continuous feedback on test results and application performance.

This feedback loop allows for proactive identification of issues and facilitates quick responses to any emerging problems.

- o Ensuring that the framework generates detailed reports and analytics helps teams understand test coverage, execution time, and defect trends, guiding future testing efforts and architectural decisions.

A well-designed test automation framework is essential for complementing software architecture principles, promoting scalability and maintainability in the development process. By aligning with principles such as modularity, separation of concerns, and reusability, the framework becomes an integral part of the software lifecycle. Ensuring the framework is scalable to match the growth of the application is critical for maintaining efficiency and effectiveness in testing practices. Embracing these concepts allows organizations to deliver high-quality software that can adapt and thrive in a rapidly changing technological landscape.

Testability as a first-class citizen

While designing test automation frameworks is critical, the ultimate success of any test automation initiative hinges on the testability of the application under test itself.

Ensuring that applications are testable is a critical aspect that can significantly impact the overall quality and reliability of the software. By prioritizing testability during the design phase, organizations can facilitate effective testing strategies that enhance both the development process and the final product.

The following are some key things that can be done to ensure testability remains a key priority in the software design process:

- **Incorporating testability in requirements:** From the initial stages of software development, it is essential to incorporate testability as part of the requirements. This involves defining clear, testable criteria for functionalities and features. By establishing these criteria early on, teams can ensure that test cases can be derived directly from the requirements, simplifying the testing process.

- **Use of design patterns:** Employing design patterns that promote testability, such as **dependency injection (DI)**[2], facilitates the decoupling of components. This allows for easier mocking and stubbing of dependencies during testing. For example, using the **Model-View-Controller (MVC)**[3] pattern separates concerns within an application, enabling isolated testing of each component without reliance on the entire system. More on these topics in later chapters.

- **Clear interfaces:** Designing components with clear and well-defined interfaces enhances testability. This enables testers to interact with the system through these interfaces, making it easier to validate behaviors and outcomes. A clear interface also allows for the creation of mock objects that can simulate real dependencies, making unit testing more straightforward and effective.

- **Fostering code readability:** Writing clean, readable, and maintainable code is fundamental for testability. Code that follows best practices and conventions is easier to understand, simplifying the creation of effective tests. This can be achieved through adherence to coding standards, consistent naming conventions, and thorough documentation, all of which contribute to a more testable codebase.

- **Automated testing in CI:** Incorporating automated testing into the CI process ensures that tests are executed regularly throughout the development lifecycle. This fosters a culture of quality and encourages developers to write testable code from the outset.

Continuous feedback from automated tests helps teams identify and resolve issues early, reinforcing the importance of testability in the development process.

Architecture decisions

It is important that testing is seen as a first-class citizen and that we need to design with testability and automation in mind. Architecture can enable testing and automation in a big way, but can also be a big hindrance, and it is important to consider when thinking about software architecture, how it can affect test automation work and the development of a decent framework. Some such architectural decisions are as follows:

- **Tightly coupled components:** Architectural decisions that lead to tightly coupled components can significantly hinder testability. When components are interdependent, it becomes challenging to isolate them for testing, resulting in complex testing scenarios and increased maintenance efforts.

  o For instance, if a service directly instantiates dependencies instead of using dependency injection, testing that service in isolation becomes difficult, requiring the entire system to be up and running.

- **Complex architectures:** While microservices and serverless architectures can offer flexibility and scalability, they can also introduce complexity that may hinder automated testing. If not designed with testability in mind, these architectures can result in a proliferation of services that complicate integration testing and increase the overhead of managing test environments.

  o It is essential to ensure that communication between services is well-defined and that each service has clear responsibilities, making it easier to test them independently.

- **State management:** Decisions regarding state management can affect testability significantly. For example, if an application relies heavily on shared state across components, it can introduce non-deterministic behavior that complicates automated testing. Using stateless designs or immutable data can enhance testability, as it reduces dependencies on shared state and enables predictable outcomes during testing.

- **Error handling and logging:** An architecture that incorporates robust error handling and logging mechanisms can enhance testability by providing valuable feedback during testing. Clear logging can help identify issues quickly, making it easier to debug failing tests.

  o Conversely, if error handling is poorly managed or inconsistent, it can obscure the root cause of failures, complicating the debugging process and hindering automation efforts.

Security and test automation

Security and test automation go hand in hand in modern software development, ensuring that vulnerabilities are identified and mitigated early in the lifecycle. By integrating security testing into automated test suites, teams can continuously scan for potential threats such as SQL injection, **cross-site scripting** (**XSS**), and insecure authentication mechanisms. Automated security tests provide a proactive defense against common exploits, reducing the risk of breaches and compliance violations. This approach, often referred to as DevSecOps, embeds security into the development pipeline, making it an integral part of the software delivery process rather than a last-minute consideration.

Beyond automated security testing, test automation also plays a crucial role in maintaining the integrity of security features over time. Regression tests ensure that updates, patches, or new features do not introduce new vulnerabilities or weaken existing security controls. Additionally, performance and load testing help identify security weaknesses under high-traffic conditions, such as **denial-of-service** (**DoS**) risks. By combining security-focused automation with traditional functional and performance testing, organizations can build robust, secure, and resilient applications while maintaining development speed and efficiency.

Test-driven and behavior-driven development

Adopting methodologies such as **test-driven development** (**TDD**)[4] and **behavior-driven development** (**BDD**)[5] encourages developers to consider testability during architectural decisions. These practices emphasize writing tests before code, which inherently drives developers to design with testability in mind. By integrating these practices into the development process, teams can create more amenable architectures to testing, leading to better overall quality.

Prioritizing testability as a first-class citizen in software design is essential for achieving high-quality and maintainable applications. By designing applications with testability in mind from the outset, organizations can simplify testing processes, reduce the likelihood of defects, and improve collaboration between development and testing teams. Additionally, architectural decisions play a pivotal role in enhancing or hindering testability. By making informed choices that align with testability principles, teams can ensure that their applications remain robust, reliable, and easy to test throughout their lifecycle. Embracing testability streamlines the development process and enhances the overall success of software projects.

Tool-agnostic frameworks and their importance

One of the biggest challenges in software test automation is the overwhelming number of tools that claim to address all of an organization's testing needs. However, the reality is that successful test automation is not about the tool—it is about the design of the framework. For this reason, much of this book focuses on a tool-agnostic approach, even as we explore various automation tools at different points.

Building a tool-agnostic framework shifts the emphasis to designing a robust test automation strategy, and this approach offers several additional significant benefits, such as the following:

- **Avoiding vendor lock-in:** Relying on a single tool for automation can introduce significant risks, especially as technology and business needs change. This section explores the risks associated with vendor lock-in and discusses strategies for building flexibility into test automation frameworks.

- **Limited flexibility:** Relying on a single automation tool can limit an organization's ability to adapt to changing technology trends or business requirements. As new tools and technologies emerge, teams may find it challenging to incorporate these advancements if they are heavily invested in one solution. This limitation can hinder innovation and prevent teams from leveraging the best tools available for specific tasks or use cases.

- **Increased costs:** Vendor lock-in may often result in increased costs over time. Organizations may face escalating licensing fees and maintenance costs associated with a single tool, which can strain budgets and reduce overall return on investment. Additionally, the costs of training and onboarding new team members to use the specific tool can add to financial burdens.

- **Dependency on vendor roadmaps:** When organizations become dependent on a single vendor, they may have to align their development timelines and strategies with the vendor's product roadmap. If the vendor fails to deliver updates or enhancements that meet the organization's needs, it can lead to stagnation and frustration. Furthermore, vendor ownership, management, or direction changes can create uncertainties and challenges for organizations that rely heavily on that vendor's tools.

- **Migration challenges:** Switching tools after becoming entrenched in a single solution can be a daunting task. Migration often involves significant time and resource investments to translate existing automation scripts and processes to the new tool, leading to potential disruptions in testing workflows. Additionally, organizations may experience a learning curve with the new tool, which can delay testing and impact product delivery timelines.

- **Reduced innovation:** When teams rely on a single vendor's tool, they may miss out on the benefits of innovative features or integrations offered by competing tools. This can result in suboptimal testing practices and reduced overall quality assurance capabilities.

  o An organization that is locked into a single tool may struggle to adopt best practices or leverage emerging technologies, putting it at a competitive disadvantage.

- **Catering to diverse technology stacks:** Modern applications are increasingly composed of diverse technology stacks that may include various front-end frameworks, back-end languages, microservices, and APIs. This diversity presents challenges for test automation, as tools may not seamlessly integrate across different components. A tool-agnostic framework addresses these challenges by ensuring compatibility across multiple technologies, promoting flexibility, and facilitating efficient testing practices.

Catering to diverse technology stacks is essential for modern software systems, and a tool-agnostic framework plays a pivotal role in ensuring compatibility across various components. By adopting design patterns and frameworks that support tool-agnostic principles, organizations can create flexible testing environments that promote efficiency and collaboration.

Future-proofing the framework

When designing a test framework, it is essential to account not only for the organization's current needs but also for future development trends and evolving requirements. Organizations must prioritize the development of test automation frameworks that can adapt to evolving industry trends, such as cloud-native architectures, containerization, and microservices. Future-proofing these frameworks is essential for ensuring their long-term viability and effectiveness in delivering quality software.

This means that an automation framework needs to cater to and adapt to the current trends in the software space while also being built in a modular enough way to easily include new technologies and approaches into the mix. The important aspects are as follows:

- **Embracing cloud-native principles:** Cloud-native development focuses on designing applications specifically for cloud environments, leveraging microservices, containers, and orchestration tools such as Kubernetes.

    o A future-proof testing framework should be capable of testing cloud-native applications by integrating with cloud service providers and CI/CD pipelines. This includes supporting the testing of microservices in distributed environments, which requires the ability to simulate various services and their interactions.

- **Containerization:** Containerization involves packaging applications and their dependencies into lightweight containers, allowing for consistent deployment across different environments.

    o A test automation framework should support running tests within containers to ensure that tests can be executed in the same environment as production. This approach mitigates the *it works on my machine* problem and enhances the reliability of test outcomes.

- **Support for microservices:** Microservices architecture involves breaking down applications into smaller, independently deployable services that communicate over APIs.

    o The test framework should provide mechanisms for testing microservices in isolation and integration with other services. This includes supporting service virtualization to simulate dependent services and API testing capabilities to validate service interactions.

- **Automation for DevOps:** DevOps emphasizes collaboration between development and operations teams, focusing on CI/CD.

    o A future-proof framework should integrate seamlessly with CI/CD tools to automate the testing process throughout the software development lifecycle. This includes running tests automatically on code changes and deployments.

- **Modularity and extensibility:** A well-architected framework should be modular, allowing teams to add or replace components without affecting the entire system. This modularity enhances maintainability and adaptability.

    o By using design patterns, such as DI and the strategy pattern, teams can create interchangeable modules that can evolve independently based on changing requirements or technology trends.

- **Separation of concerns:** Separation of concerns is critical for reducing complexity and enhancing maintainability. By organizing the framework into distinct layers (for example, test execution, reporting, and logging), teams can ensure that changes in one area do not impact others.

o Following this principle helps teams manage changes more effectively, allowing for incremental improvements and adaptations as new requirements or tools emerge.

- **Tool-agnostic design:** Focusing on tool-agnostic design enables the framework to remain adaptable to new technologies. By abstracting tool-specific functionalities, the framework can integrate with various testing tools without being locked into any single vendor.

    o Using interfaces or APIs allows teams to define how different tools will interact with the framework, enabling easy integration or replacement as technology evolves.

- **Continuous learning and improvement:** A commitment to continuous learning and improvement ensures that the framework can evolve based on feedback and emerging best practices. This involves regularly assessing the framework's effectiveness and making necessary adjustments.

    o Encouraging team members to stay updated on industry trends and participate in communities can foster an environment of innovation and adaptability.

Future-proofing a test automation framework is essential for organizations to remain competitive in an ever-changing technological landscape. By building frameworks that can evolve with changing industry trends, such as cloud-native architectures and containerization, organizations can ensure that their testing practices remain effective and relevant. Focusing on architectural principles such as modularity, separation of concerns, tool-agnostic design, and continuous improvement enhances the long-term viability of the framework, allowing it to adapt to new technologies and methodologies as they emerge. This proactive approach not only strengthens the overall quality assurance process but also positions organizations for sustained success in delivering high-quality software.

We unpack some of these modern technological trends and their impact on software testing in more detail in later chapters.

Conclusion

In today's fast-paced software development environment, test automation has emerged as a critical component in accelerating software delivery and enhancing overall quality. By automating repetitive testing tasks, organizations can significantly reduce the time and effort required for manual testing, leading to quicker release cycles and more efficient workflows. This acceleration allows development teams to respond rapidly to changing market demands and customer feedback, ultimately driving business success.

Furthermore, test automation plays a pivotal role in improving software quality. Automated tests enable early detection of bugs, ensuring that issues are identified and resolved before they reach production. This consistent and thorough testing across various environments minimizes the risk of defects, fostering a more reliable and robust application. By enabling teams to focus on exploratory and high-value testing, automation enhances the effectiveness of the quality assurance process, resulting in a superior end product.

To fully realize the benefits of test automation, it is essential for organizations to align their automation efforts with sound software architecture principles. A well-designed test automation framework that adheres to architectural best practices—such as modularity, separation of concerns, and tool-agnostic design—ensures that the framework remains adaptable to changing technologies and industry trends. This alignment not only supports the long-term viability of the testing framework but also reinforces the overall integrity and scalability of the software architecture.

Integrating test automation within the software development lifecycle is not merely a tactical decision but a strategic imperative. By prioritizing quality through automation and ensuring alignment with architectural principles, organizations can enhance their ability to deliver high-quality software efficiently and effectively, positioning themselves for sustained success in an increasingly competitive landscape.

In the next chapter, we will discuss the different attributes that make up the automation framework and how they apply across different types of testing.

Key takeaways

Test automation plays a vital role in moving software delivery, and it is important that you invest in it to gain the following benefits:

- **Accelerates development cycles:** Automated testing enables faster feedback loops, allowing teams to detect and fix defects early, reducing delays in software releases.

- **Enhances software quality and reliability:** By ensuring consistent test execution, automation reduces human error and helps maintain high-quality standards across builds and deployments.

- **Supports CI/CD and agile practices:** Test automation is a crucial enabler of CI/CD, ensuring rapid and reliable delivery of new features while maintaining system stability.

- **Improves test coverage and scalability:** Automated tests can cover more scenarios, including edge cases and large-scale regression suites, which would be impractical to execute manually.

- **Reduces long-term costs:** Although initial setup requires investment, automated tests save costs over time by reducing manual effort, catching defects earlier, and preventing expensive production failures.

- **Facilitates innovation and future-proofing:** By automating repetitive testing tasks, development teams can focus on innovation, architecture improvements, and adopting new technologies without compromising quality.

Exercises

1. How well does the framework align with your testing strategy and business goals?

2. Does the framework support multiple test types (for example, unit, API, UI, performance, security)?

3. How scalable is the framework for growing test suites and increasing complexity?

4. Is the framework modular, allowing easy updates and extensions without breaking existing tests?

5. How much effort is required to update tests when application changes occur?

6. Are test scripts reusable across different projects or teams?

7. Does the framework enforce good coding practices and avoid code duplication?

References

1. Study conducted by IBM Systems Sciences Institute. (1978). *Relative Cost of Fixing Defects*. There is also more support for these studies in the following books:

   a. *Software Engineering Economics by Boehm, B. W. (1981).*

   b. *Software Engineering: A Practitioner's Approach by Roger S. Pressman (2014).*

2. DI is a way of providing (or *injecting*) dependencies, such as objects or services that a class needs to function, from the outside, rather than having the class create them itself.

3. The MVC pattern is a software design approach that separates an application into three interconnected components: Model (data and business logic), View (user interface), and Controller (handles user input and updates Model and View), to promote organized, scalable, and maintainable code.

4. TDD is a development approach where tests are written before code, guiding the design and ensuring that functionality is validated from the start.

5. BDD extends TDD by focusing on writing tests in natural language that describe the expected behavior of the system from the user's perspective.

CHAPTER 2
Understanding Test Automation Frameworks

Introduction

In this chapter, we will explore the different elements of a test automation framework and discuss what one needs to know technically to build one that meets the needs of any organization.

A test automation framework refers to a structured set of guidelines or best practices designed to assist in the creation and design of automated test cases. It acts as a foundational layer for automating test execution, providing standardization, efficiency, and scalability to testing efforts.

At its core, a test automation framework is more than just a set of scripts or tools. It defines an organized approach to testing, ensuring consistency, reusability, and maintainability. The framework typically comprises coding standards, reporting mechanisms, test data handling, reusable functions or libraries, and test execution practices. It also provides structured guidelines for writing test scripts in a clear, consistent manner. These scripts are created using predefined conventions and methods, which help reduce complexity and minimize the risk of introducing errors. By establishing these conventions, the framework enables easier collaboration among team members, as it dictates how tests should be written, executed, and reported.

Moreover, the framework's architecture supports reusability and maintenance by allowing test components, such as scripts or functions, to be reused across multiple test scenarios. This reduces duplication of effort and streamlines the testing process. It also simplifies the task of updating and maintaining test cases when application changes occur, since the testing logic is separated from the actual test scripts.

Structure

In this chapter, we will go over the following topics:

- Foundation for automating testing
- Core components of a test automation framework
- Need for standardization in a test automation framework
- Types of test automation

- Performance and load testing

- End-to-end testing

- Balance between automation coverage and test execution time

- Traits of a well-designed framework

Objectives

By the end of this chapter, you will have gained an understanding of the key components of a test automation framework and how they apply to different types of testing. You will also learn how a test automation framework functions and how to effectively apply its design principles across various testing domains.

Foundation for automating testing

Test automation frameworks serve as the foundation for automated testing efforts, regardless of the platform (for example, web, mobile, desktop, Windows, Linux, Android, cloud). Frameworks ensure that tests can be executed consistently across different platforms, operating systems, or browsers. Other features include:

- **Cross-platform compatibility:** Many modern test automation frameworks are designed to support tests on various platforms and environments. For instance, a single test script can be executed across different web browsers, or a mobile automation framework might run tests on Android and iOS environments. This broad compatibility ensures efficiency in testing across different user bases or devices.

- **Separation of concerns:** Frameworks should encourage a modular design by separating test data, test logic, and test execution from each other. This separation allows different test teams to focus on specific parts of the framework (for example, developing the tests, managing the test environment, or analyzing the results) without overlap, improving overall productivity and organization.

- **Scalability:** Frameworks help scale test efforts efficiently. When built properly, frameworks can handle the addition of new tests or environments without needing significant rework. This adaptability is crucial for growing systems that require continuous testing as new features and updates are introduced.

- **Reporting and integration:** Most frameworks offer comprehensive reporting mechanisms and the ability to integrate with other tools, such as **continuous integration/continuous deployment (CI/ CD)** pipelines. This allows test results to be easily tracked and analyzed over time, enabling teams to identify issues and measure quality metrics rapidly.

A test automation framework provides the necessary infrastructure to manage automated test scripts, standardize processes, and facilitate consistent execution across multiple environments. This organized approach enhances test accuracy, efficiency, and maintainability throughout the software development lifecycle.

Core components of a test automation framework

The following *Figure 2.1* features the different layers of a test automation framework:

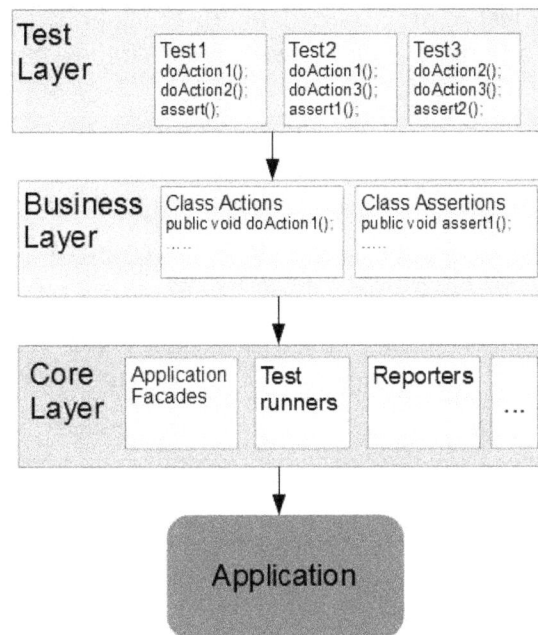

Figure 2.1: Different layers of a test automation framework

A test automation framework should be built upon several core components that work together to automate the testing process. These components ensure the testing efforts' efficiency, modularity, and scalability. Let us now examine the key elements and explain their roles within a framework:

- **Test scripts:** Test scripts are the core executable instructions written to verify that a particular feature or functionality of the software is working as expected. These scripts form the backbone of automated testing, ensuring repeatability and accuracy. They are typically written in programming languages supported by the testing tool or framework (such as Python, Java, JavaScript).

- **Modularization:** Test scripts often break down into smaller, reusable modules, allowing for flexible test design. By enabling reuse across different test cases, modular test scripts help reduce duplication and improve maintainability.

- **Parameterized test scripts:** Parameterization allows test scripts to be run multiple times with different input data sets, which is critical for covering various scenarios in functional testing.

- **Libraries:** Libraries are collections of pre-built functions and methods that support the creation of test scripts. They abstract complex operations into reusable components, improving the efficiency of writing test scripts. Libraries can include actions like handling user inputs, clicking buttons, or interacting with different user interface elements.

- **Reusable methods:** Common functionalities, such as logging in or navigating through the application, are stored in libraries, allowing test cases to focus on the specific aspects under test rather than rewriting repetitive code.

- **Third-party libraries:** Most frameworks support third-party libraries for additional functionalities, such as HTTP requests, data handling, or advanced reporting. This extensibility allows frameworks to meet the needs of various projects.

- **Test data:** Test data refers to the inputs, values, and parameters fed into test scripts during execution. In a robust framework, test data is usually externalized from the test scripts, allowing for easier maintenance and enabling data-driven testing.

- **Data-driven testing:** This approach allows the execution of test scripts with multiple sets of data, ensuring comprehensive coverage. Test data can be stored in formats such as **comma-separated values (CSV)**, JSON, XML, or databases to drive automation scripts.

- **Separation of data from test logic:** Externalizing test data enhances test maintainability. Changes in the data (for example, adding new test cases or modifying existing ones) can be handled without touching the underlying test scripts.

- **Test results:** Test results provide detailed feedback on the outcome of automated tests. A well-structured framework generates reports tracking passed, failed, or skipped tests. These results enable quick analysis and identification of issues.

- **Comprehensive reporting:** Most frameworks offer built-in reporting tools or integrate with external reporting systems to generate visual reports, including pie charts, failure logs, and traceability matrices.

- **Traceability:** Detailed logging helps trace the root cause of issues in failed tests, while success metrics provide insights into the quality and performance of the tested application.

- **Test runners:** Test runners are essential tools in the framework that are responsible for executing the test scripts. They manage the flow of test execution, including setup, execution, and teardown processes.

- **Execution control:** Test runners allow for controlling the execution order of test scripts, filtering tests based on tags, and configuring parallel or sequential execution.

- **Integration with CI/CD:** Test runners often integrate with continuous integration systems to automate test execution as part of the build process, ensuring immediate feedback on code quality.

- **Reporting tools:** Reporting tools provide mechanisms for gathering and presenting the results of automated tests. They offer visualizations, statistics, and detailed logs, making it easier for teams to understand the test outcomes and act on failures.

- **Custom reports:** Most frameworks allow the customization of reports to suit team needs, such as tailoring which metrics are displayed (for example, pass/fail ratios, execution time, error messages).

- **Dashboard integration:** Reporting tools often integrate with dashboards like Jenkins or custom-built monitoring systems for continuous feedback, allowing teams to track test results over time.

- **CI systems:** CI systems play a pivotal role in test automation frameworks by enabling automated tests to be run continuously as part of the software delivery pipeline. CI tools such as Jenkins, GitLabs, AzureDevOps, CircleCI, or Travis CI manage the automatic execution of test suites every time the codebase changes.

- **Automation of build and test:** CI systems automatically trigger test execution as part of the build process, ensuring immediate feedback on any code changes made by developers.

- **Regression testing:** CI systems, in combination with automation frameworks, enable frequent regression testing, ensuring that new changes do not negatively impact existing functionality.

In a test automation framework, these core components—test scripts, libraries, test data, test results, test runners, reporting tools, and continuous integration systems—work in harmony to deliver a structured, efficient, and scalable approach to automating testing efforts. Each component plays a crucial role in ensuring the automated tests' quality, reliability, and effectiveness, ultimately improving the speed and accuracy of software delivery.

Need for standardization in a test automation framework

Standardization is a crucial aspect of building and maintaining a practical test automation framework. It refers to the establishment of a consistent and uniform structure for test case development, execution, and maintenance. Having a standardized approach across the test automation process ensures that teams can work more efficiently and effectively, avoiding common pitfalls related to inconsistency and lack of clarity. The reasons why we need standardization in a test automation framework are as follows:

- **Consistent test case development:** Standardization in test case development ensures that all test cases follow the same design, structure, and coding practices. This consistency has multiple benefits:

  o **Improved collaboration:** When all test cases are built following a unified structure, team members can easily understand and modify each other's test scripts. This is especially useful when multiple teams or individuals are working on the same project. A standardized framework makes onboarding new team members faster since the coding practices and structures are familiar and uniform.

  o **Reduced errors:** Standardized templates for writing test cases help reduce the chances of errors introduced by manual scripting. For instance, reusing pre-defined components and methods ensures that common tasks are performed consistently, eliminating discrepancies.

  o **Scalability:** As projects grow and the number of test cases increases, maintaining a consistent structure ensures that new test cases can be added seamlessly. A well-structured framework supports scalability, allowing teams to efficiently expand test coverage without the risk of code clutter or duplication.

  o **Unified test execution:** Having a standardized framework for executing tests ensures that tests run consistently across different environments and platforms, leading to more reliable results.

  o **Platform independence:** Standardization allows for uniform execution across different platforms (for example, web, mobile, desktop) and environments (such as staging, production). Whether tests are run locally or in the cloud, a standardized framework ensures consistent results. This cross-platform capability also enables test automation teams to deploy their framework across a wide range of devices or browsers without major modifications.

- **Reproducibility of results:** By following standardized execution processes, tests can be run multiple times with the same input data, and the results will always be consistent. This reproducibility is essential when verifying bug fixes or changes in code functionality. Developers and testers can rely on these stable execution patterns to make informed decisions about the software quality.

- **Faster execution and integration:** Standardized frameworks can be easily integrated into CI/CD pipelines. With clear execution rules in place, test automation can run autonomously with minimal manual intervention, improving the speed at which testing feedback is provided to developers.

- **Streamlined maintenance:** Maintaining automated tests is one of the most significant challenges in test automation, especially as software systems evolve. A standardized framework greatly reduces the complexity of maintaining test cases by offering:

  o **Modularity:** Standardization encourages modular test design, where components such as test scripts, libraries, and data are separated and reusable. This makes it easier to update individual parts of the framework without affecting the whole system. For example, if a **user interface (UI)** changes, only the relevant UI functions in the library need to be updated, and the rest of the test suite remains untouched.

  o **Minimized technical debt:** Without standardization, test automation frameworks can quickly become cluttered, leading to technical debt where maintaining the code becomes harder and more expensive over time. Standardized practices, including modularity, parameterization, and consistent documentation, reduce technical debt and make the test suite more sustainable.

  o **Enhanced reporting and analysis:** Standardization enables more consistent and meaningful test reporting, which is vital for analyzing test outcomes and improving software quality.

  o **Uniform reporting structure:** Standardized reporting ensures that all test results are formatted similarly, making it easier for stakeholders to understand and compare. Whether test results are for functional tests, regression tests, or performance tests, a uniform structure helps stakeholders quickly review test outcomes and identify areas needing attention.

o **Actionable insights:** When test data, logs, and reports follow a consistent format, it becomes easier to extract actionable insights. Standardized error messages, timestamps, and screenshots (if applicable) help pinpoint the exact location of an issue, reducing the time needed to diagnose and fix bugs.

- **Long-term sustainability:** A standardized test automation framework ensures that the investment in automation yields long-term benefits. It provides the structure necessary to manage the complexities of evolving software and supports:

  o **Long-term reusability:** A standardized framework allows teams to reuse test scripts and modules across multiple projects and versions. This reduces the need to start from scratch every time a new project begins, saving time and resources.

  o **Continuous improvement:** When teams follow a consistent structure, it becomes easier to identify areas for improvement within the framework. By monitoring the performance and results of standardized tests, teams can improve both the framework and the quality of their automated testing.

Standardization in a test automation framework is crucial for ensuring a consistent, efficient, and maintainable approach to testing. It supports the development of reusable test components, ensures smooth test execution across various platforms, streamlines test maintenance, and enhances reporting. By adhering to standardization, teams can avoid technical debt, improve collaboration, and ensure long-term sustainability and scalability of the automated testing effort.

Types of test automation

After examining the different elements that make up a test automation framework, we will now examine the different types of frameworks available, each catering to different aspects of software testing. Refer to the following figure:

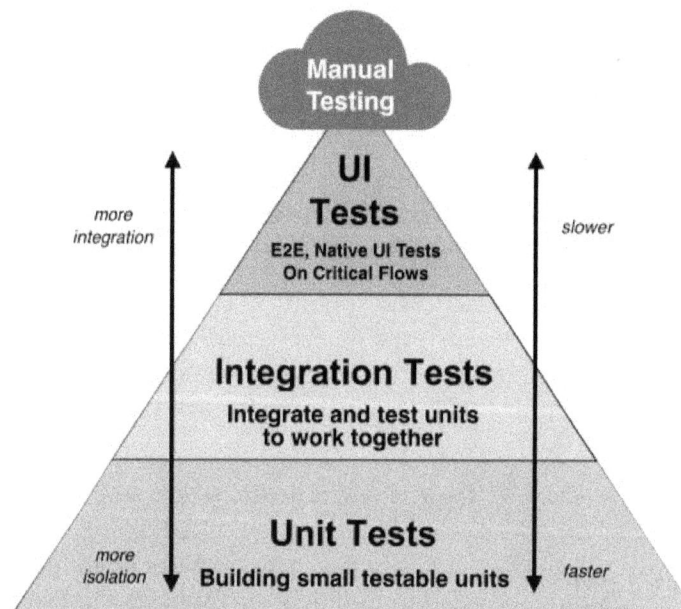

Figure 2.2: Focus of test automation with the majority of code covered at a unit level, with E2E and UI tests

Within the testing pyramid, different types of test automation ensure software quality at various levels:

- **Unit tests:** These are fast, low-level tests that validate individual functions, methods, or components in isolation. They are highly automated and provide immediate feedback to developers, ensuring that code behaves as expected at the smallest level.

- **Integration tests:** These tests verify that multiple components, services, or modules work together correctly. They focus on interactions between APIs, databases, and third-party services, catching issues like incorrect data flow or misconfigured connections. Integration tests are slower than unit tests but essential for ensuring system coherence.

- **End-to-end (E2E) tests:** These high-level tests simulate real user workflows and validate the entire application from start to finish. They ensure that all integrated components, including frontend and backend systems, function correctly under real-world conditions. While E2E tests provide high confidence, they are slower and more resource-intensive, so they should be used sparingly alongside unit and integration tests.

Balancing these automation types helps maintain an efficient, scalable, and reliable testing strategy, ensuring rapid feedback while minimizing test maintenance overhead.

Unit testing frameworks

Unit testing is the process of testing individual components or units of code, typically at the function or method level, to verify that they work as expected. A unit test isolates the smallest functional piece of code (often a single function, class, or method) to ensure that it produces the correct output for a given input and that it behaves as intended.

The core purpose of unit testing is to validate the correctness of these small, isolated pieces of functionality before they are integrated with other parts of the system. This ensures that each piece of code functions independently and can handle a variety of inputs, including edge cases, without causing errors or failures.

Focusing on lower-level tests, like unit tests, first is important because they provide fast, reliable, and cost-effective feedback on code quality. Unit tests run quickly and in isolation, allowing developers to detect and fix defects early before they propagate to higher levels of testing, where debugging becomes more complex and time-consuming.

By catching issues at the unit level, teams reduce the risk of integration and system failures, making later testing stages more efficient. Since unit tests are easier to maintain and execute frequently, they form the foundation of a solid testing strategy, ensuring a stable and scalable codebase while keeping the overall cost of defect resolution low.

Importance of unit testing

Let us now go over the reasons why unit testing is important:

- **Early bug detection:** Unit tests are executed at the earliest stages of development, allowing developers to catch and fix issues before they escalate into more complex problems at the integration or system level. Since unit tests run in isolation, they provide precise feedback, making it easier to pinpoint the exact source of an issue. This early detection reduces debugging time and lowers the cost of fixing defects compared to finding them later in the development cycle or production.

- **Code quality:** Writing unit tests forces developers to consider various edge cases and input scenarios, leading to a more thoughtful approach to coding. This often results in modular, decoupled components that are easier to understand, test, and maintain. The need to write testable code also encourages good design principles, such as single responsibility and dependency injection, ultimately improving the overall architecture of the software.

- **Refactoring confidence:** Unit tests act as a safety net when making changes to the codebase. Since they validate that individual components continue to function correctly, developers can refactor or optimize code with confidence, knowing that the tests will immediately flag any unintended side effects. Without unit tests, refactoring becomes riskier, as there is no automated way to verify that the changes have not broken existing functionality.

- **Documentation:** Unit tests provide living documentation for how a piece of code is supposed to behave. Unlike written documentation, which can become outdated, tests remain up to date as long as they are maintained. When new developers join a team, they can read unit tests to quickly understand the expected inputs, outputs, and edge cases of different functions, reducing the learning curve and improving onboarding efficiency.

Integration of unit tests in test automation framework

Unit testing forms the foundation of any comprehensive test automation framework. Although unit tests focus on small pieces of code in isolation, they play a crucial role in the overall quality assurance process. Let us now go over the following aspects:

- **Integration into CI pipelines:** Unit tests are often the first line of defense in automated testing. They are integrated into CI systems (for example, Jenkins, GitLab CI, Azure DevOps) to run automatically whenever new code is committed. This ensures that every code change is validated at the unit level before it is integrated with other parts of the system. Even if a bug existed in the code before these changes were committed, it allows developers to fix it and reduce technical debt in the process.

- **Dependency for other types of testing:** Unit tests complement higher-level tests, such as integration tests and end-to-end tests. They ensure that each unit of code works correctly, providing a solid foundation for integration testing (where multiple units are tested together) and system testing (which validates the entire system).

- **Speed and immediate feedback:** Unit tests are generally fast to execute because they test small, isolated components without requiring interaction with external systems (for example, databases or APIs). This speed makes unit tests ideal for providing immediate feedback to developers, helping them catch bugs early in the development cycle.

- **Code coverage measurement:** Many unit testing frameworks and CI systems integrate with code coverage tools (for example, JaCoCo for Java, Coverage.py for Python) to measure how much of the codebase is being tested. High code coverage ensures that most (if not all) critical pieces of code have been validated by unit tests.

- **Test-driven development:** Unit testing is a key part of **test-driven development** (**TDD**), an approach where developers write unit tests before writing the actual code. By following TDD, developers ensure that every piece of code is testable and works as expected from the outset.

- **Reusable test components:** In a broader test automation framework, unit tests often share components, such as utility functions or mock objects, with other types of tests (for example, integration or system tests). This reuse ensures consistency and reduces duplication in test code.

  o Unit testing focuses on validating the smallest units of code in isolation, helping to detect bugs early, improving code quality, and serving as a foundation for larger-scale testing efforts. Unit tests are integral to a larger test automation framework, where they are run as part of CI pipelines, provide fast feedback to developers, and ensure the reliability of individual code components before broader testing activities take place.

Integration testing

Integration testing is essential after unit testing because it verifies that individual components work together as expected. While unit tests focus on isolated functions or modules, integration tests ensure that dependencies, data flow, and interactions between different parts of the system function correctly. This helps detect issues such as misconfigured APIs, database inconsistencies, or communication failures between services, preventing defects that might not be visible in unit tests alone. By conducting integration testing, teams can catch early-stage integration problems and improve overall system reliability.

Integration testing is a key phase in the software testing lifecycle where individual modules or components are combined and tested as a group to verify their interactions and ensure they work together as expected. Unlike unit tests, which focus on the smallest, isolated pieces of functionality, integration tests evaluate how different parts of the system communicate and collaborate.

Now, let us go over the following points:

- **Testing interactions between components:** Integration tests ensure that when two or more modules interact, data flows correctly between them, and the modules function cohesively. For example, in a web application, integration tests could validate that the backend API properly handles requests from the frontend UI and returns the correct responses.

- **Identifying interface issues:** Integration testing helps detect interface mismatches, protocol errors, data format inconsistencies, or miscommunications between system components. These issues often do not surface in unit testing because unit tests do not check interactions between components, only the behavior of isolated units.

Types of integration testing

The various types of integration testing are as follows:

- **Big bang integration:** In this approach, all the system's components are integrated at once and then tested together. While this can be fast, it is also riskier because it makes it harder to pinpoint the exact cause of an issue if something fails.

- **Incremental integration:** Components are integrated and tested step-by-step, either in a top-down, bottom-up, or mixed approach. This makes it easier to identify and resolve issues early on in the integration process.

- **Top-down and bottom-up integration:** In top-down integration, higher-level modules are tested first, with lower-level modules being gradually integrated. In bottom-up integration, the opposite approach is taken, with lower-level modules being tested and integrated first, followed by higher-level ones.

Collaboration with other test types

Integration tests play a crucial role in bridging the gap between unit testing and system testing. While unit tests ensure individual components work in isolation, integration tests ensure that these components function correctly when combined.

Once integration tests pass, the system can proceed to broader end-to-end tests and system tests, which validate the entire application in real-world scenarios.

Best practices for automating integration tests

Here are some recommended best practices that should be followed when developing a framework for integration testing:

- **Use stubs and mocks for external dependencies:** Integration tests should focus on verifying the communication and collaboration between the system's components. However, external dependencies like third-party services, databases, or APIs can be mocked or stubbed to ensure tests are fast and reliable. Tools like Mockito (Java) or Sinon (JavaScript) can help simulate external components.

- **Ensure independent and isolated tests:** Each integration test should run independently without relying on the outcome of other tests. This can be achieved by resetting the environment or using database transaction rollbacks after each test to avoid data contamination.

- **Prioritize key integration points:** Integration testing should focus on the critical points where components interact, such as API endpoints, message queues, or data exchanges between the UI and backend. This ensures that the most important parts of the system are thoroughly tested.

- **Data-driven testing**: Integration tests should handle various types of input data, including edge cases, invalid data, and boundary values. This ensures robustness across different scenarios and helps identify potential integration problems early.

- **Run integration tests in CI/CD pipelines:** Automation of integration tests should be part of the CI/CD process. CI/CD tools automatically trigger integration tests whenever code is pushed to the repository, ensuring that integration issues are caught early.

- **Test in realistic environments:** For meaningful integration tests, try to use environments that closely mimic the production environment, including real databases, network configurations, and hardware setups. This helps ensure that the test results are representative of real-world usage.

- **Use version control for test data:** Ensure that the test data (for example, input datasets, mock files) used in integration tests is version-controlled. This makes it easier to track changes and maintain consistency in test results across different environments and test runs.

Integration testing plays a critical role in validating the interactions between different components of a system, ensuring that they work together as expected. It helps uncover issues that might arise when individual modules, which may work fine in isolation, fail to communicate or cooperate correctly when combined. By using popular frameworks like JUnit, Pytest, and Postman, and following best practices such as mocking external dependencies, focusing on key integration points, and integrating tests into CI pipelines, teams can effectively automate their integration testing processes and improve the reliability and performance of their software.

For example, in an e-commerce application, integration tests can be used to verify that the checkout process functions correctly by testing interactions between the payment gateway, inventory management system, and order processing service. A test might simulate a customer adding items to a cart, proceeding to checkout, and completing a payment, ensuring that the correct inventory is deducted and the order is registered in the database. These tests can be automated using tools like Selenium for front-end interactions and API testing frameworks like Postman or Rest Assured for backend validation. Running these integration tests in a CI/CD pipeline helps detect failures early, ensuring seamless communication between services before deployment to production.

UI testing frameworks

Once we have completed unit and integration test automation, there is still a need to simulate actual user behavior, and this is where UI testing comes in. UI testing frameworks focus on validating the behavior and functionality of front-end components in a web or mobile application. The goal of UI testing is to ensure that the user interface behaves as expected, with particular emphasis on user interactions, visual elements, and the correct rendering of the UI across different browsers, devices, or screen resolutions. Its other functions are as follows:

- **Validating front-end components:** UI testing involves simulating real user interactions, such as clicking buttons, entering data into forms, navigating between pages, and verifying that the UI responds as expected. Tests also ensure that elements on the page (for example, dropdowns, modals, images) are correctly displayed, and that interactive elements like buttons trigger the intended actions.

- **Rendering and layout:** UI tests also verify that front-end components render correctly on different devices, platforms, or screen resolutions, ensuring consistency in user experience. For example, responsive web design can be tested by resizing the browser window or simulating different device types in the testing environment.

- **Functional and visual testing:** UI testing frameworks can also handle visual regression testing, which checks for unintended visual changes in the UI. Functional tests focus on the behavior of UI elements, such as form validation or navigation flows, while visual testing ensures the appearance remains consistent across updates.

- **Simulating user behavior:** UI testing frameworks simulate real-world user interactions, ensuring the application behaves as a user would expect. This includes testing various scenarios like form submissions, navigation, data input validation, and error message handling.

Handling dynamic UI and asynchronous behavior

Testing dynamic UIs and handling asynchronous operations can be challenging, especially for applications that rely on JavaScript for client-side rendering, AJAX requests, or web socket communications. Here are some best practices that help ensure UI tests are reliable and maintainable:

- **Handling dynamic elements:**

  o **Explicit waits:** When working with dynamic content, it is essential to implement explicit waits, which wait for a specific condition (like an element becoming clickable or visible) before interacting with the element. This prevents tests from failing due to elements not being fully rendered before interactions. Selenium offers WebDriverWait for this purpose, while Cypress automatically waits for elements to appear.

  o **Polling and retries:** Some testing frameworks, like Cypress, automatically retry assertions and actions if an element is not found initially. This ensures that tests do not immediately fail due to timing issues, which can be especially useful for dynamic elements loaded via AJAX or after page transitions.

  o **Selectors strategy:** Using stable, reliable selectors is crucial in UI testing. Avoid relying on brittle selectors like XPath or CSS classes that may change frequently. Instead, use IDs or data-attributes specifically designed for testing.

  o **Page Object Model (POM):** The POM is a design pattern that abstracts web elements into classes or objects. This keeps the test code clean and allows for easier updates if the UI changes, reducing the maintenance burden.

- **Handling asynchronous behavior:**

  o **Automatic waiting (Cypress):** One of the key advantages of Cypress is its built-in automatic waiting mechanism. It waits for the DOM to fully load, all animations to complete, and the elements to be in an interactive state before attempting to interact with them.

  o **Async/await (JavaScript):** When writing tests in JavaScript-based frameworks (like Playwright or Cypress), use the async/await pattern to handle asynchronous operations. This ensures that API calls, animations, or dynamic content loads are completed before proceeding with test assertions.

  o **Using promises:** In Selenium and other frameworks, testing asynchronous behaviors can be tricky. Utilizing promises to synchronize your test actions ensures that the tests do not run ahead of time. For instance, waiting for an AJAX call to complete before verifying data on the page.

  o **Network mocking/intercepts:** In tests that rely heavily on network requests (such as API calls), it is useful to mock or intercept those requests. Cypress has built-in support for network request interception, allowing you to stub responses or simulate server delays to test the application's behavior under various conditions.

- **Test stability and parallel execution:**

  o **Isolate tests:** UI tests should be designed to run independently of each other. Avoid tests that depend on the outcome or state of previous tests, as this can cause false negatives when run in parallel or in a different order.

  o **Cross-browser testing:** Use tools that support multiple browsers to verify the application's compatibility. Playwright and Selenium provide excellent support for testing across a wide range of browsers.

o **CI/CD integration:** Ensure that UI tests are part of the CI/CD pipeline to catch UI bugs early. Set up nightly builds or triggers for test runs whenever code is pushed to the repository.

UI testing frameworks such as Selenium, Cypress, and Playwright provide powerful ways to automate and validate front-end components by simulating user interactions and ensuring correct functionality across browsers and platforms. By following best practices such as handling dynamic elements with explicit waits, using async/await for asynchronous operations, and maintaining stable selectors, developers can create robust and maintainable UI tests. These tests are critical in ensuring a consistent user experience and reducing manual testing efforts in modern, dynamic web applications.

Performance and load testing

Performance testing is a crucial part of the software development lifecycle, and it is aimed at evaluating how a system performs under various conditions. The primary goal is to ensure that the application remains responsive, reliable, and stable when subjected to a heavy workload or high traffic. Moreover, in the triangle mentioned at the start of this chapter; these are important at all levels in the testing triangle. Performance testing is typically divided into several key types:

- **Load testing:** This type of testing assesses how the system behaves under expected user loads. For example, load testing measures how many simultaneous users the system can handle before performance degrades. It helps identify performance bottlenecks such as slow database queries, memory leaks, or inefficient algorithms.

- **Stress testing:** Stress testing pushes the system beyond its normal operating conditions, testing its robustness under extreme traffic or resource constraints. The aim is to determine the breaking point of the system and understand how it fails (for example, crashes, slow responses, or errors).

- **Scalability testing:** Scalability testing assesses the system's ability to handle increased load by adding hardware or software resources (such as, CPU, memory, additional servers). This type of testing helps ensure that the application can scale up to meet demand without performance degradation.

- **Spike testing:** Spike testing involves subjecting the system to sudden, sharp increases in load (for example, a surge in traffic) and observing how it copes with these fluctuations. The goal is to determine whether the system can quickly recover and return to normal performance after the spike.

- **Endurance testing (Soak testing):** This type of testing evaluates how the system performs under sustained load over an extended period. The goal is to detect issues like memory leaks or resource exhaustion that may not appear during shorter tests.

Performance testing plays a critical role in ensuring that systems are scalable and performant, which is essential for user satisfaction and preventing service outages during high traffic periods (for example, Black Friday sales, product launches).

We will unpack performance and load testing frameworks in significantly more detail in *Chapter 10, Security, Performance, and Resilience Testing.*

Best practices for automating performance tests

Let us now go over some best practices:

- **Test early and often:** Performance testing should not be left until the end of development. Conducting performance tests early (for example, after key feature development) and integrating them into the CI/CD pipeline ensures that performance issues are identified and resolved quickly.

- **Set clear performance goals:** Before running performance tests, establish clear, measurable goals. Define acceptable response times, error thresholds, and throughput requirements based on business needs. This helps in interpreting results and making informed decisions.

- **Simulate realistic load scenarios:** Ensure that your load tests mimic real-world usage patterns as closely as possible. This includes simulating different types of users, load peaks, and varying data sets. For example, test both regular traffic and spikes that occur during peak times.

- **Monitor resource usage:** During performance tests, monitor key system metrics such as CPU, memory, disk I/O, and network utilization. This can help identify bottlenecks that are not obvious from the performance test results alone.

- **Use distributed testing for high loads:** If testing for high traffic scenarios, distribute the load across multiple machines. Most tools support distributed testing, which allows for realistic large-scale simulations.

- **Analyze and report:** Once the test is complete, thoroughly analyze the results, paying attention to metrics like response time, throughput, error rates, and resource utilization. Use the detailed reports generated by tools to share insights with stakeholders or build this into the framework directly. More on this in *Chapter 6, Test Orchestration and Execution.*

Performance and load testing play a critical role in assessing the scalability and reliability of a system under stress. By incorporating performance testing into the development process early and using realistic load scenarios, organizations can ensure that their systems will scale efficiently and handle high-traffic situations.

End-to-end testing

E2E testing is a comprehensive testing approach that evaluates the flow of an application from start to finish, ensuring that all integrated components and subsystems work together as expected. The purpose of E2E testing is to simulate real-world user scenarios to validate the application's behavior in a production-like environment.

The key reasons why E2E testing is essential include:

- **Full coverage of the user journey:** Unlike unit or integration testing, which tests individual components or interfaces, E2E testing focuses on how all parts of the application work together to deliver the final user experience. It verifies that critical user workflows—such as logging in, making a transaction, or checking out on an e-commerce site—are functioning correctly.

- **Validates integration between subsystems:** Many modern applications rely on multiple systems and services (databases, third-party APIs, microservices, and so on.). E2E tests ensure that these systems can integrate and communicate with each other properly, reducing the risk of integration issues slipping into production.

- **Detects high-level defects:** E2E testing helps detect issues that lower-level tests might miss, such as problems with user workflows, data flow between services, or interactions between the frontend and backend. Since it simulates how a user interacts with the application, it helps identify usability and reliability issues that could affect the end-user experience.

- **Ensures cross-platform compatibility:** Many applications are deployed across multiple platforms (for example, web, mobile, desktop), and E2E testing ensures that the app behaves consistently across these platforms. E2E tests can validate that UI and system functionalities work well on different devices, browsers, and operating systems.

- **Confidence in the application's stability:** By running comprehensive tests that mimic real-world use cases, E2E testing builds confidence that the application will work as expected when deployed to production. This is particularly important for business-critical workflows or applications with high user traffic.

- **Preventing regressions:** E2E tests can catch regressions—bugs that occur when new features or code changes unintentionally break existing functionality. This ensures that the addition of new functionality does not negatively impact the user experience.

Balance between automation coverage and test execution time

While E2E testing is crucial for validating the entire system, there are challenges associated with balancing comprehensive automation coverage with practical execution times. E2E tests can be slow and resource-intensive, especially in large and complex applications. Managing this balance effectively requires a thoughtful strategy.

Here are some key considerations:

- **Prioritize critical user journeys:** Not every feature or scenario should be tested with E2E tests. Due to the time and resources required, it is important to prioritize critical user journeys and business processes. These are the workflows that, if broken, would have the greatest negative impact on the user experience or business operations (for example, payment processing, account registration, order fulfillment).

- **Use a layered testing approach:** In addition to E2E tests, leverage a layered testing approach that includes unit, integration, and functional tests. Unit and integration tests are faster to execute and can cover most edge cases and low-level functionality. By catching most issues with lower-level tests, the E2E test suite can focus on testing high-level workflows that cannot be validated in isolation.

- **Selective E2E test suites:** Not every E2E test needs to be run on every commit or change. You can categorize your tests into different suites:

- **Smoke tests:** A subset of E2E tests that validate the most critical workflows (for example, can users log in, can transactions be completed). These are typically fast and run more frequently, such as on every deployment.

- **Full regression tests:** A larger suite that covers a broader set of E2E scenarios, which can be run less frequently (such as, nightly or before major releases). This helps ensure that you catch bugs without unnecessarily slowing down development.

- **Test coverage metrics:** Be mindful of test coverage metrics, but avoid striving for 100% E2E test coverage, as this is often not practical. Focus on achieving sufficient coverage for critical workflows while balancing time constraints and test reliability.

- **Parallelization:** To reduce execution time, run E2E tests in parallel. Most modern test frameworks (for example, Selenium Grid, Cypress, Playwright) support parallel test execution, where different test cases are executed on multiple virtual machines, containers, or browser instances simultaneously. This drastically cuts down test execution time, especially for large test suites.

- **Test flakiness:** One of the biggest challenges with E2E tests is test flakiness—tests that fail intermittently due to timing issues, environment setup, or network instability rather than actual application bugs. Flaky tests can undermine the value of E2E testing. To minimize flakiness:

  o Use proper wait mechanisms in tests to handle asynchronous events (for example, page loads, API responses, animations).

  o Avoid hardcoded wait times and prefer explicit waits (for example, wait until an element is visible).

  o Ensure that the test environment is stable and closely mimics production conditions.

- **Maintenance costs:** E2E tests require frequent updates and maintenance as the application evolves. Testers need to ensure that tests reflect the latest functionality and user interfaces. To mitigate maintenance costs:

  o Use POM or similar design patterns to decouple test scripts from UI elements, making tests more maintainable.

o   Keep tests focused on verifying user workflows, not internal implementation details, to avoid frequent changes due to minor UI updates.

- **Environment stability:** Since E2E tests depend on a fully functional test environment (for example, backend services, databases, third-party APIs), any instability in the environment can cause tests to fail. Investing in creating reliable, production-like test environments or using mock services when appropriate can improve test reliability and reduce false negatives.

End-to-end testing plays a crucial role in validating real-world user scenarios by simulating how users interact with the system. While E2E testing provides a high level of confidence in the system's overall functionality, it is important to strike a balance between comprehensive coverage and test execution time. By prioritizing critical workflows, leveraging a layered testing strategy, and optimizing test execution through parallelization and stable environments, teams can reap the benefits of E2E testing without sacrificing development velocity.

Traits of a well-designed framework

Before we conclude this chapter on test automation frameworks, it is important to highlight the benefits a well-designed framework provides and why investing the time to build it correctly is essential.

Reusability and maintainability

A well-designed test automation framework not only improves the efficiency of testing but also significantly enhances the reusability of test scripts and reduces maintenance overhead. This is how it is done:

- **Code reusability across test cases:** In a structured framework, commonly used test functions, steps, or utilities are abstracted and centralized into reusable modules or libraries. For example, tasks like logging in to the application, setting up test data, or interacting with a specific UI component can be written once and reused across multiple test cases. This reduces duplication of code, making test creation faster and easier while lowering the risk of inconsistencies.

- **Reduction in redundancy:** By centralizing key actions (such as API calls, database queries, or form submissions) into reusable libraries or helper functions, testers can avoid rewriting similar code across different test scripts. This approach cuts down on redundancy and makes the framework easier to maintain.

- **Consistency in test implementation:** A standardized framework ensures that tests follow the same structure, format, and naming conventions, making them easier to understand, update, and manage over time. As new team members join or the system evolves, this consistency simplifies onboarding and maintenance.

- **Scalability in test creation:** When the framework is modular and reusable, it allows for the rapid development of new test cases. As new features are introduced or changes are made, test cases can be added or modified by simply reusing existing components or functions, without needing to start from scratch.

- **Integration with external systems:** A good test automation framework supports integrations with external systems, such as CI/CD pipelines, reporting tools, or third-party APIs. Reusable test scripts ensure that the automation framework can be easily integrated into various environments, reducing setup time and ensuring that test results can be consistently generated, reported, and acted upon.

Importance of keeping test cases modular and decoupled

Maintaining test scripts can become challenging if they are tightly coupled or poorly organized. Modular and decoupled test cases help mitigate these challenges by ensuring that the framework is flexible, adaptable, and easy to update. Here is why this is important:

- **Decoupling of test logic from data and configuration:** Test cases should be independent of the data or configuration they rely on. By externalizing test data into data files (such as JSON, XML, or CSV), and using configuration files for environment-specific settings, test cases become more flexible and easier to manage. This allows testers to run the same tests across different environments (for example, staging, production) without modifying the test logic.

- **Modularity for ease of updates:** A modular framework breaks down test cases into smaller, reusable components, such as setup and teardown functions, page objects, or API calls. Each component is responsible for a single piece of functionality. This modularity ensures that when a feature changes (for example, the login workflow is updated), only the corresponding test module needs to be updated, rather than updating multiple test cases that perform similar actions.

- **Improved test maintenance:** Decoupled and modular tests minimize the impact of system changes on test scripts. When the underlying application evolves (for example, UI updates, new features), test cases do not need to be rewritten entirely. Instead, testers can update only the affected modules, making maintenance more efficient.

- **POM:** A commonly used pattern in UI testing is the POM, which abstracts interactions with UI elements into separate page classes. These page objects encapsulate the behavior and elements of specific web pages, allowing test scripts to interact with these objects rather than directly referencing UI elements. This way, when a UI component changes, only the corresponding page object needs to be updated, reducing maintenance across all test cases that use that page.

- **Separation of concerns:** By separating different layers of the test architecture—such as test execution, test data, and application logic—changes in one layer have minimal impact on others. For example, UI tests should not include business logic validation, which should be covered in unit or integration tests. This separation reduces the risk of widespread changes across multiple tests when a specific system part is updated.

- **Adaptability to system changes:** In fast-paced development environments where systems change frequently, having decoupled and modular test cases ensures that the framework can adapt to new changes quickly. Whether it is a new feature, a UI redesign, or changes to backend services, decoupled tests require fewer updates, allowing teams to maintain high test coverage without excessive manual work.

- **Encouraging test case reusability:** Modular test components can be reused in multiple test cases, ensuring that the same piece of code does not need to be written repeatedly. For example, if a test case requires a user to log in before performing a certain action, the login function can be a reusable module that is called in multiple test cases. This reduces the number of test scripts that need to be maintained over time.

Best practices for achieving reusability and maintainability

Let us now go over some best practices:

- **Follow SOLID principles:** In test automation frameworks, applying SOLID principles (originally from object-oriented programming) ensures that tests are well-structured and easy to maintain. The key principles—such as the Single Responsibility Principle and Open/Closed Principle—help ensure that test code is clean, modular, and flexible to changes.

- **Implement design patterns:** Design patterns like the POM (for UI testing) and factory pattern (for object creation) ensure that tests are maintainable. These patterns reduce direct dependencies and allow test logic to evolve independently of implementation details.

- **Automate test data management:** Test data should be externalized and dynamically managed to ensure tests are not hardcoded to specific values. Tools and techniques like **data-driven testing** (DDT) and keyword-driven testing enable testers to use varied data sets without modifying the underlying test logic.

- **Regularly refactor test scripts:** Like production code, test scripts should be regularly refactored to remove redundancy, improve readability, and ensure they adhere to best practices. This ongoing refactoring ensures that the test suite remains maintainable as the application grows and changes.

- **Centralize test configuration:** Centralizing test configurations and environment settings helps manage test execution across different environments. This reduces maintenance when updating environment-specific settings and allows tests to be easily scaled across environments.

- **Use version control and CI/CD:** Ensure that test automation scripts are version-controlled (for example, in Git) alongside application code. This allows for easy tracking of changes, collaborative development, and integration into CI/CD pipelines. Automated tests can then be triggered with every code change to verify that the system remains functional.

A well-structured test automation framework enhances reusability and maintainability by promoting modularity, decoupling test logic from configuration and data, and leveraging design patterns like the POM. This modularity ensures that tests can be reused across different test cases and reduces the maintenance overhead when the system evolves. By maintaining a flexible, organized framework, teams can adapt to changes faster, minimize test script duplication, and maintain high test quality with minimal effort. We will look at modularity in more detail in *Chapter 4, Designing Modular Test Frameworks*.

Scalability

As applications evolve and grow, the corresponding test automation frameworks must also scale to accommodate increasing complexity and a larger volume of test cases. Scalability in a test automation framework ensures that as new features and functionalities are added to the application, the testing efforts can keep pace without a proportional increase in maintenance overhead or test execution time.

Here are several aspects of scalability to consider:

- **Handling increased test volume:** A scalable test automation framework allows teams to add more test cases efficiently as the application grows. This includes functional tests, regression tests, and performance tests. The framework should support organized test structures, enabling easy addition and management of test scripts without impacting existing tests.

- **Complexity management:** As applications evolve, they often introduce more intricate workflows, integrations, and user interactions. A scalable framework should facilitate the testing of these complex scenarios, enabling testers to define high-level workflows that encompass various components and systems while still ensuring that lower-level tests can be executed independently. This might involve adopting patterns that support hierarchical testing approaches, where complex scenarios are composed of simpler, reusable test components.

- **Support for different testing types:** A scalable framework must support various types of testing—unit, integration, functional, UI, performance, and end-to-end testing. As the application grows, the testing landscape becomes more diverse and having a framework that can accommodate all types of tests ensures comprehensive coverage without requiring multiple disparate tools.

- **Adapting to changes in technology:** Technology and requirements are constantly changing, necessitating that the framework is adaptable. Integrating new tools, libraries, or technologies into the existing framework should be easy, allowing teams to stay current with industry trends and best practices.

- **Efficient test management:** As the number of tests grows, managing them becomes a significant challenge. A scalable framework should incorporate test management features, such as categorization, tagging, and prioritization. This makes it easier for teams to maintain a large volume of tests and ensure that the most critical tests are executed regularly.

Techniques for ensuring test execution is efficient at scale

When testing at scale, efficiency becomes critical to maintain the speed and quality of software delivery. Several techniques can be employed to optimize test execution, such as:

- **Parallelization:** Parallel test execution allows multiple tests to run simultaneously, significantly reducing overall test execution time. Most modern testing frameworks (like Selenium Grid, Cypress, and TestNG) support parallel execution, which can be configured to run tests on multiple threads, instances, or machines. Here is how to implement it effectively:

  o **Test distribution**: Group tests into smaller subsets that can run concurrently across different environments or machines. Test runners that distribute test execution based on available resources can facilitate this.

  o **Data management:** Ensure that test data is properly isolated to avoid conflicts when tests are running in parallel. This often requires managing state across different test instances to prevent interference between tests.

  o **Distributed testing:** Similar to parallelization, distributed testing involves spreading test execution across multiple machines or environments to maximize resource utilization and reduce execution time. Tools like Selenium Grid, BrowserStack, and Sauce Labs can help in distributing tests across different operating systems and browser combinations, allowing teams to achieve broader coverage while optimizing execution speed.

  o **Test prioritization:** Implementing test prioritization techniques can ensure that critical tests are run first, allowing teams to get faster feedback on high-risk areas. For example, prioritizing smoke tests that validate core functionalities can quickly indicate if the build is stable before running a full regression suite.

- **Efficient test design:** Tests should be designed to minimize dependencies and avoid complex setups. This can involve:

  o **Mocking and stubbing:** Using mocks and stubs to simulate interactions with external systems or services allows for faster execution and more reliable tests, as they eliminate the need for real-time interactions with dependencies that may introduce variability.

  o **Avoiding flaky tests:** Ensure that tests are stable and reliable, as flaky tests can lead to wasted execution time and hinder the CI/CD pipeline. Implement best practices, such as proper wait handling and environment stability, to reduce flakiness.

- **Test environment management:** Efficiently managing test environments is critical for scaling testing efforts. This includes:

  o **Containerization:** Using containers (for example, Docker) to create consistent, reproducible environments for running tests ensures that tests can be executed reliably and quickly across different stages of development.

  o **Cloud services:** Utilizing cloud-based testing platforms can provide the necessary scalability to handle a growing number of tests, enabling teams to spin up resources on demand.

- **CI/CD:** Integrating testing into the CI/CD pipeline ensures that tests are executed automatically with every code change, helping teams identify issues early in the development process. CI/CD tools facilitate efficient test execution and reporting, making it easier to manage large volumes of tests without overwhelming the team.

- **Monitoring and reporting:** Implementing robust monitoring and reporting tools helps teams effectively track test performance, execution time, and failures. Continuous monitoring quickly identifies bottlenecks and issues in the test execution process, enabling teams to optimize their testing strategy over time.

Scalability in a test automation framework is vital to keeping pace with application growth, facilitating the addition of more tests, and the handling of increasingly complex scenarios. By employing techniques such as parallelization, distributed testing, efficient test design, and effective environment management, teams can ensure that test execution remains efficient at scale. Leveraging a scalable framework not only enhances the overall testing strategy but also helps maintain high-quality software delivery in a dynamic and fast-paced development landscape.

Consistency and collaboration

In large, cross-functional organizations, ensuring consistency in testing practices across diverse teams is crucial for maintaining software quality and efficiency. A well-designed test automation framework serves as a unifying structure that promotes consistency in various ways:

- **Standardization of practices:** A well-defined framework provides standardized guidelines and best practices for writing and executing tests. This includes naming conventions, test structure, documentation, and reporting standards. By adhering to these guidelines, different teams can produce test scripts that are easier to understand and maintain, regardless of who authored them. This standardization fosters a common language across teams, minimizing miscommunication and errors.

- **Shared libraries and components:** A modular framework encourages the use of shared libraries, utilities, and components that all teams can leverage. For example, common functions for authentication, data validation, and logging can be stored in a central repository. This reduces code duplication and ensures that all teams are utilizing the same, validated logic, promoting consistency in test behavior and results.

- **Unified test environment:** A well-structured framework typically includes provisions for setting up a unified test environment where all teams can execute their tests under similar conditions. This ensures that tests run consistently across various teams and projects, reducing discrepancies in test results due to environmental differences.

- **Common reporting mechanism:** A standardized reporting mechanism allows for uniform test results presentation across teams. Using a consistent format for test reports, teams can easily compare results, identify trends, and assess overall quality metrics. This transparency helps stakeholders understand the testing outcomes and facilitates informed decision-making.

- **Cross-team visibility:** A framework that promotes consistency fosters transparency and visibility across teams. This visibility allows teams to see what tests are being executed, what issues have been encountered, and how test coverage evolves. It also enables teams to learn from each other's successes and challenges, fostering a culture of shared knowledge and continuous improvement.

Frameworks that enable collaboration

Collaboration among developers, testers, and operations teams is essential for delivering high-quality software promptly. A well-designed test automation framework can facilitate collaboration in several key ways:

- **Integrated development environments (IDEs):** A collaborative framework often integrates seamlessly with **IDEs** and tools, allowing developers and testers to work together more effectively. This integration may include shared code repositories, version control systems, and integrated testing tools that enable developers and testers to contribute to the same codebase.

- **Shared ownership of test cases:** Frameworks promote a culture of shared ownership of test cases, encouraging developers to write unit tests and testers to contribute to automated acceptance tests. This collaboration ensures that testing is considered an integral part of the development process rather than an isolated activity. When all team members feel responsible for quality, it leads to better test coverage and more robust applications.

- **CI/CD pipeline integration:** A test automation framework that integrates with CI/CD pipelines allows for seamless collaboration between development, testing, and operations teams. Automated tests can be triggered at various pipeline stages, enabling immediate feedback on code changes. This feedback loop allows developers to address issues early in the development cycle, reducing the cost of fixing bugs later.

- **Feedback loops:** Effective frameworks provide channels for rapid feedback among teams. For instance, when tests fail, the framework can automatically notify relevant team members, allowing them to investigate and resolve issues quickly. This real-time feedback fosters collaboration and prevents bottlenecks in the development process.

- **Collaboration tools:** Incorporating collaboration tools within the framework (such as issue-tracking systems, project management software, and communication platforms) enables teams to discuss testing strategies, share test results, and track progress. These tools promote communication and collaboration, ensuring everyone is aligned on testing goals and objectives.

- **Documentation and knowledge sharing:** A well-designed framework includes comprehensive documentation accessible to all team members. This documentation can cover testing strategies, guidelines, and test case examples. Regularly updated documentation fosters knowledge sharing, helping teams stay informed about best practices and new testing techniques.

- **Cross-functional workshops and training:** Frameworks that support collaboration often encourage cross-functional workshops, training sessions, or hackathons. These initiatives bring together developers, testers, and operations teams to work on testing challenges, share insights, and brainstorm solutions. Such collaborative activities strengthen team relationships and improve overall testing effectiveness.

A well-designed test automation framework is pivotal in promoting consistency and facilitating collaboration across teams in large organizations. The framework enhances consistency in testing efforts by standardizing practices, providing shared components, and establishing unified environments. Simultaneously, it enables seamless collaboration among developers, testers, and operations teams through integration with CI/CD pipelines, shared ownership of test cases, and effective communication tools. Ultimately, such a framework not only drives high-quality software delivery but also fosters a culture of collaboration and continuous improvement within the organization.

Speed and efficiency

A structured test automation framework significantly enhances the speed and efficiency of the testing process. The following are some key things that should be built into the test automation framework to enable it to operate at a quicker pace and not slow down the development process significantly:

- **Rapid test development:** A well-designed framework provides pre-built templates, reusable components, and libraries that streamline the test creation process. Testers can leverage these resources to quickly develop new test cases without needing to build everything from scratch. This rapid development capability allows teams to keep pace with fast-paced development cycles and release schedules.

- **Modular architecture:** By promoting a modular approach to test design, a structured framework allows testers to create smaller, independent test modules that can be easily combined to form more complex tests. This modularity enables teams to isolate failures quickly, facilitating faster debugging and reducing the time spent on maintenance.

- **Remove any manual steps:** Structured frameworks often incorporate automation capabilities that enable tests to be executed without manual intervention. This reduces the time and effort required to run tests, allowing for more frequent execution. Automated tests can be scheduled to run overnight or as part of a CI/CD pipeline, providing continuous feedback on the application's stability and performance.

- **Parallel and distributed testing:** By enabling parallel and distributed testing, a structured framework can significantly decrease overall test execution time. Tests can be run simultaneously across multiple environments or machines, allowing teams to cover more scenarios in less time. This efficiency is particularly crucial in large applications requiring extensive test coverage.

- **Error reduction and reliability:** Structured frameworks typically include validation checks, logging, and reporting features that enhance test reliability. These mechanisms help identify and eliminate flakiness, ensuring test results are consistent and dependable. Reliable results give teams confidence in their test outcomes, reducing the time spent investigating false positives or negatives.

Leveraging automation in the CI/CD pipeline

Integrating test automation into the CI/CD pipeline is a powerful strategy for accelerating release cycles while maintaining high quality. Here is how this integration enhances speed and efficiency:

- **Continuous testing:** Automation in the CI/CD pipeline allows for continuous testing, where tests are automatically triggered in response to code changes. This immediate feedback loop helps identify defects early in the development process, reducing the risk of issues accumulating and slowing down later stages of development.

- **Rapid feedback mechanisms:** Automated tests provide immediate feedback to developers about the quality of their changes. By running unit tests, integration tests, and regression tests automatically upon each code commit, teams can quickly ascertain whether new code introduces any issues. This rapid feedback allows for quicker iterations and minimizes the time spent fixing bugs after they are introduced.

- **Automated deployment:** A well-implemented CI/CD pipeline includes automated deployment processes to push tested code to production quickly and reliably. Automated deployment reduces the risk of human error during releases and allows for frequent and consistent delivery of new features and fixes to users.

- **Test coverage across all stages:** Leveraging automation in the CI/CD pipeline ensures that tests are executed across all stages of the software development lifecycle. This includes unit tests during the development phase, integration tests during the build process, and end-to-end tests before deployment. Comprehensive test coverage throughout the pipeline helps maintain software quality at each stage, reducing the likelihood of defects reaching production.

- **Scalability in testing:** As applications grow, the number of tests typically increases. Automation in the CI/CD pipeline allows teams to scale their testing efforts without a corresponding increase in manual testing efforts. By leveraging parallel and distributed testing strategies, teams can execute a larger suite of tests in a shorter time frame.

- **Quality gates:** Implementing quality gates within the CI/CD pipeline ensures that only code that passes automated tests can be promoted to production. This approach helps maintain quality standards and reduces the risk of introducing defects into the production environment. By enforcing these gates, organizations can confidently release new features while ensuring that critical quality checks are in place.

- **Efficient resource utilization:** Automated testing in the CI/CD pipeline allows teams to utilize resources efficiently. Organizations can optimize resource allocation by scheduling tests to run during off-peak hours or leveraging cloud-based testing solutions, ensuring that the testing process does not hinder development or deployment schedules.

A structured test automation framework significantly enhances speed and efficiency in test development and execution. By providing reusable components, modular design, and automation capabilities, it allows teams to create reliable test cases and execute them efficiently and rapidly. Integrating automation into the CI/CD pipeline further accelerates release cycles by enabling continuous testing and rapid feedback, allowing organizations to deliver high-quality software to users without compromising on speed. This combination of structured frameworks and automated processes is essential for thriving in today's fast-paced software development landscape.

Reporting and debugging

Effective reporting and debugging are critical components of a robust test automation framework. They not only help teams understand the outcomes of test executions but also facilitate quick identification and resolution of issues. Here is how detailed reporting and logging mechanisms enhance the tracking and debugging of test failures:

- **Comprehensive test reports:**

  o **Detailed results:** A well-structured reporting mechanism should provide comprehensive details of each test execution, including the status (pass/fail), execution duration, and error messages. This level of detail allows stakeholders to quickly assess the application's quality and the testing efforts' effectiveness.

  o **Historical data:** Storing historical test results enables teams to analyze trends. This data can help identify recurring issues, measure test effectiveness, and evaluate the overall stability of the application. By comparing current results with historical data, teams can pinpoint areas that require attention or further testing.

  o **Customizable reports:** Offering customizable reporting options allows teams to tailor reports to their needs. For instance, stakeholders may prefer summary reports highlighting overall test coverage, while developers might require detailed reports focusing on individual test failures. Customization improves the relevance of reports for different audiences.

- **Contextual logging:**

  o **In-depth logs:** Incorporating logging mechanisms into the framework allows teams to capture detailed logs during test execution. These logs should include the test steps taken, inputs provided, and system responses. Comprehensive logging provides a narrative of the test execution, which is invaluable for diagnosing failures.

  o **Error messages and stack traces:** When a test fails, the logs should capture clear error messages and stack traces. This information helps developers quickly understand the nature of the failure and where it occurred in the codebase. Detailed logs also reduce the time needed for troubleshooting by providing context around the failure.

  o **Variable state logging:** Capturing the state of key variables at various points during test execution can help in diagnosing issues. For instance, logging the values of inputs and outputs can provide insights into unexpected behaviors and facilitate debugging.

- **Incorporating reporting and dashboards:**

  o **Real-time dashboards:** Integrating reporting with real-time dashboards provides teams with an at-a-glance view of test execution results. Dashboards can visualize key metrics such as pass/fail rates, execution times, and defect counts, enabling stakeholders to monitor the testing progress and quality of the application in real time.

  o **Automated notifications:** Integrating automated notifications within the reporting mechanism ensures that relevant stakeholders receive timely alerts about test results. Notifications can be configured to trigger upon test failures, execution status changes, or test run completion. This proactive approach facilitates quick responses to issues and minimizes delays in addressing critical problems.

  o **Collaboration tools integration:** Integrating reporting tools with collaboration platforms (such as Slack, Microsoft Teams, or email) allows for seamless communication among team members.

For example, notifications about test failures can be automatically sent to a designated channel, ensuring that the appropriate team members are promptly informed and can take action.

- **Interactive reporting features:**

  o **Drill-down capabilities:** Interactive reporting features allow users to drill down into specific test results for more granular insights. For example, a user might click on a failed test to view the detailed execution logs, error messages, and variable states, enabling faster troubleshooting.

  o **Filter and search options:** Providing filter and search options within reports allows users to quickly locate specific tests or issues. This capability enhances usability and enables teams to focus on areas that require immediate attention.

  o **Visual representation of results:** Using graphs, charts, and other visual aids to represent test results can make the information more accessible and easier to interpret. Visual representations can highlight trends and patterns, aiding in quicker decision-making.

Incorporating detailed reporting and logging mechanisms into a test automation framework is essential for effectively tracking and debugging test failures. Comprehensive test reports, contextual logging, real-time dashboards, automated notifications, and interactive reporting features work together to provide teams with valuable insights into the testing process. By enhancing visibility into test results and facilitating rapid identification and resolution of issues, these practices ultimately contribute to higher software quality and more efficient development cycles.

Conclusion

Test automation frameworks are essential structures that enable efficient and effective testing processes across various software applications.

In conclusion, a robust test automation framework is not just a collection of tools and scripts; it is a comprehensive system that enhances the efficiency and effectiveness of testing processes. By prioritizing scalability, reusability, and maintainability, organizations can ensure that their testing efforts are aligned with their development goals, ultimately leading to higher-quality software and improved time-to-market.

Key takeaways

Test automation frameworks consist of several key components and types, each serving a distinct purpose.

Core components: Essential elements of test automation frameworks include test scripts, libraries, test data, and test results. Each component contributes to the framework's overall functionality and effectiveness, enabling teams to design, execute, and manage tests seamlessly.

Types of frameworks: Different test automation frameworks cater to various testing needs, such as unit testing, integration testing, UI testing, performance testing, and end-to-end testing. Each framework is designed with specific tools and practices to address the unique challenges associated with its respective testing domain.

Importance of scalability, reusability, and maintainability

A well-structured test automation framework is vital for several reasons:

- **Scalability:** As applications grow and evolve, the ability to scale testing efforts is crucial. A scalable framework allows teams to add more tests and manage complex scenarios efficiently, ensuring the framework can support ongoing development without becoming unwieldy.

- **Reusability:** Frameworks designed with reusability in mind enable teams to leverage existing test scripts, data, and configurations across multiple test cases. This saves time, promotes consistency, and reduces redundancy, enhancing overall testing efficiency.

- **Maintainability**: A focus on maintainability ensures that test cases can be easily updated as the application changes. By adopting best practices such as modularity and separation of concerns, teams can simplify the maintenance process, reducing the likelihood of introducing errors during updates.

Role of well-designed frameworks

Well-designed test automation frameworks are crucial in streamlining automation efforts across different testing needs. They facilitate collaboration among developers, testers, and operations teams by providing a unified structure that supports various testing activities. Moreover, by incorporating effective reporting and logging mechanisms, these frameworks enhance visibility into testing outcomes and enable faster issue identification.

Exercises

1. How well does your test automation framework integrate with your CI/CD pipeline?

2. Can your framework support multiple test types (UI, API, performance, security, etc.)?

3. How easy is onboarding new team members to use and extend the framework?

4. How modular and maintainable is your framework? Are there repeated test logic and code smells?

5. Does your framework provide clear, actionable reports for test failures?

6. How well does it handle test data management across different environments?

7. Can your framework scale to support parallel test execution?

8. Does it provide a proper abstraction to support tool-agnostic testing?

Join our Discord space

Join our Discord workspace for latest updates, offers, tech happenings around the world, new releases, and sessions with the authors:

https://discord.bpbonline.com

## CHAPTER 3

Designing with Architecture in Mind

Introduction

The approach to test automation cannot be separated from the architecture of the systems it needs to test. Whether designing the framework to capitalize on the aspects of a system's design or architecting the system for better testability and automatability, the two work hand in hand, and you cannot build a successful automation framework without having a strong understanding of the principles of software architecture.

Structure

In this chapter, we will cover the following topics:

- Introduction to software architecture principles
- Application to test automation
- Bridging software architecture and test automation
- Aligning application architecture with test automation
- Principles of software architecture applied to testing framework
- Implementing a layered approach in test automation frameworks
- Scalability in test automation
- Maintainability in test automation
- Adopting clean code practices
- Extensibility in test automation frameworks
- Architectural patterns and their relevance to test automation

Objectives

By the end of this chapter, the reader will have learned about the basic principles of software architecture, how they aid software design, and how they can be utilized to improve software testability. This chapter will also help the reader understand the important role that architecture plays in the automation of software testing and the close alignment required between architectural and test framework design to ensure the most optimal test automation outcome.

Introduction to software architecture principles

Software architecture refers to the high-level structure of a software system, encompassing the components, their relationships, and the principles and guidelines that govern its design and evolution. It serves as a blueprint for both the system and the project, developing it and guiding stakeholders through decisions about design, functionality, and performance.

The core principles of software architecture include:

- **Separation of concerns:** This principle promotes the idea that a system should be divided into distinct modules, each addressing a specific feature or functionality. This separation allows for easier maintenance, scalability, and understanding of the system.

- **Modularity:** Software should be composed of modular components that can be developed, tested, and maintained independently. This principle facilitates easier updates and enhancements while minimizing the impact on the overall system.

- **Reusability:** Encouraging the reuse of components and modules reduces redundancy and increases efficiency. Reusable components can be leveraged across different projects, leading to faster development cycles.

- **Scalability:** Software architecture must accommodate growth. A well-architected system can handle increased loads without significant modifications, ensuring consistent performance as user demand grows.

- **Flexibility and extensibility:** Well-designed architecture allows for changes and enhancements without extensive rework. This adaptability is crucial in a rapidly changing technological landscape, where new requirements frequently emerge.

Application to test automation

In the context of test automation, these principles are crucial for designing frameworks that are robust, maintainable, and effective. A well-structured test automation framework aligns with software architecture principles by promoting clear separations between test scripts, test data, and reporting mechanisms. This separation allows testers to modify tests without affecting underlying functionality, enhancing the framework's longevity and adaptability. They also help in the following aspects:

- **Enhanced maintainability:** An architecture that is thoughtfully designed enables easier maintenance of automation frameworks. When changes are required, whether due to new feature requirements or updates in technology, well-structured frameworks can be modified with minimal disruption.

- **Improved scalability:** Automation frameworks must grow with the application they are testing. By considering architecture from the outset, developers can create frameworks that easily accommodate additional tests, new testing technologies, or more complex application scenarios.

- **Increased collaboration:** Clear architectural principles foster better collaboration among development, testing, and operations teams. A shared understanding of architecture helps align efforts, ensuring everyone works towards the same goals.

- **Cost efficiency:** Investing time in proper architectural design can significantly reduce costs in the long run. A well-architected automation framework reduces technical debt, minimizes the need for extensive refactoring, and allows for more efficient use of resources.

- **Facilitated integration:** Automation frameworks often need to integrate with various tools and systems. A solid architectural foundation supports this integration, ensuring the framework can easily connect with **continuous integration and continuous deployment (CI/CD)** pipelines, test management tools, and reporting systems.

- **Early defect detection:** Considering architecture in the design of automation frameworks ultimately leads to higher-quality software. When testing is based on a well-architected framework, it is more likely to uncover defects early in the development process, leading to a more reliable final product.

Bridging software architecture and test automation

Refer to the following figure:

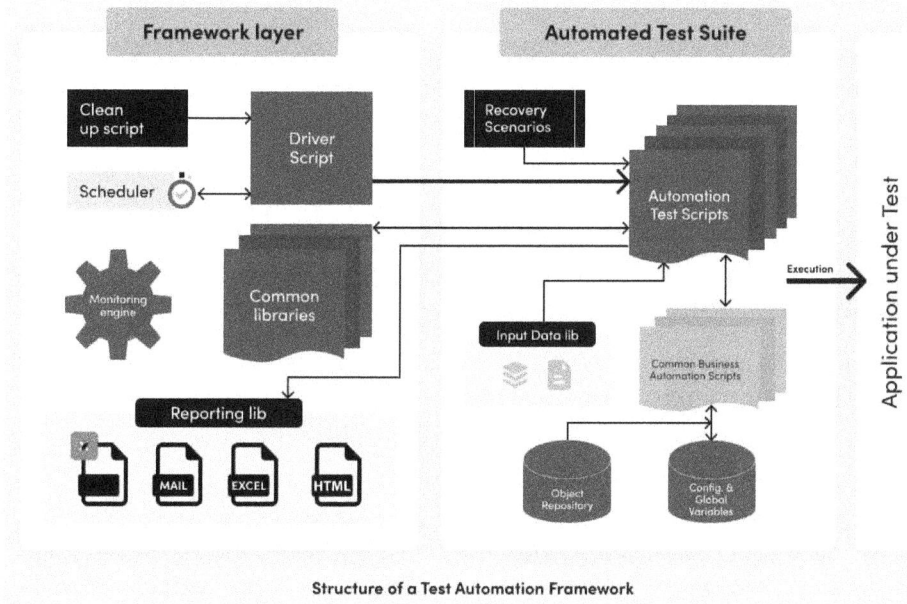

Figure 3.1: Example of modularity that can be added in an automation framework

Sound architectural decisions are fundamental to building effective and sustainable test automation frameworks. The following are several ways these decisions enhance the framework. We will just mention them briefly here before going into more detail further in the chapter:

- **Modular design:** A modular architecture allows for individual test components to be developed, executed, and maintained separately. This design means that if a specific test or set of tests requires updates, those changes can be made without impacting the entire framework. Such flexibility streamlines maintenance and facilitates faster onboarding of new team members, who can focus on specific modules rather than the whole system.

- **Clear abstraction layers:** Establishing clear abstraction layers between test scripts and the application under test improves clarity and reduces complexity. Test scripts should interact with a defined API or interface rather than the application's internals. This separation allows for changes in the application's internal structure without necessitating significant modifications to the tests themselves, enhancing longevity.

- **Consistent design patterns:** Utilizing established design patterns (for example, Page Object Model, Model-View-Controller) in the architecture of the automation framework promotes consistency and reusability. Adopting these patterns allows teams to quickly understand and modify existing tests, reducing the learning curve for new team members and improving overall productivity.

- **Scalability and performance:** Architectural decisions that consider scalability, such as selecting appropriate technologies, defining clear boundaries for testing modules, and implementing efficient data management strategies, ensure that the framework can handle increasing tests as the application grows. A scalable framework is vital for long-term success, especially in environments prioritizing CI/CD.

- **Integration capabilities:** A well-architected test automation framework should seamlessly integrate with other tools and systems, such as CI/CD pipelines, defect tracking tools, and reporting platforms. Ensuring these integration points are well-defined at the architectural level enhances the framework's usability and effectiveness in real-world scenarios.

Aligning application architecture with test automation

Aligning the architecture of the application with that of the test automation framework is crucial for maximizing effectiveness and efficiency. Here are key considerations to ensure this alignment:

- **Shared architectural vision:** Both development and testing teams should share a common architectural vision. Collaboration during the design phase ensures testing strategies align with the application's architecture. This collaboration can include regular meetings, joint planning sessions, and inclusive documentation practices that engage both teams.

- **Understanding application components:** Test automation frameworks must be designed with a comprehensive understanding of the application's architecture, including its components, interfaces, and dependencies. By mapping out the application's architecture, teams can design automation frameworks that effectively target key functionalities and areas of risk.

- **Adaptability to changes:** As the application evolves, the test automation framework should adapt accordingly. This adaptability requires close collaboration between the teams responsible for application development and test automation. Regular updates and feedback loops can ensure that the framework remains aligned with any architectural changes.

- **Testing coverage:** Ensure that the test automation framework provides adequate coverage of the application architecture. This means identifying critical paths, components, and interfaces that require rigorous testing. A well-aligned framework prioritizes the application's most important aspects, ensuring thorough validation and minimizing the risk of defects.

- **Feedback mechanism:** Implement a feedback mechanism that allows insights from test automation to influence architectural decisions in the application. For instance, if certain components prove difficult to test due to architectural choices, this feedback can inform future development efforts, leading to better designs.

- **Continuous integration:** A well-aligned automation framework should integrate seamlessly into CI/CD pipelines. This integration ensures that automated tests are executed consistently as part of the development process, providing timely feedback and promoting a quality culture across the entire development lifecycle.

Principles of software architecture applied to testing frameworks

In this section, we will look at how different principles of software architecture can be applied to the creation of a test automation framework.

Modularity and separation of concerns in test automation

Modularity is a core principle of software architecture that promotes the division of a system into smaller, independent components or modules. Applying this principle in the context of test automation involves creating reusable components that separate test logic, data, and configurations. Here is how this can be effectively achieved:

- **Reusable test components:** Building reusable test components allows teams to define common functionalities once and use them across multiple tests. For example, a login module can encapsulate the logic for logging into an application. This way, the same module can be reused whenever the login process is required in different tests, reducing redundancy and promoting consistency.

- **Separation of test logic, data, and configurations:** The separation of concerns is fundamental in modular design. Test logic (the steps that execute the test), test data (the input data used for testing), and configuration settings (environment-specific parameters) should be kept separate. By doing so:

  o **Test logic:** Focused on what needs to be tested, this can be written in a clear and concise manner without being cluttered by data handling or configuration details.

  o **Test data:** Using external data structures (like CSV, JSON, or databases) for test data enables easier updates without changing the test logic. It also promotes the use of different datasets for varied testing scenarios without rewriting the tests.

  o **Configuration files:** Storing configurations in separate files allows teams to easily manage different environments (development, testing, production). This separation ensures that configuration changes do not impact the core test logic.

- **Enhanced test maintenance:** A modular approach leads to easier maintenance of the test automation framework. When changes are necessary, whether due to application updates or enhancements to the testing strategy, only the relevant module needs to be updated. This reduces the risk of introducing errors in unrelated areas of the framework.

- **Faster onboarding and collaboration:** New team members can quickly understand the framework by focusing on specific modules instead of the entire codebase. This modularity facilitates better collaboration, as team members can work on different components simultaneously without stepping on each other's toes.

Importance of clear interfaces between components

Clear interfaces between modular components are crucial for ensuring easier maintenance and scalability in test automation frameworks. Here is why they matter:

- **Defined communication:** Clear interfaces specify how different components communicate, making it easier to understand the relationships and dependencies between modules. This clarity allows team members to modify or replace individual components without needing extensive knowledge of the entire system.

- **Encapsulation of logic:** By defining interfaces, the internal implementation details of each module can be encapsulated. This means that changes to one component's internal logic do not affect other components as long as the interface remains unchanged. This separation minimizes the risk of breaking existing tests when modifications are made.

- **Facilitating integration:** Well-defined interfaces make integrating new components or third-party tools more straightforward. If the test automation framework's architecture is modular and each component has a clear interface, developers can add or modify functionalities with minimal friction.

- **Promoting scalability:** As the application under test grows and evolves, the automation framework must adapt. Clear interfaces allow teams to scale the framework by adding or extending new modules without disrupting the overall architecture. This scalability is particularly important in environments that embrace agile methodologies and require rapid iteration.

- **Testing and validation:** When components have clear interfaces, it becomes easier to test them in isolation. This isolation allows for focused unit tests, ensuring that each component works as expected independently before integrating it into the broader framework. This practice leads to higher quality and more reliable automation.

- **Improved collaboration:** Clear interfaces foster collaboration among team members, as they provide a shared understanding of how components interact. Developers and testers can work together more effectively when they know exactly how to integrate their efforts, leading to better outcomes and reduced development time.

Designing a framework with loose coupling

Loose coupling refers to the design principle where different components of a system interact with each other in a way that minimizes dependencies. In the context of a test automation framework, this principle is critical for achieving flexibility, maintainability, and adaptability.

Here is how to implement loose coupling:

- **Component independence:** Design components to operate independently of one another. This means that changes in one component should not necessitate changes in others. For instance, if a new testing tool or library is introduced, it should not require rewriting other modules in the framework. Instead, Adapters or interfaces can be used to integrate these tools without affecting existing functionality.

- **Use of interfaces and abstract classes:** Implementing interfaces and abstract classes allows for defining contracts that components must adhere to while keeping their implementations flexible. This approach enables the framework to support multiple implementations for the same interface, allowing teams to switch out components (like reporting tools or assertion libraries) with minimal disruption.

- **Event-driven architecture:** Consider using an event-driven architecture to decouple components. In this model, components communicate through events rather than direct calls. This method allows for more flexible integration and straightforward modifications, as components can listen for specific events and act accordingly without being tightly bound to the event source.

- **Dependency injection:** Implement dependency injection to manage component dependencies. Teams can easily swap out components and manage configurations by injecting dependencies at runtime rather than hardcoding them. This technique fosters a more flexible architecture, allowing for easier updates and testing of individual components.

- **Facilitating parallel development:** Loose coupling enables teams to work on different components simultaneously without stepping on each other's toes. This capability accelerates development and encourages collaboration, as team members can focus on their respective areas of responsibility without being hindered by dependencies.

Ensuring high cohesion within components

High cohesion refers to the degree to which the elements within a module belong together. In a test automation framework, achieving high cohesion ensures that each component has a focused responsibility and performs a specific task effectively. Here is how to promote high cohesion:

- **Single Responsibility Principle (SRP):** Each component in the framework should adhere to the SRP, meaning it should have one reason to change. For example, a test data management component should focus solely on data preparation and manipulation, while a reporting component should concentrate on generating test reports. This focus enhances clarity and maintainability.

- **Organizing components by functionality:** Group related functionalities together within a module to enhance cohesion. For instance, all components related to user authentication tests (for example, login, logout, password recovery) should reside within the same module. This organization allows for more straightforward navigation and understanding of the framework, making it more intuitive for team members.

- **Clear responsibilities and interfaces:** Define clear responsibilities for each component and ensure that its interface reflects those responsibilities. This clarity helps maintain focus and prevents components from becoming bloated with multiple functions, which can lead to confusion and decreased maintainability.

- **Encouraging reuse:** High cohesion within components promotes reuse. When components are designed to perform specific tasks effectively, they can be repurposed across different testing scenarios without modification. This reuse can significantly enhance efficiency and reduce duplication of effort.

- **Facilitating testing:** Cohesive components are easier to test as they encapsulate specific functionalities. This encapsulation allows for targeted unit testing, ensuring each component works as intended before integrating into the broader framework. Such testing leads to higher reliability and quality in the automation suite.

- **Enhanced understandability:** High cohesion improves the framework's overall understandability. When team members can easily grasp the purpose and functionality of each component, it reduces new members' onboarding time and facilitates better collaboration among team members.

Implementing a layered approach in test automation frameworks

A layered architecture in a test automation framework organizes the framework into distinct layers, each responsible for specific aspects of the testing process. This design promotes a clear separation of concerns, ensuring each layer handles its designated responsibilities without overlapping with others. Refer to the following figure:

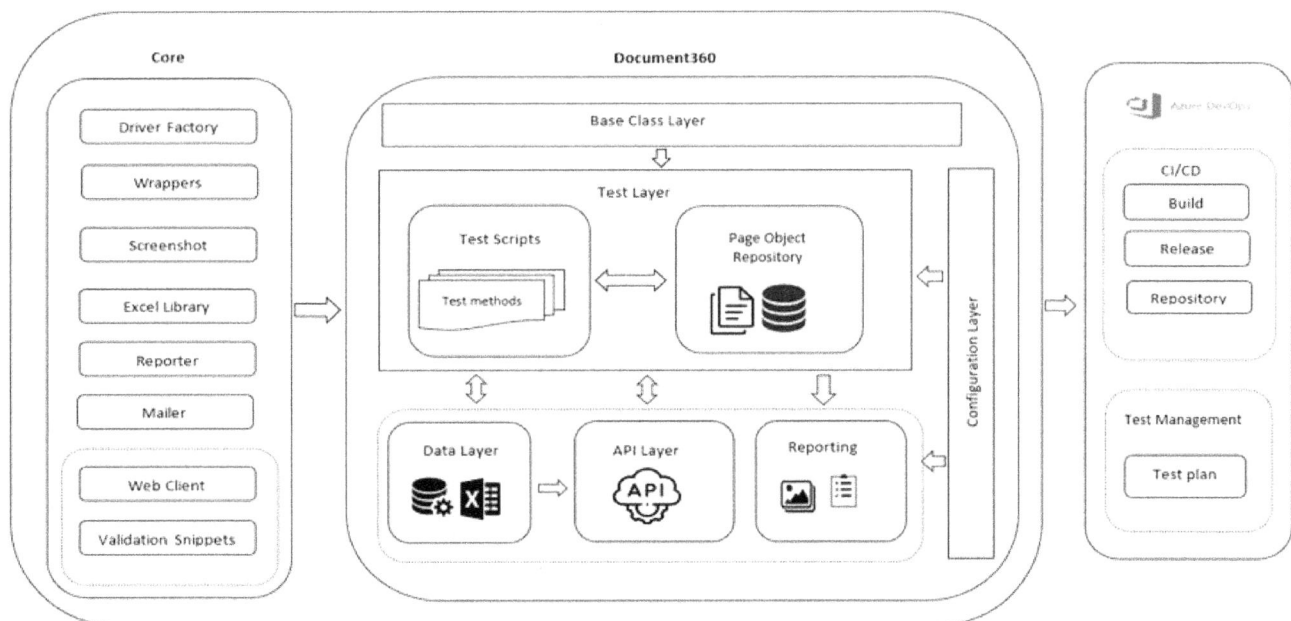

Figure 3.2: Example of a test automation framework built using a layered architecture

A typical layered architecture in a test automation framework might include the following layers:

- **Presentation layer:** This layer is responsible for interacting with the **user interface** (**UI**) of the application being tested. It includes elements such as test scripts that handle user actions and UI interactions.

- **Test logic layer:** This layer encapsulates the core logic of the tests, defining how tests are structured, executed, and reported. It is where the actual testing actions are defined, using the tools and methods appropriate for the specific test.

- **Business logic layer:** The business logic layer contains the rules and functionalities specific to the application domain. Test automation may include services that interact with the application's API or back-end processes, validating the business rules as part of the test execution.

- **Data layer:** This layer handles all data management aspects, such as data retrieval, manipulation, and storage. It isolates test data from test logic, allowing teams to manage test data separately from test execution.

- **Configuration layer:** This layer is responsible for managing environment-specific configurations, settings, and dependencies. It allows teams to adjust configurations without affecting the underlying test logic.

Benefits of a layered approach

Implementing a layered architecture in a test automation framework provides several significant benefits, particularly concerning scalability and maintenance:

- **Simplification of design:** Each layer has a distinct responsibility, reducing complexity and improving understandability. When team members can easily identify which layer handles which tasks, it promotes better collaboration and simplifies onboarding for new developers and testers.

- **Faster test maintenance:** Only the relevant layer needs to be modified when changes are required—whether due to new application features, updates to test strategies, or evolving testing requirements. For example, if new test logic is introduced, it can be added to the test logic layer without needing to alter the presentation or data layers. This modularity minimizes the risk of introducing errors during maintenance.

- **Works for organizations at scale:** As applications grow and evolve, the testing framework must adapt accordingly. A layered architecture allows for more effortless scalability, as new features can be introduced into the relevant layer without affecting the overall framework. For instance, if additional business logic needs to be tested, new components can be added to the business logic layer without requiring changes in other layers.

- **Flexibility in testing strategies:** With a layered approach, teams can adopt different testing strategies at different layers. For example, the presentation layer can utilize automated UI testing, while the business logic layer may rely on API testing. This flexibility enables teams to select the most appropriate testing methods for each layer, enhancing the effectiveness of the overall testing strategy.

- **Streamlined integration of new technologies:** Layered architectures facilitate the integration of new technologies and tools. If a new testing framework or tool is introduced, it can be incorporated into the relevant layer without disrupting other layers. This characteristic allows organizations to adopt modern testing practices more easily and stay current with industry trends.

- **Improved test reusability:** Layers that encapsulate specific functionalities can be reused across different tests or projects. For instance, test data and configuration management can be designed once and reused across various test scenarios, improving efficiency and reducing duplication of effort.

- **Simplified debugging and troubleshooting:** When issues arise, a layered architecture allows for more straightforward debugging. Teams can isolate problems within specific layers, making it easier to identify the source of an issue without having to navigate through the entire framework. This capability leads to quicker resolutions and minimizes downtime during test execution.

Scalability in test automation

Scalability in test automation refers to the ability of a testing framework to manage growing test suites effectively, accommodate diverse environments, and support large-scale applications. As applications evolve and the demand for testing increases, the framework must adapt to handle the following:

- **Growing test suites:** As software features expand and become more complex, the number of test cases typically increases. A scalable testing framework can accommodate this growth without degrading performance, ensuring that all tests can be executed efficiently.

- **Diverse environments:** Modern applications often must be tested across multiple environments (for example, different operating systems, browsers, and devices). A scalable framework should support the execution of tests in various environments simultaneously, allowing for comprehensive testing without compromising speed or reliability.

- **Large-scale applications:** Applications with a high number of users or extensive functionalities demand robust testing to ensure quality. A scalable test automation framework must handle extensive testing requirements, integrating smoothly with CI/CD processes to effectively validate functionality, performance, and security.

Techniques for ensuring scalability

To ensure that a test automation framework can scale effectively, several techniques can be implemented:

- **Parallelization:** Running tests in parallel significantly reduces overall execution time. By distributing tests across multiple threads or machines, teams can execute a larger number of tests simultaneously. Parallelization can be implemented at various levels, such as within test cases (executing multiple tests at once) or across test suites (running different suites in parallel). This approach maximizes resource utilization and accelerates feedback loops.

- **Cloud-based testing:** Leveraging cloud-based testing platforms allows teams to scale their testing efforts dynamically. Cloud services provide access to a vast array of testing environments and configurations, enabling teams to run tests in different setups without the need for significant infrastructure investment. This flexibility ensures that teams can quickly adapt to changing testing needs.

- **Distributed execution:** In distributed testing, tests are executed across multiple machines or nodes, allowing for enhanced scalability. This approach can help distribute the workload and speed up execution, particularly for large test suites. Distributed execution can also simultaneously facilitate testing in different environments, increasing the breadth of testing coverage.

- **Test prioritization and selection:** Implementing test prioritization strategies can help optimize test execution. By identifying critical tests that must be run first (for example, smoke tests or tests for frequently modified features), teams can ensure that essential functionality is validated quickly. Test selection techniques, such as only running tests affected by recent changes, can further streamline the process.

- **Modular test design:** Creating a modular test architecture allows for individual test components to be developed and executed independently. This modularity enables teams to execute specific modules based on the current testing requirements, promoting flexibility and scalability.

Ensuring efficient performance under increasing workloads

As the workload increases, ensuring that the test automation framework maintains efficient performance is crucial. Here are some strategies to minimize bottlenecks:

- **Load balancing:** In distributed testing environments, implementing load balancing techniques can help distribute the workload evenly across available resources. By monitoring resource utilization and dynamically allocating tests to different nodes, teams can prevent any single resource from becoming a bottleneck.

- **Resource optimization:** Regularly reviewing and optimizing resource allocation (such as CPU, memory, and network bandwidth) ensures that the framework can handle increasing workloads. This optimization may involve upgrading hardware, enhancing network infrastructure, or optimizing test scripts to reduce resource consumption.

- **Monitoring and analytics:** Implementing monitoring tools and analytics can help identify performance bottlenecks within the testing process. By analyzing test execution times, resource usage, and failure rates, teams can pinpoint areas for improvement and address them proactively.

- **Continuous integration:** Integrating the test automation framework into a CI pipeline allows for continuous testing and immediate feedback. This integration helps distribute the testing workload across multiple stages of development, minimizing the impact of increased testing demands on any single point in the process.

- **Regular refactoring and maintenance:** Regularly reviewing and refactoring the test automation framework is essential for maintaining performance. As tests evolve and the application changes, teams should assess the efficiency of their test cases, remove redundancies, and ensure that the framework remains agile and responsive to new requirements.

Maintainability in test automation

Maintainability refers to the ease with which a test automation framework can be updated, modified, and extended over time. It is a critical aspect of a long-term test automation strategy for several reasons:

- **Adaptation to changes:** As software applications evolve, testing requirements change. A maintainable framework allows teams to adapt quickly to these changes without extensive rework. This adaptability ensures that the testing process remains aligned with the evolving needs of the business.

- **Cost-effectiveness:** Investing in maintainability reduces long-term costs associated with test automation. A well-maintained framework minimizes the time and resources required to fix issues, update tests, and onboard new team members. This efficiency ultimately leads to a higher return on investment.

- **Quality assurance:** A maintainable test automation framework contributes to higher quality in the testing process. Regular maintenance and updates ensure that tests remain relevant and effective, helping to catch defects early and improve the overall quality of the software being developed.

- **Team collaboration:** Maintainability fosters better collaboration among team members. When the framework is easy to navigate and modify, it encourages developers and testers to work together more effectively, leading to improved communication and shared understanding of testing goals.

Best practices for ensuring maintainability

The following practices can enhance the maintainability of a test automation framework, ensuring it remains flexible and clean:

- **Regular refactoring:** Refactoring is the process of restructuring existing code without changing its external behavior. Regularly refactoring the test automation framework helps eliminate technical debt, improve code readability, and enhance performance. By continuously refining the codebase, teams can ensure that the framework remains adaptable to new requirements.

- **Code reviews:** Implementing a code review process encourages collaboration and knowledge sharing among team members. Code reviews help identify potential issues early, promote adherence to coding standards, and facilitate discussions about best practices. This collective scrutiny leads to higher-quality code and a more maintainable framework.

- **Avoiding hard-coded values:** Hard-coded values can make a framework inflexible and challenging to maintain. Instead, teams should use configuration files or environment variables to manage settings and parameters. This approach allows for easier updates and changes without modifying the core code, enhancing the framework's maintainability.

- **Modular design:** Designing the test automation framework with modularity in mind ensures that components can be added, modified, or removed independently. This modular approach simplifies maintenance, as changes in one module do not impact others, allowing teams to focus on specific areas without disrupting the entire framework.

- **Documentation:** Comprehensive documentation is essential for maintainability. Clear and up-to-date documentation helps team members understand the framework's structure, functionality, and best practices. It serves as a valuable resource for onboarding new team members and aids in maintaining the framework over time.

Adopting clean code practices

Adopting clean code practices is fundamental to ensuring the test automation framework remains maintainable and accessible for new team members. Here is how clean code practices contribute to maintainability:

- **Readability:** Clean code is easy to read and understand. By following naming conventions, using meaningful variable names, and writing self-explanatory code, teams can enhance the readability of the framework. This clarity helps new team members quickly grasp the code structure and logic, making it easier for them to contribute.

- **Consistent structure:** Clean code practices promote a consistent structure throughout the codebase. This consistency reduces team members' cognitive load, allowing them to navigate the framework with confidence. When the framework follows a uniform structure, locating and modifying specific components is easier.

- **Modularity and simplicity:** Clean code emphasizes modularity and simplicity, making it easier to isolate and fix issues. Teams can simplify maintenance efforts by breaking complex logic into smaller, manageable functions or modules. This approach allows for more straightforward testing and debugging, essential for keeping the framework in good working order.

- **Encouraging contribution:** A clean and well-structured codebase lowers the barrier to entry for new team members. When code is organized, well-documented, and easy to understand, it encourages developers and testers to contribute ideas, make enhancements, and address issues. This collaborative spirit ultimately strengthens the framework and the testing process as a whole.

Extensibility in test automation frameworks

Extensibility refers to the ability of a test automation framework to accommodate new features, technologies, or testing tools without significant rework. Designing with future enhancements in mind is crucial for several reasons:

- **Adaptation to evolving needs:** Software development practices and technologies are constantly evolving. A well-architected framework can seamlessly integrate new tools and methodologies as they emerge, ensuring that the testing process remains effective and relevant.

- **Reduced rework:** By anticipating future requirements and designing the framework to be extensible, teams can avoid extensive rework when new features or technologies are introduced. This foresight reduces the time and effort required to adapt the framework, making it easier to keep pace with changes.

- **Maximizing return on investment:** An extensible framework maximizes the return on investment by allowing organizations to leverage their existing test automation efforts while incorporating new technologies. This capability ensures that the initial investment in the framework continues to pay dividends as testing needs grow and evolve.

Strategies for enabling extensibility

To create a test automation framework that is truly extensible, the following strategies can be employed:

- **Plugin architecture:** Implementing a plugin architecture allows for modular enhancements. In this approach, core functionalities of the framework are separated from additional features that can be added as plugins. This structure enables teams to introduce new capabilities without modifying the core framework, promoting flexibility and ease of integration.

- **Abstracting tool-specific features:** To accommodate different testing tools or technologies, it is beneficial to abstract tool-specific features behind standard interfaces or abstractions. This way, teams can switch between tools or add new ones without significant disruption to the test suite. For example, instead of hard-coding interactions with a specific tool, the framework could define a standard interface for actions like clicking, typing, or asserting, allowing for easy tool replacement.

- **Configuration-driven design:** Using configuration files or settings to manage tool-specific parameters and options allows easy adaptation without code changes. By externalizing configurations, teams can adjust the framework's behavior to accommodate new tools or features simply by modifying configuration settings.

- **Use of dependency injection:** Implementing dependency injection facilitates the integration of new components and technologies. By decoupling dependencies from the code, teams can swap out implementations or introduce new services without altering the existing codebase, enhancing the framework's extensibility.

- **Documentation and guidelines:** It is essential to provide clear documentation and guidelines for extending the framework. This documentation should outline the best practices for developing plugins, contributing new features, or integrating new tools, helping maintain consistency and clarity as the framework evolves.

Balancing flexibility and complexity

While extensibility is essential, balancing flexibility and complexity when designing a test automation framework is equally important. Here are some considerations:

- **Simplicity vs. extensibility:** Extensible designs can sometimes introduce complexity, making the framework harder to understand and maintain. Teams should prioritize simplicity in the core framework while ensuring that extension points are clear and straightforward. Striking this balance can enhance usability without sacrificing extensibility.

- **Clear extension points:** Clearly defined extension points enable developers to understand where and how to extend the framework without delving into its internals. These extension points should be well-documented and intuitive, allowing for straightforward enhancements without overwhelming users with unnecessary complexity.

- **Minimizing overhead:** A framework that is too flexible may become cumbersome, introducing unnecessary overhead in terms of configuration or implementation. Teams should carefully evaluate which features genuinely need to be extensible and streamline those that do not to avoid creating a bloated architecture.

- **Incremental enhancements:** Instead of attempting to design a perfectly extensible framework from the start, teams can adopt an incremental approach to enhancements. By gradually introducing extensibility features as needs arise, teams can avoid premature complexity and ensure that the framework evolves in line with actual requirements.

- **Feedback and iteration:** Regularly gathering feedback from users of the framework can provide insights into how well it meets the needs for extensibility and usability. This feedback loop allows for continuous improvement, ensuring that the framework remains both flexible and manageable as it evolves.

Architectural patterns and their relevance to test automation

Let us now learn more about the architectural patterns and their relevance to test automation.

Factory pattern in test automation

The factory pattern is a creational design pattern that provides an interface for creating objects without specifying the exact class of the object that will be made. In the context of test automation, this pattern can be particularly useful for instantiating various types of test cases or generating test data dynamically.

There are several variations of the factory pattern, including the Simple Factory, Factory Method, and Abstract Factory. Each encapsulates object creation logic, allowing for more flexible and maintainable code.

Using the factory pattern in test automation

In test automation, the factory pattern can be utilized to instantiate different types of test cases or test data, allowing for greater flexibility and scalability. Here is how it can be implemented:

- **Test case creation:** By defining a factory class (or method) responsible for creating test case instances, teams can streamline the process of instantiating various types of tests. For example, a factory method can take parameters indicating the type of test to be created (for example, unit test, integration test, or UI test) and return the appropriate test case object. This approach decouples the test case creation logic from the test execution, promoting cleaner code.

- **Dynamic test data generation:** The factory pattern can also be applied to generate different sets of test data. By creating a data factory that can instantiate various data objects based on specific requirements (such as data types, structures, or input conditions), teams can ensure that their tests receive consistent and relevant data without hard-coding values.

- **Support for parameterized tests:** Using a factory method to generate parameterized tests can simplify the creation of test cases that require varying inputs. The factory can generate different test instances with specific parameters, enabling comprehensive testing of functions with multiple input scenarios.

Benefits of using factory methods

Implementing the factory pattern in a test automation framework provides several key benefits:

- **Consistency across test suites:** Factory methods ensure that test instances are created in a uniform manner, promoting consistency across different test suites. By centralizing the instantiation logic, teams can enforce specific creation rules and maintain a standard approach to test case creation.

- **Enhanced maintainability:** When test cases or test data are created through factory methods, it becomes easier to manage and modify the creation process. Changes to instantiation logic can be made in one location (the factory), reducing the risk of errors and simplifying maintenance efforts.

- **Decoupled design:** The factory pattern decouples test creation from the test execution logic, making modifying or extending either component easier without affecting the other. This separation of concerns leads to a more modular and maintainable codebase.

- **Increased flexibility:** The ability to create different types of test cases or data on demand allows teams to adapt their testing strategies more efficiently. For instance, if new testing requirements arise or if a new testing tool is introduced, the factory can be updated to accommodate these changes without requiring significant rework of existing tests.

- **Improved readability:** Factory methods encapsulate the object creation process, making the code more readable. The intent behind creating test cases or data is clearer, making it easier for team members to understand and work with the test framework.

- **Simplified expansion:** As testing needs evolve, teams can add new types of tests or data generation logic by simply extending the factory. This extensibility allows for the smooth integration of new functionalities without disrupting the existing framework.

Observer pattern in test automation

The Observer pattern is a behavioral design pattern that allows an object (called the subject) to notify a list of dependent objects (called Observers) when its state changes. In test automation, this pattern is particularly useful for triggering actions like logging, notifications, or reporting when certain events occur during test execution.

Its core elements are:

- **Subject:** The object observed for changes or events (for example, a test execution manager or a specific test case).

- **Observer:** The object that reacts to changes in the subject (for example, logging services, reporting tools, or notification systems).

Applying the Observer pattern to test automation

In the context of test automation, the Observer pattern can be applied to perform various actions in response to test events, such as test start, test completion, test failure, or test step execution. Here is how the pattern can be utilized effectively:

- **Logging events**: Observers can be attached to key points in the test automation framework, such as the start or end of a test case, and log important details (for example, test name, execution time, outcome). This decouples logging logic from the actual test execution code and allows for flexibility in logging implementation.

- **Real-time notifications:** When certain test conditions or failures occur, Observers can trigger notifications (for example, email, Slack, or SMS alerts). This is particularly useful for critical systems where stakeholders must be informed immediately if tests fail, allowing for quick resolution of issues.

- **Real-time reporting:** The Observer pattern can be used to implement real-time reporting, where results are updated dynamically during test execution. Each time a test is completed or a milestone is reached, an Observer could update a dashboard or report, providing continuous visibility into the testing progress.

Examples of integrating real-time reporting or error logging

Here is an example of **real-time error logging**. In a testing framework, you could have an Observer that listens for test failures. Whenever a failure occurs, the Observer triggers a logging mechanism that captures details such as the test case name, error message, and stack trace. This log could then be saved to a file, database, or monitoring tool for further analysis.

The following code examples are all written in Python:

```python
class TestObserver:
    def __init__(self, test_manager):
        self.test_manager = test_manager
        self.test_manager.register_Observer(self)

    def notify(self, event):
        if event == "test_failed":
            self.log_failure()
```

```
    def log_failure(self):
        # Logic for logging test failure
        print("Test failed. Logging details...")

class TestManager:
    def __init__(self):
        self.Observers = []

    def register_Observer(self, Observer):
        self.Observers.append(Observer)

    def notify_Observers(self, event):
        for Observer in self.Observers:
            Observer.notify(event)

    def execute_test(self):
        # Test execution logic
        # If test fails:
        self.notify_Observers("test_failed")
```

In this example, the **TestObserver** class is notified whenever a test fails, triggering the logging process.

Now, let us have an example of **real-time reporting**. Imagine a scenario where you want to display real-time test progress on a dashboard. You could have an Observer that listens for events such as test completion, test success, or test failure. Each time a test completes, the Observer could send data to update a web-based dashboard with the latest test results. Look at the following code:

```
class DashboardObserver:
    def __init__(self, test_manager):
        self.test_manager = test_manager
        self.test_manager.register_Observer(self)

    def notify(self, event, test_data):
        if event == "test_completed":
            self.update_dashboard(test_data)

    def update_dashboard(self, test_data):
        # Logic to update a dashboard with test data
        print(f"Updating dashboard with: {test_data}")

class TestManager:
    def __init__(self):
        self.Observers = []

    def register_Observer(self, Observer):
        self.Observers.append(Observer)

    def notify_Observers(self, event, test_data):
        for Observer in self.Observers:
```

```
        Observer.notify(event, test_data)

def execute_test(self, test_data):
    # Test execution logic
    self.notify_Observers("test_completed", test_data)
```

Here, the **DashboardObserver** listens for **"test_completed"** events and updates a dashboard with the relevant test data, providing a real-time view of the testing process.

Benefits of using the Observer pattern in test automation

The benefits of using the Observer pattern are as follows:

- **Decoupling of concerns:** By using the Observer pattern, the logic for test execution is separated from the logic for logging, notifications, or reporting. This separation makes the test framework more straightforward to maintain and extend, as changes to logging or reporting do not affect the core test execution code.

- **Real-time reactions to test events:** The Observer pattern allows the framework to react in real-time to specific test events, providing immediate feedback to the development and testing teams. This can help in detecting issues early and taking corrective actions promptly.

- **Scalability:** As the test automation framework grows, additional Observers can be easily added to handle new types of events or integrate with other tools. This makes it easy to extend the framework without introducing significant complexity.

- **Customization:** Observers can be customized to handle different types of events and actions. For example, some Observers might handle logging for successful tests, while others focus on error logging or sending notifications for critical failures.

Strategy pattern in test automation

The strategy pattern is a behavioral design pattern that enables selecting different algorithms or strategies at runtime, depending on the situation. It defines a family of algorithms or approaches and allows the system to choose the appropriate one without altering the underlying system's structure.

In test automation, the strategy pattern can be effectively used to implement different test execution strategies, such as local execution, remote execution, or cloud-based testing. This allows the framework to dynamically adjust its behavior based on infrastructure, test requirements, or environmental constraints.

Using the strategy pattern to define test execution approaches

By applying the strategy pattern, you can define different strategies for how tests are executed, allowing for flexibility and easy integration with various infrastructures. Here is how the pattern works in practice for test execution:

- **Local execution strategy:** The framework may define a local execution strategy where tests run on the same machine or environment where they are developed. This is ideal for quick feedback during development, unit tests, or when the full system resources are available on the local machine.

- **Remote execution strategy:** In some cases, tests need to run on a remote server or a distributed environment. A remote execution strategy defines how to execute tests on remote machines, perhaps via SSH, Docker containers, or through specific test execution services like Selenium Grid.

- **Cloud-based execution strategy:** As cloud computing has grown in popularity, cloud-based test execution is becoming more prevalent. The cloud execution strategy involves running tests on cloud infrastructure, such as AWS, Azure, or services like BrowserStack or Sauce Labs. This approach is useful for scaling tests or testing across multiple browsers and platforms.

Each of these strategies can be encapsulated within a class that implements a common interface, allowing the system to switch between them depending on the execution context.

Working of strategy pattern in test automation

The strategy pattern allows for dynamic selection of the appropriate test execution strategy. The following is an example of how the pattern could be applied:

- **Strategy interface:** The interface defines a common method for executing tests, regardless of the underlying infrastructure.

  The following code samples are all written in python:

  ```python
  class ExecutionStrategy:
      def execute(self, test_suite):
          pass
  ```

- **Local execution strategy:** Implements the logic for running tests locally.

  ```python
  class LocalExecutionStrategy(ExecutionStrategy):
      def execute(self, test_suite):
          print("Running tests locally...")
          # Logic for executing tests on the local machine
  ```

- **Remote execution strategy:** Implements the logic for running tests on a remote server or distributed environment.

  ```python
  class RemoteExecutionStrategy(ExecutionStrategy):
      def execute(self, test_suite):
          print("Running tests remotely...")
          # Logic for connecting to and executing tests on remote infrastructure
  ```

- **Cloud-based execution strategy:** Implements the logic for running tests on a cloud service or platform.

  ```python
  class CloudExecutionStrategy(ExecutionStrategy):
      def execute(self, test_suite):
          print("Running tests in the cloud...")
          # Logic for running tests on a cloud-based platform
  ```

- **Context:** The context class holds a reference to a strategy and delegates the execution to it.

  ```python
  class TestExecutor:
      def __init__(self, strategy: ExecutionStrategy):
          self.strategy = strategy

      def set_strategy(self, strategy: ExecutionStrategy):
          self.strategy = strategy

      def run_tests(self, test_suite):
          self.strategy.execute(test_suite)
  ```

- **Usage:** The test framework can select a strategy at runtime, allowing for flexible test execution paths based on infrastructure or test requirements.

  ```python
  test_executor = TestExecutor(LocalExecutionStrategy())
  test_executor.run_tests("Suite 1")  # Running locally

  test_executor.set_strategy(CloudExecutionStrategy())
  test_executor.run_tests("Suite 1")  # Running in the cloud
  ```

Benefits of using the strategy pattern

The strategy pattern provides the following benefits when applied to test automation frameworks:

- **Flexibility in execution:** The strategy pattern allows for flexible test execution based on the current requirements and available infrastructure. Whether tests need to be run locally during development or scaled up for cloud-based execution, the appropriate strategy can be chosen dynamically without modifying the core test code.

- **Separation of concerns:** By separating the logic for different execution methods into individual strategy classes, the framework becomes more modular. Each strategy is responsible for handling its specific execution logic, making it easier to maintain and extend the framework over time.

- **Easily extensible:** Adding a new execution strategy (for example, container-based execution, mobile testing) becomes simple with the strategy pattern. Developers can create a new class that implements the execution interface, without affecting the other strategies or the framework's core logic.

- **Dynamic adaptation:** The test framework can dynamically switch between different execution strategies at runtime based on environmental factors, test load, or infrastructure availability. This allows for optimal resource use and ensures that tests are executed efficiently.

Real-world example of the strategy pattern in test automation

Imagine a test automation framework that needs to support three different execution methods: local (for unit tests), remote (for integration tests), and cloud-based (for performance and cross-browser tests). By applying the strategy pattern, you can switch between these methods based on the type of test being executed or based on specific test configurations:

- **Local strategy:** Ideal for running unit tests quickly on a developer's machine.

- **Remote strategy:** Useful for testing backend services or API integrations by spinning up remote servers or containers.

- **Cloud-based strategy:** Suitable for scaling tests, running cross-browser tests, or executing performance tests on virtual machines hosted in the cloud.

Additional considerations

Here are a couple of things to consider:

- **Configuration-driven strategy selection:** Test execution strategies can be selected dynamically based on configuration files or environment settings. For example, CI/CD pipelines can configure the appropriate strategy based on the environment in which the tests are running (for example, use local for development, cloud for production).

- **Integration with existing tools:** The strategy pattern can easily integrate with existing tools such as Selenium Grid for remote execution or services like BrowserStack for cloud-based testing. Each of these tools could represent a distinct strategy in the framework, allowing teams to leverage different platforms as needed.

Decorator pattern in test automation

The decorator pattern is a structural design pattern that allows for dynamically adding behavior to an object without altering its original structure or affecting other objects of the same class. It provides a flexible alternative to subclassing for extending functionality.

In test automation, the decorator pattern can be applied to enhance test scripts or test cases by wrapping them with additional functionality, such as logging, adding preconditions or postconditions, or even dynamically changing the way tests are executed, without modifying the core test case logic.

Applying the decorator pattern to test automation

The primary advantage of using the decorator pattern in test automation is that it allows you to add features or behaviors incrementally, keeping the base test case simple and focused on its core logic. Additional behaviors can be wrapped around the test case as needed.

Some common use cases for the decorator pattern in test automation include:

- **Adding preconditions and postconditions:** You may want to ensure that certain conditions are met before a test starts or after it finishes. For example, setting up a database state before executing a test or cleaning up resources after a test completes.

- **Enhancing logging:** Test automation frameworks often require detailed logging, either for debugging or for providing real-time insights into test execution. The decorator pattern can add logging behavior around existing test cases without modifying the actual test logic.

- **Handling dynamic behavior:** Sometimes, tests need to dynamically adapt based on runtime conditions, such as retrying a failed test case or adding additional validation steps.

Example of the decorator pattern in test automation

Here is a practical example of how to apply the decorator pattern to enhance test cases by adding preconditions, postconditions, and logging.

The following code samples are all written in Python:

- **Base test case:** The core test case that contains the main test logic.

```python
class TestCase:
def execute(self):
print("Executing core test case logic.")
```

- **Abstract decorator class:** The base decorator class implements the same interface as the core test case and is responsible for wrapping the test case.

```python
class TestDecorator(TestCase):
def __init__(self, test_case):
self.test_case = test_case

def execute(self):
self.test_case.execute()
```

- **Precondition decorator:** This decorator adds preconditions to the test case, ensuring certain conditions are met before the test runs.

```python
class PreconditionDecorator(TestDecorator):
def execute(self):
self.setup_preconditions()
super().execute()

def setup_preconditions(self):
print("Setting up preconditions...")
```

- **Postcondition decorator:** This decorator adds postconditions, such as cleaning up resources or validating certain states after the test finishes.

```python
class PostconditionDecorator(TestDecorator):
def execute(self):
super().execute()
```

```
        self.teardown_postconditions()

    def teardown_postconditions(self):
        print("Cleaning up postconditions...")
```

- **Logging decorator:** This decorator adds logging around the test execution to track when a test starts and finishes.

```
class LoggingDecorator(TestDecorator):
    def execute(self):
        self.log_start()
        super().execute()
        self.log_end()

    def log_start(self):
        print("Starting test execution...")

    def log_end(self):
        print("Test execution completed.")
```

- **Usage:** Now we can dynamically apply these decorators to a test case without modifying the test's core structure.

```
# Create a basic test case
test_case = TestCase()

# Wrap it with logging, preconditions, and postconditions using decorators
test_with_logging = LoggingDecorator(test_case)
test_with_preconditions = PreconditionDecorator(test_with_logging)
test_with_postconditions = PostconditionDecorator(test_with_preconditions)

# Execute the decorated test
test_with_postconditions.execute()
```

In this example, when the decorated test case is executed, the following bash script output is produced:

```
Starting test execution...
Setting up preconditions...
Executing core test case logic.
Cleaning up postconditions...
Test execution completed.
```

As shown, the decorator pattern allows the addition of logging, preconditions, and postconditions around the core test execution without modifying the core test case's logic. This keeps the test case clean and focused while providing additional behavior flexibility.

Benefits of using the decorator pattern in test automation

The benefits are as follows:

- **Separation of concerns:** The decorator pattern allows for clean separation between the core test logic and additional behavior, such as logging or setup/teardown actions. This improves code maintainability and readability.

- **Reusability:** By using decorators, you can create reusable behaviors that can be applied to multiple test cases. For example, you can have a single logging decorator that can be applied to any test case without rewriting logging logic.

- **Extensibility:** The decorator pattern allows new behaviors to be added easily by creating new decorators, without altering existing test cases or decorators. This makes it easy to extend the framework as new requirements arise.

- **Flexible composition:** You can stack multiple decorators together to create different combinations of behaviors for a test case. For instance, some test cases may only need logging, while others might need logging, preconditions, and postconditions.

Real-world application of the decorator pattern in test automation

Imagine a large-scale automation framework where tests are run in various environments, require different levels of logging, and may need unique setup and teardown conditions. Instead of writing all this logic inside each test, decorators can be applied:

- **Retry decorator:** Adds retry logic in case of intermittent test failures.

- **Authorization decorator:** Ensures valid authentication tokens are acquired before tests that interact with secured APIs.

- **Environment setup decorator:** Prepares specific environment configurations required for certain tests, like database setup, external API stubbing, and so on.

Each of these decorators can be independently developed and applied to the appropriate test cases, making the overall framework more modular, flexible, and scalable.

Conclusion

Incorporating architectural patterns, such as decorator, factory, Observer, and strategy enhances the adaptability of test automation frameworks. These patterns allow for dynamic behavior changes, feature additions, and infrastructure integrations without altering the core structure. For instance, the decorator pattern enables the addition of responsibilities to objects dynamically, while the factory pattern provides a way to create objects without specifying their exact class, promoting flexibility and extensibility. Adopting architectural principles like separation of concerns, modularity, loose coupling, and high cohesion is crucial in building robust, scalable, and maintainable test automation frameworks. These principles ensure that the framework remains adaptable, making it easier to meet evolving business needs and technological advancements. By thoughtfully applying these patterns and principles, teams can design test automation frameworks that are not only effective in the short term but also resilient and adaptable in the face of future challenges.

In the next chapter, we take the architectural principles we learned in this chapter and apply them to building modular testing frameworks.

Key takeaways

Principled architectural design is critical to the design of test automation frameworks—the importance of which is detailed as follows:

- **Scalability:** Through well-architected frameworks, it becomes easier to handle large-scale applications, diverse environments, and expanding test suites. Techniques such as parallelization, cloud-based testing, and distributed execution enable the framework to scale while maintaining performance.

- **Maintainability:** A clear separation between test logic, data, and configurations leads to maintainable systems. Practices like regular refactoring, clean code principles, and code reviews ensure the framework remains flexible and easy to update, reducing technical debt over time.

- **Extensibility:** Designing with future requirements in mind allows frameworks to accommodate new technologies, tools, and testing methodologies. By using patterns like plugins or abstraction layers, frameworks can evolve without becoming overly complex.

Exercises

1. How well does your test automation framework align with the modularity of the application architecture?

2. Can your test automation framework scale alongside application growth and infrastructure changes?

3. Do the chosen test automation tools in your organization integrate seamlessly with the tech stack and architectural patterns?

4. Does the test automation design support long-term maintainability and adaptability to architectural changes?

5. How does test automation address cross-cutting concerns like security, logging, and observability?

6. Does the test automation strategy align with the deployment model (cloud, microservices, on-prem)?

7. Is the test automation framework optimized for distributed or parallel execution in CI/CD?

8. Does test automation validate system resilience and failure scenarios based on architectural design?

Join our Discord space

Join our Discord workspace for latest updates, offers, tech happenings around the world, new releases, and sessions with the authors:

https://discord.bpbonline.com

## CHAPTER 4

Designing Modular Test Frameworks

Introduction

In the previous chapter, we looked at the importance of architectural principles in good framework design. One of those key principles is modularity, which we will now unpack even further in this chapter. Although we will repeat some aspects of it from the previous chapter, we will explore the topic in even more detail now.

A modular test framework is a structured approach to test automation that divides the testing process into smaller, independent, reusable units called modules. Each module encapsulates a specific part of the application's functionality and is designed to be executed independently. These modules are then assembled in different combinations to create end-to-end test cases. The framework emphasizes separation of concerns, ensuring that each test module is responsible for a specific function or task, improving code organization, readability, and reusability.

The goal of modularity in test automation is to reduce code duplication, make test maintenance easier, and ensure that changes in one part of the system do not affect others. Modularity also helps to improve collaboration among teams, as different team members can work on different modules independently.

Structure

In this chapter, we will go over the following topics:

- Importance of modularity for maintainability and scalability
- Separating test logic, test data, and configurations
- Implementing reusable components
- Page Object Model
- Test hooks and setup/teardown components
- Custom assertion libraries
- Best practices for building modular frameworks

Objectives

By the end of this chapter, the readers will know the importance of modularity to automation framework design and how it enhances the testing process. Similarly, the readers will learn how to apply different principles of software architecture to design a test automation framework that allows for modularity in execution across different application areas.

Importance of modularity for maintainability and scalability

When it comes to maintainability, we have to understand that as applications evolve, many test scripts need to be updated to reflect changes. A modular test framework allows for easier updates since changes to a specific feature only require updates in the corresponding module, rather than modifying the entire test suite. This reduces the time spent maintaining tests and minimizes the risk of introducing errors.

On the other hand, when it comes to scalability, it is essential to remember that as the application grows, so does the number of test cases. A modular approach allows for efficient scaling by enabling the reuse of existing modules in new test cases. Instead of creating entirely new test scripts for every new feature, existing modules can be combined and extended, making it easier to scale the test suite to accommodate the evolving application.

Modularity helps to manage the complexity of large test suites by breaking them down into smaller, more manageable components. Each module is focused on a single task, making it easier to understand, update, and test.

Benefits of modular test frameworks

Here is a list of the key benefits modular test frameworks will offer:

- **Flexibility**: A modular test framework allows for greater flexibility in the design and execution of tests. Since modules are independent, test cases can be created by combining different modules, allowing teams to adapt their test suites to various testing needs without duplicating efforts. This flexibility also allows for easier modifications in test logic or the addition of new test scenarios.

- **Adaptability**: Modularity supports the quick adaptation of the test framework to new features or changes in the application. Instead of rewriting or duplicating test scripts, teams can update or create new modules that integrate seamlessly with existing ones. This ensures that the test framework evolves along with the application without becoming outdated or difficult to manage.

- **Ease of updating**: Since each module focuses on a specific functionality, updates to the test framework can be made in isolation. This localized updating minimizes the risk of breaking other parts of the test suite and makes it easier to maintain consistency. Teams can respond to changes in the application's functionality quickly, without affecting the overall structure of the test suite.

A modular test framework is essential for building scalable, maintainable, and flexible test automation strategies. Its modular nature enables teams to efficiently manage large test suites, reduce redundancy, and ensure that their test automation remains agile in the face of changing application requirements.

Importance of modularity

Modularity plays a crucial role in the design and success of test automation frameworks. It provides a structured way to organize test scripts, which is vital for reducing redundancy, promoting code reuse, and enabling faster test case development. This structured approach also aligns well with the core principles of software architecture, ensuring that test automation frameworks are robust, maintainable, and scalable. Now let us go over these aspects in detail:

Reduction of redundancy

In traditional and monolithic test automation frameworks, test cases often include repetitive code, especially when multiple test scripts perform similar actions such as logging in, navigating through menus, or submitting forms. This redundancy can lead to bloated codebases, making the test suite difficult to maintain and prone to errors.

Modular frameworks eliminate this problem by breaking these common actions into reusable modules. For instance, instead of writing a login procedure in multiple test scripts, the login logic is abstracted into a single module that can be reused in any test case. This reduces code duplication, ensures consistency, and cuts down on maintenance efforts. When changes are needed, they can be made in the specific module without affecting the entire test suite, making the development and updating of test cases faster and more efficient.

Faster development of test cases

Modular frameworks enable the rapid development of new test cases by allowing testers to reuse existing modules rather than building tests from scratch. This means that a new test case can be constructed by simply combining pre-existing modules in different ways, without having to rewrite common test steps. This modular structure accelerates the process of creating new tests, as the foundation is already laid out.

As a result, teams can respond quickly to new feature development or bug fixes, ensuring that the test coverage keeps pace with the application's growth. Additionally, because each module is independently tested and validated, confidence in the stability of these reusable components grows over time, which further enhances development speed.

Alignment with the principles of software architecture

We discussed many software architectural principles in the previous chapter, so we will not go into detail again about them here. The following is a modular approach in framework design that will align to see how it can be applied and benefit the system under test and overall delivery process:

- Separation of concerns
- Reusability
- Scalability and maintainability
- Encapsulation
- Testability and reliability

Modularity is key to creating efficient and scalable test automation frameworks. It reduces redundancy by promoting code reuse and modular design, which significantly accelerates the development of new test cases. Additionally, modular frameworks embody core software architecture principles such as separation of concerns, reusability, encapsulation, scalability, and maintainability. These principles ensure that the test framework not only meets current testing needs but also remains adaptable and reliable as the application evolves over time.

Separating test logic, test data, and configurations

Now let us learn more about test logic, test data, and configurations.

Test logic separation

Test logic separation is the practice of isolating the actual test scenarios from the underlying components and infrastructure in a test automation framework. By decoupling the test logic from elements like data, environment configurations, and system actions, the framework becomes more flexible, maintainable, and adaptable to application or testing requirements. This separation ensures that the focus remains on validating the behavior of the **application under test** (**AUT**), without being entangled with implementation details.

The importance of isolating test logic from other components is as follows:

- **Maintainability:** When test logic is tightly coupled with other components such as data, UI elements, or configurations, even minor changes in the application can require significant updates across multiple test scripts. Isolating test logic ensures that changes in one part of the system do not have ripple effects, making it easier to update, maintain, and extend the test suite.

- **Reusability:** Isolated test logic promotes the reuse of components across different test scenarios. For example, common actions such as logging into an application or navigating through a menu can be abstracted away into reusable functions or modules. By keeping the test logic focused only on validating specific behaviors, these reusable components can be called wherever necessary, reducing duplication and promoting efficiency.

- **Test stability:** Tight coupling between test logic and application details often leads to brittle tests, meaning that they are prone to breaking when the application undergoes changes (for example, UI updates, new database configurations). Isolating the test logic ensures that changes in non-test-related components, such as UI layouts or underlying infrastructure, do not unnecessarily break tests.

- **Improved collaboration:** Separation of concerns allows different teams or team members to work in parallel. Developers can focus on implementing application logic, while QA engineers can concentrate on designing and executing tests. By isolating the test logic from other parts of the system, it also becomes easier for non-developers to contribute to test case creation, particularly in cases where domain-specific knowledge is more important than technical implementation details.

Structuring test scripts to focus on test scenarios and expected behavior

To maintain clarity and focus on the purpose of testing, that is, validating application behavior, it is essential to structure test scripts so that they only address test scenarios and expected outcomes. This can be achieved by following the given best practices in test organization and separation:

- **Use of abstraction layers:** Implement an abstraction layer, such as a **Page Object Model** (**POM**) for UI testing or a service layer for API testing. These layers encapsulate the interaction logic with the AUT (for example, button clicks, API calls), and the test scripts themselves focus solely on asserting expected behavior. This separation ensures that test cases are not cluttered with low-level interaction details, making the logic more readable and easier to maintain.

- **Data-driven testing:** As mentioned in the previous chapter, avoid hardcoding test data directly into the test logic. Instead, externalize the data by storing it in separate files (for example, **comma-separated values** (**CSV**), **JavaScript Object Notation** (**JSON**), databases, or configuration files). This ensures that test scripts are flexible and can be executed with varying input values without modifying the underlying logic. Data-driven testing allows for greater coverage and ease of updating as new test data or scenarios arise.

- **Clear naming and structure:** Test scripts should have clear and descriptive names that reflect the behavior being tested. Organize tests in a hierarchical or modular fashion, grouping them by functionality or feature. This helps ensure that the test suite remains organized and that test cases are easy to identify and maintain.

- **Use of assertions:** Test scripts should focus primarily on making assertions about the expected outcomes. Assertions verify that the system behaves as expected under various conditions and should be placed strategically to test the key outcomes of the scenario. This keeps the test logic aligned with its core purpose: ensuring the application meets its expected behavior.

Avoiding hard-coded dependencies within test logic

Hard-coded dependencies in test logic, such as directly referencing UI elements, specific database states, or fixed environment configurations, can lead to rigid, brittle tests that are difficult to maintain. To avoid this, follow these principles:

- **Parameterization:** Instead of hardcoding values into test scripts (for example, URLs, credentials, file paths), use parameterization to inject these values at runtime. This can be achieved by using environmental variables, configuration files, or external data sources. Parameterization ensures that the same test logic can be reused across different environments (for example, development, staging, production) and with different data sets, without modification.

- **Separation of data from logic:** As mentioned earlier, externalize all test data. Test logic should only reference variables or parameters passed from external sources, allowing it to remain agnostic of the specific data it is testing. This promotes flexibility and reduces the risk of tests becoming outdated as application data evolves.

- **Avoid direct interaction with UI elements:** In UI testing, using hard-coded selectors (like XPath or CSS selectors) directly within test scripts makes the tests fragile. If the UI changes (for example, an element is moved, renamed, or restyled), the test will break. Instead, use abstraction techniques like the POM to encapsulate interactions with UI elements, making the test logic more stable and easier to maintain.

- **Mocking and stubbing external dependencies:** If the test scenario involves external services (for example, third-party APIs, databases), avoid direct reliance on these services in your test logic. Use mocking or stubbing to simulate the behavior of external systems. This not only makes the tests run faster and more reliably but also ensures that failures in external services do not affect your test suite.

Test logic separation is fundamental to creating a robust, maintainable, and scalable test automation framework. By isolating the test logic from other components, such as UI elements, data, and configurations, and focusing scripts solely on expected behaviors, the framework becomes more adaptable to change and easier to maintain. Avoiding hard-coded dependencies through parameterization, data-driven testing, and abstraction layers ensures that test scripts are resilient and flexible. This approach results in a more stable test suite aligned with software engineering best practices.

Test data separation

Test data separation refers to externalizing the data used in test automation from the test scripts themselves. Decoupling data from test logic ensures that test cases can be run with varying inputs without modifying the underlying code. This makes the test suite more flexible, maintainable, and scalable, allowing teams to test multiple scenarios and environments efficiently.

Now, let us learn more about eternalizing test data from test scripts to ensure flexibility:

- **Use of external data files:** Externalizing test data involves storing test inputs and expected outputs in separate files, such as CSV, JSON, or Excel files. The test scripts are then designed to be read from these files at runtime. This approach allows you to easily swap out data for different test cases without touching the test logic, increasing the flexibility of your tests.

- **Configuration files:** For environment-specific values (for example, URLs, credentials, or API keys), configuration files such as **Yet Another Markup Language** (**YAML**), JSON, or INI files can be used. These files allow different environment configurations to be passed into the test scripts, enabling the same test logic to be run across multiple environments (development, staging, production) by simply changing the configuration file used.

- **Environment variables:** You can leverage environment variables to pass dynamic values into your test scripts. This is particularly useful for **continuous integration and continuous deployment** (**CI/**

CD) pipelines, where different environments (for example, test, pre-production) may require different data or configurations. Using environment variables ensures that the test scripts remain flexible and adaptable without hardcoding specific values.

- **Test data management (TDM) tools:** In larger or more complex test environments, specialized TDM tools can be used to manage the creation, storage, and versioning of test data. These tools allow teams to generate test data dynamically, store it centrally, and retrieve it as needed by test scripts.

Techniques for managing test data through data-driven testing

Data-driven testing is a technique where the test data is stored separately from the test logic, and the test cases are executed with different sets of input data. This allows for greater test coverage by running the same test logic with a variety of data sets. Here are some common techniques for managing test data in a data-driven testing framework:

- **Using CSV files:** CSV files are a simple and widely supported format for storing test data. Each row in the CSV file represents a different test case, and columns represent different parameters. During execution, the test script reads the CSV file and runs the test logic for each row of data, applying the corresponding inputs.

    o **When to use:**

      - For simple, structured test data that does not require hierarchical relationships.
      - When working with legacy systems or tools that easily support CSV files.
      - When test data needs to be manually created, reviewed, or edited in a spreadsheet.

    o **Why use it:**

      - Easy to read and edit in spreadsheet applications (for example, Excel, Google Sheets).
      - Lightweight and widely supported across various testing tools.
      - Suitable for parameterized tests with flat data structures (for example, login credentials, form inputs).

    o **Limitations:**

      - Lacks support for nested or hierarchical data (such as, JSON-like structures).
      - Not ideal for complex test data requiring relationships or dynamic updates.

- **Using JSON files:** JSON is a structured format that allows for hierarchical or complex test data. JSON is particularly useful when your test data includes nested or multi-level information, such as APIs that accept payloads with multiple layers. Here is an example JSON structure for API tests:

```
[
  {
    "username": "user1",
    "password": "pass123",
    "expectedOutcome": "success"
  },
  {
    "username": "user2",
    "password": "wrongpass",
    "expectedOutcome": "failure"
  }
]
```

- o **When to use:**
  - When dealing with APIs, microservices, or any system that natively exchanges JSON.
  - For storing structured or hierarchical test data (e.g., user profiles, configurations).
  - When test data needs to be dynamically loaded or transformed at runtime.
- o **Why use it:**
  - Supports complex, nested structures, making it ideal for modern applications.
  - Readable by both humans and machines, while still being lightweight.
  - Easily integrated into automated API testing frameworks like Postman, Rest Assured, or Cypress.
- o **Limitations:**
  - More difficult to edit manually compared to CSV.
  - Can become complex if managing large datasets.

- **Using databases:** For complex or large-scale tests, you may want to store test data in a relational database (for example, MySQL, PostgreSQL) or NoSQL database (for example, MongoDB). This method allows for dynamic retrieval of data based on queries, which is especially useful for testing multiple data sets or scenarios that require large volumes of input data.

  - o With databases, test scripts query the database to fetch relevant test data before running the tests. This also enables more advanced data manipulation, such as setting up specific states or conditions before testing begins.
  - o **When to use:**
    - For large, relational, or frequently changing test data.
    - When test scenarios depend on live or transactional data (for example, banking, e-commerce).
    - When test data consistency needs to be ensured across multiple test cases.
  - o **Why use it:**
    - Allows querying specific test data dynamically, improving reusability.
    - Ensures data integrity by enforcing constraints, relationships, and dependencies.
    - Scales well for enterprise applications with extensive test data needs.
  - o **Limitations:**
    - Requires database setup, maintenance, and potential performance considerations.
    - More complex than file-based approaches (CSV, JSON).
    - Can introduce dependencies on database state, affecting test repeatability.

- **Parameterized tests:** Many testing frameworks (for example, JUnit, TestNG, Pytest) support parameterized tests, which allow you to pass test data directly into the test logic from an external source. The framework runs the same test logic multiple times, injecting different sets of data for each execution. Here is an example using JUnit with parameters:

```
@RunWith(Parameterized.class)
public class LoginTest {
    @Parameterized.Parameters
    public static Collection<Object[]> data() {
```

```
        return Arrays.asList(new Object[][] {
            { "user1", "pass123", "success" },
            { "user2", "wrongpass", "failure" }
        });
    }

    private String username;
    private String password;
    private String expectedOutcome;

    public LoginTest(String username, String password, String expectedOutcome) {
        this.username = username;
        this.password = password;
        this.expectedOutcome = expectedOutcome;
    }

    @Test
    public void testLogin() {
        // Test logic using username, password, and expectedOutcome
    }
}
```

- o **When to use:**
    - When test data needs to be injected directly into test cases via testing frameworks.
    - When using unit testing or functional testing frameworks (for example, JUnit, TestNG, Pytest).
    - For small, controlled datasets that do not require external storage.

- o **Why use it:**
    - Keeps test cases concise and avoids hardcoded values.
    - Enables fast execution without I/O overhead (compared to reading from files or databases).
    - Well-integrated into automation frameworks, making it ideal for CI/CD pipelines.

- o **Limitations:**
    - Not ideal for large-scale or frequently changing data.
    - Lacks external visibility and maintainability compared to CSV/JSON/Databases.

- **Using Excel files:** Excel files can also be used for managing test data, especially when dealing with business users or non-technical stakeholders who prefer Excel for data handling. Excel-based data can be read using libraries like Apache POI for Java or openpyxl for Python.

    - o **When to use:**
        - When working with business teams that manage test data in spreadsheets.
        - When test data needs to include formulas, formatting, or multiple sheets.
        - When dealing with structured but complex data, it is easier to review and manipulate in a tabular format.

- o **Why use it:**
  - **User-friendly:** Business users and testers can easily edit and manage data without needing technical skills.
  - **Supports multiple sheets:** Can store different types of test data (for example, login credentials in one sheet, transaction details in another).
  - **More features than CSV:** Unlike CSV, it supports formulas, conditional formatting, and comments, which can be useful for test data validation.
  - **Integration with test frameworks:** Many automation tools (for example, Selenium with Apache POI, Robot Framework, TestNG) support reading data from Excel files.
- o **Limitations:**
  - **Heavier file size:** XLSX files are bulkier compared to CSV, leading to potential performance issues.
  - **Requires external libraries:** Unlike JSON or databases, Excel files need specific libraries for parsing in automation frameworks.
  - **Not ideal for version control:** Since Excel files are binary, tracking changes in version control (for example, Git) is more challenging compared to text-based formats like JSON or CSV.

Refer to the following table:

Criteria	CSV	JSON	Database	Excel	Parameterized tests
Best for	Simple structured data	Hierarchical/ API data	Large, relational data	Business-friendly, structured data	Small, static datasets
Ease of editing	High (manual, spreadsheets)	Medium (JSON editors)	Low (requires queries)	High (spreadsheet UI)	High (within code)
Scalability	Low	Medium	High	Medium	Low
Test execution speed	Medium	Medium	Low (query overhead)	Low (parsing overhead)	High (direct injection)
Common use cases	Login forms, simple inputs	API testing, configurations	Complex business workflows	Business-driven test data, reports	Unit tests, small datasets

Table 4.1: Summarizing when different test data types should be used in a framework

The benefits of separating data include easier testing of different scenarios and environments:

- **Flexibility and reusability:** By externalizing test data, you can easily run the same test scripts with different data sets, enabling the reuse of test logic across multiple scenarios. For example, a login test can be executed with multiple sets of credentials by simply changing the input data, without altering the test logic itself. This flexibility is key for covering a wider range of test scenarios efficiently.

- **Testing multiple environments:** Separating test data allows you to run the same test cases in different environments by simply swapping configuration files or environment-specific data sets. Whether you are testing in development, staging, or production environments, the test logic remains the same, but the data adjusts according to the environment's needs. This is especially useful in CI/CD pipelines, where tests must be run in various environments with minimal manual intervention.

- **Easier maintenance:** With test data separated from test scripts, making updates becomes easier. If changes are needed to the test data (for example, new input values or expected outcomes), these changes can be made in the data source (CSV, JSON, database) without altering the underlying test logic. This improves maintainability by reducing the number of places that need to be updated when requirements change.

- **Enhanced coverage:** Data-driven testing enables broader test coverage by allowing the same test logic to be run with multiple data sets. This can help uncover edge cases and ensure that the application behaves correctly under various conditions. Separating the data from the test logic ensures that testers can focus on defining multiple scenarios without worrying about changing the core test code.

- **Improved collaboration:** When test data is separated from the test scripts, non-technical stakeholders (such as business analysts or product owners) can contribute to test design by defining input data and expected results in formats like CSV or Excel. This promotes collaboration between technical and non-technical teams, as domain experts can provide the necessary data without needing to modify the test code.

Separating test data from test scripts through data-driven testing techniques ensures flexibility, maintainability, and improved test coverage. Externalizing test data using formats like CSV, JSON, or databases allows test scripts to be run across multiple environments and with different data sets without altering the core logic. This approach simplifies maintenance, encourages reusability, and makes it easier to test a wide range of scenarios, ensuring that the test suite remains adaptable and scalable as the application evolves.

Configuration management

Configuration management is a critical component of a well-designed test automation framework, especially when dealing with multiple environments (for example, development, staging, production). By externalizing environment-specific configurations, such as URLs, browser types, and API endpoints, test automation frameworks become more flexible, scalable, and adaptable. This separation ensures that the same test scripts can be executed in different environments without modifying the test logic. Now, let us go over the following:

- **Managing environment-specific configurations:** Just as test logic should be separated from test data, environment-specific configurations like URLs, browser types, and API endpoints should also be decoupled from the test scripts. Hardcoding such values in the test scripts would limit the flexibility of the framework and make it difficult to adapt to changes in the environment. Instead, these configurations should be stored in external files, ensuring that the test logic remains environment-agnostic.

- **Dynamic configuration loading**: To ensure flexibility, test frameworks should be able to load environment-specific configurations dynamically. When the framework starts running, it can automatically detect the target environment (for example, via command-line parameters or environment variables) and load the corresponding configuration file. This approach makes it possible to switch environments, whether it is development, staging, or production, without making any changes to the test code.

- **Configuration consistency:** Consistent configuration management is important for stabilizing your test environment. Each environment, whether development, QA, staging, or production, may have different settings, but they should be managed consistently to ensure reliable testing. For instance, a testing framework may use different database instances in each environment, but how those instances are accessed and managed should follow a similar structure across environments. Proper configuration management helps ensure that switching between environments does not lead to unexpected errors or inconsistent results.

Using configuration files to store variables and credentials

Various types of configuration files can be used to externalize environment-specific configurations. Depending on the framework and programming language in use, common formats include YAML, JSON, properties files, and INI files. These configuration files store settings such as URLs, database credentials, API keys, and browser types, which test scripts can easily access. Let us now go over the configuration file types:

- **YAML files:** YAML is a popular format for configuration files due to its human-readable structure. YAML files are often used in modern CI/CD pipelines and testing frameworks, and they are highly compatible with tools like Kubernetes or Docker. Example of a YAML configuration for different environments:

```yaml
development:
  url: "https://dev.example.com"
  browser: "chrome"
  apiEndpoint: "https://dev.api.example.com"
  credentials:
    username: "devUser"
    password: "devPass"

staging:
  url: "https://staging.example.com"
  browser: "firefox"
  apiEndpoint: "https://staging.api.example.com"
  credentials:
    username: "stageUser"
    password: "stagePass"

production:
  url: "https://www.example.com"
  browser: "chrome"
  apiEndpoint: "https://api.example.com"
  credentials:
    username: "prodUser"
    password: "prodPass"
```

- **JSON files:** JSON is another widely used format for configuration files. It is especially useful when dealing with structured data and is compatible with most modern testing frameworks and tools. Here is an example of a JSON configuration file:

```json
{
  "development": {
    "url": "https://dev.example.com",
    "browser": "chrome",
    "apiEndpoint": "https://dev.api.example.com",
    "
  }
  },
  "staging": {
    "url": "https://staging.example.com",
    "browser": "firefox",
    "apiEndpoint": "https://staging.api.example.com",
"
  }
  },
  "production": {
    "url": "https://www.example.com",
```

```
      "browser": "chrome",
      "apiEndpoint": "https://api.example.com",
      }
    }
}
```

In the preceding example, you will want to manage access to these environments securely, so a **.python** file that does just that is included as:

```python
import os
import json

# Load JSON config
with open("config.json") as config_file:
    config = json.load(config_file)

# Retrieve environment-specific credentials
env = os.getenv("ENV", "development")  # Default to development if ENV is not set
username = os.getenv(f"{env.upper()}_USERNAME")
password = os.getenv(f"{env.upper()}_PASSWORD")

# Use credentials securely in your application
print(f"Running tests in {env} environment")
print(f"Using API: {config[env]['apiEndpoint']}")
print(f"Username: {username}")  # Do NOT print passwords in production
```

These environment variables are then configured as follows in PowerShell:

```
$env:DEVELOPMENT_USERNAME="devUser"
$env:DEVELOPMENT_PASSWORD="devPass"
$env:STAGING_USERNAME="stageUser"
$env:STAGING_PASSWORD="stagePass"
$env:PRODUCTION_USERNAME="prodUser"
$env:PRODUCTION_PASSWORD="prodPass"
```

- **Properties files:** In Java-based frameworks, **.properties** files are commonly used to store environment configurations. These files store key-value pairs and are simple to use in Java and other JVM-based languages. An example of a properties file for different environments:

```
url=https://dev.example.com
browser=chrome
apiEndpoint=https://dev.api.example.com
username=devUser
password=devPass
```

- **INI files:** INI files, structured with sections and key-value pairs, are also used in some systems to manage configuration settings. They are simple and easy to read, but not as powerful as JSON or YAML for more complex configurations. Here is an example of an INI file that can also be referenced similarly to the preceding environment example:

```
[development]
url = https://dev.example.com
browser = chrome
```

```
apiEndpoint = https://dev.api.example.com
username = devUser
password = devPass

[staging]
url = https://staging.example.com
browser = firefox
apiEndpoint = https://staging.api.example.com
username = stageUser
password = stagePass
```

In addition to configuration files, **environment variables** are often used to pass sensitive data, such as API keys and credentials, to test scripts. Environment variables are especially useful in CI/CD pipelines where different environments require different configurations. Here is an example usage in a Python test script:

```
import os

url = os.getenv('URL')
username = os.getenv('USERNAME')
password = os.getenv('PASSWORD')
```

Using environment variables

Let us go over the following:

- **Storing sensitive information (passwords, API keys, secrets):**
  - Avoid hardcoding credentials in source code.
  - **Example:** Database passwords, API tokens, SSH keys.
- **Configuring environment-specific settings:**
  - Define different values for development, staging, and production.
  - **Example:** `DATABASE_URL, API_ENDPOINT, LOG_LEVEL`
- **Keeping configuration outside of the source code:**
  - Avoid committing secrets to Git repositories.
  - Useful for applications deployed across multiple environments.
- **When using containerized applications (Docker, Kubernetes):**
  - Pass configuration values at runtime without modifying the container image.
  - **Example:** `docker run -e ENV=production my-app`
- **CI/CD pipelines:**
  - Store secrets securely in CI/CD tools (GitHub Actions, Jenkins, GitLab CI).
  - **Example:** Setting `AWS_ACCESS_KEY_ID` and `AWS_SECRET_ACCESS_KEY` in GitHub Actions secrets.
- **Runtime configuration:**
  - Modify behavior without changing code.
  - **Example:** Toggling a feature with `FEATURE_FLAG=true`

Not using environment variables

Let us go over the following:

- **For non-sensitive, static configuration:**
  - o If values do not change across environments, store them in configuration files.
  - o **Example:** UI timeout settings, log formats.
- **For large configuration data:**
  - o Environment variables should be simple key-value pairs, not large JSON/YAML data.
  - o Store complex configurations in config files, databases, or secrets managers instead.
- **When you need version-controlled configurations:**
  - o Environment variables are not stored in source control, making it hard to track changes.
  - o Use `.env` files (in development) or infrastructure-as-code tools for consistency.
- **If security policies require centralized secret management:**
  - o Some organizations mandate AWS Secrets Manager, HashiCorp Vault, or Azure Key Vault instead.
  - o These provide better access control, auditing, and rotation.

Best practices

Some best practices are as follows:

- **Use .env files for local development:**
  - o Store environment variables in a `.env` file and load them using tools like **dotenv** (Python, Node.js).
- **Use secret management services in production:**
  - o Avoid storing secrets directly in environment variables; use a vault or secret manager.
- **Do not print or log sensitive variables:**
  - o Prevent exposure by avoiding `print(os.environ["SECRET_KEY"])`.
- **Limit environment variables to essential configs:**
  - o Avoid cluttering with non-sensitive settings that could go in a config file.

Ensuring adaptability to different environments without code changes

It is important to limit the code changes in your test automation framework every time environments or system configuration changes occur. The following points help to ensure your framework can withstand these changes effectively:

- **Configuration-based execution:** To make the framework adaptable to different environments, the test execution process should allow for selecting which configuration to use at runtime. This can be done using command-line arguments, environment variables, or selecting the configuration file at the start of the test suite. The test logic should be environment-agnostic, meaning that it does not change, no matter which environment the tests are run in. Here is an example command-line parameter for selecting the environment:

```
python test_suite.py --env=staging
```

The test framework can then load the appropriate configuration file based on the **--env** parameter and apply it dynamically during test execution.

- **Flexible test environments:** When your configuration management is done properly, the same test suite can be executed across different environments without altering the codebase. This is especially useful in continuous testing pipelines, where the same tests need to be run in various environments, such as local development, staging, and production, to verify application behavior in each.

  This adaptability ensures that the testing framework remains robust and scalable, regardless of changes in the environment. For instance, if the test suite needs to run in a production environment, only the configuration file for that environment would need to be updated, while the test scripts remain unchanged.

- **Sensitive data management:** When handling sensitive information (for example, passwords, API keys), avoid storing them directly in the configuration files or test scripts. Instead, use environment variables or secret management tools to manage sensitive data securely. This reduces the risk of exposing critical information and ensures that configurations can be shared without compromising security. In CI/CD pipelines, secret management tools such as Vault, AWS Secrets Manager, or Azure Key Vault can be used to securely store and retrieve sensitive data at runtime.

- **Validation and testing:** It is important to validate that each environment-specific configuration is correct and complete before executing the tests. Misconfigured environments can lead to false test results, which could delay the testing process. Test the configurations separately, ensuring the application connects to the right environment with the correct credentials and URLs.

Effective configuration management is essential for building a scalable and maintainable test automation framework. By externalizing environment-specific configurations in files like YAML, JSON, or properties files, and using environment variables to pass sensitive information, you ensure that the test logic remains flexible and adaptable across different environments. This separation of concerns allows you to manage configurations without modifying the core test code, making it easier to test in multiple environments, handle sensitive data securely, and maintain a consistent testing process.

Implementing reusable components

Reusable test functions are essential for building efficient, maintainable, scalable test automation frameworks. By designing test functions and methods that can be reused across multiple test cases, you avoid redundancy, simplify maintenance, and improve test coverage. Reusable functions streamline common tasks such as login actions, API calls, and database connections, enabling you to focus on the unique aspects of each test case while leveraging consistent, well-tested functionality.

To design test functions and methods for reuse, we have to consider the following:

- **Abstract common functionality:** Identify common tasks that are repeated across multiple test cases, such as logging in, navigating to specific pages, interacting with databases, or making API requests. These tasks should be abstracted into reusable functions or methods that can be called by any test case needing the functionality. This way, if the underlying logic needs to be updated, it can be changed in one place rather than across multiple test scripts.

- **Use parameterized functions:** To ensure that test functions can handle varying inputs or outputs, design them to be parameterized. This allows the same function to be used in different scenarios with different data, avoiding the need to create separate functions for each test case. For example, a login function can accept username and password parameters, making it reusable for different sets of credentials. Here is an example of a reusable login function:

```python
def login(username, password):
    # Navigate to login page
    navigate_to_login_page()
```

```
# Enter credentials
enter_text("username_field", username)
enter_text("password_field", password)
# Submit login form
click_button("login_button")
```

This function can be called in different test cases with different credentials:

```
login("user1", "pass123")
login("admin", "adminpass")
```

- **Modularize code:** Breaking down test code into smaller, modular units ensures that individual functions can be reused in various contexts. Each function should have a clear, singular responsibility and perform one well-defined task. By separating concerns into smaller modules, test functions become more composable, allowing them to be combined in various ways to fit different test scenarios. For example, modularizing page interactions:

```
def navigate_to_page(url):
    driver.get(url)


def enter_text(field_id, text):
    driver.find_element_by_id(field_id).send_keys(text)


def click_button(button_id):
    driver.find_element_by_id(button_id).click()
```

Creating utility libraries for common actions

Let us now understand the following:

- **Utility libraries:** Common actions that are frequently needed across test cases, such as making API calls, connecting to a database, or performing UI interactions (for example, login or logout), should be placed in utility libraries. These libraries can be imported and reused throughout the test suite, reducing code duplication and centralizing maintenance. Here is an example structure for utility libraries:

```
/utilities
    /api.py          # Common API call functions
    /db.py           # Database connection functions
    /ui_actions.py   # Common UI interactions (e.g., login, logout)
```

- **API call utilities:** For tests that involve interacting with APIs, create utility functions for making HTTP requests (for example, GET, POST). These functions can be designed to accept different endpoints, payloads, and headers, making them reusable for various API calls across different test cases. Here is an example of a reusable API function:

```
import requests


def api_call(method, endpoint, data=None, headers=None):
    if method == "GET":
        response = requests.get(endpoint, headers=headers)
    elif method == "POST":
        response = requests.post(endpoint, json=data, headers=headers)
    return response
```

This utility can then be reused in test cases:

```
response = api_call("GET", "https://api.example.com/users")
response = api_call("POST", "https://api.example.com/login", data={"username":
"user", "password": "pass"})
```

- **Database connection utilities:** When interacting with databases, create reusable functions for connecting to the database, executing queries, and closing connections. These functions ensure test cases can access database data or perform database validation consistently and efficiently. Here is an example of a reusable database function:

```
import psycopg2

def db_connect():
    conn = psycopg2.connect(database="testdb", user="user", password="password",
host="localhost", port="5432")
    return conn

def execute_query(query):
    conn = db_connect()
    cursor = conn.cursor()
    cursor.execute(query)
    results = cursor.fetchall()
    conn.close()
    return results
```

This utility can be called in test cases to verify data:

```
results = execute_query("SELECT * FROM users WHERE id=1")
```

- **UI interaction utilities:** For UI test automation, create utility functions for common interactions like navigating to a page, filling forms, clicking buttons, and capturing screenshots. These utilities ensure consistency in handling UI elements and can be reused across multiple UI-related test cases. Here is an example of a utility function for UI interactions:

```
def fill_form(fields):
    for field, value in fields.items():
        driver.find_element_by_id(field).send_keys(value)

def submit_form(button_id):
    driver.find_element_by_id(button_id).click()
```

Ensuring generic functions for flexibility

To ensure that test functions are flexible and reusable across different test cases, they should be generic enough to handle different inputs, outputs, or contexts. Here are some key strategies for achieving this:

- **Parameterization:** Parameterizing functions allows them to handle a wide variety of inputs. Instead of hardcoding values inside the function, pass the inputs as arguments so the function can be reused in different scenarios. For example, a function for checking API responses should accept the expected status code and data as parameters. Here is an example:

```
def verify_api_response(response, expected_status_code, expected_data=None):
    assert response.status_code == expected_status_code
    if expected_data:
        assert response.json() == expected_data
```

- **Handle dynamic data:** Functions should be able to handle dynamic inputs or outputs, such as varying data formats, error codes, or exceptions. For instance, a function interacting with a database might need to handle different schemas or table structures. Here is an example of handling dynamic data:

```python
def fetch_data(query, expected_columns=None):
    results = execute_query(query)
    if expected_columns:
        assert len(results[0]) == len(expected_columns)
    return results
```

- **Error handling and validation:** Generic functions should include error handling and validation mechanisms to make them robust across different use cases. For example, if a database connection fails or an API request returns an error, the function should be designed to handle these scenarios gracefully, providing helpful feedback or retries. Here is an example of error handling:

```python
def api_call_with_retry(method, endpoint, retries=3):
    attempt = 0
    while attempt < retries:
        try:
            response = api_call(method, endpoint)
            if response.status_code == 200:
                return response
        except Exception as e:
            print(f"Attempt {attempt + 1} failed: {e}")
        attempt += 1
    raise Exception("API call failed after multiple retries")
```

- **Reusable assertions:** Create reusable assertion functions for validating different conditions, such as checking for element visibility in UI tests, comparing API responses, or verifying database records. These assertion functions can be used across test cases to ensure that tests follow a consistent validation pattern. Here is an example of a reusable assertion function:

```python
def assert_element_visible(element_id):
    element = driver.find_element_by_id(element_id)
    assert element.is_displayed(), f"Element {element_id} is not visible"
```

Reusable test functions are essential for creating efficient, maintainable, and scalable test automation frameworks. By abstracting common functionality, parameterizing functions, and creating utility libraries, you can avoid redundancy and make your test suite more adaptable. Whether handling UI interactions, database connections, or API calls, reusable functions ensure your framework remains flexible and easier to maintain. Moreover, by ensuring that test functions are generic enough to handle varying inputs and outputs, your tests can cover a broader range of scenarios with minimal effort.

Page Object Model

The POM is a design pattern widely used in UI test automation to enhance the maintainability, readability, and organization of test scripts. POM promotes the separation of the page structure from the test logic by creating an object-oriented representation of the web pages within an application. This approach allows testers to create a clear, structured way to interact with the user interface, making it easier to maintain and update tests as the application evolves. Let us now go over the following:

- **Separating page structure from test logic:** The key aspect of the POM design pattern is the separation of the application changes at either a frontend or API layer from the test itself, reducing the maintenance of the framework when application changes do occur.

- **Encapsulation of page elements:** In POM, each web page in the application is represented by a separate class (commonly referred to as a Page Object). This class encapsulates all the elements (UI components) and actions associated with that page, allowing test scripts to interact with the page without being concerned about its internal implementation details. For example, a **LoginPage** class can be created to handle all interactions related to the login page of an application:

```python
class LoginPage:
    def __init__(self, driver):
        self.driver = driver
        self.username_field = driver.find_element_by_id("username")
        self.password_field = driver.find_element_by_id("password")
        self.login_button = driver.find_element_by_id("login")

    def enter_username(self, username):
        self.username_field.send_keys(username)

    def enter_password(self, password):
        self.password_field.send_keys(password)

    def click_login(self):
        self.login_button.click()
```

- **Reduced duplication:** The Page Object classes encapsulate page interactions, minimizing code duplication. Test scripts can invoke methods from these classes to perform actions on the UI, thus reducing the need to repeat element locators or interaction logic throughout the test suite. Here is an example of a test script using the LoginPage class:

```python
def test_login_success(driver):
    login_page = LoginPage(driver)
    login_page.enter_username("user")
    login_page.enter_password("password")
    login_page.click_login()
    # Further assertions can be added here
```

- **Improved readability:** Tests written using POM are generally more readable and maintainable. The test logic focuses on the high-level actions being performed rather than the intricate details of how those actions are implemented, making it easier for testers to understand what the tests do at a glance.

Creating page classes for interactions

Here are some examples of how page classes can be created. For the benefits of these examples, we have focused purely on frontend components, but a similar approach can be followed to apply to backend components as well.

- **Designing page classes:** Each Page Object class should represent a single page of the application and include all the necessary methods and attributes for interacting with that page. This includes locating elements, performing actions, and verifying expected outcomes. Here is an example of a page class for a dashboard:

```python
class DashboardPage:
    def __init__(self, driver):
        self.driver = driver
        self.logout_button = driver.find_element_by_id("logout")
```

```
def click_logout(self):
    self.logout_button.click()
```

- **Method for actions:** Each page class should provide methods for common actions performed on that page. These methods should encapsulate the logic for interacting with the UI elements, making the tests simpler and more focused on their goals. If the way an action is performed changes (for instance, the locator for a button changes), it only needs to be updated in the Page Object class, not in every test case. Here is an example of combining actions:

```
class LoginPage:
    # Existing methods...

    def login(self, username, password):
        self.enter_username(username)
        self.enter_password(password)
        self.click_login()
```

```
The corresponding test can be simplified:
def test_login_success(driver):
    login_page = LoginPage(driver)
    login_page.login("user", "password")
    # Further assertions
```

- **Page navigation:** Page Object classes can also include methods for navigating to related pages. For example, if a user needs to navigate from the login page to the dashboard after a successful login, you can include a method for that transition. Here is an example of a navigation method:

```
class LoginPage:
    # Existing methods...

    def navigate_to_dashboard(self):
        self.click_login()
        return DashboardPage(self.driver)
```

- **Combining multiple pages:** If your application has a complex flow that involves interacting with multiple pages, you can create methods that navigate through these pages seamlessly. This reduces the complexity in your test scripts, as the navigation logic is encapsulated within the Page Objects. Here is an example of a workflow:

```
def test_user_flow(driver):
    login_page = LoginPage(driver)
    dashboard_page = login_page.login("user", "password")
    assert dashboard_page.is_displayed()
    dashboard_page.click_logout()
```

- **Encapsulating assertions:** While POM primarily focuses on separating page interactions from test logic, you can also include assertion methods within your Page Object classes. This can help further encapsulate the verification logic associated with a particular page. Here is an example of assertions:

```
class DashboardPage:
    # Existing methods...

    def verify_user_logged_in(self, username):
```

```
        welcome_message = self.driver.find_element_by_id("welcome_message").text
        assert username in welcome_message, f"Expected username '{username}' not
found."
```

This allows for more compact tests:

```
def test_login_success(driver):
    login_page = LoginPage(driver)
    dashboard_page = login_page.login("user", "password")
    dashboard_page.verify_user_logged_in("user")
```

Benefits of using POM

Here is a list of benefits of using the POM design principle in your framework:

- **Maintainability:** The POM design pattern greatly enhances the maintainability of the test automation framework. If the UI changes (for example, a button ID changes), updates are localized to the Page Object class instead of needing to modify multiple test scripts.

- **Reusability:** Page Object classes can be reused across different test cases. This promotes code reuse and prevents duplication, as common functionalities can be implemented once and used throughout the test suite.

- **Readability:** Tests become more readable and self-explanatory when they utilize Page Objects. Test logic focuses on the actions being performed rather than the technical details of how they are executed, which is beneficial for both developers and non-developers.

- **Scalability:** As applications grow in complexity, the POM structure allows for easy scaling of test cases. New Page Object classes can be added as new pages or features are introduced, and existing tests can be updated with minimal effort.

- **Ease of collaboration:** A well-structured POM can improve collaboration among team members. Developers, testers, and other stakeholders can work on different parts of the test suite without stepping on each other's toes, since the logic is clearly separated.

The POM is a powerful design pattern for UI test automation that promotes the separation of page structure from test logic. By encapsulating interactions with web pages in dedicated Page Object classes, POM improves maintainability, readability, and reusability of test scripts. This design pattern not only helps in organizing test code but also adapts to changes in the application under test, making it a vital practice in building robust and scalable test automation frameworks.

Test hooks and setup/teardown components

Test hooks and setup/teardown components are essential elements of a robust test automation framework. They allow for the modularization of the setup and cleanup processes that are necessary for executing test cases consistently and reliably. By designing reusable hooks for common preconditions and postconditions, testers can ensure a cleaner, more organized, and maintainable test suite.

Modularizing setup and teardown processes

Setup refers to the actions taken to prepare the test environment before executing a test case. This might involve initializing test data, creating user sessions, or configuring the environment.

Teardown involves cleaning up resources and reverting the environment to its original state after running a test case. This could include deleting test data, closing connections, or logging out users.

Creating reusable setup/teardown methods

Modularizing these processes allows you to define reusable setup and teardown methods that can be invoked across multiple test cases, reducing code duplication and increasing maintainability. Here is an example of reusable setup and teardown methods:

```python
def setup_user_session(driver):
    # Code to create a user session
    driver.get("https://example.com/login")
    login_page = LoginPage(driver)
    login_page.login("user", "password")


def teardown_user_session(driver):
    # Code to log out and clean up the user session
    dashboard_page = DashboardPage(driver)
    dashboard_page.click_logout()
```

Integrating setup and teardown in test cases

By integrating these reusable setup and teardown methods into your test cases, you ensure that every test starts with a clean slate and ends with the proper cleanup. Here is an example of using setup and teardown in a test case:

```python
def test_user_profile_update(driver):
    setup_user_session(driver)  # Setup
    try:
        # Test actions for updating user profile
        profile_page = ProfilePage(driver)
        profile_page.update_profile("New Name", "newemail@example.com")
        assert profile_page.verify_update_success()
    finally:
        teardown_user_session(driver)  # Teardown
```

Designing hooks for common preconditions and postconditions

Preconditions are necessary states or conditions that must be satisfied before a test case can run. Common preconditions include creating user accounts, setting up test data, or initializing specific settings. Here is an example of a precondition hook:

```python
def create_test_user(driver):
    # Code to create a test user in the application
    admin_page = AdminPage(driver)
    admin_page.add_user("testuser", "password", "testuser@example.com")
```

This precondition can be reused in multiple test cases:

```python
def test_user_login(driver):
    create_test_user(driver)
    # Continue with test logic
```

Postconditions ensure that the test environment remains clean and consistent after a test case has executed. This might include deleting any test data created during the test or resetting application states. Here is an example of a postcondition hook:

```
def cleanup_test_user(driver):
    # Code to delete the test user after the test runs
    admin_page = AdminPage(driver)
    admin_page.delete_user("testuser")
```

This can also be integrated into test cases to ensure proper cleanup:

```
def test_user_deletion(driver):
    create_test_user(driver)
    try:
        # Test logic for user deletion
        user_page = UserPage(driver)
        user_page.delete_user("testuser")
        assert user_page.verify_user_deleted("testuser")
    finally:
        cleanup_test_user(driver)
```

Using before and after hooks

Many testing frameworks provide mechanisms to define hooks that automatically run before and after test cases. These hooks can be configured to ensure consistency and to prevent test data corruption across tests.

For example, in a framework like **pytest**, you can use fixtures:

```
import pytest

@pytest.fixture
def user_session(driver):
    setup_user_session(driver)  # Setup
    yield  # Test runs here
    teardown_user_session(driver)  # Teardown
```

The test case can then leverage this fixture:

```
def test_user_profile_update(user_session, driver):
    profile_page = ProfilePage(driver)
    profile_page.update_profile("New Name", "newemail@example.com")
    assert profile_page.verify_update_success()
```

Let us now go over the following points:

- **Ensuring consistency:** Using before and after hooks ensures that each test runs in a consistent state, with all necessary preconditions satisfied and postconditions applied. This helps prevent issues related to test data corruption and provides a clean slate for each test case.

- **Reducing boilerplate code:** By centralizing the setup and teardown logic in hooks, you reduce boilerplate code within your test cases. This allows you to focus on writing meaningful tests rather than repetitive setup and cleanup code.

Implementing test hooks and modularizing setup and teardown processes significantly enhances the robustness and maintainability of test automation frameworks. By designing reusable methods for common preconditions and postconditions, testers can ensure that test cases execute consistently while preventing data corruption. Utilizing before and after hooks further streamlines the test execution process, allowing for clean, efficient, and reliable test cases that are easier to maintain and scale over time. This structured approach contributes to a more organized and effective test automation strategy.

Custom assertion libraries

Custom assertion libraries play a crucial role in enhancing the expressiveness and readability of test cases in automation frameworks. By extending the capabilities of built-in testing frameworks, these libraries allow testers to implement reusable assertions tailored to their specific testing needs. This not only promotes consistency across tests but also improves the overall quality of test validations.

Implementing reusable assertions

Custom assertions are specialized validation functions designed to check specific conditions that may not be directly supported by a testing framework's built-in assertions. They encapsulate common verification logic, making it easier to express complex conditions in a readable manner.

Creating custom assertion functions

When designing custom assertions, the goal is to encapsulate common validation logic into functions that can be reused across multiple test cases. This improves code reuse and minimizes duplication.

Example of a custom assertion in Python:

```python
def assert_user_logged_in(driver, username):
    """Custom assertion to verify that the user is logged in."""
    welcome_message = driver.find_element_by_id("welcome_message").text
    assert username in welcome_message, f"Expected username '{username}' not found in
'{welcome_message}'"
```

This custom assertion can then be reused in multiple test cases:

```python
def test_login_success(driver):
    # Assume successful login logic here
    assert_user_logged_in(driver, "testuser")
```

Encapsulating complex logic

Custom assertions can encapsulate more complex verification logic involving multiple steps or checks. For example, a statement that verifies a user profile update may need to check multiple fields. Here is an example of a more complex custom assertion:

```python
def assert_user_profile_updated(driver, username, expected_email):
    """Custom assertion to verify that the user profile has been updated correctly."""
    profile_page = ProfilePage(driver)
    actual_email = profile_page.get_email()
    assert actual_email == expected_email, f"Expected email '{expected_email}', but got
'{actual_email}'"
    assert_user_logged_in(driver, username)
```

Ensuring modularity and applicability

Custom assertions should be designed to be modular and independent, meaning they can be used across different test cases without relying on specific test setups or contexts. This ensures flexibility and reusability. Here is an example of a modular assertion library:

```python
class CustomAssertions:
    @staticmethod
    def assert_element_visible(driver, element_id):
```

```
    """Asserts that a specific element is visible on the page."""
    element = driver.find_element_by_id(element_id)
    assert element.is_displayed(), f"Element with ID '{element_id}' is not visible."


@staticmethod
def assert_text_in_element(driver, element_id, expected_text):
    """Asserts that a specific text is present in an element."""
    element = driver.find_element_by_id(element_id)
    assert expected_text in element.text, f"Expected text '{expected_text}' not found
in element with ID '{element_id}'."
```

Improving readability and consistency

By using custom assertions, the readability of test cases improves significantly. Instead of verbose and repetitive validation logic, assertions become concise and expressive, clearly conveying the intent of the test. Here is an example of using the custom assertions:

```
def test_profile_update(driver):
    # Assume logic for updating profile here
    CustomAssertions.assert_element_visible(driver, "success_message")
    CustomAssertions.assert_text_in_element(driver, "success_message", "Profile updated
successfully.")
```

Creating a centralized assertion library

A centralized assertion library can be beneficial for organizing all custom assertions in one place. This makes it easy to manage and update assertions and ensures that any changes propagate throughout all tests that utilize them. Here is an example of a centralized assertion library:

```
class AssertionLibrary:
    @staticmethod
    def assert_element_present(driver, locator):
        element = driver.find_element(*locator)
        assert element is not None, f"Element {locator} should be present."


    @staticmethod
    def assert_status_code(response, expected_status):
        assert response.status_code == expected_status, f"Expected status code {expected_
status}, but got {response.status_code}."
```

Testing custom assertions

It is essential to ensure that the custom assertions themselves are thoroughly tested. This can be accomplished by writing unit tests for each assertion function, verifying that they behave as expected in various scenarios. Here is an example of a simple test for a custom assertion:

```
def test_assert_user_logged_in(driver):
    # Setup a user session
    setup_user_session(driver)
    try:
        # Test the custom assertion
        assert_user_logged_in(driver, "testuser")
    finally:
        teardown_user_session(driver)
```

Implementing custom assertion libraries significantly enhances the effectiveness and readability of test automation frameworks. By encapsulating common validation logic in reusable assertion functions, testers can improve code consistency and reduce duplication across test cases. Ensuring that these assertions are modular and applicable across various tests not only makes the test suite more organized but also fosters better collaboration among team members. By centralizing custom assertions in a well-structured library, organizations can maintain high-quality testing practices and adapt quickly to application changes.

Best practices for building modular frameworks

We have examined many principles for designing a modular test automation framework, but the following are a few more best practices to help you get the most out of your framework:

- **Avoiding duplication in test automation frameworks:** Avoiding duplication in test automation frameworks is essential for creating efficient, maintainable, scalable test suites. By identifying opportunities to abstract common patterns and functionalities, teams can streamline their testing processes, improve code consistency, and simplify ongoing maintenance efforts.

- **Identifying opportunities to abstract common patterns:**

  o **Recognizing repetitive code:** The first step in avoiding duplication is to recognize areas where similar code patterns appear across multiple test cases. This can include repeated setup logic, assertion statements, or common test workflows. For example, if multiple tests perform similar actions, such as logging in to the application, the login logic should be abstracted into a reusable function or method.

    ```python
    def login_user(driver, username, password):
        login_page = LoginPage(driver)
        login_page.enter_username(username)
        login_page.enter_password(password)
        login_page.click_login()
    ```

  o **Creating utility functions:** Utility functions can be created to handle repetitive tasks that are common across different tests. This reduces redundancy and improves readability. For example, if several tests require verifying user profiles, a utility function can handle this.

    ```python
    def verify_user_profile(driver, username, expected_email):
        profile_page = ProfilePage(driver)
        actual_email = profile_page.get_email()
        assert actual_email == expected_email, f"Expected {expected_email}, got {actual_email} for user {username}."
    ```

  o **Using test data management:** Centralizing test data management can eliminate duplication related to data setups. Instead of hardcoding data in multiple tests, consider externalizing data in configuration files or using data-driven approaches. For example: Store user credentials in a configuration file, allowing multiple tests to access the same data without duplication.

    ```json
    {
        "users": [
            { "username": "testuser", "password": "password123" }
        ]
    }
    ```

  o **Implementing design patterns:** Utilizing design patterns such as POM, factory pattern, or strategy pattern can help encapsulate common functionality and reduce redundancy. For example, the POM allows for the creation of a single class representing a web page, reducing the need to repeat locators and interactions across test cases.

- **Helping ensure consistency by reducing duplication:**

  o **Improved consistency across tests:** By abstracting common functionality, teams can apply the same logic uniformly across multiple tests. This minimizes the risk of discrepancies or errors that may arise from having multiple implementations of similar logic. For example, if login logic is defined in one place, any updates to the login process must only be made in that single location, ensuring all tests are updated consistently.

  o **Easier debugging and issue resolution:** When duplication is minimized, debugging becomes more manageable. If an issue arises with a particular function, there is only one implementation to investigate rather than multiple instances spread across various tests. For example, if a login method fails, a team can quickly identify the issue in the utility function rather than hunting through several tests for differing implementations.

  o **Reduced maintenance effort:** Maintaining a test suite with minimal duplication simplifies updates and enhancements. When required, they can be made in one location, significantly reducing the time and effort spent on maintenance. For example, if the login process changes, the team only needs to update the login utility function, and all tests relying on that function will automatically use the updated logic.

- **Simplifying maintenance:**

  o **Streamlined test code:** Reducing duplication results in cleaner, more concise test code. This clarity enhances readability, making it easier for team members (new or existing) to understand the tests and their purposes. For example, simplified test cases allow testers to focus on the business logic of the tests rather than being bogged down by repetitive code.

  ```
  def test_user_login(driver):
      login_user(driver, "testuser", "password123")
      assert_user_logged_in(driver, "testuser")
  ```

  o **Encouraging code reuse:** When functions and methods are reusable, the test suite becomes more modular. This modularity allows for easy adaptation and expansion of the test suite as new features are added to the application. For example, if a new feature requires similar login functionality, testers can easily leverage existing utility functions, reducing the time spent writing new code.

  o **Facilitating collaboration:** A well-structured, duplication-free test suite makes it easier for team members to collaborate. Each member can focus on specific aspects of the framework or on creating new tests without worrying about duplicating existing functionality. For example, with a centralized login function, new team members can quickly implement tests without needing to understand the intricacies of the login process.

Avoiding duplication in test automation frameworks is a critical practice for enhancing efficiency, consistency, and maintainability. By identifying opportunities to abstract common patterns, creating utility functions, and leveraging design patterns, teams can significantly reduce redundancy in their test suites. This leads to improved consistency across tests, simplified maintenance, and streamlined code that is easier to read and understand. In turn, this allows teams to adapt quickly to changes in the application, fostering a more agile and effective testing environment.

Managing through version control

Managing reusable components effectively through version control and integrating them into a CI/CD pipeline is crucial for maintaining the stability and reliability of test automation frameworks. These practices ensure that changes are tracked, tested, and validated before integration, allowing teams to deliver high-quality software efficiently.

Importance of version control

Version control systems (**VCS**) like Git enable teams to track changes in their codebase, facilitating collaboration and maintaining a history of modifications. This is especially important for reusable components in test automation, as they often serve as foundational elements across multiple tests. Now, let us go over the following:

- **Tracking changes:** By using version control, teams can manage updates to reusable components effectively. Each change can be documented with descriptive commit messages, making it easier to understand the evolution of the codebase. For example, when modifying a utility function, a team member can commit the changes with a message explaining the reason for the modification. This provides context for future developers.

  ```
  git commit -m "Refactor login_user function to handle two-factor authentication."
  ```

- **Branching strategies:** Implementing a branching strategy, such as GitFlow or feature branching, allows teams to work on new features or fixes in isolation without disrupting the main codebase. This is particularly beneficial when developing new reusable components. For example, a developer can create a new branch to implement a new assertion method, ensuring that ongoing work on other parts of the framework remains unaffected.

- **Code reviews:** Utilizing **pull requests** (**PR**) in conjunction with version control fosters collaboration and quality assurance. Code reviews allow team members to evaluate changes before merging into the main branch, ensuring that new reusable components adhere to coding standards and best practices. For example, before merging a new utility function, a developer can request a code review from peers, leading to constructive feedback and enhancements.

Integrating reusable components into a CI/CD pipeline

Some of these components are as follows:

- **CI:** Integrating reusable components into a CI pipeline ensures that changes are automatically tested whenever new code is committed. This helps detect issues early in the development cycle and maintains the stability of the test automation framework. For example, when a developer pushes changes to the repository, the CI pipeline can trigger automated tests that validate the functionality of the modified reusable components, such as utility functions or custom assertions.

- **Automated testing:** Implementing automated tests for reusable components is critical to verify their behavior before they are integrated into the main test suite. This can include unit tests, integration tests, and end-to-end tests. For example, each time a change is made to a utility function, a suite of unit tests can verify that the function behaves as expected under various conditions.

- **Build and deployment:** The CI pipeline should include steps to build and deploy the test automation framework to a test environment. This process can validate that the framework remains stable and functional after integrating new reusable components. For example, after successful test execution, the pipeline can deploy the test framework to a staging environment for further validation before moving to production.

- **CD:** In a fully automated CI/CD pipeline, successful builds and tests can lead to automatic deployment of the latest version of the test framework. This approach allows teams to quickly implement updates and improvements to reusable components, ensuring they are readily available for testing new application features. For example, if a new assertion method is added and passes all tests, it can be automatically deployed to the test environment for immediate use.

- **Monitoring and reporting:** Monitoring the performance and stability of the test automation framework after integrating new components is vital. CI/CD pipelines can provide reports on test results, code coverage, and build status, helping teams identify and address issues promptly. For example, if a newly integrated component causes test failures, the CI/CD system can notify the team, allowing for quick investigation and resolution.

Effectively managing reusable components through version control and integrating them into a CI/CD pipeline is essential for ensuring the stability and reliability of test automation frameworks. Teams can maintain high-quality reusable components by tracking changes, implementing automated testing, and fostering collaboration through code reviews. Moreover, integrating these components into a CI/CD pipeline allows for early detection of issues and continuous delivery of updates, ultimately supporting faster and more efficient software development processes. This approach leads to enhanced testing effectiveness and improves overall software quality.

Documentation and code standards in test automation frameworks

Maintaining clear documentation for reusable components and establishing coding standards are critical practices in developing and sustaining effective test automation frameworks. These practices not only facilitate team collaboration and understanding but also contribute to the overall quality and maintainability of the codebase. Let us go over the following:

- **Importance of documentation:** Clear documentation is a vital resource for teams, enabling them to quickly understand and adopt reusable components. Well-documented code helps reduce onboarding time for new team members and ensures consistent usage of the framework.

- **Comprehensive component descriptions:** Each reusable component should have a detailed description that outlines its purpose, functionality, and how it fits into the larger test framework. This can include explanations of inputs, outputs, and any dependencies. For example, for a utility function that handles login, the documentation might include:

```
## `login_user(driver, username, password)`
```

This function automates the login process for a given user.

```
**Parameters:**
- `driver`: The web driver instance controlling the browser.
- `username`: The username of the user to log in.
- `password`: The password of the user.


**Returns:**
- None


**Usage:**
```python
login_user(driver, "testuser", "password123")
```

- **Code comments:** In-line comments within the code can provide context and clarity for complex logic or decisions made during implementation. Comments should explain the why behind certain approaches rather than the what, which is often evident from the code itself. For example:

```
def login_user(driver, username, password):
    # Wait for the login form to be visible before interacting
    WebDriverWait(driver, 10).until(EC.visibility_of_element_located((By.ID, "login_
form")))
    driver.find_element(By.ID, "username").send_keys(username)
    driver.find_element(By.ID, "password").send_keys(password)
    driver.find_element(By.ID, "login_button").click()
```
```

- **Usage examples:** Including usage examples in the documentation helps users understand how to implement and utilize the components effectively. These examples should illustrate typical use cases and specific scenarios where the component may be beneficial.

- **API documentation tools:** Utilizing documentation tools like Sphinx, JSDoc, or Swagger can help automate the generation of documentation based on code annotations. This ensures that the documentation remains up to date with changes in the codebase. For example, using Sphinx, developers can generate HTML documentation from docstrings in the code, making it accessible and easy to navigate.

- **Versioning documentation:** As reusable components evolve, their documentation should also be versioned to reflect changes accurately. This helps teams understand the history of a component and any modifications that may impact its usage.

Establishing coding standards

Much like all code in an enterprise, coding standards need to be created or adhered to help ensure the framework remains easy to maintain and update. Let us go over the following:

- **Importance of coding standards:** Establishing coding standards ensures that the modular framework remains coherent, clean, and easy to understand. Consistency in code style fosters collaboration and reduces the cognitive load for team members when navigating the codebase.

- **Define style guidelines:** Coding standards should include style guidelines that specify conventions for naming, indentation, spacing, and structure. Common guidelines can be based on widely accepted standards like **Python Enhancement Proposal 8 (PEP 8)** for Python or the Google Java Style Guide. For example, adopting consistent naming conventions, such as using `snake_case` for function names in Python or camelCase for variable names in Java, helps improve readability.

- **Code structure and organization:** Establishing a clear directory structure for organizing reusable components, tests, and documentation is essential. This organization allows team members to quickly locate files and understand the project structure. For example:

```css

├── tests/
│   ├── test_login.py
│   └── test_profile.py
├── utils/
│   ├── login_util.py
│   └── assertion_util.py
├── docs/
│   └── README.md
└── main.py
```

- **Consistent formatting:** Utilizing code formatting tools like Prettier or Black can help maintain consistent formatting across the codebase. These tools automatically format code according to defined standards, reducing manual effort and the potential for style discrepancies.

- **Linting and static analysis:** Implementing linting and static analysis tools, such as ESLint for JavaScript or Pylint for Python, can help identify and enforce coding standards in real-time. This encourages developers to adhere to best practices and catch potential issues early in the development process.

- **Code reviews for compliance:** Incorporating code reviews as part of the development workflow ensures that coding standards are consistently applied. Team members can provide feedback on adherence to standards and suggest improvements, fostering a culture of quality and collaboration.

- **Documentation of standards:** Documenting coding standards and making them easily accessible to the team is crucial. This documentation should outline the established guidelines and provide examples to clarify expectations. For example, a coding standards document might include sections on naming conventions, code organization, commenting guidelines, and examples of both good and bad practices.

Maintaining clear documentation for reusable components and establishing coding standards are essential practices in developing a robust test automation framework. Comprehensive documentation enables teams to quickly understand and adopt reusable components, while coding standards ensure consistency and clarity throughout the codebase.

Conclusion

In today's rapidly evolving software development landscape, modular test frameworks have emerged as a cornerstone for achieving maintainability, scalability, and flexibility in test automation. By adopting a modular approach, teams can significantly enhance the efficiency of their testing processes and the overall quality of their software products.

In conclusion, modular test frameworks offer substantial benefits in terms of maintainability, scalability, and flexibility. By emphasizing the importance of separating test logic, test data, and configurations, teams can create clean and adaptable frameworks. Moreover, leveraging reusable components fosters efficiency and reduces maintenance overhead, ultimately contributing to the success of test automation efforts in delivering high-quality software.

We have had a look at the architecture of good framework design, and now in the next chapter, we will look at testability in the design process and the vital role it plays in making your software easier to test and automate.

Key takeaways

Here are the key takeaways of the benefits of modular framework design:

- **Maintainability:** Modular test frameworks facilitate easier updates and modifications by allowing teams to isolate and manage individual components. This isolation reduces the complexity of maintaining the test suite and enables faster adaptation to changes in the application under test.

- **Scalability:** The modular design supports the growth of the test suite as new features are added or existing functionalities evolve. Teams can easily extend the framework by incorporating new reusable components without overhauling the entire testing structure, thus promoting a scalable testing environment.

- **Flexibility:** A modular framework allows for the quick adaptation of tests to changing requirements. Test cases can be easily modified or replaced without impacting the overall framework, enabling teams to respond promptly to shifts in business needs or application changes.

- **Efficiency improvement:** Reusable components, such as utility functions, custom assertions, and page objects, streamline the development of test cases. By leveraging these components, teams can avoid redundancy, reduce the time spent writing tests, and focus on higher-level testing strategies.

- **Reducing maintenance overhead:** Centralizing reusable components minimizes the maintenance burden on teams. When a component requires an update, it can be modified in one location, automatically reflecting changes across all tests that utilize it. This leads to a more manageable codebase and allows teams to devote resources to improving the overall quality of their tests.

Exercises

1. How well are test execution, reporting, and data management separated in your test frameworks?

2. Can new tools, test types, or integrations be added without major refactoring?

3. Are test components (for example, assertions, utilities, setup/teardown) reusable across different test cases and suites?

4. How effectively does the framework abstract tool-specific code to maintain flexibility?

5. Are there defined patterns (for example, Page Object Model, Screenplay, or Adapter patterns) to ensure consistency?

6. How does the framework handle dependencies between modules to prevent tight coupling?

7. Is test data managed in a modular way to support different environments and scenarios?

8. Can configurations be easily modified without changing test logic?

9. Does the framework support concurrent test execution without bottlenecks?

10. How are test modules versioned and managed to avoid breaking dependencies?

11. Can the framework adapt to new technologies (for example, APIs, mobile, cloud-native systems)?

Join our Discord space

Join our Discord workspace for latest updates, offers, tech happenings around the world, new releases, and sessions with the authors:

https://discord.bpbonline.com

## CHAPTER 5

Testability and Software Design

Introduction

In this chapter, we continue our exploration from *Chapter 3, Designing with Architecture in Mind*, and *Chapter 4, Designing Modular Test Frameworks*, to explore aspects of testability in software design and the impact they have on the ability to script automated tests for the system under test. A software architecture that prioritizes testability enables faster feedback loops, reduces maintenance overhead, and enhances system reliability. Integrating testability into architecture requires designing modular, loosely coupled components with clear boundaries, leveraging principles such as separation of concerns, dependency injection, and decoupling from external systems to minimize test fragility.

As we will explore in this chapter, best practices include creating clear and consistent interfaces, enabling isolated testing through mocking and stubbing, and maintaining simplicity and predictability in design. Robust logging and monitoring further support debugging and failure analysis. To enable continuous testing, teams should adopt tools for unit testing, test data management, end-to-end validation, and static analysis. A well-structured, testable system ensures rapid iteration, release confidence, and long-term maintainability.

Structure

In this chapter, we will go over the following topics:

- Testability
- Relationship between software architecture and testability
- Designing for testability
- Separation of concerns
- Dependency injection
- Decoupling from external systems
- Best practices for ensuring systems are testable
- Isolated testing

- Simplicity and predictability
- Logging and monitoring
- Enabling continuous testing
- Best practices for automating tests
- Tools and techniques to support testing
- Mocking and stubbing
- Test data management
- End-to-end testing tools
- Code coverage and static analysis tools

Objectives

By the end of this chapter, the readers will understand how testability in the design of an application allows for better testing and easier automation. We will also look at how testability can be achieved in software design, enabling earlier involvement in the software design process to ensure that testability can be achieved. The readers will also learn about how a variety of different testing techniques can be applied to different levels of software architecture to enhance their testability and test automation outcome.

Testability

Testability is a critical software quality attribute that refers to the ease with which a software system can be tested. It encompasses various factors that influence the ability to verify and validate that a system meets its requirements and performs as expected. Testability is not merely about the presence of tests but is fundamentally tied to the design, architecture, and implementation of the software.

The key aspects of testability are as follows:

- **Observability:** The degree to which the internal state of a system can be observed through its outputs. A system that produces clear and understandable outputs makes it easier to determine whether it is functioning correctly.

- **Controllability:** The ability to control the inputs and state of the system to facilitate testing. A testable system allows testers to manipulate various conditions to evaluate different scenarios.

- **Decomposability:** The ability to break the system down into smaller, manageable components that can be tested independently. This aspect allows for targeted testing, making it easier to isolate and diagnose issues.

- **Isolation:** The capacity to test components in isolation from one another. This minimizes dependencies and interactions that can complicate testing and obscure the root cause of issues.

Significance of testability in modern software development

In the context of modern software development, testability plays a vital role in the following ways:

- **Facilitating agile development:** As agile methodologies gain popularity, the emphasis on quick iterations and rapid delivery underscores the importance of testability. High testability allows for continuous integration and deployment, enabling teams to deliver features quickly and confidently.

- **Enhancing quality assurance:** Testable systems are easier to validate and verify, leading to higher quality software. By ensuring that software is designed with testability in mind, teams can catch defects early in the development process, reducing costs associated with post-release bug fixes.

- **Supporting automation:** Testability is crucial for effective test automation. Automated tests rely on clear inputs, outputs, and predictable behaviors. Systems designed with testability in mind facilitate the creation of automated test scripts that can be executed repeatedly with confidence.

- **Improving collaboration:** Testable systems encourage collaboration between developers, testers, and other stakeholders. When a system is easily testable, all team members can contribute to the testing process, leading to a shared understanding of the software's behavior and requirements.

Impact of ease of testing on overall efficiency and effectiveness

The ease of testing directly impacts the efficiency and effectiveness of the overall testing process in the following ways:

- **Reduced time to test:** Highly testable systems streamline the testing process, allowing teams to identify and execute tests more quickly. When testing is efficient, teams can focus on broader testing strategies rather than getting bogged down in debugging and investigation.

- **Increased coverage:** Systems designed with testability in mind enable more comprehensive testing coverage. When it is easy to test individual components and scenarios, teams can ensure that various conditions are evaluated, leading to more robust software.

- **Faster feedback loops:** High testability leads to quicker feedback on software changes. Developers can validate their code more rapidly, reducing the likelihood of introducing defects into the production environment. This responsiveness supports a more agile development process.

- **Higher quality deliverables:** Testable systems yield better quality software. When teams can effectively verify the functionality of components, they can be more confident in their releases, reducing the risk of post-deployment issues and increasing customer satisfaction.

- **Cost efficiency:** Investing in testability during the design and development phases reduces costs associated with later-stage bug fixes and maintenance. By catching issues early, teams minimize the time and resources spent on addressing defects.

Testability is a fundamental software quality attribute that significantly impacts modern software development. By defining and prioritizing testability, teams can enhance the efficiency and effectiveness of their testing processes. The ease of testing directly influences the overall quality, cost, and agility of software delivery, ultimately contributing to successful software products that meet user expectations and business objectives.

Relationship between software architecture and testability

Software architecture plays a crucial role in determining the testability of a system. Architectural choices can significantly influence how easily and effectively a system can be tested, impacting both the development process and the final product's quality.

The key architectural aspects affecting testability are as follows:

- **Modularity:** A modular architecture breaks down a system into smaller, independent components or modules. This decomposition allows for isolated testing of each module, making it easier to identify and resolve issues. Higher modularity enhances both observability and controllability, two critical factors of testability.

- **Layered architecture:** Implementing a layered architecture (such as the classic presentation, business logic, and data access layers) can improve testability by clearly separating concerns. This separation enables targeted testing of each layer independently, reducing the complexity of tests and allowing for easier validation of functionality.

- **Loose coupling and high cohesion:** Designing components with loose coupling and high cohesion facilitates easier testing. Loose coupling minimizes dependencies between components, allowing them to be tested in isolation. High cohesion ensures that components are focused on a single responsibility, making their behavior more predictable and easier to verify.

- **Design patterns:** Utilizing design patterns, such as the **Page Object Model (POM)** for UI testing or **dependency injection (DI)**, can enhance testability. These patterns promote better organization of code, allowing for more straightforward and maintainable tests. For example, DI allows for the easy replacement of dependencies with mocks or stubs during testing.

- **Configurability:** An architecture that allows for easy configuration of components (for example, using configuration files or environment variables) can enhance testability. This flexibility enables testers to simulate different scenarios and environments without changing the codebase, facilitating more comprehensive testing.

Benefits of designing for testability early in the SDLC

Designing for testability early in the **software development life cycle (SDLC)** offers several advantages that can lead to improved software quality and reduced costs, such as:

- **Early defect detection:** By incorporating testability into the architectural design, teams can detect and address defects early in the development process. This proactive approach reduces the likelihood of issues being discovered later in the lifecycle, where they can be more costly and time-consuming to fix.

- **Streamlined testing process:** Early design considerations for testability lead to a more straightforward testing process. With a well-architected system that promotes easy testing, teams can create effective test cases more quickly, reducing the overall time spent on testing.

- **Increased test coverage:** When systems are designed with testability in mind, it becomes easier to cover a broader range of test scenarios. This increased coverage ensures that various conditions and edge cases are tested, resulting in higher-quality software.

- **Enhanced collaboration:** Involving testers in the architectural design phase fosters collaboration between development and testing teams. This collaboration leads to a shared understanding of the system's requirements and functionality, ultimately improving the quality of the software.

- **Cost efficiency:** Designing for testability reduces costs associated with late-stage testing and bug fixing. By catching issues early and ensuring the system is easier to test, teams can minimize the resources spent on addressing defects after deployment.

- **Better documentation and maintainability:** A focus on testability often leads to better documentation and maintainability of the system. When components are designed to be testable, their behaviors and interactions are typically well-documented, making it easier for future developers to understand and modify the system.

- **Facilitated automation:** Designing for testability supports the implementation of automated testing frameworks. A well-architected system makes it easier to create and maintain automated tests, which can significantly enhance the efficiency of the testing process and provide faster feedback.

The relationship between software architecture and testability is profound, as architectural choices directly impact the ease with which systems can be tested. By prioritizing testability in the architectural design phase, teams can reap significant benefits, including early defect detection, streamlined testing processes, and improved overall software quality. Emphasizing testability throughout the SDLC ultimately leads to more efficient, effective, and high-quality software products.

Designing for testability

When designing software systems, it is crucial to prioritize testability from the outset. Architectural patterns and principles such as modularity, loose coupling, and high cohesion play a significant role in enhancing testability, as explained:

- **Modularity:** Modularity refers to breaking down a system into smaller, self-contained components or modules that can be developed, tested, and maintained independently. This approach allows for more focused testing, as each module can be validated separately before integrating it into the larger system. Additionally, modularity aids in isolating faults, making it easier to identify and fix issues.

- **Loose coupling:** Loose coupling means that components or modules within a system have minimal dependencies on one another. This principle enhances testability by allowing individual components to be tested in isolation. When components are loosely coupled, changes in one module are less likely to affect others, which simplifies both testing and maintenance. Techniques such as dependency injection and event-driven architecture can help achieve loose coupling.

- **High cohesion:** High cohesion refers to the degree to which the elements within a module belong together. A cohesive module focuses on a single responsibility, making it easier to understand, test, and maintain. When modules are highly cohesive, the interactions between them become clearer, leading to more straightforward integration and testing processes.

Breaking systems into smaller, independent, and testable units

Breaking down systems into smaller, independent, and testable units is vital for improving overall system testability. This approach offers several benefits:

- **Enhanced focus:** Testing smaller units allows teams to concentrate on specific functionalities, leading to more thorough and effective tests. Developers can write unit tests that cover various scenarios, edge cases, and error conditions, ensuring that each unit behaves as expected.

- **Faster feedback:** Smaller, independent units enable quicker testing cycles. Developers can run unit tests locally before integrating changes into the main codebase, reducing the time it takes to identify and address issues.

- **Parallel development:** When a system is divided into independent components, different teams can work on separate modules simultaneously. This parallel development accelerates the overall delivery process while maintaining high testability standards.

- **Ease of refactoring:** Smaller units are easier to refactor or replace when needed. If a module requires changes or enhancements, developers can modify it without risking unintended side effects in other parts of the system, leading to safer and more efficient refactoring.

Designing APIs, services, and interfaces for testability

To ensure APIs, services, and interfaces are easily testable, several design considerations should be implemented, such as:

- **Clear contracts:** APIs should define clear contracts, outlining the expected inputs, outputs, and behavior. Well-defined contracts facilitate the creation of comprehensive tests that validate compliance with these expectations. Tools such as OpenAPI can help in documenting and validating API contracts.

- **Use of mocking and stubbing:** Designing APIs with testability in mind involves enabling the use of mocking and stubbing frameworks. By allowing dependencies to be replaced with mock objects during testing, developers can isolate the unit under test and simulate various scenarios without relying on actual implementations.

- **Granular endpoints:** For RESTful services, creating granular endpoints that correspond to specific operations or resources enhances testability. Each endpoint can be tested individually, ensuring that the service behaves as expected under different conditions.

- **Versioning:** Implementing versioning for APIs allows for backward compatibility while enabling teams to introduce changes or improvements. This flexibility reduces the risk of breaking existing functionality, making it easier to test new features in isolation.

- **Comprehensive error handling:** APIs should incorporate robust error handling mechanisms, providing meaningful error messages and status codes. Testing various error scenarios becomes easier when APIs are designed with predictable and consistent error handling.

- **Support for testing frameworks:** APIs and services should be designed to integrate seamlessly with popular testing frameworks. This includes providing endpoints for health checks, mock data, and test configurations that facilitate automated testing.

Designing for testability is essential for ensuring the reliability and maintainability of software systems. By embracing architectural patterns and principles such as modularity, loose coupling, and high cohesion, teams can create systems that are easier to test and validate. Breaking systems into smaller, independent units improves testability by allowing focused testing, faster feedback, and easier maintenance. Furthermore, designing APIs, services, and interfaces with testability enables efficient unit, integration, and end-to-end testing, ultimately leading to higher-quality software.

Separation of concerns

Separation of concerns (SoC) is a fundamental design principle in software engineering that advocates for dividing a program into distinct sections, each addressing a separate concern or functionality. By isolating different aspects of software, developers can create more manageable, maintainable, and testable components. This approach is especially valuable for ensuring software systems evolve without becoming tangled or overly complex.

Designing independently testable software components

By applying the principle of separation of concerns, software components can be designed to be independently testable. This involves creating clear boundaries between different responsibilities within the application, allowing each component to be tested in isolation. Here is how this principle facilitates independent testability:

- **Encapsulation of functionality:** When concerns are separated, each component encapsulates specific functionality. For example, a module responsible for user authentication can be developed and tested without involving the user interface or data storage layers. This encapsulation allows developers to focus on the behavior of each module, ensuring thorough testing.

- **Simplified testing scenarios:** With concerns separated, developers can create focused test scenarios for each component. For instance, unit tests can validate a business service's logic without invoking the database or user interface, leading to faster and more effective testing cycles.

- **Reduced complexity:** A well-structured application with separated concerns reduces the complexity of testing. Developers can isolate failures and determine the root cause of issues easily when the functionality is neatly compartmentalized.

- **Facilitation of mocking and stubbing:** When components are independent, mocking and stubbing become more straightforward. Dependencies can be easily replaced with test doubles, allowing developers to simulate various states and behaviors during testing without needing the actual implementations.

Separating business logic, data access, and user interfaces

The following *Figure 5.1* features how the different layers in an application can work:

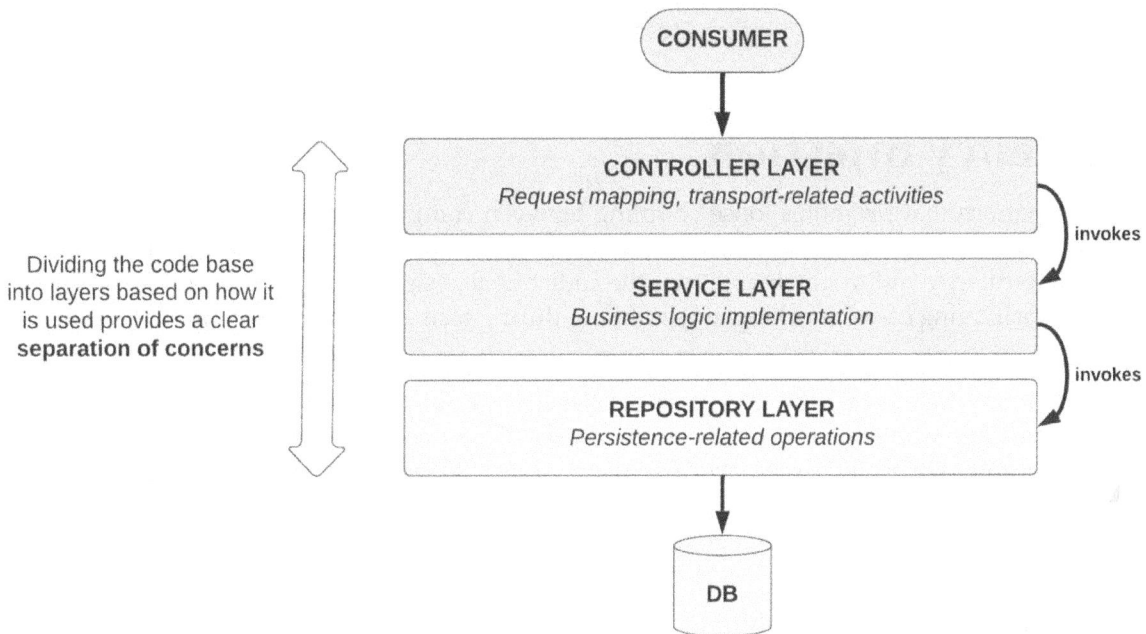

Figure 5.1: Image of how different layers in an application can work

Separating different layers of an application, such as business logic, data access, and user interfaces, significantly enhances the testability of the application. Here is how each layer benefits from this separation:

- **Business logic layer:**

  o **Independence from data access and UI:** The business logic layer encapsulates the core functionality of the application, such as calculations, decision-making, and rules. By keeping it independent from data access and user interfaces, it can be tested without worrying about external dependencies.

  o **Focused unit testing:** Since business logic is centralized, developers can write comprehensive unit tests to validate all possible scenarios and edge cases, ensuring the application behaves as expected.

- **Data access layer:**

  o **Isolation of database concerns:** By isolating data access, the application can implement various data storage strategies without impacting the business logic or user interface. This allows for testing of data retrieval and manipulation independently.

  o **Mocking database interactions:** During testing, developers can mock data access methods, enabling them to simulate different database states and behaviors without needing a live database connection. This leads to faster and more reliable tests.

- **User interface layer:**

  o **Testing user interactions:** The user interface layer can be designed to interact with the business logic without being tightly coupled. This separation allows for testing user interactions and interface behavior without involving the underlying logic or data access.

  o **Integration testing:** With a clear boundary, integration tests can be created to ensure that the user interface correctly communicates with the business logic, validating the entire flow of the application while still allowing the individual layers to be tested in isolation.

The principle of separation of concerns is vital for designing independently testable software components. Developers create a more structured and manageable application architecture by separating business logic, data access, and user interfaces. This separation enhances testability by allowing focused unit tests, simplifying the testing process, and reducing complexity. Overall, applying the principle of SoC results in higher-quality software that is easier to maintain, extend, and test, ultimately contributing to improved software development practices.

Dependency injection

DI is a design pattern that promotes loose coupling between components in software systems by injecting dependencies from the outside rather than having components create them internally. This pattern not only improves the modularity and maintainability of the code but also significantly enhances the testability of the application by facilitating easier mocking and stubbing during tests. Let us understand the following:

- **Decoupling components:** One of the primary benefits of DI is that it decouples the components of an application. When a class (or component) relies on interfaces rather than concrete implementations, it becomes agnostic to the specific classes it uses. This decoupling allows for easy substitution of dependencies, which is particularly useful in testing scenarios. For example, a service class that depends on a repository interface can be injected with different implementations, whether real or mocked, without needing to change the service's code. This separation promotes cleaner design and easier testing.

- **Facilitating mocking and stubbing:** DI makes it straightforward to use mocking frameworks to create test doubles (mocks or stubs) that simulate the behavior of real dependencies. During unit tests, developers can provide these test doubles instead of actual implementations, allowing them to isolate the component under test. By injecting a mock repository into a service, for instance, a developer can simulate various scenarios (for example, returning a successful result or throwing an exception) without relying on the actual database. This flexibility enables comprehensive testing of the service's logic in different conditions.

Replacing real dependencies with test doubles

Dependency injection allows for the seamless replacement of real dependencies with test doubles during automated testing. Here is how this process works:

- **Injection of dependencies:** Dependencies are injected into components through constructor injection, property injection, or method injection. By specifying the dependencies externally, the component does not need to instantiate them internally.

  o For instance, in a web application, a controller may require a service to handle business logic. Instead of creating an instance of the service, the controller receives the service instance through its constructor.

- **Using mocking frameworks:** With DI in place, developers can easily use mocking frameworks (like Mockito for Java or Moq for .NET) to create test doubles. These frameworks provide the functionality to set up expectations, define return values, and verify interactions with the dependencies.

  o When writing tests, developers can configure the DI container or directly inject the mocked dependency into the component being tested. This allows for testing without the overhead or complications of real dependencies.

- **Automated testing scenarios:** During automated tests, the use of DI enables the testing of various scenarios by swapping out the real dependencies for appropriate test doubles. This process allows teams to simulate edge cases, error conditions, or specific data states easily.

  o For example, in testing a payment processing service, a mock payment gateway can be injected instead of integrating with a live payment gateway that simulates successful and failed

transactions. This allows for comprehensive testing of the service's behavior under different conditions.

DI is a powerful pattern that significantly improves testability by decoupling components and facilitating the use of test doubles in testing scenarios. By leveraging DI, developers can easily swap actual dependencies with mocks or stubs, allowing for focused and efficient testing of individual components. This not only enhances the application's reliability and maintainability but also promotes better software design practices, resulting in higher-quality software that is easier to test, maintain, and extend.

Decoupling from external systems

Decoupling from external systems is a crucial design principle in software engineering that emphasizes minimizing the reliance on external dependencies, such as databases, APIs, or third-party services, especially during unit testing. By designing systems that are less dependent on these external components, developers can create more reliable, maintainable, and testable software. This approach ensures that tests run quickly and consistently, without the complications of network latency, data inconsistencies, or service availability.

Designing systems to minimize reliance on external dependencies

Let us understand the following:

- **Use of local testing environments:** Designing applications to function well in local testing environments minimizes reliance on external systems. For instance, applications can be configured to use in-memory databases (like H2 for Java) or local mock services during testing. This setup allows developers to execute tests without needing to connect to actual databases or external APIs.

- **Configurable endpoints:** Applications should allow the configuration of external service endpoints. During testing, these endpoints can be redirected to mock services or local implementations. By configuring these dependencies, developers can ensure their unit tests do not rely on external services being available.

- **Environment profiles:** Implementing environment profiles (such as development, testing, and production) allows teams to specify different configurations for each environment. For example, in a testing environment, the application could connect to a mock API or a test database instead of a live service, ensuring tests run in isolation from external systems.

- **Fallback mechanisms:** Incorporating fallback mechanisms allows applications to handle scenarios where external systems may be temporarily unavailable. This design not only improves resilience in production but also aids testing by ensuring that unit tests can simulate failure conditions without relying on external systems.

Using abstractions, interfaces, or mocks

Let us understand the following:

- **Creating abstractions:** Abstractions, such as interfaces or abstract classes, can be used to define the expected behavior of external systems. For example, rather than directly interacting with a database or an API, an application can define an interface that encapsulates the necessary operations. This abstraction allows for easy replacement of the actual implementation with a mock or stub during testing.

  o By coding against interfaces rather than concrete implementations, developers can change the underlying logic without impacting the rest of the application, promoting flexibility and easier testing.

- **Mocking frameworks:** Mocking frameworks (such as Mockito, Moq, or Sinon) can be employed to create test doubles that simulate the behavior of external systems. These frameworks allow developers to define expectations, specify return values, and verify interactions with the mocks during test execution.

  o For instance, when testing a service that retrieves data from an external API, developers can create a mock of the API client that returns predefined responses. This setup enables thorough testing of the service logic without making real network requests.

- **Simulating external systems:** In cases where complex external systems need to be simulated, tools like WireMock or MockServer can be employed. These tools allow developers to create mock HTTP services that respond like the real services they are designed to replace, enabling more realistic testing scenarios.

  o By simulating external systems, teams can test how their application behaves under various conditions, such as different response times or error codes, without being affected by the actual external service's state.

Decoupling from external systems is an essential design principle that minimizes reliance on external dependencies for unit testing. Developers can create more reliable, maintainable, and testable applications by designing systems to operate independently of these components. Utilizing abstractions, interfaces, and mocking techniques enables teams to simulate external systems during test execution, allowing for focused and efficient testing without the complications of network latency or service availability. Ultimately, this approach leads to higher-quality software that is easier to develop, test, and maintain.

Best practices for ensuring systems are testable

In order to ensure the best testable design in your software systems, it is important to consider the following best practices.

Clear and consistent interfaces

In software design, having clear and consistent interfaces between modules and components is critical for ensuring the system is easy to understand, maintain, and test. Well-defined interfaces act as contracts that specify how different parts of a system interact, leading to better collaboration among team members and more reliable testing outcomes as follows:

- **Clear specifications:** Interfaces should have clearly defined methods, parameters, and expected return types. This clarity allows developers to understand how to use the interface without ambiguity. For example, an interface for a payment processing system might specify methods for processing payments, refunding transactions, and checking payment statuses, all with clear documentation on expected input and output.

  o By providing thorough documentation, including examples and edge cases, developers can more easily implement and test against the interface, leading to fewer misunderstandings.

- **Consistent naming conventions:** Using consistent naming conventions across interfaces helps convey their purpose and functionality. For instance, developers can quickly identify their roles if all data access interfaces begin with I (for example, IDataRepository). Consistent naming reduces cognitive load, making it easier to remember and utilize different interfaces throughout the codebase.

  o Establishing and adhering to interface naming standards enhances readability and discoverability, which can significantly benefit testing.

- **Versioning and change management:** Interfaces should be versioned, allowing for backward compatibility while introducing new functionality. This versioning ensures that existing tests remain valid even when the interface evolves, making it easier to manage changes and maintain reliability in test cases.

o   Providing clear deprecation notices and transition guides helps developers adjust their implementations and tests without significant disruptions.

Reducing complexity and increasing reliability of test cases

Let us go over the following:

- **Simplified testing scenarios:** With clear and consistent interfaces, testing becomes more straightforward, as developers can write tests that focus on the contract defined by the interface rather than the underlying implementation details. This separation allows unit tests to validate that a module behaves as expected when interacting with the interface.

  o   When tests are designed around interfaces, they can be reused across different implementations, ensuring that the expected behavior is maintained regardless of changes in the underlying code.

- **Mocking and stubbing made easier:** We have mentioned this several times already, but it only goes to highlight how important mocking and stubbing are to ensure the testability of an application. Clear interfaces facilitate the creation of mocks and stubs, which are essential for unit testing. When interfaces are well-defined, mocking frameworks can easily create test doubles that adhere to the same contracts, allowing for precise simulation of various scenarios.

  o   Developers can focus on testing interactions with the interface without needing to know how the actual implementations work, reducing the complexity involved in setting up tests.

- **Improved reliability of test cases:** Standardized interfaces increase the reliability of test cases by ensuring that tests are consistent across different components. If every component adheres to the same interface structure, it reduces the likelihood of discrepancies or errors in how tests are executed.

  o   With well-defined interfaces, regression testing becomes more effective, as tests can consistently verify that components interact correctly with each other, thus maintaining the integrity of the entire system.

- **Clearer error handling:** Consistent interfaces also contribute to clearer error handling. By standardizing how errors are communicated through the interface (for example, using exceptions, return codes, or specific error objects), developers can write more effective tests to validate that errors are handled correctly.

  o   This clarity in error management leads to more robust test cases, ensuring that failure scenarios are adequately covered and understood.

Establishing clear and consistent interfaces between modules and components is essential for improving testability and reliability in software systems. By ensuring that interfaces are well-defined, consistently named, and documented, developers can create a testing environment that is straightforward and less complex. This standardization simplifies the process of writing and executing test cases and increases their reliability, resulting in higher-quality software that is easier to maintain and evolve over time. Embracing this practice leads to more robust applications and a smoother development workflow, ultimately benefiting the entire development lifecycle.

Isolated testing

Isolated testing refers to the practice of designing software components so that they can be tested independently from the rest of the system. This approach ensures that dependencies do not interfere with the execution of individual unit tests, allowing developers to focus on the specific functionality of each component. By facilitating isolated testing, teams can achieve higher test coverage, improve reliability, and simplify the debugging process.

Designing components to be testable in isolation

To enable isolated testing, it is essential to adhere to the principle of SoC. This principle encourages developers to break down the application into distinct components, each responsible for a specific function. By minimizing the interdependencies between components, developers can isolate the testing of individual modules.

For example, a web application could separate its business logic, data access, and presentation layers. This separation allows each layer to be tested independently, ensuring that issues in one layer do not affect the others. Let us go over the following:

- **Minimal external dependencies:** Components should be designed to rely minimally on external systems or shared resources. By avoiding tight coupling with databases, APIs, or other components, developers can create modules that are easier to test in isolation.

  o For instance, a service that processes data should not directly query a database but rather rely on an abstraction (such as an interface) for data retrieval. This approach allows the service to be tested independently by providing a mock implementation of the data access layer.

- **Clear input and output definitions:** Well-defined input and output parameters for components make it easier to test them in isolation. When a component's interface clearly states what it expects as input and what it returns, developers can create focused unit tests that verify the component's behavior under various scenarios.

  o For example, a function that calculates tax should accept inputs (income, tax rate) and return a specific output (calculated tax). Clear definitions facilitate targeted testing of the function's logic.

- **Mocking frameworks:** Mocking frameworks (such as Mockito, Moq, or Sinon) are essential tools for creating isolated testing environments. These frameworks allow developers to create test doubles that simulate the behavior of external dependencies, enabling the testing of individual components without invoking real implementations.

  o For example, when testing a service that relies on an external API, a mock of the API client can be created to return predefined responses. This setup allows the service to be tested in isolation, validating its logic without the complications of real network interactions.

- **Dependency injection:** DI plays a vital role in isolating tests by allowing developers to inject mock dependencies into components during testing. By relying on interfaces instead of concrete implementations, DI makes it easy to substitute real dependencies with test doubles.

  o For instance, a service that sends emails can accept an email client interface as a dependency. In unit tests, a mock email client can be injected to simulate sending emails without triggering the email-sending process.

- **Setting up isolated testing environments:** With the combination of DI and mocking frameworks, developers can create isolated testing environments for each module. This setup allows for focused unit tests that validate the functionality of individual components without interference from external systems.

  o For example, when testing a data processing service, developers can mock all the dependencies it interacts with (like data access and external APIs) and verify that the service processes data correctly based on various inputs and conditions.

Isolated testing is a crucial practice in software development that allows components to be tested independently, ensuring that dependencies do not hinder the execution of individual unit tests. By designing components to minimize external dependencies and using mocking frameworks alongside dependency injection, developers can create isolated testing environments for each module. This approach leads to more focused and reliable tests, ultimately resulting in higher-quality software that is easier to maintain, debug, and extend. Embracing isolated testing practices promotes better software design and a more efficient development process, benefiting both development teams and end-users.

Simplicity and predictability

In software development, simplicity and predictability are foundational principles that enhance the overall quality of the codebase and its associated tests. By favoring simple designs, developers can create software that is easier to write, execute, and maintain tests. Simpler designs not only streamline the testing process but also foster predictable behavior, making it easier to detect, reproduce, and fix issues during testing.

Favouring simplicity in software design

Let us go over the following:

- **Keep It Simple, Stupid (KISS) principle:** The KISS principle advocates for simplicity in design, encouraging developers to avoid unnecessary complexity. When software components are straightforward and focused on a single responsibility, they become easier to understand, implement, and test.

    o For example, a user authentication function should focus solely on that task without mixing in unrelated concerns like logging or user notification. This separation simplifies the logic and enhances testability.

- **Minimalist design:** Adopting a minimalist design philosophy helps reduce the number of features and interactions within a component. By eliminating unnecessary complexity, developers create modules that are easier to reason about and test.

    o For instance, a user registration component might include only the essential fields (like username and password) rather than overwhelming users with additional optional fields at the outset. This approach streamlines the logic, making the component easier to test.

- **Avoiding premature optimization:** Developers should refrain from premature optimization, focusing instead on building simple and clear solutions first. Complex optimizations can introduce unnecessary difficulties in testing and maintenance.

    o By concentrating on clear functionality and a simple design, developers can create a solid foundation that can be optimized later without complicating the initial implementation.

Simpler designs leading to predictable behavior

Let us go over the following:

- **Easier detection of issues:** Simpler designs typically result in fewer pathways and edge cases to consider, making it easier to detect issues. When a component has straightforward logic, identifying the root cause of a problem becomes more manageable during testing.

    o For instance, if a function has only a few conditional branches, it is easier to trace the execution path and understand why a particular outcome was produced.

- **Reproducible test scenarios:** Predictable behavior in software components leads to reproducible test scenarios. When a component consistently produces the same output for the same input, tests can reliably verify its functionality.

    o For example, a function that calculates discounts should return the same result for the same input values every time it is executed. This predictability ensures that tests can be run repeatedly without variations in behavior.

- **Simplified debugging process:** Simpler designs facilitate a more straightforward debugging process when issues arise. Developers can more easily analyze the code, identify where things went wrong, and apply fixes.

  o For instance, if a complex function throws an error, pinpointing the source of the problem can be daunting. However, a simpler implementation with clear logic makes it easier to trace the error's origin and implement an effective solution.

- **Increased test coverage:** Simpler designs encourage better test coverage. When components are easier to understand and test, developers are more likely to write comprehensive unit tests that cover various scenarios, including edge cases.

  o For example, if a class is designed to handle user input, simpler logic encourages tests that
   • validate all possible input combinations, leading to higher confidence in the system's reliability.

Emphasizing simplicity in software design is crucial for creating components that are easier to write, execute, and maintain tests. Simpler designs lead to more predictable behavior, facilitating easier detection, reproduction, and fixing of issues during testing. By adopting principles like KISS, minimalist design, and avoiding premature optimization, developers can create robust systems that foster reliability and maintainability. Ultimately, embracing simplicity and predictability in software design not only enhances the testing process but also contributes to the overall quality and success of the software development lifecycle.

Logging and monitoring

Logging and monitoring are critical practices in modern software development that enhance application observability. Integrating logging and monitoring tools into a system allows developers and testers to capture real-time information about the application's state during testing and production. This capability is essential for diagnosing issues, understanding application behavior, and ensuring the overall health of the system.

Integrating logging and monitoring tools

Let us go over the following:

- **Choosing the right tools:** Selecting appropriate logging and monitoring tools is the first step in establishing effective observability. Popular logging frameworks (like Log4j, SLF4J, or Serilog) and monitoring solutions (like Prometheus, Grafana, or ELK Stack) should align with the application's technology stack and requirements.

  o These tools should support structured logging, enabling logs to be formatted in a way that facilitates querying and analysis. Additionally, they should integrate well with the application and provide real-time monitoring and alerting capabilities.

- **Incorporating logging into the application:** Logging should be integrated throughout the application at key points where important events occur, such as function entry and exit, error handling, and significant state changes. This comprehensive coverage helps capture the application's behavior during testing.

  o Developers should use appropriate log levels (for example, DEBUG, INFO, WARN, ERROR) to categorize log messages based on their importance and severity. This categorization makes it easier to filter and analyze logs during testing and production.

- **Monitoring application metrics:** In addition to logging, implementing monitoring solutions to capture key performance metrics (such as response times, error rates, and resource utilization) provides valuable insights into the application's behavior.

Monitoring tools can track real-time metrics, alerting developers to anomalies or performance issues as they arise. This capability allows for immediate investigation during testing, ensuring that potential issues are identified and addressed promptly.

Robust logging aiding debugging and root-cause analysis

Let us go over the following:

- **Detailed contextual information:** Robust logging provides detailed contextual information about the application's state during test execution. By capturing relevant data (such as variable values, user inputs, and timestamps), logs offer insights that help developers understand the circumstances surrounding a failure.

  o For instance, when a test fails, the logs can reveal what inputs were processed, what external services were called, and what errors occurred, enabling developers to quickly narrow down the root cause.

- **Reproducing test failures:** Detailed logs enable developers to reproduce test failures by providing a comprehensive account of the execution flow leading up to the failure. By analyzing the logs, developers can retrace the steps the application took and replicate the conditions that caused the test to fail.

  o This reproducibility is crucial for diagnosing intermittent failures or complex issues that may not surface consistently.

- **Identifying patterns and trends:** Logging can reveal patterns and trends in application behavior that may not be immediately apparent during testing. By analyzing logs over time, developers can identify recurring issues, such as specific error messages or performance bottlenecks, enabling proactive improvements to the system.

  o For example, if a particular API consistently returns errors during specific tests, developers can investigate and address the underlying issue before it affects end users.

- **Facilitating collaboration:** Robust logging fosters collaboration among team members by providing a common reference point for diagnosing issues. Detailed logs serve as a shared resource for discussing and resolving problems when multiple developers are involved in testing and debugging.

  o Additionally, when issues are documented with clear logs, it becomes easier for new team members to understand the application's behavior and contribute to resolving ongoing challenges.

- **Enhancing post-mortem analysis:** After a test failure, robust logging facilitates effective post-mortem analysis. Developers can review logs to assess what went wrong, how it impacted the system, and what corrective actions should be taken.

  o This analysis helps improve the overall testing process, as lessons learned from failures can inform future test designs, logging strategies, and application enhancements.

Integrating logging and monitoring tools into a software system is essential for capturing real-time information about the application's state during testing. Robust logging aids in debugging and root-cause analysis by providing detailed contextual information, enabling reproducibility of test failures, and identifying patterns and trends. By fostering collaboration among team members and enhancing post-mortem analysis, effective logging and monitoring practices ultimately lead to higher-quality software and a more efficient development lifecycle. Embracing these practices empowers teams to proactively address issues and continuously improve their applications, ensuring reliability and performance in production.

Enabling continuous testing

Continuous testing is a crucial practice in modern software development that aims to improve software quality and accelerate delivery by executing tests automatically throughout the development lifecycle. By designing systems to facilitate continuous testing and integrating them seamlessly into **continuous integration/ continuous deployment** (**CI/CD**) pipelines, teams can ensure that testing becomes an integral part of the development process. This approach enables early defect detection, faster feedback loops, and a more reliable software delivery process.

Designing systems for continuous testing

Let us go over the following:

- **Test-driven development (TDD):** Adopting TDD encourages developers to write tests before implementing functionality. This practice not only ensures that tests are an integral part of the design but also promotes a focus on testability from the outset.

    o   In TDD, developers write a failing test, implement the minimal code required to pass the test, and then refactor. This cycle reinforces the creation of testable components and supports continuous testing.

- **Modular architecture:** Designing systems with a modular architecture allows for easier testing of individual components in isolation. This modularity supports continuous testing by enabling focused tests for each module without the need to set up the entire system.

    o   For instance, microservices architectures facilitate testing by allowing teams to deploy and test each service independently, making it easier to integrate continuous testing into CI/CD pipelines.

- **Integration with CI/CD pipelines:** Continuous testing should be seamlessly integrated into CI/CD pipelines to ensure that tests are automatically executed with each code change. This integration can be achieved through configuration management tools, build automation tools, and CI/CD platforms (like Jenkins, GitLab CI, CircleCI, or Azure DevOps).

    o   By triggering tests on specific events (for example, code commits, pull requests, or scheduled builds), teams can catch issues early in the development process.

Best practices for automating tests

Let us go over some best practices now:

- **Test automation strategy:** Establish a clear test automation strategy that defines what types of tests to automate (for example, unit tests, integration tests, end-to-end tests) and how to prioritize them. Prioritizing critical tests that provide the most value helps optimize testing efforts.

    o   Aim for a balanced test suite, where unit tests cover the core logic, integration tests validate interactions between components, and end-to-end tests ensure the overall system works as expected.

- **Pre-commit testing:** Implement pre-commit hooks to run quick checks and validations (such as linting and unit tests) before committing code. This practice helps catch issues early, reducing the likelihood of introducing defects into the codebase.

    o   Tools like Husky or Git hooks can facilitate the execution of these checks automatically when changes are committed.

- **Pre-merge testing:** During the **pull request (PR)** process, run a comprehensive suite of tests, including unit tests, integration tests, and any relevant functional tests. This step ensures that all code changes are validated against the existing codebase before merging into the main branch.

    o   Configure CI/CD tools to run the test suite on each PR, providing immediate feedback to developers about the impact of their changes.

- **Post-deployment testing:** After deploying to production or staging environments, execute smoke tests and sanity checks to validate that the deployment was successful and that critical functionalities are working as expected. This practice helps catch any issues arising during the deployment process.

    o   Implement automated rollback mechanisms if critical tests fail post-deployment, ensuring that the system can quickly recover from issues.

- **Continuous monitoring and feedback:** Integrate monitoring tools to capture metrics and logs during test execution and production usage. This data can inform teams about test performance, code coverage, and the application's overall health.

  o Establish a feedback loop where developers receive insights on test results, system performance, and any failures encountered during testing. This will enable continuous improvement of the testing process.

Enabling continuous testing is essential for modern software development, as it fosters a culture of quality and accelerates delivery. By designing systems that support continuous testing and integrating it seamlessly into CI/CD pipelines, teams can automate testing at various stages of development. Implementing best practices for automating tests, such as TDD, pre-commit and pre-merge testing, and post-deployment validation, helps ensure that software remains reliable and meets quality standards throughout its lifecycle. Embracing continuous testing enhances the efficiency of the development process and improves the overall quality of the software, ultimately leading to better outcomes for both developers and end-users.

Tools and techniques to support testing

Let us go over some tools and techniques now.

Unit testing tools

Unit testing is a fundamental practice in software development that involves testing individual components or functions of an application in isolation to ensure they behave as expected. To facilitate this process, various tools and frameworks have been developed, providing developers with the necessary resources to write, execute, and manage unit tests efficiently. Some of the most widely used unit testing frameworks include JUnit for Java, NUnit for .NET applications, and Pytest for Python.

JUnit: JUnit is a popular open-source testing framework for Java that provides annotations, assertions, and test runners to simplify the process of writing and running unit tests. It is widely used in Java projects and is often integrated with build tools like Maven and Gradle. The key features are:

- Annotations for defining test cases, setup, and teardown methods.
- Assertions for verifying expected outcomes.
- Support for parameterized tests to run the same test with different inputs.

NUnit: NUnit is a widely used unit testing framework for .NET applications that allows developers to write tests in C#. It provides similar functionality to JUnit, including test case definitions, assertions, and support for various test runners.

The key features are:

- Rich set of attributes for defining tests and test fixtures.
- Assertion libraries for verifying test outcomes.
- Support for data-driven tests to run multiple scenarios with different inputs.

Pytest: Pytest is a versatile testing framework for Python that supports both simple unit tests and complex functional testing. It is known for its ease of use and powerful features, including fixtures, parameterized testing, and plugin support.

The key features are:

- Simple syntax for writing tests and assertions.
- Fixture support for managing test setup and teardown.
- Extensive plugin ecosystem for extending functionality.

Writing testable code

To achieve maximum code coverage and facilitate early defect detection, it is essential to write testable code. This involves adhering to principles like SoC and Single Responsibility Principle, and ensuring that code is modular and loosely coupled.

Aim for well-defined interfaces and use dependency injections to decouple components, making them easier to test in isolation.

Establishing a testing strategy

Develop a clear testing strategy that outlines the types of tests to be written (unit tests, integration tests, and so on) and the level of coverage desired. This strategy should prioritize critical components and functionalities for testing.

Consider using tools like SonarQube or Codecov to measure and report on code coverage, helping teams identify untested areas of the codebase.

Using test coverage tools

Most unit testing frameworks offer built-in tools or plugins for measuring code coverage. For example:

- JUnit can be integrated with tools like Jacoco for Java to generate coverage reports.

- NUnit can utilize Coverlet or ReportGenerator for .NET applications to analyze coverage.

- Pytest supports coverage measurement through the pytest-cov plugin, which reports on code coverage when running tests.

These tools help developers visualize which parts of the codebase are covered by tests and identify areas that require additional testing.

Writing comprehensive test cases

Each unit test should focus on a single behavior or functionality of the component being tested. Tests should be clear, concise, and well-documented to ensure that their purpose is easily understood.

Aim to cover various scenarios, including:

- **Positive tests:** Valid inputs that the function should handle correctly.

- **Negative tests:** Invalid inputs that should trigger appropriate error handling.

- **Edge cases:** Boundary conditions or unusual inputs that may cause unexpected behavior.

Automating test execution

Integrate unit tests into the CI/CD pipeline to automate their execution whenever code changes are made. This practice ensures that tests are run consistently and frequently, allowing for early defect detection.

Use tools like Jenkins, GitHub Actions, or GitLab CI to configure automated test execution and provide immediate feedback to developers.

Regular refactoring and maintenance

Regularly refactor tests to keep them up to date with changes in the codebase. As the application evolves, test cases may become outdated or irrelevant, so maintaining their relevance is essential.

Review and improve test cases based on feedback from test results, focusing on enhancing coverage and clarity.

Unit testing tools like JUnit, NUnit, and Pytest provide developers with the frameworks necessary to write, execute, and manage unit tests effectively. By setting up unit tests for maximum code coverage and early defect detection, teams can ensure that their code is reliable, maintainable, and high-quality. Adopting best practices such as writing testable code, establishing a testing strategy, utilizing coverage tools, and automating test execution contributes to a robust testing process that enhances the overall software development lifecycle. Embracing these practices empowers teams to deliver reliable software with confidence, ultimately leading to improved user satisfaction and business success.

Mocking and stubbing

Mocking and stubbing are essential techniques in software testing that allow developers to simulate the behavior of complex or external dependencies, enabling more effective unit and integration testing. By using mocking frameworks and test doubles, developers can isolate components, reduce test execution time, and improve the reliability of tests.

Role of mocking frameworks

Mocking frameworks facilitate the creation of test doubles, which are objects that mimic the behavior of real objects in a controlled way. These frameworks allow developers to define how dependencies should behave during tests, enabling them to focus on testing the component under scrutiny without being affected by its dependencies.

Mockito: Mockito is a popular mocking framework for Java that allows developers to create mock objects and define their behavior using a fluent API. It is widely used in combination with JUnit for unit testing. Its key features are:

- Easy to create mocks and define behavior with simple syntax.

- Support for verifying interactions and method calls on mock objects.

- Allows for argument matchers and custom return values.

Moq: Moq is a powerful mocking framework for .NET applications that enables developers to create and manipulate mock objects easily. It integrates well with NUnit and other testing frameworks. Its key features are:

- Simple and intuitive syntax for creating mocks and defining behavior.

- Support for verifying method calls and property accesses.

- Ability to set up callbacks for more complex scenarios.

FakeIt: FakeIt is a lightweight mocking framework for .NET that allows for the creation of fake objects to simulate dependencies during testing. It emphasizes simplicity and ease of use. Its key features are:

- Minimalistic syntax for creating fake objects.

- Flexibility in defining behavior for methods and properties.

- Support for asynchronous programming and LINQ queries.

Using test doubles to replace complex components

Test doubles, including mocks, stubs, fakes, and spies, serve various purposes in testing by replacing complex or slow components with simpler, faster alternatives. Here is a breakdown of different types of test doubles:

- **Mocks:** Mocks are objects that simulate the behavior of real objects in a way that allows verification of interactions. They are used to ensure that the tested component interacts with its dependencies as expected. For example, when testing a service that calls an external API, a mock can simulate the API's responses without making actual network calls.

- **Stubs:** Stubs are objects that provide predefined responses to method calls, allowing tests to proceed without relying on the real implementations of dependencies. Stubs do not verify interactions; they simply return data as configured. For example, if a component relies on a database connection, a stub can return mock data instead of querying the actual database, speeding up the testing process.

- **Fakes:** Fakes are lightweight implementations of interfaces or classes that provide the necessary functionality without the complexity of real objects. Fakes can maintain state and can be used when the actual implementation is too slow or complex. For instance, a fake repository can simulate data access in memory, allowing for faster tests without the overhead of interacting with a real database.

- **Spies:** Spies are test doubles that record information about how they were interacted with, allowing developers to verify whether certain methods were called with specific parameters. They are useful when the primary focus is on interaction rather than state. For example, a spy can be used to track calls to a logging service, ensuring that the correct log messages are generated.

Advantages of mocking and stubbing

The advantages are:

- **Isolation:** Mocking and stubbing allow for the isolation of the component under test, ensuring that tests focus solely on its behavior. This isolation reduces the complexity of testing and leads to more reliable results.

- **Speed:** Tests that rely on mocks and stubs execute faster because they eliminate the need for complex operations, such as network calls or database queries. This speed is crucial in large test suites, where execution time can become a bottleneck.

- **Determinism:** Mocks and stubs can provide consistent, predictable behavior, making it easier to test edge cases and failure scenarios. This determinism enhances the reliability of tests, as they can reproduce specific conditions without interference from external factors.

- **Simplicity:** By replacing complex components with simpler alternatives, developers can focus on testing the logic of the component without being bogged down by dependencies. This simplification leads to clearer and more maintainable tests.

Mocking frameworks like Mockito, Moq, and FakeIt play a crucial role in unit and integration testing by enabling developers to simulate dependencies and isolate components effectively. By using test doubles, developers can replace complex or slow components with more straightforward, faster alternatives, enhancing the reliability and performance of tests. Embracing mocking and stubbing techniques empowers teams to write practical unit tests, leading to higher-quality software and a more efficient development process. By integrating these practices into their testing strategies, teams can ensure that their applications are robust, maintainable, and deliver user value.

Test data management

Test data management (TDM) is a critical aspect of software testing that involves creating, maintaining, and utilizing test data. Efficient TDM ensures that testing processes are reliable, reproducible, and relevant to real-world scenarios. With applications' increasing complexity and the need for comprehensive testing, effective TDM becomes essential for validating software quality and performance.

Managing test data efficiently

Numerous tools are available to assist in generating, storing, and resetting test data. These tools help streamline the management process and ensure data consistency across various testing environments.

Data generation tools

The tools are:

- **Mockaroo:** An online tool that allows users to create realistic mock data sets based on specified schemas. It can generate large volumes of data in multiple formats (CSV, JSON, SQL, and so on) and is useful for populating databases with representative test data.

- **Faker:** A library available in various programming languages (such as Python, Java, and Ruby) that generates fake data. It can create realistic names, addresses, emails, and other types of data, making it easy to simulate real-world scenarios.

- **dbForge data generator:** A powerful tool for generating test data for SQL databases. It provides a user-friendly interface and a variety of pre-defined data generation templates to simplify the process.

Data masking tools

The tools are:

- **Informatica data masking:** A tool that helps protect sensitive information by replacing real data with fictional but realistic data. It is crucial for maintaining data privacy and compliance during testing.

- **Delphix:** A data management platform that includes data masking features to secure sensitive data while providing developers and testers with access to realistic data sets.

Data refresh tools

The tools are:

- **Redgate SQL clone:** A tool that allows for fast, space-efficient database cloning. It enables teams to quickly refresh test environments with up-to-date production data without affecting production systems.

- **Talend:** An **extract, transform, load** (ETL) tool that can be used to extract test data from production systems, transform it to meet testing requirements, and load it into test environments.

Resetting test data

Regularly resetting test data ensures that tests are conducted in a consistent environment. This can be achieved through automation scripts that restore databases to a known state or tools that facilitate data refreshes.

Implementing automated data setup and teardown processes in CI/CD pipelines can help maintain a clean testing environment, minimizing issues related to stale or inconsistent data.

Synthetic data generation

Synthetic data is artificially generated data that mimics the characteristics of real-world data without exposing sensitive information. It can be created using algorithms or statistical methods that replicate data distributions and relationships.

Synthetic data is beneficial for load testing and performance testing, as it allows teams to simulate a wide variety of scenarios without relying on production data.

Data subsetting

Data subsetting involves creating a smaller, representative set of test data from a larger production database. This technique allows teams to work with relevant data while ensuring that sensitive information is masked or anonymized.

By selecting only the necessary data for testing purposes, teams can improve test execution times and resource utilization.

Data obfuscation

Data obfuscation techniques modify sensitive data in a way that retains its format and structure while removing any identifiable information. This approach allows teams to use realistic data for testing without compromising data privacy.

Examples of obfuscation techniques include data masking, shuffling, and encryption, ensuring that the data remains usable while protecting sensitive information.

Creating scenarios based on user stories

Developing test data based on user stories and acceptance criteria helps ensure that the data is relevant and representative of real-world scenarios. This approach allows teams to cover a variety of test cases, including edge cases and error conditions.

Collaborating with stakeholders to understand business requirements can help identify the necessary data sets and conditions needed for effective testing.

Using production data with caution

While production data can provide valuable insights, it should be used cautiously in testing environments. Always ensure that sensitive information is protected through masking or anonymization before utilizing production data.

Consider creating a data retention policy that defines how long test data should be retained, when it should be refreshed, and how sensitive data should be handled.

Effective test data management is essential for ensuring reliable and comprehensive testing processes. By leveraging tools for generating, storing, and resetting test data, teams can streamline their testing efforts and maintain data consistency across environments. Employing techniques such as synthetic data generation, data subsetting, data obfuscation, and scenario-based data creation allows for the development of reliable and representative test data that mimics real-world scenarios without compromising production data. Embracing these practices not only enhances the quality of testing but also ensures compliance with data protection regulations, ultimately leading to more robust and trustworthy software products.

End-to-end testing tools

End-to-end (E2E) testing is a critical phase in the software testing lifecycle. It aims to validate an application's complete functionality from start to finish by simulating real user scenarios. This type of testing ensures that all integrated components work together as intended. Several tools and frameworks are designed to facilitate E2E testing, particularly for UI testing, such as:

- **Selenium:** Selenium is one of the most widely used open-source frameworks for automating web applications. It supports multiple programming languages (Java, C#, Python, etc.) and can run tests across various browsers (Chrome, Firefox, Safari). The key features are:

  o Browser automation through WebDriver, allowing interaction with web elements like buttons, forms, and links.

o   Support for parallel test execution using Selenium Grid, enabling faster feedback cycles.

o   Extensive community support and numerous integrations with CI/CD tools.

- **Playwright**: Developed by Microsoft, Playwright is a relatively new open-source automation framework that provides powerful features for E2E testing of web applications. It supports multiple languages (JavaScript, Python, Java, C#) and can automate interactions across multiple browsers. The key features are:

o   Built-in support for headless browsing, making tests run faster and consume fewer resources.

o   Support for testing across different browser contexts and devices, allowing for comprehensive cross-browser testing.

o   Automatic waiting for elements, reducing the need for manual wait conditions in test scripts.

- **Cypress:** Cypress is a modern JavaScript-based testing framework designed specifically for web applications. It operates directly in the browser and provides an intuitive interface for writing and executing tests. The key features are:

o   Real-time reloads and a user-friendly interface for writing and debugging tests.

o   Time travel feature, which allows developers to see what happened at each step of the test execution.

o   Built-in waiting and retry mechanisms to handle asynchronous operations smoothly.

Strategies for testing across the full application stack

To ensure comprehensive E2E testing coverage across the entire application stack, consider the following strategies:

- **Test planning and design:** Develop a detailed test plan that outlines the objectives, scope, and user flows to be tested. This plan should include test cases that cover critical user interactions, edge cases, and integration points across the application.

o   Identify user stories and acceptance criteria to guide the development of test scenarios, ensuring that tests align with real-world usage.

- **Modular test architecture:** Structure test cases into reusable and modular components that can be combined to create complex user flows. This modular approach simplifies test maintenance and enhances code reusability.

o   Implement POM design patterns to encapsulate the UI elements and interactions for different pages in the application, promoting better organization and reducing duplication.

- **Cross-browser testing:** Use tools like Selenium Grid, Playwright, or cloud-based services such as BrowserStack or Sauce Labs to execute tests across multiple browsers and devices. This ensures that the application behaves consistently for all users, regardless of their environment.

o   Establish a matrix of browser and device combinations to cover different platforms, screen sizes, and operating systems.

- **Data-driven testing:** Implement data-driven testing techniques to run the same test with multiple data sets, covering a variety of scenarios and user inputs. This approach helps identify potential issues in the application logic and enhances overall test coverage.

o   Use external data sources (for example, CSV files, databases, or APIs) to supply different input values and expected outcomes for the tests.

- **API testing integration**: Include API testing in the E2E testing strategy to validate the communication between the frontend and backend components. Tools like Postman, RestAssured, or SoapUI can be used to test API endpoints before integrating them into E2E tests.

    o   Ensure that API responses are correctly handled in the UI tests, verifying that the application reacts appropriately to various API responses.

- **Continuous testing in CI/CD pipelines:** Integrate E2E tests into CI/CD pipelines to ensure that tests are executed automatically whenever code changes are made. This practice enables teams to identify defects early in the development process and maintain a high level of quality throughout the software lifecycle.

    o   Use tools like Jenkins, GitHub Actions, or GitLab CI to automate test execution, generate reports, and notify teams of test results.

- **Monitoring and maintenance:** Regularly review and update E2E tests to ensure they remain relevant and effective as the application evolves. This includes modifying tests to accommodate new features or changes in the UI.

    o   Monitor test execution results to identify flaky tests and investigate their causes. Implement retry mechanisms or use tools like Cypress to manage unstable tests more effectively.

End-to-end testing is a vital component of the software development lifecycle that ensures the complete functionality of an application is validated against real-world user scenarios. Tools such as Selenium, Playwright, and Cypress provide robust frameworks for automating UI testing, enabling teams to simulate user interactions effectively. Teams can ensure comprehensive coverage across the full application stack by employing strategies such as modular test architecture, cross-browser testing, data-driven testing, API testing integration, and continuous testing in CI/CD pipelines. Embracing these practices leads to higher-quality software, improved user satisfaction, and more efficient development processes.

Code coverage and static analysis tools

Code coverage and static analysis are essential practices in software development that enhance code quality, ensure thorough testing, and mitigate potential issues before they manifest in production. By measuring how much of the codebase is tested and analyzing the code for potential defects or vulnerabilities, teams can maintain high standards of software quality and security.

Using code coverage tools

Code coverage tools are designed to measure the extent to which the source code is executed during testing. These tools provide insights into which parts of the code are tested and help identify areas that may require additional test cases. Here are some popular code coverage tools:

- **Java Code Coverage (JaCoCo):** JaCoCo is an open-source tool for measuring code coverage in Java applications. It provides detailed reports on code coverage metrics, such as line, branch, and instruction coverage. The key features are:
  - o   Integration with build tools like Maven and Gradle for seamless code coverage analysis.
  - o   HTML and XML reporting to visualize coverage data.
  - o   Support for both unit tests and integration tests.

- **Istanbul:** Istanbul is a popular JavaScript code coverage tool that works with various testing frameworks (like Mocha and Jasmine). It provides coverage reports for both front-end and back-end applications. The key features are:
  - o   Supports multiple output formats (HTML, JSON, LCOV) for easy visualization and integration with CI/CD pipelines.
  - o   Instrumentation of code to collect coverage data during test execution.
  - o   Integration with tools like Jest for an improved testing experience.

- **Cobertura:** Cobertura is another code coverage tool for Java that provides insights into test coverage and helps identify untested parts of the codebase. It integrates with popular build tools and CI systems. The key features are:

  o Line coverage metrics along with visual representations of covered and uncovered lines in the code.

  o Integration with Maven, Ant, and Gradle for automated coverage analysis.

  o HTML reporting for easy navigation and understanding of coverage results.

Integrating static analysis tools

Static analysis tools analyze source code without executing it, helping to identify potential defects, security vulnerabilities, and adherence to coding standards before tests are run. This proactive approach enhances code quality and reduces the likelihood of introducing issues into production. Here are some popular static analysis tools:

- **SonarQube:** SonarQube is a widely used open-source platform for continuous inspection of code quality. It supports multiple languages and provides comprehensive reports on code smells, bugs, vulnerabilities, and test coverage. The key features are:

  o Integrates with CI/CD pipelines to provide real-time feedback on code quality.

  o Customizable quality gates to enforce coding standards and ensure code quality is maintained.

  o Extensive reporting features to visualize code quality trends over time.

- **ESLint:** ESLint is a static analysis tool specifically designed for identifying and fixing problems in JavaScript code. It helps enforce coding conventions and best practices, improving code readability and maintainability. The key features are:

  o Configurable rules and presets to suit different project needs and coding styles.

  o Integration with various IDEs and build tools for real-time linting during development.

  o Support for plugins to extend functionality and include additional rules.

- **Checkstyle:** Checkstyle is a static analysis tool for Java that helps enforce coding standards and best practices. It provides reports on code formatting and structure, making it easier to maintain consistent code quality. The key features are:

  o Customizable rules to enforce project-specific coding standards.

  o Integration with build tools and IDEs for seamless feedback during development.

  o Reporting features to visualize code quality issues and trends.

Benefits of code coverage and static analysis

The benefits are as follows:

- **Improved test coverage:** Code coverage tools help identify untested areas of the codebase, allowing teams to create targeted test cases. This leads to higher test coverage and better assurance that critical functionalities are validated.

- **Early detection of issues:** Static analysis tools catch potential defects, vulnerabilities, and code smells early in the development process. This proactive approach minimizes the cost and effort associated with fixing issues later in the lifecycle.

- **Enhanced code quality:** By enforcing coding standards and best practices, static analysis tools contribute to improved code quality. This leads to more maintainable and readable code, reducing the likelihood of introducing bugs.

- **Security assurance**: Static analysis tools can identify security vulnerabilities in the codebase, helping teams address potential threats before they can be exploited in production. This proactive security posture is essential for safeguarding sensitive data and maintaining user trust.

- **Informed decision-making:** The insights gained from code coverage and static analysis tools empower teams to make informed decisions about code quality, test strategy, and resource allocation. This data-driven approach enhances overall development efficiency.

Code coverage and static analysis are vital practices in modern software development that ensure high-quality, reliable, and secure applications. Tools like JaCoCo, Istanbul, and SonarQube provide valuable insights into code coverage and potential defects, enabling teams to enhance their testing strategies and maintain high code quality standards. By integrating these tools into the development process, teams can proactively identify issues, improve test coverage, and deliver robust software solutions that meet user needs and expectations. Embracing these practices enhances software quality and contributes to a more efficient and effective development lifecycle.

Conclusion

Integrating testability into software architecture from the very beginning is crucial for ensuring the long-term success and reliability of software systems. A testable architecture allows teams to quickly identify defects, validate functionality, and adapt to changes, ultimately leading to higher quality products and improved development efficiency.

By emphasizing all the aforementioned best practices and leveraging essential tools and techniques, organizations can create a robust testing environment that enhances the overall quality and reliability of their software products. Integrating testability into the architecture not only improves testing efficiency but also lays the foundation for sustainable software development and continuous delivery.

In the next chapter, we will look at the approach to orchestration and execution that helps you optimize execution speed, reduce flakiness, and lead to quick and reliable feedback.

Key takeaways

Here are some of the important aspects of testability that we have explored in this chapter:

- **Importance of integrating testability:**

  o **Early detection of issues:** By considering testability in the architecture, teams can identify and resolve issues early in the development lifecycle, reducing the cost and effort associated with fixing defects later.

  o **Facilitating continuous improvement:** A focus on testability enables teams to implement continuous testing practices, ensuring that code quality is maintained as the application evolves.

  o **Enhanced collaboration:** Testable architecture fosters collaboration among team members, as clear interfaces and modular components make it easier to work in parallel and integrate different parts of the system.

- **Best practices for ensuring testability:**

  o **Dependency injection:** Leveraging dependency injection decouples components and simplifies the testing process by allowing for easy replacement of real dependencies with test doubles. This facilitates easier mocking and stubbing in automated tests.

  o **Separation of concerns:** By separating business logic, data access, and user interfaces, teams can design software components that are independently testable. This approach increases the testability of different layers of the application and reduces complexity.

- o **Modular design:** Implementing a modular design allows systems to be broken into smaller, independent, and testable units. This improves overall system testability and simplifies maintenance and scalability.

- **Essential tools and techniques:**

  - o **Code coverage tools:** Utilizing tools like JaCoCo and Istanbul helps measure code coverage, ensuring that critical parts of the codebase are adequately tested.

  - o **Static analysis tools**: Integrating static analysis tools such as SonarQube and ESLint enables teams to identify potential defects and security vulnerabilities before running tests, enhancing code quality.

  - o **End-to-end testing frameworks:** Tools like Selenium, Playwright, and Cypress facilitate comprehensive E2E testing, simulating real user scenarios and validating the full functionality of applications.

  - o **Test data management:** Efficiently managing test data through tools and techniques ensures that tests are conducted in a consistent environment, mimicking real-world scenarios without affecting production data.

Exercises

1. Can your test framework easily detect and diagnose failures in the system?

2. How easily can different parts of your systems be isolated and tested independently?

3. How well does architecture separate concerns to allow focused testing at each layer?

4. Are dependencies managed in a way that minimizes test complexity and setup?

5. Can components be tested independently without relying on full system execution?

6. Is there a clear strategy for replacing external dependencies in tests?

7. Do you have adequate coverage at unit, integration, and end-to-end levels in your different systems?

Join our Discord space

Join our Discord workspace for latest updates, offers, tech happenings around the world, new releases, and sessions with the authors:

https://discord.bpbonline.com

## CHAPTER 6

Test Orchestration and Execution

Introduction

In modern software development, test orchestration and execution play a crucial role in ensuring efficient, scalable, and reliable test automation. Test execution refers to running automated tests, where test scripts interact with the system under test to validate functionality, performance, and security. On the other hand, test orchestration involves the coordinated scheduling, sequencing, and management of these test executions across different environments, tools, and pipelines.

In this chapter, we will examine these areas and how to create a test framework that can successfully deliver in orchestration and execution to achieve successful test automation results.

Structure

In this chapter, we will go over the following topics:

- Test orchestration
- Impact of a well-designed execution strategy
- Designing a custom test runner
- Managing test suites and orchestration
- Test orchestration tools and techniques
- Orchestrating cross-environment tests
- Handling parallelization, reporting, and test scheduling
- Reporting and test results
- Test scheduling and execution frequency

Objectives

By the end of this chapter, the reader will gain a deep understanding of test automation frameworks, including their inner workings and design principles. They will learn how to build a framework capable of transforming test scripts into executable actions that run in parallel. Additionally, the chapter will cover integrating reporting and scheduling mechanisms to enhance test execution and management.

Test orchestration

Test orchestration refers to systematically coordinating various testing processes and tools within a software testing framework. It encompasses the management of test execution, environments, data, and resources to ensure that tests are executed efficiently and effectively. The primary goal of test orchestration is to streamline the testing workflow, facilitating seamless integration between different testing stages, such as unit, integration, system, and acceptance testing, while ensuring that all components work together harmoniously.

In essence, test orchestration acts as a conductor of an orchestra, managing the various instruments (or testing tools) to produce a cohesive output (or test results). This approach enhances collaboration among different teams, reduces redundancy, and optimizes resource utilization.

Role in the efficient execution of tests

The role of test orchestration in the efficient execution of tests can be summarized as follows:

- **Automation and integration:** Orchestration allows for the automation of test execution across various environments and platforms. By integrating different testing tools (for example, test management tools, **continuous integration/continuous deployment (CI/CD)** systems), teams can create a streamlined testing process that minimizes manual intervention and reduces the likelihood of human error.

- **Test planning and scheduling:** Effective orchestration facilitates strategic test planning and scheduling. It allows teams to determine the optimal timing for test execution based on dependencies, resource availability, and project milestones. This proactive approach ensures that testing aligns with the overall development timeline.

- **Enhanced visibility and reporting:** Orchestration tools often provide dashboards and reporting capabilities, giving teams real-time insights into the testing process. This visibility allows stakeholders to monitor progress, identify bottlenecks, and make data-driven decisions to improve testing strategies.

Managing the complexity of large test suites

As software applications grow in complexity, managing large test suites can become a daunting task. Test orchestration helps mitigate this complexity through several key mechanisms:

- **Test scheduling:** Orchestration tools enable teams to schedule tests based on priority and dependencies. This ensures that critical tests are executed first, while less critical tests can be run later, optimizing the overall testing timeline. Additionally, scheduling can be automated based on CI/CD pipeline triggers, allowing for timely feedback on code changes.

- **Parallel execution:** One significant advantage of test orchestration is the parallel execution of tests. By distributing tests across multiple environments or machines, teams can significantly reduce the time required for test execution. This is particularly beneficial for large test suites, as it allows for faster feedback cycles and enables teams to promptly identify and address issues.

- **Resource management:** Effective orchestration involves the dynamic allocation and management of resources, such as test environments and hardware. By monitoring resource utilization and automatically scaling resources up or down as needed, orchestration ensures that testing processes are efficient and cost-effective. This helps teams avoid delays caused by resource constraints while maximizing the use of available infrastructure.

- **Dependency management:** In complex applications, tests often have dependencies on specific components or data. Test orchestration tools help manage these dependencies by ensuring that the necessary components are available before tests are executed. This prevents failures caused by missing or incompatible dependencies and enhances the overall reliability of the testing process.

Test orchestration is critical to modern software testing, providing the framework necessary for efficiently executing and managing tests in complex environments. By automating processes, facilitating collaboration, and optimizing resource utilization, orchestration empowers teams to navigate the challenges of large test suites while ensuring high-quality software delivery. As organizations continue to embrace agile and DevOps methodologies, the importance of test orchestration will only grow, making it an essential focus for software development teams.

Impact of a well-designed execution strategy

A well-designed test execution strategy is crucial for ensuring the quality and reliability of software products. It significantly influences various aspects of the development workflow, including speed, reliability, and overall efficiency, as given:

- **Test speed:** An effective execution strategy optimizes testing speed by employing techniques such as parallel execution, test prioritization, and automation. Teams can achieve faster feedback cycles by running tests concurrently and focusing on critical test cases first. This speed is vital in agile environments, where rapid iterations and frequent releases are the norm. A quicker testing process enables developers to identify and address issues promptly, reducing the time to release software.

- **Reliability:** Reliability in test execution is paramount for maintaining software quality. A well-structured execution strategy minimizes the risk of flaky tests and false positives or negatives. It includes robust error handling, explicit test dependencies, and effective management of test data and environments. By ensuring that tests consistently produce accurate results, teams can build confidence in their software, leading to more reliable releases and fewer production issues.

- **Overall development workflow:** An effective execution strategy enhances the workflow by facilitating collaboration between development and testing teams. By integrating testing into the development process, teams can adopt a shift-left approach, where testing occurs earlier in the development cycle. This proactive strategy fosters a quality culture, enabling teams to catch defects early, reduce rework, and streamline the entire software delivery process.

Additionally, clear communication and well-defined roles in the execution strategy help minimize misunderstandings and ensure that everyone is aligned with the project goals.

Integrating test orchestration into CI/CD pipelines for continuous testing

Test orchestration plays a pivotal role in the integration of testing within CI/CD pipelines, facilitating continuous testing throughout the software development lifecycle, as explained:

- **Automated test execution:** In CI/CD pipelines, test orchestration automates the execution of tests triggered by code changes. Whenever developers push code to the repository, the CI/CD system can automatically initiate a suite of tests to verify that the changes do not introduce defects. This automation reduces the reliance on manual testing, speeds up feedback, and ensures that testing is consistently applied to every code change.

- **Feedback loops:** Test orchestration enables rapid feedback loops by providing immediate results from automated tests. This quick feedback is essential for developers to address issues before they progress further down the pipeline. If a test fails, the orchestration tool can halt the pipeline, alert the developers, and provide detailed logs and reports, allowing for swift remediation.

- **Integration with development tools:** Test orchestration tools seamlessly integrate with various development and deployment tools within the CI/CD ecosystem. They can connect to version control systems and build servers and deployment platforms, creating a cohesive workflow. This integration ensures that testing is integral to the CI/CD process, aligning testing with other development activities and promoting collaboration across teams.

- **Dynamic resource management:** Test orchestration optimizes resource utilization within CI/CD pipelines by dynamically allocating resources based on testing requirements. For instance, during peak development periods, orchestration tools can scale up testing environments to handle increased test loads. Conversely, resources can be scaled down during quieter periods, ensuring cost-effectiveness while maintaining testing capabilities.

- **Comprehensive reporting and analytics:** Orchestration tools provide insights and analytics on test execution within the CI/CD pipeline. By tracking test performance, code coverage, and defect density over time, teams can identify trends, optimize testing strategies, and improve overall software quality. These insights enable data-driven decision-making and continuous improvement of testing practices.

The importance of effective test execution cannot be overstated in today's fast-paced software development landscape. A well-designed execution strategy enhances test speed and reliability, significantly improving the overall development workflow. By integrating test orchestration into CI/CD pipelines, organizations can achieve continuous testing, ensuring that quality is maintained throughout the development lifecycle. This integration fosters a culture of collaboration, agility, and continuous improvement, ultimately leading to more robust and reliable software products.

Designing a custom test runner

A test runner is a critical component in the software testing process. It is responsible for executing test cases and reporting their outcomes. The test runner serves as the interface between the testing framework and the actual test scripts, managing the entire lifecycle of test execution.

The primary purposes of a test runner include:

- **Test execution:** The test runner identifies, loads, and executes test cases defined within the testing framework. It systematically runs each test, ensuring they are executed in the correct order and under the appropriate conditions.

- **Reporting results:** After executing tests, the runner collects the results and generates reports that indicate which tests passed, which failed, and any relevant error messages. This reporting functionality provides immediate feedback to developers and testers, allowing for the timely identification and resolution of issues.

- **Test management:** Test runners often include features for managing test suites, allowing users to group tests logically, run specific subsets of tests, and control execution based on various parameters (for example, tags, test types, or environments).

- **Integration:** Test runners facilitate integration with other tools, such as CI systems and code quality analyzers. This integration is vital for automating the testing process within a broader development workflow.

- **Configuration and setup:** A test runner can handle configuration settings, such as environment variables, test data, and dependencies, ensuring that tests run in a consistent environment.

Benefits of custom versus built-in test runners

While many testing frameworks come with built-in test runners, there are several benefits to designing a custom test runner tailored to the specific needs of a project or organization:

- **Tailored functionality:** A custom test runner can be designed to meet specific requirements that built-in runners may not address. For example, it can incorporate unique reporting formats, logging mechanisms, or additional features such as retry logic for flaky tests.

- **Enhanced integration:** Custom test runners can be better integrated into existing development workflows and tools. They can facilitate seamless communication with other components of the software development lifecycle, such as deployment pipelines, monitoring systems, and project management tools.

- **Control over execution:** By building a custom test runner, developers gain complete control over how tests are executed, including the order of execution, parallelization strategies, and resource management. This control can lead to optimizations that improve performance and reduce testing time.

- **Better resource management:** Custom runners can implement sophisticated resource management strategies that align with an organization's specific infrastructure and environments. For instance, they can dynamically allocate resources based on current load or optimize execution based on available hardware.

- **Specialized reporting:** A custom test runner allows for the generation of tailored reports highlighting specific metrics important to the organization. These reports can include custom dashboards, visualizations, and integration with analytics tools for in-depth test results analysis.

- **Flexibility and extensibility:** Custom test runners can be designed with extensibility in mind, allowing teams to add new features or capabilities as their testing needs evolve. This flexibility can be particularly beneficial in fast-paced development environments where requirements frequently change.

- **Simplicity and clarity:** Built-in runners can sometimes be complex or overloaded with features that may not be necessary for all projects. A custom test runner can be streamlined to focus on the project's specific needs, making it easier for teams to understand and use.

A test runner is a fundamental component of any testing framework, serving the essential function of executing tests and reporting their outcomes. While built-in test runners offer convenience and standardization, designing a custom test runner can provide significant advantages, including tailored functionality, enhanced integration, and improved resource management. By investing in a custom test runner, organizations can better align their testing processes with their unique needs, ultimately leading to more efficient and effective software quality assurance.

Core responsibilities of a test runner

A test runner is a critical tool in the testing framework, with several core responsibilities that ensure efficient and effective test execution. The key components include:

- **Loading test cases:**
  - **Discovery:** The test runner must be capable of discovering test cases within the specified directory or module. This involves scanning the codebase for defined test functions or classes that adhere to specific naming conventions (for example, prefixed with **test_** in Python or annotated with **@ Test** in Java).
  - **Organization:** Once discovered, the test runner should categorize the test cases into logical groups or suites for better management and execution. This organization can be based on various criteria, such as functionality, component, or testing type (unit, integration, end-to-end).

- **Managing configurations:**
  - **Setup and teardown:** The test runner is responsible for executing any setup (initialization) and teardown (cleanup) procedures required before and after test execution. This can include configuring test environments, initializing databases, or resetting application states.
  - **Configuration handling:** Test runners must handle various configurations, such as environment variables, test parameters, and options that influence tests' execution. This flexibility allows testers to customize execution without modifying test code.

- **Executing test logic:**

  o **Execution:** The primary function of a test runner is to execute the test cases. It should run each test in isolation, track their results, and ensure that tests are executed in the correct order, especially if there are dependencies among them.

  o **Error handling:** During execution, the test runner must capture errors and exceptions, providing meaningful feedback and stack traces for failed tests. This information is crucial for developers to diagnose and fix issues promptly.

  o **Result reporting:** After executing tests, the test runner should summarize the results, indicating which tests passed, which failed, and any associated error messages. It may also provide additional metrics, such as execution time, code coverage, and test suite statistics.

Structuring the runner to handle test cases dynamically

To effectively manage test cases based on input parameters or environment configurations, a test runner can be structured in the following ways:

- **Dynamic test case loading:**

  o **Parameterization:** The test runner can support parameterized tests, allowing users to run the same test logic with different inputs. This capability can be achieved through decorators or specific syntax, enabling easy modification of input values without duplicating test code.

  o **Configuration files:** The runner can read from configuration files (for example, JSON, YAML, or XML) that specify which tests to run, along with their parameters. This allows users to define test scenarios externally, making adapting tests to different environments or conditions easier.

- **Conditional execution:**

  o **Environment-based logic:** The test runner can implement logic that determines which tests to execute based on the current environment (for example, development, testing, production). For instance, specific tests might be skipped or included depending on the environment configurations, such as specific database connections or feature flags.

  o **Command-line arguments:** Incorporating command-line arguments allows users to specify which tests to run, modify execution parameters, or enable/disable specific features. This flexibility enables quick adjustments without modifying the runner's source code.

- **Test suite management:**

  o **Dynamic test suites:** The test runner can support creating dynamic test suites that can be composed based on specific criteria (for example, all tests that contain a specific tag). This allows users to quickly assemble and execute relevant tests tailored to their current needs.

  o **Hierarchical organization:** Structuring tests hierarchically enables more complex configurations and executions. For example, users can define parent suites, including child suites or individual test cases, providing clear organization and modularity.

- **Logging and debugging:**

  o **Enhanced logging:** Incorporating detailed logging capabilities within the runner allows for better tracking of the execution process, capturing essential information like the start and end times of tests, input parameters used, and any errors encountered during execution.

  o **Debugging support:** The test runner can provide debugging tools or hooks, allowing users to step through test execution or examine variables during runtime. This feature can be beneficial for diagnosing issues in complex test scenarios.

The key components of a test runner, loading test cases, managing configurations, and executing test logic, are essential for efficient and effective test execution. Structuring the runner to handle test cases dynamically based on input parameters or environment configurations enhances its flexibility and adaptability, enabling teams to execute tests that align with their specific needs. Organizations can significantly improve their testing processes by implementing these strategies, leading to higher software quality and faster development cycles.

Designing the runner for extensibility and maintainability

Creating an extensible test runner requires careful design and architectural choices to ensure that it can adapt to future needs without extensive refactoring. Here are key principles and strategies for designing a test runner that is both extensible and maintainable:

- **Modular architecture:**
  - **Separation of concerns:** Organize the test runner into distinct modules, each responsible for a specific functionality, such as test discovery, execution, reporting, and configuration management. This modular approach allows developers to make changes or add new features without affecting other components.
  - **Interfaces and abstract classes:** Define clear interfaces or abstract classes for key components (for example, test executors and reporters). This approach allows different implementations to be created and plugged into the runner, facilitating future enhancements.

- **Plug-in system:**
  - **Plugin architecture:** Implement a plugin system that enables users to extend the test runner with custom functionality. By allowing external modules (plugins) to be registered and loaded at runtime, developers can introduce new test types, reporting mechanisms, or execution strategies without modifying the core runner code.
  - **Configuration-based plugin loading:** Allow plugins to be loaded based on configuration files, environment variables, or command-line arguments. This flexibility makes enabling or disabling plugins easy based on the current project requirements.

- **Flexible configuration:**
  - **Dynamic configuration management:** Utilize configuration files (for example, JSON, YAML) to specify settings related to test execution, such as which tests to run, test parameters, and reporting preferences. This approach allows users to modify the runner's behavior without changing the codebase.
  - **Customizable execution strategies:** Design the runner to support different execution strategies, such as parallel execution, sequential execution, or prioritized execution. This flexibility allows teams to adapt the runner to their specific testing needs.

- **Extensible reporting mechanisms:**
  - **Multiple reporting options:** Create a reporting module that supports various output formats (for example, console logs, HTML reports, JSON outputs). By allowing users to select or plug in different reporting mechanisms, the runner can cater to diverse stakeholder needs.
  - **Custom reporters:** Provide a framework for creating custom reporters, enabling users to define how test results should be displayed or stored. This can include visual dashboards, integration with third-party reporting tools, or specialized formats for different audiences.

Designing for adaptability

To ensure that the test runner can accommodate different testing frameworks (for example, unit tests, UI tests, or performance tests), consider the following design principles:

- **Abstracting test execution:**

  o **Generic test execution interface:** Define a generic interface for test execution that can be implemented by various testing frameworks. This interface should encapsulate everyday actions such as starting tests, stopping tests, and retrieving results. By adhering to this interface, different testing frameworks can be easily integrated into the runner.

  o **Adapter pattern:** The Adapter pattern creates specific Adapters for various testing frameworks. These Adapters translate calls from the test runner into calls specific to the underlying testing framework, allowing the runner to work with multiple test types seamlessly.

- **Unified test discovery:**

  o **Common discovery mechanism:** Implement a common test discovery mechanism that can identify tests from various frameworks. This mechanism should handle different conventions for test naming and organization, allowing it to adapt to the structure of different test types without requiring modifications.

  o **Annotation or convention-based discovery:** Support annotation-based and convention-based test discovery methods. For example, a user might use annotations to mark test methods in a unit testing framework or rely on naming conventions for UI tests.

- **Configurable test execution flow:**

  o **Dynamic execution flow:** Allow the execution flow of tests to be configured based on the type of tests being run. For instance, performance tests might require additional warm-up phases or specialized setup procedures that differ from unit tests or UI tests.

  o **Execution strategies:** Implement execution strategies that can be configured at runtime to suit different testing contexts. This may include strategies for how tests are run in parallel or how resources are managed during execution.

- **Extensible framework integration:**

  o **Integration with third-party tools:** Design the test runner to easily integrate with other tools in the testing ecosystem, such as test management tools, CI/CD systems, or code quality analyzers. Users can build a more comprehensive testing solution by providing APIs or hooks for integration.

  o **Support for different test types:** Ensure that the runner can accommodate various test types, including unit tests, functional tests, UI tests, performance tests, and security tests. This adaptability allows organizations to maintain a single test runner while supporting diverse testing needs.

Creating an extensible test runner requires thoughtful design and a focus on modularity, flexibility, and adaptability. By implementing a plugin architecture, abstracting test execution, and ensuring dynamic configuration management, developers can create a runner that is easy to maintain and enhance over time. Designing for adaptability allows the runner to support various testing frameworks, making it a valuable tool in diverse testing environments. This approach ultimately leads to a more efficient testing process and improved software quality.

Example of a custom test runner

This section will walk through the design and implementation of a simple custom test runner in Python. This example will cover the essential components of executing test cases, managing configurations, and programmatically reporting results:

1. **Define the test runner structure:** We will start by defining the basic structure of our custom test runner, which will include classes for managing test cases, executing them, and reporting results, including execution times, which are tracked in the following examples to identify how long tests take to execute. This is useful for identifying potential performance issues in your code if specific performance tests execute outside of the expected time.

```
import os
import time

class TestCase:
    def __init__(self, name, test_function):
        self.name = name
        self.test_function = test_function
        self.passed = False
        self.error_message = None

    def run(self):
        try:
            self.test_function()
            self.passed = True
        except Exception as e:
            self.error_message = str(e)
            self.passed = False

class TestRunner:
    def __init__(self):
        self.test_cases = []
        self.results = []

    def add_test_case(self, test_case):
        self.test_cases.append(test_case)

    def run_tests(self):
        for test_case in self.test_cases:
            start_time = time.time() //tracks execution time of test
            test_case.run()
            duration = time.time() - start_time
            self.results.append((test_case, duration))

    def report_results(self):
        print("\nTest Results:")
        for test_case, duration in self.results: //test will only pass if doesn't
exceed specific benchmark
            if test_case.passed:
                print(f"√ {test_case.name} - Passed (Duration: {duration:.4f}s)")
            else:
                print(f"X {test_case.name} - Failed (Duration: {duration:.4f}s) -
Error: {test_case.error_message}")
```

2. **Create sample test cases:** Next, we will create some sample test cases to demonstrate how to use our custom test runner:

```
# Sample test functions
def test_success():
    assert 1 + 1 == 2
```

```
def test_failure():
    assert 1 + 1 == 3

def test_exception():
    raise ValueError("This is an intentional error.")

# Create instances of TestCase
test1 = TestCase("Test Success", test_success)
test2 = TestCase("Test Failure", test_failure)
test3 = TestCase("Test Exception", test_exception)
```

3. **Execute test cases using the custom test runner:** Now, we will use our **TestRunner** class to execute the test cases and report the results:

```
# Instantiate the test runner
runner = TestRunner()

# Add test cases to the runner
runner.add_test_case(test1)
runner.add_test_case(test2)
runner.add_test_case(test3)

# Run the tests
runner.run_tests()

# Report the results
runner.report_results()
```

Full example:

Here is the complete code, combining all the steps:

```
import os
import time


class TestCase:
    def __init__(self, name, test_function):
        self.name = name
        self.test_function = test_function
        self.passed = False
        self.error_message = None

    def run(self):
        try:
            self.test_function()
            self.passed = True
        except Exception as e:
            self.error_message = str(e)
            self.passed = False
```

```python
class TestRunner:
    def __init__(self):
        self.test_cases = []
        self.results = []

    def add_test_case(self, test_case):
        self.test_cases.append(test_case)

    def run_tests(self):
        for test_case in self.test_cases:
            start_time = time.time()
            test_case.run()
            duration = time.time() - start_time
            self.results.append((test_case, duration))

    def report_results(self):
        print("\nTest Results:")
        for test_case, duration in self.results:
            if test_case.passed:
                print(f"✓ {test_case.name} - Passed (Duration: {duration:.4f}s)")
            else:
                print(f"X {test_case.name} - Failed (Duration: {duration:.4f}s) - Error:
{test_case.error_message}")

# Sample test functions
def test_success():
    assert 1 + 1 == 2


def test_failure():
    assert 1 + 1 == 3


def test_exception():
    raise ValueError("This is an intentional error.")

# Create instances of TestCase
test1 = TestCase("Test Success", test_success)
test2 = TestCase("Test Failure", test_failure)
test3 = TestCase("Test Exception", test_exception)

# Instantiate the test runner
runner = TestRunner()

# Add test cases to the runner
runner.add_test_case(test1)
runner.add_test_case(test2)
runner.add_test_case(test3)
```

```
# Run the tests
runner.run_tests()
```

```
# Report the results
runner.report_results()
```

Explanation of the code

Here is a brief explanation of the code:

- **TestCase class:** This class encapsulates a test case, holding its name and the test function. The run method executes the test and records whether it passed or failed, along with any error messages.

- **TestRunner class:** This class manages a collection of test cases. It provides methods to add test cases, run them, and report the results.

- **Sample test functions:** We create three test functions: one that passes, one that fails, and one that raises an exception.

- **Execution and reporting:** Finally, we instantiate the test runner, add the test cases, execute them, and report the results.

This simple custom test runner demonstrates how to execute test cases and report results programmatically. It can be expanded upon to include additional features such as configuration management, logging, support for different test types, and integration with CI/CD pipelines. You can create a tailored testing solution that meets your specific needs by building a custom runner.

Managing test suites and orchestration

A test suite is a collection of test cases grouped together for execution as a single unit. The primary role of a test suite is to organize and manage related tests, making it easier to run them efficiently and effectively. Test suites can be structured based on various criteria, such as:

- **Functionality:** Tests can be grouped by the features or modules they are designed to validate. For example, a suite may contain all tests related to user authentication, while another suite focuses on payment processing.

- **Priority:** Test cases can be organized based on their priority levels, helping teams determine which tests to execute first. High-priority tests that cover critical functionalities may be grouped to ensure they are run frequently.

- **Execution order:** Test suites can define the order in which tests should be executed. This is particularly important when there are dependencies between tests, where one test's outcome may affect another test's execution.

- **Test type:** Test cases can be categorized by their types, such as unit tests, integration tests, or end-to-end tests, enabling a structured approach to testing that aligns with the development workflow.

Importance of categorizing tests by type

Categorizing tests by type, such as smoke tests, regression tests, and performance tests, plays a crucial role in effective orchestration and scheduling. Here is how this categorization enhances testing processes:

- **Efficient execution:**
  - **Smoke tests:** These are a subset of tests that verify whether the most critical functionalities of an application are working correctly. By grouping smoke tests into a separate suite, teams can quickly validate the application's health after each build or deployment.

- o **Regression tests:** Regression test suites are designed to ensure that new changes do not adversely affect existing functionalities. By maintaining a dedicated suite for regression tests, teams can efficiently run these tests after every significant code change or release, ensuring the software remains stable.

- o **Performance tests:** Grouping performance tests into their own suite allows teams to focus on evaluating the system's responsiveness and stability under varying load conditions. This separation ensures that performance-related issues are identified and addressed without the noise of unrelated test failures.

- **Better resource management:**

  - o **Selective execution:** Categorization allows for selective execution of test suites based on the current context, such as development stage or specific user stories being tested. For example, during early development, teams may prioritize running unit tests while deferring more extensive regression or performance tests until later in the cycle.

  - o **Structured results:** By organizing tests into suites based on their types and priorities, teams can generate clearer and more structured reports. This organization allows stakeholders to quickly identify areas of concern and understand which functionalities are stable or require further attention.

- **Enhanced CI/CD integration:**

  - o **Automated scheduling:** In CI/CD pipelines, categorizing tests allows for automated scheduling based on triggers. For example, smoke tests can run on every commit, while regression tests might be executed nightly or before major releases, ensuring an efficient testing workflow that aligns with development cycles.

A test suite serves as a fundamental organizational structure for managing test cases effectively. By grouping tests based on functionality, priority, or execution order, teams can enhance the efficiency of their testing processes. Furthermore, categorizing tests by type, such as smoke tests, regression tests, and performance tests, provides a framework for better orchestration, scheduling, and resource management, ultimately contributing to higher software quality and more effective development practices.

Managing large-scale test suites

Managing large-scale test suites can be challenging, especially as software projects grow in complexity and size. Effective management strategies are crucial for maintaining the testing process's efficiency, reliability, and effectiveness. Here are key techniques and considerations for managing and organizing large test suites:

- **Techniques for managing and organizing large test suites:**

  - o **Dynamic metadata:** Use tags to annotate test cases with relevant metadata, such as functionality, test type, priority, or intended execution context. Tags enable testers to quickly filter and select tests based on specific criteria. For example, a test case for user authentication could be tagged with labels like smoke, regression, and authentication, allowing it to be easily identified and executed when needed.

  - o **Hierarchical structure:** Organize tests into a hierarchical structure based on functional areas, types, or business objectives. This structure can facilitate navigation and help teams understand the scope of testing coverage. For example, create separate directories or namespaces for different functionalities (for example, `user_management`, `payment_processing`, `reporting`), with subcategories for various test types (for example, `unit_tests`, `integration_tests`, `e2e_tests`).

  - o **Functional grouping:** Group tests based on their objectives, such as feature sets or user stories. This approach ensures that related tests are executed together, facilitating comprehensive validation of specific functionalities. For example, group all tests related to user registration, login, and password recovery into a `UserAuthenticationSuite` to ensure that changes to user management features are adequately validated.

- **Utilizing test framework features:**

  o **Built-in features:** Many modern test frameworks (for example, JUnit, TestNG, pytest) offer features such as parameterized tests, test suites, and test filters. Leverage these features to organize and manage tests effectively.

  o **Parameterized tests:** Create parameterized tests to run the same test logic with different inputs, reducing duplication and enhancing maintainability.

- **Maintaining a test coverage matrix:**

  o **Tracking coverage:** Develop and maintain a test coverage matrix that maps test cases to requirements or functionalities. This matrix can help identify gaps in testing and inform decisions on test prioritization. For example, regularly review and update the matrix to ensure all critical functionalities are covered by relevant test cases, enabling focused efforts on areas with inadequate coverage.

- **Defining execution logic:** Defining effective execution logic is essential for ensuring that the correct tests run at the right times. Consider the following strategies:

  o **Automated triggers:** Set up automated triggers based on specific events, such as code commits, pull requests, or nightly builds. This automation ensures that tests are executed consistently and reduces manual intervention. For example, configure CI/CD tools (for example, Jenkins, GitLab CI, CircleCI) to automatically run smoke tests on every commit, while more comprehensive regression tests run nightly.

  o **Filtering logic:** Implement filtering logic that dynamically selects which tests to execute based on the context or current state of the codebase. This approach allows teams to optimize test execution based on relevance. For example, use tags or configuration files to specify which tests should run for different scenarios, such as running only regression tests for a scheduled nightly build or specific tests related to the feature being developed for a pull request.

  o **Execution order:** Define the execution order of tests based on their priority. Critical tests should run first, while less critical tests can be executed later or in parallel. For example, in a CI/CD pipeline, configure the execution flow to run smoke tests first, followed by regression tests and performance tests, ensuring immediate feedback on the most critical functionalities.

  o **User-triggered tests:** Allow developers and testers to execute specific test suites or test cases on demand, facilitating quick validation during development. This can be achieved through command-line interfaces or **integrated development environments** (IDE). For example, provide commands to trigger specific test suites via the command line, such as `run_tests --suite=smoke`, enabling team members to quickly validate critical functionalities without running the entire test suite.

  o **Parallel execution:** Implement parallel test execution to reduce the overall test runtime. Proper resource management ensures that tests can run concurrently without resource contention. For example, use tools like `pytest-xdist` or built-in features of CI/CD systems to run tests in parallel across multiple threads or machines, speeding up feedback loops.

Effectively managing large-scale test suites requires a combination of strategic organization and well-defined execution logic. Techniques such as tagging, categorization, and grouping by test objectives can help streamline the testing process, making it easier to navigate and execute relevant tests. Defining execution logic based on triggers, dynamic selection, and priority ensures that the correct tests are run at the right times, ultimately leading to improved software quality and more efficient development workflows.

Test orchestration tools and techniques

Test orchestration tools are essential for automating the execution of tests across different environments and platforms. They help streamline the testing process, ensuring that tests run efficiently and effectively within CI/CD pipelines.

Techniques to optimize test orchestration

Optimizing test orchestration involves ensuring efficient execution while maintaining coverage and reliability. Here are key techniques for maximizing the orchestration of test suites:

- **Risk-based testing**: Identify and prioritize tests that cover critical functionalities or areas with a history of defects. By focusing on high-risk tests, teams can ensure that the most important aspects of the application are validated first. For example, in a financial application, prioritize tests related to transaction processing and data integrity, as failures in these areas could have severe consequences.

- **Change detection:** Implement mechanisms to detect changes in the codebase and execute only the tests relevant to those changes. This approach reduces unnecessary test executions and speeds up feedback loops. For example, use Git commit messages or branch names to trigger specific test suites. Only the tests related to that module should run if a developer modifies the user authentication module.

- **Splitting large test suites:** Break down large test suites into smaller, more manageable ones based on functionality, type, or execution context. This division allows for faster execution and easier maintenance. For example, separate integration tests from unit tests, enabling quicker feedback on unit-level changes while running more extensive integration tests at scheduled intervals.

- **Test impact analysis:** Analyze past test results to determine the reliability of specific tests. Remove or reduce the frequency of tests that frequently fail without valid reasons (flaky tests) to optimize execution times. For example, if certain tests consistently fail due to environmental issues rather than code changes, consider marking them as *ignored* until they can be stabilized.

- **Dynamic resource management:** Use orchestration tools to allocate resources based on current testing needs dynamically. This approach can help maximize resource utilization and minimize bottlenecks. For example, automatically scale up testing resources during peak times (for example, before a release) and scale down during quieter periods.

- **Running tests in parallel:** Configure orchestration tools to execute tests across multiple nodes or containers. This strategy significantly reduces the overall testing time. For example, utilize cloud services or local test environments to run different test suites simultaneously, maximizing resource use and speeding up the testing process.

Test orchestration tools such as Jenkins, CircleCI, and GitLab CI play a vital role in automating and managing test execution across various environments and platforms. By leveraging these tools alongside techniques such as prioritizing high-risk tests, conditional execution based on code changes, and optimizing test suite management, teams can ensure that their testing processes are efficient, reliable, and aligned with the fast-paced nature of modern software development. These strategies not only enhance the quality of software but also contribute to faster delivery cycles and more effective development workflows.

Orchestrating cross-environment tests

Orchestrating tests across different environments ensures that applications behave as expected in various scenarios, from development to production. This orchestration involves systematically managing the execution of tests while ensuring that each environment is set up correctly. Here is how to effectively manage cross-environment tests and ensure proper setup and teardown.

Managing the execution of tests across different environments

Managing tests across different environment requirements and needs is one of the biggest challenges of effective test execution. Here, we look at different best practices that can assist in achieving this:

- **Environment consistency:**

    o **Use of containers:** Containerization (for example, using Docker) helps create consistent environments across development, staging, and production. Containers encapsulate the application and its dependencies, ensuring that tests run in the same environment regardless of the underlying infrastructure.

    o **Infrastructure as code (IaC):** Tools like Terraform or Ansible can be used to define and provision environments programmatically. This approach ensures that all environments (development, staging, production) are consistently configured, reducing discrepancies during test execution.

- **Test environment configuration:**

    o **Environment-specific configuration files:** Maintain separate configuration files for each environment. These files can define settings such as database connections, API endpoints, and feature flags specific to that environment.

    o **Dynamic environment variables:** Use environment variables to configure tests dynamically based on the environment in which they are running. This practice allows for flexible configurations without hardcoding values in the tests.

- **Pipeline integration:**

    o **CI/CD integration:** Integrate your testing strategy into your CI/CD pipeline to automate test execution across environments. This setup can automatically trigger tests based on specific events, such as code commits or pull requests, across development and staging environments before promoting changes to production.

    o **Environment promotion:** Implement an environment promotion strategy in which tests are first executed in development, then in staging, and finally in production. This step-wise approach allows teams to catch issues early in less critical environments before they affect production.

- **Environment-specific test suites:**

    o **Grouping tests by environment**: Organize your test suites to run specific tests based on the target environment. For example, specific integration tests may only be relevant for staging or production environments, while unit tests can run in development.

    o **Conditional execution logic:** Use conditional logic in your orchestration tool to decide which tests to run based on the environment. For example, run performance tests only in staging or production, where the application's performance can be accurately assessed.

- **Ensuring proper setup and teardown of test environments:** Allow execution across different environments. To ensure environment costs are reduced, it is important that your test execution framework also deals with the setup and teardown of your environments so that test environments are not running when unused and causing unnecessary cloud or server costs.

- **Automated environment setup:**

    o **Scripted setup processes:** Create scripts to automate the setup of testing environments. This may include provisioning servers, installing dependencies, and configuring databases. Automating these tasks reduces the risk of human error and ensures consistency.

    o **Pre-built images:** Use pre-built images for environments that can be quickly deployed. For example, container images that include all necessary dependencies and configurations can be instantiated quickly for testing.

- **Teardown procedures:**

  o **Automated teardown:** Implement automated teardown procedures to clean up resources after executing tests. This includes shutting down containers, removing temporary files, and reverting databases to their original states.

  o **Resource monitoring:** Monitor resource usage during testing to identify any lingering processes or resources that could cause conflicts in subsequent test runs. Automated scripts can check for and clean up any leftover resources.

- **Isolation of test environments:**

  o **Dedicated test environments:** Use dedicated test environments for different stages of the development lifecycle (for example, separate environments for unit tests, integration tests, and user acceptance tests). This separation prevents conflicts between tests and minimizes the risk of tests affecting each other.

  o **Database snapshots:** Utilize database snapshots to revert the database to a known state before each test execution. This approach ensures that tests run in a clean state, avoiding contamination from previous tests.

- **Environment cleanup strategies:**

  o **Scheduled cleanup:** Implement a scheduled cleanup strategy to regularly remove unused test environments or resources that are no longer needed. This practice helps maintain system performance and prevents resource exhaustion.

  o **Logging and monitoring:** Keep logs of environment setups, test executions, and teardowns to track any issues that arise during tests. Monitoring tools can alert teams to configuration issues or resource conflicts.

Orchestrating cross-environment tests is vital for ensuring that applications perform reliably in various settings. By effectively managing the execution of tests across development, staging, and production environments, teams can catch issues early and improve overall software quality. Implementing robust setup and teardown procedures helps maintain clean and isolated environments, reducing the risk of conflicts during test orchestration. By leveraging containerization, IaC, and automation, teams can streamline their testing processes and achieve greater confidence in their software releases.

Handling parallelization, reporting, and test scheduling

Parallel test execution is a critical practice in modern software development, particularly when dealing with large test suites. By executing tests simultaneously, teams can significantly reduce the overall testing time, enabling faster feedback and more efficient development cycles. This section discusses the importance of parallel test execution, techniques for its implementation, and the challenges that may arise.

Let us now understand the importance of parallelizing tests for faster feedback:

- **Reduced test execution time:**

  o **Faster feedback loops:** By running tests in parallel, teams can drastically decrease the time it takes to execute all tests, allowing for quicker identification of issues. This is especially important in agile environments where rapid iterations are essential.

  o **Increased development velocity:** With faster feedback, developers can address failures more promptly, leading to a more efficient development workflow and a shorter time-to-market for new features.

- **Scalability:**

  o **Handling large test suites**: As applications grow, so do their test suites. Parallel execution allows teams to scale their testing efforts without a proportional increase in execution time, making it feasible to maintain high test coverage.

  o **CI support**: In CI pipelines, where tests need to be executed after every change, parallel execution ensures that the build-and-test cycle remains quick, keeping the integration process smooth.

- **Resource utilization:**

  o **Maximizing hardware efficiency:** Parallel execution leverages available computational resources more effectively. Running tests on multiple cores, CPUs, or containers ensures that the hardware capacity is fully utilized, leading to faster overall execution times.

Techniques for implementing parallel test execution

With tests often reaching into the thousands and the need to get feedback as early as possible on potential failures, it is important that frameworks and runners are designed to operate in parallel. The following tips will help to maximize a framework's ability to operate in parallel:

- **Splitting test suites:**

  o **Thread-based execution:** Many testing frameworks (for example, JUnit, pytest) support running tests in parallel using threads. Configuring the framework to use multiple threads allows tests to be executed concurrently within the same process.

  o **Process-based execution:** Consider using multiple processes instead of threads for test cases that are not thread-safe. Tools like **pytest-xdist** or TestNG provide mechanisms to run tests in separate processes, avoiding issues related to shared state.

  o **Containerization:** Use container orchestration platforms (for example, Kubernetes) to run tests in isolated containers. This method allows for easy scaling and resource allocation while ensuring that tests do not interfere with each other.

- **Test sharding:**

  o **Dividing tests by characteristics:** Implement test sharding, where the entire test suite is divided into smaller subsets based on certain criteria, such as test type or execution time. Each subset can then be assigned to different threads or processes.

  o **Dynamic sharding:** Utilize tools that automatically analyze test durations and dynamically allocate tests to threads or processes based on their execution time to optimize resource usage.

- **CI/CD integration:**

  o **Pipeline configuration:** Integrate parallel test execution into CI/CD pipelines by configuring jobs to run tests concurrently. Most CI/CD tools (for example, Jenkins, CircleCI, GitLab CI) support parallel job execution, allowing for easy setup.

  o **Matrix builds:** Some CI/CD platforms allow the creation of matrix builds, where the same set of tests can be run in parallel across different environments or configurations, further speeding up the testing process.

Challenges of parallelization

Parallelization makes test automation far more efficient and dynamic but is not without its challenges. Some of them are as follows:

- **State management:** When tests run in parallel, they may attempt to access shared resources or data, leading to conflicts. For example, tests that write to the same database or file may interfere with each other.

- **Isolation:** Ensure that tests run in isolated environments where possible. Use separate databases, configurations, or mock data to avoid conflicts.

- **Transaction rollbacks:** Use database transactions that can be rolled back after tests, ensuring that tests do not leave residual data that could affect others.

- **Resource contention:** Running multiple tests simultaneously may lead to resource contention, where multiple tests compete for limited resources, causing performance degradation.

- **Resource allocation:** Monitor resource usage and dynamically allocate resources based on demand. Use resource limits in containers to prevent one test from monopolizing resources.

- **Load balancing:** Distribute tests evenly across available resources to optimize performance and minimize contention.

- **Interdependent tests:** If tests depend on the order of execution, running them in parallel can lead to failures. This is often seen with tests that rely on a specific sequence of actions.

Parallel test execution is a powerful technique that enhances the efficiency and speed of testing processes, particularly for large test suites. By implementing effective strategies such as test sharding, thread/process-based execution, and CI/CD integration, teams can maximize resource utilization and reduce feedback times. However, it is essential to be aware of the challenges associated with parallelization, including shared data conflicts, resource management, and test order dependencies. By proactively addressing these challenges with appropriate strategies, teams can successfully implement parallel test execution and achieve faster, more reliable software delivery.

Reporting and test results

Effective test reporting is crucial for understanding the outcomes of test executions and assessing the overall health of a system. Well-designed reports provide actionable insights, help identify trends, and guide team decision-making processes. This section discusses designing effective test reporting, customizing reports with key metrics, and ensuring real-time reporting for quicker issue detection.

Designing effective test reporting

The following are important traits that good test reports should have and how frameworks can contribute towards them:

- **Clear structure and presentation:**
  - **Organized layout:** Structure test reports logically, grouping results by test suites, categories, or functionality. This organization makes it easier for stakeholders to navigate and understand the results.
  - **Visualizations:** Use charts, graphs, and tables to present data visually. Visual representations of data can quickly convey information about trends, pass/fail rates, and execution times, making it easier for team members to grasp the results at a glance.

- **Actionable insights:**
  - **Root cause analysis:** Include sections highlighting failed tests, relevant logs, error messages, and stack traces. Providing context helps teams quickly identify the root cause of issues and facilitates faster resolution.

o **Historical comparison:** Compare current results with historical data to identify trends. This analysis can reveal whether the overall system health is improving or deteriorating and help teams focus on areas needing attention.

- **Stakeholder relevance:**

o **Tailored reports**: Design reports that target different stakeholders, such as developers, QA engineers, and management. Customize the level of detail and focus of the report based on the audience's needs. For instance, management might prefer high-level summaries, while developers might need detailed logs and metrics.

Customizing test reports with key metrics

Key metrics to include are as follows:

- **Pass/Fail rates:** Display the percentage of tests that passed versus failed. This metric provides a quick overview of the test suite's health.

- **Execution times:** Record and present the total time taken for test execution and the average time per test. Identifying long-running tests can help optimize test performance.

- **Flakiness:** Track and report on test flakiness, which refers to tests that sometimes pass and sometimes fail without changes to the code. This metric helps identify unreliable tests that may need attention.

- **Test coverage:** Include metrics on code coverage to indicate how much of the codebase is being tested. This information helps assess the adequacy of the tests.

Ensuring real-time reporting

Tests are often executed multiple times a day, and teams often need to make quick decisions on whether software is good enough for releases. It is important that test data is not delayed but kept as up to date as possible, preferably with real-time execution results built in. Let us go over the following:

- **Immediate feedback:**

o **Live reporting dashboards:** Implement real-time dashboards that update automatically during test execution. These dashboards can display live metrics, such as current pass/fail rates and execution progress, allowing teams to monitor the testing process actively.

o **Webhooks and notifications:** Use webhooks to trigger notifications in chat platforms (for example, Slack, Microsoft Teams) when tests pass or fail. This integration ensures that team members are promptly informed of test results without manually checking reports.

- **Centralized logging:**

o **Log aggregation:** Use centralized logging systems (for example, ELK Stack, Splunk) to collect and aggregate logs from various test runs. This practice allows teams to analyze logs in real time and correlate them with test results, enhancing the ability to detect and diagnose issues quickly.

o **Error tracking tools:** Integrate error tracking tools (for example, Sentry, Rollbar) with the testing framework to capture and report errors automatically. This integration ensures that failures are logged and can be addressed without manual intervention.

- **Post-test analysis:**

o **Automated analysis tools:** Use tools that analyze test results after execution and provide insights into trends and issues. For example, these tools can highlight patterns of flakiness or identify tests that consistently fail.

     o **Continuous feedback loops:** Establish a culture of continuous feedback where test results are discussed in regular team meetings. This practice ensures that insights from testing are shared promptly and acted upon.

Effective reporting and analysis of test results are essential for maintaining the health of a software system and facilitating timely issue resolution. By designing clear, actionable reports with key metrics, teams can gain valuable insights into their testing efforts and system performance. Integrating reporting tools and ensuring real-time reporting further enhances the ability to detect issues quickly and maintain high-quality software. A robust reporting strategy ultimately contributes to more efficient development cycles and improved collaboration among team members.

Test scheduling and execution frequency

Effective test scheduling is essential for maintaining high software quality while optimizing resource usage and minimizing delays in the development process. This section outlines best practices for scheduling tests, techniques for optimizing execution schedules, and methods for implementing intelligent test scheduling.

Best practices for scheduling tests

With so many different types of tests and a need to execute them frequently, it is important that a framework deals with ways of scheduling tests differently based on priorities and relevant to the changes made in the application under test. Let us now go over the following:

- **Run smoke tests with every commit:**
  - o **Purpose of smoke tests:** Smoke tests are a subset of tests that validate the basic functionality of an application. They ensure that the critical features work as expected and help catch major issues early.
  - o **Continuous feedback:** Running smoke tests with every commit provides immediate feedback to developers, allowing them to identify and fix problems before they propagate further into the development process. This practice helps maintain code quality and reduces the chances of introducing defects into the main branch.
- **Schedule full regression tests nightly or weekly:**
  - o **Full regression suite:** A full regression suite consists of comprehensive tests designed to verify that existing functionalities work after code changes. Given their scope, these tests can take a significant amount of time to execute.
  - o **Timing execution:** Scheduling full regression tests to run nightly or weekly ensures that they do not disrupt the development flow during the day. Nightly runs allow for thorough testing after the day's work is completed, providing a complete overview of the system's health before the next day's development begins.
- **Utilize test suites based on release cycles:**
  - o **Pre-release testing:** In addition to regular schedules, consider running full regression and additional tests before significant releases or deployments. This pre-release testing ensures that all functionalities are working correctly before reaching users.
  - o **Feature branch testing:** For feature branches, run targeted tests that are relevant to the changes made in that branch. This approach reduces the overall testing time and focuses efforts on the areas most likely to be impacted.

Techniques for optimizing test execution schedules

The following are some techniques that will help ensure tests are scheduled effectively for quicker and more effective feedback:

- **Categorize tests by type and importance:**

  o **Test prioritization:** Classify tests based on their importance and the likelihood of failure. Critical tests should be run more frequently, while lower-priority tests can be scheduled less often. This practice ensures that the most impactful tests receive attention during every execution cycle.

  o **Risk-based testing:** Implement a risk-based testing approach, where tests are scheduled based on the risk associated with the features being tested. High-risk areas should have more frequent test coverage, while lower-risk features can be tested less often.

- **Monitor execution times and outcomes:**

  o **Execution metrics:** Track execution times and failure rates for tests over time. Identify tests that consistently take longer than average or those that frequently fail. Use this data to refine execution schedules, potentially moving problematic tests to a separate schedule or addressing underlying issues.

  o **Scheduled maintenance windows:** Allocate time for maintenance of tests, such as refactoring long-running tests, improving performance, and resolving flakiness. Scheduled maintenance can help ensure the test suite remains efficient and reliable.

- **Leverage CI/CD tools:**

  o **Integration with CI/CD:** Use CI/CD tools to automate test scheduling based on project needs. Configure your CI/CD pipeline to trigger specific tests based on events, such as commits, pull requests, or merge events.

  o **Configurable scheduling:** Many CI/CD tools allow for configurable schedules. Utilize these features to set up test execution plans that align with project milestones and deliverables.

- **Implementing intelligent test scheduling:**

  o **Dynamic test execution:**

    ▪ **Dependency mapping**: Create a mapping of dependencies between tests and code changes. Only the tests related to that area should be executed when a change is made in a particular module or feature. This targeted approach reduces unnecessary test executions.

    ▪ **Change detection:** Use change detection tools or mechanisms that analyze recent commits to determine which tests are relevant. By focusing on tests related to modified code, teams can save time while ensuring quality.

  o **Historical data analysis:**

    ▪ **Utilize past test results:** Analyze historical test results to identify patterns in failures and successes. If certain tests consistently fail after specific changes, prioritize their execution whenever those changes are made.

    ▪ **Flakiness detection:** Implement metrics to track flaky tests, which may pass in one execution and fail in another. Use historical data to determine the reliability of tests and adjust the execution schedule accordingly.

  o **Adaptive scheduling:**

    ▪ **Feedback loops:** Implement feedback mechanisms where test execution results influence future scheduling. For example, if a test consistently passes, it could be run less frequently, while tests that frequently fail should be run more often.

    ▪ **User-defined rules:** Allow teams to define rules for test execution based on specific project needs. These rules can consider factors like the severity of changes, time since the last execution, or the impact of recent releases.

Effective test scheduling and execution frequency are vital for ensuring software quality while optimizing resource usage. By implementing best practices, such as running smoke tests with every commit and scheduling complete regression tests nightly, teams can maintain a healthy development workflow. Techniques like test categorization, execution metrics, and CI/CD integration further enhance scheduling efficiency. Finally, intelligent test scheduling that dynamically adapts based on recent code changes and historical data ensures that only relevant tests are executed, leading to faster feedback and improved software reliability.

Conclusion

Efficient test orchestration and execution are crucial components of a successful test automation framework. They not only streamline the testing process but also enhance the overall quality of software delivery. By effectively organizing and managing test executions, teams can identify issues earlier in the development lifecycle, ultimately leading to faster and more reliable software releases.

A custom test runner plays a pivotal role in this landscape by managing test cases and ensuring flexibility in the execution process. It allows teams to tailor the testing environment to their specific needs, providing the capability to handle various test types, configurations, and reporting requirements. The extensibility of a custom test runner enables organizations to adapt to changing testing demands and integrate with different frameworks seamlessly.

Parallel execution, robust reporting, and intelligent test scheduling further enhance the efficiency and effectiveness of the testing process. Parallel execution accelerates feedback loops by running tests simultaneously, allowing teams to receive quicker insights into system health. Comprehensive and actionable reporting helps stakeholders make informed decisions based on key metrics, while smart test scheduling ensures that only relevant tests are executed based on recent code changes and historical results. Together, these elements contribute to improving the speed and accuracy of testing, fostering a culture of continuous improvement and high-quality software development.

In the next chapter, we tackle the critical aspect of test data and how to best manage it execute tests that are meaningful and relevant.

Key takeaways

Here are some things to consider when looking at designing a framework to handle effective test orchestration and execution:

- **Test orchestration enhances efficiency:** Orchestrating test execution ensures that large test suites are managed effectively, reducing execution time and optimizing resource usage.

- **Custom test runners provide flexibility**: A well-designed test runner can dynamically load test cases, manage configurations, and support multiple test types, making it a crucial component of an adaptable test automation framework.

- **Parallel execution speeds up testing:** Running tests concurrently across threads, processes, or containers improves feedback loops but requires careful handling of shared data and resources.

- **Smart test scheduling optimizes execution:** Intelligent scheduling techniques prioritize relevant tests based on code changes and execution history, ensuring efficient and timely test runs.

- **Comprehensive reporting drives insights:** Effective test reports should include key metrics such as pass/fail rates, execution times, and flakiness, enabling teams to make data-driven decisions and detect issues early.

- **CI/CD integration enables continuous testing:** Seamless integration with CI/CD pipelines ensures automated, consistent, and scalable test execution across development environments.

- **Cross-environment testing prevents deployment issues:** Managing test execution across different environments (for example, staging, production) ensures that tests reflect real-world conditions, reducing post-deployment risks.

- **Scalability and extensibility are crucial:** A test framework should be designed to support evolving needs, allowing integration with different test frameworks and execution strategies.

Exercises

1. Are your test executions optimized for speed and reliability, or are there bottlenecks?

2. How do you handle test dependencies and avoid execution conflicts?

3. Are you using a built-in test runner or a custom-built one? What are the reasons for your choice?

4. How flexible is your test execution setup? Can you easily integrate different types of tests (unit, UI, performance)?

5. Are you running tests in parallel? If not, what are the blockers preventing you from doing so?

6. How do you manage shared resources and test data when executing tests in parallel?

7. Are you using intelligent test execution (for example, running only impacted tests based on code changes)?

Join our Discord space

Join our Discord workspace for latest updates, offers, tech happenings around the world, new releases, and sessions with the authors:

https://discord.bpbonline.com

CHAPTER 7
Test Data Management

Introduction

Test data management (TDM) refers to the processes and techniques used to create, maintain, and manage test data necessary for testing software applications. TDM plays a crucial role in ensuring the accuracy, reliability, and repeatability of tests by providing testers with the appropriate data they need to simulate real-world scenarios and assess applications' functionality, performance, and security.

In software testing, the quality of the test data significantly influences the outcome of the tests. TDM involves several key activities that contribute to effective testing practices. One essential activity is data creation, which focuses on generating realistic test data that mirrors production environments and adequately covers a range of use cases and edge scenarios. Closely related is data provisioning, which involves distributing this data to various testing environments to ensure that testers have timely and reliable access to the data they need.

Equally important is data maintenance, which consists of regularly updating and refreshing test data to reflect changes in the production environment—this helps preserve the relevance and accuracy of the tests over time. Finally, data management encompasses the implementation of policies and procedures that control access to test data, ensure its quality, and support secure and efficient data retrieval. Together, these activities form the foundation of a well-structured TDM process that enhances test effectiveness and supports overall software quality.

Structure

In this chapter, we will go over the following topics:

- Importance of using realistic and well-structured test data
- Approaches to test data generation and management
- Test data versioning
- Externalizing test data
- Managing state across tests
- Data-driven testing principles

- Creating reusable data sets
- Improving test coverage through DDT
- Test data security and anonymization
- Best practices in test data management
- Data management in CI/CD pipelines

Objectives

By the end of this chapter, the reader will learn the importance of test data in the test process and the different approaches to utilizing data to improve test automation. This includes balancing the need for comprehensive test data sets to allow for more effective testing while also looking at ways of managing it more effectively, securely, and optimally for CI/CD development.

Importance of using realistic and well-structured test data

When it comes to testing and especially automation, there is a fine balance between dealing with simple and stubbed data sources to improve efficiency and predictability, and using more complex but realistic data, which may be difficult to source and add complexity to your final solution to get right. However, with the software world increasingly reliant on data, it is more critical than ever to include representative data in your testing and automation.

Using realistic and well-structured test data is essential for several reasons:

- **Reflecting real-world scenarios:** Tests based on accurate data can better mimic how end-users interact with the software, leading to more reliable results. When test data is structured to reflect actual user behaviours and data distributions, it helps identify potential issues that may arise in production.

- **Improved test coverage:** Well-structured test data allows for comprehensive testing across various conditions, ensuring that both common and edge cases are evaluated. This enhances the likelihood of discovering defects and performance bottlenecks before the software is deployed.

- **Increased confidence in results:** Tests performed with realistic data yield more trustworthy outcomes. This instils confidence in stakeholders about the software's readiness for production, as they can rely on the results to make informed decisions.

- **Facilitating compliance and audit trails:** In regulated industries, using test data that meets compliance standards is vital. Structured test data can help organizations demonstrate adherence to regulations during audits.

Challenges associated with TDM

Despite its importance, TDM presents several challenges, such as:

- **Data consistency:** Maintaining consistency across various testing environments can be difficult. Discrepancies in test data can lead to false negatives or positives, making it challenging to ascertain the true quality of the software.

- **State management:** Different tests may require the system to be in specific states (for example, user logged in, data populated). Managing these states effectively while ensuring the underlying test data remains valid can be complex.

- **Security concerns:** Handling sensitive data is one of the most significant challenges in TDM. Organizations must ensure that test data in non-production environments does not expose sensitive information, such as **personally identifiable information** (**PII**) or financial data. Techniques like data masking, anonymization, and tokenization are often employed to protect sensitive information while allowing for realistic testing.

- **Scalability**: As software applications evolve and become more complex, the volume and variety of required test data grow. Scaling TDM processes to meet these demands without compromising quality or performance can be a daunting task.

- **Automation and integration:** Integrating TDM practices with existing CI/CD pipelines and test automation frameworks is crucial for efficient testing. However, achieving this integration can be challenging, especially when dealing with disparate tools and technologies.

TDM is a critical component of effective software testing. By ensuring the accuracy, reliability, and repeatability of tests through realistic and well-structured test data, organizations can enhance their software quality and reduce the risk of defects in production. However, overcoming the challenges associated with TDM, particularly in areas of data consistency, state management, security, scalability, and automation, is essential for successful implementation. Proper TDM practices can lead to improved testing outcomes and contribute significantly to the overall success of software development initiatives.

Approaches to test data generation and management

Let us understand the difference between static and dynamic test data.

Static test data refers to pre-defined data that is created and stored before the testing process begins. This type of data remains unchanged during the test execution and is often used for tests that require consistency and repeatability. Static test data can be generated based on known requirements or scenarios and is typically stored in files, databases, or as part of the testing framework.

Dynamic test data, on the other hand, is generated at runtime during the execution of the tests. This data is often created on the fly based on specific test conditions, inputs, or user interactions. Dynamic test data is useful for simulating a wide range of scenarios, particularly those that involve variability and unpredictability.

Use cases for static test data

Here are some specific use cases where utilising static data can be helpful in different forms of testing:

- **Regression testing:** Static test data is particularly useful in regression testing, where the goal is to verify that recent code changes have not adversely affected existing functionality. By using a consistent set of pre-defined test data, testers can reliably compare the outcomes of tests over time, making it easier to identify any new defects introduced by recent changes.

- **Smoke testing:** For smoke tests, which are preliminary tests to check the basic functionality of an application, static test data can provide a quick and consistent means to ensure that the core features are working as expected.

- **Unit testing:** Static data is often used in unit tests to isolate specific components of the codebase. By providing consistent input, testers can verify the behaviour of individual functions or methods without the influence of external factors.

- **Compliance and security testing:** In situations where consistent data is crucial, such as compliance audits or security testing, static test data ensures that tests can be reliably repeated to verify compliance with regulations or security standards.

Use cases for dynamic test data

Here are some specific use cases where utilizing dynamic data can be useful in different forms of testing:

- **Performance testing:** Dynamic test data is essential for performance testing, where the goal is to evaluate how the application behaves under various loads. Generating data at runtime allows for simulating different user scenarios, such as multiple concurrent users accessing the application with varying data sets, which provides a more realistic representation of production environments.

- **Stress testing:** Similar to performance testing, stress testing examines how an application handles extreme conditions or heavy loads. Dynamic test data enables testers to create unpredictable scenarios, such as sudden spikes in user traffic or unexpected data inputs, helping identify potential bottlenecks and failure points.

- **User acceptance testing (UAT):** In UAT, stakeholders test the application to ensure it meets their requirements. Dynamic test data can mimic real-world user behavior, allowing testers to explore different paths and interactions, which enhances the validity of the testing process.

- **Data-driven testing:** In data-driven testing, multiple test cases are executed with varying input data. Dynamic test data generation allows for efficient execution of these tests, as different combinations of inputs can be created and applied without the need for extensive manual setup.

Both static and dynamic test data have their respective strengths and use cases within the software testing lifecycle. While static test data offers consistency and repeatability, making it ideal for regression, smoke, and unit testing, dynamic test data is vital for performance, stress, and user acceptance testing, where variability and unpredictability are essential. Understanding when to utilize each type of test data allows organizations to optimize their testing processes and ensure a comprehensive evaluation of their software applications.

Test data generation approaches

Test data generation is a crucial aspect of software testing that involves creating the data required for testing applications. Depending on the testing needs and scenarios, it can be approached in various ways. This section discusses three primary approaches: using predefined datasets, generating dynamic test data, and synthetic data generation.

Creating and maintaining static datasets

Predefined datasets are useful when consistency and repeatability are essential for testing. Static datasets are typically created in advance and stored in formats such as **comma-separated values (CSV)**, **JavaScript Object Notation (JSON)**, or within databases. Here are the steps required to create static datasets for your testing purposes:

1. **Identify test cases:** Begin by determining the scenarios that need to be tested, including typical use cases and edge cases.

2. **Data collection:** Collect relevant data that reflects the necessary input for the identified test cases. This can be done by extracting data from production databases, user input logs, or existing application logs.

3. **Data formatting:** Structure the data in a format that is easy to use in tests, such as CSV files for tabular data or JSON for hierarchical data.

Maintaining static datasets

Here are some best practices to manage the data within your test cases:

- **Version control:** Use version control systems to track changes to the datasets over time. This helps ensure the correct dataset version is used for each test cycle.

- **Regular updates:** Schedule regular reviews and updates of the datasets to ensure they reflect any application changes or requirements.

- **Documentation:** Maintain clear documentation on the dataset structure, the purpose of each dataset, and how to update it, facilitating easier onboarding for new team members.

Generating dynamic test data

Dynamic test data generation is essential for scenarios where variability is required. Several tools and libraries facilitate this process, such as:

- **Faker:**

  o **Overview:** Faker is a popular Python library that generates fake data for various purposes, such as names, addresses, dates, and emails.

  o **Usage:** It allows testers to create random data easily and can be customized to suit specific needs. For example:

  ```
  from faker import Faker
  fake = Faker()
  name = fake.name()
  email = fake.email()
  ```

- **Mockaroo:**

  o **Overview:** Mockaroo is a web-based tool that provides a user-friendly interface for generating realistic test data in various formats, including CSV, JSON, and SQL.

  o **Usage:** Users can define the schema for the data they need and specify data types, constraints, and relationships between fields. Mockaroo can generate large datasets quickly, making it ideal for performance and stress testing.

Custom data generators

In cases where predefined tools do not meet specific needs, creating custom data generators can be beneficial. This involves writing scripts or functions that generate data based on specific rules or patterns, particularly for edge cases. For example, a custom generator can be implemented to create test data for a system that handles financial transactions, ensuring scenarios like negative balances, invalid account numbers, or boundary conditions are tested.

Synthetic data generation

Synthetic data generation involves creating data that mimics real-world production data while avoiding the risks associated with using actual sensitive data. Techniques for generating synthetic data include:

- **Data masking:**

  o **Overview:** Data masking involves obfuscating sensitive information within a dataset. For example, names, social security numbers, and credit card details can be replaced with fictitious but realistic-looking values.

  o **Benefits:** This method allows for the use of realistic data patterns while protecting sensitive information.

- **Data simulation:**

  o **Overview:** Data simulation involves creating models that generate data based on statistical patterns observed in production data. This method uses algorithms to create synthetic datasets that maintain the same statistical properties as the original data.

  o **Benefits:** This approach ensures that the synthetic data is representative of actual data distributions, allowing for more accurate testing.

- **Generative adversarial networks (GANs):**

    o **Overview:** GANs are a type of machine learning model used to generate new data instances that resemble training data. They consist of two networks: a generator that creates synthetic data and a discriminator that evaluates the authenticity of the generated data.

    o **Benefits:** GANs can create high-quality synthetic data that is difficult to distinguish from real data, making it useful for various testing scenarios.

Choosing the appropriate test data generation approach is critical for effective software testing. Predefined datasets offer consistency for tests such as regression, while dynamic test data generation tools and custom generators provide flexibility for performance and stress testing. Meanwhile, synthetic data generation techniques help mitigate security risks while ensuring that the test data remains representative of production environments. By leveraging these approaches effectively, organizations can enhance the quality and reliability of their testing processes.

Test data versioning

Test data versioning is an essential practice in software testing that involves managing different versions of test data to ensure reproducibility and consistency across various environments. Maintaining accurate and relevant test data becomes increasingly important as applications evolve rapidly. This section discusses strategies for managing test data versions and updating datasets over time.

Managing test data versions

One of the biggest obstacles to working with test data is that the relevancy of certain data may change as frequently as the code itself. As a result, it is critical to version test data correctly based on the needs of your test scenarios. The following are different examples of managing the versioning of your test data:

- **Version control systems (VCS):**

    o **Overview:** Utilize VCS (like Git) to track changes in test data files, similar to how source code is managed. By committing changes to test datasets, teams can keep a history of modifications, enabling easy rollback to previous versions if necessary.

    o **Benefits:** This approach allows teams to collaborate effectively, maintain clear documentation of changes, and ensure that all testers are working with the correct version of the data.

- **Semantic versioning:**

    o **Overview:** Apply semantic versioning (for example, `MAJOR.MINOR.PATCH`) to test data sets. Each change in the dataset can be categorized based on its impact on the tests: significant changes may affect existing tests. In contrast, minor changes add new data or modify existing entries without breaking existing tests.

    o **Benefits:** This system of versioning helps stakeholders understand the implications of changes to test data and facilitates communication within the team.

- **Environment-specific versioning:**

    o **Overview:** Maintain separate versions of test data for different environments (for example, development, testing, staging). This ensures that the data used in one environment does not inadvertently affect others, providing clarity about which version of data corresponds to which environment.

    o **Benefits:** Environment-specific versioning enhances control over the testing process and minimizes potential disruptions caused by changes in test data across environments.

Strategies for updating and managing test data sets

Here are some best practices to help ensure your test data sets remain updated and relevant to provide reliable test outcomes that match the behaviors of a production environment:

- **Regular review and update cycles:**

  o **Overview:** Establish regular intervals for reviewing and updating test datasets, especially after significant application changes, new feature releases, or bug fixes. This could involve assessing whether the existing data still reflects real-world scenarios and user interactions.

  o **Benefits:** Regular updates ensure that test data remains relevant and accurate, thereby improving the reliability of test results.

- **Automated data generation:**

  o **Overview:** Implement automated data generation techniques to create new test data as needed, particularly when existing data is outdated or insufficient. Tools like Faker, Mockaroo, and custom data generators can help automate this process.

  o **Benefits:** Automation reduces the manual effort involved in maintaining test data and allows for rapid adjustments to keep pace with evolving application requirements.

- **Data dependency mapping:**

  o **Overview:** Maintain a mapping of data dependencies to understand how different pieces of test data interact with each other. This mapping can help identify which datasets need to be updated when changes occur in the application.

  o **Benefits:** By visualizing data dependencies, teams can prioritize updates and avoid introducing inconsistencies that could affect test results.

- **Backward compatibility testing:**

  o **Overview:** When updating test data, conduct backward compatibility tests to ensure that new data does not break existing tests. This may involve running regression tests to verify that the application behaves as expected with the updated datasets.

  o **Benefits:** Backward compatibility testing helps maintain stability in the testing process, ensuring that existing functionalities continue to work correctly even as the test data evolves.

- **Stakeholder involvement:**

  o **Overview:** Engage stakeholders, including developers, testers, and product owners, in discussions about test data management. Gather input on necessary changes and updates, and establish a shared understanding of how test data relates to application functionality.

  o **Benefits:** Collaboration fosters a sense of ownership and accountability around test data, leading to better practices and higher-quality datasets.

Effective test data versioning and management are critical for ensuring reproducibility and consistency in software testing, particularly in rapidly evolving systems. By leveraging VCS, applying semantic versioning, and maintaining separate data sets for different environments, organizations can enhance their testing processes. Moreover, implementing strategies for regularly updating and managing test datasets, such as automated data generation, data dependency mapping, backward compatibility testing, and involving stakeholders, can ensure that test data remains relevant and reliable throughout the software development lifecycle. Through these practices, teams can significantly improve the quality of their testing efforts and the overall success of their applications.

Externalizing test data

Externalizing test data refers to the practice of separating test data from test scripts, allowing for greater flexibility, maintainability, and reusability in testing processes. By externalizing test data, teams can create test scripts that are independent of the specific data they consume, making it easier to update or modify test data without impacting the test logic.

This section outlines best practices for externalizing test data and strategies for storing and managing test data in dedicated repositories or cloud-based data services.

Best practices for externalizing test data

Let us now go over the various best practices:

- **Use of data-driven testing (DDT):**

  o **Overview:** Implement DDT methodologies, where test scripts are designed to execute with various sets of data. In DDT, test data is stored externally (for example, in CSV, Excel, or JSON files), allowing the same test script to run multiple times with different inputs.

  o **Benefits:** This approach enhances reusability and reduces duplication of test scripts, making it easier to maintain and update the testing framework.

- **Clear data format standards:**

  o **Overview:** Establish clear standards for the format and structure of external test data files. Define consistent naming conventions, data types, and structures that all team members should follow when creating or updating test data.

  o **Benefits:** Consistency in data formatting minimizes confusion, reduces errors, and streamlines the process of integrating new test data into existing scripts.

- **Centralized data management:**

  o **Overview:** Maintain a centralized repository for all test data files, making it easy for team members to access, modify, and update data as needed. This can be a version-controlled system (for example, Git) or a shared network drive.

  o **Benefits:** Centralization enhances collaboration, ensures that all testers work with the latest data, and allows for easy tracking of changes over time.

- **Parameterized tests:**

  o **Overview:** Use parameterization in test scripts to allow external inputs to be passed into the tests. This enables flexibility in test execution and allows for easy modification of input values without changing the test logic.

  o **Benefits:** Parameterized tests promote independence between test logic and test data, enabling more efficient test maintenance.

- **Documentation:**

  o **Overview:** Document the external test data structure, including field descriptions, data types, and sample values. Additionally, provide guidelines for how to create, update, and manage test data.

  o **Benefits:** Comprehensive documentation serves as a reference for team members and helps ensure consistent practices when handling test data.

Storing and managing test data

Let us go over the following:

- **Dedicated repositories:**

    o **Overview:** Store test data in dedicated repositories designed specifically for managing test assets. This could involve using version-controlled repositories (for example, GitHub, GitLab) or specialized database systems for structured data storage.

    o **Benefits:** Dedicated repositories enhance data organization, facilitate collaboration, and provide robust version control to track changes over time.

- **Cloud-based data services:**

    o **Overview:** Leverage cloud-based data services (for example, Amazon S3, Google Cloud Storage, Azure Blob Storage) to store and manage test data. These services offer scalable storage solutions that can be easily accessed from various testing environments.

    o **Benefits:** Cloud-based solutions provide flexibility, high availability, and the ability to integrate with other cloud services, such as CI/CD pipelines, facilitating automated testing processes.

- **Data cataloguing:**

    o **Overview:** Implement data cataloguing practices to track and manage test data assets. A data catalogue provides a centralized inventory of test data, including metadata such as data lineage, usage, and version history.

    o **Benefits:** Data cataloguing improves visibility into available test data and assists teams in identifying suitable datasets for specific testing scenarios.

- **Access control and security:**

    o **Overview:** Establish access control policies to restrict who can view or modify test data. This may involve setting up user roles, permissions, and auditing mechanisms to ensure data integrity and security.

    o **Benefits:** Implementing robust access controls protects sensitive test data and ensures that only authorized personnel can make changes, reducing the risk of errors and unauthorized access.

Externalizing test data is a best practice that promotes flexibility, maintainability, and reusability in testing processes. Organizations can enhance the efficiency of their testing efforts by implementing strategies such as data-driven testing, centralized data management, parameterized tests, and comprehensive documentation. Additionally, utilizing dedicated repositories and cloud-based data services for storing and managing test data ensures scalability, availability, and security. By embracing these practices, teams can create a more agile and responsive testing environment, ultimately contributing to higher-quality software outcomes.

Managing state across tests

Test state refers to the specific condition or configuration of the system or application under test at a given point in time during the testing process. It encompasses various aspects, including the data in use, the environment configuration, the application's status, and any dependencies or interactions with external systems. Managing the test state is crucial for ensuring that tests yield consistent and reliable results, especially when testing complex applications that involve multiple components.

Importance of the test state in maintaining consistency

Test states are important to maintain consistency for the following reasons:

- **Reproducibility:** Test state ensures that the conditions under which a test is executed are consistent each time the test is run. This reproducibility is vital for diagnosing issues, as it allows testers to reliably recreate test conditions when analyzing test failures. By maintaining a controlled test state, teams can easily identify whether a failure is due to changes in the code or variations in the test environment.

- **Isolation of tests:** Test state management allows for the isolation of individual tests, preventing one test's execution from affecting another. This isolation is especially important when tests modify shared resources or interact with external systems. By controlling the state before and after each test, teams can ensure that tests do not interfere with one another, leading to more accurate test results.

- **Data integrity:** Managing test state helps maintain the integrity of test data. When tests are run with pre-defined data states, it ensures that the data remains consistent throughout the testing process. Proper state management prevents scenarios where tests accidentally modify data in unexpected ways, leading to erroneous outcomes.

Ensuring reliability in scenarios with external systems

Let us go over the following points now:

- **Interaction with external systems:** Many applications interact with external systems, such as databases, APIs, or third-party services. Test state management becomes critical in these scenarios to ensure that tests correctly represent the state of the system being interacted with. By controlling the state of external systems or mocking their behaviour, testers can validate how the application handles various scenarios, such as successful responses, failures, or timeouts.

- **Database state management:** When tests interact with databases, managing the database state is essential. This includes setting up known data states before tests are run and ensuring that any changes made during tests are rolled back or cleaned up afterward. Strategies such as database snapshots, transactions, or in-memory databases can be employed to manage the database's state effectively, ensuring that tests do not leave residual data that could affect subsequent test runs.

- **Environmental consistency:** The test state also encompasses the configuration of the testing environment, including server settings, application versions, and infrastructure dependencies. Managing this state is crucial to maintaining consistency across different test executions. Automated deployment tools and configuration management systems can help ensure that the test environment is consistently set up, reducing variability in test results.

- **State recovery:** In situations where tests fail, managing the test state allows for recovery mechanisms to restore the system to a known good state. This can involve resetting the application, clearing caches, or restoring databases to their initial state. Effective state recovery strategies enable teams to quickly rerun tests without needing to manually reset the environment, thus improving efficiency.

Test state plays a critical role in ensuring the reliability and consistency of software testing. By clearly defining and managing the test state, teams can achieve reproducibility, isolate tests, and maintain data integrity. In scenarios involving interactions with external systems, robust state management is essential for ensuring accurate test outcomes and minimizing the risk of errors. By implementing best practices for test state management, organizations can enhance the quality of their testing processes and ultimately deliver more reliable software products.

Using mocks, stubs, and fakes

In software testing, mocks, stubs, and fakes are essential techniques used to simulate components of a system. These tools help isolate the unit being tested, allowing for focused testing and improved reliability. Here is a detailed overview of each technique, including its definitions and practical applications.

Mocks

Mocks are simulated objects that mimic the behaviour of real objects in controlled ways. They are particularly useful for testing interactions between components, especially when dealing with external systems or services.

Simulating external systems or services: Mocks are often used to simulate APIs, databases, or third-party services. By creating mock versions of these components, developers can isolate the code being tested from external dependencies. For instance, when testing a function that retrieves data from an external API, a mock can be used to simulate the API's response without making actual network calls.

Techniques for mocking

Let us now go over some techniques for mocking:

- **Using mocking libraries:** Libraries such as Mockito (Java), unittest.mock (Python), and Jest (JavaScript) provide built-in capabilities for creating mocks. These libraries allow developers to define expected behaviours and verify interactions during tests. Here is an example in Python using **unittest.mock**:

```
from unittest.mock import Mock

# Create a mock object
api_mock = Mock()
api_mock.get_data.return_value = {'key': 'value'}

# Use the mock in a test
response = api_mock.get_data()
assert response == {'key': 'value'}
```

- **Verification of interactions:** Mocks can verify that specific methods were called with the expected parameters, which helps ensure that the code interacts correctly with external services. For example:

```
api_mock.get_data.assert_called_once_with(expected_param)
```

Stubs

Stubs are simplified implementations of a component that return predetermined responses. Unlike mocks, stubs focus on providing fixed responses and do not track interactions.

Replacing components with simplified implementations: Stubs replace components in the system to isolate the unit under test, providing a controlled environment for testing. They are typically used in unit tests where specific functionality needs to be tested without involving the complete system. For example, when testing a service that interacts with a database, a stub can be used to return fixed data without accessing the actual database.

Providing fixed responses for certain calls: Stubs can be configured to return specific values based on their input. This makes them ideal for scenarios where the behaviour of the system can be predetermined. Here is an example in Python:

```
class DatabaseStub:
    def fetch_user(self, user_id):
        return {'id': user_id, 'name': 'Test User'}

# Using the stub in a test
db_stub = DatabaseStub()
user = db_stub.fetch_user(1)
assert user['name'] == 'Test User'
```

Fakes

Fakes are lightweight, in-memory implementations of components that emulate the behavior of real services or databases. Unlike mocks and stubs, fakes are more complex and can have actual implementations.

Creating lightweight in-memory implementations: Fakes provide a functional implementation that behaves similarly to the real component but operates in memory instead of relying on external systems. This is useful for integration testing or when the overhead of using real services is too high. For instance, a fake database can store data in memory, allowing for tests to run without the need for a real database connection.

Avoiding real services or databases: Fakes allow developers to avoid the complexities of real services or databases, such as authentication, network latency, and data consistency issues. This can lead to faster tests and more straightforward debugging. Here is an example of a simple fake database:

```python
class FakeDatabase:
    def __init__(self):
        self.users = {}

    def add_user(self, user_id, name):
        self.users[user_id] = name

    def get_user(self, user_id):
        return self.users.get(user_id, None)


# Using the fake database in a test
fake_db = FakeDatabase()
fake_db.add_user(1, 'Test User')
assert fake_db.get_user(1) == 'Test User'
```

Using mocks, stubs, and fakes effectively is crucial for building reliable and maintainable test suites. Mocks help simulate and verify interactions with external systems, while stubs provide fixed responses for isolated testing. Fakes offer lightweight, in-memory implementations that avoid dependencies on real services or databases. By employing these techniques, teams can enhance their testing strategies, leading to more robust and efficient software development processes.

Test isolation techniques

Test isolation techniques are crucial in ensuring that tests are independent and do not interfere with one another. This independence is essential for producing reliable and reproducible test results. The following sections discuss managing shared state across tests and using setup and teardown methods to maintain clean execution environments:

- **Identifying shared state:** The first step in managing shared state is to identify any global or shared data that might be accessed or modified by multiple tests. This could include variables, database entries, files, or configurations that, if altered, could impact other tests. By recognizing these shared states, teams can develop strategies to isolate or reset them as needed.

- **Avoiding global state:** Whenever possible, avoid using global variables or shared states that can be modified during tests. Instead, utilize instance variables or local variables that are scoped to individual test cases. This approach reduces the risk of unintended side effects caused by changes made in one test affecting another.

- **Test data management:** Implement strategies for managing test data to prevent data contamination. This includes using separate databases or schemas for testing or utilizing mocks and fakes to simulate interactions without altering real data. For example, using an in-memory database for tests can help ensure that changes made during testing do not persist beyond the lifecycle of a single test.

- **Isolation through containers:** Utilize containerization technologies (for example, Docker) to create isolated environments for tests. Each test can run in its own container, ensuring that dependencies and states do not bleed into one another. This method allows for a consistent testing environment that can be easily reset, making it ideal for integration and end-to-end testing.

Using setup and teardown methods

Let us now look at the following two methods:

- **Setup methods:**

  - **Definition:** A setup method is executed before each test to prepare the test environment. This may involve initializing variables, configuring services, or populating databases with required test data.

  - **Example:** In Python's **unittest** framework, the **setUp()** method can be used to set up the necessary context before each test.

    ```python
    import unittest
    class TestExample(unittest.TestCase):
    def setUp(self):
    self.test_data = {'key': 'value'}  # Prepare test data
    def test_example(self):
    self.assertEqual(self.test_data['key'], 'value')
    ```

- **Teardown method:**

  - **Definition:** A teardown method is executed after each test to clean up the environment. This may include resetting states, removing test data, or closing service connections.

  - **Example:** In Python's **unittest** framework, the **tearDown()** method can be used to clean up after each test.

    ```python
    def tearDown(self):
        self.test_data = {}  # Reset test data
    ```

Ensuring clean execution environments: By using setup and teardown methods, teams can ensure that each test starts with a clean slate, preventing state leakage from previous tests. This is particularly important when tests modify shared resources, such as databases or files. This practice promotes reliable and consistent test results, as each test is executed in isolation from others.

Parameterized tests: When using parameterized tests, the setup and teardown methods can be employed to handle different input scenarios while still maintaining isolation. This ensures that each parameterized instance is treated independently, with its setup and teardown executed for each set of parameters.

Test isolation techniques are vital for maintaining the integrity and reliability of software testing. By managing shared state effectively and using setup and teardown methods, teams can ensure that tests are independent, reproducible, and data contamination-free. These practices contribute to a more robust testing framework, ultimately leading to higher-quality software and reduced risk of bugs in production.

Handling stateful systems

Testing stateful systems, which maintain a record of interactions, sessions, or transactions, presents unique challenges. These systems may have dependencies on previous interactions or data, making it crucial to manage state effectively to ensure reliable and consistent test outcomes. This section outlines strategies for dealing with stateful systems during testing and how to use state-resetting techniques to ensure that each test starts with a clean slate.

Now let us go over the following:

- **Understanding the state model:** Before testing a stateful system, it is essential to understand its state model, including how states are maintained, transitioned, and persisted. This includes knowing how sessions are created and terminated, how data is stored and retrieved, and the impact of user interactions. Mapping out state transitions can help identify critical points where testing needs to occur, allowing for a targeted testing strategy.

- **Isolation of tests:** Ensure that each test case is isolated from others to avoid unintended side effects. This can be achieved by using unique identifiers for sessions or transactions in each test run. For example, if testing user sessions, each test could generate a unique session token to ensure that no shared state persists between tests.

- **Utilizing mocks and stubs:** Employ mocks and stubs to simulate the behaviour of stateful components without relying on actual state. This is particularly useful for components that maintain complex states, such as databases or user authentication services. By replacing real interactions with simulated ones, teams can avoid side effects and focus on testing specific functionality.

- **Transactional testing:** Use transactional testing techniques, where tests are executed within transactions that can be rolled back at the end of each test. This approach allows tests to change the state without persisting those changes beyond the test scope. For example, in a database context, a transaction can be started at the beginning of a test, and any changes made can be rolled back to restore the database to its original state.

- **Session management:** For systems that maintain sessions, consider using session management techniques to create and destroy sessions programmatically. This allows tests to set up the necessary state for each test without manual intervention. For example, an API test could log in programmatically at the start of each test to establish a fresh session.

State-resetting techniques

Let us go over some state-resetting techniques now:

- **Setup and teardown methods:** As previously mentioned, using setup and teardown methods is essential for managing state in tests. In the setup phase, initialize the required state, and in the teardown phase, reset or clean up any changes made during the test. This practice ensures that each test starts with a known state, preventing dependencies between tests.

- **Use of snapshots**: Create snapshots of the system's state before tests are run, allowing for a quick reset after each test. This can be particularly effective in complex systems where restoring the original state manually would be cumbersome. For example, database snapshots can be used to restore the database to a known good state before each test execution.

- **Environment configuration:** Leverage configuration management tools to maintain consistent environments for testing. Tools like Docker or Kubernetes can create isolated environments that reset automatically after each test run. This ensures that tests run against a clean and controlled environment, minimizing variability in test results.

- **In-memory databases:** For systems that rely heavily on databases, consider using in-memory databases for testing. These databases can be quickly initialized and cleared, providing a fresh state for each test without the overhead of interacting with a real database. For example, using SQLite in memory mode or using tools like H2 can allow rapid testing without persistent state issues.

- **Test containers:** Utilize test containers that spin up and tear down for each test suite or test case. These containers can contain all dependencies, including databases, external services, and application instances, providing a clean slate for every test. Tools like Testcontainers for Java or Pytest's Docker integration for Python can facilitate this process.

Handling stateful systems during testing requires careful consideration of state management strategies and effective state-resetting techniques. By isolating tests, using mocks and stubs, and employing transactional testing, teams can mitigate the challenges associated with stateful systems. Additionally, utilizing setup and teardown methods, snapshots, and containerization techniques ensures that each test starts with a clean slate, ultimately leading to more reliable and consistent test outcomes. Adopting these practices will enhance the quality of testing efforts, reduce the likelihood of test failures, and improve overall software quality.

Data-driven testing principles

DDT is a testing methodology that emphasizes the separation of test logic from test data. It allows the same test script or scenario to be executed with multiple sets of data, enabling comprehensive testing of different input combinations and conditions without duplicating the test code. This approach enhances testing efficiency and coverage, particularly in scenarios where the same functionality needs to be validated under various conditions.

In DDT, test scripts are designed to read input data from external sources such as databases, spreadsheets, or configuration files. The test logic remains constant, while the data sets can vary, allowing for a wide range of test cases to be executed systematically. The general process of DDT includes:

1. **Test design:** Developing a test case outlining the testing functionality.

2. **Data preparation:** Creating a data source containing input combinations and expected outcomes.

3. **Test execution:** Running the same test script with different data sets pulled from the data source.

4. **Result validation:** Comparing the actual outcomes against expected results for each data set.

Advantages of data-driven testing

The advantages of DDT are as follows:

- **Separation of test logic and test data:** By separating test logic from test data, teams can maintain cleaner and more organized test scripts. This modular approach allows for easier updates to test cases without modifying the underlying code. For example, if a business rule changes, testers can update the corresponding data in the external data source without altering the test scripts.

- **Increased test coverage:** DDT enables comprehensive test coverage by allowing a single test case to be executed with multiple data sets. This approach helps ensure that the application behaves as expected across a wide range of scenarios, including edge cases and negative test cases. For instance, when testing a login function, various combinations of usernames and passwords can be tested without writing separate test cases for each combination.

- **Enhanced maintainability:** Test maintenance is simplified because changes to test data do not require corresponding changes to the test scripts. This flexibility is especially beneficial in agile environments where requirements frequently evolve. Maintaining a central repository for test data makes updating, adding, or removing test cases easy, leading to faster testing cycles.

- **Reusability of test scripts:** Test scripts can be reused across different projects or modules, as they are designed to work with various data sets. This reduces redundancy in test development and accelerates the testing process. For instance, a test script for an order processing function can be reused with different datasets for various products or customer scenarios.

- **Reduced manual effort:** Automated data-driven tests can execute many test cases with minimal manual intervention, freeing up testers to focus on more complex scenarios or exploratory testing. This efficiency can lead to significant time savings, especially in regression testing cycles where many test cases need to be executed repeatedly.

- **Better validation of business rules:** DDT allows testers to validate business rules against a variety of scenarios, helping to ensure that the application meets all functional requirements. By testing different data combinations, teams can identify edge cases that might not be covered in traditional testing approaches, enhancing the overall quality of the software.

DDT is a powerful methodology that enhances testing efficiency and coverage by separating test logic from test data. This approach allows the same test to be executed with multiple data sets, improving maintainability, reusability, and reducing manual effort. By leveraging DDT, organizations can achieve more comprehensive test coverage and ensure that their applications perform as expected under various conditions, ultimately leading to higher-quality software and better user experiences.

Implementing data-driven tests

DDT is an effective strategy for improving the breadth and efficiency of your testing efforts. Implementing DDT involves techniques for reading data from external sources and leveraging tools and frameworks that support the methodology. This section outlines key techniques for implementing data-driven tests and highlights tools and frameworks that facilitate DDT.

Techniques for implementing data-driven testing

Let us now learn about these techniques.

Reading data from external sources

CSV files: CSV files are a common format for storing tabular data. They are easy to read and write, making them a popular choice for data-driven tests. Here is a Python example using the **csv** module:

```python
import csv

with open('test_data.csv', newline='') as csvfile:
    reader = csv.DictReader(csvfile)
    for row in reader:
        product = row['product']
        expected_price = row['expected_price']
        # Execute test for product pricing logic
```

JSON files: JSON is a lightweight format for data interchange that is easy to read and write. It is beneficial for structured data. Here is a Python example using the **json** module:

```python
import json

with open('test_data.json') as jsonfile:
    test_data = json.load(jsonfile)
    for case in test_data['test_cases']:
        product = case['product']
        expected_price = case['expected_price']
        # Execute test for product pricing logic
```

eXtensible Markup Language (XML) files: XML is another format used for storing structured data. While less common than JSON for DDT, it is still utilized in various applications. Here is a Python example using **xml. etree/ElementTree**:

```python
import xml.etree.ElementTree as ET

tree = ET.parse('test_data.xml')
root = tree.getroot()
for case in root.findall('test_case'):
    product = case.find('product').text
    expected_price = case.find('expected_price').text
    # Execute test for product pricing logic
```

Databases: Databases can provide a dynamic source of data for data-driven tests. By querying a database, testers can retrieve the necessary test data. Here is a Python example using **sqlite3**:

```python
import sqlite3

conn = sqlite3.connect('test_data.db')
```

```
cursor = conn.cursor()
cursor.execute('SELECT product, expected_price FROM product_tests')
for row in cursor.fetchall():
    product, expected_price = row
    # Execute test for product pricing logic
```

APIs: Test data can also be fetched from APIs, allowing for real-time data retrieval for testing. This approach is beneficial for integration testing. Here is a Python example using requests:

```python
import requests

response = requests.get('https://api.example.com/testdata')
test_data = response.json()
for case in test_data['cases']:
    product = case['product']
    expected_price = case['expected_price']
    # Execute test for product pricing logic
```

Tools and frameworks that support DDT

Let us now go over some tools and frameworks that support DDT.

JUnit

JUnit provides support for DDT through parameterized tests for the Java programming language. This allows the same test method to be run with different sets of parameters.

```java
import org.junit.Test;
import org.junit.runner.RunWith;
import org.junit.runners.Parameterized;

@RunWith(Parameterized.class)
public class LoginTest {
    @Parameterized.Parameter
    public String username;
    @Parameterized.Parameter(1)
    public String password;

    @Parameterized.Parameters
    public static Collection<Object[]> data() {
        return Arrays.asList(new Object[][] {
            {"user1", "pass1"},
            {"user2", "pass2"},
            {"user3", "pass3"},
        });
    }

    @Test
    public void testLogin() {
        // Perform login test with username and password
    }
}
```

TestNG

TestNG supports DDT through data providers, which allow you to pass multiple data sets to a test method. Like JUnit, this is also for the Java programming language, as:

```java
import org.testng.annotations.DataProvider;
import org.testng.annotations.Test;

public class LoginTest {
    @DataProvider(name = "loginData")
    public Object[][] createData() {
        return new Object[][] {
            {"user1", "pass1"},
            {"user2", "pass2"},
            {"user3", "pass3"},
        };
    }

    @Test(dataProvider = "loginData")
    public void testLogin(String username, String password) {
        // Perform login test with username and password
    }
}
```

Pytest

Pytest provides a simple way to parameterize tests, allowing you to define multiple sets of data for a single test function in the Python programming language, as:

```python
import pytest

@pytest.mark.parametrize("username,password", [
    ("user1", "pass1"),
    ("user2", "pass2"),
    ("user3", "pass3"),
])
def test_login(username, password):
    # Perform login test with username and password
```

Robot Framework

Robot Framework supports data-driven testing through its keyword-driven approach. You can define test cases with external data sources, including CSV, JSON, and Excel, as:

```robotframework
*** Settings ***
Library     OperatingSystem

*** Variables ***
${DATA_FILE}    test_data.csv

*** Test Cases ***
Login Test
```

```
[Documentation]    Run login tests using data from a CSV file
@{data}    Get CSV Data    ${DATA_FILE}
:FOR    ${row}    IN    @{data}
\    Log    Username: ${row}[0], Password: ${row}[1]
```

Implementing DDT involves leveraging various techniques for reading data from external sources, such as files, databases, and APIs. Tools and frameworks like JUnit, TestNG, Pytest, and Robot Framework provide robust support for DDT, allowing testers to execute the same tests with multiple data sets efficiently. By employing DDT, teams can enhance their testing strategies, improve coverage, and streamline the testing process, ultimately leading to higher-quality software.

Creating reusable data sets

Reusable data sets are essential for effective DDT, allowing teams to efficiently manage and apply test data across different test cases and suites. By implementing best practices for organizing and managing these data sets, teams can improve test efficiency and maintainability. This section outlines best practices for creating reusable data sets and ensuring adaptability for various environments, platforms, or configurations.

Best practices for organizing and managing reusable data sets

Let us go over some best practices now:

- **Centralized data repository:** Maintain a centralized repository for test data sets, which can be accessed by all test cases. This could be a dedicated database, file system, or cloud storage solution. Organizing test data in one location simplifies updates, promotes consistency, and makes it easier for team members to locate and use the data.

- **Structured data formats:** Store test data in structured formats such as CSV, JSON, or XML. These formats make data easier to read, write, and manipulate, allowing for efficient parsing and usage in tests. Ensure that the structure is consistent across data files to simplify data processing in your test scripts.

- **Naming conventions:** Implement clear naming conventions for data sets and files. Use descriptive names that indicate the purpose of the data, such as **user_credentials.csv** or **order_data.json**. This helps testers quickly understand the contents of the data sets. Consider including version numbers in file names (for example, **user_credentials_v1.csv**) to track changes and updates to data sets.

- **Modular data sets:** Organize data sets into smaller, modular components that can be combined as needed. For example, create separate data files for user information, product details, and transaction data that can be reused across various test cases. This modular approach promotes reusability and reduces redundancy, as different tests can pull data from the same modular sources.

- **Documentation:** Document the purpose, structure, and usage of each data set, including examples of how to use them in tests. This documentation can be included in a **README** file or as comments within the data files themselves. Clear documentation helps new team members understand the data sets quickly and reduces the learning curve.

- **Version control:** Use version control systems (for example, Git) to manage changes to test data sets. This allows teams to track changes over time, revert to previous versions if needed, and collaborate effectively on data set updates. Keeping test data under version control ensures that any updates are logged and reviewed, promoting accountability and traceability.

- **Automated data generation:** When applicable, use automated data generation tools and scripts to create reusable data sets. This can help generate large volumes of data quickly and consistently while adhering to defined patterns and structures. Tools like Faker or custom scripts can help populate data sets with realistic data that can be reused across tests.

Ensuring adaptability for different environments, platforms, or configurations

Let us go over the following:

- **Environment-specific configuration:** Structure test data to include environment-specific configurations, such as URLs, credentials, or API keys. Use placeholders or variables that can be replaced with the appropriate values for each environment (for example, development, staging, production). For example, store environment variables in a separate configuration file and reference them in your data sets to ensure the correct settings are applied.

- **Parameterized data sets:** Design data sets to be parameterized, allowing for easy adaptation to different configurations. Use a single data file with various combinations of parameters that can be dynamically loaded during test execution. For example, a single JSON file could contain different user roles, access levels, or configurations that are loaded based on the test scenario being executed.

- **Using data mapping:** Implement data mapping techniques to translate test data to the appropriate format or structure for different platforms or configurations. This approach helps maintain consistency while accommodating variations in data requirements. For instance, if a test case requires different field names for different API versions, create a mapping file that defines how to transform the data accordingly.

- **Reusable data utilities:** Develop utility functions or classes that facilitate the retrieval and manipulation of test data. These utilities can handle data loading, transformation, and environment-specific adaptations, streamlining the process of working with test data across different scenarios. By encapsulating data access logic, these utilities promote code reusability and reduce duplication in test scripts.

- **Testing environment profiles:** Create environment profiles that specify which data sets and configurations to use for each testing environment. This could be managed through configuration files or environment variables that dictate the data source based on the execution context. By defining profiles, teams can ensure that the appropriate data sets are used for each test run without manual intervention.

Creating reusable data sets is a vital aspect of effective data-driven testing. By following best practices for organizing and managing these data sets, teams can enhance test efficiency and maintainability. Additionally, ensuring adaptability for different environments, platforms, or configurations helps promote flexibility in testing, allowing for comprehensive coverage and effective validation of software across various scenarios. Implementing these practices will lead to more robust testing processes, ultimately contributing to higher-quality software.

Improving test coverage through DDT

DDT significantly enhances test coverage by allowing testers to validate multiple scenarios with varying inputs. This approach enables a comprehensive evaluation of the software's functionality and robustness, ensuring that it meets the diverse needs of users and performs well under different conditions. This section discusses how DDT contributes to broader test coverage and explores techniques for automating the generation of edge cases and corner cases.

Achieving broader test coverage through DDT

Let us go over the following:

- **Validation of multiple scenarios:** Single test logic, multiple inputs: With DDT, a single test script can be executed with various data sets. This means that a single test can cover multiple scenarios, reducing the need for repetitive code and allowing for a more extensive exploration of functionality.

- **Comprehensive input combinations:** DDT enables the testing of various combinations of input values, configurations, and conditions. For example, when testing a login feature, you can validate different combinations of usernames and passwords, including valid, invalid, and edge-case inputs. This thorough examination helps identify potential issues that might not surface with limited input testing.

- **Flexibility and adaptability:** Easy updates and maintenance: When requirements change or new scenarios need to be tested, data-driven tests can be easily updated by modifying the input data sets rather than rewriting the test logic. This adaptability allows teams to respond quickly to changes, ensuring that test coverage remains relevant.

- **Separation of concerns:** By separating test data from test logic, teams can maintain clearer boundaries between what is being tested and how it is being tested. This separation enhances readability and maintainability, making it easier to understand which scenarios are covered and where gaps might exist.

- **Increased test efficiency:** Focusing more testing at the unit level allows automated tests to run faster, while reducing the number and fragility of higher-level tests. This is because unit tests are more isolated, quicker to execute, and less dependent on complex system interactions, making them more reliable and easier to maintain.

- **Automated test execution:** DDT allows for automated execution of tests with multiple data sets, significantly reducing manual testing efforts. Automation tools can iterate through data sets, executing the same test logic against different inputs without human intervention, resulting in faster testing cycles.

- **Parallel execution:** Many testing frameworks support parallel execution of data-driven tests. This capability enables multiple test instances to run simultaneously, further speeding up the testing process and expanding coverage within limited time frames.

Techniques for automating the generation of edge cases

The following techniques can be used to help identify the data required for appropriate edge cases where errors are likely to occur in the testing process:

- **Defining edge cases and corner cases:**

  o **Edge cases:** These are scenarios that occur at the extreme ends of input ranges or boundaries. For example, if a function accepts a numeric input between 1 and 100, edge cases would include inputs like 1 and 100.

  o **Corner cases:** These refer to scenarios that involve combinations of different edge cases, often leading to unexpected behaviour. For instance, testing the function with an input of 0 (which may be outside the accepted range) alongside another parameter at its maximum limit.

- **Using automated data generation tools:**

  o **Faker and similar libraries:** Libraries such as Faker can be employed to automatically generate random test data, including edge cases. Testers can define rules to ensure generated data falls within specific ranges or adheres to certain formats.

  o **Custom data generators:** Create custom scripts or functions that generate edge and corner cases based on defined criteria. For example, you can write a script that generates input values around the boundaries of valid inputs and includes a combination of maximum and minimum values.

- **Algorithmic techniques for data generation:**
  - o **Boundary value analysis:** This technique focuses on generating test cases at the boundaries of input ranges. For example, if a function accepts integers between 1 and 100, generate test cases for values 0, 1, 100, and 101.
  - o **Equivalence partitioning:** This technique involves dividing input data into equivalent classes where the system should behave similarly. Testers can create test cases from each partition, including both valid and invalid values. Edge cases are typically derived from these partitions.

- **Randomized testing:**
  - o **Fuzz testing:** Fuzz testing involves providing random data inputs to the system to uncover vulnerabilities or unexpected behaviour. Automated fuzz testing tools can generate a wide variety of inputs, including edge cases, to explore the robustness of the system.
  - o **Monte Carlo simulation:** This technique involves generating a large number of random inputs to statistically analyse the system's behavior. By running multiple simulations, testers can identify potential edge cases and corner cases that might not have been explicitly defined.

- **Parameterized testing frameworks:**
  - o **Utilizing test frameworks:** Frameworks like JUnit, TestNG, and Pytest allow parameterized tests, enabling easy generation of edge cases and corner cases by feeding various inputs directly into the test functions. For example, a test can be parameterized with edge case values, and the framework will execute the test for each input.
  - o **Data providers:** Use data providers in frameworks like TestNG to supply different sets of edge case data. This not only automates the generation but also simplifies the execution of tests across various scenarios.

DDT plays a crucial role in improving test coverage by validating multiple scenarios through varying inputs. By leveraging DDT, teams can execute comprehensive tests that uncover potential issues across a wide range of conditions. Additionally, automating the generation of edge cases and corner cases through techniques like boundary value analysis, fuzz testing, and parameterized testing helps ensure the robustness of the system under test. Ultimately, the effective implementation of DDT contributes to higher-quality software and greater user satisfaction.

Test data security and anonymization

In software testing, the management of test data is crucial, particularly when it involves handling sensitive or **personally identifiable information** (PII). Ensuring data security and compliance with data protection regulations, such as the **General Data Protection Regulation** (GDPR), is essential for maintaining user trust and meeting legal requirements. This section discusses how to handle sensitive information in test data and explores techniques for anonymizing production data or generating synthetic data that mirrors real-world usage.

Handling sensitive or PII in test data

Let us go over the following:

- **Identifying sensitive data:**
  - o **Data inventory:** Conduct a thorough inventory of the data being used in testing environments to identify sensitive information, including names, addresses, social security numbers, email addresses, financial data, and health records. Understanding what constitutes sensitive data helps in implementing appropriate safeguards.
  - o **Data classification:** Classify data based on sensitivity levels, such as public, internal, confidential, and regulated data. This classification assists in determining the necessary security measures for each category.

- **Access control and permissions:**
  - o **Role-based access control (RBAC):** Implement RBAC to restrict access to sensitive test data based on the roles and responsibilities of team members. Only authorized personnel should have access to PII or sensitive data, minimizing the risk of unauthorized exposure.
  - o **Audit trails:** Maintain logs of who accesses sensitive data and when. Regular audits can help identify potential security breaches and ensure compliance with data protection policies.

- **Data minimization:**
  - o **Minimal data usage:** Limit the amount of sensitive data used in testing environments. Instead of using full production data sets, only pull the data necessary for specific tests to reduce exposure to sensitive information.
  - o **Subsetting:** Create subsets of production data that include only essential fields for testing. For example, if testing a billing feature, include only the necessary financial information without exposing full customer details.

- **Data anonymization techniques:**
  - o **Masking:** Data masking replaces sensitive information with fictional or scrambled values. For instance, names can be replaced with random names from a list, and credit card numbers can be replaced with randomly generated numbers that maintain the same format but are not real.
  - o **Tokenization:** Tokenization involves replacing sensitive data with unique identifiers (tokens) that retain essential information without revealing the actual data. For example, a social security number might be replaced with a token that is mapped to the original number in a secure environment.

- **Data perturbation:**
  - o **Adding noise:** Introduce small random variations to sensitive data to obscure its true values while still maintaining its usefulness for testing. For instance, modifying ages by adding or subtracting a few years can obscure exact values while still allowing for realistic testing scenarios.
  - o **Aggregation:** Aggregate data to a level where individual records cannot be identified. For example, instead of using individual transaction details, use total sales figures for a region or demographic group.

- **Synthetic data generation:**
  - o **Using generative models:** Employ machine learning algorithms to create synthetic data that mirrors real-world usage patterns while ensuring no actual sensitive information is used. Generative models can learn the distribution of the original data and produce new data points that retain the statistical characteristics without revealing PII.
  - o **Faker libraries and custom generators:** Utilize libraries such as Faker or custom data generators to produce synthetic data that mimics the structure and variety of production data. These tools can create realistic names, addresses, dates, and other fields without using actual user data.

- **Compliance with data protection regulations:**
  - o **Regulatory awareness:** Stay informed about relevant data protection regulations, such as GDPR, CCPA, or HIPAA. Ensure that all data handling practices align with these regulations, including how sensitive data is collected, processed, and stored during testing.
  - o **Data processing agreements:** If using third-party services or tools for data handling, ensure that appropriate data processing agreements are in place that outline responsibilities for data protection and compliance.

- **Testing with anonymized data:**
  - o **Validation of data anonymization:** Implement procedures to verify that data anonymization techniques effectively protect sensitive information. Regularly test the anonymization process to ensure that it complies with relevant regulations and retains the necessary data utility for testing.

o **Environment segregation:** Maintain separate environments for development, testing, and production. Ensure that anonymized data is used exclusively in testing environments to prevent accidental exposure of sensitive production data.

Managing test data security and anonymization is critical for protecting sensitive information and complying with data protection regulations. By implementing strategies to handle PII, including access control, data minimization, and classification, organizations can safeguard against unauthorized exposure. Additionally, utilizing techniques for data anonymization and synthetic data generation enables teams to conduct thorough testing without compromising user privacy. Adhering to these practices fosters user trust and aligns with regulatory requirements, ultimately contributing to the development of secure and reliable software.

Best practices in test data management

Let us now go over the best practices:

- **Maintaining data consistency:** Maintaining data consistency across different environments, such as development, staging, and production, is crucial for ensuring reliable and accurate testing. Inconsistent data can lead to misleading test results, making it challenging to identify bugs and assess the performance of applications. This section explores strategies for ensuring test data consistency and techniques to synchronize test data across different teams and pipelines.

- **Standardized data models:**

  o **Data schema definition:** Establish a clear and standardized data model that defines the structure, format, and constraints of test data across all environments. This ensures that all environments use the same data structure, reducing the risk of discrepancies.

  o **Version control for schemas:** Use version control systems to manage changes to data schemas. By keeping track of schema changes, teams can ensure that all environments remain aligned with the latest data model.

- **Environment configuration management:**

  o **Configuration files:** Use configuration files to specify environment-specific settings, including database connections and data sources. This approach allows teams to maintain consistency while accommodating different environments' configurations.

  o **Infrastructure as code (IaC):** Implement IaC tools, such as Terraform or Ansible, to manage environment setups. IaC ensures that all environments are provisioned identically, minimizing variations in test data configurations.

- **Data migration and synchronization tools:**

  o **Automated data migration:** Utilize data migration tools to replicate data across environments. These tools can automate the process of moving data from production to staging or development environments, ensuring that each environment reflects the most recent production state.

  o **Database replication:** Implement database replication strategies to synchronize data between environments. This can include techniques like point-in-time recovery or continuous data replication to keep data consistent across environments.

- **Regular data refreshes:**

  o **Scheduled data refreshes:** Establish a schedule for regularly refreshing test data from production to other environments. This can involve periodic updates that ensure test environments have the most up-to-date data, reflecting real-world scenarios.

  o **Data subsetting:** When refreshing data, consider using subsetting techniques to reduce the size of the data set while maintaining its relevance. This helps ensure that the test environment is populated with representative data without the overhead of full production data.

Techniques to keep test data synchronized

Managing test data becomes increasingly complex in environments with interconnected systems that share information. A deliberate strategy is essential to ensure that test data is properly synchronized across multiple systems, enabling comprehensive coverage for end-to-end testing efforts. Let us go over the following:

- **Centralized test data management:**

  o **Single source of truth:** Maintain a centralized repository for test data that can be accessed by all teams involved in testing. This repository serves as the single source of truth, ensuring everyone uses the same data sets and configurations.

  o **Version control for test data:** Implement version control for test data files, similar to code. By managing changes to test data through version control, teams can track updates, revert to previous versions, and collaborate effectively.

- **Data synchronization tools:**

  o **Data sync services:** Utilize data synchronization services that can automatically keep test data in sync across different environments. These services can be configured to detect changes in one environment and propagate those changes to others, ensuring consistency.

  o **API-driven data updates:** Employ APIs to facilitate data synchronization. By using APIs, teams can create automated processes to push updates from one environment to another, ensuring that test data is always aligned.

- **Automated CI/CD pipelines:**

  o **Integrate data management into CI/CD:** Incorporate test data management processes into continuous CI/CD pipelines. Automated scripts can be created to refresh or synchronize test data during build or deployment processes, ensuring that the correct data is available at all stages of testing.

  o **Environment-specific data generation:** Use CI/CD pipelines to generate environment-specific test data as part of the build process. This can include automated generation of synthetic data that adheres to the structure and constraints of the application's data model.

- **Collaboration and communication:**

  o **Cross-functional teams:** Foster collaboration between development, testing, and operations teams to ensure everyone knows the data requirements and changes. Regular meetings and updates can help keep teams aligned on data management strategies.

  o **Documentation:** Maintain thorough documentation of data management processes, including data sources, refresh schedules, and synchronization techniques. This documentation is a reference for teams to ensure they follow consistent practices.

- **Monitoring and validation:**

  o **Data quality checks:** Implement data quality checks to validate the consistency and accuracy of test data across environments. Automated tests can be created to verify that data in different environments matches expected values, alerting teams to discrepancies.

  o **Logging and auditing:** Maintain logs of data synchronization activities, including timestamps, data sources, and changes made. This auditing helps teams track data movement and resolve any issues related to data consistency.

Maintaining data consistency across different environments is vital for ensuring reliable and accurate testing outcomes. Organizations can effectively manage test data and keep it synchronized by implementing standardized data models, utilizing data migration tools, and fostering collaboration between teams. Automated processes, CI/CD integration, and regular data refreshes contribute to a robust data management strategy that enhances testing efficiency and improves overall software quality. Ultimately, achieving data consistency leads to more effective testing processes, better identification of defects, and improved confidence in the software being delivered.

Data management in CI/CD pipelines

Effective data management in CI and CD pipelines ensures that software is tested thoroughly and consistently. Proper handling of test data during these processes enables teams to achieve repeatability, reliability, and, ultimately, a higher-quality product. This section discusses strategies for managing test data in CI/CD pipelines and outlines best practices for handling test data refreshes between builds or deployments.

Managing test data effectively in CI/CD pipelines

Here are some best practices to help manage test data within a CI/CD pipeline:

- **Incorporating data management in CI/CD processes:** Ensure that test data management is a core part of the CI/CD pipeline. This includes defining how and when test data will be created, updated, or refreshed as part of the build and deployment processes.

- **Automated test data provisioning:** Utilize scripts or tools to automate the provisioning of test data. This could involve creating databases, loading data sets, or setting up mock services, all triggered as part of the CI/CD pipeline.

- **Environment as code:** Use IaC tools, such as Terraform or Ansible, to create and configure environments consistently across development, staging, and production. Ensuring that the same data sources and configurations are used in all environments minimizes discrepancies and facilitates accurate testing.

- **Containerization:** Leverage container technologies like Docker to package applications along with their required test data and dependencies. This ensures that the application runs consistently across different environments and simplifies data management.

- **Version control for test data:** Implement version control for test data, similar to how code is managed. This allows teams to track changes, roll back to previous data sets when necessary, and ensure that the correct data version is used for testing.

- **Branch-specific test data:** Consider maintaining different branches of test data for feature branches or releases. This enables teams to work on features independently, ensuring that tests remain relevant and consistent with the specific code branch.

- **Dynamic data sources:** Configure test environments to dynamically pull from different data sources based on the context. For instance, test data can be pulled from a production-like data set for staging while using a mocked or synthetic data set in development.

- **Parameterized builds:** Use parameterized builds in CI/CD tools to specify which test data set to use for a particular build. This enables flexibility and allows different test scenarios to be executed based on the build's specific needs.

Handling test data refreshes between builds or deploys

The following are some of the things that can be done to manage the refreshing of data between builds or code deployments. Something critical for CI/CD execution is where execution is frequent, and data often needs to be refreshed rapidly in between executions.

- **Scheduled data refreshes:**
  - **Regular refresh intervals:** Establish a schedule for refreshing test data in various environments. This could be daily, weekly, or aligned with specific release cycles. Regular refreshes ensure that test data remains relevant and reflects the current state of production.

o **Event-driven refreshes:** Implement event-driven mechanisms to refresh test data based on specific triggers, such as a new deployment or the completion of a build. This can help keep environments in sync with the latest production data.

- **Data subsetting and masking:**

o **Subsetting production data:** When refreshing test data, consider using subsets of production data that capture the necessary characteristics without duplicating the entire data set. Subsetting can speed up the refresh process while ensuring data relevance.

o **Data masking for privacy:** Use techniques to protect sensitive information during the refresh process. Masked data can replace actual values with anonymized versions, ensuring compliance with data protection regulations while maintaining the integrity of test scenarios.

- **Continuous data integration:**

o **Integrate data refresh with CI/CD tools:** Leverage CI/CD tools to automate data refresh processes. For example, integrate scripts that automatically refresh test data during build or deployment steps, ensuring that the latest data is always available for testing.

o **Database migration scripts:** Use migration scripts to update and refresh databases automatically as part of the deployment process. These scripts can ensure that the test database is populated with the correct data as the application evolves.

- **Validation and consistency checks:**

o **Data validation after refresh:** Implement validation checks to verify the integrity and consistency of test data after it has been refreshed. This could involve automated tests that check for data completeness, accuracy, and adherence to expected formats.

o **Continuous monitoring:** Monitor test data usage and consistency across environments. Implement logging and reporting mechanisms to track when data is refreshed and any issues that arise during the process.

- **Rollback strategies:**

o **Backup and restore procedures:** Establish backup procedures to save snapshots of test data before refreshes. This allows teams to quickly roll back to a previous state if issues arise after a data refresh.

o **Automated rollback scripts:** Create scripts that can automatically restore data from backups or revert to a previous version in case of failure during the data refresh process.

Effective data management in CI/CD pipelines is essential for maintaining the reliability and accuracy of software testing. Teams can ensure that test data is consistent and relevant by integrating test data management into the CI/CD process, utilizing automated provisioning, and implementing version control. Furthermore, handling test data refreshes between builds through scheduled updates, data subsetting, and continuous integration techniques allows for repeatability and reliability in testing outcomes. By adhering to these practices, organizations can achieve higher quality software and deliver value to their users with confidence.

Minimizing test data dependencies

Minimizing test data dependencies is crucial for maintaining a robust, efficient, and reliable testing framework. Complex test data can lead to bloated tests, increased fragility, and longer execution times, making it challenging to maintain and scale test suites. This section outlines techniques for reducing reliance on complex test data and emphasizes lightweight solutions for unit and integration tests to ensure faster, more isolated execution.

Let us go over some techniques for minimizing reliance on complex test data:

- **Mock external dependencies:** Use mocking frameworks (for example, Mockito, Moq) to simulate interactions with external systems or services. By replacing real data with mock responses, tests can run independently of the actual data state and eliminate the need for complex test setups.

- **Stub simplified implementations:** Implement stubs to provide fixed responses for certain method calls during tests. Stubbing allows you to isolate the component under test while avoiding the complexity of managing intricate data setups.

- **Targeted data generation:** Instead of relying on comprehensive data sets, create specific test data tailored to the scenarios being tested. This targeted approach minimizes the volume of data needed and reduces the risk of data-related issues during testing.

- **Parameterized tests:** Utilize parameterized tests to run the same test logic with different sets of lightweight data. This allows for comprehensive testing of various scenarios without duplicating test cases or maintaining complex data configurations.

- **Utilize in-memory databases:** For integration tests, consider using in-memory databases (for example, H2, SQLite) that can be easily reset and populated with lightweight test data. This approach reduces overhead and avoids dependencies on external data sources, leading to faster execution and simplified management.

- **Temporary data setup:** Set up and tear down test data within the same test execution context. This minimizes dependencies on pre-existing data, ensuring that tests remain isolated and repeatable.

- **Use simple data models:** Opt for simplified data structures that capture the essence of the data needed for testing without unnecessary complexity. This makes creating, understanding, and maintaining test data easier, reducing reliance on extensive setups.

- **Data normalization:** Normalize test data to reduce duplication and dependencies. By creating reusable data sets that can be referenced across tests, teams can avoid bloated data structures and streamline data management.

- **Decouple test logic from data:** Implement DDT to separate test logic from test data. This approach allows teams to maintain a clear distinction between what is being tested and the data used, minimizing dependencies and facilitating easier updates.

- **Centralized test data repository:** Store test data in a centralized repository that can be accessed by different tests. This ensures consistency while reducing duplication and complexity in managing test data across multiple tests.

Lightweight test data solutions for unit and integration tests

Data strategies are not all the same, though, and there are some things to consider depending on the test type. Let us go over the following:

- **Unit tests:**

  o **Use minimalistic data:** For unit tests, rely on minimalistic test data that captures only the essential characteristics needed for the test. This keeps tests fast and focused on specific functionality without the burden of extraneous data.

  o **Factory patterns:** Implement factory patterns to create lightweight test data objects quickly. Factories can generate objects with default values that can be easily overridden for specific test cases, promoting consistency while minimizing complexity.

- **Integration tests:**

  o **Lightweight test fixtures:** Use lightweight test fixtures that set up only the necessary context for integration tests. This may involve creating only the relevant entities or data points required for the test without populating the entire database.

  o **Setup and teardown methods:** Implement setup and teardown methods to establish and clean up test data quickly. This approach ensures that each test starts with a clean slate, avoiding reliance on previous test data states and reducing potential side effects.

o **Leverage test containers:** Utilize test containers (for example, Testcontainers) to create isolated environments for running tests with lightweight configurations. Test containers can provide a fresh environment with minimal setup, ensuring tests run quickly and consistently without complex data dependencies.

o **Integrate with CI/CD pipelines:** Incorporate lightweight test data solutions into CI/CD pipelines to ensure tests run efficiently and consistently across environments. Automated tests that utilize lightweight data can execute faster, facilitating quicker feedback loops and enhancing development productivity.

o **Frequent feedback:** Focus on providing frequent feedback to developers by maintaining fast-running tests with minimal dependencies. This encourages developers to run tests often and make iterative improvements without the overhead of complex data management.

Minimizing test data dependencies is essential for maintaining efficient and reliable testing practices. By adopting techniques such as mocking, simplified data generation, and leveraging lightweight test data solutions, teams can avoid bloated tests and fragile test suites. Emphasizing lightweight strategies for unit and integration tests enhances execution speed and isolation, leading to a more agile development process. Ultimately, reducing reliance on complex test data fosters a more manageable testing environment, improves test quality, and accelerates the delivery of high-quality software.

Conclusion

Effective test data management is pivotal in ensuring the accuracy, reliability, and speed of automated tests. Implementing robust data management strategies can significantly enhance organizations' testing processes, leading to higher-quality software delivery and improved confidence in deployment outcomes.

Utilizing various test data generation techniques, along with mocks, stubs, and data-driven testing approaches, enables teams to create scalable and adaptable test automation solutions. These methodologies not only reduce dependencies on complex data setups but also enhance the flexibility and comprehensiveness of testing efforts. By leveraging mocks and stubs, testers can isolate components, simulate external interactions, and streamline test execution, while data-driven testing allows for extensive coverage across multiple scenarios with minimal overhead.

Maintaining data consistency, effectively handling state across tests, and adhering to best practices are essential for improving test efficiency. Implementing version control for test data, using lightweight data solutions, and employing setup and teardown methods ensures that tests are reliable, repeatable, and less prone to failures. By emphasizing these principles, organizations can foster a more agile and efficient testing environment, leading to faster feedback cycles and higher-quality software products.

In the next chapter, we will look at Quality Gates, the role they play in ensuring the quality of software, and how they can be integrated into the CI/CD pipelines.

Key takeaways

The key takeaways from the chapter are as follows:

- Using realistic and well-structured test data is essential for ensuring test scenarios closely mimic real-world usage. It helps identify defects that might not be apparent with synthetic or static data, reducing false positives and negatives while improving the overall reliability of tests.

- There are several approaches to test data generation and management. Synthetic data generation creates artificial yet meaningful data sets, while production data masking allows teams to use real data while anonymizing sensitive details. Database seeding involves preloading test data before execution, and test data on demand generates or fetches data dynamically as needed.

- Test data versioning is crucial in maintaining consistency across test runs and environments. It allows teams to roll back to previous states when debugging issues and supports parallel development and testing by ensuring data compatibility. Versioning ensures that test cases always use appropriate and reliable data sets.

- Externalizing test data improves maintainability by decoupling test logic from data. This makes it easier to update test cases without modifying the underlying scripts. Additionally, it allows different configurations to be supported, such as localization or environment-specific data, ensuring flexibility in test execution.

- Managing state across tests is critical for ensuring test independence and repeatability. Strategies such as database transaction rollbacks, isolated test environments, and proper session management help prevent data pollution between test cases. Ensuring that each test runs clean and predictable reduces flaky test results and improves overall test reliability.

- **Data-driven testing** (**DDT**) is a key principle that increases test coverage by executing the same test logic with different input values. This approach reduces redundancy by eliminating the need for multiple test cases covering similar scenarios. DDT also supports parameterized testing, enabling external data sources like CSV files, JSON, or databases to feed inputs into test cases dynamically.

- Creating reusable data sets minimizes duplication and maintenance effort while ensuring consistency across test cases. A well-designed data set can be shared across multiple test suites, making the testing process more scalable and efficient. By centralizing test data management, teams can maintain high consistency in test execution.

- Test coverage can be significantly improved through data-driven testing by efficiently validating various edge and corner cases. Instead of writing separate test cases for each data variation, the same test logic can be executed with different inputs. This reduces test script maintenance overhead while maximizing test coverage.

- Ensuring test data security and anonymization is critical for protecting sensitive user information. Data masking and encryption help prevent unauthorized access to personal or confidential data. Compliance with regulations like GDPR and HIPAA is necessary to avoid legal risks, and organizations must implement strict access controls to safeguard test data.

- Best practices in test data management include separating test data from test logic to improve maintainability. Versioning test data allows teams to track changes and roll back if necessary. Automated test data generation and cleanup strategies help maintain consistency, and ensuring that test data is reusable, modular, and scalable enhances long-term test efficiency.

Exercises

1. Does your test data accurately represents real-world scenarios?

2. If using production data, how do we handle data privacy concerns?

3. What methods do we use to generate test data (synthetic, masked production data, database seeding, and so on)?

4. How is test data versioning managed and tracked, and is the management process automated?

5. How do teams ensure that different teams or test environments use the correct version of test data?

6. Is our test data decoupled from test scripts to improve maintainability?

7. How do we manage test data across different environments (for example, dev, staging, production)?

8. Are teams leveraging DDT to maximize test coverage with minimal test script duplication?

9. How do teams ensure that sensitive production data is not exposed in test environments?

10. What anonymization techniques (for example, masking, tokenization, encryption) are in place?

11. Is test data automatically provisioned as part of our CI/CD pipeline?

CI/CD Integration and Quality Gates

Introduction

Continuous integration (CI) and **continuous deployment/delivery** (CD) are essential practices in modern software development that enhance collaboration, improve code quality, and accelerate delivery timelines.

CI frequently merges code changes into a shared repository, ideally several times daily. Each integration triggers an automated build process, which includes compiling the code and running tests. This early detection of integration issues helps developers identify problems quickly, reducing the risk of significant disruptions during later stages of development. CI encourages collaboration and ensures that every team member's change works seamlessly with the codebase.

CI and CD extend the principles of CI into the deployment phase. Continuous delivery ensures that code is always in a deployable state. After passing automated tests, the code is ready for deployment, but the actual deployment to production is a manual decision.

Continuous deployment takes it a step further by automatically deploying every change that passes the automated tests directly to production, without manual intervention. This leads to more frequent releases, allowing users to receive new features and bug fixes rapidly.

Structure

In this chapter, we will go over the following topics:

- Importance of automation in CI/CD
- Introducing automation in the CI/CD pipeline
- Setting up automated tests in CI pipelines
- Test execution strategies in CI/CD
- Implementing quality gates for build success/failure
- Configuring quality gates
- Handling failed quality gates
- Ensuring seamless integration with different CI tools

- Handling flaky tests in CI/CD
- Monitoring and reporting in CI/CD

Objectives

By the end of this chapter, the reader will learn about the importance of CI/CD pipelines to the development process, how to best introduce them into projects, and how to design for optimal testing and quality assurance. In this chapter, we will explore the topic of quality gates, what they are in the CI/CD space, and how they can be applied to these pipelines to enhance quality software delivery throughout the entire development process.

Importance of automation in CI/CD

Automation plays a pivotal role in enhancing the effectiveness of CI/CD pipelines. Organizations can significantly improve software quality, speed, and reliability by automating various stages of the development and release process, as explained:

- **Early detection of issues:** Automation in CI/CD pipelines facilitates immediate feedback on code changes. Automated builds and tests run as soon as code is committed, allowing developers to identify integration issues, bugs, and performance problems early in the development process. This reduces the chances of serious issues arising later, which can be more challenging and costly to fix.

- **Frequent testing:** Automated testing allows teams to run a wide range of tests (unit, integration, and system tests) frequently throughout the development cycle. This frequent validation ensures that the new code does not introduce regressions, thus maintaining the overall stability of the application.

- **Increased coverage:** Automation enables teams to execute more tests than would be feasible through manual testing alone. This broad test coverage helps in identifying edge cases and potential issues that might otherwise be overlooked, resulting in higher-quality software releases.

- **Reduced manual testing:** Automated testing minimizes the reliance on manual testing efforts, which can be time-consuming and prone to human error. This allows QA teams to focus on more complex testing scenarios and exploratory testing, improving overall testing efficiency.

- **Faster feedback loops:** Automation provides instant feedback to developers, enabling them to address issues as they arise. Quick identification of bugs leads to shorter development cycles and a more agile response to changes, allowing teams to adapt to user needs and market demands swiftly.

- **Streamlined release cycles:** Automated processes significantly accelerate the release cycle. By integrating automated tests into the CI/CD pipeline, teams can ensure that code is always in a deployable state. This enables frequent and reliable releases, allowing organizations to deliver new features and fixes to users faster.

- **Enhanced collaboration:** Automation fosters a culture of collaboration between development and operations teams (DevOps). With shared goals and automated processes, teams can work more cohesively, leading to improved communication and faster issue resolution.

- **Scalability:** As the project grows, automated tests can quickly scale to cover new features and components without a proportional increase in testing effort. This scalability is crucial for managing complex applications and accommodating continuous growth.

- **Consistency and reliability:** Automated tests are executed consistently, reducing variability in test results. This reliability ensures that tests yield the same outcomes regardless of when or where they are run, contributing to a more stable and trustworthy release process.

Automation in CI/CD pipelines is essential for detecting issues early and ensuring high-quality software releases. The incorporation of test automation not only reduces manual testing efforts but enhances feedback loops and streamlines release cycles, ultimately leading to better collaboration and more robust software products.

CHAPTER 8

Introducing automation in the CI/CD pipeline

Effectively integrating automated tests into a CI/CD pipeline is crucial for maintaining software quality and accelerating the development lifecycle. Here is a guide on how to do this across different stages of the CI/CD pipeline and where to run these tests:

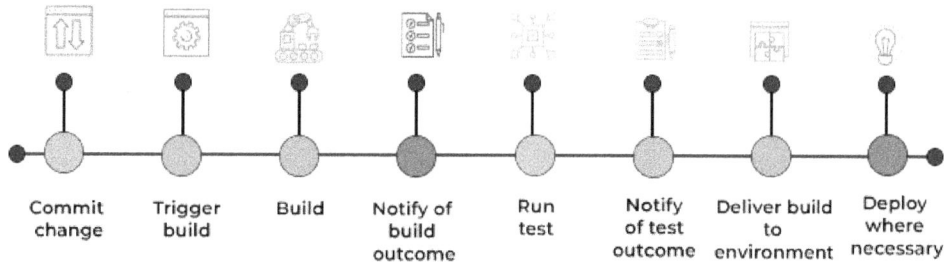

Figure 8.1: *Steps of a CI/CD pipeline*

Integrating automated tests at various stages of the CI/CD pipeline

Now, let us go over the following:

- **Unit tests:** Unit tests should be integrated at the earliest stage of the CI pipeline, typically immediately after code commit.

  o **Purpose:** They verify the smallest parts of the application in isolation, ensuring that individual components function correctly.

  o **Best practices:** Some best practices are:

    - Use mocking frameworks to isolate the unit tests.

    - Aim for high code coverage to ensure that most code paths are tested.

    - Run unit tests on every commit to catch issues early.

- **Integration tests:** Integration tests should run after unit tests, ideally as part of the build process.

  o **Purpose:** They test the interactions between different components or modules to ensure they work together as expected.

  o **Best practices:** Some best practices are:

    - Use a staging environment that mimics production for testing integrations.

    - Keep integration tests focused on critical workflows to manage execution time.

    - Schedule these tests to run after a successful unit test phase.

- **End-to-end (E2E) tests:** End-to-end tests should be integrated after successful integration tests and can run in a pre-deployment phase.

  o **Purpose:** They validate the entire application flow from start to finish, simulating user interactions and ensuring that the system works as a whole.

  o **Best practices:** Some best practices are:

    - Use dedicated test environments to avoid interference with production data.

    - Run E2E tests less frequently due to their longer execution times, ideally during nightly builds or before significant releases.

    - Ensure that test data is consistent and representative of real-world scenarios.

Defining where automated tests should run

We have looked at the different types of testing and the value they bring to the CI/CD pipelines, but now we will look at when certain test types should be run in different phases of the pipeline process as follows:

- **During code commit:**
  - o **Tests:** Unit tests.
  - o **Purpose:** To catch basic issues and errors immediately after code changes are made.
  - o **Benefits**: Immediate feedback for developers, reducing the likelihood of introducing bugs into the shared codebase.

- **Pre-deployment:**
  - o **Tests:** Integration tests and E2E tests.
  - o **Purpose:** To ensure that the code functions correctly in conjunction with other components and to validate overall application behavior before it goes live.
  - o **Benefits:** Minimizes the risk of critical issues affecting users when deploying new changes.

- **Post-deployment:**
  - o **Tests:** Smoke tests and monitoring checks.
  - o **Purpose:** To verify that the application is running correctly in the production environment and to check for major functionality after deployment.
  - o **Benefits:** Quickly identifies any issues that may have occurred during deployment, allowing for rapid rollback or fixes if necessary.

- **Scheduled tests:**
  - o **Tests:** Performance tests, security scans, and comprehensive E2E tests.
  - o **Purpose:** To assess system performance and security on a regular basis without disrupting the development workflow.
  - o **Benefits:** Ensures long-term stability and security of an application.

Integrating automated tests at various stages of the CI/CD pipeline and defining the appropriate points for their execution is essential for maintaining high software quality. By effectively incorporating unit, integration, and end-to-end tests and scheduling them at strategic points in the development lifecycle, teams can ensure rapid and reliable releases while minimizing the risk of introducing defects into production.

Setting up automated tests in CI pipelines

Incorporating automated tests into a CI pipeline is vital for ensuring software quality and speeding up development cycles. Here are best practices for setting up automated tests in CI pipelines, along with strategies for handling different types of tests:

- **Version control integration:** Ensure that all automated tests are stored in the same version control system as the application code. This guarantees that tests are versioned alongside the code, making it easier to manage changes and updates.

- **Trigger tests based on code changes:** Use webhooks or CI tools to trigger automated tests whenever code is committed or a pull request is created. This ensures that tests run consistently and provide immediate feedback. Configure the CI pipeline to detect changes in specific directories or files to run only relevant test suites, optimizing execution time.

- **Create a modular test suite:** Organize tests into modular suites based on functionality (for example, unit tests, integration tests, end-to-end tests). This modularity allows for selective test execution, depending on the nature of the changes. Implement a tagging or labelling system to categorize tests, enabling targeted runs for specific branches or features.

- **Maintain test dependencies**: Ensure that all test dependencies are documented and included in the build environment. Use dependency management tools to automate this process, ensuring consistency across different environments.

- **Run tests in isolated environments:** Use containerization (for example, Docker) or virtual environments to create isolated testing environments. This reduces conflicts between different test dependencies and maintains consistency.

- **Monitor test results:** Implement logging and reporting mechanisms to track test results and provide insights into test failures. Integrate notification systems (for example, emails, Slack messages) to alert team members of any issues.

Setting up automated tests in CI pipelines requires careful planning and adherence to best practices. By integrating tests based on code changes, modularizing test suites, and effectively managing different types of tests, teams can ensure a smooth and efficient CI/CD process. This ultimately leads to higher software quality, faster feedback, and more reliable releases.

Test execution strategies in CI/CD

Various strategies can be employed to execute different types of tests to ensure efficient testing within CI/CD pipelines. These strategies help optimize resource utilization and improve feedback speed, leading to higher-quality software. Let us now go over them in detail.

Parallelization

Parallelization involves running multiple tests simultaneously across different environments or processes. This significantly reduces overall test execution time. Refer to the following:

- **Test frameworks:** Use testing frameworks that support parallel execution, such as JUnit with parallel execution settings, `pytest` with `pytest-xdist`, or TestNG.

- **CI/CD configuration:** Configure your CI/CD tool to allocate multiple runners or containers to execute different tests in parallel. For example, in Jenkins, you can use multiple executors, while in CircleCI, you can define various parallel jobs.

- **Benefits:** Faster feedback loops and improved resource utilization, allowing teams to run comprehensive test suites without delaying the development process.

Sharding

Sharding involves dividing a test suite into smaller, manageable pieces (shards) and executing them in parallel across different environments or CI/CD runners. Refer to the following:

- **Test distribution:** Use tools like tox (for Python) or Jest's sharding capabilities to distribute tests evenly among shards based on factors like test duration or resource requirements.

- **Configuration:** Set up your CI/CD pipeline to allocate shards based on test metadata, ensuring balanced and efficient execution.

- **Benefits:** Reduces bottlenecks caused by long-running tests and allows for more scalable testing as the project grows.

Running tests in isolated environments

Running tests in isolated environments helps eliminate interference between tests, ensuring that each test executes in a clean state with consistent dependencies. Refer to the following:

- **Containerization:** Use Docker to create isolated containers for each test environment, ensuring that tests run with the same configuration and dependencies every time.

- **Virtual environments:** For languages like Python, use virtual environments (for example, **venv**, **virtualenv**) to isolate dependencies per test suite.

- **Benefits:** Minimizes flakiness in test results and allows for better control over the testing environment.

Implementing effective test execution strategies in CI/CD pipelines is essential for improving software quality and speeding up development cycles. Teams can execute tests more efficiently by utilizing parallelization, sharding, and isolated environments.

Implementing quality gates for build success/failure

Refer to the following figure:

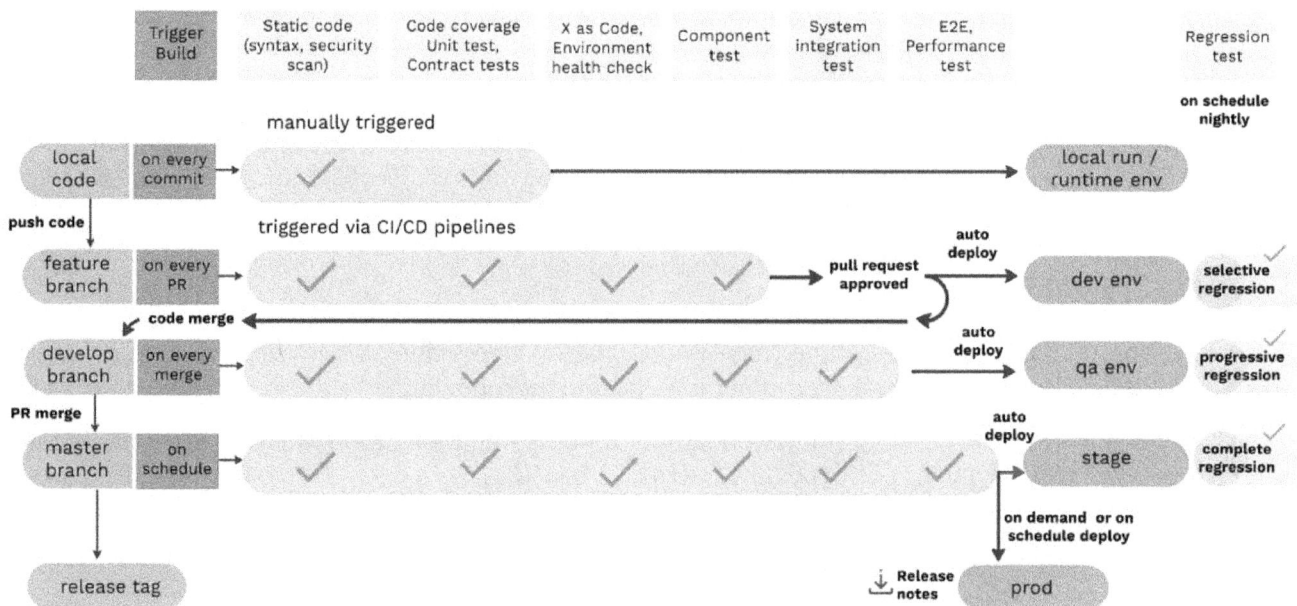

Figure 8.2: *Quality gates ensure testing is sufficient before moving on to the next environment*

Quality gates are predefined criteria and standards that must be met at various stages of a CI/CD pipeline for the build to succeed and progress to the next stage. They serve as checkpoints that assess the quality of the code before it is deployed to production.

The key elements of quality gates are as follows:

- **Criteria:** These can include metrics such as code coverage, static code analysis results, code complexity, and the number of critical bugs identified by testing tools.

- **Integration:** Quality gates are integrated into the CI/CD pipeline to ensure that code changes meet specific quality standards before being merged or deployed.

- **Failing builds:** If a code change does not meet the established criteria, the build fails, and developers are notified to address the issues before proceeding.

Role of quality gates in improving code quality

Here are some of the key benefits that quality gates will provide to the software development process:

- **Enhancing code quality:** Quality gates enforce coding standards and best practices by requiring developers to adhere to specific metrics before their code can be merged or released. This promotes a culture of quality within the development team and leads to more maintainable and robust code.

- **Catching regressions early:** By integrating automated tests and code quality checks into the quality gates, teams can identify and address regressions or bugs early in the development process. This proactive approach reduces the risk of introducing defects into the production environment and minimizes the cost and effort needed to fix issues later.

- **Preventing problematic code from being released:** Quality gates act as a safety net by preventing code that does not meet quality standards from reaching production. This significantly reduces the likelihood of deploying problematic code, leading to fewer production incidents, improved system stability, and higher user satisfaction.

- **Encouraging continuous improvement:** Establishing quality gates fosters a culture of continuous improvement. Teams can regularly assess and refine the criteria based on lessons learned from previous projects or incidents, ensuring that the quality gates evolve to meet the changing needs of the project and the organization.

- **Providing clear feedback:** Quality gates provide developers with clear and actionable feedback on their code. By setting specific quality thresholds, developers know exactly what needs to be addressed before their code can be merged or released, leading to quicker iterations and reduced frustration.

Quality gates play a crucial role in CI/CD pipelines by establishing clear criteria that must be met for code to proceed through the development lifecycle. They improve code quality, catch regressions early, and prevent problematic code from being released, thereby enhancing software applications' overall reliability and stability. By integrating quality gates into the development process, teams can foster a culture of quality and continuous improvement, leading to better outcomes for developers and end-users.

Key metrics for quality gates

Quality gates rely on specific metrics to assess the quality of code at various stages of the CI/CD pipeline. These metrics provide measurable criteria that teams can use to ensure that their code meets predefined quality standards before proceeding. Here are some commonly used metrics, along with guidance on setting appropriate thresholds.

The following examples of metrics commonly used in quality gates are crucial for implementing quality gates within a CI/CD pipeline, accompanied by suggested thresholds. However, solely relying on metrics poses the risk of them being manipulated. To address this, we include key considerations to keep in mind:

- **Code coverage:**
  o **Definition:** Code coverage measures the percentage of code that is tested by automated tests. It indicates how much of the codebase is validated through tests, highlighting untested areas.
  o **Purpose:** Higher code coverage suggests better-tested code, reducing the risk of undetected bugs.
  o **Threshold example:** Set a minimum code coverage threshold of 80%. This means that at least 80% of the code must be executed by the tests.
  o **Consideration:** Balance between coverage and meaningful tests. High coverage with poorly written tests may not improve code quality.

- **Pass/Fail test results:**
  o **Definition:** This metric tracks the outcome of automated tests, indicating whether they have passed or failed.

- o **Purpose:** Consistently passing tests ensure that code changes do not introduce new defects or regressions.
- o **Threshold example:** Limit the maximum number of allowed test failures to 2 in the pipeline before the build fails.
- o **Consideration:** Ensure that test failures are promptly addressed to maintain build stability and confidence in the codebase.

- **Static code analysis results:**
  - o **Definition:** Static code analysis examines the source code for potential errors, vulnerabilities, and adherence to coding standards without executing the code.
  - o **Purpose:** It helps identify code smells, security vulnerabilities, and maintainability issues early in development.
  - o **Threshold example:** Set a threshold for critical and significant issues identified by static code analysis tools, allowing 0 critical issues and a maximum of 5 significant issues.
  - o **Considerations:** Tailor thresholds based on the team's ability to address issues. Start with stricter limits and adjust as necessary.

- **Performance metrics:**
  - o **Definition:** Performance metrics assess the application's responsiveness, resource usage, and scalability under specific conditions.
  - o **Purpose:** Ensuring code changes do not negatively impact performance is critical for user satisfaction and application efficiency.
  - o **Threshold example:** Define acceptable performance benchmarks, such as response times under 200ms for key user interactions.
  - o **Consideration:** Ensure performance thresholds align with user expectations and application requirements. Regularly review and adjust based on real user data.

- **Cyclomatic complexity:**
  - o **Definition:** Cyclomatic complexity measures the number of linearly independent paths through a program's source code. It provides an indication of code complexity.
  - o **Purpose:** Lower cyclomatic complexity suggests simpler, more maintainable code. High complexity may indicate code that is harder to test and understand.
  - o **Threshold example:** Establish a maximum cyclomatic complexity threshold of 10 for functions or methods. This encourages developers to write simpler, more maintainable code.
  - o **Consideration:** Adjust thresholds based on the team's experience and the complexity of the project. More complex applications may require higher thresholds.

Key metrics are fundamental to establishing quality gates in CI/CD pipelines. By using metrics like code coverage, pass/fail test results, static code analysis outcomes, performance metrics, and cyclomatic complexity, teams can assess the quality of their code effectively. Setting appropriate thresholds for these metrics ensures that only code meeting quality standards progresses through the pipeline, thereby enhancing overall software quality and stability. Regularly reviewing and adjusting these thresholds helps teams adapt to changing project needs and maintain high-quality code.

Configuring quality gates

Configuring quality gates in CI/CD tools involves integrating static analysis and testing tools into the CI/CD pipeline to ensure code quality is maintained. Here is a step-by-step guide for configuring quality gates in popular CI/CD tools, along with examples of defining custom rules and conditions.

In this section, we will look at an example using GitHub Actions on setting up quality gates in a CI/CD pipeline. Due to the length of the code, we will only be focusing on one tool example for now, but the logic can be easily transferred to other CI/CD tools in YAML.

The following code covers the following areas:

- **Code coverage:** This ensures that a specified percentage of your codebase is covered by automated tests. Tools such as JaCoCo, Coveralls, or Codecov can generate the coverage report.

  o **Example threshold:** Code coverage must be above 80%.

- **Security scans:** Security gates ensure the code is free of high-severity vulnerabilities using tools like Snyk, Trivy, or OWASP Dependency-Check.

  o **Example threshold:** No high or critical vulnerabilities are allowed.

- **Testing quality:** This checks that automated tests meet specified quality criteria. Tools like JUnit, Mocha, or Allure can analyze test results.

  o **Example threshold:** All tests must pass, and the pipeline should fail if any flaky tests or errors occur.

The following code example is in YAML using GitHub. The job names have been made bold to showcase how they align with the three aforementioned measures.

```yaml
name: Quality Gates Pipeline

on:
  push:
    branches:
      - main
  pull_request:

jobs:
  code-coverage:
    runs-on: ubuntu-latest
    steps:
      - name: Checkout Code
        uses: actions/checkout@v3

      - name: Set up Java
        uses: actions/setup-java@v3
        with:
          java-version: '17'

      - name: Run Tests with Coverage
        run: |
          ./gradlew test jacocoTestReport
          bash <(curl -s https://codecov.io/bash) -t ${{ secrets.CODECOV_TOKEN }}

      - name: Check Code Coverage Threshold
        run: |
          coverage=$(grep -oP 'TOTAL\s+\d+\s+\d+\s+\d+\s+\d+\.\d+' build/reports/jacoco/
test/jacocoTestReport.csv | awk '{print $4}')
```

```
        if (( $(echo "$coverage < 80.0" | bc -l) )); then
          echo "Code coverage is below threshold: $coverage%"
          exit 1
        fi
      shell: bash


security-scan:
  runs-on: ubuntu-latest
  steps:
    - name: Checkout Code
      uses: actions/checkout@v3

    - name: Run Security Scan
      uses: snyk/actions/cli@v3
      with:
        args: test
      env:
        SNYK_TOKEN: ${{ secrets.SNYK_TOKEN }}

    - name: Fail on High/Critical Vulnerabilities
      run: |
        if snyk_output=$(snyk test --severity-threshold=high); then
          echo "No high/critical vulnerabilities found."
        else
          echo "High/critical vulnerabilities detected:"
          echo "$snyk_output"
          exit 1
        fi
      shell: bash


testing-quality:
  runs-on: ubuntu-latest
  steps:
    - name: Checkout Code
      uses: actions/checkout@v3

    - name: Run Tests
      run: |
        ./gradlew test
      continue-on-error: false

    - name: Analyze Test Results
      run: |
        if grep -q 'FAILED' build/test-results/test/TEST-*.xml; then
          echo "Test failures detected."
          exit 1
        else
```

```
        echo "All tests passed successfully."
      fi
    shell: bash
```

The preceding code is the full piece of code, but we will break down the steps in more detail in the following to make sense of what they do:

```
name: Quality Gates Pipeline

on:
  push:
    branches:
      - main
  pull_request:
```

Purpose: Defines when the pipeline should run.

Explanation:

- The pipeline triggers on push events to the main branch.

- It also triggers pull requests, enforcing quality gates before merging changes.

Code coverage job

Let us go over the following steps:

1. **Checkout code:**

    a. **Purpose**: Fetch the repository code so the pipeline can work with it.

    b. **Key tool:** The actions/checkout action clones the repository.

    ```
    jobs:
      code-coverage:
        runs-on: ubuntu-latest
        steps:
          - name: Checkout Code
            uses: actions/checkout@v3
    ```

2. **Set up Java (For Java-based projects):**

    a. **Purpose:** Prepares the environment for running Java code.

    b. **Key option:** Specifies the Java version (17 in this case).

    ```
      - name: Set up Java
        uses: actions/setup-java@v3
        with:
          java-version: '17'
    ```

3. **Run tests and generate code coverage:**

    a. **Purpose:**

        i. Runs tests using Gradle and generates a JaCoCo coverage report.

        ii. Upload the report to Codecov for visualization.

    b. **Secrets:** The **CODECOV_TOKEN** is securely stored in the repository's secrets to authenticate with Codecov.

```
- name: Run Tests with Coverage
  run: |
    ./gradlew test jacocoTestReport
    bash <(curl -s https://codecov.io/bash) -t ${{ secrets.CODECOV_TOKEN }}
```

4. **Enforce code coverage threshold:**

   a. **Purpose:** Checks if the total code coverage is above 80%.

   b. **How it works:**

      i. Extracts the coverage percentage from the JaCoCo report.

      ii. Compares it to the threshold (80%) and fails the pipeline if the condition is not met.

```
- name: Check Code Coverage Threshold
  run: |
    coverage=$(grep -oP 'TOTAL\s+\d+\s+\d+\s+\d+\s+\d+\.\d+' build/reports/
    jacoco/test/jacocoTestReport.csv | awk '{print $4}')
    if (( $(echo "$coverage < 80.0" | bc -l) )); then
      echo "Code coverage is below threshold: $coverage%"
      exit 1
    fi
  shell: bash
```

Security scan job

Let us go over the following steps now:

1. **Checkout code:** Same as the code-coverage job; fetches the repository code.

```
security-scan:
  runs-on: ubuntu-latest
  steps:
    - name: Checkout Code
      uses: actions/checkout@v3
```

2. **Run security scan:**

   a. **Purpose:** Runs Snyk to scan for vulnerabilities.

   b. **Key option:** The **args:** test ensures only tests are run without modifying anything.

   c. **Secrets:** The **SNYK_TOKEN** is securely stored for authenticating with Snyk.

```
- name: Run Security Scan
  uses: snyk/actions/cli@v3
  with:
    args: test
  env:
    SNYK_TOKEN: ${{ secrets.SNYK_TOKEN }}
```

3. **Enforce security threshold**

   a. **Purpose:** Fails the pipeline if high/critical vulnerabilities are found.

   b. **How it works:**

      i. Runs snyk test with a severity threshold set to high.

      ii. Exits with an error if any vulnerabilities are detected.

```
- name: Fail on High/Critical Vulnerabilities
```

```
    run: |
      if snyk_output=$(snyk test --severity-threshold=high); then
        echo "No high/critical vulnerabilities found."
      else
        echo "High/critical vulnerabilities detected:"
        echo "$snyk_output"
        exit 1
      fi
    shell: bash
```

Testing quality job

Refer to the following steps:

1. **Run tests:**

   a. **Purpose:** Executes the test suite.

   b. **Key option:** The **continue-on-error: false** ensures the pipeline fails if any tests fail.

   ```
   testing-quality:
     runs-on: ubuntu-latest
     steps:
       - name: Checkout Code
         uses: actions/checkout@v3

       - name: Run Tests
         run: |
            ./gradlew test
         continue-on-error: false
   ```

2. **Analyze test results:**

   a. **Purpose**: Reads the test result XML files to check for failures.

   b. **How it works:**

      i. Scans the test result files for the word **FAILED**.

      ii. Exits with an error if any test failure is found.

   ```
   - name: Analyze Test Results
     run: |
       if grep -q 'FAILED' build/test-results/test/TEST-*.xml; then
         echo "Test failures detected."
         exit 1
       else
         echo "All tests passed successfully."
       fi
     shell: bash
   ```

Summary of steps from the preceding code sample

The following is a brief explanation of the key automated checks defined in the preceding code sample:

- **Code coverage job:** Runs tests, generates coverage, and enforces an 80% threshold.

- **Security scan job:** Scans dependencies for vulnerabilities and enforces no high/critical issues.

- **Testing quality job:** Runs tests and ensures all tests pass successfully.

This modular structure ensures high-quality code, secure dependencies, and reliable tests before changes are merged or deployed.

Handling failed quality gates

Quality gates are great at enforcing quality in the development process. However, when they fail, it can lead to frustration, as if it is slowing down the development process, if the failures are not managed effectively.

Managing build failures caused by failed quality gates is crucial for maintaining code quality and ensuring a smooth development process. Quick feedback mechanisms and effective techniques can help developers address issues without significantly impacting the speed of delivery.

The following are some of the things teams can do to effectively manage build failures as a result of failed quality gates.

Importance of quick feedback

Here are some key attributes that highlight the importance of getting quick feedback on a CI/CD pipeline:

- **Immediate awareness:** When a quality gate fails, developers need to be immediately notified of the issue so they can address it promptly. Delays in feedback can lead to further complications, such as more significant regressions or increased difficulty in pinpointing the cause of the failure.

- **Contextual information:** Providing detailed feedback about the specific criteria that caused the failure (for example, code coverage, static analysis errors) allows developers to understand and rectify the problem efficiently.

- **Collaboration and accountability:** Quick feedback encourages developers to collaborate on fixing issues and fosters a culture of accountability, where team members take ownership of code quality.

Steps to handle build failures

Let us go over these steps now:

1. **Automated notifications:** Configure CI/CD tools to send automated notifications (for example, emails, Slack messages) when a quality gate fails. Include details about the failure to help developers address issues quickly.

2. **Build logs and reports:** Provide developers access to detailed build logs and quality reports, which outline the reasons for the failure. This enables them to diagnose and resolve issues efficiently.

3. **Prioritize fixes:** Encourage teams to prioritize addressing quality gate failures as part of their workflow. This can be done by integrating the resolution of quality gate issues into sprint planning or daily stand-ups.

4. **Temporary workarounds:** If critical deadlines are approaching, consider allowing temporary workarounds while maintaining transparency. For example, a developer can request a temporary bypass of specific quality gates, provided they agree to address the issues promptly.

Techniques for enforcing quality gates in agile environments

While enforcing quality gates is essential, agile environments often prioritize speed and flexibility. Here are some techniques to balance quality enforcement with fast delivery:

- **Run critical tests early:** Prioritize running only a subset of critical tests (for example, unit tests) in the early stages of the pipeline. This provides quick feedback on foundational functionality without delaying the build.

- **Incremental testing:** Implement incremental testing strategies where only tests affected by recent code changes are executed. This can be achieved using tools that analyze code dependencies and impact.

- **Feature flags:** Use feature flags to control the release of new features. This allows teams to merge code even if certain features are not yet complete or if they do not meet all quality gate criteria. It ensures that only stable code is deployed while enabling rapid iterations.

- **Test prioritization:** Categorize tests into different priorities (for example, critical, important, and non-essential). Run essential tests of the CI/CD pipeline while deferring longer-running or less critical tests to later stages or separate pipelines.

- **Quality gate batching:** Implement a batching approach where quality gates are checked at different stages of development. For instance, strict quality gates should be checked when merging to the main branch, but allow looser criteria during development branches.

- **Continuous improvement:** Review quality gate thresholds regularly and adjust them based on team performance and feedback. This helps teams balance maintaining quality and ensuring fast delivery.

- **Training and documentation:** Provide training and clear documentation on quality gate processes and expectations. Empowering developers with knowledge ensures they understand the importance of quality gates and how to address issues effectively.

Handling failed quality gates requires a proactive approach to providing quick feedback and efficient resolution processes. By prioritizing communication, access to information, and collaborative problem-solving, teams can minimize disruptions caused by quality gate failures. Employing techniques like running critical tests early, using feature flags, and implementing incremental testing allows agile teams to enforce quality gates effectively while maintaining the speed of delivery, ensuring that high-quality software is delivered without compromising agility.

Ensuring seamless integration with different CI tools

To keep your test automation framework flexible and CI tool-agnostic, consider the following best practices:

- **Use standardized command-line interfaces:** Design the test automation framework to accept command-line arguments for configurations (for example, environment variables, test reports). This allows easy integration regardless of the CI/CD tool used.

- **Abstract CI/CD-specific code:** Isolate any CI/CD-specific scripts or configurations from your main test automation framework. Use configuration files or environment variables to manage settings that may change across CI environments.

- **Leverage plugins and extensions:** Utilize plugins or extensions that allow your framework to integrate with various CI/CD tools without modifying the core code. For example, tools like Maven, Gradle, or npm scripts can be used to manage dependencies and test execution.

- **Containerization:** Use containerization technologies (for example, Docker) to encapsulate the test environment. This ensures consistency across different CI environments, allowing your tests to run in the same environment regardless of the CI/CD tool.

- **Cross-platform compatibility:** Ensure that your test automation framework is compatible with multiple operating systems (Windows, macOS, Linux). This can help streamline integration across different CI/CD tools that may run on various platforms.

- **Maintain comprehensive documentation:** Document the integration process for each CI/CD tool clearly, including any configurations needed for your test automation framework. This documentation should be kept up to date to facilitate onboarding and maintenance.

- **Use version control:** Keep your automation scripts, configuration files, and related documentation in version control. This helps maintain a history of changes and enables easy collaboration among team members.

- **Automate testing setup:** Create scripts to automate the setup of your testing environment, including installing dependencies and configuring the environment. This can reduce setup time and make the framework easier to use across different CI tools.

Integrating a test automation framework with CI/CD tools like Jenkins, GitLab CI, Travis CI, CircleCI, and Azure DevOps ensures continuous testing and high-quality software delivery. By following integration strategies specific to each tool and adhering to best practices for maintaining a CI tool-agnostic framework, teams can streamline their testing processes and enhance their development workflows, ensuring flexibility and efficiency across multiple CI environments.

Tool-specific configurations

When integrating a test automation framework with various CI/CD tools, it is crucial to establish specific configurations that handle environment variables, secrets, and test dependencies. The following are some examples of configurations for popular CI/CD tools and guidelines for creating modular and reusable configurations.

Jenkins

Handling environment variables:

```
pipeline {
    agent any
    environment {
        NODE_ENV = 'test'
        API_KEY = credentials('my-secret-api-key')
    }
    stages {
        stage('Build') {
            steps {
                sh 'npm install'
            }
        }
        stage('Test') {
            steps {
                sh 'npm test'
            }
        }
    }
}
```

Handling secrets: Use Jenkins Credentials Plugin to store secrets securely. Reference secrets in the pipeline using the credentials function, as shown previously.

Test dependencies: Include dependencies in the **package.json** file and run **npm install** in the build stage to install them.

GitLab CI

Handling environment variables:

```
NODE_ENV: "test"
API_KEY: "${MY_SECRET_API_KEY}"
```

```
stages:
  - build
  - test

build:
  stage: build
  script:
    - npm install

test:
  stage: test
  script:
    - npm test
```

Handling secrets: Store secrets in GitLab CI/CD settings under Settings | CI/CD | Variables. Reference them in the **.gitlab-ci.yml** file, as shown previously.

Test dependencies: Manage dependencies using **package.json** and ensure to run **npm install** in the build stage.

Travis CI

Handling environment variables:

```
env:
  global:
    - NODE_ENV=test
    - secure: "MY_SECRET_API_KEY"

script:
  - npm install
  - npm test
```

Handling secrets: Use Travis CI's encrypted environment variables feature to store secrets. Use the Travis CLI to encrypt and add them to your repository.

Test dependencies: Include a **package.json** file for dependencies, and Travis will automatically run **npm install**.

CircleCI

Handling environment variables:

```
version: 2.1
jobs:
  build:
    docker:
      - image: circleci/node:latest
    environment:
      NODE_ENV: test
      API_KEY: $MY_SECRET_API_KEY
    steps:
```

```
      - checkout
      - run:
          name: Install Dependencies
          command: npm install
      - run:
          name: Run Tests
          command: npm test

workflows:
  version: 2
  build:
    jobs:
      - build
```

Handling secrets: Store secrets in CircleCI under Project Settings | Environment Variables and reference them as shown in the preceding code.

Test dependencies: Use a **package.json** file to manage dependencies.

Azure DevOps

Handling environment variables:

```
trigger:
  branches:
    include:
      - main
pool:
  vmImage: 'ubuntu-latest'

variables:
  NODE_ENV: 'test'
  API_KEY: $(MY_SECRET_API_KEY)

steps:
  - script: |
      npm install
      npm test
    displayName: 'Install Dependencies and Run Tests'
```

Handling secrets: Use Azure Key Vault to manage secrets and access them as pipeline variables using **$(VARIABLE_NAME)** syntax.

Test dependencies: Manage dependencies using **package.json** and run **npm install** in the pipeline.

Creating modular and reusable CI/CD configurations

Creating modular and reusable CI/CD configurations can greatly enhance productivity and maintainability. Here are some best practices for achieving this:

- **Use shared configuration files:** Create a common configuration file for your CI/CD pipeline (for example, a template **.yml** file) that can be included in different pipeline definitions across various CI tools.

- **Parameterize your configurations:** Utilize parameters or variables within your CI/CD configurations to allow customization based on the environment or specific use cases. For example, use a **${CI_ ENVIRONMENT}** variable to determine the environment (development, testing, production) and adjust settings accordingly.

- **Modularize build steps:** Break down your CI/CD configurations into reusable build steps or jobs. Each job should handle a specific task (for example, build, test, deploy) and can be referenced across different pipelines. For example, define a testing job that can be reused (using **yaml** code):

```
test_job:
  script:
    - npm test
```

- **Environment-specific configurations:** Maintain separate configuration files for different environments (for example, **test.yml**, **prod.yml**) and include the relevant file in your main CI/CD configuration based on the context.

- **Centralized secret management:** Use centralized secret management tools (for example, AWS Secrets Manager, HashiCorp Vault) to handle secrets across different CI tools. Ensure your CI/CD configurations consistently reference these secrets.

- **Documentation:** Maintain thorough documentation of your CI/CD configurations, including details on how to set up environments, manage dependencies, and handle secrets. This aids in onboarding new team members and reduces reliance on individual knowledge.

Tool-specific configurations for integrating test automation frameworks with CI/CD tools are essential for smooth and effective software delivery. By following the outlined examples and best practices, teams can create modular and reusable configurations that adapt across various environments and CI tools, promoting efficiency and consistency in their development workflows.

Ensuring cross-tool compatibility

Building CI/CD pipelines that work across different tools and platforms requires careful design and implementation. By employing certain techniques, teams can ensure their pipelines and tests are adaptable and robust enough to handle changes in CI tools or environments without requiring significant modifications.

Here are some techniques for building CI/CD pipelines across different tools:

- **Use a common configuration format:** Leverage common configuration formats such as YAML or JSON for defining pipelines. This makes it easier to translate configurations between different CI/CD tools, as many tools support these formats. For instance, use a common **.ci-config.yml** file to maintain environment settings, dependencies, and scripts, which can be referenced or included in tool-specific configurations.

- **Adopt containerization:** Use containerization (for example, Docker) to create a consistent build environment across different CI/CD tools. This eliminates environment discrepancies and ensures the same code runs identically regardless of the CI/CD platform. Define a Dockerfile that includes all necessary dependencies and configurations. CI pipelines can then run tests in a containerized environment, ensuring consistency.

- **Define clear APIs for interactions:** Implement well-defined APIs for tools that interact with your CI/CD pipeline. For example, if you have custom scripts that need to run during the pipeline, ensure they can be invoked easily with command-line arguments or HTTP requests. This reduces the dependency on any specific CI tool's features and allows the same scripts to be used across various environments.

- **Use CI/CD agnostic tools:** Opt for CI/CD tools and frameworks that are designed to be agnostic and support integrations across multiple platforms. For instance, tools like Jenkins, GitLab CI, and CircleCI can often integrate with various testing frameworks and deployment tools seamlessly.

- **Implement version control for configuration files:** Keep all CI/CD configurations in version control (for example, Git). This allows for easy tracking of changes and the ability to roll back configurations as needed. It also facilitates collaboration among team members. Use branches to experiment with different configurations without impacting the main pipeline.

- **Develop wrapper scripts:** Create wrapper scripts for CI/CD tasks that can be executed regardless of the underlying tool. For instance, you can develop shell scripts or Python scripts to run tests, build applications, and deploy code, which can be called from any CI tool. This abstracts away tool-specific commands and provides a unified interface.

Ensuring robustness in tests and pipelines

Having tests and pipelines fail regularly can be frustrating for teams to work with. This leads to more time being spent fixing and maintaining tests and pipelines than getting feedback from them. The following steps will help provide more stability in executing your automated testing in a CI/CD pipeline:

- **Modular and reusable code:** Design tests and pipelines in a modular way, breaking them into reusable components (for example, functions or classes). This allows for easy updates and modifications when adapting to a new CI tool or environment. For example, use a separate module for handling dependencies, which can be called in any test or pipeline without rewriting code.

- **Environment-variable driven configuration:** Use environment variables to define key parameters for your CI/CD pipelines, such as database connection strings, API keys, and environment-specific settings. This allows you to change configurations without modifying the pipeline code itself.

- **Implement feature flags:** Use feature flags to enable or disable specific features or tests in your codebase. This helps in managing changes to the pipeline or tests without deploying new code. Feature flags allow for gradual rollouts and quick reversions if needed.

- **Continuous monitoring and logging:** Integrate monitoring and logging within your CI/CD pipelines to capture detailed information about builds, tests, and deployments. This data can be invaluable for troubleshooting and adapting to changes. Use tools like Prometheus, Grafana, or **Elasticsearch, Logstash, Kibana (ELK)** Stack to gather and visualize logs and metrics, allowing for quick identification of issues when transitioning between tools.

- **Regularly review and update configurations:** Establish a process for regularly reviewing and updating your CI/CD configurations to ensure they remain relevant and functional as tools evolve. This can be part of your sprint retrospectives or team reviews. Encourage team members to share feedback and experiences when working with different CI tools to identify areas for improvement.

- **Documentation and training:** Maintain comprehensive documentation of your CI/CD processes, configurations, and any tool-specific nuances. This helps onboard new team members and provides guidance when transitioning to new tools. Provide training sessions or resources for team members to familiarize them with various CI/CD tools and best practices, ensuring everyone is equipped to handle changes.

Ensuring cross-tool compatibility in CI/CD pipelines is essential for maintaining flexibility and adaptability in a rapidly changing development landscape. By employing techniques such as using common configuration formats, containerization, and modular code design, teams can create robust pipelines that can easily adapt to changes in CI tools or environments. Additionally, maintaining thorough documentation, implementing monitoring strategies, and fostering a culture of continuous improvement will help ensure the long-term success of CI/CD processes across different platforms.

Optimizing for speed and reliability

Along with stability in your pipelines, you also need tests to execute quickly to provide rapid feedback. We will now look at approaches that can help you optimize the speed of your test execution without compromising its reliability.

Balancing speed and quality in CI/CD

Balancing the need for quick feedback with the requirement for comprehensive testing is a crucial challenge in CI/CD pipelines. Achieving this balance ensures that teams can deliver high-quality software rapidly without sacrificing the thoroughness of testing. Here are strategies and techniques to optimize CI/CD pipelines for speed while maintaining quality:

- **Balancing quick feedback with comprehensive testing:**

  o **Establish a testing pyramid:** Implement a testing pyramid strategy that prioritizes the types of tests based on their speed and reliability.

    ▪ **Unit tests:** Base the pyramid on a high volume of unit tests. They are fast, and running them often provides immediate feedback on the code's correctness.

    ▪ **Integration tests:** Use fewer integration tests that validate interactions between components. These tests are slower but crucial for identifying issues in component interactions.

    ▪ **End-to-end tests:** At the top of the pyramid, maintain a limited number of end-to-end tests. These are the slowest and most complex, but are essential for validating complete workflows.

- **Create a testing strategy:** Define a clear strategy for when and what to test, ensuring that critical paths are constantly tested. Regularly review which tests are essential to your workflow and adapt as needed. Use exploratory testing in conjunction with automated tests to cover areas that automated tests may miss.

- **Encourage a culture of testing:** Foster a culture where testing is integrated into the development process, encouraging developers to write tests alongside their code changes. This practice can lead to better code quality and fewer bugs.

Techniques to optimize CI/CD pipelines for speed

The following techniques can help tests execute quickly and load faster:

- **Run tests in parallel:** Utilize parallel test execution to reduce overall testing time. Many CI/CD tools support running tests concurrently, allowing multiple tests to be executed simultaneously.

- **Containerized environments:** Use containerization (for example, Docker) to create isolated and consistent testing environments. Containerized environments can be spun up quickly and are less prone to discrepancies between development and production.

- **Selective test execution:** Implement selective test execution by running only tests that are affected by recent code changes. This can be achieved by analyzing the codebase to identify impacted tests based on modified files.

- **Use caching mechanisms:** Leverage caching in CI/CD pipelines to speed up the build and test phases. For instance, cache dependencies or build artifacts to avoid redundant downloads or rebuilds.

- **Optimize test suite:** Regularly review and refactor your test suite to remove flaky tests, redundant tests, or slow tests. This practice helps to keep the test suite efficient and effective.

- **Implement pre-commit hooks:** Use pre-commit hooks to run quick tests (for example, linters, unit tests) locally before code is pushed to the repository. This practice can catch simple issues early, reducing the feedback cycle.

- **Continuous monitoring and reporting:** Implement monitoring and reporting systems to keep track of pipeline performance and test execution times. Analyzing this data can help identify bottlenecks and optimize the pipeline further.

- **Prioritize tests based on risk:** Prioritize tests that cover the most critical and high-risk features. By focusing on these areas, you can ensure that essential functionality is always tested thoroughly without overwhelming the pipeline.

Balancing speed and quality in CI/CD pipelines requires strategic planning and implementation of efficient testing practices. By establishing a testing pyramid, leveraging parallel test execution, utilizing containerized environments, and optimizing test execution through selective testing and coaching, teams can achieve quick feedback without compromising the comprehensiveness of their testing. Regularly reviewing and adjusting these strategies ensures that teams can continue to deliver high-quality software rapidly and effectively.

Handling flaky tests in CI/CD

Flaky tests pose a significant challenge in CI/CD pipelines, as they can lead to false positives or negatives, disrupt the development workflow, and undermine confidence in the testing process. Effectively managing flaky tests requires a combination of strategies aimed at isolating their causes, automating reruns, and enhancing overall test stability.

Dealing with flaky tests

The following are a few things that can be quickly implemented to help identify and reduce flaky tests in a pipeline:

- **Identify and acknowledge flaky tests:** Recognize that flaky tests exist and can disrupt the CI/CD process. Maintain a dedicated list of known flaky tests to monitor their behavior over time.
- Use test reporting tools to track and analyze test outcomes, identifying tests that fail intermittently.
- **Root cause analysis:** Investigate the underlying causes of flaky tests. Common reasons include:
  - **Timing issues:** Tests that depend on asynchronous operations may fail if the timing is not consistent.
  - **Resource contention:** Tests that run in parallel may compete for shared resources, leading to failures.
  - **Environment sensitivity:** Tests that depend on external services or environmental conditions may experience variability.
- Utilize logging and debugging tools to capture detailed information when tests fail to help pinpoint the issue.

Strategies for isolating flaky tests

Along with identifying and reducing these flaky tests, it is also important to build measures into your framework that can isolate these failing tests and prevent them from being effective throughout the execution run. Let us go over the following:

- **Isolate tests:** Run tests in isolation to identify whether the failure is caused by interactions with other tests. This can be done by:
  - **Segregating tests:** Organize tests into groups (unit, integration, end-to-end) and run them in separate environments.
- **Mocking dependencies**: Use mocking frameworks to isolate tests from external dependencies, reducing variability.
- **Run tests sequentially:** Temporarily run tests sequentially to determine if running them in parallel contributes to their flakiness. This approach helps identify resource contention issues.

- **Increase test timeout:** If tests fail due to timing issues, consider increasing their timeout settings to allow more time for operations to complete, especially for integration and end-to-end tests.

Rerunning failed tests automatically

Let us go over the following:

- **Implement automatic reruns:** Configure CI/CD pipelines to automatically rerun tests that fail. This helps to confirm whether a failure is genuine or a result of flakiness.

  o Set a threshold for reruns (for example, rerun failed tests up to two additional times) to avoid infinite loops of failing tests.

- **Use test retry plugins:** Many CI/CD tools have plugins or built-in support for retrying failed tests. For example:

  o In Jest, use the `--retries` option to automatically rerun failing tests.

  o In JUnit, use the `@Retry` annotation to specify retries for specific tests.

- **Report and analyze rerun outcomes:** Maintain detailed logs of test reruns, capturing information on the number of reruns and the outcomes. This data can help assess tests' reliability and make informed decisions about their stability.

Improving test stability

The preceding strategies will reduce the impact flaky tests have on the CI/CD pipeline, but there are still some additional things that can be done to improve test stability overall, such as:

- **Refactor flaky tests:** Regularly refactor flaky tests to improve their stability. This may include:

  o **Reducing dependencies:** Minimize reliance on external services or shared resources.

  o **Simplifying logic:** Simplify test logic to reduce potential points of failure.

  o **Adding wait conditions:** Implement explicit waits for asynchronous operations to ensure that tests do not fail due to timing issues.

- **Adopt a retry mechanism:** Implement a robust retry mechanism within tests that allows certain tests to automatically retry on known flaky conditions (for example, network errors) while maintaining overall stability.

- **Integrate test stability metrics:** Monitor test stability metrics to track the flakiness of tests over time. Key metrics include:

  o **Flaky test rate:** Percentage of tests identified as flaky over a given period.

  o **Failure rate:** Number of test failures relative to total test runs.

  Use these metrics to identify trends and prioritize efforts to stabilize flaky tests.

- **Regularly review and maintain tests:** Establish a process for regularly reviewing and maintaining the test suite. This includes removing obsolete tests, refactoring existing tests, and ensuring all tests remain relevant and effective. Schedule periodic reviews as part of the development cycle to focus on improving test quality.

Effectively handling flaky tests in CI/CD pipelines is essential for maintaining the integrity of the testing process and ensuring reliable software delivery. By identifying and acknowledging flaky tests, isolating their causes, implementing automatic reruns, and improving overall test stability, teams can minimize disruptions caused by flaky tests and enhance confidence in their testing processes. Regular monitoring and maintenance of the test suite will contribute to sustained quality and reliability in CI/CD workflows.

Monitoring and reporting in CI/CD

Effective reporting in CI/CD pipelines is crucial for ensuring transparency, enabling quick decision-making, and maintaining high quality in software development. Generating and integrating detailed reports from test automation frameworks provides insights into test results, build statuses, and quality metrics that are valuable for both development teams and stakeholders. The following are strategies for achieving this integration.

Generating and integrating reports from test automation frameworks

Here are some steps that will help with generating reports from the test automation framework that will support your CI/CD execution:

- **Generate reports during CI/CD runs:** Configure your CI/CD pipelines to automatically generate reports after tests are executed. This can be done by:

  o Adding report generation commands in the CI/CD pipeline configuration file (for example, `.gitlab-ci.yml`, `Jenkinsfile`).

  o Ensuring that the output reports are saved in a designated directory for easy access.

- **Publish reports as artifacts:** Many CI/CD tools allow for publishing test reports as build artifacts. This ensures that reports are accessible for review after the build process is completed. For example:

  o In Jenkins, use the `archiveArtifacts` step to store reports.

  o In GitLab CI, use the `artifacts` keyword to specify which files should be retained after a job is completed.

- **Integrate with CI/CD dashboards:** Leverage built-in dashboards or third-party dashboard solutions to visualize test results and metrics. Tools such as Grafana, Kibana, or specific CI/CD dashboards (for example, Jenkins Blue Ocean) can provide real-time insights into pipeline performance and test outcomes.

Ensuring visibility into test results, build statuses, and quality metrics

The following steps will help ensure that teams are kept aware of quality gate failures or successes, and provide them with meaningful metrics to address improvement and quality issues:

- **Implement notifications and alerts:** Set up notifications to alert development teams and stakeholders about build statuses, test results, and quality metrics. This can be done using:

  o Email notifications are configured in CI/CD tools.

  o Integration with messaging platforms (for example, Slack, Microsoft Teams) to send real-time updates.

  o Customize notifications based on severity (for example, send immediate alerts for failed builds, daily summaries for overall health).

- **Use dashboard widgets:** Utilize dashboard widgets that summarize key metrics, such as:

  o Total tests run, passed, and failed.

  o Code coverage percentages.

  o Build history and trends over time.

  o Ensure that dashboards are tailored to meet the needs of both technical and non-technical stakeholders.

- **Visualize test trends and patterns:** Create visualizations that display trends over time, such as:
  - o The number of tests passing/failing over the last several builds.
  - o Code coverage changes over time.
  - o Use tools like Grafana or Google Data Studio to aggregate data and provide visual insights.

- **Generate summary reports:** Create summary reports at regular intervals (for example, daily or weekly) that provide insights into the overall health of the codebase, including:
  - o Build stability and success rates.
  - o Test results and coverage metrics.
  - o Any outstanding issues or regressions.
  - o Distribute these summary reports to relevant stakeholders to keep everyone informed about project status.

- **Integrate static code analysis results**: Include results from static code analysis tools (for example, SonarQube, CodeClimate) in your reports. These tools can provide insights into code quality, maintainability, and potential vulnerabilities.
  - o Ensure that code quality metrics are part of your CI/CD dashboard, enabling visibility alongside test results.

- **Define key performance indicators (KPIs):** Establish KPIs for your CI/CD process to measure and evaluate performance. Common KPIs include:
  - o **Mean time To Recovery (MTTR)** for failed builds.
  - o Test pass rate and code coverage metrics.
  - o Deployment frequency and lead time to changes.
  - o Regularly review these KPIs with the team and stakeholders to assess the effectiveness of the CI/CD process and identify areas for improvement.

Integrating detailed reporting from test automation frameworks into CI/CD pipelines is essential for ensuring visibility into test results, build statuses, and quality metrics. By generating and publishing reports, utilizing dashboards, and implementing notifications, development teams and stakeholders can stay informed about the health of the codebase and make data-driven decisions. Establishing clear KPIs and regularly reviewing these metrics fosters continuous improvement in the CI/CD process and enhances the overall quality of software delivery.

Real-time monitoring of builds

Real-time monitoring of builds and test execution is crucial for maintaining high software quality and ensuring that teams can quickly respond to issues as they arise. By utilizing various tools and techniques, development teams can gain immediate visibility into the CI/CD process, enabling them to identify and resolve problems swiftly. Here are some effective strategies for implementing real-time monitoring in CI/CD pipelines.

Tools for monitoring test execution and build results

Let us now go over some important tools:

- **CI/CD platform dashboards:** Most CI/CD tools (for example, Jenkins, GitLab CI, CircleCI, Travis CI) offer built-in dashboards that provide real-time visibility into the status of builds and tests. These dashboards typically display:
  - o Current build status (success, failure, in progress).

o Test results and code coverage metrics.

o Historical data on build durations and success rates.

- **Third-party monitoring tools:** Use specialized monitoring tools that can integrate with CI/CD platforms to provide enhanced visibility. Popular tools include:

  o **Grafana:** An open-source platform for monitoring and observability that can visualize data from multiple sources.

  o **Prometheus:** A monitoring and alerting toolkit designed for reliability and scalability. It works well with Grafana for visualization.

  o **New Relic:** Provides **application performance monitoring (APM)** along with CI/CD insights to monitor builds and deployments.

- **Log aggregation tools:** Implement log aggregation tools like ELK Stack or Splunk to collect and analyze logs from various sources, including CI/CD pipelines. These tools allow for real-time search and visualization of logs, helping to pinpoint issues during the build process.

Techniques for real-time monitoring

The following techniques will help to ensure metrics are gathered quickly and tracked in real-time, providing teams with accurate and up-to-the-minute information for decision-making:

- **Alert systems:** Set up alerting mechanisms to notify the team of build failures, test failures, or other critical events. Alerting can be done through:

  o **Email notifications:** Configure your CI/CD tool to send emails upon build success or failure.

  o **Instant messaging integrations:** Integrate with communication platforms like Slack, Microsoft Teams, or Discord to send real-time alerts and notifications.

  o Customize alert thresholds to avoid alert fatigue, ensuring that only significant events trigger notifications.

- **Live build logs:** Utilize CI/CD tools that provide live streaming of build logs. This allows developers to monitor the progress of builds and tests in real-time and identify issues as they happen. In tools like Jenkins, use the Blue Ocean plugin for an improved UI that displays real-time logs and insights.

- **Visual dashboards:** Create visual dashboards that aggregate data from multiple sources to provide a comprehensive view of the CI/CD pipeline's health. Key elements to include:

  o Build status overview (for example, pie charts showing the proportion of successful vs. failed builds).

  o Real-time test execution status and results.

  o Key metrics such as build duration, test pass rates, and deployment frequency.

- **Health checks and metrics:**

  o Implement periodic health checks to verify the availability and performance of your CI/CD services and tools.

  o Monitor KPI like:

    ▪ Build success rates and trends.

    ▪ MTTR from failures.

    ▪ Test coverage and pass rates over time.

Integration with issue tracking systems

Integrate CI/CD monitoring with issue tracking tools (for example, Jira, Trello) to create tickets automatically when build failures or test issues occur.

This integration streamlines tracking and resolving problems, allowing teams to focus on fixing issues quickly.

Performance dashboards

Use performance monitoring tools to visualize your applications' performance during and after deployments. These dashboards can provide insights into application health, user experience, and any regressions introduced by new builds.

Real-time monitoring of builds and test execution is essential for maintaining the quality and reliability of software delivery in CI/CD pipelines. By leveraging built-in CI/CD dashboards, third-party monitoring tools, alert systems, and live log streaming, teams can gain immediate insights into the state of their builds. Implementing these tools and techniques enhances visibility and enables quicker responses to issues, ultimately leading to more efficient and reliable software development processes.

Post-execution reporting

Post-execution reporting is vital to the CI/CD process, providing teams with actionable insights into build and test outcomes. Effective reports help identify issues, track progress, and maintain the overall health of the codebase. Therefore, generating impactful post-execution reports is important. The following are some reports that should be gathered based on metrics gathered during the CI/CS process:

- **Build and test summary reports:** Create comprehensive summary reports that include:
  - o **Build status**: Indicate whether the build was successful or failed and the reason for failure.
  - o **Test results**: Summarize the number of tests run, passed, failed, and skipped. Include details on failed tests, such as error messages and stack traces.
  - o **Duration metrics:** Show how long the build and tests took to execute, helping to identify any performance issues.
- **Detailed failure reports:** Generate detailed reports for failed builds and tests that include:
  - o **Error logs:** Capture and present relevant error logs or output from the CI/CD tool to facilitate debugging.
  - o **Screenshots or artifacts:** Attach screenshots or other artifacts (for example, logs, reports) from failed tests to provide context for failures.
  - o **Regression information:** Highlight any regressions or changes compared to the last successful build, allowing teams to quickly assess what might have caused the failure.
- **Trends and historical data:** Include historical data and trends in reports to show:
  - o **Build and test success rates:** Track success rates over time to identify patterns or persistent issues.
  - o **Code coverage changes**: Monitor changes in code coverage to ensure that new code is adequately tested.
  - o **Performance trends:** Analyze build times and test execution times to identify areas for optimization.
- **Actionable insights and recommendations:** Provide clear recommendations based on the data presented in the reports. For example:

    o   Suggest refactoring flaky tests that frequently fail.

    o   Recommend increasing test coverage for critical components of the application.

    o   Highlight any potential bottlenecks in the CI/CD process based on build or test duration.

- **Key insights on the health of the codebase**:

    o   **Code quality metrics:** Include metrics related to code quality, such as:

        ■   **Static code analysis results:** Summarize findings from tools like SonarQube or ESLint that identify code smells, vulnerabilities, and maintainability issues.

        ■   **Cyclomatic complexity:** Highlight areas of the code that may be overly complex and suggest refactoring.

- **Dependency health:** Monitor the health of external dependencies and libraries. Include insights such as:

    o   **Outdated dependencies:** List any outdated libraries and recommend updates to mitigate security risks and improve performance.

    o   **License compliance:** Ensure that all dependencies comply with licensing requirements.

- **User feedback and bug tracking**: Integrate feedback from users or bug-tracking systems to provide a holistic view of code health. Including:

    o   **User reports:** Summarize feedback from users regarding recent releases, including any critical bugs or feature requests.

    o   **Bug trends:** Analyze trends in reported bugs to identify areas of the codebase that may require additional testing or attention.

- **Custom reporting dashboards:** Create custom dashboards using tools like Grafana or Kibana to visualize, build, and test data in real time. These dashboards can provide interactive insights into code health and CI/CD performance.

Post-execution reporting is essential for maintaining visibility into build and test outcomes, providing actionable insights that help teams improve the quality of their codebase. By generating detailed failure reports, tracking trends, and including key quality metrics, teams can quickly identify issues and make informed decisions. Utilizing automated reporting tools and integrating reporting features within CI/CD platforms enhances the efficiency and effectiveness of the reporting process, ultimately leading to better software quality and faster delivery cycles.

Conclusion

In the fast-paced world of software development, CI and CD have become indispensable practices for achieving high-quality, rapid releases. The integration of CI/CD processes streamlines test automation and enhances collaboration among development, testing, and operations teams.

CI/CD integration is essential for achieving efficient, reliable, and high-quality software delivery. By emphasizing the importance of quality gates, leveraging automation, and adopting tool-agnostic strategies, organizations can streamline their development processes and foster a culture of quality. Adhering to best practices ensures that CI/CD pipelines remain robust and adaptable, ultimately leading to faster releases and enhanced software quality.

Now that we have looked at ideal practices for building quality into the CI/CD pipelines, we will next look at how the test frameworks can be further enhanced to cater to more complicated asynchronous and distributed systems.

Key takeaways

CI/CD integration facilitates the automation of testing, ensuring that tests are executed consistently and efficiently throughout the development lifecycle. This integration provides several benefits:

- **Rapid feedback:** Automated tests are triggered automatically with each code change, enabling teams to detect issues early and make timely adjustments.

- **Continuous improvement:** Regularly executed tests contribute to a culture of continuous improvement, as teams can address bugs and improve code quality iteratively.

- **Efficiency gains:** Automation minimizes manual testing efforts, allowing teams to focus on higher-value tasks, such as feature development and user experience enhancements.

Importance of quality gates and automation integration

Quality gates play a critical role in maintaining the integrity of the codebase and ensuring that only high-quality code is deployed. Key takeaways include:

- **Quality assurance:** Quality gates provide defined criteria that must be met for builds to succeed, helping to catch regressions and prevent problematic code from being released.

- **Automated testing:** Integrating automated tests within the CI/CD pipeline allows for consistent enforcement of quality gates, leading to improved code quality and faster identification of issues.

- **Tool-agnostic strategies:** Employing tool-agnostic strategies ensures that test automation frameworks can integrate seamlessly with various CI/CD tools, providing flexibility and reducing vendor lock-in.

Best practices for seamless CI/CD integration

To ensure successful CI/CD integration across different tools and environments while maintaining a focus on speed, stability, and quality, consider the following best practices:

- **Modular configuration:** Create modular and reusable CI/CD configurations that can easily adapt to different environments and tools. This approach promotes consistency and reduces the complexity of managing multiple configurations.

- **Test execution strategies:** Implement strategies like parallelization and selective test execution to optimize test runs, achieving faster feedback without sacrificing thoroughness.

- **Continuous monitoring:** Establish real-time monitoring of builds and test executions to provide immediate visibility into the health of the CI/CD pipeline. This allows teams to respond promptly to any issues that arise.

- **Post-execution reporting:** Generate actionable post-execution reports that highlight key insights, build failures, and test results. These reports should focus on delivering value by helping teams make informed decisions.

Exercises

1. How frequently do you deploy changes to production?

2. Do you have automated unit, integration, and end-to-end tests running in the pipeline? If so, at which stages?

3. Are there any manual approval steps before a release can proceed? If so, what criteria must be met?

4. Do you enforce static code analysis, security scans, or dependency checks as part of your pipeline? If so, what thresholds or benchmarks must be met for tests, code coverage, or performance before a build is promoted?

5. How do you handle secret management and avoid exposing sensitive data in the pipeline?

6. Are compliance or regulatory checks automated in the pipeline? If so, how are they enforced?

7. Do you include performance and load testing in your pipeline? If so, at which stage?

8. How do you monitor the health of deployments after they reach production?

9. Do you have rollback strategies in place if deployment fails?

10. How do you track pipeline failures and identify bottlenecks?

11. Do you collect and analyze CI/CD pipeline metrics such as build success rates, deployment frequency, or MTTR?

12. How do you ensure that new features in your pipeline do not introduce regressions or increase technical debt?

Join our Discord space

Join our Discord workspace for latest updates, offers, tech happenings around the world, new releases, and sessions with the authors:

https://discord.bpbonline.com

## CHAPTER 9

Handling Asynchronous and Distributed Systems

Introduction

We have already uncovered several key testing and automation principles that should apply to most applications. The demand for accelerated development cycles is driving the shift toward modular, maintainable, and more compact applications. This shift introduces added complexity, as testing must now address broader, distributed, and asynchronous communication. Given the intricacy and importance of this aspect, it warrants a dedicated chapter to explore its challenges and role in ensuring the success of modern test automation efforts.

In this chapter, we will explore the significance of asynchronous systems in modern software development and the challenges they introduce to testing. Many companies struggle to balance modularity with tightly coupled dependencies, making it difficult to adopt modern software design principles. As a result, some organizations abandon these practices due to the complexity of addressing related testing challenges.

However, these challenges also present valuable opportunities for test automation frameworks to integrate these design principles. By doing so, they can better support distributed and microservices architectures while maintaining confidence in end-to-end testing approaches.

Structure

In this chapter, we will go over the following topics:

- Asynchronous systems
- Distributed systems
- Rise of microservices, event-driven architectures, and cloud-native applications
- Challenges of testing asynchronous and distributed systems
- Testing microservices
- Challenges in event-driven architectures
- Communication patterns in microservices
- Techniques for testing distributed systems

- Contract testing
- Strategies for testing performance and scalability
- Managing dependencies and orchestration in complex environments
- Handling failures and recovery in distributed systems
- Chaos engineering principles
- Monitoring and observability in testing distributed systems
- Design for testability in distributed systems
- Handling flaky tests in distributed systems

Objectives

By the end of this chapter, we will understand how distributed systems operate and the benefits/challenges they introduce to the software testing space. You will also learn concepts like contract testing and chaos engineering, and how different testing approaches like this can better equip teams for microservices testing.

Asynchronous systems

Asynchronous systems are designed to allow components to operate independently and concurrently, enabling them to perform tasks without waiting for others to complete. In such systems, components communicate primarily through messaging or events. This design promotes flexibility and scalability, as different parts of the system can be developed, deployed, and scaled independently. Refer to the following figure:

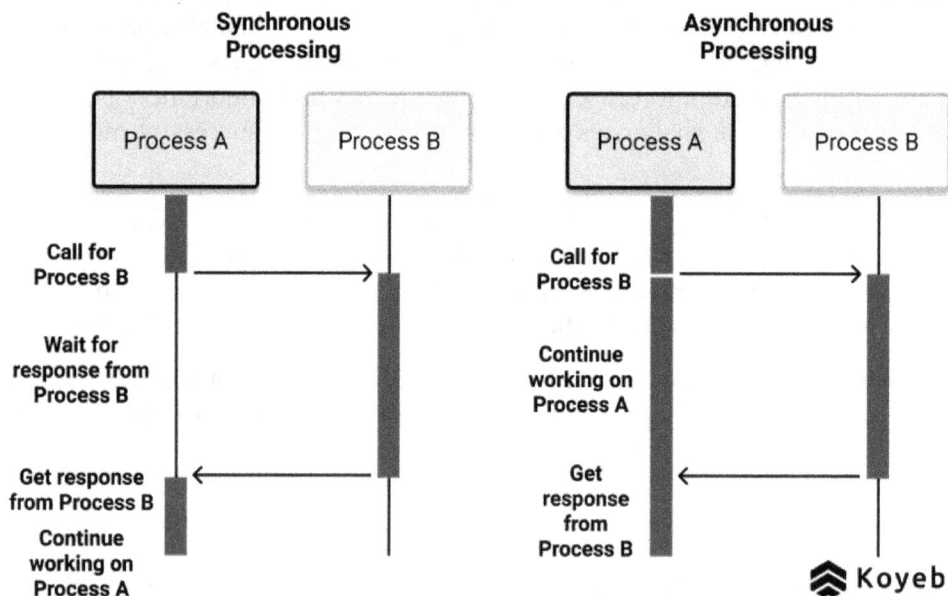

Figure 9.1: Showcase of the differences between synchronous and asynchronous communication

The key characteristics of asynchronous systems include:

- **Non-blocking communication:** Components send messages or events and continue their processing without waiting for a response, allowing for better resource utilization and responsiveness.

- **Loose coupling:** Components interact through well-defined interfaces, reducing dependencies and making it easier to modify or replace individual components.

- **Event-driven architecture:** Systems can respond to events dynamically, enabling real-time processing and enhanced user experiences.

Distributed systems

Distributed systems consist of multiple independent components (or services) that interact over a network. These systems are characterized by their decentralized nature, where no single entity controls the entire system. Each component can reside on different machines, in the cloud, or even on different public cloud providers distant from one another. Refer to the following figure:

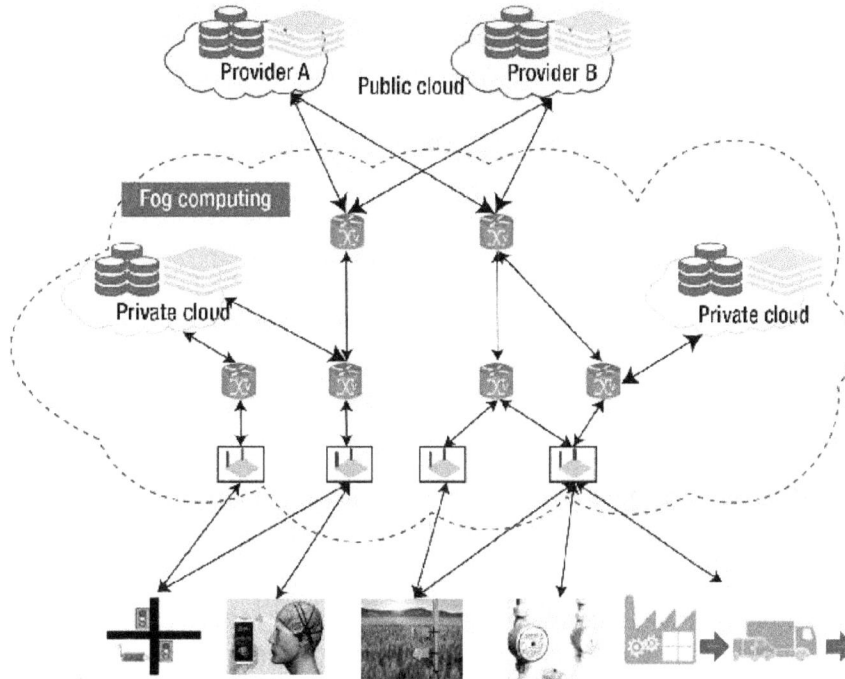

Figure 9.2: A distributed system across the internet and different types of devices

The key aspects of distributed systems include:

- **Resource sharing:** Distributed systems leverage resources from multiple nodes, enabling efficient processing and storage.

- **Scalability:** These systems can scale horizontally by adding more nodes to handle increased load, which is often more cost-effective than vertical scaling.

- **Fault tolerance:** Distributed systems can continue to function even when individual components fail, as other components can take over the work.

Rise of microservices, event-driven architectures, and cloud-native applications

The most common types of distributed and asynchronous systems are cloud-native applications that often tend to follow a microservice or **event-driven architecture** (**EDA**). The increasing adoption of these types of applications has significantly impacted the design and complexity of asynchronous and distributed systems. We will now explain how they work before discussing the testing element in more detail:

- **Microservices:** This architectural style breaks down applications into small, independently deployable services. Each service focuses on a specific business capability, allowing teams to work on different services simultaneously. While microservices promote flexibility and scalability, they also introduce challenges in service orchestration, data consistency, and network latency, complicating testing and integration.

- **EDA:** In an EDA, components communicate by emitting and responding to events. This model enhances responsiveness and decouples services, but can create challenges in tracking the flow of events and managing state across distributed components. Testing in such environments requires new strategies to simulate events and verify the correct handling of asynchronous operations.

- **Cloud-native applications:** Designed to leverage cloud computing, cloud-native applications are typically built using microservices and are designed for dynamic environments. They utilize containerization and orchestration tools (like Kubernetes) to manage deployments. The complexity of cloud-native applications comes from managing state, scaling services dynamically, and ensuring resilient communication between distributed components.

Challenges of testing asynchronous and distributed systems

Testing asynchronous and distributed systems presents a unique set of challenges due to their inherent complexities. The following points outline the key difficulties faced in these environments:

- **Reliance on non-blocking communication:** Asynchronous systems often rely on non-blocking communication, allowing components to operate independently and simultaneously. This introduces several challenges:

  o **Timing issues:** The non-deterministic nature of asynchronous communication can lead to timing issues. Events may be processed in unpredictable orders, making it difficult to reproduce specific scenarios during testing.

  o **Race conditions:** Parallel processing can result in race conditions, where multiple components attempt to access shared resources simultaneously, potentially leading to inconsistent states or unexpected behaviors.

  o **Event handling:** Verifying that components correctly handle events, including edge cases and error conditions, requires robust testing strategies. The complexity of event flows can make it challenging to ensure all possible interactions are covered.

- **Dealing with failures, delays, retries, and timeouts:** While they may be designed to be more resilient and scalable, distributed systems are inherently susceptible to various failure modes, including network latency, service outages, and component failures. Testing must account for these unpredictable conditions:

  o **Failure scenarios:** Simulating failures (for example, service unavailability or network partitioning) is crucial to test how the system behaves under stress. This includes validating retries and fallback mechanisms, ensuring they function correctly when components are down.

  o **Delay handling:** Network delays can affect communication between services. Testing must evaluate how the system handles delays and whether it can recover gracefully from slow responses.

  o **Timeout management:** Implementing and testing appropriate timeout settings is vital to prevent components from waiting indefinitely for responses, which could lead to resource exhaustion or cascading failures.

- **Managing distributed state and ensuring data consistency:** In distributed systems, managing state across multiple components adds another layer of complexity:

  o **State management:** Each service may maintain its state, making it challenging to track and validate the overall system state. Testing must ensure that state transitions occur as expected across distributed components.

o **Data consistency:** Ensuring data consistency is particularly difficult in systems that adopt eventual consistency models. Testing must account for scenarios where data updates may not be immediately visible across all services, which can lead to discrepancies and errors.

o **Eventual consistency testing:** Validating eventual consistency requires testing strategies that allow for time and potential delays. Ensuring that all components eventually converge to a consistent state involves creating test cases that simulate various timing and interaction patterns.

Testing asynchronous and distributed systems presents significant challenges due to the complexities of asynchronous communication, parallel processing, failure handling, and data consistency. Organizations must adopt innovative testing strategies and tools to effectively manage these challenges, ensuring that systems are robust, resilient, and capable of delivering consistent performance in real-world scenarios. This may involve using simulation tools, automated testing frameworks, and comprehensive monitoring to verify the behavior of distributed components under diverse conditions.

Testing microservices

Now that we have looked at some of the challenges involved with these systems, let us look at how to test them to solve these challenges.

Microservices architecture is an approach to software development that structures an application as a collection of small, independent services. Each service focuses on a specific business capability and can be developed, deployed, and scaled independently. This modularity promotes flexibility, faster development cycles, and easier maintenance. However, it also introduces a range of challenges in testing, as outlined.

Challenges in testing microservices

The challenges in testing microservices are as follows:

- **Testing in isolation:** A crucial aspect of testing microservices is achieving high test coverage for the microservice's operations in isolation while ensuring it can be effectively tested with its dependencies, all while maintaining its independence.

- **Independent deployment:** Each microservice can be developed and deployed independently, which means that testing must be conducted in isolation to ensure that each service functions correctly on its own. This requires setting up test environments that accurately reflect the individual service's functionality without relying on other services.

- **Mocking dependencies:** Since microservices often depend on one another, testing a service in isolation requires mocking or stubbing dependencies. This can lead to incomplete tests if the mocks do not accurately represent the behavior of the real services.

Service-to-service communication

An essential aspect of isolation testing is establishing contracts and communication patterns that enable services to interact independently and asynchronously, as explained:

- **API contracts:** Microservices typically communicate through well-defined APIs. Testing these API contracts to ensure that services can interact as intended is crucial. Changes in one service's API can have ripple effects on other services, so thorough testing is required to catch any issues early.

- **Network resilience:** Asynchronous communication between services can lead to unpredictable behavior, especially in scenarios involving network latency or failures. Testing must simulate these conditions to ensure that services can handle communication issues gracefully.

The following figure provides an example of service-to-service communication in a checkout-aggregator solution:

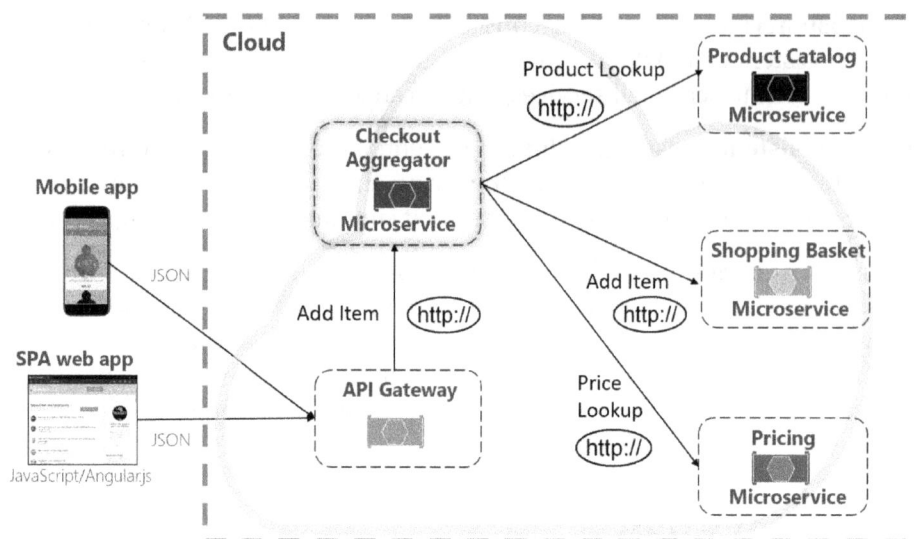

Figure 9.3: Example of service-to-service communication in a checkout aggregator solution

Testing as part of a larger system

While the primary focus of microservice testing is on its operation in isolation from the broader system, it must also function as an integral part of the overall system. This necessitates incorporating traditional integration and end-to-end testing alongside isolated testing, which can be explained as follows:

- **Integration testing:** While isolated testing is essential, integration testing is equally important to verify that the services work together as expected. This involves testing service interactions and ensuring that data flows correctly through the system.

- **End-to-end testing:** Testing the complete workflow of an application requires testing all microservices as a cohesive unit. This adds complexity as it necessitates coordinating multiple services and managing their dependencies, which can lead to challenges in setting up test environments and executing tests.

Data consistency and flow

One of the challenges in integrated testing is managing the sharing of data between services, which is explained as follows:

- **Data sharing**: Microservices often share data, and ensuring consistency across services is critical. Testing must verify that data changes in one service are accurately reflected in others, which is especially challenging in systems that use eventual consistency models.

- **Event-driven communication:** In EDAs, testing must include the validation of events emitted by one service and consumed by others. Ensuring that events trigger the expected behaviors in subscriber services is vital for maintaining system integrity.

Testing microservices presents unique challenges due to the architecture's inherent complexities, such as the need to test services in isolation and as part of a larger system. Emphasizing the interactions between services, including service-to-service communication and APIs, is crucial for ensuring that microservices function correctly both independently and collectively.

Challenges in event-driven architectures

Event-driven communication is seen as a large part of making microservices work. So, it is important to under some of the challenges related to this architectural pattern as well.

EDA are designed to enable services to communicate through asynchronous events, facilitating decoupled interactions between components. While this approach provides numerous benefits, including increased scalability and responsiveness, it also introduces significant challenges in testing.

Complexity of asynchronous communication

In an EDA, services communicate using mechanisms like message queues (for example, RabbitMQ, Kafka) to publish and subscribe to events. This asynchronous nature complicates testing in several ways:

- **Decoupling of components:** Services operate independently, making it challenging to test them in conjunction with others. Each service must be able to send and receive events without requiring the immediate presence of other services, complicating integration testing.

- **Event-driven flow:** The non-linear flow of events requires testing strategies that can account for various event sequences and the conditions under which events are triggered. This adds complexity to test case design and execution.

Testing event producers and consumers independently

When working with event-driven systems, it is essential to independently test both event producers (the services that emit events) and consumers (the services that listen for and process those events). Key challenges include:

- **Mocking event interfaces:** When testing producers, it is often necessary to mock the event-handling interfaces of consumers. This can lead to incomplete tests if the mocks do not accurately simulate the behavior of real consumers.

- **Verifying event processing:** For consumer testing, ensuring that events are processed correctly can be challenging. Tests must verify that consumers correctly handle various event payloads, including error conditions, and maintain the expected state in the system.

Dealing with real-time events and message ordering

EDAs often handle real-time data and events, presenting unique challenges:

- **Message ordering:** In systems where the order of events is significant, testing must ensure that events are processed in the correct sequence. This can be particularly challenging in distributed environments where messages may arrive out of order due to network latency or failures.

- **Real-time processing:** Testing real-time event processing requires simulating the timing and volume of events that services will encounter in production. This includes stress testing to assess how well the system handles high event throughput and ensuring that processing latency meets performance expectations.

Event-driven failures

Failure scenarios in EDAs can be complex, making them difficult to test:

- **Failure handling:** Services must be capable of handling failures gracefully, such as when an event consumer crashes while processing an event. Testing must verify that systems can recover from these failures without losing events or compromising data integrity.

- **Idempotency:** Events may be delivered multiple times due to retries or failures in processing. Testing must ensure that consumers handle duplicate events correctly without causing unintended side effects, requiring careful design of consumer logic.

Testing in EDAs introduces several challenges, including the complexity of asynchronous communication, the need to test producers and consumers independently, and the difficulties posed by real-time events and message ordering.

Communication patterns in microservices

In microservices architectures, various communication patterns dictate how services interact with each other. Understanding and testing these patterns is crucial for ensuring system reliability and performance. The primary communication patterns include request-response, publish-subscribe, and fire-and-forget. Each pattern presents unique challenges and testing strategies.

Testing communication patterns between services

Let us now learn more about testing.

Request-response pattern

In this synchronous pattern, a service (the client) sends a request to another service (the server) and waits for a response before proceeding. This is commonly used in RESTful APIs.

Testing strategies:

- **Unit testing:** Verify that the client sends the correct request and that the server processes the request accurately, returning the expected response.

- **Integration testing:** Test the complete interaction between client and server, ensuring that the request and response cycle functions correctly under various scenarios, including error handling.

- **Load testing:** Assess how the system handles multiple concurrent request-response interactions, identifying bottlenecks and performance issues.

Publish-subscribe pattern

In this asynchronous pattern, services emit events (publish) without waiting for responses, while other services listen to these events (subscribe) and react accordingly. This decouples services and enhances scalability.

Testing strategies:

- **Event contract testing:** Verify that published events adhere to predefined contracts, ensuring subscribers can correctly interpret the event data.

- **Consumer testing:** Validate that subscribers correctly process events, including edge cases where events may contain unexpected or malformed data.

- **End-to-end testing:** Simulate the entire event flow, from publication to consumption, to ensure that events propagate through the system as intended.

Fire-and-forget pattern

In this asynchronous pattern, a service sends an event or message and does not wait for a response. This approach is often used for logging, notifications, or background processing.

Testing strategies:

- **Simulated load testing:** Evaluate how the system behaves under high volumes of fire-and-forget messages, ensuring that message queues can handle the load without loss or delay.

- **Failure handling testing:** Assess how the system handles failures in consumers, ensuring that the service sending the message can continue to function without waiting for confirmation.

Strategies for testing synchronous vs. asynchronous calls

Let us now go over the following strategies.

Synchronous calls

Blocking nature: In synchronous calls, the caller waits for the callee to respond, which can introduce latency and impact overall system performance.

Testing strategies:

- **Performance testing:** Measure response times and system performance under various load conditions to identify potential bottlenecks caused by blocking calls.

- **Timeout scenarios:** Test how the system behaves when a synchronous call times out, ensuring proper error handling and recovery mechanisms are in place.

Asynchronous calls

Non-blocking nature: In asynchronous calls, the caller does not wait for a response, allowing for parallel processing and improved responsiveness.

Testing strategies:

- **Event flow testing:** Verify that events are published, processed, and responded to in the correct order, especially when dealing with multiple services.

- **State management testing:** Assess how the system maintains state during asynchronous processing, ensuring that all components converge to a consistent state after events are handled.

Understanding the impact on the overall system

Synchronous vs. asynchronous trade-offs: Each communication pattern and call type has trade-offs. Synchronous calls simplify testing but can introduce latency, while asynchronous calls enhance responsiveness but complicate testing and require careful handling of event flows and states.

System architecture considerations: Understanding the chosen communication patterns is crucial for designing an architecture that meets performance and scalability requirements. Testing strategies should align with these patterns to ensure the system functions reliably under real-world conditions.

Testing the various communication patterns in microservices, request-response, publish-subscribe, and fire-and-forget, requires tailored strategies that consider each pattern's specific challenges. Organizations can ensure their microservices architectures' reliability, performance, and scalability by implementing robust testing practices for synchronous and asynchronous calls.

Techniques for testing distributed systems

Now that we have looked at some of the challenges around testing microservices, their EDA, and the different communication patterns required, let us look at testing in more detail.

Isolated testing vs. end-to-end testing

In microservices architectures, testing is a critical phase in the development process to ensure that both individual components and the entire system function as intended. This involves two primary testing strategies: isolated testing and end-to-end testing. Each serves a different purpose and addresses specific challenges in the software development lifecycle.

Importance of isolated testing

Isolated testing focuses on verifying the functionality of individual services or components without the influence of external dependencies. This approach typically involves unit tests and integration tests. We have already discussed these topics in previous chapters, but we will unpack them again here in terms of how they apply to the topic of distributed systems.

Unit testing: Unit tests validate the smallest parts of an application (for example, functions or classes) in isolation. They ensure that each component behaves as expected and catch bugs early in the development process. The benefits are:

- Fast execution, allowing for quick feedback.
- Easier to pinpoint the source of failures.
- Encourages modular design and promotes code quality.

Integration testing: Integration tests verify the interactions between different components or services, ensuring they work together as intended. While integration tests do not cover the entire system, they help confirm that communication between service functions is correct. The benefits are:

- Identifies issues related to data formats, communication protocols, and external dependencies.
- Helps catch integration-related bugs before deploying to production.
- Isolated testing is crucial for ensuring that each component is robust and reliable, laying the foundation for a stable system.

Balancing the need for both isolated and end-to-end testing

Finding the right balance between isolated testing and end-to-end testing is crucial for an effective testing strategy:

- **Complementary approaches:** Isolated testing provides quick feedback and ensures that individual components function correctly, while end-to-end testing validates the entire system's behavior. Together, they create a comprehensive testing strategy.

- **Resource management:** End-to-end tests are often more resource-intensive and time-consuming than isolated tests. Therefore, they should be used judiciously to avoid slowing down the development cycle.

- **Prioritize critical paths:** Focus end-to-end testing efforts on critical user paths and high-risk areas of the application while relying on isolated tests for most functionality.

- **Continuous feedback loop:** Utilize CI/CD pipelines to integrate both types of testing, providing a continuous feedback loop that helps identify issues early and ensures that the application remains stable as changes are made.

Isolated testing and end-to-end testing are both essential components of a robust testing strategy in microservices architectures. Isolated testing ensures that individual services function correctly, while end-to-end testing validates the overall system's behavior. Balancing these approaches allows organizations to maintain code quality, reduce the risk of failures, and deliver reliable software that meets user needs. By implementing a comprehensive testing strategy that leverages both isolated and end-to-end testing, teams can enhance their development processes and ensure a seamless user experience.

Contract testing

Contract testing is a testing methodology designed to validate interactions between services, ensuring that service interfaces behave as expected without requiring full system integration. This approach is particularly useful in microservices architectures, where services are often developed and deployed independently.

Introduction to contract testing

Contract testing focuses on the agreements (or contracts) made between service providers (those that offer services) and service consumers (those that consume services). A contract defines the expectations around service interactions, including:

- **Request format:** The structure and content of requests that a service expects to receive.

- **Response format:** The expected structure and content of responses that a service provides.

- **Behavioral expectations:** The expected behavior of services under various conditions, such as handling error scenarios or specific data formats.

By validating these contracts, organizations can ensure that changes in one service do not break the functionality of dependent services, reducing integration issues and enhancing overall system reliability.

Ensuring expected behavior without full system integration

One of the key benefits of contract testing is that it allows teams to verify service interactions independently without requiring the entire system to be integrated. This has several advantages:

- **Early feedback:** Contract tests can be executed alongside unit and integration tests, providing early feedback on interface changes and ensuring that services meet their contractual obligations.

- **Decoupled development:** Teams can develop and test services independently, reducing the need for coordinated release schedules. As long as the contract is honored, changes can be made without risking the integrity of dependent services.

- **Reduced integration overhead:** By validating contracts before integration, teams can avoid many common integration issues, leading to smoother deployment processes and faster development cycles.

Tools and libraries supporting contract testing

Several tools and libraries facilitate contract testing, helping teams implement and maintain contracts between services effectively. Some of them are:

- **Pact:** Pact is a popular framework for contract testing that supports consumer-driven contracts. It allows developers to define contracts for interactions simply and expressively. Pact works by generating a contract file from the consumer's perspective, which the provider then uses to validate its implementation. This process helps ensure that the provider adheres to the expectations set by the consumer.

- **Spring Cloud Contract:** Spring Cloud Contract is a Spring ecosystem project that supports contract testing. It allows developers to define contracts in a Groovy DSL or YAML, which can be automatically converted into tests for both consumers and providers. It integrates seamlessly with Spring applications, enabling teams to validate service interactions in a consistent manner.

- **Postman:** While primarily an API testing tool, Postman can also be used for contract testing. Users can define collections that outline expected request and response formats, ensuring that services adhere to specified contracts during development.

- **Pactflow:** Pactflow is a hosted service for managing contracts and integrations. It provides a centralized contract repository, enabling teams to collaborate more effectively and manage versioning, security, and documentation for contracts across services.

Contract testing is a vital methodology in modern software development, especially within microservices architectures. By validating interactions between services without requiring full system integration, contract testing helps ensure that service interfaces behave as expected, minimizing the risk of integration issues and promoting smoother development cycles.

Testing asynchronous workflows

Asynchronous workflows are integral to modern applications, particularly in microservices and event-driven architectures, where services communicate through events or messages without waiting for immediate responses. While this approach enhances responsiveness and scalability, it also presents unique challenges in testing. Here are techniques and best practices for effectively testing asynchronous workflows:

- **Waiting for events or messages:** When testing asynchronous systems, one of the primary challenges is ensuring that the system correctly processes events or messages after they are published or sent. Techniques to manage this include:

  o **Polling:** Implement polling mechanisms in tests to repeatedly check for expected events or messages. This can be useful for verifying that events have been emitted or that specific actions have occurred.

  o **Event listeners:** Utilize event listeners to capture emitted events within the test environment. This allows tests to verify that the appropriate events are triggered in response to specific actions or inputs.

  o **Timeouts:** Set reasonable timeouts for waiting for events. This prevents tests from running indefinitely and provides clear failure messages if the expected events are not observed within the specified timeframe.

- **Using mocks and stubs:** Mocks and stubs are essential tools in testing asynchronous systems, enabling developers to simulate the behavior of services or message queues:

  o **Mocks:** Mocks can be used to simulate the behavior of dependent services, allowing tests to verify how a service interacts with its dependencies without relying on the actual implementations. For example, a mock service can simulate an external API's response or a queue's behavior.

  o **Stubs:** Stubs provide predefined responses to calls made during tests. They can simulate specific scenarios, such as returning error codes or success responses, allowing developers to test how the system handles various outcomes.

  o **Frameworks**: Tools like Mockito (for Java), Sinon (for JavaScript), and others provide extensive support for creating mocks and stubs, making it easier to isolate components and test their interactions effectively.

- **Dealing with eventual consistency:** In asynchronous systems, achieving immediate consistency can be challenging. Eventual consistency means that the system guarantees that, given enough time, all updates will propagate and all nodes will converge to the same state. Testing for data correctness in such scenarios involves:

  o **State validation:** Validate the final state of the system after a series of events have been processed. This often involves checking that data is consistent across different services or components and that it meets the expected criteria.

  o **Data snapshots:** Capture snapshots of the data at various points in time during the workflow. This helps ensure that the system is progressing towards the expected final state.

  o **Retry mechanisms:** Implement retry logic in tests to handle transient failures or delays. If an expected event or data state is not achieved, retrying the operation can help validate eventual consistency.

  o **Assertions with delays:** In tests, use assertions with a delay mechanism to check for data correctness over time. This allows the test to wait for a brief period to allow the asynchronous processes to complete before validating the state.

Testing asynchronous workflows requires a unique set of techniques and strategies to manage the inherent complexities of asynchronous communication. Organizations can ensure that their systems function reliably under asynchronous conditions by employing techniques for waiting on events, utilizing mocks and stubs to simulate the behavior, and addressing the challenges of eventual consistency.

Latency and performance testing

Latency and performance testing are crucial for ensuring that distributed systems can handle varying loads and maintain responsiveness under different conditions. Given the nature of distributed architectures, it is essential to simulate real-world scenarios, including network latency, message delays, and system failures. This write-up discusses strategies for testing the performance and scalability of distributed systems, along with the use of load testing tools.

Strategies for testing performance and scalability

There can be a lot of complexities that can affect distributed systems. As such, here are some strategies that can help with this against these different challenges:

- **Simulating network latency:**

  o **Network emulators:** Use network emulators to introduce artificial latency into the system. Tools like Clumsy or Network Link Conditioner can simulate different network conditions, allowing teams to observe how their systems respond to latency.

  o **Environment configuration:** Adjust configuration settings in test environments to replicate real-world network conditions, including bandwidth limitations and packet loss. This helps in assessing how the system behaves when faced with network-related issues.

- **Introducing message delays:**

  o **Delay injection:** Implement delay injection mechanisms in the message brokers or services to simulate message processing delays. This can be done by configuring the message queue settings (for example, RabbitMQ or Kafka) to introduce processing delays or using middleware to enforce delays.

  o **Asynchronous task testing:** In asynchronous workflows, explicitly introduce delays in the execution of tasks or events to evaluate how the system manages delayed operations and eventual consistency.

- **Simulating system failures:**

  o **Chaos engineering:** Adopt chaos engineering principles by intentionally introducing failures in the system to test its resilience. Tools like Chaos Monkey can be used to terminate instances, simulate network outages, or introduce high latency in certain components, helping teams understand how the system behaves under stress.

  o **Error injection:** Simulate errors by modifying response statuses from dependent services. For example, return 500 error codes or timeouts from mocked services to observe how the system handles such scenarios.

- **Best practices for latency and performance testing:**

  o **Define clear objectives:** Establish performance goals and **service level agreements (SLA)** to guide testing efforts. This includes defining acceptable latency thresholds and expected throughput.

  o **Test in production-like environments:** Whenever possible, conduct tests in environments that closely mimic production to get accurate results. This includes using similar hardware, configurations, and network settings.

  o **Analyze and optimize:** After conducting load tests, analyze the results to identify bottlenecks or performance issues. Use profiling tools to investigate areas of high resource usage or long response times and optimize accordingly.

o **Monitor resource utilization:** Keep track of system resources (such as CPU, memory, disk I/O) during tests to understand how the system scales and where limitations may occur.

Latency and performance testing are vital for ensuring that distributed systems can handle high loads and respond effectively under various conditions. Implementing these practices will lead to robust, resilient applications that can meet user expectations and perform reliably in real-world scenarios.

Managing dependencies and orchestration in complex environments

In distributed systems, services often rely on one another to function properly. These service dependencies can significantly impact the testing process, making it essential for teams to understand and manage them effectively. This write-up explores the nature of service dependencies, techniques for isolating them during testing, and strategies for managing external dependencies.

Understanding the impact of service dependencies

In a microservices architecture, services typically communicate over a network and rely on one another for data and functionality. Each service may consume APIs from other services, access shared databases, or integrate with third-party systems. The challenges are:

- **Cascading failures:** A failure in one service can lead to cascading failures in dependent services, complicating debugging and testing efforts.

- **Increased complexity:** The interconnected nature of services introduces complexity, making it difficult to test individual components in isolation.

- **Variability:** External service behavior may vary due to factors like network latency, downtime, or changes in response formats, leading to unreliable tests.

We have already discussed many different testing techniques that can solve these dependencies, but the orchestration of the different testing techniques is essential in applying any testing technique.

Orchestration and choreography testing

In distributed systems, the patterns of orchestration and choreography determine how services interact and collaborate to complete tasks. Testing these patterns is essential to ensure that workflows function correctly and reliably. This write-up explores the concepts of orchestration and choreography, along with strategies for testing each pattern.

Testing service orchestration patterns: Orchestration refers to a pattern where a central component or orchestrator coordinates the interactions and actions across multiple services. Workflow engines like Apache Airflow and Camunda are commonly used to manage these orchestrated workflows.

Some testing strategies are as follows:

- **Unit testing:** Test individual orchestration components to verify that they initiate and manage service interactions correctly. This includes checking that the orchestrator handles various inputs and scenarios correctly.

- **Integration testing:** Verify that the orchestrator can communicate with all dependent services as expected. This includes validating the data formats, protocols, and error-handling mechanisms.

- **Mocking dependencies:** Use mocks or stubs to simulate the behavior of services that the orchestrator interacts with. This allows you to focus on testing the orchestration logic without relying on the actual implementations of external services.

Testing service choreography patterns: Choreography refers to a pattern where services operate independently, reacting to events or state changes without a central orchestrator. Each service knows how to respond to events it receives, creating a decentralized approach to workflow management.

Some testing strategies are:

- **Unit testing:** Test each service independently to ensure it responds correctly to incoming events. This includes validating the event handling logic and verifying that the service maintains its state correctly.

- **Contract testing:** Implement contract testing to define and validate the expectations for events and messages between services. This ensures that services adhere to agreed-upon interfaces, reducing the risk of integration issues.

- **Event-driven testing:** Use event-driven testing techniques to simulate event emissions and verify that services react appropriately. This may involve using mocking frameworks or event simulators to generate events and validate responses.

- **Chaos testing:** Apply chaos testing to verify how services handle unexpected failures or network issues. This is particularly important in a choreographed environment, where services must be resilient to changes in state and availability.

Validating complex workflows

Complex workflows often span multiple services or events, making them challenging to test. Here are some strategies for validating these workflows:

- **End-to-end testing:** Conduct end-to-end tests that cover the entire workflow, validating that all services involved collaborate correctly to achieve the desired outcome. This consists in simulating various paths through the workflow, including success and failure scenarios.

- **State verification:** Check the state of the system after the completion of workflows to ensure that all services have reached the expected state. This may include querying databases or service endpoints to confirm that data is consistent and accurate.

- **Monitoring and logging:** Implement monitoring and logging mechanisms to capture the behavior of services during workflow execution. This data can be invaluable for debugging issues and understanding how services interact in real time.

- **Test automation:** Use test automation frameworks to streamline the testing process for complex workflows. Automated tests can help verify that workflows behave correctly over time, especially as changes are made to individual services.

Testing orchestration and choreography patterns is critical for ensuring the reliability and correctness of workflows in distributed systems. By employing various testing strategies, including unit testing, integration testing, and event-driven testing, teams can validate the behavior of orchestrators and services operating independently. Additionally, strategies for validating complex workflows, such as end-to-end testing, state verification, and monitoring, enable teams to maintain robust and resilient systems.

Handling failures and recovery in distributed systems

Due to the complexity and interconnectivity of services in distributed systems, failures are inevitable. Ensuring that the system behaves correctly under failure conditions and has effective recovery mechanisms is crucial for maintaining reliability and user satisfaction. This write-up explores strategies for testing system behavior during failures, techniques for evaluating recovery mechanisms, and the principles of chaos engineering for enhancing resilience.

Testing the system's behavior under failure conditions

When testing distributed systems, it is essential to simulate various failure scenarios to observe how the system responds. Common failure conditions include:

- **Service crashes:** Simulate service crashes to test how the system behaves when one or more services become unavailable. This can involve terminating service instances or introducing random failures during testing.

- **Message loss:** Introduce scenarios where messages sent between services are lost or delayed. This can help evaluate how the system handles missing or out-of-order messages and whether it can recover from them.

- **Partial failures:** Test scenarios where some services function correctly while others do not. This can include verifying that the system continues to operate and provides essential functionality even when some components are experiencing issues.

Some testing strategies are as follows:

- **Unit and integration tests:** Develop unit and integration tests that intentionally induce failure conditions. For example, you can simulate network timeouts or service unavailability to verify that components handle these situations correctly.

- **Failure scenarios in test cases:** Create specific test cases to cover various failure conditions, ensuring that each scenario is tested systematically.

Techniques for testing recovery mechanisms

Effective recovery mechanisms are crucial for maintaining the integrity and availability of distributed systems. Key techniques include:

- **Retries:** Implement retry logic in the system to automatically attempt failed operations. Test this mechanism by inducing transient failures and verifying that the system retries operations as expected. Use configurable parameters (for example, backoff strategies) to control the retry behavior, and test various configurations to understand their impact on performance and success rates.

- **Circuit breakers:** A circuit breaker prevents the system from attempting operations that are likely to fail, allowing it to recover and reduce unnecessary load. Test circuit breaker behavior by simulating failures and observing how it opens and closes under different conditions. Validate that the circuit breaker accurately reflects the health of services and that the fallback mechanisms work as intended when the circuit is open.

- **Compensating transactions:** In distributed systems, especially with eventual consistency, compensating transactions can help reverse the effects of a previous transaction that has failed. Test these mechanisms by inducing failures and ensuring that compensating actions are executed correctly to restore system integrity.

Chaos engineering principles

Chaos engineering involves intentionally introducing failures into a system to test its resilience and fault tolerance. By doing so, organizations can identify weaknesses and improve overall system robustness. Its features are as follows:

- **Controlled failures:** Use chaos engineering tools like Chaos Monkey to introduce controlled failures, such as terminating instances of services or introducing latency. This helps validate the system's behavior under real-world failure conditions. Set up experiments to monitor system performance and response during these controlled failures. This will allow teams to identify potential issues and areas for improvement.

- **Hypothesis-driven testing:** In chaos engineering, hypotheses about how the system should behave under specific failure conditions should be formulated. For example, *If Service A fails, Service B should still function correctly and handle requests from clients.* Conduct experiments to validate or invalidate these hypotheses, using metrics and logging to assess system behavior during failures.

- **Feedback loops:** Establish feedback loops to continuously improve the system based on findings from chaos engineering experiments. Analyze the results of each experiment, identify weaknesses, and implement improvements to enhance fault tolerance.

Handling failures and recovery in distributed systems is critical to ensuring reliability and resilience. Organizations can build robust systems that can withstand real-world challenges by testing the system's behavior under various failure conditions and evaluating recovery mechanisms like retries, circuit breakers, and compensating transactions. Employing chaos engineering principles also allows teams to proactively identify weaknesses and enhance fault tolerance. By adopting these strategies, organizations can deliver high-quality distributed applications that meet user expectations, even in the face of failures.

Monitoring and observability in testing distributed systems

In distributed systems, observability is a crucial aspect that enhances the ability to understand and test complex environments. It encompasses logging, monitoring, and tracing, enabling teams to gain insights into system behavior, identify issues, and ensure that the system functions as intended. This write-up explores the importance of observability in distributed systems and the role of distributed tracing tools in enhancing system testability and performance.

Importance of observability in distributed systems

Observability refers to the ability to measure and analyze the internal states of a system based on its external outputs. In complex, distributed environments, observability helps ensure testability through the following aspects:

- **Improved debugging:** Effective logging and monitoring provide valuable context when diagnosing issues. When a failure occurs, developers can refer to logs and metrics to understand what went wrong, making it easier to identify the root cause of problems.

- **Real-time insights:** Monitoring tools allow teams to observe system performance and behavior in real-time. This enables proactive identification of anomalies and issues before they escalate into significant problems, thus ensuring higher system reliability.

- **Enhanced test coverage:** With better observability, teams can gain insights into how different components interact. This helps identify gaps in test coverage and areas that require additional testing, leading to more robust test strategies.

- **Data-driven decision making:** Observability data provides a foundation for making informed decisions about system changes, optimizations, and scaling efforts. Teams can prioritize improvements effectively by understanding how components perform under load or during failures.

Role of distributed tracing tools

Distributed tracing tools play a critical role in enhancing observability by allowing teams to track requests as they flow through various services. Tools like Jaeger and Zipkin are commonly used for this purpose, offering valuable insights into system performance and behavior. The other functions are:

- **Tracking requests across services:** Distributed tracing enables teams to visualize a request's path as it traverses multiple services. Each segment of the request journey is tracked, providing a clear view of how services interact and where delays or bottlenecks occur.

- **Identifying bottlenecks:** Teams can identify performance bottlenecks in their systems by analyzing traces. If a particular service consistently exhibits latency, it can be flagged for optimization. This data helps teams prioritize performance improvements based on actual usage patterns.

- **Troubleshooting failures:** When a failure occurs, distributed tracing allows teams to trace the request path and pinpoint the service or component responsible for the failure. This accelerates troubleshooting efforts and reduces the time required to resolve issues.

- **Latency analysis:** Distributed tracing tools can provide detailed latency information for each request segment. This granularity allows teams to assess where the most time is spent processing requests, enabling targeted optimizations.

- **Contextual information:** Traces can carry metadata that provides context about the request, such as user identifiers or transaction details. This contextual information enhances the understanding of system behavior and improves the relevance of observability data.

Adding observability to distributed systems is vital for ensuring their reliability and testability. Organizations can gain valuable insights into system behavior and performance by implementing effective logging, monitoring, and tracing strategies. Distributed tracing tools such as Jaeger and Zipkin facilitate tracking requests across services, enabling teams to identify bottlenecks, troubleshoot failures, and enhance overall system performance. Embracing observability improves the ability to test and debug distributed systems and also fosters a culture of continuous improvement and operational excellence.

Using metrics and alerts for testing

In the context of distributed systems, leveraging metrics, logs, and alerts during testing is essential for monitoring system health and behavior under various scenarios. By implementing a robust monitoring strategy, teams can proactively identify issues, assess performance, and ensure the system meets its requirements. This write-up explores how to use metrics and alerts for testing purposes effectively.

Utilizing metrics, logs, and alerts during testing

Metrics are quantitative measurements that provide insights into system performance and behavior. Logs capture detailed information about system events, while alerts notify teams of critical issues that require immediate attention. Together, they form a comprehensive monitoring strategy. Let us now go over the functions:

- **Monitoring system health:**

    o **Performance metrics:** Track KPI such as response times, error rates, throughput, and resource utilization (CPU, memory, and so on). This allows teams to assess the system's behavior under various load conditions and identify performance bottlenecks.

    o **Event logs:** Collect and analyze logs generated by the system during testing. This can include information about requests, errors, state changes, and interactions between services. Logs provide context for understanding the system's behavior and diagnosing issues.

- **Behavior under different scenarios:**

    o **Load testing:** During load testing, monitor metrics to observe how the system performs as traffic increases. Look for thresholds that trigger alerts, such as increased response times or elevated error rates.

    o **Stress testing:** Implement metrics to capture the system's behavior under stress, simulating high loads or failures. Analyze how the system responds to these conditions and use logs to track errors and failures.

o **Regression testing:** Use metrics to compare current performance with historical benchmarks during regression tests. This helps identify any degradation in performance or unexpected behavior resulting from code changes.

Implementing custom alerts

Custom alerts capture performance degradation, errors, or unexpected behaviors in test environments. Here is how to implement them effectively:

- **Defining alert conditions:**

  o **Performance degradation:** Set up alerts for metrics that exceed predefined thresholds. For example, if the average response time for an API exceeds a certain limit, an alert should trigger.

  o **Error rates:** Implement alerts for error rates that exceed acceptable levels. For instance, if the percentage of failed requests rises above a specified threshold, the alert system should notify the team.

  o **Unexpected behaviors:** Define alerts for unexpected behaviors, such as unusual resource utilization spikes or unexpected traffic pattern changes. This can help catch issues early before they escalate.

- **Alerting mechanisms:**

  o **Real-time notifications:** Configure alerts to send real-time notifications through channels such as email, Slack, or other communication platforms. This ensures that the relevant team members are promptly informed of critical issues.

  o **Centralized dashboard:** Use monitoring tools to create a centralized dashboard that visualizes metrics and alerts. This provides a comprehensive view of system health and allows teams to quickly assess the status of their applications.

- **Actionable alerts:** Ensure that alerts are actionable and provide enough context to facilitate quick resolution. For example, instead of simply alerting on high response times, include details about which service is affected and any relevant log entries.

Using metrics and alerts during testing is vital for maintaining the health and performance of distributed systems. By monitoring system behavior and defining custom alerts, teams can proactively identify and address issues, ensuring their applications meet performance requirements. This approach enhances the effectiveness of testing efforts and fosters a culture of continuous improvement, enabling organizations to deliver high-quality software that meets user expectations. A robust monitoring strategy can lead to more resilient systems and improved user experiences.

Best practices for testing asynchronous and distributed systems

We have looked at several approaches to testing distributed systems in this chapter, but we will now look at some of the additional best practices that should be considered to maximize the most out of testing.

Test environment setup

Creating reliable and scalable test environments that closely replicate production is crucial for effective testing in distributed systems. A well-configured test environment allows teams to simulate real-world conditions, identify issues early, and ensure the software meets quality standards before deployment. This write-up provides recommendations for setting up such environments and discusses the role of containerization and orchestration platforms.

Some recommendations for setting up reliable and scalable test environments are as follows:

- **Environment parity:** Ensure that the test environment closely mirrors the production environment in terms of configuration, dependencies, and data. This includes using the same operating systems, libraries, and service versions to minimize discrepancies that could lead to issues in production.

- **IaC:** Utilize IaC tools (for example, Terraform, AWS CloudFormation) to define and provision test environments programmatically. This approach ensures consistency across environments and allows for easy replication and scaling.

- **Data management:**

  o **Test data:** Use realistic test data that mimics production data to test various scenarios, including edge cases. To comply with privacy regulations, avoid using sensitive production data in the test environment.

  o **Data refreshing:** Implement strategies to refresh test data regularly, ensuring that the testing process reflects the latest production conditions. This could involve automated scripts or tools to create or anonymize data.

  o **Isolation and independence:** Create isolated test environments to ensure that testing activities do not interfere with each other or with production systems. This isolation enables parallel testing and reduces the risk of environmental interference.

  o **Scalability:** Design test environments to scale easily in response to varying testing needs. This includes adding more instances or resources when conducting load or performance testing.

  o **CI:** Integrate the test environment setup with CI pipelines to automate the provisioning and configuration of environments for each test run. This ensures that tests are executed in consistent environments and provides immediate feedback on code changes.

Role of containerization and orchestration platforms

Containerization and orchestration platforms play a vital role in creating flexible and reproducible test environments, enhancing the efficiency and reliability of the testing process. Let us now go over them:

- **Containerization (for example, Docker):**

  o **Lightweight isolation:** Containers provide lightweight isolation for applications, allowing multiple instances to run on the same host without conflicts. This is particularly beneficial for testing multiple versions or configurations of a service simultaneously.

  o **Environment consistency:** Docker containers encapsulate all dependencies, libraries, and configurations required to run an application. This ensures that the application behaves the same way in both development and testing environments.

  o **Ease of replication:** With Docker, teams can easily replicate test environments across different machines or stages of development, ensuring consistency and reducing setup time.

- **Orchestration platforms (for example, Kubernetes):**

  o **Scalability and management:** Kubernetes automates containerized applications' deployment, scaling, and management. It can dynamically allocate resources based on load, allowing teams to simulate production-scale scenarios during testing.

  o **Service discovery and load balancing:** Kubernetes provides built-in service discovery and load balancing, essential for testing microservices architectures. This helps replicate production conditions more accurately and tests service interactions effectively.

  o **Environment configuration:** Kubernetes allows for easy configuration of different environments (dev, test, staging, production) through ConfigMaps and Secrets. This simplifies managing environment-specific settings and ensures consistency.

o **Integration with CI/CD pipelines:** Containerization and orchestration tools can be integrated into CI/CD pipelines to automate the setup and teardown of test environments. This enables rapid feedback and facilitates continuous testing throughout the development lifecycle.

Setting up reliable and scalable test environments is crucial for ensuring software quality in distributed systems. Teams can create effective testing conditions by following recommendations for environment parity, infrastructure as code, and effective data management. Containerization (using Docker) and orchestration platforms (with Kubernetes) further enhance this process by providing lightweight, consistent, and easily scalable environments. By leveraging these technologies, organizations can improve their testing practices, leading to higher-quality software and more robust applications in production.

Design for testability in distributed systems

Designing distributed systems with testability in mind is essential for ensuring that applications can be thoroughly and efficiently tested. By incorporating monitoring, logging, and test hooks into the architecture, teams can enhance the ability to validate system behavior. Additionally, ensuring that services are loosely coupled facilitates independent testing, leading to more reliable and maintainable systems. This write-up explores strategies for designing distributed systems for testability.

Building in monitoring, logging, and test hooks

Monitoring and logging are critical components for understanding system behavior and diagnosing issues, while test hooks facilitate testing by allowing specific interactions or observations within the system. Let us go over them now:

- **Monitoring:** Integrate monitoring solutions (for example, Prometheus, Grafana) into the system architecture to provide real-time insights into service performance and health. This enables teams to observe key metrics such as response times, error rates, and resource utilization during testing.

  o Implement health checks for services to provide early warnings about potential issues. These health checks should be easily accessible and configurable, allowing for proactive problem identification.

- **Logging:** Design services to generate detailed logs that capture relevant events, errors, and state changes. Logs should be structured (for example, JSON) to facilitate easier querying and analysis, enabling teams to trace issues back to their source.

  o Ensure that logging levels (for example, DEBUG, INFO, WARN, ERROR) are configurable so that teams can adjust the verbosity of logs based on testing needs without requiring code changes.

- **Test hooks:** Introduce test hooks or APIs that allow interactions with the service during testing. These hooks can enable specific behaviors or expose internal states that facilitate testing without compromising the system's security or integrity.

  o Use dependency injections to provide mock implementations for external services, enabling isolated testing of components without needing to interact with real dependencies.

Ensuring loose coupling for independent testing

Loose coupling between services is essential for enabling independent testing in a distributed system. This can be achieved through the following practices:

- **Service interfaces:** Define clear and stable APIs for each service, ensuring that service interactions are well-documented. This allows teams to test services independently by mocking or stubbing their dependencies during unit and integration testing.

o　Adopt versioning strategies for APIs to ensure backward compatibility. This allows teams to test new features without disrupting existing functionality.

- **Event-driven architecture:** Leverage event-driven architecture where services communicate through events or messages rather than direct calls. This decouples service dependencies, enabling teams to test services independently by simulating events.

    o　Implement message queues (for example, RabbitMQ, Kafka) to facilitate asynchronous communication. This allows for more flexible testing scenarios where services can be tested in isolation while still interacting with the overall system.

Configuration management

Use configuration management tools to externalize service configurations, allowing each service to be independently configured for different testing environments. This ensures that services can be tested in isolation without requiring changes to the codebase.

Mocking and stubbing: Implement mocking and stubbing frameworks to simulate the behavior of dependencies during testing. This enables teams to isolate services and validate their functionality without needing the full system or external services to be present.

Use service virtualization tools to create mock versions of services, allowing for realistic testing scenarios without relying on actual implementations.

Designing distributed systems for testability involves building in monitoring, logging, and test hooks while ensuring that services are loosely coupled. By integrating these elements into the architecture, teams can enhance their ability to test and validate system behavior effectively. Clear service interfaces, event-driven communication, and configuration management contribute to independent testing of services, leading to more maintainable and reliable applications. Ultimately, prioritizing testability in the design phase facilitates smoother testing processes, faster identification of issues, and higher quality software.

Handling flaky tests in distributed systems

We spoke about flaky tests in the previous chapter and how to deal with them in the CI/CD pipelines. Flaky tests are also a common challenge in asynchronous and distributed environments, often arising due to timing issues, transient states, or environmental inconsistencies. These tests can lead to false positives or negatives, undermining confidence in the testing process and complicating continuous integration efforts. This write-up explores strategies for identifying and mitigating flaky tests and best practices for stabilizing them within distributed systems.

Identifying and mitigating flaky tests

The following are repeated examples of some of the basic things that can help identify and mitigate flaky tests in distributed systems:

- **Monitoring test results:** Track test results over time to identify tests that frequently fail without changes to the codebase. Create metrics to monitor the pass/fail rate of individual tests, highlighting those that exhibit flaky behavior.

- **Test logging:** Enhance logging within tests to capture detailed information about test execution, including timings, states, and interactions. This data can help pinpoint the cause of flakiness and identify patterns related to failures.

- **Environment consistency:** Ensure that tests are run in consistent environments. Variability in the environment can lead to flaky tests, so using containers or virtualized environments can help minimize differences.

- **Run tests in isolation:** Execute tests in isolated environments to reduce dependencies on other tests or system states. This can help identify tests that rely on shared resources, which may contribute to flakiness.

- **Mocking and stubbing:** Use mocks or stubs for external services or dependencies to control their behavior during tests. This reduces the influence of unpredictable external factors, such as network latency or availability, which can lead to flaky tests.

Best practices for stabilizing tests

Let us go over some best practices now:

- **Addressing race conditions:**

    o **Explicit synchronization:** Use synchronization mechanisms (for example, locks, semaphores) to manage concurrent access to shared resources. This helps prevent race conditions that can lead to intermittent failures.

    o **Wait strategies:** Implement explicit wait strategies that allow tests to wait for specific conditions to be met before proceeding (for example, waiting for elements to be visible in UI tests or ensuring that data is available in a database). This reduces the likelihood of timing-related issues causing test failures.

- **Handling retries:**

    o **Retry logic:** Implement retry logic for tests that fail due to transient issues, such as temporary network failures or timing-related problems. Use exponential backoff strategies to minimize the load on systems during retries.

    o **Limit retries:** Set a maximum number of retries to avoid masking underlying issues. If a test continues to fail after the specified retries, it should be flagged for review and investigation.

- **Managing test dependencies:**

    o **Decoupling tests:** Aim to decouple tests from each other to minimize dependencies that can lead to flakiness. Each test should be able to run independently without relying on the outcome or state of other tests.

    o **Using test fixtures:** Implement test fixtures to set up and tear down the necessary state for tests consistently. This ensures that tests start from a known state and reduces the chances of state-related issues affecting outcomes.

- **Regular maintenance:**

    o **Refactoring flaky tests:** Regularly review and refactor flaky tests to improve their reliability. This can involve simplifying complex tests, improving the clarity of test logic, or rewriting tests prone to failure.

    o **Continuous monitoring:** Continue to monitor the stability of tests over time, adjusting strategies as needed based on ongoing performance and results.

Handling flaky tests is essential for maintaining confidence in automated testing, especially in asynchronous and distributed environments. By identifying flaky tests through monitoring and logging and implementing strategies to mitigate their occurrence, teams can improve the reliability of their test suites. Best practices such as addressing race conditions, handling retries, managing test dependencies, and conducting regular maintenance contribute to stabilizing tests. A proactive approach to managing flaky tests ultimately leads to higher-quality software and more efficient testing processes.

Conclusion

Testing asynchronous and distributed systems presents unique challenges that require careful consideration and tailored approaches. This summary recaps the key challenges, techniques, and best practices for ensuring effective testing in these complex environments.

By addressing these challenges, employing effective testing techniques, and adhering to best practices, organizations can improve their ability to test asynchronous and distributed systems successfully. This leads to more reliable, resilient software that meets user expectations and performs well in production environments.

In the next chapter, we turn away from the functional aspects of software testing and start to look at the cross functional concerns of security, performance and resilience and how they can be included in the framework design and testing processes.

Key takeaways

Let us go over some key facts now.

- **Key challenges in testing asynchronous and distributed systems:**

  o **Handling service dependencies:** As systems grow in complexity, managing the dependencies between microservices can lead to issues during testing. Changes in one service can affect others, complicating the testing process.

  o **Ensuring event correctness:** In event-driven architectures, ensuring that events are produced and consumed correctly is crucial. Testing must account for the asynchronous nature of communication and the potential for event loss or duplication.

  o **Dealing with failures:** Distributed systems are inherently more prone to failures, such as network issues, service outages, and message loss. Testing must address these scenarios to ensure systems recover gracefully and maintain functionality.

- **Key techniques for testing microservices and event-driven systems:**

  o **Contract testing:** This technique involves defining and validating contracts between services to ensure they adhere to expected behaviors. Contract tests help mitigate integration issues by verifying that service interfaces remain compatible over time.

  o **Orchestration testing:** Testing service orchestration patterns focuses on validating the interactions between multiple services coordinated by a central component. This ensures workflows function as intended, particularly in complex scenarios spanning various services.

  o **Chaos engineering:** This approach intentionally introduces failures into the system to test its resilience. By simulating real-world disruptions, teams can identify weaknesses and improve the overall reliability of distributed systems.

- **Best practices for ensuring testability, reliability, and resilience:**

  o **Design for testability:** Incorporate monitoring, logging, and test hooks into the architecture to facilitate effective testing. Ensure that services are loosely coupled and designed to be tested independently.

  o **Stabilizing tests:** Implement strategies to identify and mitigate flaky tests, such as addressing race conditions, handling retries, and managing test dependencies. Regular maintenance and monitoring of tests contribute to their reliability.

  o **Creating robust test environments:** Use containerization and orchestration platforms to set up reliable and scalable test environments that closely mimic production. This helps ensure consistent testing conditions and reduces environmental discrepancies.

o **Emphasizing observability:** Integrate observability practices, including distributed tracing and logging, to gain insights into system behavior during testing. This allows for better diagnosis of issues and enhances overall system reliability.

Exercises

1. How do your services communicate—synchronously (REST/gRPC) or asynchronously (events, messaging)?

2. What orchestration or choreography patterns are used in your system? How do you handle inter-service dependencies?

3. Are you using contract testing (for example, Pact, Spring Cloud Contract) to verify service integrations? If so, how do you ensure contract consistency?

4. Do you perform end-to-end tests across your distributed system? How do you handle data consistency across services?

5. How do you test event-driven flows and message processing? Do you use event simulation or replay mechanisms?

6. Do you use synthetic data generation or mocks for testing distributed components in isolation?

7. Have you implemented chaos engineering practices (for example, Chaos Monkey, Gremlin) to test system resilience?

8. How do you ensure your system gracefully handles event duplication, message loss, or out-of-order processing?

9. Do you have circuit breakers or fallback mechanisms in place for failing services?

10. Do you deploy services independently, or do you require coordinated releases?

11. How do you validate compatibility between different versions of services?

Join our Discord space

Join our Discord workspace for latest updates, offers, tech happenings around the world, new releases, and sessions with the authors:

https://discord.bpbonline.com

CHAPTER 10

Security, Performance, and Resilience Testing

Introduction

Cross-cutting concerns like security, performance, and resilience are aspects of a system that impact multiple areas or layers, affecting the system's overall behavior. These are not confined to a single functional area but influence the application across different modules. In the context of test automation, cross-cutting concerns must be integrated into the testing strategy to ensure system-wide quality.

Security involves ensuring that the system is resilient to security vulnerabilities across all modules. Performance focuses on validating that the system performs efficiently under various loads, irrespective of the feature being tested. Resilience ensures that the system can recover from failures affecting different components in the stack. Logging refers to standardizing how information is logged for traceability across various modules. Error handling involves providing consistent error reporting mechanisms for a clearer understanding of system issues.

Structure

In this chapter, we will go over the following topics:

- Improving quality by addressing cross-cutting concerns
- Challenges of non-functional testing
- Integrating non-functional concerns
- Integrating security testing in a tool-agnostic framework
- Performance testing within the same framework
- Common performance testing metrics
- Types of performance tests
- Chaos testing and resilience validation
- Integrating chaos testing into CI/CD workflows
- Best practices for non-functional testing

- Creating a unified testing strategy
- Tooling and infrastructure considerations

Objectives

By the end of this chapter, the reader will learn about the different types of cross-cutting non-functional concerns and the impact they have on software delivery. We will then look at each of those areas in more detail and unpack security, performance, and resilience in detail at both a strategy and tooling perspective, and how they can be incorporated into a testing framework.

Improving quality by addressing cross-cutting concerns

Incorporating non-functional concerns into a test automation framework is essential for achieving comprehensive, reliable, and maintainable tests. These concerns influence overall system quality in several ways:

- **Consistency across tests:** Cross-cutting concerns ensure that every layer or module of the application is tested uniformly, avoiding gaps in coverage. For example, security tests should be embedded at multiple stages, ensuring that different modules adhere to the same security protocols.

- **System-wide risk mitigation:** Neglecting cross-cutting concerns could result in significant vulnerabilities being missed because they span multiple areas. For instance, resilience testing ensures that a system gracefully handles failure, even when different parts interact.

- **Improved maintenance and scalability:** By integrating these concerns into the framework, future updates are simpler. For example, if performance benchmarks need adjustments, they can be updated globally without rewriting tests for individual modules.

- **Comprehensive quality assurance:** Ensuring that security, performance, and resilience are included in tests helps teams measure system quality holistically, not just feature-by-feature.

- **Standardization:** By addressing cross-cutting concerns in the framework itself, all teams using the automation suite will adhere to common standards, reducing the likelihood of inconsistencies in testing practices.

Cross-cutting concerns are critical to the success of test automation because they ensure that the system's non-functional aspects, like security and performance, are thoroughly tested across all components. This ensures not only feature-level validation but also a focus on overall system quality and robustness.

Challenges of non-functional testing

Security, performance, and resilience often pose unique challenges in test automation because they require specialized testing approaches that differ significantly from standard functional tests. Each of these concerns involves different criteria for validation, varying testing environments, and often, more complex tools and methodologies. Let us go over the following:

- **Security:** Security testing goes beyond typical functional validation. It involves vulnerability assessments, penetration testing, and compliance checks to ensure data protection and safe user interactions. The complexity of securing an entire system means that security testing must cover authorization, encryption, and injection attacks across all modules. It often requires tools like **Static Analysis Security Testing (SAST)** or **Dynamic Analysis Security Testing (DAST)**, which are highly specialized.

- **Performance:** Performance testing must evaluate how the system behaves under varying loads and stress conditions, which can differ significantly from module to module. Performance bottlenecks can occur due to network issues, database handling, or resource limitations. Simulating realistic traffic, measuring response times, and ensuring acceptable throughput often requires tools like JMeter or LoadRunner, making it a distinct area from regular test cases.

- **Resilience:** Testing for resilience involves ensuring the system can withstand and recover from failures, including hardware crashes, network issues, and unexpected system loads. This requires simulating failure scenarios, such as terminating instances or disconnecting services, and ensuring that the system can recover gracefully. Chaos engineering tools like Chaos Monkey are often used for such testing.

Each of these areas demands tailored strategies, tools, and methodologies to identify and mitigate potential issues effectively.

Integrating non-functional concerns

While specialized testing approaches are necessary for cross-cutting concerns, incorporating them into a test automation framework should not create fragmented or siloed tests. Instead, these concerns need to be seamlessly integrated into a unified, tool-agnostic, reusable, and maintainable test automation framework. This brings several advantages:

- **Tool-agnostic flexibility:** A framework that is tool-agnostic can adapt to various testing environments and tools, making it easier to switch or upgrade tools without needing to rewrite tests. For instance, if a team shifts from using one security tool to another, the test automation framework should support that transition with minimal rework.

- **Reusability across modules:** Cross-cutting concerns often require tests that need to be reused across different parts of the system. A well-designed framework enables the creation of reusable components that can be applied across multiple areas, ensuring consistent testing for security, performance, and resilience.

- **Maintainability:** The need for specialized testing approaches often means that these areas require ongoing maintenance, updates, and enhancements. A maintainable framework allows for easily adding or modifying tests as the system evolves. For instance, if new performance metrics need to be introduced, the framework should allow for seamless integration of those metrics without disrupting the existing structure.

- **Systematic incorporation:** By embedding cross-cutting concerns into the core of the automation framework, testing becomes part of the development process rather than an afterthought. This ensures that every deployment, code change, or system update is consistently evaluated for security, performance, and resilience. A centralized, modular framework allows for the continuous integration of these concerns into the CI/CD pipeline, ensuring that every aspect of the system is constantly monitored.

Incorporating non-functional concerns into a tool-agnostic and maintainable framework ensures the system's overall quality and resilience without locking the development team into specific tools or methodologies. This approach provides both flexibility and scalability as systems and requirements evolve.

Integrating security testing in a tool-agnostic framework

Security testing is the process of identifying vulnerabilities, risks, and threats in a system to ensure that data remains protected and the application is secure from attacks. Its primary goal is to uncover weaknesses that could be exploited by malicious actors, compromising the system's integrity, confidentiality, and availability.

Common security vulnerabilities include:

- **SQL injection:** This occurs when an attacker can execute arbitrary SQL queries on a database through insecure input fields. It can lead to data theft, deletion, or manipulation.

- **Cross-site scripting (XSS):** XSS vulnerabilities allow attackers to inject malicious scripts into web pages viewed by other users, potentially leading to session hijacking or defacement.

- **Cross-site request forgery (CSRF):** CSRF attacks trick users into executing unintended actions on a website, such as changing account details or making purchases without their knowledge.

- **Authentication and authorization flaws:** Issues in the authentication process or user roles can enable unauthorized users to access sensitive areas of an application.

- **Insecure data storage:** Poorly secured data at rest (for example, passwords stored in plain text) makes the system vulnerable to data theft.

By identifying these vulnerabilities, security testing helps ensure system robustness and protects against data breaches, reputational damage, legal consequences, and financial losses.

Role of test automation in security testing

Test automation is crucial in proactively detecting and mitigating security issues, making it a vital component of a robust security testing strategy. While some aspects of security testing, like penetration testing, require manual effort and deep expertise, automation can help scale security efforts and integrate them into the software development lifecycle.

Let us now discuss the roles of test automation:

- **Early detection and continuous monitoring:** By automating security tests as part of the CI/CD pipeline, teams can detect vulnerabilities early in the development cycle. For example, automated static code analysis tools can identify common coding errors, such as unsanitized inputs, before they make it into production.

- **Automated vulnerability scanning:** Automated tools such as **Open Web Application Security Project Zed Attack Proxy (OWASP ZAP)** and Burp Suite can scan for common vulnerabilities like SQL injection, XSS, and insecure headers. Regular scans can be scheduled to ensure new vulnerabilities are detected as code changes occur.

- **Simulating attacks:** Automation allows for the simulation of various attack scenarios, such as brute force attacks or CSRF attempts, to evaluate how well the system responds. These tests help assess the system's resilience to external threats.

- **Regression security testing:** Every time new features are introduced or code is changed, automated security tests can ensure that existing vulnerabilities are not reintroduced. This is crucial in maintaining a secure codebase over time.

- **Faster feedback loop:** Automated security testing provides rapid feedback to developers, allowing them to address security flaws immediately. This reduces the lack of opportunity for attackers to exploit vulnerabilities that might otherwise be left unaddressed for more extended periods.

- **Scalability:** Manual security testing can be time-consuming and resource-intensive, especially for large applications with frequent updates. Automation allows for continuous security coverage across large codebases and multiple releases.

Security testing is vital for uncovering potential vulnerabilities in a system and safeguarding it against threats. By integrating automated security tests into the development process, organizations can proactively identify and mitigate risks, ensuring that the system remains robust against evolving security threats.

Types of security tests

Security is quite technical and extensive, and while we will not be able to go into detail here, the following is a high-level overview of the different types of security testing that can be done.

Static Application Security Testing

SAST is a white-box testing method that analyzes an application's source code, bytecode, or binary code to identify security vulnerabilities without executing the code. SAST tools scan the codebase for patterns and signatures of known vulnerabilities such as SQL injection, buffer overflows, and insecure data handling.

Examples of vulnerabilities found are as follows:

- **Hardcoded credentials:**

  o **Example**: A developer might accidentally commit API keys or database passwords directly in source code:

    ```
    String dbPassword = "P@ssw0rd123";
    ```

  This exposes sensitive information and can lead to unauthorized access if the code is leaked or reused.

- **Unsanitized input (Injection attacks):**

  o **Example**: A web application constructs SQL queries directly from user input:

    ```
    SELECT * FROM users WHERE username = '" + input + "'";
    ```

  This is vulnerable to SQL injection, allowing attackers to manipulate the query.

- **Poor encryption practices:**

  o **Example**: An application uses weak or outdated encryption algorithms like MD5 or DES:

    ```
    MessageDigest md = MessageDigest.getInstance("MD5");
    ```

  These algorithms are known to be cryptographically broken and should not be used for secure hashing or encryption.

Tools

Some tools are as follows:

- **SonarQube**: An open-source platform for continuous inspection of code quality, detecting bugs, code smells, and security vulnerabilities using static code analysis.

- **Checkmarx**: A SAST tool that scans source code to identify security flaws early in the development lifecycle.

- **Veracode**: A cloud-based platform offering static and dynamic application security testing (SAST and DAST), helping teams find and fix vulnerabilities across the **software development life cycle** (**SDLC**).

- **Fortify**: An enterprise-grade security tool from OpenText that provides static and dynamic code analysis to detect and remediate software vulnerabilities.

Dynamic Application Security Testing

DAST is a black-box testing method that evaluates the security of a running application by simulating external attacks. Unlike SAST, DAST does not require access to the source code; instead, it interacts with the application, scanning for vulnerabilities in real-time.

Some examples of vulnerabilities found are as follows:

- **SQL injection:**

  o **Vulnerability**: User input is directly used to build SQL queries without sanitization.

  ```
  # Vulnerable Python example
  username = input("Enter username:")
  query = "SELECT * FROM users WHERE username = '" + username + "';"
  ```

  o **What an attacker might input**:

  ```
  ' OR '1'='1
  ```

  o **Result**: This input could cause the query to always return true, bypassing authentication or exposing data.

- **XSS:**

  o **Vulnerability**: User input is rendered on a webpage without proper encoding or escaping.

  ```
  <!-- Vulnerable HTML snippet -->
  <p>Welcome, <?php echo $_GET['name']; ?></p>
  ```

  o **What an attacker might input**:

  ```
  <script>alert('Hacked!');</script>
  ```

  o **Result**: The attacker's script runs in the browser of any user who visits the page.

- **Authentication issues:**

  o **Vulnerability**: Weak logic or misconfiguration in authentication checks.

  ```
  // Client-side-only authentication check (bad practice)
  if (localStorage.getItem("auth") === "true") {
  showAdminPanel();
  }
  ```

  o **Result**: An attacker can manipulate local storage or cookies to gain unauthorized access.

Other common examples are:

- On login forms, enabling brute-force attacks.

- **Default credentials not changed:** `admin/admin`.

Tools

Some tools are as follows:

- **OWASP ZAP:** A free and open-source DAST tool designed to find security vulnerabilities in web applications during runtime.

- **Burp Suite:** A popular web vulnerability scanner and proxy tool used for manual and automated testing of web applications, especially by penetration testers.

- **Acunetix:** A commercial DAST tool that automatically scans websites and APIs for a wide range of security vulnerabilities, including SQL injection and XSS.

- **Netsparker:** A dynamic security scanner that identifies exploitable web vulnerabilities with proof-based scanning to minimize false positives.

Penetration testing

Penetration testing, or pen testing, is a more manual process where ethical hackers attempt to exploit vulnerabilities within a system, mimicking real-world attack scenarios. This can involve automated tools, but it often requires human insight to explore complex attack vectors.

Some examples of vulnerabilities include:

- **Logic flaws:**

    o **Vulnerability**: A mistake in the application's business logic allows unintended behavior.

    o **Example**: An e-commerce site lets users apply discount coupons without validation:
    ```
    if (couponCode) {
    totalPrice = totalPrice - 50;
    }
    ```

    o **Issue**: Users can reuse or guess coupons (for example, **SAVE50**) and get discounts multiple times, even when ineligible.

    o **Impact**: Financial loss, abuse of features, or bypassing payment logic.

- **Insecure APIs:**

    o **Vulnerability**: APIs lack proper authentication, authorization, or data validation.

    o **Example**: A mobile app's API allows any user to fetch other users' data:
    ```
    GET /api/users/12345
    ```

    No token or authorization check is performed.

    o **Issue**: An attacker can enumerate user IDs and access personal data.

    o **Impact**: Data leakage, violation of privacy regulations (for example, GDPR).

- **Privilege escalation opportunities:**

    o **Vulnerability**: Users can gain access to features or data beyond their role.

    o **Example**: A regular user can change their role via a client-side request:
    ```
    POST /api/updateUser
    {
    "username": "bob",
    "role": "admin"
    }
    ```

    o **Issue**: The server blindly trusts the input without validating the user's current permissions.

    o **Impact**: Unauthorized users can access admin dashboards or perform restricted operations.

Tools

Some tools are as follows:

- **Metasploit**: A powerful penetration testing framework used to develop, test, and execute exploits against target systems.

- **Nmap**: A network scanning tool used to discover hosts, services, and vulnerabilities on a network.

- **Kali Linux**: A specialized Linux distribution packed with tools for penetration testing, ethical hacking, and security research.

Integrating security tests into automated frameworks and CI/CD pipelines

Most organizations reserve security testing for special phases in the delivery process, but it can and should be integrated into the CI/CD process to allow for quicker feedback and remediation of any security issues and ensure that code is secure before it even makes it into any form of exposed environment.

SAST in CI/CD pipelines

SAST tools can be integrated early in the development cycle, often during the coding phase. As part of the CI/CD pipeline, SAST scans the code with every code commit, pull request, or merge, providing instant feedback on potential security flaws. This allows developers to fix issues before progressing further in the pipeline, ensuring code quality from the start.

Integration: SAST tools can be configured to run automatically as part of build processes. If vulnerabilities are detected, the build can fail, prompting developers to review and correct the issue.

Automation framework: SAST results can be incorporated into reporting frameworks that track security health over time, providing visibility into trends.

DAST in CI/CD pipelines

DAST tools can be integrated later in the pipeline once the application is deployed to a test or staging environment. Automated DAST tests run scans against the running application, identifying vulnerabilities in real time. They can also be part of nightly builds or integrated into post-deployment tests for constant monitoring of new or ongoing security issues.

Integration: DAST can be scheduled to run at specific stages, like post-deployment in test environments, where it automatically tests the application for security vulnerabilities. Feedback from DAST tools can trigger alerts or fail a deployment if critical vulnerabilities are detected.

Automation framework: DAST findings can be fed into the same reporting and dashboarding tools used for other tests, providing a unified view of functional and security health.

Penetration testing in CI/CD pipelines

While pen testing is largely manual and cannot be fully automated, there are ways to incorporate parts of it into the pipeline. For example, penetration testing scripts or tools like Metasploit can be used to automate testing of known vulnerabilities during the pipeline's later stages, especially before a production release.

Integration: In pre-production environments, automated portions of pen tests, like scans or brute force attempts, can be part of security regression tests. While not fully automated, pen testing results can be captured and tracked alongside automated tests to assess the system's security readiness.

Automation framework: Penetration testing results can be stored in vulnerability management tools and reviewed periodically as part of a comprehensive security audit.

Benefits of integrating security tests into the CI/CD pipeline

The benefits are as follows:

- **Shift-left approach:** Integrating security testing into the CI/CD pipeline allows for a shift-left strategy, meaning security concerns are addressed earlier in the development lifecycle, reducing the time and cost of fixing vulnerabilities later.

- **Continuous feedback:** Automated security tests provide continuous feedback to developers and QA teams, ensuring that security is constantly focused on in every deployment.

- **Early and frequent detection:** SAST identifies issues before the code is even compiled, while DAST catches vulnerabilities in running applications. Together, they ensure comprehensive coverage of both code and runtime vulnerabilities.

- **Automated governance:** Security tests can be automated to ensure they are run with every build or deployment, preventing security neglect in fast-paced release cycles.

Incorporating SAST, DAST, and parts of penetration testing into the test automation framework enhances the system's overall security posture and provides confidence that the application is resilient to security threats as it evolves.

Incorporating security testing into a tool-agnostic framework

Building a tool-agnostic security testing framework means designing a system that can integrate with multiple security testing tools and adapt to technological changes. It ensures flexibility and scalability and prevents vendor lock-in, allowing teams to adopt new tools as needed. Here are some approaches to achieving this:

- **API-based integration**: Many security tools, both commercial and open-source, offer APIs that can be leveraged for tool-agnostic integration. By creating an API-driven test automation framework, you can interact with different security tools programmatically, regardless of the specific tool in use. For instance, you can run security scans, retrieve reports, and analyze results through the tool's API without relying on any proprietary interfaces.

  o Abstract security testing operations (for example, scan initiation, vulnerability retrieval) into functions or services that can communicate with any tool that supports APIs. This enables you to switch tools easily without affecting the overall automation framework.

- **Scripting-based approach:** Scripting languages such as Python, JavaScript, or Bash can make your framework adaptable to different security tools. Scripting provides flexibility to control and automate security tests across various tools, and you can integrate different test suites by invoking **command-line interfaces (CLI)** or APIs from your scripts.

  o Write modular, reusable scripts that can interface with different security tools (for example, calling OWASP ZAP for dynamic testing or executing Snyk for static analysis). This ensures that switching or combining tools remains seamless.

- **Open-source tools with standardized output**: A tool-agnostic approach can be achieved by using open-source tools that adhere to common standards or provide standardized output formats (for example, JSON, XML, CSV). By processing these outputs uniformly, you can integrate multiple tools and consolidate their results in a unified reporting mechanism. This approach allows for easy integration of new tools into the automation pipeline without significant rework.

  o Design the framework to parse output from various tools (for example, vulnerability reports from ZAP, SAST results from SonarQube) into a common format, allowing you to compare results and maintain a consistent reporting structure.

- **Modular and plug-and-play architecture:** Implement a modular architecture in the test automation framework where each security tool is treated as a pluggable module. This allows new tools to be added or replaced without impacting the overall structure of the framework. Each module can handle the specific configuration and execution logic for the corresponding tool, while the framework maintains a consistent workflow and reporting layer.

  o Create a base interface or abstract class for security testing within the framework. Each tool can then have its implementation, allowing easy swaps or additions without breaking existing functionality.

Example frameworks and tools for tool-agnostic security testing

Refer to the following figure:

Where Does DAST Come in SDLC?

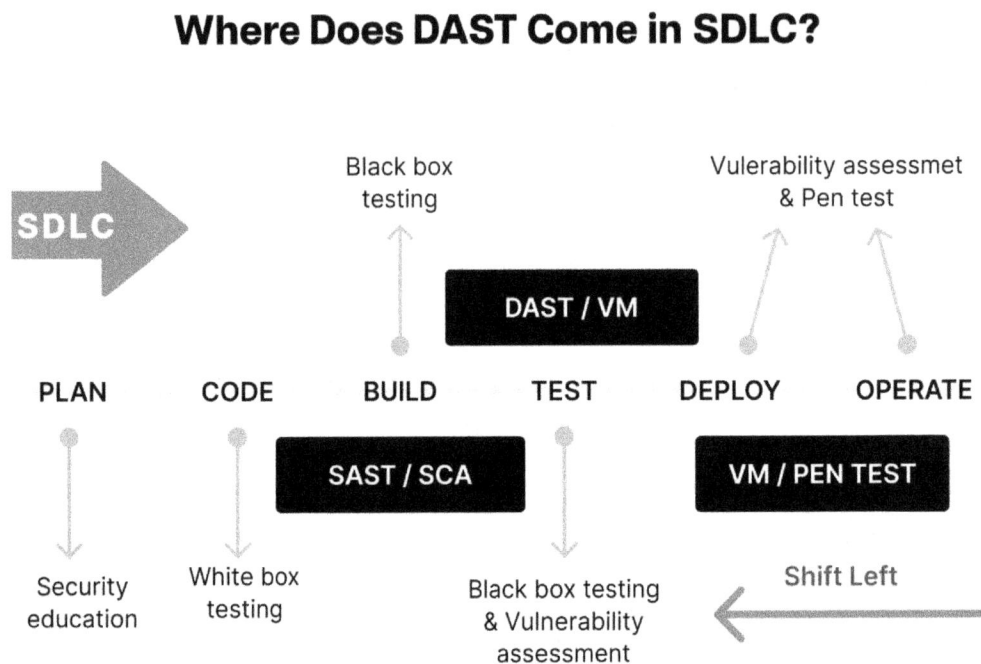

Figure 10.1: Diagram showing the different types of security scanning and where they fit into the SDLC

Let us now go over these examples:

- **OWASP ZAP:**

  o **Type:** Dynamic Application Security Testing.

  o **Features:** OWASP ZAP is a popular open-source tool for DAST, capable of simulating various attacks (for example, XSS, SQL injection) against running applications. It supports an API that allows for tool-agnostic integration, making it suitable for inclusion in any automation framework.

  o **Tool-agnostic use:** ZAP's REST API can be called from scripts or frameworks to automate security scans, retrieve results, and trigger alerts. It can easily fit into any CI/CD pipeline or custom framework through its API, CLI, or Docker container.

- **Burp Suite:**

  o **Type:** Dynamic Application Security Testing.

  o **Features:** Burp Suite is another popular tool for performing comprehensive web security assessments. It offers both a graphical interface and a CLI, making it suitable for tool-agnostic scripting and integration.

  o **Tool-agnostic use:** The CLI (in the professional version) and Burp's extensions (via APIs) allow for automated, headless security testing. The results can be captured in formats parsed and processed by custom scripts or reporting tools.

- **Snyk:**
  - o **Type:** Static Application Security Testing.
  - o **Features:** Snyk is an open-source tool that focuses on identifying vulnerabilities in dependencies, code, and container images. It provides CLI and API-based integration for flexible use in various automation frameworks.
  - o **Tool-agnostic use:** By using Snyk's CLI or REST API, you can easily integrate it into any automation workflow, scan projects for vulnerabilities, and export the results into a standardized format for further processing.

- **SonarQube:**
  - o **Type:** Static Application Security Testing.
  - o **Features:** SonarQube is widely used for code quality analysis, including security checks for potential vulnerabilities in the source code. It provides a rich API for extracting results, making it suitable for tool-agnostic use.
  - o **Tool-agnostic use:** The SonarQube API can be used to trigger scans, fetch results, and monitor code quality trends in a custom automation framework. It can be integrated into CI/CD pipelines with standardized reporting.

- **Nmap:**
  - o **Type:** Network security scanning.
  - o **Features:** Nmap is a widely used open-source tool for network discovery and vulnerability scanning. It is typically used in penetration testing scenarios and provides CLI and scripting options.
  - o **Tool-agnostic use:** Nmap can be executed from scripts to run network scans, and its results (in XML or other formats) can be parsed for further analysis. This makes it easy to integrate into a larger automation framework.

- **Bandit:**
  - o **Type:** Static Application Security Testing.
  - o **Features:** Bandit is an open-source Python tool that checks for common security vulnerabilities in Python code. It is lightweight and can be integrated into Python-based projects as part of a tool-agnostic security testing strategy.
  - o **Tool-agnostic use:** Bandit can be executed via CLI or integrated into build scripts, and its results can be exported in multiple formats (for example, JSON, CSV) for processing in a common framework.

Tool-agnostic security testing provides flexibility, scalability, and the ability to future-proof your security testing efforts. By focusing on APIs, scripting, and open-source tools with standardized output, you can create an adaptable framework that integrates various security tools without being dependent on any specific one. Tools like OWASP ZAP, Burp Suite, and Snyk can be used modular and tool-agnostic to ensure that your automation framework remains flexible and easily maintainable over time.

Automating security testing in the CI/CD pipeline

Automating security testing within the CI/CD pipeline is crucial for maintaining the security of an application throughout its development lifecycle. By embedding security tests directly into CI/CD workflows, organizations can continuously assess code for vulnerabilities as it evolves, providing early detection and remediation.

Shift-left security testing

Shifting security testing to the left means integrating security checks early in the SDLC, particularly during the coding and build phases. This ensures that vulnerabilities are identified as soon as code is written, significantly reducing the cost and complexity of fixing issues later.

Code analysis: As developers commit code, SAST tools such as SonarQube, Checkmarx, or Snyk can automatically scan the code for vulnerabilities. These tools integrate into the CI/CD pipeline, providing real-time feedback on potential security risks before the code proceeds to further stages.

Dependency scanning: Tools like Snyk and OWASP Dependency-Check can automatically scan third-party libraries or dependencies for vulnerabilities. These scans are triggered during the build phase to ensure that vulnerable components are not introduced into the project.

Security as code

Security tests can be treated like any other test, versioned and stored alongside application code. This allows security testing to evolve as the application grows, ensuring that new vulnerabilities and risks are addressed in a scalable manner.

Automated tests: Write security tests in code, using tools like OWASP ZAP or custom scripts, and integrate them into the CI/CD pipeline using scripting or APIs. Automated DAST can simulate attacks against the running application and provide feedback in real-time.

Continuous feedback: Security issues discovered during automated scans are reported directly to the developers via CI/CD systems (for example, Jenkins, GitLab CI). Developers can be notified of vulnerabilities immediately, and security reports can be integrated into dashboards for visibility.

Automated compliance checks

Many security tests, such as compliance checks for data protection regulations (for example, GDPR, HIPAA), can be automated. These checks ensure the application adheres to security policies and standards by validating configurations, logging practices, and encryption methods.

Example: Automated compliance tools, such as CIS-CAT, can be integrated into the CI/CD pipeline to regularly audit the application's security configuration. These tools check against predefined standards and ensure compliance before the code proceeds to production.

Configuring security gates in CI/CD pipelines

Security gates are automated checkpoints embedded into the CI/CD pipeline that ensure only secure and compliant code advances to production. By configuring security gates, organizations can prevent builds with critical vulnerabilities from being deployed, ensuring that security is an integral part of the release process.

Defining security gates in CI/CD

Security gates evaluate the results of automated security tests and decide whether the build can proceed to the next stage of the pipeline. These gates are configured based on severity thresholds, ensuring that high-risk vulnerabilities block deployments.

Example: If a SAST tool identifies a SQL injection vulnerability with a critical severity level, the security gate will prevent the pipeline from advancing until the issue is resolved.

Customizable criteria: Security gates can be customized based on project requirements. For example, a critical security vulnerability might halt the pipeline, while lower severity issues (for example, informational or minor warnings) could allow the pipeline to proceed with a warning.

Integration with CI/CD tools

Most CI/CD tools (for example, Jenkins, GitLab CI, CircleCI) support the integration of security testing tools, allowing the configuration of security gates directly within the pipeline. These tools provide flexibility to automate testing for different stages, during code integration, build, and deployment.

Example: In Jenkins, a post-build action can be configured to automatically fail the build if a SAST tool reports vulnerabilities above a certain severity threshold. Similarly, GitLab CI allows security scanning results to be automatically reviewed and blocks deployment if critical vulnerabilities are found.

Pipeline stages with security gates

Security gates can be applied at various stages in the pipeline to ensure continuous security checks throughout the SDLC:

- **Pre-commit stage:** Tools like pre-commit hooks can run lightweight static analysis checks and code linters before code is even committed, blocking vulnerable code from entering the repository.

- **Build stage:** During the build phase, SAST tools can analyze the code, and dependency scanners can identify vulnerabilities in third-party components. The security gate prevents the build from progressing if critical issues are found.

- **Post-deployment stage:** Once the application is deployed to a test or staging environment, DAST tools like OWASP ZAP or Burp Suite can run dynamic security tests, simulating attacks against the live application. If vulnerabilities are detected, the deployment of production can be blocked until the issues are resolved.

Fail-fast vs. fail-later strategy

Security gates can be configured to enforce a fail-fast or fail-later strategy:

- **Fail-fast:** This strategy blocks the pipeline immediately when critical vulnerabilities are detected. It ensures that only secure code advances, but it may slow down the development process.

- **Fail-later:** This strategy allows the pipeline to proceed but generates warnings and requires a security review before production deployment. It provides faster feedback but increases the risk of security vulnerabilities reaching production if not carefully managed.

Continuous monitoring and feedback loops

Security gates should not be a one-time checkpoint. Instead, they should support continuous monitoring, running regular security scans on pre-production environments, and alerting developers of any new vulnerabilities as the code evolves.

Monitoring tools: Continuous monitoring tools like WhiteSource or Snyk can continuously scan for new vulnerabilities in dependencies, even after the application has been deployed. These tools provide alerts and prevent further deployments until issues are remediated.

Automating security testing within the CI/CD pipeline ensures that security is continuously monitored throughout the development lifecycle, from code commit to production. By embedding security gates at critical points in the pipeline, organizations can prevent high-severity vulnerabilities from progressing into production, enhancing the security posture of the entire system. This approach enables the seamless integration of security into DevOps workflows, fostering a culture of DevSecOps where security is a shared responsibility across development, operations, and security teams.

Performance testing within the same framework

Performance testing is essential in ensuring that applications meet expected performance benchmarks under various conditions. It evaluates how well an application behaves under normal and stressful conditions, identifying potential bottlenecks and performance issues before they reach production. For modern distributed systems and cloud-native applications, the complexity and scale of the infrastructure make performance testing even more crucial for the following reasons:

- **Scalability and elasticity in distributed systems:** Modern distributed systems and cloud-native applications often need to handle a high volume of traffic and scale dynamically. Performance testing ensures that the system can scale horizontally (adding more instances) or vertically (increasing resources per instance) while maintaining optimal performance. This is critical for applications hosted in the cloud or relying on microservices architectures, where components interact across multiple nodes and services.

  o **Example:** Testing a cloud-native e-commerce platform during peak shopping periods to ensure it scales seamlessly without performance degradation.

- **Cloud-native architectures and containerization:** Cloud-native applications are typically built using containers (for example, Docker) and orchestrated by platforms like Kubernetes. These architectures are designed to be distributed, with services communicating over a network. Performance testing validates how network latency, service discovery, and inter-service communication affect the application's overall performance.

  o **Example:** Testing Kubernetes pods to ensure they are dynamically created and scaled based on workload demand, without introducing excessive latency.

- **Ensuring optimal user experience:** In today's competitive environment, users expect fast, responsive applications. Performance testing measures critical factors, such as page load times, responsiveness to user input, and system stability under load. Poor performance leads to a degraded user experience, resulting in reduced customer satisfaction, application abandonment, and potential revenue loss.

  o **Example:** Testing a streaming platform to ensure smooth video playback without buffering under various bandwidth conditions.

- **Cost optimization in cloud environments**: Cloud environments operate on a pay-as-you-go model, where costs are tied to resource consumption. Performance testing helps optimize resource usage by identifying the most efficient ways to run workloads, reducing unnecessary compute, memory, and network overhead. By testing various configurations, teams can find the balance between performance and cost efficiency.

  o **Example:** Running performance tests on different instance sizes to determine the optimal resource allocation for cost-effective scaling.

- **Resilience and fault tolerance**: Performance testing is also crucial for ensuring resilience in distributed systems. Applications must handle failures gracefully without impacting performance. For example, if a microservice goes down, performance testing validates that the system can reroute traffic or scale up other services to maintain performance.

  o **Example:** Testing a failover scenario in a microservices architecture to verify that performance remains consistent during service outages.

Common performance testing metrics

Performance tests focus on measuring specific key metrics to ensure that applications meet performance requirements. These metrics help identify performance bottlenecks, assess system behavior under various conditions, and guide optimization efforts.

Response time

Response time refers to the total time it takes for a system to respond to a request. It measures the time it takes from when a user sends a request (for example, clicking a button or submitting a form) to when the system delivers the result (for example, page load or data retrieval). Let us look at the following details:

- **Importance:** Response time directly impacts user experience. Longer response times result in frustration and decreased engagement, especially in interactive applications.

- **Test scenario:** Testing the response time of an API under different loads to ensure it meets the acceptable time limits for user interaction.

Throughput

Throughput measures the number of transactions or requests a system can process in a given amount of time. It reflects the system's capacity to handle concurrent requests without degradation in performance. Let us look at the following details:

- **Importance:** High throughput is essential for applications that handle large volumes of traffic, such as e-commerce platforms, social media sites, or online banking systems. It ensures that the system can handle peak loads without slowing down.

- **Test scenario:** Testing how many orders an e-commerce platform can process per second during a flash sale.

Latency

Latency refers to the time it takes for a request to travel from the user's system to the server and back. It is particularly critical in distributed systems and cloud-native applications, where requests often traverse multiple networks and services. Let us look at the following details:

- **Importance:** Low latency is vital for real-time applications like online gaming, video streaming, or live data processing, where even minor delays can severely impact the user experience.

- **Test scenario:** Testing a real-time messaging app to ensure messages are delivered instantly, even under heavy network conditions.

Resource utilization

Resource utilization measures the consumption of system resources, such as CPU, memory, disk I/O, and network bandwidth, during the test. It indicates how efficiently the application uses its resources under different loads. Let us look at the following details:

- **Importance:** High resource utilization can indicate inefficiencies in the code or infrastructure, leading to performance degradation and higher costs (especially in cloud environments). Monitoring resource utilization helps teams optimize their application for better performance and cost management.

- **Test scenario:** Testing the memory and CPU usage of a microservice when handling different workloads, identifying potential memory leaks or inefficiencies.

Error rate

Error rate is the percentage of failed requests compared to the total number of requests sent. It reflects an application's stability and reliability under various load conditions. Let us look at the following details:

- **Importance:** High error rates during peak load indicate system instability, which can lead to downtime or data loss. Monitoring the error rate helps determine the system's failure points and ensures that error-handling mechanisms are effective.

- **Test Scenario:** Testing an API under high concurrent load and monitoring the error rate to ensure that failures are within acceptable limits.

Concurrency

Concurrency measures the number of users or requests the system can handle simultaneously without a noticeable drop in performance. This metric is crucial for systems designed to support many concurrent users or processes. Let us look at the following details:

- **Importance:** High concurrency levels are critical for applications like online services, multiplayer games, or social media platforms, where many users interact with the system simultaneously.

- **Test scenario:** Testing the number of users a web application can handle simultaneously during peak traffic without declining response time or throughput.

Performance testing is a vital part of the test automation lifecycle, especially for modern distributed and cloud-native applications that require high levels of scalability, resilience, and efficiency. By measuring key performance metrics such as response time, throughput, latency, and resource utilization, performance testing helps ensure optimal system behavior under varying loads. It not only protects the user's experience but also enables cost-efficient resource usage and system reliability, making it an indispensable component of modern software delivery.

Types of performance tests

Performance testing encompasses various techniques to evaluate how an application behaves under specific conditions. These different types of performance tests help identify performance bottlenecks, system limitations, and overall stability.

Load testing

Definition: Load testing measures how an application performs under expected user load. The goal is to verify that the system can handle the anticipated number of concurrent users, transactions, or data volumes within acceptable performance thresholds.

Purpose: To ensure the system performs optimally under normal, expected traffic conditions.

Metrics: Response time, throughput, latency, resource utilization, and error rate.

Example: Testing an e-commerce site with 10,000 concurrent users during regular business hours to ensure the checkout process works smoothly without performance degradation.

Stress testing

Definition: Stress testing evaluates how an application performs beyond its expected limits by gradually increasing the load until the system fails or exhibits unacceptable performance. The goal is to identify the breaking point and determine how the system behaves under extreme conditions.

Purpose: To assess the system's robustness and identify potential failure points under heavy traffic or resource exhaustion.

Metrics: Maximum throughput, error rate, response time, resource utilization at peak load, and system recovery time.

Example: Testing a financial application with a load 10 times higher than usual, simulating a sudden surge in transactions to see how long the system can maintain performance before failure.

Spike testing

Definition: Spike testing evaluates how an application handles a sudden, dramatic increase in load, followed by an immediate drop back to normal levels. This type of test checks the system's ability to scale up quickly and recover gracefully from a sharp rise in traffic.

Purpose: To measure how well the system can handle unexpected traffic spikes without crashing or becoming unresponsive.

Metrics: Response time during and after the spike, error rate, and system recovery time.

Example: Testing a media streaming platform's ability to handle a sudden increase in viewers when a viral video is released, followed by a rapid decline once the initial surge ends.

Endurance testing

Definition: Endurance testing, also known as soak testing, evaluates the system's performance over an extended period, often under a sustained load. It tests the application for memory leaks, resource exhaustion, and performance degradation over time.

Purpose: To ensure the system can maintain performance and stability during prolonged operation without deteriorating.

Metrics: Memory usage, CPU usage, resource exhaustion, throughput, and response time over time.

Example: Running an endurance test on a cloud-native application for 48 hours with continuous traffic to detect memory leaks or performance drops due to resource exhaustion.

Scalability testing

Definition: Scalability testing measures how well an application can scale up (increase system resources) or scale out (add more nodes) to accommodate higher loads without impacting performance. It evaluates the system's capacity to handle growing traffic or data volumes while maintaining acceptable performance levels.

Purpose: To ensure the system can scale efficiently when traffic increases and maintain performance across different configurations.

Metrics: Response time, throughput, resource utilization, and system performance at various load levels.

Example: Testing an application hosted on Kubernetes by simulating a gradual increase in user load to evaluate how well it scales as more pods are added.

Comparing test types and their implementation across the SDLC phases

Each type of performance test serves a specific purpose in evaluating different aspects of system behavior. Understanding how they differ and when to apply them is crucial for optimizing performance across the software development lifecycle.

Placement in the SDLC

Let us now go over the following:

- **Early development (unit and integration testing phase):** Some basic performance tests, such as load testing on individual modules or services, can be integrated into the early stages of the SDLC. This helps ensure that each component meets performance benchmarks before integration.

- **System testing and pre-production:** Most performance testing types (load, stress, spike, endurance, scalability) occur during the system testing phase after functional testing is complete. This ensures that the fully integrated system can handle expected and unexpected traffic patterns.

- **Post-deployment and production monitoring:** While most performance testing is conducted before production, ongoing performance monitoring in production environments (using observability tools) can ensure the system continues to meet performance requirements and scale as needed.

Each type of performance test serves a specific role in ensuring system robustness, stability, and scalability under different conditions. By strategically incorporating load, stress, spike, endurance, and scalability tests into the software development lifecycle, organizations can detect and resolve performance issues early, delivering applications that perform optimally under real-world conditions. These tests are especially critical for cloud-native, distributed systems, where performance requirements vary widely based on usage patterns and system complexity.

Designing tool-agnostic performance tests

A tool-agnostic approach to performance testing ensures that the tests are reusable across various environments and platforms, independent of the tools used. This design philosophy focuses on flexibility, scalability, and portability, ensuring that performance tests are adaptable, whether running tests in a local development environment, a staging server, or a production-level cloud setup. To achieve this, the following are necessary:

- **Abstraction of testing logic:** Design tests in a way that abstracts the core testing logic from the underlying tools or infrastructure. By separating the test scenarios (for example, API calls, user flows, transaction loads) from specific tool implementations, you create reusable test scripts that can be executed using different performance testing tools or environments without modification.

  o **Example:** Instead of hardcoding tool-specific configurations, store your test inputs (for example, URLs, request parameters) in configuration files or environment variables that can be dynamically loaded at runtime.

- **Parameterization:** Parameterization is key to making performance tests adaptable to different environments. By externalizing inputs such as the number of users, test duration, target URLs, and data sets, you can run the same test scripts in various scenarios by simply changing the parameter values.

  o **Example:** Running the same API load test in development with 100 users, and in production with 10,000 users, without changing the core test script.

- **Cross-platform compatibility:** When designing performance tests, it is important to ensure they can run in any environment, whether it is a local machine, a virtual machine, or a cloud-based container. This is accomplished by using open formats and standard protocols and by avoiding proprietary features tied to specific tools or platforms.

  o **Example:** Creating performance tests that use standard protocols such as HTTP, WebSockets, or gRPC, which are supported across multiple performance testing tools.

Using open-source tools in a tool-agnostic framework

Several open-source performance testing tools allow for flexibility and tool-agnostic testing. These tools offer powerful testing capabilities while remaining adaptable to different platforms, CI/CD pipelines, and environments.

We unpacked testing tools in more detail in *Chapter 11, Overview of Tools Used in Test Automation*, but will briefly mention the popular tools here as well.

JMeter

Apache JMeter is a widely used open-source tool for load testing a wide range of applications, including web services, databases, and APIs. Due to its command-line interface and compatibility with CI/CD tools, JMeter can be easily integrated into various environments and automated workflows. Let us look at the following details:

- **Advantages:** Extensible, supports multiple protocols (HTTP, JDBC, FTP), and integrates well with CI/CD tools like Jenkins or GitLab.

- **Tool-agnostic usage:** JMeter scripts can be reused across environments by storing test plans as XML files and using properties or environment variables for dynamic test data.

Gatling

Gatling is an open-source tool designed for high-performance load testing of web applications. It is particularly useful for testing large-scale web systems and APIs, and due to its focus on automation, it integrates well into CI/CD pipelines. Let us look at the following details:

- **Advantages:** High scalability, detailed real-time metrics, and support for complex scenarios. Gatling's test scripts are written in Scala, which offers strong flexibility and integration with other frameworks.

- **Tool-agnostic usage:** Gatling's test scenarios are stored in code (as Scala scripts), which can be parameterized for different environments and reused across multiple platforms without modification.

k6

k6 is a modern, open-source load-testing tool for developers and performance engineers. It focuses on making performance testing as code, allowing easy integration into modern development workflows, including CI/CD. Let us look at the following details:

- **Advantages:** Lightweight, easy to write test scripts in JavaScript, and integrates well with cloud infrastructure and containerized environments like Docker and Kubernetes.

- **Tool-agnostic usage:** k6 scripts can be easily parameterized and run across different environments. Its ability to generate real-time metrics and export data in common formats like JSON makes it highly versatile.

Other open-source tools

Let us now look at a couple of other open-source tools:

- **Locust:** Another Python-based load-testing tool that can simulate millions of users and integrates well with distributed environments.

- **Artillery:** A modern load testing toolkit for developers focused on ease of use and built to handle cloud-native applications.

In the next chapter on automation tooling, we will examine a list of different tools for automation and performance.

Structuring performance tests for modularity

Modular test design ensures that individual test components (for example, user scenarios, load profiles, request patterns) are isolated and reusable across different test suites and environments. This modularity is crucial for integrating performance tests into diverse CI/CD pipelines and environments while maintaining test consistency.

Test segmentation

Break down performance tests into smaller, reusable components. For instance, you can separate user behavior scenarios (for example, login, search, purchase) from load profiles (for example, 100 concurrent users for 1 hour). Doing so allows you to mix and match these components to create different performance test configurations without rewriting test logic.

Example: Have separate modules for simulating user authentication, browsing, and checkout flows. Depending on the test case, combine these modules into different scenarios (for example, a login-heavy test or a shopping-heavy test).

Reusable test templates

Create performance test templates that define common test structures (for example, load distribution, concurrency patterns) that can be reused across various test suites. This allows you to quickly adapt to different test scenarios without creating new test plans from scratch.

Example: A template that defines a test for simulating 10,000 users over a 5-minute period with ramp-up and ramp-down phases, which can be applied to multiple endpoints or scenarios.

Integration into CI/CD pipelines

Modularity makes it easier to plug performance tests into CI/CD pipelines. Using parameterized test scripts and modular components, you can trigger specific performance tests automatically as part of the CI/CD process, depending on the deployed changes.

Example: Automatically triggering a specific API load test after every deployment to a staging environment by pulling the latest configuration from a centralized repository.

Environment-specific configurations

Use environment-specific configurations to adjust test parameters (for example, base URLs, user credentials, database connections) without modifying the core test logic. This approach allows the same test suite to run in development, staging, and production environments with minimal effort.

Example: Use environment variables or configuration files to specify different endpoint URLs for development, staging, and production while keeping the test scripts the same across all environments.

Designing tool-agnostic performance tests provides flexibility, scalability, and reusability across different environments and platforms. By using open-source tools like JMeter, Gatling, and k6, you can create tests that are independent of the tools and easily integrated into CI/CD pipelines. Modularity and parameterization further ensure that tests are adaptable and reusable, helping organizations maintain performance consistency throughout the software development lifecycle.

Integrating performance testing into the CI/CD pipeline

Performance testing in CI/CD pipelines is crucial for ensuring that each release maintains optimal performance under various conditions. Integrating performance tests into the CI/CD workflow allows teams to catch performance degradations early in the development cycle. The following are the key best practices to ensure effective automation of performance tests in CI/CD pipelines:

- **Shift left: Run performance tests early and often**: Running performance tests early in the development lifecycle (shifting left) ensures that issues are caught before they escalate. To detect performance regressions early, integrate lightweight performance tests, such as API load tests or low-traffic simulations, into every code commit or build.

o **Strategy:** Include basic performance tests in the continuous integration phase to check for changes in response time, latency, and throughput after each code push.

- **Gradual load testing in stages:** Performance tests should be run at different stages of the pipeline, with increasing levels of complexity and load. Start with basic load tests at the integration level and scale up to more intensive stress or endurance tests in pre-production or staging environments.

  o **Strategy:** Configure tests to start with light loads (for example, simulating 50 users) in earlier stages and gradually increase the load (for example, to 5,000 or 10,000 users) in later stages of the pipeline before a release.

- **Use parameterized and environment-specific configurations**: Create performance tests that are flexible and environment-specific. Use parameterization to run tests in different environments (for example, development, staging, production)' without modifying the test code. Use environment variables or configuration files to specify key test inputs, such as the number of users, target URLs, and request payloads.

  o **Strategy:** Design tests that automatically adjust the load parameters and endpoints depending on the environment they are executed in.

- **Performance testing as code**: Treat performance tests like code, storing them in version control systems (for example, Git) alongside application code. This allows for better traceability and ensures that performance tests are updated and maintained as part of the development process.

  o **Strategy:** Store JMeter, Gatling, or k6 scripts in the same repository as the application code and trigger them during specific CI/CD pipeline stages.

- **Containerized testing environments**: Use containerized environments (for example, Docker) to ensure consistency in performance test execution. Containerizing the test environment removes discrepancies between different machines or configurations and allows the same tests to run in identical conditions across all stages.

  o **Strategy:** Package performance test tools like JMeter or k6 in Docker containers, ensuring that the environment is consistent from local testing to production pipelines.

- **Run tests in parallel**: To avoid performance testing becoming a bottleneck, run tests in parallel. Distribute test scenarios across multiple nodes or containers to speed up execution while maintaining accuracy.

  o **Strategy:** Distribute performance tests using Kubernetes or cloud infrastructure, allowing different components (for example, APIs, databases, and services) to be tested simultaneously under load.

- **Automate test data management:** Performance tests often require large sets of test data to simulate real-world scenarios. Automate the creation, updating, and management of test data to ensure consistency and prevent manual effort.

  o **Strategy:** Use scripts or tools to automatically generate test data before executing performance tests and clean up after tests are completed.

- **Monitor infrastructure and application metrics during tests:** Performance testing should not only focus on response times or throughput. Monitor server resource utilization (CPU, memory, network) alongside application-level metrics (for example, database query times, API response times) to comprehensively view system performance.

  o **Strategy:** Integrate monitoring tools like Prometheus, Grafana, or **Elasticsearch, Logstash, Kibana** (**ELK**) to collect and visualize performance metrics in real-time.

Strategies for ensuring consistent review of performance test results

Getting effective information and consistent, measurable results out of your performance tests is often a challenge, but the following best practices will help to address it.

Establish performance thresholds and SLAs

Define clear performance thresholds for key metrics such as response time, error rate, and throughput. These thresholds should be based on **service level agreements** (**SLA**) or customer expectations. When a test exceeds these thresholds, the pipeline should automatically fail or trigger alerts. Let us look at the following details:

- **Strategy:** Configure the pipeline to evaluate test results against pre-defined thresholds, automatically flagging builds that fail to meet performance criteria.

- **Example:** Set a threshold of 95% of requests responding in less than 200 milliseconds. If the threshold is exceeded, the CI/CD pipeline should halt further deployments.

Set up quality gates

A performance quality gate is a checkpoint within the CI/CD pipeline that ensures performance standards are met before moving forward. Integrating performance quality gates into the CI/CD workflow helps prevent performance regressions from reaching production. Let us look at the following details:

- **Strategy:** Set up gates at different pipeline stages, particularly after heavy-load tests in staging environments. These gates assess performance metrics such as response times, error rates, and resource utilization.

- **Example:** Implement a quality gate in Jenkins or GitLab that evaluates whether the application can handle 10,000 concurrent users with no more than a 1% error rate before allowing the release to proceed.

Automate reporting and notification

After performance tests are executed, automatically generate detailed reports and send notifications to relevant stakeholders. This helps ensure that performance test results are reviewed consistently, even if the tests are passed. Let us look at the following details:

- **Strategy:** Use integrated reporting tools to automatically generate reports that include key performance metrics, trends, and comparisons to previous test results. Set up email or Slack notifications for test outcomes.

- **Example:** Generate automated reports in Jenkins or GitLab CI with JMeter or k6, summarizing response times, error rates, and throughput, and send them to the performance team.

Trend analysis and historical comparisons

Performance test results should not be reviewed in isolation. Compare current test results with previous runs to detect performance trends over time. This approach helps identify gradual performance degradation or improvements across multiple releases. Let us look at the following details:

- **Strategy:** Store performance test results in a centralized database and use visualization tools like Grafana or Kibana to analyze performance trends across different builds and releases.

- **Example:** Use Grafana dashboards to monitor historical performance metrics, highlighting trends that may indicate growing resource usage or degradation of response time.

Define actionable insights and remediation plans

Performance test results should be actionable. When thresholds or quality gates are breached, ensure that remediation steps are clearly defined and root-cause analysis is performed. Let us look at the following details:

- **Strategy:** For each failed performance test, link the failure to specific application changes and assign teams to investigate and resolve issues. Track resolution progress through issue-tracking tools such as Jira.

- **Example:** When a performance test for database throughput fails, automatically create a Jira issue for the database team to investigate and provide recommendations.

Integrating performance testing into CI/CD pipelines is essential for maintaining consistent application performance across releases. By automating performance tests and embedding them into the pipeline, teams can detect and fix performance issues early, prevent regressions, and ensure that applications meet the required performance standards. Establishing quality gates and automating reporting ensures that performance test results are consistently reviewed and acted upon, helping organizations maintain high system performance across the development lifecycle.

Chaos testing and resilience validation

Chaos engineering is a proactive approach to software testing that involves intentionally introducing failures or disruptive events into a system to evaluate its resilience and fault tolerance. This practice emerged from the need to ensure that modern, complex distributed systems can withstand unexpected failures and continue to operate effectively. By simulating real-world problems in a controlled manner, organizations can identify weaknesses and improve their systems before failures occur.

The concept of chaos engineering can be traced back to the tech culture at companies like Netflix, where developers recognized that failure was common in distributed architectures. They introduced chaos engineering practices to help build more robust and resilient systems, allowing their applications to handle various types of disruptions without significant service degradation or outages.

Key aspects of chaos engineering include:

- **Controlled experiments:** Chaos engineering involves running controlled experiments to intentionally induce faults in a system while closely monitoring its behavior. These experiments help teams observe how the system responds and identify areas for improvement.

- **Automated tools:** Various tools and frameworks, such as Chaos Monkey, Gremlin, and Litmus, are available to facilitate chaos engineering experiments. These tools can automate the process of introducing failures, making it easier for teams to execute chaos engineering systematically.

- **Hypothesis-driven:** Teams formulate hypotheses about how the system will behave under specific adverse conditions before conducting chaos experiments. This structured approach helps teams understand expectations and measure outcomes effectively.

Importance of validating system behavior under adverse conditions

Validating systems behave as expected under adverse conditions is crucial for several reasons such as:

- **Building resilience:** Systems today are often built using microservices and cloud-based architectures, which can be susceptible to various failures, including hardware malfunctions, network disruptions, and service outages. By testing these scenarios, organizations can identify potential weaknesses and enhance the resilience of their applications.

- **Preventing downtime:** Unforeseen failures can lead to significant downtime and revenue loss. By proactively identifying vulnerabilities through chaos engineering, teams can implement mitigation strategies before actual outages occur, reducing the risk of service disruptions and ensuring higher availability.

- **Enhancing customer trust:** Users expect high levels of service reliability. By validating system resilience through chaos engineering, organizations can ensure a consistent user experience, even in the face of failures. This fosters customer trust and satisfaction, as users are less likely to encounter issues during their interactions with the application.

- **Improving incident response:** Chaos engineering helps organizations develop better incident response strategies. By simulating failures, teams can practice their response to different scenarios, refining their procedures and ensuring that they can quickly address issues when they arise in production.

- **Validating redundancy and failover mechanisms:** Many systems incorporate redundancy and failover mechanisms to maintain service availability. Chaos engineering allows teams to test these mechanisms under real-world conditions, ensuring that they function as intended when needed.

- **Encouraging a culture of continuous improvement:** Implementing chaos engineering fosters a culture of continuous improvement and learning within development teams. It encourages teams to regularly test their systems, identify areas for enhancement, and adapt to changing conditions in the software landscape.

Chaos engineering is essential for modern software development, particularly in complex, distributed systems. By intentionally introducing failures, organizations can validate their applications' resilience and fault tolerance, ensuring that they continue to function as expected under adverse conditions. This proactive approach ultimately leads to improved system reliability, enhanced customer trust, and a robust incident response strategy, making chaos engineering a valuable component of a comprehensive software testing and quality assurance strategy.

Chaos testing principles

As previously explained (albeit briefly) in *Chapter 9, Handling Asynchronous and Distributed Systems*, chaos testing is grounded in specific principles that guide the design and execution of chaos engineering experiments. These principles ensure that the experiments yield meaningful insights into the system's resilience and help teams improve the overall reliability of their applications. Here are the key principles of chaos testing:

- **Start small and gradually scale up**: Begin chaos experiments on a small scale within a controlled environment. This allows teams to observe system behavior without causing significant disruptions. As confidence grows in the system's resilience, gradually increase the complexity and scale of experiments.

  o **Implementation:** Start with a single microservice or component and gradually expand to multiple services. Monitor the impact at each stage.

- **Hypothesis-driven experimentation**: Before conducting an experiment, teams should formulate a hypothesis regarding the expected system behavior when a failure occurs. This hypothesis guides the experiment's design and helps teams focus on specific outcomes.

  o **Example:** A team may hypothesize that a particular service will maintain its performance despite the failure of one of its dependencies.

- **Monitor system behavior:** Monitoring is crucial during chaos experiments. Teams must gather metrics and logs to understand how the system responds to failures. This includes performance metrics, error rates, and system health indicators.

  o **Tools:** Utilize monitoring tools such as Prometheus, Grafana, or Datadog to track metrics in real time.

- **Automate experiments:** Automating chaos experiments allows teams to run them consistently and repeatably. Automated chaos testing tools can simulate failures without manual intervention, ensuring that experiments are run systematically.

  o **Example:** Use tools like Gremlin or Chaos Monkey to automate the introduction of faults into the system.

- **Learn and adapt:** After conducting chaos experiments, teams should analyze the results to gain insights into system behavior and identify areas for improvement. Learning from these experiments fosters a culture of continuous improvement.

  o **Outcome:** Use insights gained from chaos testing to make architectural changes, improve incident response plans, and enhance overall system design.

- **Ensure safety and control:** Safety should be a priority in chaos testing. Implement safeguards to prevent experiments from causing widespread disruptions. This may involve running tests in non-production environments or during off-peak hours.

  o **Implementation:** Establish rollback procedures or limit the scope of experiments to reduce potential impacts.

- **Involve stakeholders:** Engage cross-functional teams in the chaos engineering process, including developers, operations, and security. This collaborative approach ensures a comprehensive understanding of system behavior and promotes a culture of shared ownership of reliability.

  o **Example:** Conduct post-experiment reviews with stakeholders to discuss findings and necessary actions.

Examples of potential chaos experiments

Chaos experiments can take various forms, depending on the specific aspects of the system being tested. Here are some common types of chaos experiments:

- **Killing instances:** Randomly terminate instances of a microservice to evaluate how the system handles instance failures. This tests the service's ability to recover and ensure that other instances can handle the load.

  o **Example:** Use a tool to randomly kill EC2 instances running a particular service and monitor how quickly the system recovers.

- **Severing network connections:** Simulate network disruptions by severing connections between services or between clients and services. This helps evaluate the system's resilience to network failures and ability to reroute traffic.

  o **Example:** Use a chaos tool to introduce latency or packet loss between microservices and monitor the impact on overall system performance.

- **Overloading services:** Artificially increasing the request rate to a service beyond its capacity simulates an overload scenario. This tests how the service responds under extreme load and whether it can scale effectively.

  o **Example:** Implement a load testing tool to send a high volume of requests to an API endpoint and observe how the service handles the load.

- **Introducing resource constraints:** Simulate resource exhaustion by limiting CPU, memory, or disk I/O for specific instances or services. This tests the system's behavior under constrained resources and its ability to prioritize critical operations.

  o **Example:** Use resource control tools to restrict CPU usage for a service and observe how it affects response times and error rates.

- **Dependency failure:** Simulate the failure of an external dependency, such as a database or third-party API. This helps teams understand how the system handles cascading failures and whether appropriate fallback mechanisms are in place.

  o **Example:** Use chaos engineering tools to simulate the unavailability of a critical database service and monitor how the application reacts.

- **Configuration changes:** Introduce unexpected configuration changes to test how the system reacts to changes in parameters, such as timeouts or feature flags. This ensures that the system can adapt to changes in its environment.

  o **Example:** Randomly change configuration values for a service and monitor whether it can adapt without disruption.

Chaos testing is a powerful practice for validating system resilience and improving overall reliability. By adhering to the key principles of chaos engineering and conducting a variety of chaos experiments, organizations can gain valuable insights into their systems' behavior under adverse conditions. This proactive approach not only enhances system robustness but also fosters a culture of continuous learning and improvement within development and operations teams.

Tool-agnostic chaos testing

Chaos testing is essential for validating the resilience of modern systems, and integrating it into a tool-agnostic framework enhances flexibility and adaptability across various environments. By utilizing open-source chaos engineering tools and following best practices, organizations can ensure their chaos experiments are portable and practical regardless of the underlying infrastructure.

To integrate chaos testing into a tool-agnostic framework, follow the given steps:

1. **Choose open-source chaos engineering tools:** Start by selecting open-source chaos engineering tools that offer flexibility and compatibility with different systems. Some popular tools include:

   a. **Chaos Monkey:** Developed by Netflix, it randomly terminates instances in production to ensure that applications are resilient to instance failures.

   b. **Gremlin:** Provides a user-friendly interface for running chaos experiments and supports a wide range of failure scenarios, such as resource exhaustion and network issues.

   c. **Litmus:** A cloud-native chaos engineering framework that integrates seamlessly with Kubernetes environments and provides a wide variety of chaos experiments.

2. **Abstract experiment configuration:** Create an abstraction layer for chaos experiment configurations, allowing teams to define experiments using a standard interface. This approach makes it easier to manage different tools and adapt experiments across various environments.

   a. **Implementation:** Define experiment templates using a configuration language (like YAML or JSON) that outlines parameters such as failure types, target services, and expected outcomes. Use a controller that translates these templates into specific commands for each chaos tool.

3. **Use APIs and scripting for flexibility:** Leverage the APIs provided by chaos tools to run experiments programmatically. This allows you to integrate chaos experiments into CI/CD pipelines, ensuring that tests can be executed consistently across different development and deployment stages.

   a. **Example:** Write scripts in Python or Bash that invoke chaos experiments through the APIs of Chaos Monkey or Gremlin, enabling automated execution in a CI/CD pipeline.

4. **Implement environment-driven configurations:** Structure your chaos experiments to be environment-specific. This allows teams to customize the behavior of chaos tests based on the infrastructure (for example, cloud provider, on-premises setup) and environment (such as staging, production) where the tests are executed.

a. **Implementation:** Use environment variables or configuration files to dynamically adjust parameters such as service endpoints, instance IDs, or resource limits based on the execution environment.

5. **Leverage containerization for portability:** Containerize chaos engineering tools to ensure that they can run consistently across different environments. By packaging tools such as Gremlin or Litmus in Docker containers, you can easily deploy them regardless of the underlying infrastructure.

a. **Example:** Create Docker images for chaos engineering tools and deploy them in your Kubernetes cluster or any other orchestration platform, ensuring the same environment setup for chaos experiments.

Ensuring chaos experiments are portable

To ensure that chaos experiments are portable, ensure the following:

- **Design modular chaos experiments:** Modular design allows chaos experiments to be easily reused and adapted across various contexts. Break down chaos scenarios into smaller, reusable components, such as scripts or templates that can be combined to form complete experiments.

    o **Implementation:** Create a library of common failure scenarios (e.g., instance termination, network latency) that can be parameterized and reused in different experiments.

- **Document experiment dependencies:** Clearly document any dependencies or prerequisites required for chaos experiments to run successfully. This includes specifying any necessary configurations, access permissions, or tools that must be present in the environment.

    o **Outcome:** A well-documented set of dependencies ensures that teams can replicate chaos experiments in different environments without missing critical setup steps.

- **Support multiple cloud providers and on-premises environments:** Design chaos experiments to support multiple cloud providers (for example, AWS, Azure, Google Cloud) and on-premises setups. Use cloud-agnostic APIs and tools to minimize vendor lock-in and enhance portability.

    o **Implementation:** Create abstraction layers that interact with cloud provider APIs or on-premises infrastructure, enabling the same chaos experiments to be executed regardless of where the application is hosted.

- **Enable rollback mechanisms:** Implement rollback mechanisms that allow teams to revert changes made during chaos experiments quickly. This ensures that any disruptions caused by the experiments can be mitigated, maintaining system stability.

    o **Strategy:** Use orchestration tools like Kubernetes to manage deployments and easily roll back to previous versions if an experiment causes issues.

- **Conduct post-experiment reviews:** After executing chaos experiments, conduct post-experiment reviews to evaluate their effectiveness and identify areas for improvement. Involve stakeholders from various teams to gather feedback and refine the chaos testing process.

    o **Outcome:** Continuous feedback loops enable teams to adapt chaos experiments to better fit different environments and improve their overall effectiveness.

Integrating chaos testing into a tool-agnostic framework enhances flexibility and adaptability across diverse environments and infrastructure setups. By utilizing open-source chaos engineering tools, designing modular experiments, and employing best practices for portability, organizations can effectively validate the resilience of their systems. This proactive approach strengthens system reliability and fosters a culture of continuous improvement and innovation within development and operations teams.

Integrating chaos testing into CI/CD workflows

Incorporating chaos testing into CI/CD workflows is crucial for ensuring the resilience and reliability of modern applications at scale. Organizations can proactively detect vulnerabilities and minimize the risk of service disruptions by automating resilience testing and establishing effective response strategies. This section outlines how to integrate chaos testing into CI/CD workflows effectively. Let us learn how to incorporate chaos testing into the CI/CD pipeline:

- **Define chaos testing objectives:** Before integrating chaos testing into CI/CD workflows, establish clear goals for what you want to achieve. This may include validating system resilience, testing failover mechanisms, or measuring recovery times.

- **Implementation:** Define specific metrics (for example, response time, error rates) and outcomes for each chaos experiment that will be executed as part of the CI/CD process.

- **Select appropriate stages for chaos testing:** Identify the right stages in the CI/CD pipeline where chaos testing should be incorporated. Common stages include:

  o **Pre-deployment testing:** Run chaos experiments in staging environments before deploying to production.

  o **Post-deployment testing:** Conduct chaos testing in production after a successful deployment to validate resilience under real-world conditions.

  o **Example:** Configure chaos tests to run automatically after unit and integration tests during the CI phase.

Integrate chaos testing tools

Use automation tools and scripts to seamlessly integrate chaos testing tools into the CI/CD pipeline. This may involve leveraging plugins or APIs provided by CI/CD platforms such as Jenkins, GitLab CI, or CircleCI.

Implementation: Create CI/CD pipeline stages that invoke chaos testing tools (for example, Chaos Monkey, Gremlin) using scripts or dedicated plugins.

Automating resilience testing in CI/CD workflows

Let us now understand the following.

Use automation frameworks

Employ automation frameworks to execute chaos tests within the CI/CD pipeline. These frameworks should facilitate the scheduling, execution, and monitoring of chaos experiments.

Example: Utilize tools like Jenkins or GitLab CI to create pipeline jobs that run chaos tests at specified intervals or as part of specific branches or tags.

Set up monitoring and alerts

Implement monitoring tools to track system performance during chaos tests. Establish alerting mechanisms to notify teams of failures or performance degradation in real time.

Implementation: Integrate monitoring tools such as Prometheus, Grafana, or Datadog into the CI/CD pipeline to visualize metrics and trigger alerts when predefined thresholds are breached.

Review and analyze results

After chaos tests are run, automate the analysis of results to determine whether the system met resilience criteria. This analysis can be automated using reporting tools that generate insights based on the collected metrics.

Outcome: Create dashboards to visualize chaos testing outcomes, enabling teams to quickly identify trends, issues, and areas for improvement.

Automating rollback or compensating actions

Let us go over the following.

Establish rollback procedures

Create predefined rollback procedures to automatically revert changes when chaos tests detect failures. This may involve restoring previous application versions, scaling down services, or activating failover mechanisms.

Implementation: Use IaC tools such as Terraform or AWS CloudFormation to automate the deployment and rollback processes.

Integrate with orchestration tools

Leverage orchestration tools (for example, Kubernetes) to manage service deployments and facilitate automatic rollbacks or scaling based on the outcomes of chaos tests.

Example: Set up Kubernetes deployment strategies (for example, rolling updates or blue-green deployments) that automatically revert to a stable version if chaos tests indicate a failure.

Define compensating actions

In addition to rollbacks, outline compensating actions that can be triggered in response to failures detected during chaos tests. These may include routing traffic away from failing services, activating backup services, or adjusting resource allocations.

Implementation: Use service mesh tools (for example, Istio) to implement traffic management strategies that can dynamically adjust routing based on the health of services during chaos tests.

Implement testing gates

Integrate testing gates within the CI/CD pipeline to prevent deployments from proceeding if chaos tests fail. This adds a layer of assurance that only resilient systems are promoted to production.

Outcome: Use tools like Jenkins or GitHub Actions to enforce gate conditions that halt the pipeline when chaos tests do not meet predefined success criteria.

Integrating chaos-testing into CI/CD workflows is essential for validating the resilience of modern applications at scale. Organizations can proactively manage risks and ensure high system reliability by automating chaos experiments, monitoring results, and establishing rollback or compensating actions. This proactive approach enhances application resilience and fosters a culture of continuous improvement and innovation within development and operations teams.

Best practices for non-functional testing

Integrating security, performance, and resilience testing into a cohesive and comprehensive testing strategy is essential for ensuring robust, reliable, and secure applications. By aligning these critical testing aspects, organizations can enhance their overall quality assurance efforts while avoiding duplication of efforts. This section outlines practical strategies for combining these testing methodologies.

Strategies for an integrated testing strategy

Let us now go over the following.

Adopt a shift-left approach

Implement a shift-left strategy by integrating security, performance, and chaos testing early in the software development lifecycle. This proactive approach enables teams to identify and address potential issues before they escalate into costly problems later in the process.

Implementation: Involve security, performance, and chaos engineers in design reviews and early architecture discussions. This ensures that testing considerations are embedded from the outset.

Define cross-disciplinary testing teams

Form cross-functional teams that include security experts, performance engineers, and chaos engineers. This encourages collaboration and knowledge sharing among different testing disciplines, fostering a holistic approach to application quality.

Example: Create a quality assurance team comprising members from different backgrounds who can contribute to security, performance, and chaos testing efforts.

Establish common testing frameworks

Utilize a common testing framework or tool chain that supports security, performance, and chaos testing. This reduces complexity and streamlines the testing process, allowing teams to manage all aspects of testing through a unified interface.

Implementation: Choose open-source tools or frameworks (for example, JMeter for performance, OWASP ZAP for security, and Gremlin for chaos) that can be integrated into a single testing pipeline.

Develop comprehensive test plans

Create test plans that encompass security, performance, and chaos testing. Ensure that these plans outline objectives, testing methodologies, success criteria, and roles and responsibilities for each testing aspect.

Outcome: A well-defined test plan helps teams stay aligned to goals and ensures that all critical areas are addressed without redundancy.

Implement continuous monitoring

Establish continuous monitoring practices to track application performance, security vulnerabilities, and system resilience in real time. This helps teams identify and respond to issues across all three domains.

Tools: Use monitoring tools like Prometheus, Grafana, and Datadog to visualize metrics related to security, performance, and chaos testing.

Integrate testing early in the design phase

Collaborate with architects and developers during the design phase to identify potential security, performance, and resilience challenges. This enables teams to design systems that inherently address these concerns, minimizing the need for extensive post-development testing.

Example: Conduct threat modeling sessions to assess security risks and performance bottlenecks early in the architecture design process.

Create shared requirements and acceptance criteria

Develop shared requirements incorporating security, performance, and resilience into acceptance criteria for features and functionalities. This ensures that all testing disciplines work toward common goals and metrics.

Implementation: Use user stories and acceptance criteria that explicitly mention security, performance, and chaos testing requirements.

Leverage automation for testing

Automate testing processes to facilitate seamless integration of security, performance, and chaos tests into CI/CD pipelines. Automation reduces manual effort and ensures that all testing aspects are executed consistently across environments.

Tools: Implement tools that support automated testing, such as Selenium for functional testing, JMeter for performance, and OWASP ZAP for security, within the same CI/CD pipeline.

Conduct regular test reviews and retrospectives

Organize regular reviews and retrospectives to evaluate the effectiveness of the integrated testing strategy. Encourage team members to share insights and identify areas for improvement, ensuring continuous refinement of testing processes.

Outcome: Regular feedback loops help teams identify any duplication of efforts and make necessary adjustments to streamline testing activities.

Utilize risk assessment frameworks

Implement risk assessment frameworks that evaluate security, performance, and resilience risks in a unified manner. This enables teams to prioritize testing efforts based on risk profiles, ensuring that critical areas receive adequate attention.

Implementation: Use frameworks like OWASP Top Ten for security risks and performance risk matrices to guide testing priorities and strategies.

Combining security, performance, and chaos testing into a cohesive, integrated testing strategy is essential for delivering robust, reliable, and secure applications. By adopting a shift-left approach, fostering collaboration, and leveraging automation, organizations can ensure that all critical testing aspects are addressed efficiently and effectively. This integrated strategy not only enhances overall application quality but also promotes a culture of continuous improvement and innovation within development and operations teams.

Creating a unified testing strategy

To create a unified testing strategy that incorporates security, performance, and resilience testing, organizations must ensure that these aspects are integral to the development lifecycle. By following best practices and establishing clear metrics, thresholds, and gates, teams can enhance the quality and reliability of their applications while minimizing risks.

Embed testing into the development lifecycle

Integrate security, performance, and resilience testing into every phase of the development lifecycle, from requirements gathering to design, implementation, and deployment. This shift-left approach ensures that these aspects are considered from the outset rather than treated as afterthoughts.

Implementation: Involve testing specialists in early design discussions and create checklists for each phase to ensure all three aspects are covered.

Adopt an agile methodology

Use agile methodologies that promote iterative development and continuous feedback. This fosters a culture where security, performance, and resilience testing are continuously assessed and improved throughout the development process.

Outcome: Encourage teams to incorporate testing tasks into sprint planning and allocate time for security and performance reviews in each iteration.

Foster cross-disciplinary collaboration

Create cross-functional teams that include members from development, security, performance engineering, and operations. This collaboration encourages knowledge sharing and ensures that all perspectives are considered during development.

Example: Organize regular meetings where team members discuss ongoing challenges and collaborate on solutions related to security, performance, and resilience.

Promote a culture of accountability

Establish a culture where all team members understand the importance of security, performance, and resilience. Encourage developers to take ownership of these aspects by providing training, resources, and incentives for identifying and addressing issues early in development.

Outcome: Empower team members to prioritize these aspects in their daily work, creating a shared responsibility for application quality.

Incorporate automated testing

Automate security, performance, and resilience testing to ensure that these processes are consistently executed throughout the development lifecycle. Automated tests can be easily integrated into CI/CD pipelines, allowing for continuous validation of these aspects.

Tools: Use testing tools such as Selenium for functional testing, OWASP ZAP for security testing, and JMeter for performance testing within the same pipeline.

Establishing clear metrics, thresholds, and gates

In order for these cross-cutting testing techniques to work effectively, there needs to be clear measurement of the different parameters so that clear failures or exceptions can be identified. The following are some ways that these can be defined, measured, and built into quality gates.

Define KPIs

Establish KPI for security, performance, and resilience testing that align with business objectives. These metrics should be measurable and relevant to the application's specific goals. Some example metrics are:

- **Security:** Number of vulnerabilities detected, time to remediate vulnerabilities.
- **Performance:** Response time, throughput, error rates under load.
- **Resilience: Mean Time to Recovery (MTTR)**, percentage of successful chaos tests.

Set thresholds for acceptable performance

Define clear thresholds for each metric, specifying acceptable ranges for performance and security metrics. These thresholds should be informed by industry standards, user expectations, and business requirements.

Implementation: Use historical data and benchmarking to establish realistic thresholds that reflect the desired performance and security levels.

Implement quality gates in CI/CD pipelines

Establish quality gates in CI/CD pipelines that enforce compliance with security, performance, and resilience thresholds before code can be promoted to production. This ensures that only code meeting predefined criteria is deployed.

Example: Configure CI/CD tools to automatically halt the deployment process if any security vulnerabilities exceed a defined severity level or performance metrics fall below acceptable thresholds.

Conduct regular reviews and adjustments

Regularly review metrics, thresholds, and gates to ensure they remain relevant and effective as applications evolve. Use insights from testing and real-world performance to adjust criteria as needed.

Outcome: Continuous refinement of metrics and thresholds allows teams to adapt to changing requirements and improve overall testing effectiveness.

Create a dashboard for visualization

Implement a centralized dashboard to visualize key metrics and thresholds for security, performance, and resilience. This visibility enables teams to track progress, identify trends, and respond quickly to issues.

Tools: Utilize tools such as Grafana, Kibana, or custom dashboards that aggregate data from various testing tools to provide a comprehensive view of application health.

Creating a unified testing strategy that integrates security, performance, and resilience testing into the development lifecycle is essential for delivering high-quality applications. Organizations can proactively manage risks and enhance overall application reliability by embedding these aspects into every development phase and establishing clear metrics, thresholds, and gates. This comprehensive approach not only improves software quality but also fosters a culture of continuous improvement and accountability among development teams.

Tooling and infrastructure considerations

When developing a unified testing strategy that encompasses security, performance, and resilience testing, selecting the right tools and frameworks, along with robust infrastructure, is critical. These considerations ensure that testing can be executed effectively, flexibly, and on a scale, supporting the needs of complex and distributed systems.

Choosing tools and frameworks

While we will unpack different testing tools and how to select them in *Chapter 11, Overview of Tools Used in test Automation*, the following is a list of key criteria to consider for your performance and security tooling.

Flexibility and integration

Opt for tools and frameworks that can integrate seamlessly with existing development and CI/CD pipelines. Flexibility allows teams to adapt testing tools to various environments, platforms, and programming languages. Some examples of flexible tools are:

- **Security testing:** OWASP ZAP, Burp Suite, Snyk (for static and dynamic analysis).
- **Performance testing:** JMeter, Gatling, k6 (supporting various protocols and load scenarios).
- **Chaos testing:** Gremlin, Chaos Monkey (allowing easy integration with cloud and microservices environments).

Scalability

Choose tools that can scale according to the complexity and size of your applications. As applications grow, the tools should handle increased load and provide meaningful insights without performance degradation.

Implementation: Evaluate tools that support distributed testing and can manage thousands of virtual users or extensive datasets efficiently.

Comprehensive functionality

Select tools that provide comprehensive functionality covering multiple testing aspects. This reduces the number of tools required, minimizing overhead and complexity.

Example: Tools like JMeter can be used for both performance and load testing, while Snyk provides security analysis throughout the development lifecycle.

Support for automation

Ensure the chosen tools support automation features that can be integrated into CI/CD pipelines. Automated testing allows for continuous security, performance, and resilience validation without manual intervention.

Outcome: Look for APIs or CLI interfaces that enable scripting and automation of test execution and reporting.

Community and support

Consider the community and vendor support for the tools you select. Strong community backing can lead to better documentation, frequent updates, and shared experiences that enhance tool usability.

Implementation: Evaluate open-source tools with active communities and commercial tools that offer dedicated support options.

Ensuring robust infrastructure

Let us go over the following.

Cloud-native infrastructure

Leverage cloud-native infrastructure to support testing activities. Cloud environments provide flexibility to scale resources on demand and can simulate various real-world scenarios more effectively.

Implementation: Use cloud platforms (for example, AWS, Azure, GCP) to dynamically provision resources for testing, ensuring environments mimic production conditions.

Containerization and orchestration

Utilize containerization technologies (for example, Docker) and orchestration platforms (such as Kubernetes) to create isolated and repeatable testing environments. This setup helps manage dependencies and versions consistently across testing stages.

Outcome: Containerized testing environments can be easily replicated and scaled, providing reliable conditions for conducting tests.

Load balancing and redundancy

Design infrastructure with load balancing and redundancy to ensure high availability during testing. This is particularly crucial for performance and resilience testing, where the goal is to simulate real-world load conditions.

Implementation: Use load balancers and redundant systems to distribute testing workloads and prevent single points of failure.

Monitoring and logging

Implement robust monitoring and logging solutions to track the performance and behavior of applications during testing. Comprehensive logging aids in diagnosing issues and understanding system behavior under stress.

Tools: Use monitoring tools like Prometheus, Grafana, or ELK stack to visualize metrics and logs.

Data management

Ensure that your infrastructure can handle test data management effectively. This includes generating, storing, and cleaning up test data without compromising production data integrity.

Implementation: Use data masking techniques and synthetic data generation tools to create realistic test data while maintaining compliance with data protection regulations.

Security considerations

Integrate security measures into the testing infrastructure. This includes ensuring that testing environments are secure, with access controls, encryption, and network security measures in place to protect sensitive data.

Outcome: Regularly audit the security of your testing infrastructure and adapt policies to align with industry best practices and compliance requirements.

Choosing the right tools and frameworks, along with a robust infrastructure, is essential for supporting security, performance, and resilience testing in a unified strategy. Organizations can enhance their testing capabilities by focusing on flexibility, scalability, comprehensive functionality, and strong support. Additionally, ensuring that the infrastructure is designed to handle complex and distributed systems will allow teams to conduct effective testing that simulates real-world conditions, ultimately leading to higher-quality applications and improved user satisfaction.

Conclusion

Addressing concerns such as security, performance, and resilience within a tool-agnostic test automation framework is crucial for delivering high-quality software. These aspects not only contribute to the overall robustness of applications but also enhance user satisfaction and compliance with industry standards. By integrating these concerns into a unified strategy, organizations can mitigate risks and ensure their systems perform reliably under various conditions.

In the next chapter, we will look at how to select the right testing tools for your automation framework and unpack some of the popular tools in more detail.

Key takeaways

The following are the key takeaways from the chapter:

- **Integrating security testing:** Security testing should be embedded throughout the development lifecycle, utilizing automated tools and frameworks to detect vulnerabilities early. Employing a variety of testing methods, such as SAST, DAST, and penetration testing, ensures comprehensive coverage against potential threats.

- **Performance testing**: Regular performance testing is vital for understanding how applications behave under different loads. Key metrics, such as response time, throughput, and resource utilization, should be defined and monitored continuously. Types of performance tests, including load, stress, and endurance testing, must be integrated into the CI/CD pipeline for ongoing validation.

- **Resilience engineering:** Implementing chaos engineering practices allows teams to validate system resilience by intentionally introducing failures and observing system behavior. This proactive approach ensures that applications can withstand unexpected disruptions, making resilience a key aspect of overall system design.

- **Best practices for a unified framework:**

  o **Tool-agnostic approach:** Choose tools that support a flexible and scalable testing strategy without being locked into a specific technology. This promotes reusability and adaptability across different environments.

  o **Continuous testing:** Ensure that security, performance, and resilience testing are conducted continuously within CI/CD workflows. Setting clear quality gates based on defined thresholds helps prevent vulnerabilities and performance bottlenecks from reaching production.

  o **Cross-functional collaboration:** Foster collaboration among teams responsible for development, security, performance, and operations. A culture of shared responsibility for quality encourages early identification and resolution of potential issues.

  o **Robust infrastructure:** Invest in infrastructure that can handle the complexities of modern applications, such as cloud-native and containerized environments. This infrastructure should support automated testing and provide the resources necessary for comprehensive testing scenarios.

  o **Regular reviews and adaptation:** Conduct regular reviews of testing strategies, metrics, and practices. Use insights gained from testing to refine and improve the framework, ensuring it remains effective as application requirements evolve.

By implementing these strategies and best practices, organizations can create a resilient, high-performing system that continuously meets the demands of security, performance, and resilience testing. This integrated approach ultimately leads to improved application quality, reduced risk, and greater overall user satisfaction.

Exercises

1. How are cross-cutting concerns (performance, security, resilience, and so on) identified and prioritized during development and testing?

2. How are cross-cutting concerns incorporated into the SDLC from design to deployment?

3. How is performance testing integrated into CI/CD pipelines?

4. What key performance metrics (for example, response time, throughput, resource utilization) are monitored?

5. Are performance baselines and SLAs defined for applications? How are they enforced?

6. What security testing is integrated into your development lifecycle (for example, SAST, DAST, dependency scanning)?

7. How do you manage secrets, credentials, and access controls in development and testing environments?

8. Are there automated security gates in CI/CD pipelines that prevent insecure code from being deployed?

9. How do you test system resilience against failures, outages, and unexpected loads?

10. Do you perform chaos engineering or fault injection testing to assess system robustness?

11. How does your system handle graceful degradation under high load or partial failures?

12. What backup and disaster recovery strategies are in place? How often are they tested?

13. How do you validate failover and high availability mechanisms?

14. What strategies are in place for handling distributed system failures, including retry policies and circuit breakers?

15. How do you monitor and respond to real-time incidents affecting resilience?

CHAPTER 11
Overview of Tools Used in Test Automation

Introduction

In the software testing world, there is a lot of debate around testing tools. Whether it be the merits of Selenium vs. Cypress vs. Playwright, a comparison between UI automation tools, or the many tools out there that are designed to help a team with various stages of test and defect management. This list of tools continues to grow, and if you were to believe a lot of the vendors out there, almost all of them are going to revolutionize your testing approach.

However, the reality could not be more off. Not only are any of these tools unlikely to offer the value you expect from a testing and automation perspective, but there is a good chance you probably will not even need them, or at least most of the features they offer.

It is not the tool that determines your success, but rather your testing approach and automation frameworks, which will form the foundation of your testing and quality successes. Tools are simply a means to achieve that success, and how you use them is what counts.

This is why this book is based around building frameworks, rather than using specific tooling, and applies to a tool-agnostic approach. That does not mean tools are not needed. They are vital to the process as you need to leverage the power of tools to interact with the different elements of applications and provide features that can help speed up the process significantly.

Structure

In this chapter, we will cover the following topics:

- Tips to evaluate testing tools
- Test automation tools
- Testing tools for performance and load testing

Objectives

By the end of this chapter, the reader will know how best to evaluate different testing tools that can be used in your organization, before looking at specific testing tools in more detail, with some of the pros and cons of each.

Tips to evaluate testing tools

One of the biggest mistakes that many companies make is starting out their tool search with a preconceived notion in mind. Whether it be the desire to choose an open-source or commercial suite or to choose the latest popular tools just to appear popular and trendy to their development teams, too often companies end up making detrimental tool decisions because they simply rush the process or fail to understand what they really need.

The following guidelines guide how to evaluate different testing tools effectively and whether they suit your needs, before we look at a breakdown of tools in more detail. These steps are important because all tools have strengths and weaknesses, and it is best for all companies and teams to evaluate the right tool for their needs rather than just trying to go with the most common or popular option.

Define the testing requirements

Much like you need to fix the bigger issues in your testing space and take the time to fully understand your processes and frameworks, you also need to take the time to understand the tool requirements. It is only once you have fixed the gaps in those sections that you can perhaps understand why and where you may need a tool to help you.

In all situations, though, the problem you are trying to solve needs to be clear, and there needs to be a clear set of priorities and requirements for the things that matter to you. Some questions that you need to explore are:

- What types of applications and platforms do you need your tooling to support?
- Is your automation more backend or frontend focused?
- Do you want something that runs on the cloud, or does it need to be on-premise?
- How necessary are traceability and meeting audit requirements in your testing?
- Do you need your tool to fit into any existing CI pipelines or other existing development and testing tools?
- What about programming language requirements, existing skills within the team, or migration features?

Often, it can also be a little more specific, such as a need to automate a specific type of application, object, or track a specific performance or security measurement. Having a clear understanding of what you are looking for is key, and you need to identify all these things before moving on to the next step.

Prioritize the requirements

While you may have a clear idea of your requirements, not all features hold the same level of importance. For example, audit and security requirements are typically non-negotiable areas where investing in the best solution is essential. In contrast, you might save costs in other areas to accommodate these priorities.

A practical approach is to associate a potential cost with each risk, should it materialize. For instance, consider the hypothetical costs of a security breach versus a performance bottleneck, a failed audit, or delays caused by excessive maintenance cycles due to inadequate automation. While these costs may not always be easily quantifiable, this exercise can help prioritize critical requirements and identify areas where compromises might be acceptable.

It is essential to acknowledge that no tool is perfect or excels at everything. During your evaluation, focus on understanding your must-have features versus the ones you can compromise on. Avoid getting distracted by tools that boast the most features, claim to offer the best value for money, or are fully open-source without thoroughly assessing how their specific capabilities align with your organization's needs and goals.

Know your budget

Every company has budget constraints, even for critical areas such as security. Understanding the financial limits and available funding is crucial for determining where to allocate resources effectively and where cost-saving measures can be applied.

However, this goes beyond simply knowing the dollar amount available. It is essential to consider broader factors such as the overall development costs of various projects, hardware, servers, or existing cloud expenses, as well as staffing salaries. These elements provide a clearer picture of the total investment required. Additionally, this comprehensive view allows you to calculate the **return on investment** (**ROI**) for any tool you plan to implement, helping you assess where the tool can contribute to cost savings in the long run.

Identify the available testing tools

This step might seem straightforward, but it is also one where time can be easily wasted. While researching features and requirements of testing tools online or reading blog posts may seem productive, it often leads to encountering tools with oversold claims or features that are not specific enough for your needs. Unfortunately, it is nearly impossible to know whether a tool will truly meet your requirements without testing it.

So, how do you identify the right tools to trial among the overwhelming number of options, many claiming to offer similar capabilities? The key lies in leveraging the requirements analysis you completed in the first step. It should help you narrow your list down to three potential tools if done thoroughly. Suppose you are unable to narrow the list. In that case, it may be worth revisiting your requirements to add more details, especially around technical or business needs, to make the decision-making process clearer.

This is also where your prioritization and budget insights play a critical role. Knowing your most important requirements and budget constraints will help identify tools that align with those priorities.

Even if one tool stands out as a strong contender, avoid narrowing your choice to just one. Constantly evaluate at least three tools. It is only when you test them against your existing frameworks and processes that you will uncover their true capabilities and feasibility.

Evaluate the testing tools

Now comes the critical step of testing the tools. This is where involving key architects and technical stakeholders becomes essential—not only for the initial setup and configuration, but also for running the tools through a short mock project or even an actual sprint iteration if feasible.

Selecting the right team and use case

Choosing the right people and team to conduct the evaluations is crucial. While standardizing tools and processes across the organization is ideal, not all teams face the same challenges. For instance, if one team struggles with automating tests or adapting to the current tools, involving them, under the guidance of a key architect, may yield better insights than engaging a team without such challenges.

Similarly, it is important to select a specific use case for each tool. Define clear actions to be performed and measurable outcomes to compare how each tool meets your needs. This will make the evaluation process structured and meaningful.

Key evaluation criteria

Once the right people and use case are in place, the tools should be evaluated across the following criteria. While this list is a guideline, your specific requirements may dictate additional focus areas, so use discretion in tailoring your evaluation. Let us now go over this list:

- **Functionality:** The tool must perform the required tests and deliver the desired outcomes based on your use case and criteria. For example, if you are evaluating a performance testing tool, ramp up scripts with a consistent sample size and assess which tool provides the most accurate data and insights.

- **Installation and setup:** Evaluate the ease of installation and setup. For on-premises tools, how straightforward is the installation and integration with existing processes and tooling? For cloud-based tools, assess the ease of configuration, compatibility with security protocols, and integration with your organization's systems.

- **Integration:** The tool should seamlessly integrate with your existing tools, processes, and workflows. For example, if your organization relies on CI/CD pipelines, the tool must integrate effectively with CI/CD systems. Consider compatibility with your development cycle, programming languages, and frameworks.

- **Ease of use:** A tool's usability is critical for adoption and effectiveness. The tool should have a user-friendly interface and require minimal training. While it is ideal for the tool to align with existing skill sets, avoid tying yourself to legacy approaches. The tool should also be intuitive for those with appropriate expertise.

- **Cost:** Even if you have shortlisted tools within budget, it is worth comparing costs against features to determine which tool offers the best value. Consider not only licensing costs but also maintenance, training, and support. Sometimes, a tool with fewer features but greater ease of use can result in long-term cost savings.

- **Support:** Strong support and maintenance are essential. During the evaluation, log support tickets, explore documentation, and assess the vendor's or community's responsiveness. For open-source tools, the strength of documentation and community support becomes even more critical.

- **Data, security, and privacy:** Evaluate how each tool handles sensitive data, test data, and privacy. Assess the tool's security protocols to ensure no vulnerabilities could compromise your systems. Verify compliance with security standards and scrutinize older versions for potential issues.

Testing tools in real scenarios with the right team and clearly defined use cases ensures you uncover their true capabilities. By evaluating across multiple dimensions, you can make an informed decision that aligns with your technical as well as business needs.

Select and implement the testing tool

After evaluating the testing tools based on various criteria, the team selects the tool that best aligns with the most important requirements. However, the work does not end with this decision. The team must now prepare for a broader rollout and implementation, which includes any necessary training for different teams.

A phased approach is often the most effective strategy, rolling out the tool to one or two teams simultaneously to ensure proper support during implementation. Critical issues should be logged and tracked throughout this process on a dedicated implementation board. These issues should be addressed by a designated team or support resources (some vendors may offer specialized assistance) to ensure prompt resolution. If any critical issues arise that cannot be resolved, the company may decide to pause or discontinue the full implementation of the tool.

Monitor and evaluate the testing tool

At this stage, with the considerable effort invested in selecting and implementing the tool, it is expected that it will integrate well with the organization and fulfil its intended purpose. However, the evaluation does not stop here. It is important to track the tool's effectiveness over time to ensure it continues to meet the organization's evolving needs and delivers the expected ROI. This monitoring process typically includes pre-established performance metrics and additional measures specific to the tool's implementation.

In the early stages, performance improvements may not be immediately noticeable, and there might even be a temporary dip in effectiveness, as teams adjust during the adoption phase. However, steady progress should become apparent over a 3 to 12-month period, after which the tool's impact may plateau as it reaches its maximum effectiveness.

During this time, it is crucial to assess tool adoption as well. Teams may revert to old habits or fail to utilize the tool fully, or the organization's needs may shift, rendering the tool less effective. In such cases, the team should reassess whether the tool should continue to be used or if a new evaluation process should be initiated.

Test automation tools

Now that we have looked at the evaluation criteria for different tools, let us look at the tools themselves. Note this is not an exhaustive list by any means, but merely a look at the most popular tools at the time of writing. For a more complete list of these tools and any newer tools that are developed post the publication of this book, BrowserStack provides a comprehensive overview of this every year: **https://www.browserstack.com/guide/best-test-automation-frameworks**. Though they do sometimes confuse the principle of a framework and a tool, it is still a very comprehensive and detailed list worth reading through.

This section also focuses on tools that perform the actual automation and not tools that act as a framework instead (like Robot Framework). We have also excluded low-code and AI-driven tools from this list because many of them are new and untested in long-term framework implementation at the time of writing.

We will go deep on three very popular test automation frameworks, while then explaining some of the others in more detail.

Selenium

Selenium is an open-source suite of tools designed for automating web browsers. It allows developers and testers to write scripts in multiple programming languages (for example, Java, Python, C#, Ruby) to perform automated testing of web applications. Selenium supports multiple browsers such as Chrome, Firefox, Edge, and Safari, and works across various operating systems. Refer to the following figure:

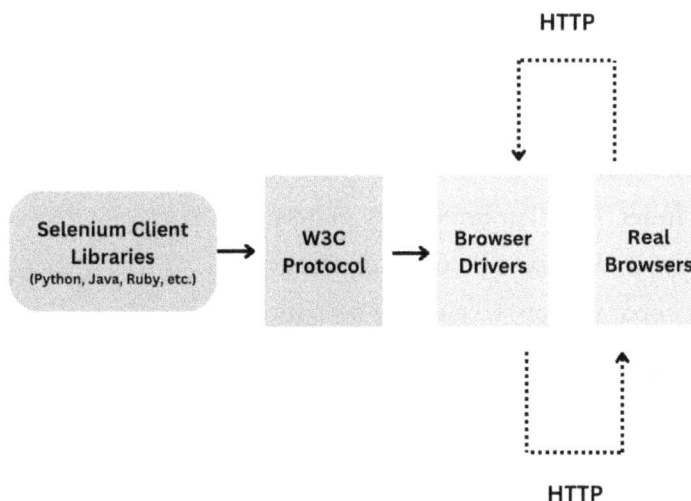

Figure 11.1: Example of how Selenium works against different web browsers

Selenium architecture

Selenium (at a high-level) operates on a client-server architecture comprising three main components:

- **Test Script/Client Layer:** Your test code (in Java, Python, and so on) interacts with the Selenium library bindings. This is where you write commands like `driver.findElement(...)`.

- **WebDriver API:** A language-specific interface that sends commands to the browser via the WebDriver protocol (JSON Wire Protocol/W3C WebDriver Protocol). Each browser has its own WebDriver implementation (for example, ChromeDriver, GeckoDriver).

- **Browser driver/Server layer:** Acts as a bridge between your test script and the actual browser. Receives HTTP requests from the WebDriver API, translates them into browser-native commands (for example, click, navigate), and returns the response.

- **Browser**: Executes the commands in the actual browser instance (headless or full UI), simulating a real user.

Architectural flow

The flow is:

[Test Code] | [Selenium Bindings] | [WebDriver API] | [Browser Driver] | [Browser]

       ←   JSON Wire / W3C Commands   ←

Embedding Selenium into a framework

To embed Selenium into a scalable, maintainable test automation framework, it should be encapsulated, abstracted, and modularized. Here is how you typically structure that:

- **Driver management layer:** We have:
    - Singleton or Factory pattern to manage WebDriver lifecycle.
    - Capable of supporting multiple browsers (Chrome, Firefox, and so on).
    - Config-driven (browser type, headless mode, grid, timeouts).

    The following Java code sample explains how to include a web driver into a framework:

```java
public class DriverManager {
public static WebDriver getDriver() {
        // Return WebDriver instance per configuration
}
}
```

- **Test the abstraction layer:** We have:
    - **Page Object Model** (**POM**) or Screenplay pattern.
    - Encapsulate element locators and user actions.
    - Keep test logic separate from UI element definitions.

    Refer to the following:

```java
java
CopyEdit
public class LoginPage {
private WebDriver driver;
```

```java
public void login(String user, String pass) {
        driver.findElement(userField).sendKeys(user);
        driver.findElement(passField).sendKeys(pass);
        driver.findElement(loginButton).click();
    }
}
```

- **Test orchestration layer:** We have:
    o Integrates with test runners (for example, JUnit/TestNG, pytest, NUnit).
    o Manages test setup/teardown, parameterization, and retries.
    o Parallel execution with Selenium Grid or cloud providers.

Cross-cutting concerns

Some cross-cutting concerns are as follows:

- **Logging and reporting**: Hooks to log browser actions, attach screenshots.
- **Exception handling**: Wrapper methods to handle stale elements, retries.
- **Configuration management**: Read from `.properties`, `yaml`, or JSON.
- **Data management**: Externalize test data (CSV, Excel, DB, API).
- **Execution modes**: Local, remote, Dockerized, CI/CD integrated.

Integration points

Some integration points are:

- **CI/CD pipelines**: Triggered via Jenkins, GitHub Actions, and so on.
- **Cloud grids**: BrowserStack, SauceLabs, LambdaTest, and so on.
- **Test management tools**: XRay, Zephyr, Allure, and so on.

Here is an example modular stack:

```
test-framework/
├── driver
│   └── DriverManager.java
├── pages
│   └── LoginPage.java
├── tests
│   └── LoginTests.java
├── utils
│   └── WaitHelper.java
│   └── ConfigReader.java
├── reports
│   └── ExtentReportManager.java
├── data
│   └── loginTestData.json
└── testng.xml / junit config / pytest.ini
```

The pros of Selenium are:

- **Open source and free**: Selenium is free to use, making it accessible for teams of any size.

- **Multi-browser and multi-OS support**: Compatible with all major browsers and operating systems.

- **Programming language flexibility**: Supports many popular programming languages, offering flexibility to testers.

- **Community support**: A vast, active community provides updates, plugins, and troubleshooting help.

- **Integration**: Easily integrates with CI/CD tools (for example, Jenkins) and other testing frameworks (such as TestNG, JUnit).

The cons of Selenium are:

- **No built-in reporting**: Lacks built-in reporting capabilities; requires integration with third-party tools for detailed reporting.

- **Limited mobile testing**: Selenium is primarily designed for web testing and does not natively support mobile apps (though it can integrate with Appium for mobile testing).

- **Steep learning curve**: Requires programming knowledge, making it less beginner-friendly than other tools.

- **Maintenance overhead**: As applications evolve, maintaining Selenium scripts can become complex and time-consuming.

- **No built-in test management**: Selenium does not provide features for test case management or test planning.

Playwright

Playwright is an open-source, modern testing tool developed by Microsoft for end-to-end automation of web applications. It supports multiple programming languages such as JavaScript, Python, C#, and Java, and provides cross-browser automation for major browsers (Chromium, Firefox, and WebKit). Playwright is designed to handle modern web application complexities, including dynamic content, **single-page applications** (**SPA**), and multi-tab interactions. Refer to the following figure:

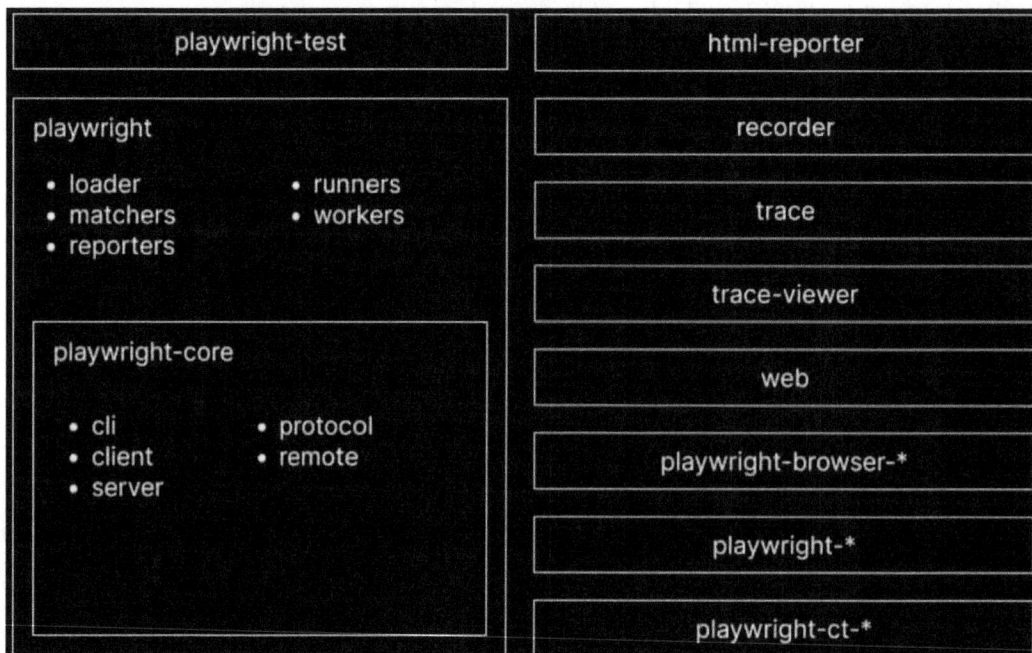

Figure 11.2: Example of the key components found in the Playwright architecture

Playwright architecture

Playwright has a **client-server architecture**, but it is more compact and modern than Selenium. It operates via a persistent WebSocket connection instead of stateless HTTP requests.

Core components

The core components are:

- **Test code/client layer:**
  - o Test scripts written in Node.js, Python, Java, or .NET using Playwright bindings.
  - o Interacts with the Playwright API.
- **Playwright driver (Core):**
  - o A unified driver that handles browser automation via a **WebSocket** connection.
  - o Abstracts browser-specific protocol differences (Chrome DevTools Protocol, Firefox protocol).
- **Browser engines:**
  - o Embedded or installed versions of Chromium, Firefox, WebKit (downloaded via Playwright).
  - o Can run in headless or headed mode.

Architectural flow

The flow is:

[Test Code] | [Playwright API] ⇄ [Playwright Driver] ⇄ [Browser Engine]

   ⇄   Persistent WebSocket   ⇄

We have:

- The WebSocket allows faster bi-directional communication than Selenium's RESTful model.
- All actions (click, type, wait, and so on) are queued and executed in strict order, supporting auto-waiting, retries, and tracing.

Embedding Playwright into a framework

Playwright is modular by design, and so it is relatively straightforward to embed into a test automation framework. Here is how you can structure that:

- **Browser context management:** Here, we have:
  - o Encapsulate Browser, Context, and Page initialization.
  - o Handle headless mode, viewport settings, context reuse (isolated sessions), and so on.

  The TypeScript code is as follows:

```
export class BrowserManager {
static async getContext(): Promise<BrowserContext> {
const browser = await chromium.launch();
return await browser.newContext();
}
}
```

- **Test the abstraction layer:** Here, we have:

  o Use the POM to isolate UI logic.

  o Since Playwright supports multiple tabs and frames, consider splitting logic by user journey or functional module.

  Here is an example:

```
export class LoginPage {
constructor(private page: Page) {}

async login(user: string, pass: string) {
await this.page.fill('#username', user);
await this.page.fill('#password', pass);
await this.page.click('#login');
}
}
```

- **Test the orchestration layer:** We have:

  o Integrate with native Playwright Test Runner, or third-party runners like Jest, Mocha, pytest, or TestNG (Java).

  o Support tagging, retries, parallelism, slow-mo, and test config via **playwright.config.ts**.

  Look at the following:

```
test.describe('Login Suite', () => {
test('should log in successfully', async ({ page }) => {
const loginPage = new LoginPage(page);
await loginPage.login('admin', 'admin123');
});
});
```

Cross-cutting concerns

Some cross-cutting concerns are as follows:

- **Auto-waiting and resilience**: Playwright waits for UI stability (no explicit waits usually needed).
- **Tracing**: Built-in support for recording traces (screenshots, steps, network).
- **Screenshots and videos**: Easy hooks for capturing on failure.
- **Environment config**: Driven through **playwright.config** or external files.
- **Parallelism and sharding**: Native support without external grid (via worker processes).

Integration points

Refer to the following:

- **CI/CD**: GitHub Actions, Jenkins, Azure DevOps, and so on, with one-line Playwright test execution.
- **Containerized execution**: Supports Docker-based headless testing.
- **Reporters**: Allure, HTML Reporter, JSON, JUnit XML.
- **Third-party integration**: TestRail, XRay, Slack alerts, and so on.

Here is an example modular stack:

```
playwright-framework/
├── tests
│   └── login.spec.ts
├── pages
│   └── LoginPage.ts
├── utils
│   └── BrowserManager.ts
│   └── Config.ts
├── reports
│   └── playwright-report/
├── fixtures
│   └── loginData.json
├── playwright.config.ts
└── package.json / requirements.txt / pom.xml (based on language)
```

The pros of Playwright are:

- **Cross-browser testing with a single API**: Simplifies multi-browser testing with a unified API across Chromium, Firefox, and WebKit.

- **Auto-waiting**: Reduces flaky tests by automatically waiting for elements and network conditions.

- **Built-in features for debugging**: Supports debugging with video recording, screenshots, and tracing, all natively included.

- **Parallel execution by default**: Optimized for parallel execution to improve test speed and efficiency.

- **Supports modern web features**: Handles complex scenarios such as iframes, multiple tabs, and network interception out of the box.

- **Headless mode**: Allows running tests in headless mode for faster execution.

The cons of Playwright are:

- **Smaller community compared to Selenium**: While growing rapidly, it has less community support and fewer third-party plugins than Selenium.

- **Relatively new**: As a newer tool, it may not have all the ecosystem maturity or integrations that Selenium offers.

- **Limited mobile support**: Primarily focused on web testing, and mobile testing requires integration with tools like Appium.

- **Steeper learning curve for new users**: Advanced features can be overwhelming for beginners or teams new to modern test automation.

- **Heavier dependency on Node.js**: Though it supports other languages, its core is built around Node. js, which might not suit all teams.

Unified Functional Testing

Unified Functional Testing (UFT), formerly known as **QuickTest Professional** (QTP), is a commercial test automation tool developed by Micro Focus. It is widely used for functional, regression, and API testing of desktop, web, and mobile applications. UFT supports various application technologies, including web, Windows, SAP, Oracle, and .NET, making it suitable for enterprise applications. It uses VBScript as its scripting language. Refer to the following figure:

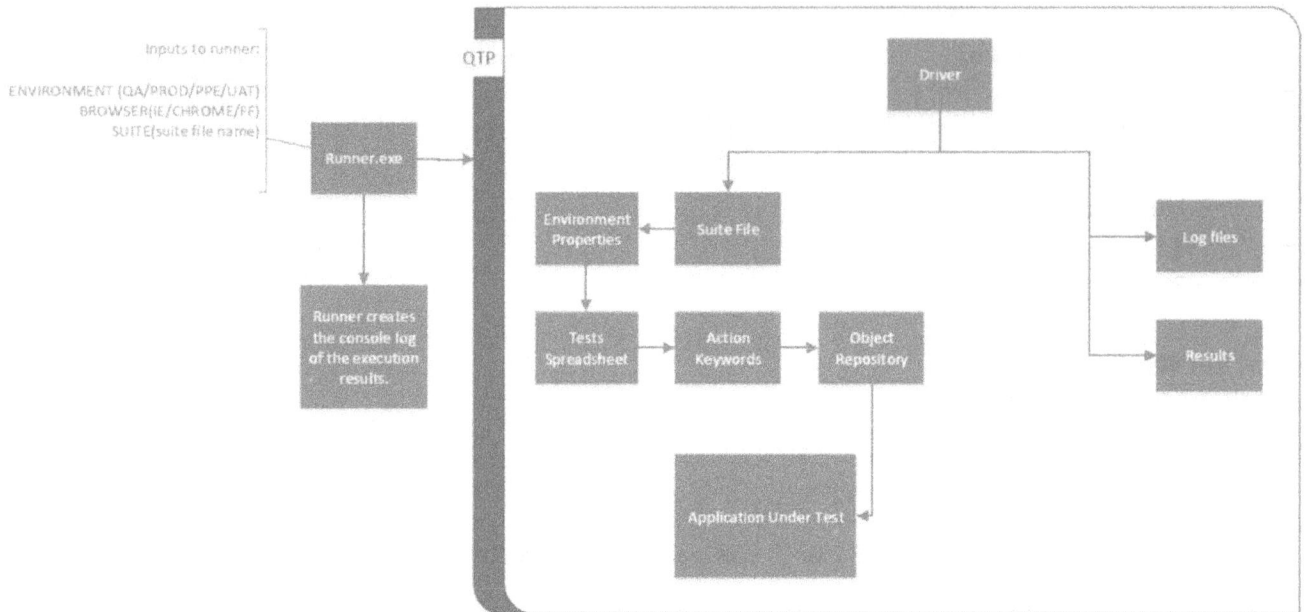

Figure 11.3: *Example of UFT architecture*

Unified Functional Testing architecture

UFT follows a component-based, desktop-driven architecture that is heavily reliant on Windows and **Component Object Model** (**COM**) interfaces. It is primarily a GUI-based tool but also supports code-behind (VBScript) for automation logic.

Core components

The core components are as follows:

- **Test scripts (VBScript):**
  - o User-defined test logic written using VBScript (procedural or modular).
  - o Interacts with the **Object repository** and **Test objects**.

- **Object repository:**
  - o Centralized or per-action store of UI object definitions and properties.
  - o Used by test scripts to recognize and interact with application objects.

- **Test execution engine:**
  - o Parses VBScript, accesses the Object Repository, and drives test execution via the UFT runtime.
  - o Interfaces with **Application Under Test** (**AUT**) via COM-based test objects and native plug-ins.

- **Automation Object Model (AOM):**
  - o Programmatic API (VBScript/COM) to control UFT externally (for example, from CI pipelines or external scripts).
  - o Enables launching UFT, running tests, generating reports, and so on.

- **Add-ins:**
  - o Plug-ins for recognizing objects of specific technologies (Web, SAP, .NET, Java, and so on)
  - o Must be loaded at startup depending on application type.

Architectural flow

The flow is:

[Test Script] → [Object Repository / Descriptive Programming]

↓

[Test Execution Engine] ⇄ [Add-ins/Plugins] ⇄ [Application Under Test (AUT)]

↓

[Results Viewer / Logs]

When UFT is run programmatically via AOM or via **Application Lifecycle Management** (**ALM**), it looks like this:

[CI Tool / ALM] → [UFT via AOM] → [Test Execution Engine] → [AUT]

Embedding UFT into a framework

Despite its GUI roots, UFT can be embedded into a framework through VBScript modularization, external control via AOM, and integration with CI tools. Here is how you can structure that:

- **Test modularity:** We have:

  o   Use *Function Libraries* (**.vbs** files) to define reusable logic.

  o   **Implement action-based modularization:** split test flows into shared or reusable actions.

  Here is a code sample in VBScript:

```
' Function Library
Function Login(username, password)
Browser("App").Page("Login").WebEdit("User").Set username
Browser("App").Page("Login").WebEdit("Password").Set password
Browser("App").Page("Login").WebButton("Login").Click
End Function
```

- **Centralized object repositories:** We have:

  o   Shared ORs for maintainability.

  o   Or, use descriptive programming for dynamic, code-based object recognition.

  Here is a code sample in VBScript:

```
Browser("micClass:=Browser").Page("micClass:=Page").WebButton("name:=Login").Click
```

- **Configuration and test data management:** We have:

  o   **External data sources:** Excel, CSV, XML, or DataTables (UFT built-in).

  o   Drive tests using **data-driven testing (DDT)** via global/local data sheets.

- **Execution control and orchestration:** We have:

  o   Control UFT from the outside using AOM (VBScript or another automation language via COM).

  Here is a code sample in VBScript:

```
Set qtApp = CreateObject("QuickTest.Application")
qtApp.Launch
qtApp.Open "C:\Tests\LoginTest", True
Set qtTest = qtApp.Test
```

```
qtTest.Run
qtTest.Close
```

This allows UFT to be triggered from batch scripts, Jenkins jobs, or CI/CD platforms.

- **Reporting:** We have:

  o   UFT auto-generates HTML test reports and logs.

  o   Custom logging can be added via Reporter utility or exported to external systems.

  Here is a sample:

```
Reporter.ReportEvent micPass, "Login", "Login successful"
```

- **Integration points:** We have:

  o   **ALM/Quality center**: Deep native integration for test management, scheduling, and execution.

  o   **Jenkins/Azure DevOps**: UFT tests can be triggered via the command line or plugins.

  o   **Git**: UFT supports Git for version control in recent versions (with UFT Developer/LeanFT support).

  o   **Hybrid testing**: Can be extended with API tests via **UFT API** or via REST calls using VBScript.

Here is an example modular stack (UFT directory layout):

```
UFT_Framework/
├── Tests
│   └── LoginTest/
│       ├── LoginTest.brs
│       └── LoginTest.tsr (OR)
├── FunctionLibraries
│   └── CommonFunctions.vbs
├── Data
│   └── LoginTestData.xlsx
├── Reports
│   └── TestResults/
├── Scripts
│   └── RunAllTests.vbs (AOM Orchestrator)
```

The pros of UFT are:

- **Wide technology support**: Works with a vast range of applications and platforms, including legacy systems and packaged applications.

- **Built-in test management integration**: Integrates natively with Micro Focus ALM for end-to-end test management.

- **Easy-to-use interface**: User-friendly UI and keyword-driven testing make it accessible to non-programmers.

- **API and GUI testing in one tool**: Supports both API and GUI testing, reducing the need for multiple tools.

- **Rich reporting features**: Provides detailed and customizable reports out of the box.

- **Enterprise-level support**: Backed by Micro Focus, it offers professional support and regular updates.

The cons of UFT are:

- **Commercial licensing costs**: UFT is expensive, which can be prohibitive for smaller teams or organizations.

- **VBScript limitation**: Relies on VBScript, which is less popular and modern compared to other scripting languages such as Python or Java.

- **Limited cross-browser testing**: While it supports multiple browsers, its capabilities are less robust than modern tools like Selenium or Playwright.

- **Slow execution**: Tests can be slower compared to lightweight, open-source tools.

- **High resource requirements**: Consumes significant system resources, which can impact performance during test execution.

- **Less flexible for agile environments**: Its heavier framework and slower test creation process may not align well with agile and DevOps workflows.

Architectural highlights comparing Selenium, Playwright, and UFT

Here is a brief summary of some of the key differences in the architecture of UFT, Selenium, and Playwright:

Feature	UFT	Selenium	Playwright
Language	VBScript	Java, Python, C#, JS	JS/TS, Python, .NET, Java
Test runner	Built-in GUI runner	External (JUnit, TestNG, etc.)	Native Playwright Test
Object handling	Object Repository + Add-ins	DOM Locators via browser drivers	Direct DOM access via DevTools
Extensibility	Limited (COM-based)	High	High
Parallelism	Manual setup, limited	Grid-based	Native worker-based
CI/CD integration	Via AOM or ALM plugins	High flexibility	Seamless and native
Platform dependency	Windows only	Cross-platform	Cross-platform

Table 11.1: Key differences in the architecture of UFT, Selenium, and Playwright

Tosca

Tosca is a commercial, enterprise-level test automation tool developed by Tricentis. It is designed for end-to-end testing, including functional, regression, and API testing, with strong support for modern, enterprise, and legacy systems. Tosca focuses on model-based testing, enabling scriptless automation, which makes it highly accessible for non-programmers. It integrates seamlessly with agile and DevOps workflows and supports continuous testing.

The key features include:

- **Model-based testing**: Creates reusable models of application elements for automation instead of writing code.

- **Scriptless automation**: Eliminates the need for scripting, making it user-friendly for testers without coding skills.

- **End-to-end testing**: Covers web, desktop, mobile, API, and packaged applications like SAP, Oracle, and Salesforce.

- **CI/CD integration**: Built for agile and DevOps workflows, integrating with CI/CD tools like Jenkins, Azure DevOps, and Jira.

The pros of Tosca are:

- **Scriptless automation**: Reduces the learning curve and allows non-technical users to participate in automation efforts.

- **Broad application support**: Supports web, desktop, API, mobile, and packaged enterprise apps, making it versatile for enterprise environments.

- **Reusability and maintenance**: Model-based testing ensures that changes to the application are easy to adapt without rewriting scripts.

- **Integration with enterprise tools**: Works well with CI/CD pipelines, test management tools, and agile project management tools.

- **Risk-based testing**: Prioritizes test cases based on business risk, improving test efficiency.

- **Built-in reporting and analytics**: Provides out-of-the-box reporting and dashboards for test execution insights.

- **Strong support for SAP and enterprise systems**: One of the leading tools for testing SAP and other complex enterprise applications.

The cons of Tosca are:

- **High licensing costs**: As a commercial tool, its cost is significant, making it less accessible for smaller organizations.

- **Complex setup for beginners**: While scriptless, its setup and configuration for large systems can still be complex.

- **Resource-intensive**: Requires powerful infrastructure for smooth execution, especially in large-scale environments.

- **Limited flexibility**: The scriptless, model-based approach can sometimes be restrictive for highly custom or edge-case scenarios.

- **Dependency on vendor support**: Strong reliance on Tricentis support and training to fully leverage the tool.

- **Smaller community**: Compared to open-source tools like Selenium or Playwright, Tosca has a smaller community, limiting free troubleshooting resources.

Cypress

Cypress is a modern, open-source test automation tool designed for end-to-end testing of web applications. It is particularly well-suited for testing modern, dynamic, and JavaScript-heavy applications. Unlike traditional tools that operate outside the browser, Cypress runs directly within the browser, allowing it to have more control and insight into application behavior. Cypress is built on JavaScript/TypeScript, making it a favorite among developers familiar with these languages.

The key features include:

- **Real-time reloading**: Automatically reloads tests as you make changes.

- **Time travel debugging**: Captures snapshots during test execution, enabling users to travel back in time to debug issues.

- **Built-in mocking and stubbing**: Easily control and manipulate network requests and responses.

The pros of Cypress are:

- **Developer-friendly**: Designed with developers in mind, featuring fast setup and easy integration into JavaScript workflows.

- **Built-in debugging tools**: Features like time travel, screenshots, and readable error messages make debugging straightforward.

- **Fast execution**: Runs directly in the browser, making test execution fast and efficient.

- **All-in-one tool**: Includes built-in features like mocking, stubbing, and assertions without needing external libraries.

- **Interactive test runner**: Provides a visually intuitive test runner that shows test steps and results in real time.

- **Active community**: A vibrant and growing community provides extensive documentation, plugins, and support.

- **Supports modern frameworks**: Optimized for modern web technologies, including React, Angular, and Vue.js.

The cons of Cypress are:

- **Limited browser support**: While it supports Chromium-based browsers, Firefox, and Edge, it does not support WebKit (for example, Safari) natively.

- **Not for non-web applications**: Focused entirely on web applications, so it cannot test desktop, mobile, or enterprise apps like SAP.

- **Single programming language**: Only supports JavaScript/TypeScript, which might limit its adoption in non-JS-heavy teams.

- **Lacks true parallel execution**: Parallelism requires configuration with third-party services like Cypress Dashboard.

- **Limited cross-domain testing**: Has restrictions when testing across different domains due to its browser-native architecture.

- **Resource-intensive**: Running tests within the browser can consume significant memory and CPU resources.

Puppeteer

Puppeteer is an open-source Node.js library developed by Google that provides a high-level API to control Chromium-based browsers (including Chrome) using the DevTools Protocol. It is primarily used for browser automation tasks such as web scraping, generating PDFs, and automated UI testing. While Puppeteer is commonly associated with automation, it does not natively provide testing features like assertions or a test runner, but can be integrated into testing workflows with additional libraries.

The key features include:

- **Headless and headed browser automation**: Supports running tests in both headless and full-browser modes.

- **DevTools Protocol**: Provides profound control over browser features such as network interception and performance monitoring.

- **Fast and reliable**: Offers rapid execution by working closely with Chromium browsers.

The pros of Puppeteer are:

- **Powerful browser control**: Direct access to the Chrome DevTools Protocol enables advanced automation capabilities such as tracing, network interception, and performance profiling.

- **Fast and lightweight**: Optimized for Chromium-based browsers, making it highly performant and lightweight.

- **Full control of browser**: Allows manipulation of browser features such as cookies, caching, and screen emulation.

- **Ease of use with JavaScript**: Designed for Node.js, making it ideal for teams already working with JavaScript/TypeScript.

- **Headless browser support**: Built for fast headless automation, making it efficient for tasks like web scraping or rendering.

- **Customizable**: Provides granular control over browser automation, making it flexible for specific use cases.

The cons of Puppeteer are:

- **Chromium-only**: Supports Chromium-based browsers only, with no native support for other browsers like Firefox, Safari, or Edge (though there is an experimental Firefox support).

- **No built-in testing features**: Lacks features such as assertions, test runners, or reporting; requires integration with libraries like Jest, Mocha, or Jasmine for testing.

- **Limited community compared to Selenium**: While growing, Puppeteer's ecosystem is smaller than mature tools like Selenium.

- **No cross-browser testing**: Cannot natively test across different browser engines, unlike tools such as Playwright or Selenium.

- **Requires JavaScript knowledge**: Being a Node.js library, it is not ideal for teams unfamiliar with JavaScript/TypeScript.

- **Lack of enterprise features**: Missing enterprise-friendly features like built-in reporting, dashboards, or CI/CD integrations found in other tools.

Appium

Appium is an open-source test automation framework designed for testing mobile applications (native, hybrid, and mobile web) across iOS and Android platforms. It supports a wide range of programming languages such as Java, Python, JavaScript, and C#, making it versatile for teams with different language preferences. Appium operates on the principle of *Write Once, Run Anywhere*, allowing a single script to run on multiple platforms. It uses the WebDriver protocol, like Selenium, for automation.

The key features include:

- **Cross-platform support**: Works with iOS and Android, including simulators, emulators, and real devices.

- **Language agnostic**: Supports a variety of programming languages via client libraries.

- **Open source**: No licensing costs, making it accessible for teams of all sizes.

The pros of Appium are:

- **Cross-platform testing**: Enables reusability of test scripts for Android and iOS, reducing duplication efforts.

- **Language and framework flexibility**: Works with multiple programming languages and test frameworks, offering great flexibility.

- **Supports real devices and emulators**: Tests can run on physical devices, emulators, and cloud-based device farms like BrowserStack and Sauce Labs.

- **Open-source community**: A large, active community provides support, plugins, and integrations.

- **No modifications to the app**: Does not require modifying the application under test (for example, adding custom hooks).

- **WebDriver protocol**: Familiar for teams already using Selenium, easing the learning curve.

The cons of Appium are:

- **Slow test execution**: Tests may execute slower compared to tools specifically optimized for mobile testing.

- **Complex setup**: Initial setup, especially for iOS, can be challenging due to dependencies like Xcode and provisioning profiles.

- **Limited advanced gesture support**: Complex gestures and animations may require workarounds or additional libraries.

- **Reliability issues**: Flaky tests can occur, especially in environments with inconsistent devices or network conditions.

- **No built-in reporting**: Lacks built-in reporting and requires integration with external tools for test analytics.

- **Maintenance overhead**: As mobile OS versions and devices evolve, test maintenance can become resource-intensive.

TestComplete

TestComplete is a commercial, enterprise-grade test automation tool developed by SmartBear. It supports functional UI and end-to-end web, desktop, and mobile application testing. It is known for its flexibility in scripting and scriptless testing, offering a choice between keyword-driven or record-and-playback methods and the ability to write scripts in various programming languages like JavaScript, Python, or VBScript. TestComplete is widely used for applications built on modern and legacy technologies.

The key features include:

- **Cross-platform support**: Allows web, desktop, and mobile application testing across different operating systems.

- **Scripted and scriptless options**: Enables technical and non-technical users to create and execute tests.

- **Integration with CI/CD**: Works with tools like Jenkins, Azure DevOps, and Git for continuous testing.

The pros of TestComplete are:

- **Broad technology support**: Covers web, mobile, and desktop applications built with frameworks like Angular, React, .NET, Java, and others.

- **Flexible test creation**: It supports scriptless testing with record-and-playback features and scripting in multiple languages, accommodating testers of all skill levels.

- **Built-in object recognition**: Uses AI-driven object recognition to handle dynamic UI elements effectively.

- **Reusable test components**: Enables modular test design for easier test maintenance and scalability.

- **Enterprise-friendly features**: Provides built-in reporting, test coverage metrics, and integrations with CI/CD pipelines.

- **Support for multiple languages**: Offers flexibility in scripting with options like Python, JavaScript, and VBScript.

- **Parallel test execution**: Allows running tests concurrently on multiple machines to reduce execution time.

The cons of TestComplete are:

- **High licensing cost**: Its commercial nature makes it less accessible for small teams or startups with budget constraints.

- **Resource-intensive**: It can be heavy on system resources and requires robust hardware for smooth execution.

- **Limited community support**: While it has strong vendor support, the open-source community around TestComplete is smaller compared to tools like Selenium.

- **Steep learning curve for complex scenarios**: Advanced features may require more time to master, especially for testers without coding experience.

- **Dependency on vendor updates**: Heavily reliant on vendor updates to keep pace with emerging technologies and browser updates.

- **Less popular for mobile testing**: While it supports mobile, it is not as widely adopted for mobile testing compared to tools like Appium.

Jest

Jest is a popular, open-source testing framework primarily used for testing JavaScript and TypeScript applications. Developed by Facebook, Jest is widely adopted for testing applications built with frameworks like React, Angular, and Node.js. It is known for its simplicity, ease of use, and built-in features that eliminate the need for external libraries. Jest supports unit, integration, and snapshot testing and is optimized for performance with features like parallel test execution and intelligent test selection.

The key features include:

- **Zero configuration**: Works out-of-the-box for most JavaScript/TypeScript projects, reducing setup time.

- **Snapshot testing**: Captures snapshots of components and helps detect unintended UI changes.

- **Rich API**: Provides extensive matchers and utilities for testing.

The pros of Jest are:

- **Ease of use**: Minimal configuration needed, making it beginner-friendly and quick to adopt.

- **Snapshot testing**: Simplifies UI regression testing by comparing component snapshots.

- **Fast execution**: Built-in parallelism and test filtering ensure quick test execution.

- **Great for front-end frameworks**: Especially suited for testing React applications due to tight integration and tools like react-testing-library.

- **Comprehensive built-in features**: Includes mocking, spying, assertions, and test coverage without the need for additional libraries.

- **Active ecosystem**: Backed by Facebook and a large community, ensuring continuous updates and extensive support.

- **Supports TypeScript**: Offers seamless integration with TypeScript projects.

The cons of Jest are:

- **JavaScript-focused**: Primarily designed for JavaScript and TypeScript, making it less suitable for non-JS ecosystems.

- **Not ideal for E2E testing**: Focused on unit and integration testing; lacks the browser automation capabilities of tools like Selenium or Cypress.

- **Limited support for non-React frameworks**: While it can work with other frameworks like Angular or Vue.js, it may require additional setup compared to React.

- **Performance overhead in large projects**: Optimizing performance in large-scale applications with thousands of tests may require careful configuration.

- **Steep learning curve for complex features**: Mastering advanced features like custom matches or mocking complex modules can take time.

Postman

Postman is a widely-used API testing tool designed to simplify the creation, testing, and management of APIs. It offers a user-friendly interface for sending requests, analyzing responses, and automating API workflows. Postman supports a wide range of protocols such as REST, SOAP, and GraphQL, making it versatile for testing modern and legacy APIs. Its features are designed for developers, QA engineers, and teams working collaboratively on API development and testing.

The key features include:

- **Request creation and testing**: Send requests with customizable parameters, headers, and bodies, and easily analyze responses.

- **Collection management**: Organize and share API requests in collections for better reusability and collaboration.

- **Automation with Newman**: Automate API testing in CI/CD pipelines using the command-line tool, Newman.

- **Pre/post request scripts**: Write JavaScript for dynamic request configurations or response validation.

The pros of Postman are:

- **User-friendly interface**: Provides an intuitive UI for quickly creating and testing APIs without needing coding skills.

- **Collaboration tools**: Teams can share collections, environments, and documentation for seamless collaboration.

- **Extensive API support**: Handles REST, SOAP, and GraphQL APIs, offering flexibility for different protocols.

- **Automated testing**: Built-in test scripts enable the automation of functional and regression testing.

- **Environment management**: Use environments and variables to simplify testing across multiple API environments (for example, dev, QA, production).

- **Integrated mock servers**: Quickly mock APIs for testing without needing the actual backend.

- **CI/CD integration**: Supports API testing in CI/CD pipelines through Newman and integrations with tools like Jenkins and GitHub Actions.

The cons of Postman are:

- **Resource-intensive**: The desktop application can consume significant system resources, especially with large collections or environments.

- **Limited for E2E testing**: Focused on API testing, making it less suitable for complete end-to-end testing scenarios involving UI.

- **Learning curve for advanced features**: Features like pre/post-request scripting and collection runners can be complex for beginners.

- **Subscription costs for advanced features**: While the basic version is free, team collaboration, API monitoring, and advanced analytics require a paid plan.

- **Limited version control**: While it supports some versioning, it is not as robust as using Git or other VCS tools for managing changes.

- **Script execution limited to JavaScript**: Scripts for pre/post-request processing are JavaScript-only, which might be restrictive for teams unfamiliar with it.

Testing tools for performance and load testing

Here is a set of tools that are very effective at assisting with load and performance testing. While these tools can be used for other automation testing as well, they are better suited for performance testing given their feature set.

JMeter

Apache JMeter is an open-source testing tool designed primarily for performance and load testing. It simulates multiple users sending requests to a server, enabling teams to measure the performance, scalability, and stability of applications, APIs, and services. Though initially focused on load testing, JMeter also supports functional testing of APIs, web applications, and databases. It is a Java-based tool with a graphical interface and scriptable functionality.

The key features include:

- **Performance and load testing**: Simulates high traffic to evaluate system performance.

- **Protocol support**: Works with a wide range of protocols, including HTTP(S), FTP, SOAP, REST, JDBC, and more.

- **Extensibility**: Highly customizable with plugins and support for scripting in Groovy and Java.

The pros of JMeter are:

- **Open source**: Free to use, with no licensing costs.

- **Scalable**: Can simulate thousands of concurrent users for large-scale performance testing.

- **Extensive protocol support**: Beyond HTTP, it supports FTP, SOAP, REST, database queries (via JDBC), and more.

- **Customizable testing**: Allows test plans to include dynamic variables, custom scripts, as well as logic controllers like loops and conditions.

- **Rich reporting**: Offers detailed reports and graphs for analyzing performance metrics such as response time, throughput, and error rates.

- **Integration with CI/CD**: Compatible with Jenkins, GitLab CI, and other tools for automated performance testing.

- **Active community**: A large user base contributes plugins, tutorials, and support.

The cons of JMeter are:

- **Steep learning curve**: The interface and setup can be intimidating for beginners, especially for advanced scenarios.

- **Resource-intensive**: Running large-scale tests requires significant hardware resources, often requiring distributed testing.

- **Not ideal for modern UI testing**: Limited to backend and performance testing, making it unsuitable for front-end or visual validations.

- **Outdated UI**: The interface is less modern and user-friendly, compared to newer tools.

- **Limited real-time monitoring**: Lacks robust real-time monitoring capabilities without third-party integrations.

- **Requires scripting for complex scenarios**: Advanced features may require knowledge of Groovy or Java for custom scripting.

- **Manual correlation for dynamic data**: Handling dynamic session data (for example, tokens) can require manual correlation and setup.

k6

k6 is an open-source, developer-centric performance testing tool, built for testing APIs, web applications, and microservices. Unlike traditional performance testing tools, k6 focuses on simplicity, performance, and integration into modern CI/CD pipelines. Test scripts are written in JavaScript, making it accessible to developers familiar with modern programming languages. k6 is often used for load testing, stress testing, and endurance testing.

The key features include:

- **JavaScript scripting**: Test scripts are written in JavaScript, enabling easy adoption by developers.

- **CLI-based execution**: Lightweight and command-line-driven, making it suitable for automation and integration with CI/CD workflows.

- **Built for scalability**: Designed to handle high-performance testing scenarios.

The pros of k6 are:

- **Developer-friendly**: Test scripts use JavaScript, a familiar language for most modern developers, making it accessible and easy to write tests.

- **High performance**: Optimized for high concurrency, capable of handling large-scale load tests with minimal resource consumption.

- **Modern CI/CD integration**: Seamlessly integrates with CI/CD tools like Jenkins, GitLab, and GitHub Actions, enabling automated performance testing.

- **Rich metrics and reporting**: Provides detailed metrics and integrates with monitoring tools like Grafana and Prometheus for real-time analysis.

- **Cross-platform**: Runs on Windows, macOS, and Linux without requiring a complex setup.

- **Lightweight and fast**: Minimal overhead, ensuring efficient execution.

- **Extensive protocol support**: Supports HTTP, WebSocket, and gRPC protocols, making it versatile for different testing scenarios.

The cons of k6 are:

- **No GUI**: Operates entirely via the command line, which might be challenging for testers accustomed to graphical interfaces.

- **Limited protocol support**: While it supports HTTP, WebSocket, and gRPC, it lacks built-in support for other protocols such as FTP or SMTP.

- **JavaScript-only scripting**: While JavaScript is developer-friendly, teams unfamiliar with it may face a learning curve.

- **Not ideal for functional testing**: Primarily designed for performance testing, not end-to-end or UI testing.

- **No built-in distributed execution**: Requires external tools like k6 Cloud or Kubernetes for distributed load testing scenarios.

- **Paid cloud services for advanced features**: While the tool is free, features like distributed testing and managed monitoring require the use of the paid k6 Cloud.

Gatling

Gatling is an open-source performance testing tool designed for testing APIs and web applications. Known for its developer-friendly nature, Gatling allows users to create expressive test scenarios using Scala or JavaScript-like **Domain Specific Language (DSL)**. It focuses on high performance and scalability, making it ideal for testing applications under heavy load. Gatling also offers a commercial version, Gatling Enterprise, which provides advanced features like team collaboration and CI/CD integrations.

The key features include:

- **Scala-based DSL**: Enables expressive and flexible scripting for test scenarios.

- **Asynchronous architecture**: Handles large-scale concurrent users efficiently with minimal hardware requirements.

- **Comprehensive reporting**: Generates detailed, interactive HTML reports.

The pros of Gatling are:

- **High performance**: Its asynchronous architecture allows it to handle thousands of virtual users with minimal resource consumption.

- **Rich reporting**: Automatically generates detailed, interactive reports with metrics like response times, throughput, and error rates.

- **Extensive protocol support**: Built-in support for HTTP, WebSocket, and JMS protocols.

- **Developer-friendly**: Scripting with Scala DSL offers flexibility and allows complex scenarios to be expressed elegantly.

- **Scalable and lightweight**: Efficiently simulates high traffic without the need for distributed systems for most scenarios.

- **Integration-friendly**: Works well with CI/CD tools like Jenkins, GitLab, and Bamboo, enabling automated performance testing pipelines.

- **Open source and enterprise options**: Free for small-scale projects, with an enterprise version offering advanced features for teams.

The cons of Gatling are:

- **Learning curve for Scala**: Writing test scripts requires knowledge of Scala, which might be unfamiliar to testers or developers not using JVM-based languages.

- **Limited UI**: Gatling is CLI-driven and does not have a graphical interface, which might deter users who prefer GUI tools.

- **Protocol support gaps**: Focuses on HTTP-based protocols and lacks support for others such as FTP, SMTP, or SOAP out of the box.

- **No real-time monitoring**: Does not provide real-time monitoring natively; external integrations like Grafana are needed.

- **Java-based environment**: Requires Java runtime, which may be an overhead for teams unfamiliar with JVM tools.

- **Distributed testing requires setup**: For large-scale, distributed load testing, additional setup or enterprise solutions are required.

Locust

Locust is an open-source performance testing tool focused on load testing web applications, APIs, and other systems. It is highly scalable and allows users to define test scenarios in Python, making it accessible and flexible for developers. Locust is event-driven, meaning it can simulate thousands of users with minimal resource consumption. Its distributed architecture makes it suitable for testing large-scale applications.

The key features include:

- **Python-based scripting**: Test scenarios are written in Python, a widely used and beginner-friendly programming language.

- **Web-based UI**: Includes a web interface for managing and monitoring tests in real time.

- **Distributed load testing**: Supports distributed execution for simulating millions of users.

The pros of Locust are:

- **Developer-friendly**: Uses Python, which is easy to learn and allows for highly customizable and readable test scripts.

- **Scalable**: Can handle thousands or even millions of concurrent users by distributing the load across multiple machines.

- **Real-time monitoring**: Offers a web-based UI to monitor test progress, response times, and error rates during execution.

- **Lightweight and efficient**: Designed to run efficiently with minimal resource consumption.

- **Protocol flexibility**: Although primarily HTTP-based, custom protocols can be tested by extending Locust with Python.

- **Open source**: Free to use, with an active community contributing plugins and improvements.

- **CI/CD friendly**: Works well in automated testing pipelines and integrates with tools like Jenkins, GitHub Actions, and GitLab.

The cons of Locust are:

- **Limited built-in protocol support**: Focuses on HTTP/HTTPS, requiring additional scripting to support other protocols like WebSocket or gRPC.

- **No detailed reporting by default**: Offers basic metrics in the web UI; external tools like Grafana or Prometheus must be integrated for advanced reporting.

- **Requires Python knowledge**: While Python is beginner-friendly, teams unfamiliar with it may face a learning curve.

- **Not ideal for complex scenarios**: Handling highly complex workflows or scenarios may require significant custom scripting.

- **No GUI for test design**: Test scenarios must be coded, which may deter non-technical testers.

- **Distributed setup can be challenging**: While Locust supports distributed testing, setting up and managing multiple worker nodes can be complex.

Conclusion

When it comes to software test automation, there is certainly no shortage of tools. New tools are constantly being built while these existing tools continue to be refined, so this chapter in this book may not age very well. However, rather than trying to be exhaustive, the purpose of this chapter is to instead provide you with an overview of the types of significant tools out there and how to evaluate them across different criteria best so that you can make your own decisions in identifying the right tool to solve specific testing issues in your organization.

Test automation tools differ across specialization in API, UIs, web, and mobile, while others are better at performance and load more than just pure functional automation. Regardless of the tool you use and its purpose, the strength of your automation will lie not in the tool you use, but rather in the framework you build and ensuring that it can best adapt the test cases from your testing team into an executable test suite that can work across all aspects of your application and be successfully embedding in your CI/CD pipelines.

In the next chapter, we will start our first case study, looking at ways to build a scalable framework from scratch.

Key takeaways

Evaluating tools is an important, yet complex thing that companies need to do when looking at varying ways of introducing new tools into their software testing approach. The following are some key takeaways when approaching tool evaluation across test automation tools:

- **Align with business and testing needs**: Choose a tool that meets current and future testing requirements, supports various test types, and integrates well with your development ecosystem.

- **Ease of adoption matters**: A tool with a steep learning curve or poor documentation can slow down adoption. Prioritize tools with good community support, training resources, and intuitive usability.

- **Performance and scalability are critical**: Ensure the tool can handle large test suites, parallel execution, and distributed testing without compromising speed or stability.

- **Flexibility and extensibility**: A good testing tool should be customizable and support third-party integrations, API testing, and service virtualization for long-term adaptability.

- **Security and compliance considerations**: Look for tools with built-in security features, encrypted credential management, and compliance support for industry standards (for example, GDPR, SOC2).

- **Total cost of ownership (TCO) matters**: Consider licensing, infrastructure, maintenance, and hidden costs before committing. Open-source tools can reduce costs but may require additional support and customization.

- **Robust reporting and debugging features**: A tool that provides detailed logs, real-time reporting, and actionable insights helps in faster test failure analysis and debugging.

Exercises

1. What are the primary testing needs and goals that the tool must support?

2. Is the tool compatible with our current tech stack, CI/CD pipelines, and deployment environments?

3. Does it support multiple testing types (for example, unit, integration, functional, performance, security)?

4. How well does the tool scale with increasing test volume and complexity?

5. How easy is it to learn and integrate into existing workflows?

6. Does the tool have active community support or vendor-provided customer support?

7. Does the tool support parallel execution and distributed testing for faster test runs?

8. Can it handle data-driven testing and test parameterization efficiently?

9. How does the tool impact test execution speed and resource consumption?

10. Does it have built-in security features (for example, secure handling of credentials, compliance support)?

11. Can the tool be customized or extended to meet specific needs?

12. Does it support API testing and service virtualization for microservices-based architectures?

13. How well does it integrate with other testing tools, monitoring, and logging systems?

14. What is the total cost of ownership, including licensing, infrastructure, and maintenance?

15. Does the pricing model align with the budget and long-term testing strategy?

## CHAPTER 12

Case Study: Building a Scalable Framework From Scratch

Introduction

The purpose of this case study is to walk through the complete process of designing and implementing a scalable, tool-agnostic test automation framework from the ground up. By focusing on real-world scenarios, it will provide practical insights into the strategic decisions, challenges, and solutions faced when developing a framework that meets the diverse needs of modern software projects.

This case study serves as a roadmap for teams and organizations seeking to build a robust test automation strategy that transcends tool-specific constraints and embraces a holistic approach, covering design principles, modularity, and cross-cutting concerns. In evaluating the case study, though, we will take a broad approach, looking at multiple solutions, rather than going into detail about its specific use case to highlight the different approaches that can be taken.

Structure

In this chapter, we will cover the following topics:

- Overview of the case study
- Scenario
- Defining the requirements
- Single execution engine for all test types
- Implementation of a framework
- Key challenges and solutions
- Lessons learned

Objectives

By the end of this chapter, the reader will learn how to apply many of the principles we have learned in prior chapters to build an automation framework from scratch. We will look at ways of identifying the requirements for the framework you want to build, how to approach architecture design, and then look at ways to build the execution engine and implement it across an organization.

Overview of the case study

This chapter adopts a practical, hands-on approach, following a hypothetical project that aims to develop a scalable test automation framework. By highlighting key design choices, the case study illustrates the complex, iterative nature of framework development. Each phase will be discussed in detail, from initial planning and tool selection to addressing critical challenges such as maintainability, modularity, and integration into CI/CD pipelines.

The case study aims to equip readers with actionable insights by describing real challenges faced during the process, such as balancing scalability with flexibility and adapting to team-specific needs. Practical examples of overcoming common roadblocks and making critical decisions will ensure that readers understand the theory as well as the practical aspects of creating a sustainable test automation solution.

Scenario

The case study centers around a mid-size e-commerce platform undergoing rapid expansion to accommodate increasing traffic and an evolving product architecture. As the system grows, distributed services become crucial, with multiple teams contributing to different parts of the platform, each working on independent microservices.

This complexity introduces the need for a test automation framework that scales with the platform's growth and remains maintainable and modular enough to support ongoing development efforts across diverse teams and services.

Key requirements for the framework include:

- **Scalability:** As the platform grows, so will the need to efficiently run tests across various microservices without significant overhead or bottlenecks.

- **Modularity:** Teams must be able to extend the framework as needed for their specific services without causing interdependencies or breaking existing functionality.

- **Wide range of test types:** The framework must support various test types, including unit, integration, performance, security, and end-to-end tests, to ensure comprehensive coverage across the platform.

- **Tool-agnostic design:** Given the varying needs of different teams, the framework needs to remain tool-agnostic. This ensures that it can be integrated with a variety of testing tools and technologies and adapts to different development stacks.

By walking through this e-commerce platform's scenario, the case study will explore the real-world decisions to balance these requirements, ensuring that the framework meets the company's current and future testing needs while being flexible enough to evolve alongside the platform.

Defining the requirements

Let us now understand and define the requirements for this case study.

Identifying core needs

To build a scalable and efficient test automation framework, it is essential to address the following core needs upfront, ensuring the framework can evolve with the product while maintaining high-quality testing standards:

Support for multiple test types

The framework must handle a diverse array of test types, including:

- Unit tests to validate the smallest components of the system in isolation.
- Integration tests to ensure that various services work together seamlessly.
- End-to-end tests to simulate user interactions with the platform.
- Performance tests to assess the system's behavior under heavy loads.
- Security tests to identify vulnerabilities and ensure compliance with security standards.

By catering to multiple types of tests, the framework guarantees comprehensive test coverage across all aspects of the platform.

Tool-agnostic flexibility

To accommodate various teams and services within the e-commerce platform, the framework must be tool-agnostic. This flexibility allows different teams to plug in the tools they are familiar with or that best suit their specific needs (for example, JUnit for unit testing, Selenium for end-to-end testing, JMeter for performance testing, and so on). The framework should not be tightly coupled to any one tool, ensuring adaptability as testing tools evolve or as teams require new integrations.

Support for parallel execution

As the number of tests grows with the platform's expansion, the ability to execute tests in parallel is critical. Parallel execution reduces the time required to run the full test suite and is crucial for maintaining fast feedback loops, especially when integrating tests into CI/CD pipelines. This ensures continuous, real-time validation of code changes without delaying the release process.

Maintainability

With frequent product updates and team contributions, the test automation framework must remain maintainable. This includes being easy to extend, update, and modify without introducing test breakage or maintenance overhead. The framework should incorporate best practices such as modular design and reusable components, allowing tests to be updated as the platform evolves. The framework ensures long-term viability and smooth scaling across teams by prioritizing maintainability.

Non-functional requirements

Several non-functional requirements need to be prioritized to ensure the test automation framework remains adaptable and efficient as the platform grows. These requirements will enhance the framework's ability to scale, evolve, and integrate into the broader development lifecycle. Let us now go over these non-functional requirements:

- **Scalability:** As the platform expands and the number of microservices increases, the volume of tests will grow significantly. The framework must be designed to scale effortlessly, allowing for the efficient addition of new tests without degrading performance or increasing execution time. This includes ensuring that test infrastructure, such as test environments and data management, can handle large-scale test execution.

- **Extensibility:** The framework should be built with extensibility in mind. As the product evolves, new features, services, and microservices will be added, necessitating the creation of new test suites. The framework must be designed to accommodate these changes quickly, with minimal setup required to add new tests. This could involve supporting service-specific test modules or templates that allow teams to integrate swiftly, tests for new components without disrupting existing workflows.

- **Reporting mechanisms:** Effective test automation is not just about running tests but also about delivering actionable insights to multiple stakeholders. The framework should include robust reporting mechanisms capable of generating detailed, meaningful reports for different audiences. Refer to the following:

    o   Developers need detailed, granular reports to identify the root causes of failures.

    o   QA teams require insights into test coverage and pass/fail rates to gauge the overall health of the system.

    o   Management benefits from high-level overviews, such as trends in testing performance, defect rates, and test coverage metrics over time, which help inform strategic decisions.

    o   Customizable reporting dashboards or integrations with existing reporting tools can help achieve this goal, ensuring each stakeholder has access to the information they need.

- **Ease of integration with continuous integration (CI) tools:** Seamless integration with popular CI tools is critical for embedding the test automation framework into the broader development pipeline. The framework should easily integrate with CI/CD platforms such as Jenkins, GitLab CI, CircleCI, and others. This ensures that automated tests are triggered on code commits, merges, or releases, providing immediate feedback on the quality and stability of the codebase.

    o   Additionally, the integration should support the configuration of test triggers (for example, running a full test suite for major releases versus a subset of tests for minor commits), allowing teams to tailor the testing process based on their development and release schedules.

Core design considerations

Several core considerations are necessary when designing a test automation framework to ensure it remains flexible, maintainable, and scalable. A modular design is at the heart of this, enabling clear separation of responsibilities, better reuse, and easier updates as the platform evolves. Next, we will discuss the key elements of the modular design approach.

Modular design

A well-architected modular design ensures that various components of the framework are decoupled, allowing teams to modify, extend, or reuse parts of the framework without affecting others. The primary benefit of modularity is that it promotes maintainability, making it easier to update the framework as new features or services are added to the platform. This is especially important in a microservices architecture where different teams may be working on separate components.

The framework will be built with distinct layers, each responsible for a specific aspect of test automation. This layered architecture supports a clear division of responsibilities and enables efficient scaling. Let us now go over the layers:

- **Test orchestration (test execution engine):** The orchestration layer is responsible for managing the overall test execution process. This includes selecting the appropriate test cases, managing test suites, and handling test execution in a controlled environment. The orchestration engine must be flexible enough for different test types (for example, unit, integration, performance) and support parallel execution for faster feedback.

- **Test data management (mocks, stubs, and so on):** Managing test data is critical, especially in complex systems with multiple dependencies. This layer will handle the setup, management, and cleanup of test data, including mocks, stubs, and simulated environments where necessary. By decoupling test data from the test logic itself, this layer ensures that tests can run reliably and independently of external dependencies, enabling repeatability and reducing flaky tests.

- **Reporting and logging:** Comprehensive reporting and logging are essential for understanding the outcomes of test executions and troubleshooting failures. This layer will focus on generating detailed logs and structured reports for different stakeholders. Reports should provide granular insights for developers and testers while offering high-level summaries for management. This separation allows each stakeholder to get the level of detail they need without overwhelming others with unnecessary information.

- **Parallel execution and result collection:** To support faster feedback loops, the framework must be capable of executing tests in parallel, particularly as the volume of tests grows. The parallel execution layer will manage the distribution of tests across different environments or threads and handle the collection of results in real time. This is particularly valuable for large-scale systems where tests need to run across multiple microservices concurrently. Efficient result aggregation and collection ensure that stakeholders can review results quickly, reducing downtime between code commits and deployments.

By separating the framework into these modular layers, each aspect of the test automation process is streamlined, allowing for independent development, scaling, and maintenance. Teams can focus on improving or modifying specific parts of the framework without risking the stability of the entire system, ensuring long-term sustainability.

Language and tooling choices

The choice of language and tools for the test automation framework is a critical decision that should align with the team's expertise, existing development ecosystem, and the needs of the product. Selecting the right combination of language and tooling ensures the framework is powerful and easy for the team to maintain and extend over time.

Language selection

The test automation framework's language should be chosen based on the following considerations:

- **Team's expertise:** Leveraging a language the team is already familiar with will reduce the learning curve and make adoption smoother. If most of the development team works in Python, Java, or JavaScript, choosing a corresponding language for the framework ensures consistency and faster implementation.

- **Existing ecosystem:** The chosen language should integrate well with the tools, libraries, and CI/CD pipelines already in use. For example, if the organization has a strong Java-based ecosystem, integrating Java with tools like Maven or Gradle will make for a more seamless process. Similarly, Python's rich ecosystem of testing and data libraries makes it an excellent choice for teams that prioritize quick test development and versatility.

In the context of the case study, the following languages were evaluated as the most commonly used in our e-commerce company, and thereby the framework needed to be written in one of these languages, and tools needed to support these languages, to maximize adoption in the organization:

- **Python:** Known for its readability and simplicity, Python is ideal for teams looking to quickly build and maintain test suites. It has strong community support, especially for testing, with frameworks like pytest, which is versatile and can handle various test types.

- **Java:** Often favored by large enterprise systems, Java provides robust options for test automation. It is highly compatible with enterprise tools and integrates well with many CI/CD platforms. Frameworks like TestNG and JUnit are well-suited for large-scale projects.

- **JavaScript/TypeScript:** As front-end development often relies on JavaScript, many teams prefer to keep their test automation in the same language to reduce context switching. Tools like Mocha, Jest, and Cypress are powerful options for JavaScript-based test automation.

Tooling choices for test orchestration

For test orchestration, it is essential to choose libraries and tools that are flexible, mature, and capable of handling multiple test types, including unit, integration, performance, and end-to-end tests. These libraries should also support parallel execution, reporting, and be easily extensible to meet the growing needs of the product.

Common test orchestration libraries for our three chosen languages would include:

- **pytest (Python):** A highly popular and versatile testing framework, pytest supports a wide range of test types, from unit and integration tests to more complex scenarios. It also integrates well with various reporting and logging tools, making it an excellent choice for Python-based frameworks.

- **TestNG (Java):** A robust testing framework for Java, TestNG supports parallel test execution, data-driven tests, and integrates seamlessly with continuous integration systems. It is a great fit for teams building enterprise-level test automation in Java.

- **Mocha (JavaScript):** A flexible and simple testing framework for JavaScript, Mocha is designed to work well with Node.js applications but can handle other types of testing with the right setup. It is often paired with assertion libraries like Chai for full testing support.

Each of these orchestration tools brings flexibility to the table, allowing teams to set up and configure their testing frameworks in a way that aligns with their project needs. This tool-agnostic approach ensures that the test automation framework can evolve alongside the team's toolset, remaining adaptable as new requirements emerge.

Handling tool-agnosticism

One of the key principles in designing a scalable and maintainable test automation framework is ensuring it remains tool-agnostic. This approach allows teams to integrate various testing tools and technologies without tightly coupling the framework to any single one. By adopting a tool-agnostic strategy, the framework becomes more flexible, future-proof, and adaptable to changing requirements, allowing teams to select the best tool for each type of test.

Framework independence from specific tools

The framework should be built in a way that enables it to support various types of tests using a wide range of tools, each chosen based on the team's needs and the nature of the tests. This flexibility allows teams to use the right tool for the job, whether it is security testing, performance testing, or any other type. The goal is to create a framework where the core execution and orchestration engine can run tests without being locked into any specific tool. Examples of this flexibility include the following:

- **Security testing:** Security tests can vary widely in scope, and different tools may be preferred based on the organization's needs or expertise. The test automation framework should allow for integration with tools like:

  o **OWASP ZAP:** An open-source tool for identifying vulnerabilities in web applications, particularly useful for detecting common security issues such as **cross-site scripting** (**XSS**) and SQL injection.

  o **Burp Suite:** A more advanced security testing tool offering features like vulnerability scanning, manual testing, and penetration testing, often used by security professionals.

  o The framework should ensure that security tests using OWASP ZAP or Burp Suite can be triggered within the same test pipeline without requiring tool-specific code.

- **Performance testing:** Similar to security testing, performance tests should integrate seamlessly into the framework, leveraging tools best suited for load and stress testing. Popular tools include:

- o **JMeter:** A widely used open-source tool for load and performance testing, particularly in enterprise systems.

- o **k6:** A modern, developer-friendly tool for performance testing, designed to be scalable and efficient.

- o The test orchestration layer must allow performance tests, whether conducted via JMeter or k6, to be executed alongside other test types within the same framework.

Single execution engine for all test types

The core of the test automation framework should be powered by a single execution engine, such as pytest (for Python) or TestNG (for Java), that can handle triggering and managing multiple types of tests. The execution engine will serve as the backbone, managing test orchestration and ensuring that all test types, unit, integration, security, performance, and so on, are triggered in a consistent and organized manner.

Our e-commerce company has decided to consider this approach as a way of allowing the framework to scale across the organization and increase the adoption of automation, having their teams use one core framework across all teams rather than looking to maintain multiple frameworks across different teams.

The benefits of using a single execution engine include:

- **Simplified test execution:** Testers do not need to worry about switching between tools or running different commands for various test types. The same engine triggers all types of tests from a single point of control.

- **Unified reporting:** Regardless of the type of test or the tool used to run it, all results can be collected and reported in a unified format, providing consistency for stakeholders.

- **Scalability:** As the product grows and new types of tests are added, the execution engine remains the same, allowing the framework to evolve without significant overhead or rework.

For example, a test run might involve triggering unit tests via pytest, security tests via OWASP ZAP, and performance tests via JMeter, all orchestrated and executed by the same engine. This approach ensures consistency, reduces complexity, and allows the framework to handle various test types and tools as needed.

Parallel execution and scalability

As test suites grow in size and complexity, parallel execution becomes essential to maintain fast feedback loops and ensure that testing does not become a bottleneck in the development and deployment process. Efficient parallelization allows teams to run multiple tests simultaneously, reducing execution time. Coupling parallel execution with cloud-based infrastructure ensures that the framework can handle increased loads as the product and testing requirements scale.

Parallel execution techniques

To achieve efficient parallel execution, the test automation framework can leverage various techniques depending on the architecture and the environment in which tests are run. For this e-commerce company, where they may have multiple processes being used at the same time in production on certain core services, it has been decided to include this in the framework. This will also allow the tests to run quicker and be implemented into a pipeline more easily, taking less time to execute. The techniques are as follows:

- **Threading:** In frameworks such as pytest (Python) or TestNG (Java), threading allows multiple tests to be executed concurrently within the same process. Threading is particularly useful when the tests are IO-bound or depend on external services, such as API calls or database interactions, where waiting time can be parallelized to optimize efficiency. For example:

o pytest can use plugins like **pytest-xdist** to run tests in parallel across multiple CPU cores or even across machines, reducing test execution time significantly.

o TestNG can use its built-in parallel execution capabilities to run test methods, classes, or suites concurrently, optimizing for both unit and integration tests.

- **Multiprocessing:** Multiprocessing is often more effective than threading for CPU-bound tests, such as performance testing or tests involving complex calculations. Multiprocessing allows each test to run in its process, taking full advantage of multi-core systems to speed up execution.

- **Containerization:** Another powerful approach, especially in microservices-based architectures, is using containers (for example, Docker) to isolate and run tests in parallel. Each test can run in its container, simulating the real-world environment and eliminating conflicts between tests that might otherwise share the same resources. Containerization also provides the advantage of environment consistency, allowing the framework to execute tests in environments identical to production, further improving reliability.

Leveraging cloud-based infrastructure for scalability

As the number of tests increases, scaling locally may no longer be feasible. At this point, leveraging cloud infrastructure becomes essential to ensure that the test automation framework can scale dynamically to meet the demands of growing test volumes. Cloud infrastructure offers virtually unlimited resources and can be tailored to handle parallel execution at a massive scale, making it an ideal solution for scalability challenges. Let us now go over the following:

- **AWS Lambda:** Serverless technologies like AWS Lambda can be utilized to run individual tests or test batches in a serverless environment. This eliminates the need for managing physical or virtual servers, allowing the framework to scale automatically based on the number of tests. Lambda functions are ideal for small, independent test executions, such as unit tests or lightweight integration tests, where rapid spin-up and tear-down of test environments are key.

- **Kubernetes:** Kubernetes will provide an excellent solution for running large test suites at scale in our e-commerce company. An e-commerce company might choose Kubernetes to execute tests because of its powerful scalability and orchestration capabilities. During peak periods like sales events or new feature rollouts, testing demands can spike dramatically. Kubernetes enables the dynamic scaling of test environments, allowing the company to run many tests in parallel across multiple containers. This not only speeds up test execution but also ensures timely feedback for developers working in fast-paced delivery cycles.

  Kubernetes also ensures consistency across testing environments by running containers that encapsulate all necessary dependencies and configurations. This eliminates environment-related issues and increases the reliability and reproducibility of test results. Additionally, the platform is well-suited for integration with modern CI/CD pipelines, allowing automated tests to be triggered as part of build and deployment workflows, critical for maintaining quality in a continuous delivery model.

  Given that our e-commerce system has adopted a microservices architecture, Kubernetes provides an ideal foundation for orchestrating complex integration tests. It allows teams to spin up isolated, production-like environments on demand, including the necessary services and data dependencies. Combined with efficient resource utilization and cost control, Kubernetes offers a flexible, scalable, and robust solution for managing and executing automated tests across all layers of an e-commerce platform.

  o By running tests in a Kubernetes environment, the framework can dynamically allocate resources based on current testing needs:

  ▪ Performance and load testing, where multiple instances of the same test need to be run simultaneously to simulate high traffic.

- Large integration tests, where multiple microservices need to be tested together in a complex, distributed environment.
  - o Kubernetes also integrates with popular CI/CD tools, enabling fully automated test runs as part of a continuous delivery pipeline.

Dynamic resource allocation

One of the significant advantages of cloud-based infrastructure is dynamic resource allocation. Depending on the size and complexity of the test suite, the framework can automatically request more resources (for example, additional containers or server instances) from the cloud provider to accommodate the increased load. This ensures that tests always run in optimal conditions, minimizing execution time and reducing the risk of resource-related failures.

Scaling beyond local infrastructure

While parallel execution techniques like threading and multiprocessing can provide significant speed improvements, they are limited by the capacity of local infrastructure (for example, CPU cores, memory). By integrating with cloud services, the test automation framework gains the ability to scale beyond the limitations of local hardware, ensuring that even the most extensive test suites can be executed in a timely manner.

Implementation of a framework

Let us go over the steps for the implementation of a framework.

Setting up the project structure

This is the first step. A well-defined folder structure is essential for maintaining organization, clarity, and modularity within a test automation framework. A clear project structure not only makes it easier for teams to navigate the codebase but also fosters collaboration and scalability as the project grows.

Defining the folder structure

The following is a recommended folder structure for a tool-agnostic test automation framework:

```
/test-framework
├── /tests
│   ├── /unit_tests/
│   ├── /integration_tests/
│   └── /performance_tests/
├── /configs
│   ├── config.yaml
│   └── /environments/
├── /data
│   └── test_data.json
├── /orchestration
│   ├── test_runner.py
│   └── parallel_executor.py
└── /reports
    ├── /html_reports/
    └── /logs/
```

Folder descriptions

The folders are as follows:

- **/tests**: This directory contains all test cases organized by type. By separating test types into distinct subfolders, the framework promotes clarity and modularity, making it easy to locate specific tests. These tests do not need to all be in one folder, but can be broken up into each functional area and team to better replicate the architecture for that specific team.

    o **/unit_tests/**: Holds unit tests that verify the functionality of individual components or functions in isolation. The unit tests here should be mapped according to the architecture of the underlying code and run in alignment with that, so when code changes are made, only the appropriate unit tests are run.

    o **/integration_tests/**: Contains integration tests that check the interactions between multiple components or services to ensure they work together as expected.

    o **/performance_tests/**: Includes performance tests that assess the responsiveness, speed, scalability, and stability of the application under various conditions.

- **/configs**: This directory stores configuration files required for the framework.

    o **config.yaml**: A main configuration file that defines parameters and settings for running tests, such as test timeouts, logging levels, and other environment-specific variables.

    o **/environments/**: A subdirectory for environment-specific configuration files. This can include configurations for different stages (development, testing, production) and can help facilitate smooth transitions between environments.

- **/data**: This directory is used for storing test data files, which can be used as input for various tests.

    o **test_data.json**: A sample JSON file that contains test data used across different tests, ensuring data consistency and ease of management. For the pipeline tests, to ensure tests run quickly, the company has decided to place their test data here to allow for quick loading and execution in a pipeline.

    o For integration tests, an integration with an actual test database will be used that will provide a large sample-set of production-like data.

- **/orchestration**: This directory includes the core components responsible for managing test execution and orchestration.

    o **test_runner.py**: The main script for executing tests, orchestrating the running of different test suites, and managing dependencies.

    o **parallel_executor.py**: A script or module that implements the logic for executing tests in parallel, enhancing efficiency and reducing overall execution time.

- **/reports**: This directory is dedicated to storing the results of test executions and generating reports.

    o **/html_reports/**: A subdirectory for storing HTML reports generated after test runs, providing a user-friendly view of test results, including pass/fail rates, execution times, and detailed logs. HTML was decided for this as it loads into a web browser and allows for easy reading for stakeholders. These reports can then be stored in a storage location like an s3 bucket for easy access and display.

    o **/logs/**: A subdirectory for storing log files, capturing runtime information and error messages during test execution, which can aid in debugging and performance analysis.

Separation and modularity

The defined folder structure ensures clear separation and modularity within the framework, allowing teams to work on different components without interfering with one another. This modularity also facilitates easier updates and maintenance; for example, if a specific type of test requires changes, only the relevant folder and files need to be modified.

Additionally, a well-structured framework promotes reusability of code and test data, as well as easier integration with CI/CD pipelines, enhancing the overall development and testing process.

Creating the test runner

This is the second step. The test runner is a critical component of the test automation framework, responsible for managing the execution of different types of tests and generating reports. A custom test runner allows for flexibility and modularity, enabling the framework to adapt to various testing requirements as they evolve.

Developing the test runner

The following is an example of a custom test runner implemented in Python using the **pytest** framework. This test runner will handle unit, integration, and performance tests, while allowing for easy expansion to include additional test types such as security and resilience tests.

```python
import pytest
import sys


def run_tests(test_type):
    match test_type:
        case "unit":
            pytest.main(["-v", "--html=reports/unit_report.html", "tests/unit_tests"])
        case "integration":
            pytest.main(["-v", "--html=reports/integration_report.html", "tests/
integration_tests"])
        case "performance":
            pytest.main(["-v", "--html=reports/performance_report.html", "tests/
performance_tests"])
        case _:
            print(f"Unknown test type: {test_type}")
            sys.exit(1)


if __name__ == "__main__":
    if len(sys.argv) < 2:
        print("Please provide a test type: unit, integration, or performance.")
        sys.exit(1)

    run_tests(sys.argv[1])
```

How the test runner works

Let us now understand how the test runner works:

- **Importing required libraries:** The script begins by importing the necessary libraries. The **pytest** library is used for running the tests, while the **sys** library allows for interaction with command-line arguments.

- **Defining the run_tests function:** The **run_tests** function accepts a parameter, **test_type,** to determine which set of tests to execute. Based on the value of **test_type**, the function calls **pytest. main()** with appropriate arguments:

- o **-v** enables verbose output during test execution.

- o **--html** specifies the path where the generated HTML report will be saved.

- o The final argument indicates the path to the respective test directory.

- **Handling unknown test types:** If an unsupported **test_type** is provided, the script prints an error message and exits with a non-zero status, indicating failure.

- **Executing the script:** When the script is run directly, it captures the command-line argument (the type of test to run) and calls the **run_tests** function with that argument.

- **Extending the test runner:** This test runner can be easily expanded to support additional test types by adding more **elif** clauses within the **run_tests** function. For example, to include security tests or resilience tests, you could add:

```
elif test_type == "security":
    pytest.main(["-v", "--html=reports/security_report.html", "tests/security_
tests"])
elif test_type == "resilience":
    pytest.main(["-v", "--html=reports/resilience_report.html", "tests/resilience_
tests"])
```

The benefits of a custom test runner are:

- **Modularity:** A custom test runner allows for a modular design, making it easy to manage and execute different types of tests based on their specific needs.

- **Reporting:** By generating HTML reports for each type of test, stakeholders can easily review test results and track quality over time.

- **Flexibility:** The runner can be modified and expanded as new testing requirements arise, ensuring that the framework remains adaptable to the evolving needs of the development and QA teams.

Implementing test data management

This is the third step. Effective test data management is crucial for maintaining the reliability and flexibility of a test automation framework. By decoupling tests from hard-coded data, teams can easily update test cases without modifying the underlying logic, allowing for better maintainability and scalability.

Decoupling tests from hard-coded data

To achieve this, we introduce a structured approach to managing test data. By utilizing configuration files (for example, YAML or JSON) to manage different environments and their corresponding data sources, tests can dynamically retrieve the necessary data at runtime from the different environments.

Using configuration files

An example of a configuration file in YAML format is as follows:

```
default_environment: "staging"
environments:
  staging:
    base_url: "https://staging.example.com"
    db_connection: "staging-db"
  production:
    base_url: "https://prod.example.com"
    db_connection: "prod-db"
```

The key components are:

- **default_environment**: Specifies the default environment to be used when running tests. This can be easily changed to switch between different environments (for example, staging or production).

- **environments**: This section defines various environments and their configurations:

- **staging:** Contains the **base_url** and **db_connection** specific to the staging environment.

- **production**: Defines the corresponding values for the production environment.

Creating helper functions

To retrieve test data dynamically from a JSON file, we can create a helper function in Python. Here is an example:

```
import json

def load_test_data(file_path):
    with open(file_path, 'r') as file:
        return json.load(file)
```

Here is the function explanation:

- **load_test_data(file_path)**: This function accepts the path to a JSON file containing test data. It opens the file, reads its contents, and returns the data as a Python dictionary.

  This function can be used throughout the test framework to load test data as needed, ensuring that test cases are not reliant on hard-coded values.

The benefits of test data management are:

- **Flexibility:** By using configuration files, you can easily switch between environments without altering the test code. This makes it simpler to run tests in different contexts (for example, staging vs. production).

- **Maintainability:** Separating test data from test logic allows for easier updates. When changes are required (for example, updating URLs or database connections), only the configuration file needs modification, reducing the risk of introducing bugs.

- **Scalability:** As the application grows and requires more tests, the test data can be expanded within the configuration files without impacting existing tests.

- **Reusability:** Test data loaded from JSON or YAML files can be reused across multiple tests, promoting **Don't Repeat Yourself** (**DRY**) principles within the codebase.

Example usage in tests

To utilize the helper function and configuration in tests, you might do something like this:

```
import pytest
import os

# Load the environment configuration
environment = load_test_data('configs/config.yaml')

# Example test case using the configuration
@pytest.mark.parametrize("url", [environment['environments'][environment['default_
environment']]['base_url']])
```

```
def test_example(url):
    response = requests.get(url)
    assert response.status_code == 200
```

In this example, the test dynamically retrieves the base URL from the configuration file, ensuring that the test is adaptable to different environments.

Key challenges and solutions

Let us now go over some challenges and their respective solutions.

Challenge 1: Handling scalability

Problem: As the e-commerce product expands to accommodate multiple microservices, the volume of tests will inevitably increase. This growth can lead to longer test execution times, making it difficult to maintain a fast and efficient development pipeline. To ensure that testing remains effective and timely, the system must be able to scale up test runs dynamically, addressing both the number of tests and the resources required to execute them.

Solution: To address this challenge, we can implement parallel execution techniques and utilize orchestration tools. Two viable approaches are:

- **Parallel testing with pytest-xdist: pytest-xdist** is a popular plugin for the **pytest** framework that enables the execution of tests in parallel, significantly reducing overall test run times. By distributing tests across multiple CPU cores, **pytest-xdist** allows the test suite to leverage the full capabilities of the available hardware. For implementation, install **pytest-xdist** in your testing environment using pip:

  pip install pytest-xdist

  o **Execute tests in parallel**: Modify the test execution command in the test runner to include the **-n** option to specify the number of CPU cores to utilize. For example:

    pytest -n auto --html=reports/unit_report.html tests/unit_tests

  o The **-n auto** option tells **pytest** to automatically determine the number of available CPU cores and use them for parallel execution.

- **Distributed testing with Kubernetes:** As the product scales, it may be necessary to distribute test execution across multiple containers, particularly in microservices architectures. Kubernetes is an excellent solution for orchestrating these containers, allowing for scalable and efficient test execution. The implementation steps are:

  o **Containerization:** First, containerize the test framework and its dependencies using Docker. This ensures that the environment is consistent across all testing instances.

  o **Kubernetes configuration:** Create Kubernetes manifests (YAML files) to define the deployment of the test containers. This includes specifications for resources (CPU, memory) and environment variables.

  o **Test distribution:** Use a job or deployment in Kubernetes to spin up multiple instances of the test container. Each instance can run a subset of the test suite, effectively distributing the workload.

  o **Monitoring and scaling:** Utilize Kubernetes' Horizontal Pod Autoscaler to automatically scale the number of pods based on the CPU utilization or custom metrics, ensuring that the system can handle varying loads efficiently.

The benefits of the solutions are as follows:

- **Efficiency:** Implementing parallel execution drastically reduces the time required to run tests, allowing quicker feedback during development and integration processes.

- **Resource optimization:** Utilizing tools like Kubernetes allows for better resource management, enabling the system to dynamically allocate resources as needed based on current demand.

- **Scalability:** Both approaches are designed to scale easily with the application as new microservices and corresponding tests are introduced, ensuring the testing infrastructure remains robust and responsive to growth.

By addressing the scalability challenge through parallel testing with **pytest-xdist** and distributed testing using Kubernetes, our test automation framework will be well-equipped to handle the increasing demands of our growing microservices architecture that our e-commerce company will need. This approach not only improves the efficiency of test execution but also enhances the overall robustness and reliability of the testing process.

Challenge 2: Tool-agnostic design

Problem: In the rapidly evolving landscape of software development, various testing tools may be preferred for different types of tests (performance, security, functional). However, tightly coupling the test automation framework to a specific tool can create significant challenges, especially with a company that is still growing and may need to adapt and evolve its underlying architecture over time as it encounters different business challenges. This approach can lead to increased maintenance overhead, hinder flexibility, and limit the ability to adapt to new tools as technology evolves.

Solution: To address the challenge of maintaining a tool-agnostic design, our framework must be structured in a way that allows for the easy integration and swapping of various testing tools. Here are key strategies for achieving this:

- **Abstract test interfaces:** Define clear interfaces for different types of tests within the framework. These interfaces will act as contracts that any tool must adhere to in order to be integrated. For example, a performance test interface might require methods like **setup()**, **execute()**, and **teardown()**. This abstraction allows the framework to interact with any performance testing tool that implements these methods, regardless of its underlying technology.

```
class PerformanceTest:
    def setup(self):
        raise NotImplementedError

    def execute(self):
        raise NotImplementedError

    def teardown(self):
        raise NotImplementedError
```

- **Dependency injection:** Use dependency injection to manage the selection of testing tools at runtime. This allows you to inject different tool implementations based on the configuration or environment without changing the underlying test execution logic. For example, if using **JMeter** for performance testing, the framework can instantiate the JMeter-specific implementation of the **PerformanceTest** interface and invoke its methods without being tightly coupled to the **JMeter** tool itself.

- **Configuration management:** Utilize configuration files to specify which tools to use for different testing types. This setup allows teams to easily switch tools by modifying configuration settings rather than altering code. Here is an example YAML configuration:

```
tests:
  performance:
    tool: "JMeter"
```

```
    configuration: "path/to/jmeter/config.jmx"
  security:
    tool: "OWASP ZAP"
    configuration: "path/to/zap/config.yaml"
```

- **Wrapper classes:** Implement wrapper classes around third-party tools to standardize interactions. These wrappers can translate framework calls into tool-specific commands, allowing the core framework to remain independent of any specific tool's API. Here is an example wrapper for **JMeter**:

```
class JMeterPerformanceTest(PerformanceTest):
    def __init__(self, config):
        self.config = config

    def setup(self):
        # Code to prepare JMeter for execution

    def execute(self):
        # Code to run JMeter tests

    def teardown(self):
        # Code to clean up after tests
```

- **Plugin architecture:** Consider designing the framework with a plugin architecture that allows for easy integration of new tools. By implementing a plugin system, you can enable users to add or replace tools with minimal disruption to the overall framework.

Benefits of tool-agnostic design are as follows:

- **Flexibility:** The ability to swap tools easily means teams can adopt the best tools for their specific needs without being locked into one solution.

- **Maintainability:** As new tools and technologies emerge, the framework can adapt without requiring significant refactoring or redevelopment efforts.

- **Scalability:** The organization's tool-agnostic design supports its growing needs, allowing it to scale testing efforts across multiple types of tests and services without being constrained by existing tool dependencies.

By implementing a tool-agnostic design, the test automation framework can accommodate a variety of testing tools without locking the system into a specific technology. This flexibility enhances the framework's adaptability and longevity and ensures that teams can leverage the best tools available to maintain high-quality standards in their software development processes.

Challenge 3: Managing test data and configuration

Problem: One of the most significant challenges in test automation that our e-commerce framework will need to address is effectively managing test data and configuration. Tests that rely on static data or hard-coded configuration are prone to frequent breakage as the product evolves. Changes in application behavior, data formats, or environmental conditions can lead to test failures, making maintenance burdensome and time-consuming. This reliance on static configurations can hinder the agility of development teams, slowing down the feedback loop and impacting overall product quality.

Solution: To mitigate the issues associated with static test data and configuration, we can adopt a dual strategy involving dynamic test data generation techniques and the use of separate configuration files for different environments. Here is how to implement this solution:

- **Dynamic test data generation:** Utilize data generation libraries and tools to create test data dynamically rather than relying on fixed datasets. This approach allows tests to adapt to changing application states and reduces the chances of failures due to outdated data. Consider using libraries such as Faker (for generating fake data) or custom scripts to generate data that simulates real-world scenarios. Here is an example using the Faker library in Python:

```python
from faker import Faker

fake = Faker()

def generate_user_data():
    return {
        'name': fake.name(),
        'email': fake.email(),
        'address': fake.address(),
    }

# Example of generating test data for a user
user_data = generate_user_data()
print(user_data)
```

This approach allows for the generation of realistic and varied data for testing, reducing dependencies on static datasets.

- **Configuration management:** Implement configuration management practices by separating environment-specific configurations into dedicated files. This approach allows the testing framework to load the appropriate configuration based on the current environment (for example, development, staging, production). Use formats like YAML or JSON to store environment configurations, making it easier to modify settings without changing the underlying test code. Here is an example YAML configuration file:

```yaml
default_environment: "staging"
environments:
  staging:
    base_url: "https://staging.example.com"
    db_connection: "staging-db"
    api_key: "staging-api-key"
  production:
    base_url: "https://prod.example.com"
    db_connection: "prod-db"
    api_key: "prod-api-key"
```

In this setup, tests can load the configuration dynamically based on the specified environment, ensuring that the correct settings are applied during execution.

- **Environment-specific data:** In addition to environment configurations, consider maintaining environment-specific datasets that can be loaded as needed. This ensures that tests can adapt to variations in data requirements across different environments. Implement a system for versioning test data, allowing for the tracking of changes over time and facilitating easy rollbacks if needed.

- **Centralized test data management:** Develop a centralized test data management system that allows for easy access and management of test data. This could involve a combination of APIs, databases, and file storage systems to manage and retrieve test data efficiently. Here is an example of a helper function to load environment configurations:

```python
import yaml

def load_config(environment):
```

```
    with open(f'configs/{environment}.yaml', 'r') as file:
        return yaml.safe_load(file)

# Load configuration for the staging environment
config = load_config('staging')
print(config['base_url'])
```

The benefits of managing test data and configuration are:

- **Reduced test breakage:** By using dynamic data generation and separating configurations, tests become more resilient to changes in the application and its environment, leading to fewer failures.

- **Enhanced agility:** Teams can adapt quickly to changes in requirements, ensuring that tests remain relevant and practical without extensive rewrites.

- **Improved maintainability:** Separating test data and configuration from the test logic promotes cleaner code and easier maintenance, allowing teams to focus on delivering quality software.

- **Environment flexibility:** Using distinct configuration files for different environments ensures that tests can run seamlessly across various stages of development, reducing the risk of environmental inconsistencies.

The test automation framework can effectively manage test data and configuration challenges by adopting dynamic test data generation techniques and utilizing separate configuration files for different environments. This approach enhances test reliability and maintainability and supports agile development practices, ensuring that testing keeps pace with the rapid evolution of software products.

Lessons learned

One of the critical lessons learned from the case study is the paramount importance of designing a test automation framework that is modular, scalable, and tool-agnostic.

Modularity ensures that the framework is composed of distinct, self-contained components that can be developed, tested, and maintained independently. This separation of concerns fosters reusability, making it easier to adapt specific parts of the framework without impacting the entire system. For instance, teams can introduce new types of tests or integrate new tools simply by adding or replacing modules, rather than overhauling the entire framework.

Scalability is essential as the product evolves and the volume of tests increases. A scalable framework can handle the growing demands of testing without a corresponding increase in execution time. This capability is achieved through strategies such as parallel execution and cloud-based infrastructure, enabling teams to maintain efficiency as the product and its test suite expand.

Tool-agnostic design facilitates flexibility in testing approaches, allowing teams to choose the best tools for their specific needs without being locked into a single solution. This adaptability is crucial in a rapidly changing technology landscape, where new tools and best practices are continuously emerging. Organizations can evolve their testing strategies without significant overhead or disruption by decoupling the framework from specific tools.

Best practices to ensure smooth integration into CI/CD pipelines

Integrating the test automation framework into CI/CD pipelines is essential for ensuring continuous delivery and maintaining high-quality standards. Here are some best practices that emerged from the case study:

- **Automation of test execution:** Ensure the framework supports automated test execution as part of the CI/CD pipeline. This involves configuring the pipeline to trigger test runs on code commits, pull requests, or at scheduled intervals, enabling rapid feedback on code quality.

- **Reporting and feedback mechanisms:** Implement robust reporting mechanisms to provide immediate feedback on test results. This can include generating reports in various formats (HTML, JSON, and so on) and integrating them into the CI/CD dashboard. Clear visibility into test outcomes helps developers identify issues early and facilitates informed decision-making.

- **Environment consistency:** Use containerization (for example, Docker) to ensure that the test environment is consistent across development, staging, and production. This consistency reduces the likelihood of discrepancies between environments, helping to avoid *works on my machine* problems.

- **Parallel test execution:** Leverage parallel execution capabilities to minimize test run times within the CI/CD pipeline. This practice accelerates the feedback loop and ensures that test execution does not become a bottleneck in the deployment process.

- **Version control for test scripts:** Store test scripts and configurations in version control systems alongside application code. This practice promotes collaboration, traceability, and easy rollback of test changes in response to issues.

- **Regular maintenance and refactoring:** Establish a routine for maintaining and refactoring test scripts to ensure that they remain relevant and efficient. This includes removing obsolete tests, updating test data, and refining configurations in response to changes in the application.

The insights gained from this case study underscore the importance of a thoughtful approach to test automation framework design and implementation. A modular, scalable, and tool-agnostic framework is foundational to long-term success, while a well-defined architecture lays the groundwork for adaptability and growth. By adhering to best practices for CI/CD integration, organizations can enhance their testing processes, ensuring that they deliver high-quality software rapidly and efficiently.

Conclusion

In this case study, we explored the journey of designing and implementing a scalable, tool-agnostic test automation framework for a mid-size e-commerce platform.

In conclusion, designing and implementing a test automation framework is a complex but rewarding endeavor. By applying these principles and decisions, organizations can build a robust testing infrastructure that meets current needs and adapts to future challenges, ultimately driving software quality and innovation.

In the next chapter, we will look at another case study and how we can convert a tool-specific framework to a tool-agnostic approach.

Key takeaways

Throughout this process, several key decisions and architecture choices significantly shaped the framework's effectiveness and adaptability, such as:

- **Modular architecture:** The decision to adopt a modular architecture allowed us to compartmentalize the framework into distinct layers—test orchestration, data management, reporting, and execution. This design promoted code reusability and maintainability and facilitated easier updates as the product evolved.

- **Tool-agnostic flexibility:** By ensuring that the framework did not depend on any specific testing tool, we were able to incorporate a wide range of test types (unit, integration, performance, security, and so on) seamlessly. This flexibility empowered teams to select the best tools suited for their unique requirements without being constrained by the framework.

- **Scalability and parallel execution:** Implementing parallel execution techniques allowed the framework to handle increased test volumes efficiently as the system expanded into multiple microservices. Leveraging cloud-based infrastructure provided the necessary scalability to support extensive test runs without sacrificing performance.

- **Dynamic test data management:** Addressing the challenges associated with static data, we introduced dynamic test data generation and environment-specific configuration management. This approach minimized test breakage and improved the reliability of test outcomes.

- **Integration into CI/CD pipelines:** Ensuring seamless integration of the framework into CI/CD pipelines was essential for achieving continuous delivery. We established automated test execution, robust reporting mechanisms, and version control practices to support rapid feedback and maintain high quality throughout development.

Throughout the implementation, we faced various challenges, including managing scalability, ensuring tool-agnostic design, and maintaining effective test data management. Each challenge prompted thoughtful solutions that enhanced the framework's overall resilience and adaptability.

Final thoughts on applying principles and design decisions to other projects

The principles and design decisions highlighted in this case study can serve as a valuable framework for any organization looking to implement a scalable and flexible test automation solution. Here are some key takeaways that can be applied to other projects:

- **Prioritize modularity:** Emphasizing a modular design from the outset will enable teams to adapt to changing requirements and facilitate collaboration among diverse skill sets. This approach ensures that different framework components can evolve independently, promoting overall agility.

- **Maintain tool-agnosticism:** Organizations can future-proof their testing strategies by focusing on a tool-agnostic design. This flexibility allows for easy integration of new tools and technologies as they emerge, ensuring that the testing framework remains relevant in a rapidly changing landscape.

- **Plan for scalability:** When designing the framework, consider scalability from the start. Implement parallel execution and leverage cloud resources to accommodate growing test volumes without compromising performance. This foresight can help prevent bottlenecks in testing as the product grows.

- **Manage test data wisely:** Invest in dynamic test data generation and separate configuration management to minimize reliance on static data. This practice will enhance test reliability and reduce maintenance efforts as the application evolves.

- **Seamless CI/CD integration:** Make CI/CD integration a core focus during framework development. Establishing transparent processes for automated test execution, reporting, and version control will ensure that the framework supports continuous delivery and fosters a culture of quality.

Exercises

1. What are the main drivers for building a custom test automation framework instead of using an existing one?

2. What key challenges or pain points are you trying to solve with this framework?

3. What types of applications will the framework support (for example, web, mobile, APIs, microservices, desktop, cloud-native)?

4. What programming languages and tech stack will the framework be built on?

5. Will the framework be tool-agnostic, or will it be designed around specific automation tools?

6. How will the framework support modularity and extensibility to accommodate future changes?

7. What design patterns will be used (for example, Page Object Model, Screenplay, keyword-driven, BDD)?

8. How will the framework support parallel execution and distributed testing?

9. How will the framework integrate with CI/CD pipelines?

10. What mechanisms will be used for automatic test execution, reporting, and notifications?

11. How will test results be stored and analysed over time?

12. How will the framework integrate with test data management solutions?

## CHAPTER 13

Case Study: Migrating to a Tool-agnostic Framework

Introduction

As organizations strive to deliver quality software rapidly, the testing landscape has evolved dramatically. Traditional, tool-specific test automation frameworks, such as those based on Selenium or JUnit, may offer immediate benefits but can quickly become limitations as teams adopt a wider array of tools. This write-up explores the growing need for flexibility, the importance of avoiding vendor lock-in, and a case study of a mid-sized organization transitioning to a tool-agnostic framework.

Structure

In this chapter, we will cover the following topics:

- Growing need for flexibility
- Case study: Transitioning from tool-specific to tool-agnostic framework
- Lessons from transitioning between tools
- Identifying the need for change
- Planning and executing the migration
- Managing team adoption and buy-in
- Pilot projects
- Key challenges and solutions
- Benefits of migrating to a tool-agnostic automation framework

Objectives

By the end of this chapter, the readers will learn how to apply many of the design principles discussed earlier in the book to migrate from a tool-specific framework to one that is more tool-agnostic. We discuss the best ways to transition between them and build a framework around those challenges, along with different migration approaches, both from a technical perspective and also how to train and ensure teams can support the new framework.

Growing need for flexibility

In today's fast-paced software development environment, teams often use a diverse set of tools tailored to specific testing needs. For instance:

- **Unit testing:** Due to their specialized capabilities, frameworks like JUnit and NUnit are commonly employed for unit testing.

- **Performance testing:** Tools such as JMeter or Gatling provide insights into application performance under various load conditions.

- **Security testing:** Solutions like OWASP ZAP are essential for identifying vulnerabilities in applications.

This diversity allows teams to optimize their testing processes for different contexts. However, when frameworks are tightly coupled with specific tools, teams can struggle to integrate and adapt. A tool-agnostic framework provides flexibility to incorporate any tool seamlessly into the testing ecosystem, promoting a more dynamic and responsive testing strategy.

Avoiding vendor lock-in

Vendor lock-in is a significant concern for organizations relying on tool-specific frameworks. When teams invest heavily in a particular vendor's tool, transitioning away can be complex, time-consuming, and costly. This lock-in can hinder the organization's ability to adopt emerging technologies or adjust to changes in business requirements.

By migrating to a tool-agnostic framework, organizations can:

- **Choose best-of-breed tools:** Teams can select the most suitable tools for their specific needs without being constrained by a particular vendor.

- **Easily adapt to change:** As technology evolves, organizations can adapt their testing frameworks and tools swiftly, ensuring they remain competitive and efficient.

- **Facilitate knowledge transfer:** A tool-agnostic framework enables team members to develop skills across various tools, enhancing team resilience and reducing dependency on specific individuals.

Case study: Transitioning from tool-specific to tool-agnostic framework

When it comes to the background, consider a mid-sized organization, *Tech Innovations*, that previously relied on a Selenium-based test automation framework. While Selenium served its purpose well for web application testing, the organization faced several challenges as it expanded its testing scope to include performance and security testing.

The challenges faced are as follows:

- **Integration issues:** The existing Selenium framework made it difficult to integrate performance and security testing tools, leading to fragmented testing processes.

- **Maintenance overhead:** As new tools were introduced, maintaining compatibility became increasingly burdensome, resulting in delays and reduced test coverage.

- **Resistance to change:** The reliance on a single vendor made the organization hesitant to explore better options available in the market.

Migration journey

To address these challenges, Tech Innovations embarked on a migration to a tool-agnostic, modular architecture. The process included:

- **Assessment of current tools:** A thorough evaluation of existing testing tools and processes was conducted using a structured framework that included criteria such as integration capability, ease of use, execution speed, reporting features, scalability, and support for CI/CD pipelines. Each tool was scored across these dimensions using stakeholder feedback, benchmark tests, and historical defect detection rates. The features are:

  o **Integration with CI/CD:** Only 60% of tools had seamless integration with the CI pipeline, resulting in manual test triggers and increased release times.

  o **Ease of use:** Testers reported a steep learning curve for legacy tools, with a usability rating of 5.8/10.

  o **Execution speed:** Regression test suites took over 3 hours to complete on average due to a lack of parallel execution capabilities.

  o **Reporting and diagnostics:** Many tools lacked actionable reporting, with test failure logs requiring manual parsing, slowing down defect triage.

  o **Tool overlap and duplication:** Multiple tools were being used for similar functions (for example, UI vs. API test automation), resulting in maintenance overhead and inconsistency.

  o **Scalability:** Some tools struggled under increased load when run in parallel environments, especially during peak release cycles.

  The results revealed clear opportunities to streamline the toolset, consolidate overlapping functionality, and adopt modern, more scalable, and CI-friendly tools.

- **Modular framework design:** The new framework was intentionally designed with modularity at its core, enabling seamless plug-and-play integration with various tools (for example, reporting, test runners, data sources) without requiring major rewrites. This contrasts with older non-modular frameworks that were:

  o **Tightly coupled:** making changes or upgrades to one component (like the test runner or reporting tool) often broke others.

  o **Hard to scale:** lacked support for distributed execution or running tests across different environments easily.

  o **Difficult to maintain:** required deep knowledge of intertwined code bases, increasing onboarding time, and error-proneness.

  o **Tool-locked:** heavily reliant on specific vendors or tools, making it hard to adopt newer, more efficient alternatives.

  o **Slow to evolve:** adapting to new technologies (for example, microservices, containers, cloud testing) required significant rework or redesign.

  o **Lacking in reusability:** test logic and utilities were not easily reusable across projects or teams, leading to duplication and inconsistency.

- **Training and knowledge sharing:** A structured training program was rolled out to onboard team members to the new modular test automation framework. This included:

  o Interactive workshops covering core framework architecture, tool integrations, and design principles.

  o Hands-on labs for writing and refactoring tests using the new modular components.

  o Internal documentation and video walkthroughs to support asynchronous learning.

  o Knowledge-sharing sessions where early adopters demonstrated best practices and lessons learned.

This initiative helped reduce onboarding time for new team members by 40%, improved framework adoption across multiple squads, and established a shared language around automation practices. It also encouraged ongoing contributions to framework enhancements and documentation.

- **Pilot implementation:** A focused pilot project was launched to validate the new modular framework in a real-world setting. A representative application was selected, and a small, cross-functional team of testers and developers used the framework to automate a subset of regression and API tests. This allowed the team to:

  o Evaluate the ease of onboarding and learning curve for new users.

  o Measure improvements in test execution speed and stability.

  o Identify how easily components (like logging, reporting, or data sources) could be swapped or extended.

  o Compare test maintainability and readability against the legacy framework.

  o Collect qualitative feedback on usability, integration with CI/CD, and collaboration between roles.

  Results from the pilot showed a 30% reduction in test maintenance effort, faster test execution in CI pipelines, and positive feedback from users on modular design and configurability. These insights were used to refine the framework before wider rollout.

Results

The migration yielded significant benefits for *Tech Innovations*, such as:

- **Enhanced flexibility:** By moving away from a tool-specific framework (such as one tightly coupled to Selenium), the new tool-agnostic architecture enabled teams to plug in different testing tools, such as Playwright for modern web automation, REST-assured for API testing, or Appium for mobile, without overhauling the entire framework.

  o This shift reduced dependency risks and allowed teams to select the best-fit tools for their specific testing needs.

  o Test layers were decoupled from execution engines, enabling teams to switch between local runs, headless executions, and cloud-based solutions with minimal changes.

  o As a result, automation coverage improved across platforms, and the average test execution time decreased by 30%, thanks to smarter tool choices and parallel execution capabilities.

- **Reduced maintenance efforts:** The modular architecture decoupled tool-specific logic from core test components, making it easier to swap or update tools without affecting the entire framework. This significantly decreased the time spent on maintaining brittle test code, enabled parallel updates across modules, and allowed teams to dedicate more effort to designing robust, business-aligned test scenarios rather than resolving tool compatibility issues. Here,

  o Tool-specific logic was abstracted into independent modules, reducing the impact of tool upgrades or replacements.

  o Version updates became localized, allowing individual tools or libraries to be upgraded without breaking the entire framework.

  o Test scripts were insulated from low-level tool changes, enabling better reuse across different execution environments.

  o Troubleshooting became easier, as issues could be traced to specific modules rather than sprawling across the whole framework.

  o Engineers could focus more on test design and coverage, rather than spending time fixing compatibility or configuration issues.

- o Onboarding new tools or libraries required minimal changes, supporting continuous improvement without excessive rework.

- **Empowered teams:** By reducing tool lock-in, team members felt empowered to explore new tools and methodologies, driving innovation and improving the organization's competitive edge. Here,

  - o Experimentation was encouraged, as the framework supported plug-and-play integration with emerging technologies.

  - o Team autonomy increased, allowing squads to make independent tooling decisions within a consistent architectural boundary.

  - o Confidence grew among engineers, knowing their choices wouldn't require extensive framework rewrites.

  - o Innovation cycles accelerated, as teams could trial new methodologies (e.g., contract testing, visual testing) without bureaucratic blockers.

  - o Cross-functional collaboration improved, as Dev, QA, and DevOps could all contribute to evolving and optimizing the toolchain.

  - o The organization gained a competitive edge, driven by faster adoption of modern practices and reduced dependency on legacy tooling.

As demonstrated by the case study of Tech Innovations, such a transition can lead to significant enhancements in the testing process, ultimately contributing to the organization's success in delivering high-quality software. By embracing a tool-agnostic approach, teams can position themselves for long-term growth and sustainability in an ever-evolving technological landscape.

Background and initial setup

Let us now learn more about the setup.

Tool-specific framework limitations

Tech Innovations initially adopted a Selenium-based framework for UI testing, providing a solid foundation for their testing needs. In the early stages of development, Selenium's robust capabilities allowed the team to automate web application testing effectively. However, as the organization expanded its testing scope, several limitations became apparent, such as:

- **Lack of scalability:** As the volume of tests grew, the existing Selenium framework struggled to keep pace with increased demands. The complexity of maintaining an extensive suite of UI tests became a significant bottleneck, leading to longer test execution times and delayed releases. Other issues included:

  - o **UI-centric bottleneck**: The framework relied heavily on Selenium for UI tests, making it difficult to scale test coverage across layers (API, integration, performance).

  - o **Long execution times**: As test suites grew, UI test runs became slower due to browser startup overhead and rendering time, limiting parallelization options.

  - o **High flakiness**: Selenium tests were prone to flakiness from minor UI changes or asynchronous page behavior, requiring frequent maintenance and re-runs.

  - o **Difficult parallel execution**: Limited built-in support for distributed test execution without significant infrastructure setup hinders scalability.

  - o **Resource-intensive infrastructure**: Scaling up meant provisioning more VMs or containers for browser instances, increasing CI/CD costs.

  - o **Monolithic architecture**: Tool-specific design made it hard to decouple test logic from execution engine, preventing reuse and optimization across layers.

o **Inflexibility to adapt**: Integrating newer or faster tools (like Playwright or Cypress) was difficult without rewriting large portions of the framework.

o **Delayed feedback**: Slow and brittle test runs reduced the speed of feedback loops, impacting developer productivity and delaying releases.

- **Integration challenges:** Tech Innovations sought to diversify its testing efforts beyond UI automation. However, the tool-specific nature of the framework made it difficult to integrate other types of testing, such as performance and security testing. This fragmentation resulted in silos of testing efforts, limiting the overall effectiveness of the testing strategy. Other issues included:

o **Limited extensibility:** The Selenium-centric framework was not designed to support non-UI testing, such as API, performance, or security testing, making cross-domain integration cumbersome.

o **Fragmented tooling landscape:** Different teams adopted separate tools for API, load, or security testing, leading to isolated test strategies and duplicated efforts.

o **Lack of centralized reporting:** Each testing tool produced its results, with no unified reporting or dashboards, making it difficult to gain a holistic view of test health.

o **Complex CI/CD integration:** Integrating multiple tools into CI pipelines required custom scripts and workarounds, increasing maintenance overhead.

o **Duplication of test coverage:** Teams often recreate similar test logic across different tools due to a lack of interoperability, wasting effort and increasing inconsistency.

o **Hard to enforce standards:** Without a unified framework, standardizing test design, naming conventions, and tagging across toolsets was difficult.

o **Delayed risk identification:** Security and performance issues were often discovered late in the cycle due to the separation of test disciplines, affecting release quality.

o **Stifled innovation:** Teams were reluctant to explore newer tools that didn't fit the existing framework, reducing adaptability to emerging testing needs.

Aim for a flexible and extensible framework

Recognizing these challenges, Tech Innovations set out to redefine its testing approach with the following goals in mind:

- **Flexibility:** The new framework needed to accommodate a variety of testing tools, allowing teams to choose the best solutions for their specific needs without being constrained by a single vendor or technology.

- **Extensibility:** The framework should be designed to integrate seamlessly with various testing types, including performance testing (e.g., JMeter), security testing (e.g., OWASP ZAP), and unit testing (e.g., JUnit). This extensibility would enable the organization to expand its testing capabilities over time.

- **Consistency and robustness:** Despite the diversity of tools, the new framework must maintain a consistent and robust testing process. This consistency would ensure that teams could rely on a unified approach to testing, minimizing confusion and improving collaboration across different testing domains.

By focusing on these goals, Tech Innovations aimed to create a tool-agnostic test automation framework that would empower teams to enhance their testing efforts and drive continuous improvement in software quality.

Lessons from transitioning between tools

Let us understand the challenges of a tool-specific framework. While Tech Innovations initially benefited from its Selenium-based test automation framework, the organization soon encountered several significant challenges that hindered its testing efforts and overall software quality. Let us go over these challenges now.

Technical debt accumulation

The reliance on a tool-specific framework led to the accumulation of technical debt over time. Key issues included:

- **Tightly coupled tests:** The framework's design encouraged the creation of tightly coupled tests that depended heavily on Selenium's specific functionalities. This coupling made it difficult to modify or enhance tests without extensive rework, limiting agility and responsiveness to application changes. Some examples are:

    o **High coupling to tool-specific APIs:** Tests were written using direct Selenium calls, embedding low-level interactions (like findElement, waits, selectors) throughout test logic, making tests brittle and hard to maintain.

    o **Low abstraction and reuse:** There was minimal separation between test logic and implementation, resulting in duplicated code across multiple test cases and reduced maintainability.

    o **Difficulty adapting to UI changes:** Even small UI updates (for example, element ID changes) required widespread modifications across numerous tests, consuming significant time and effort.

    o **Inhibited modularization:** The lack of a clear separation between test orchestration, interaction, and data layers hindered reuse across test scenarios.

    o **Prolonged onboarding and ramp-up:** New team members faced steep learning curves due to dense, non-standardized code intertwined with tool-specific logic.

    o **Accumulated workaround logic:** Over time, the test codebase grew with patches and conditional logic to accommodate UI inconsistencies or test flakiness, exacerbating technical debt.

    o **Poor scalability for parallel testing:** Tightly coupled code often assumes sequential execution, making it difficult to isolate test environments or run tests concurrently.

    o **Slow feedback loops:** The cost of updating tests meant regression suites were not consistently kept up-to-date, reducing confidence in test results and delaying issue detection.

- **Difficulty maintaining code:** As the test suite grew, maintaining the code became increasingly challenging. The complexity of intertwined tests led to confusion, making it harder for team members to understand and modify the codebase. Consequently, new team members faced a steep learning curve, further slowing down the development and testing efforts. Examples include:

    o **Lack of clear structure or conventions**: The legacy framework lacked standardized patterns or architecture, resulting in inconsistent code styles, naming, and test flows across the suite.

    o **Interdependent test logic**: Many tests shared data setups, environment configurations, or utility functions in a non-isolated way, meaning changes in one test could unintentionally break others.

    o **Inadequate documentation and onboarding support**: Key architectural decisions, test strategies, and helper methods were undocumented or tribal, increasing reliance on a few experienced individuals.

    o **Manual maintenance of locators and test data**: There was no central repository for UI element locators or reusable test data, making updates error-prone and time-consuming.

    o **Duplication of logic across tests**: Without reusable components or abstraction layers, logic for actions like login or form submission was repeated in multiple tests, inflating maintenance effort.

    o **Test flakiness and debugging challenges**: Poor separation of concerns and inconsistent state handling led to frequent test failures with ambiguous root causes, requiring time-intensive investigations.

o **Limited IDE support and code readability**: The monolithic structure and long, procedural test scripts made it harder for modern development tools to provide effective navigation, autocompletion, or linting.

o **Delayed incorporation of improvements**: Refactoring was avoided due to risk of breakage, leading to stagnation in code quality and missed opportunities to modernize or simplify logic.

Tool limitations

The organization faced significant limitations when attempting to expand its testing capabilities, such as:

- **Incorporating new test types:** Tech Innovations aimed to adopt additional testing types, such as API testing and performance testing. However, the existing Selenium framework was not designed to accommodate these needs as UI driven testing was the only testing done at the time and now that the testing has shifted, the framework is not robust enough to adapt to these different test types. The team struggled to integrate new tools effectively, resulting in fragmented testing efforts and a lack of comprehensive coverage.

- **Inflexibility to change:** The rigidity of the tool-specific framework meant that adapting to new technologies or methodologies was cumbersome. As the industry evolved, the inability to easily incorporate best-of-breed tools hindered the organization's competitiveness and innovation.

Maintenance overhead

As the project matured, the maintenance overhead associated with the tool-specific framework became unmanageable:

- **High test flakiness:** Many tests became flaky due to dependencies on the Selenium framework's specific behaviors. This unreliability led to increased time spent on identifying and fixing false positives, diverting resources away from actual development and testing efforts.

- **Brittle test scripts:** The tightly coupled nature of the tests resulted in brittle scripts that frequently broke with minor changes to the application. This fragility required constant attention from the testing team, contributing to frustration and burnout.

These challenges underscored the need for Tech Innovations to transition to a tool-agnostic framework. By doing so, the organization aimed to reduce technical debt, enhance integration capabilities, and streamline maintenance efforts, ultimately fostering a more efficient and effective testing process.

Identifying the need for change

As Tech Innovations continued to evolve, it became increasingly clear that the existing tool-specific framework was inadequate for meeting the organization's growing testing demands. Several key issues highlighted the need for a strategic change in their approach to test automation. Let us go over these issues now.

Cross-team friction

One of the most significant challenges was the cross-team friction that arose from the use of various tools:

- **Diverse toolsets:** Different teams employed different tools to fulfill their specific testing needs. For instance, the performance testing team relied on JMeter, while the functional testing team used Selenium. This diversity created silos within the organization, making it challenging to integrate testing efforts cohesively. While this is not a technical limitation on the previous framework, it drove the need to consolidate and ensure that a more purpose-built framework was developed.

- **Communication barriers:** As teams struggled to align their testing strategies, communication barriers emerged. Without a unified framework, knowledge sharing became difficult, leading to duplicated efforts and inconsistent testing practices across the organization.

Incompatibility with CI/CD pipelines

The organization also faced incompatibility issues with CI/CD pipelines, which hindered the automation of the testing process:

- **Tool dependencies:** The reliance on multiple tool-specific frameworks created challenges in automating all test types within a single CI/CD pipeline. Each tool had its own setup requirements and execution environments, complicating integration efforts and slowing down the deployment process.

- **Fragmented testing:** This incompatibility led to fragmented testing cycles, where different types of tests could not run seamlessly together. As a result, the organization struggled to achieve comprehensive test coverage within its CI/CD process, undermining the benefits of continuous integration and deployment.

Slow execution and limited parallelism

Another critical issue was the slow execution and limited parallelism offered by the existing tool-specific framework:

- **Bottlenecks in testing:** The old framework's inability to support parallel test execution led to significant bottlenecks in the testing process. As the test suite expanded, execution times grew longer, delaying feedback loops and slowing down overall development. And while newer versions of Selenium supported parallel execution, the framework could not support it. Additionally, the team sought to explore alternative, headless approaches to parallelism to further improve execution speed. This would require potentially different tooling and for the team to look at a more tool-agnostic approach.

- **Inefficient resource utilization:** The lack of parallel execution capabilities severely limited the efficiency of the testing process by preventing teams from distributing test execution across multiple machines or threads. This shortcoming meant that even though the infrastructure, such as build agents, virtual machines, or cloud resources, was capable of handling concurrent workloads, it remained underutilized. As a result, tests were executed sequentially, significantly increasing overall execution time. This not only delayed feedback loops but also caused bottlenecks in the CI/CD pipeline, ultimately slowing down release cycles. Developers and testers had to wait longer for test results, reducing their ability to respond quickly to failures or code changes. Over time, this inefficiency contributed to reduced team velocity, higher operational costs, and mounting frustration due to idle compute resources and elongated delivery timelines.

These challenges underscored the urgent need for Tech Innovations to transition to a tool-agnostic test automation framework. By addressing cross-team friction, enhancing compatibility with CI/CD pipelines, and improving test execution efficiency, the organization aimed to create a more cohesive and agile testing environment that could adapt to the complexities of modern software development.

Planning and executing the migration

Let us go over the steps for planning and executing the migration now.

Step 1: Establishing migration goals

In embarking on the transition from a tool-specific test automation framework to a tool-agnostic framework, Tech Innovations recognized the importance of establishing clear migration goals. These goals would serve as a guiding framework throughout the migration process and help ensure that the new approach effectively addressed the organization's challenges.

The key objectives are:

- **Tool-agnostic framework**: The primary objective was to create a tool-agnostic framework that would support the integration of various testing tools tailored to different testing needs. This flexibility would empower teams to select the best tools for their specific requirements, whether for UI, performance, security, or API testing.

- **Maintain or improve speed of execution and CI/CD integration:** Another key goal was to maintain or even improve the speed of test execution and ensure seamless integration into CI/CD pipelines. The new framework is needed to enable efficient test execution and facilitate automated testing processes, thereby minimizing delays in the software delivery lifecycle.

- **Reusability and adaptability of existing tests:** The organization aimed to ensure that existing tests from the old tool-specific framework could be reused or adapted without extensive rewriting. This objective was crucial for minimizing disruption during the transition and preserving the value of previously developed test assets.

Defining success metrics

To measure the success of the migration, Tech Innovations established several key success metrics, such as:

- **Reduced test execution time:** A core success metric of the new framework was its ability to significantly reduce test execution time. Under the old Selenium-based system, the average end-to-end test suite execution time was approximately 4 hours, largely due to sequential execution and a monolithic structure. After migrating to the modular, tool-agnostic framework with built-in support for parallel test execution and distributed runs via CI tools like Jenkins and GitLab CI, the average execution time should drop to around 1 hour and 15 minutes—a 70% reduction. This improvement will be tracked using CI pipeline logs and automated execution time dashboards integrated with Grafana. Quicker execution will directly improve feedback cycles: teams will be able to identify and fix issues earlier in the development process, with a planned reduction in the average bug resolution time from 2.3 days to 0.9 days and increasing deployment frequency by 30% within three sprints.

- **Improved test coverage across multiple tools:** The new framework would enable testing across multiple domains—including UI, API, performance, and security—using a unified structure. Previously, coverage was limited to about 42% of critical business functionality, focused almost exclusively on the UI layer. After rollout, teams are expected to expand coverage to include API contract testing (via Postman and REST Assured), load testing (via JMeter), and basic security checks (via OWASP ZAP). As a result, test coverage of critical functionalities should increase to 85%, with 15% of new tests focused on non-functional aspects like performance and vulnerability scanning. These coverage improvements will be monitored using tools like SonarQube, code coverage plugins, and a custom test gap analysis dashboard that aligns test results with application features.

- **Easier maintenance for future teams:** Maintainability will be measured through both objective metrics and subjective team feedback. Objectively, the average time to onboard a new team member to the framework should drop from 3 weeks to 5 days, owing to a clear modular structure, inline documentation, and prebuilt templates for common test types. Pull request analysis should reveal a 45% decrease in the average number of lines changed per test enhancement, indicating that small, modular changes are easier to implement without large-scale rewrites. Subjectively, regular internal surveys (conducted at the end of each sprint) should show that 90% of engineers reported improved maintainability, and 85% noted a significant reduction in the number of regressions caused by test modifications. Technical debt tickets related to test flakiness and brittle test design are required to drop by 60% over two quarters.

By clearly defining these migration goals and success metrics, Tech Innovations set the stage for a structured and effective transition to a tool-agnostic test automation framework. This strategic approach would help ensure that the new framework addressed the existing challenges while positioning the organization for future growth and adaptability in its testing efforts.

Step 2: Designing the new framework

With the migration goals established, Tech Innovations proceeded to the crucial phase of designing the new tool-agnostic test automation framework. The design aimed to create a robust, flexible, and extensible architecture that would facilitate seamless integration of diverse testing tools while promoting maintainability and scalability.

Modular and extensible design

A fundamental principle of the new framework was to adopt a modular and extensible design:

- **Separation of concerns:** The framework was structured to separate different concerns, such as test orchestration, reporting, and test data management. This separation ensured that each module could be developed, maintained, and updated independently, minimizing interdependencies that could complicate future enhancements.

- **Plug-and-play integration:** By designing the framework with modularity in mind, Tech Innovations enabled easy plug-and-play integration of various tools. Teams could add or replace tools as needed without significant rework or disruption, allowing for greater flexibility in adapting to new testing requirements or technologies.

Abstracting tool-specific code

To further enhance the framework's adaptability, the organization focused on abstracting tool-specific code:

- **Abstraction layer for test execution:** The new framework included an abstraction layer that allowed for the orchestration of tests using different tools. This abstraction enabled the framework to manage various test types, such as using Selenium for some existing UI testing for older legacy applications with little change, JMeter for performance testing, and Playwright for functional testing of APIs and newly built micro frontends without being tightly coupled to any specific tool.

- **Unified interface:** A major advantage of introducing an abstraction layer in the tool-agnostic framework was the creation of a unified interface that decoupled test logic from underlying tool implementations. Previously, testers had to learn and manage multiple tool-specific syntaxes, configurations, and execution workflows, for instance, writing separate scripts and runners for Selenium (UI), Postman (API), and JMeter (performance). This fragmentation not only increased onboarding time and cognitive load but also introduced inconsistencies in how tests were structured and executed.

With the abstraction layer in place, all test types—regardless of tool—could be registered, configured, and executed using standardized interfaces and commands, typically via a CLI or configuration-driven runner. For example, executing a UI test and an API test both followed the pattern:

```
./run-tests --type=ui --tag=smoke
./run-tests --type=api --tag=regression
```

Tool-specific details (like WebDriver setup, REST endpoints, or JMX configurations) were handled internally by dedicated Adapter modules that implemented a common execution contract. This was achieved using design patterns like the Adapter and Facade, which wrapped each tool's unique logic behind common test lifecycle operations (`setup()`, `execute()`, `teardown()`).

The impact was measurable:

- Onboarding time for new test engineers dropped by 60%, as they no longer needed to learn each tool's syntax upfront.

- Code duplication reduced by 40%, since shared logic (for example, environment setup, reporting, and logging) was centralized in the core framework layer.

- CI pipeline configuration became simpler, with unified test steps regardless of test type, enabling teams to create reusable pipeline templates across projects.

This abstraction significantly improved developer experience, encouraged adoption of a wider variety of tools, and made the framework far more maintainable and extensible in the long term.

Retrofitting existing tests

To transition from a legacy Selenium-based framework to a new modular, tool-agnostic test automation framework, the organization adopted a gradual and prioritized migration strategy. This ensured continuity of testing operations while realizing the benefits of the new architecture.

Compatibility layer to bridge old and new

A compatibility Adapter was introduced to allow legacy Selenium tests to run within the new framework environment. This layer abstracted Selenium-specific logic behind the new tool-agnostic API surface.

For example:

```
# Legacy call
driver.find_element(By.ID, "submit").click()


# Abstracted version
ui.click("submit")  # Internally uses the correct tool based on config
```

This let teams migrate individual tests gradually without breaking CI pipelines or retraining everyone up front.

Prioritizing high-impact tests

Before initiating the migration, a test value assessment was performed. Tests were evaluated based on:

- Business criticality (for example, login, payments, onboarding).
- Execution frequency (for example, tests run in every build).
- Historical flakiness or failure impact.

Based on this, ~10–15% of the test suite, representing critical smoke and regression scenarios, was selected for initial migration.

For example:

- Login and registration tests were migrated first, as they often blocked deployments.
- Checkout flow tests were prioritized next, due to their direct impact on revenue.

Pilot implementation in CI

Migrated tests were executed in parallel with the legacy suite during CI runs. Flags were used to control test selection:

```
--runLegacyTests=true --runNewFrameworkTests=true
```

The benefits include:

- Side-by-side performance and stability comparisons.
- Early detection of issues in the migrated test logic.
- No risk to release schedules.

Iterative migration by sprint

Each sprint included a migration target, such as converting 20 tests in a functional area or replacing a full test category (for example, user profile settings).

Example sprint goal:

- **Sprint 5:** Migrate all Order Management tests (38 test cases).
- **Sprint 6:** Migrate flaky Payment Gateway tests to improve reliability.

Progress tracking:

- % of total tests migrated.

- Reduction in average test execution time.

- Number of tests eliminated due to redundancy or obsolescence.

Simplified maintenance for retrofitted tests

Newly migrated tests followed strict modular design, shared common utilities, and eliminated direct tool dependencies. This:

- Reduced duplication.

- Increased reusability across teams.

- Simplified onboarding of new QA engineers.

Final migration and legacy decommissioning

When over 85% of tests were running under the new framework:

- Legacy Selenium test runners were retired.

- Remaining low-priority tests were either migrated or archived.

- The compatibility layer was removed, and build pipelines were cleaned up.

The key metrics tracked during migration can be seen in the following table:

Metric	Before migration	After 3 months
Avg. test execution time	4 hours	75 minutes
% tests migrated	0%	72%
High-impact tests migrated	N/A	100%
Avg. test flakiness rate	11%	3%
Test onboarding time for new QAs	~5 days	2 days

Table 13.1: Key metrics tracked during migration

By implementing a modular and extensible design, abstracting tool-specific code, and planning for the gradual retrofitting of existing tests, Tech Innovations established a strong foundation for its new tool-agnostic test automation framework. This strategic design addressed the challenges of the previous tool-specific framework and positioned the organization for future growth and adaptability in its testing practices.

Managing team adoption and buy-in

As Tech Innovations embarked on its transition to a tool-agnostic test automation framework, a robust communication strategy was essential for ensuring alignment among all stakeholders and facilitating a smooth migration process. The organization recognized that clear and effective communication would help address concerns, foster collaboration, and drive enthusiasm for the new framework.

Clear communication of benefits

A key component of the communication strategy was to articulate the following benefits of a tool-agnostic framework to various stakeholders, including developers, QA teams, and management:

- **Enhanced flexibility:** Stakeholders were informed that the new framework would allow teams to select the best tools for their specific testing needs, promoting agility and responsiveness to changing project requirements.

- **Improved efficiency:** The framework's modular design and ability to integrate diverse testing tools would streamline testing efforts, leading to reduced execution times and improved turnaround for feedback.

- **Lower maintenance overhead:** The abstraction layer and separation of concerns would simplify maintenance, making it easier for teams to manage tests and adapt to future changes without significant rework.

Aligning the migration plan with business goals

To ensure buy-in from all stakeholders, Tech Innovations worked to align the migration plan with broader business goals:

- **Improving product quality:** The organization emphasized how the tool-agnostic framework would contribute to higher product quality through comprehensive test coverage and the ability to integrate various testing methodologies.

- **Speeding up releases:** By streamlining testing processes and improving efficiency, the new framework would enable faster releases, allowing the organization to respond more quickly to market demands and customer needs.

- **Reducing maintenance overhead:** Highlighting the reduction in maintenance overhead as a direct result of the new framework would reassure stakeholders that the transition would not only improve testing effectiveness but also enhance resource allocation and team productivity.

Implementation of the communication strategy

Tech Innovations employed various methods to communicate these benefits and align the migration plan with business goals, such as:

- **Stakeholder meetings:** Regular meetings with stakeholders provided an opportunity to present the migration strategy, discuss benefits, and address any concerns.

- **Workshops and training:** Organizing workshops and training sessions helped teams familiarize themselves with the new framework and its advantages, fostering engagement and collaboration.

- **Documentation and resources:** Providing detailed documentation outlining the migration process, expected benefits, and alignment with business objectives ensured that all stakeholders had access to the information they needed to support the transition.

By effectively communicating the benefits of a tool-agnostic framework and aligning the migration plan with business goals, Tech Innovations aimed to foster a collaborative environment that would facilitate a successful transition. This communication strategy was critical for gaining support from stakeholders, ensuring that the organization was well-prepared to embrace this new framework and align all teams on its adoption and implementation.

Training and skill development

As Tech Innovations prepared to migrate to a tool-agnostic test automation framework, a comprehensive training and skill development strategy was essential for ensuring a smooth transition. The organization recognized that equipping team members with the necessary knowledge and skills would be critical for maximizing the benefits of the new framework and minimizing disruptions during the migration process.

Conducting workshops and training sessions

To facilitate the learning process, Tech Innovations organized workshops and training sessions tailored to various teams:

- **Hands-on workshops:** Interactive workshops provided team members with hands-on experience using the new framework. These sessions allowed participants to explore their features, experiment with different tools, and understand how to effectively integrate them into their testing processes.

- **Role-specific training:** Training sessions were tailored to specific roles, such as developers, QA engineers, and team leads. This approach ensured that each group received relevant information and practical skills pertinent to their responsibilities within the new framework.

- **Question and answer (Q&A) sessions:** To address questions and concerns, Tech Innovations included Q&A sessions in the training program, allowing team members to seek clarification on specific aspects of the framework and share their insights or challenges.

Creating comprehensive documentation and tutorials

In addition to live training, Tech Innovations prioritized the development of comprehensive documentation and tutorials to support ongoing learning and ensure that it was easy for all staff to understand the operation and usage of the framework:

- **Detailed documentation:** Comprehensive documentation was created to outline the new framework's architecture, components, and best practices. This resource served as a reference guide for team members adapting to the new system.

- **Step-by-step tutorials:** To facilitate the transition, step-by-step tutorials were developed, guiding team members through the process of executing tests, integrating tools, and utilizing framework features. These tutorials were designed to accommodate varying skill levels, ensuring accessibility for all team members.

- **Resource library:** Tech Innovations established a resource library containing additional materials, such as videos, FAQs, and troubleshooting guides. This library aimed to provide ongoing support and enable team members to quickly find solutions to any challenges they encountered during the transition.

Ensuring a smooth transition

By conducting workshops and training sessions, alongside creating comprehensive documentation and tutorials, Tech Innovations aimed to foster a supportive learning environment that would enable team members to adapt to the new tool-agnostic test automation framework effectively. This focus on training and skill development was crucial for reducing the learning curve, enhancing team confidence, and ensuring that the organization could fully leverage the benefits of the new framework in its testing efforts.

Collaborative approach

To ensure a successful transition to a tool-agnostic test automation framework, Tech Innovations emphasized a collaborative approach that involved engaging team members throughout the migration process. This strategy was designed to foster a culture of teamwork and open communication, allowing for the identification of challenges and the reinforcement of confidence in the new framework.

Gathering feedback

Tech Innovations implemented a systematic process for gathering feedback from the engineering and QA teams:

- **Regular feedback sessions:** Scheduled feedback sessions were established to create a structured environment where team members could voice their concerns, share insights, and discuss any challenges they encountered during the migration. These sessions provided a platform for open dialogue, allowing the organization to address issues promptly.

- **Identifying bottlenecks and challenges:** These feedback sessions enabled the organization to identify specific bottlenecks or challenges in the migration process. By actively listening to the teams' experiences, Tech Innovations could make informed adjustments to the migration strategy, improving the overall transition experience.

Pilot projects

To ensure a smooth and sustainable migration from the legacy Selenium-based framework to the newly designed tool-agnostic architecture, Tech Innovations initiated the process with a focused pilot project. This strategic decision allowed the organization to validate assumptions, reduce risk, and gather feedback before embarking on a broader rollout.

Minimizing disruption with targeted scope

The pilot was deliberately limited to a specific product line, Tech Innovations' Customer Profile Management module, which had a manageable number of critical tests (~50 test cases) and minimal external dependencies. This scoped implementation ensured that:

- Day-to-day release cycles were not disrupted.
- Any teething issues in the new framework could be contained and resolved without affecting the entire QA operation.
- The learning curve for teams could be addressed in a lower-pressure environment.

This isolation helped teams explore the new framework safely, experiment with its features, and gradually adapt their testing mindset from tool-specific scripting to modular, abstracted test design.

Demonstrating capabilities through real use cases

Within the pilot, teams implemented several different types of tests, such as, functional UI checks, API validations, and data integrity assertions, using tools like Playwright and REST Assured, all plugged into the unified, tool-agnostic interface.

For instance:

- The same login test could be executed using either Playwright or Cypress based on runtime configuration.
- API smoke tests were triggered as part of the same suite without additional tooling overhead.

The pilot successfully demonstrated key benefits:

- Execution time dropped by 35%, due to better parallelization and faster tools.
- Test failures decreased by 60%, thanks to standardized setup/teardown logic.
- Testers reported a 40% reduction in time spent debugging or rewriting failed tests.

These wins not only proved the value of the framework but also helped showcase its flexibility, maintainability, and future scalability in front of stakeholders and engineering leadership.

Fostering ownership and building momentum

Team members involved in the pilot became early champions of the framework. Their direct involvement led to:

- Increased trust in the design principles.
- Faster knowledge sharing across other QA squads.
- Collaborative refinement of reporting, configuration, and test data strategies.

The hands-on experience gave these team members a strong sense of ownership, and their feedback led to several early improvements, such as refining CLI commands and updating test scaffolding templates for easier adoption.

Building confidence for broader adoption

As pilot teams gained proficiency and began reporting tangible productivity gains, Tech Innovations used this momentum to:

- Organize brown-bag sessions and demos for other QA and development teams.
- Document best practices, pitfalls, and migration strategies from the pilot.
- Launch onboarding workshops based on pilot learnings.

The successful completion of the pilot phase became a catalyst for broader migration efforts. With clear metrics and team testimonials, leadership gained the confidence that the framework was not only viable for niche use cases but was ready to scale to large, cross-domain test suites.

The key pilot outcomes can be seen in the following table:

Outcome	Pilot result
Avg. execution time (per suite)	Reduced from 22 min → 14 min
Setup time for new tests	Cut from ~90 mins to ~35 mins
Flaky test frequency	Dropped from 1 in 5 runs to 1 in 12
Team sentiment (survey)	92% positive feedback on maintainability & speed
New teams onboarded post-pilot	3 additional squads in the next 4 weeks

Table 13.2: Key pilot outcomes

This pilot-first strategy allowed Tech Innovations to de-risk the migration, demonstrate real-world benefits, and build the internal momentum required to successfully roll out the tool-agnostic framework across the enterprise.

Tech Innovations aimed to create an inclusive environment that encouraged team participation and engagement throughout the migration process by adopting a collaborative approach that focused on gathering feedback and implementing pilot projects. This strategy not only helped identify and address challenges but also built confidence among team members, setting the stage for a successful transition to the tool-agnostic test automation framework.

Maintaining backward compatibility

Recognizing the importance of legacy tests, Tech Innovations made it a priority to ensure backward compatibility:

- **Running critical legacy tests:** For critical tests that remained vital to ongoing operations, the new framework was designed to run these legacy tests until they could be fully migrated. This measure helped mitigate risk and ensured that existing testing coverage was maintained during the transition.

- **Transition strategy:** Tech Innovations developed a transition strategy that allowed for the gradual replacement of legacy tests with their tool-agnostic counterparts. This approach provided teams with the flexibility to adapt without sacrificing the reliability of their testing processes.

By employing a phased approach to migration that included pilot migration, gradual rollout, and maintaining backward compatibility, Tech Innovations set a solid foundation for a successful transition to a tool-agnostic test automation framework. This strategic method minimized disruption, managed risk, and allowed for continuous learning and adaptation throughout the migration process, ultimately leading to a more effective and efficient testing environment.

Mitigating risk during migration

To ensure a smooth and risk-managed transition to a tool-agnostic test automation framework, Tech Innovations implemented several key strategies to minimize disruptions and maintain testing integrity. These strategies focused on fallback options and integrating robust version control and CI processes.

Fallback strategy

A critical aspect of mitigating risk during migration was the establishment of a fallback strategy:

- **Execution in the old framework:** Tech Innovations ensured that if a test failed in the new framework, it could still be executed in the old framework. This fallback mechanism provided a safety net, allowing the team to maintain release schedules without interruption.

- **Minimizing disruption to releases:** By maintaining the ability to run tests in the legacy system, the organization could quickly resolve issues and validate functionality without delaying product releases. This approach not only safeguarded the testing process but also bolstered team confidence during the transition.

Version control and CI integration

To further enhance risk management, Tech Innovations leveraged version control and CI integration:

- **Tracking migration progress:** Version control systems were employed to track the migration progress meticulously. This included documenting changes made to test cases, maintaining a history of adaptations, and ensuring that team members could easily reference prior versions of tests if necessary.

- **Running frameworks in parallel:** CI/CD pipelines were configured to run both the old and new frameworks in parallel during the transition period. This dual execution allowed for real-time comparison of results, helping to identify discrepancies and validate the new framework's performance against the legacy system.

- **Immediate feedback loop:** The integration of version control and CI provided an immediate feedback loop, enabling teams to address any issues that arose during testing quickly. By monitoring results from both frameworks, the organization could ensure that the new system met or exceeded the standards set by the legacy framework.

By implementing a fallback strategy and using version control combined with CI integration, Tech Innovations effectively mitigated risks associated with migrating to a tool-agnostic test automation framework. These strategies provided a safety net to safeguard release schedules, ensure consistent testing outcomes, and facilitate a smoother transition, ultimately supporting the organization's goal of achieving greater flexibility and adaptability in its testing processes.

Key challenges and solutions

Let us now go over some key challenges and their respective solutions.

Challenge 1: Legacy code and test rewriting

As Tech Innovations embarked on migrating to a tool-agnostic test automation framework, one significant challenge was dealing with legacy code and test rewriting. The transition involved migrating large amounts of existing test code, some of which was incompatible with the new framework. This presented a unique set of hurdles that required careful planning and execution.

Problem: Migrating legacy test code

The primary issue at hand was the migration of legacy test code, which posed several challenges, such as:

- **Incompatibility:** Many legacy tests were tightly coupled with the specific tool used in the old framework, making them incompatible with the new tool-agnostic architecture. This incompatibility meant that running the old tests in the new environment would not yield accurate results or functionality.

- **Volume of code:** The sheer volume of legacy test scripts added complexity to the migration effort. Manually reviewing and rewriting these tests would be time-consuming and prone to errors, potentially leading to gaps in testing coverage during the transition.

Solution: Mapping strategy and automation

To address the challenges associated with legacy code, Tech Innovations developed a systematic approach:

- **Mapping strategy:** A comprehensive mapping strategy was established to identify and categorize legacy tests based on their functionality, complexity, and relevance. This strategy involved determining which tests could be directly adapted, which required refactoring, and which could be deprecated altogether.

- **Systematic adaptation and refactoring:** The mapping strategy enabled teams to systematically adapt or refactor old tests to be compatible with the new architecture. The organization could maintain essential testing coverage by prioritizing critical tests for immediate migration while gradually addressing less critical tests.

- **Leveraging automated tools:** Tech Innovations leveraged automated tools to facilitate the migration process wherever possible. These tools could help convert legacy test scripts into a format compatible with the new framework, significantly reducing the amount of manual rewriting required. Automation also minimized human error and increased efficiency, allowing the team to focus on more complex refactoring tasks.

The challenge of migrating legacy code and rewriting tests was a significant hurdle during Tech Innovations' transition to a tool-agnostic test automation framework. By developing a mapping strategy and leveraging automation tools, the organization was able to systematically address these challenges, ensuring a smoother migration process and preserving the integrity of its testing efforts throughout the transition.

Challenge 2: Tool compatibility and integration

As Tech Innovations transitioned to a tool-agnostic test automation framework, one of the key challenges was ensuring tool compatibility and integration. With various testing tools being used for different purposes, such as UI testing, API testing, and performance testing, there was a pressing need to create a cohesive and seamless integration within the new framework.

Problem: Ensuring smooth integration of different tools

The primary challenge in this phase was:

- **Diverse tools:** Different teams were using specialized tools tailored for specific testing needs and ways of working (for example, Selenium for UI testing, Postman for API testing, and JMeter for performance testing). While the modularity of the new framework solved this, teams still had to adapt the way they had worked around previous tools, and this change management and migration needed to be managed in a manner that was not too time-intensive.

- **Consistency in execution:** Without a standardized approach, integrating these tools could lead to inconsistencies in test execution, making it difficult to maintain an effective testing strategy.

Solution: Implementing an Adapter pattern

To address the challenge of tool compatibility and integration, Tech Innovations employed an Adapter pattern:

- **Standardizing test execution:** The Adapter pattern served as a design solution to standardize how tests were executed, regardless of the tool being used. By creating an abstraction layer, the framework could communicate with various testing tools without needing to understand their specific implementations.

- **Easy tool switching:** This design allowed for easy switching between tools. For instance, if a new tool needed to be integrated into the testing process, it could be added with minimal disruption. The framework would simply require a new Adapter, which would handle the specifics of the new tool while keeping the core test orchestration consistent.

- **Maintaining consistent test orchestration:** By using the Adapter pattern, Tech Innovations ensured that all tests could be orchestrated in a consistent manner. This facilitated a unified testing experience, where teams could run and manage tests across multiple tools without encountering compatibility issues.

The challenge of tool compatibility and integration was effectively addressed through the implementation of an Adapter pattern during Tech Innovations' migration to a tool-agnostic test automation framework. This approach standardized test execution, allowed for seamless integration of diverse tools, and maintained consistency in test orchestration, ultimately contributing to a more flexible and adaptable testing environment.

Challenge 3: Team resistance to change

As Tech Innovations progressed with the migration to a tool-agnostic test automation framework, one of the significant challenges faced was team resistance to change. Many team members were accustomed to using familiar tools, even when those tools exhibited limitations. Overcoming this resistance was essential for ensuring a successful transition.

Problem: Resistance to familiarity

The main issues surrounding team resistance included:

- **Comfort with existing tools:** Teams had developed a comfort level with their existing tools and workflows, which made them hesitant to adopt a new system. This resistance was extreme among team members who had invested significant time in mastering their current tools.

- **Concerns about disruption:** Team members expressed concerns about the potential disruption a new framework could bring to their established processes. They feared the migration could lead to increased workload, a steeper learning curve, and possible setbacks in project timelines.

Solution: Highlighting long-term benefits and offering training

To address this resistance, Tech Innovations implemented several strategies:

- **Highlighting long-term benefits:** The organization emphasized the long-term advantages of transitioning to a tool-agnostic framework. By showcasing benefits such as reduced maintenance, faster execution times, and greater flexibility in testing, management aimed to align the teams' perspectives with the broader organizational goals. Real-world examples and case studies demonstrating the positive impact of similar transitions were shared to illustrate potential outcomes.

- **Offering training sessions:** Tech Innovations organized comprehensive training sessions for team members to ease the transition. These sessions included workshops, hands-on demonstrations, and interactive tutorials designed to familiarize teams with the new framework and tools. By investing in skill development, the organization aimed to alleviate fears and build confidence in the new system.

- **Encouraging feedback and participation:** To further encourage acceptance, the organization fostered an open dialogue, allowing team members to share their concerns and suggestions during the migration process. Involving team members in discussions and decision-making helped create a sense of ownership and partnership in the transition.

Overcoming team resistance to change was a critical challenge during Tech Innovations' migration to a tool-agnostic test automation framework. By highlighting the new system's long-term benefits and offering targeted training sessions, the organization successfully addressed concerns and fostered a positive attitude toward the transition. This proactive approach ensured that team members felt supported and prepared for the changes ahead, ultimately contributing to the successful implementation of the new framework.

Benefits of migrating to a tool-agnostic automation framework

Migrating to a tool-agnostic test automation framework offers several significant advantages that enhance testing capabilities and align with the evolving needs of organizations. Here are some of the key benefits:

- **Improved flexibility and future-proofing:** One of the standout benefits of a tool-agnostic framework is its flexibility:

  o **Integration of new tools:** The framework allows for the seamless integration of new tools or the replacement of old ones without requiring a complete rewrite of existing tests. This capability ensures that the testing framework remains relevant as technology evolves, enabling organizations to adopt innovative solutions that best fit their needs.

  o **Adapting to changing requirements:** As organizations grow and their requirements change, the ability to quickly adapt testing strategies becomes crucial. A tool-agnostic framework provides the agility to pivot as necessary, ensuring teams can respond to emerging challenges without significant overhead.

- **Reduced maintenance and easier upgrades:** Another critical advantage of a tool-agnostic approach is the reduction in maintenance efforts:

  o **Less dependency on specific tools:** By minimizing reliance on specific tools, the framework simplifies the process of upgrades and maintenance. Teams can focus on enhancing the testing process rather than managing the complexities associated with a particular vendor or technology stack.

  o **Mitigating vendor lock-in risks:** The risk of vendor lock-in is significantly reduced, allowing organizations to maintain control over their technology choices. This independence enhances the strategic decision-making process, as teams can select the tools that best align with their objectives without being constrained by existing dependencies.

- **Seamless integration into CI/CD pipelines:** A tool-agnostic framework supports a more efficient CI/CD process:

  o **Abstracting tool execution:** By abstracting the execution of tools, the new framework facilitates streamlined integration into CI/CD pipelines. This abstraction enables teams to run tests across various tools within a unified process, enhancing the efficiency of continuous testing.

  o **Enhancing continuous testing:** The integration of diverse testing types, such as unit tests, integration tests, and performance tests, into the CI/CD pipeline becomes straightforward. As a result, organizations can achieve faster feedback cycles and improve the overall quality of their software products.

Migrating to a tool-agnostic test automation framework provides organizations with enhanced flexibility, reduced maintenance burdens, and seamless integration into CI/CD pipelines. By embracing this approach, organizations position themselves to adapt to evolving technologies, streamline their testing processes, and ultimately deliver higher-quality software more efficiently. The strategic benefits of this transition make it a vital consideration for any organization looking to modernize its testing efforts.

Conclusion

The migration from a tool-specific to a tool-agnostic test automation framework at Tech Innovations involved a carefully orchestrated process, encompassing several key steps and critical decisions.

The journey began with identifying the need for change by recognizing the limitations of the existing tool-specific framework, including challenges related to scalability, tool integration, and team resistance to change. Clear migration goals were then established, focusing on creating a flexible framework that supports multiple tools, improves execution speed, and ensures minimal disruption to ongoing testing efforts.

To design the new framework, a modular and extensible architecture was implemented using an Adapter pattern to standardize test execution. This design enabled the integration of various tools while maintaining consistent test orchestration.

To address team resistance, comprehensive training sessions were conducted, accompanied by ongoing communication that emphasized the long-term benefits of the new framework. This proactive approach encouraged acceptance and collaboration among team members.

A phased approach to migration was adopted, beginning with pilot projects and gradually rolling out the new framework across various test types. This ensured that critical legacy tests could continue to run until they were fully adapted to the new system. Throughout the process, efforts were made to mitigate risks, such as establishing fallback strategies and maintaining backward compatibility with legacy tests.

By addressing these challenges through strategic decisions and solutions, Tech Innovations successfully transitioned to a tool-agnostic framework, enhancing flexibility and adaptability in their testing processes.

In the next chapter, we will look at another case study, this time focusing on the continuous improvement of a testing framework.

Key takeaways

For teams considering a similar migration journey, several insights and best practices emerged from Tech Innovations' experience:

- **Prioritize clear communication:** Regular updates and transparent discussions about the benefits and goals of the migration can help alleviate concerns and foster team buy-in.

- **Involve stakeholders early:** Engaging various stakeholders in the decision-making process can create a sense of ownership and collaboration, facilitating a smoother transition.

- **Emphasize training and support:** Providing comprehensive training and resources helps teams build confidence in the new framework and reduces resistance to change.

- **Adopt a phased approach:** Gradual migration allows for iterative feedback and adjustments, minimizing disruptions and ensuring ongoing testing coverage.

- **Focus on flexibility and future-proofing:** Design the new framework with adaptability in mind, ensuring that it can accommodate new tools and technologies as they emerge.

By applying these best practices, teams can enhance their chances of successfully migrating to a tool-agnostic test automation framework, positioning themselves for greater agility and efficiency in their testing efforts.

Exercises

1. What are the primary reasons for migrating to a tool-agnostic framework (for example, avoiding vendor lock-in, scalability, maintainability)?

2. What challenges have been faced with the current tool-specific framework faced that the new framework must address?

3. What are the expected benefits of a tool-agnostic approach in terms of flexibility, cost, maintainability, and integration?

4. What functionalities and features must be retained or improved from the existing framework?

5. How much existing test code needs to be migrated, and what percentage can be reused versus rewritten?

6. Are there any legacy dependencies that might hinder the transition?

7. How will you measure success criteria for the migration (for example, reduced execution time, improved maintainability, ease of adoption)?

8. What is the planned timeline for the migration, and how will it be aligned with ongoing software development?

9. What risks and mitigation strategies have been identified for this transition?

CHAPTER 14

Case Study: Framework Evolution and Continuous Improvement

Introduction

In the fast-paced world of software development, the necessity for continuous evolution in test automation frameworks cannot be overstated. This evolution is driven by several critical factors that underscore the need for adaptability in our testing approaches.

Structure

In this chapter, we will go over the following topics:

- Evolving nature of software development
- Overview of the case study
- Adapting to changing requirements and technologies
- Framework evolution cycle
- Balancing technical debt and architectural improvements
- Architectural improvements to reduce debt
- Strategies for continuous improvement
- Incorporating feedback loops
- Upgrading tooling and integrations
- Key challenges and solutions
- Lessons from the framework evolution process

Objectives

By the end of this chapter, the reader will learn how to apply lessons from previous chapters to help ensure the test automation framework is continuously maintained and improved to ensure it does not become obsolete and continues to support new tooling and testing approaches.

Evolving nature of software development

Software development is an inherently dynamic field, characterized by rapid advancements in methodologies, tools, and practices. The shift towards agile, DevOps, and **continuous integration/continuous deployment (CI/CD)** paradigms emphasizes speed and flexibility. In this environment, test automation frameworks must evolve to align with these changing methodologies, ensuring they can support faster development cycles and more frequent releases. A framework that does not adapt can become a bottleneck, hindering the overall efficiency and agility of the development process.

Changing technologies

As new technologies emerge, such as cloud computing, microservices, and containerization, testing requirements also evolve. The tools and techniques that were once effective may no longer be suitable for modern architectures. For example, testing strategies that focus on monolithic applications might not suffice in a microservices architecture, where services must be tested independently and collaboratively. A rigid framework that fails to accommodate these technological shifts risks becoming obsolete, limiting the team's ability to leverage the latest innovations and maintain a competitive edge.

Shifting testing requirements

Testing requirements are not static; they evolve in response to changing business needs, user expectations, and regulatory landscapes. The rise of user-centered design principles means testing must incorporate more usability and performance assessments. Additionally, with increasing security concerns, frameworks must adapt to integrate security testing practices from the outset. A test automation framework that cannot evolve with these changing requirements risks providing inadequate coverage and increasing the likelihood of defects reaching production.

System architecture changes

Modern software systems often have diverse components, including APIs, databases, third-party services, and user interfaces. As system architectures evolve, the testing framework must also adapt to accommodate these complexities. A flexible framework allows teams to incorporate various testing types within a single structure, such as unit, integration, and end-to-end testing, facilitating better collaboration and ensuring comprehensive test coverage. Failing to evolve may lead to fragmented testing efforts and an inability to validate the entire system effectively.

The evolution of test automation frameworks is essential to keep pace with the rapidly changing landscape of software development. By embracing change and fostering adaptability, organizations can ensure their testing strategies remain adequate, relevant, and capable of supporting the demands of modern software development. A commitment to evolving frameworks not only enhances the quality of software products but also contributes to the overall success of the development process.

Overview of the case study

This case study delves into a company's transformative journey to adapt its test automation framework in response to evolving project requirements, expanding systems, and emerging technologies. As the software landscape continually shifts, the company recognized the need to rethink its testing strategy to enhance efficiency and ensure product quality.

Key focus

The primary focus of this case study is to explore how the organization effectively strikes a balance between addressing immediate project needs and preserving long-term architectural integrity. This balance is crucial, as the pressures of rapid development cycles and shifting priorities can often lead to quick fixes that compromise the robustness of the overall framework.

To achieve this, the company employed several strategic approaches:

- **Continuous feedback loops:** By establishing regular communication channels among developers, testers, and stakeholders, the team ensured that immediate needs were clearly understood and prioritized. This allowed for timely adaptations without losing sight of long-term goals.

- **Modular architecture:** The team adopted a modular approach to the test automation framework, enabling them to implement changes incrementally. This strategy addressed immediate requirements and ensured that each modification aligned with the overarching architectural principles.

- **Integration of emerging technologies:** The company invested in research and development to explore new technologies, such as cloud-based testing tools and AI-driven automation solutions. This proactive stance enabled them to remain competitive and responsive to current and future needs.

- **Long-term vision:** The leadership team emphasized the importance of maintaining a long-term vision for the test automation framework. By defining clear architectural guidelines and success metrics, the organization navigated the complexities of immediate demands while ensuring sustainable growth and adaptability.

Through this case study, we aim to illustrate the challenges and successes encountered during the company's journey. It serves as a valuable reference for other organizations seeking to evolve their test automation frameworks in a similarly dynamic environment, highlighting the importance of maintaining a delicate balance between immediate responsiveness and long-term integrity.

Adapting to changing requirements and technologies

As organizations adopt modern architectural practices, such as microservices and APIs, they face new testing requirements that were not previously necessary. This shift introduces several critical areas of focus:

- **API testing:** The proliferation of APIs necessitates robust testing capabilities to ensure that services interact seamlessly. API testing involves validating APIs' functionality, performance, and security to confirm they meet specifications and deliver the expected results. A test automation framework must incorporate specialized tools and practices for effective API testing, including automated endpoint verification and contract testing.

- **Load testing:** With the introduction of new microservices, understanding how these services perform under varying levels of load becomes essential. Load testing simulates concurrent users and transactions to assess how well the system handles increased demand. Incorporating load testing into the test automation framework allows teams to identify bottlenecks and scalability issues early, ensuring the system can sustain expected traffic levels.

Adoption of new technologies

The transition to cloud-native and containerized architecture presents unique challenges for testing, particularly in managing distributed systems and asynchronous processes:

- **Testing distributed systems:** In a microservices architecture, components may reside on different servers or cloud environments, making testing interactions across these distributed systems crucial. A robust test automation framework should support testing strategies that accommodate service-to-service communication, including the ability to simulate network latency and failures.

- **Handling asynchronous processes:** Many cloud-native applications utilize asynchronous communication, where services interact without waiting for responses. Testing these asynchronous processes requires specialized approaches, such as event-driven testing and message queues. The automation framework must be equipped to handle these complexities, ensuring comprehensive coverage of all interaction scenarios.

Regulatory and security requirements

As organizations navigate a landscape increasingly influenced by security concerns and regulatory mandates, integrating compliance and security testing into the test automation framework is critical:

- **Security testing:** The rise of cyber threats necessitates a proactive approach to security testing. Organizations must incorporate security testing into their automation processes to identify vulnerabilities early in the development lifecycle. This can include static and dynamic analysis, penetration testing, and continuous monitoring to ensure that security measures are consistently applied.

- **Regulatory compliance:** Regulations such as GDPR, POPIA, and HIPAA impose stringent requirements on data handling and privacy. Knowing how these apply to your industry, company, and the different global rules is critical. Testing for compliance must be seamlessly integrated into the test automation framework to ensure that applications meet legal standards. This involves validating data protection mechanisms, access controls, and audit logging features to demonstrate adherence to regulatory requirements.

By addressing these new testing needs, organizations can enhance their test automation frameworks to better support modern development practices. This proactive adaptation not only ensures high-quality software delivery but also strengthens the organization's position in an increasingly competitive and regulated environment.

Framework evolution cycle

In the journey of adapting a test automation framework, regular evaluation is paramount to ensure its ongoing effectiveness and relevance. This evaluation focuses on several key aspects:

- **Framework performance:** The organization must consistently assess the test automation framework's performance, examining factors such as execution speed, reliability, and resource utilization. Performance metrics provide insights into whether the framework meets the demands of current testing processes and can handle increasing workloads.

- **Ease of maintenance:** As the framework evolves, it is essential to evaluate its maintainability. This involves assessing how easily new tests can be added, existing tests can be modified, and bugs can be addressed. A maintainable framework minimizes technical debt and reduces the time and effort required for ongoing support.

- **Ability to meet new testing needs:** Software development's dynamic nature means that testing requirements can change rapidly. Regular evaluations should focus on the framework's adaptability to incorporate new types of tests (for example, security testing, performance testing) and support for emerging technologies. This proactive approach ensures the framework remains aligned with business goals and user expectations.

Some of the metrics that are useful to track on these measures include:

- **Execution speed metrics:**
  - **Average test suite duration:**
    - **What it is:** Time taken to execute the full test suite (for example, nightly or pre-release).
    - **Why it matters:** Helps track performance regressions and efficiency improvements.
  - **Time per test case:**
    - **What it is:** Mean duration of individual test cases, useful for spotting long-running or inefficient tests.
    - **How to measure:** Collect timing logs in CI/CD tools (e.g., GitHub Actions, Jenkins).

- **Test reliability metrics:**
  - **Flakiness rate:**
    - **What it is:** % of tests that pass or fail inconsistently across runs without code changes.
    - **Why it matters:** High flakiness undermines trust and delays releases.
    - **How to measure:** Use historical test run data to identify non-deterministic behavior.
  - **Pass rate consistency:**
    - **What it is:** Variability in pass rates across multiple runs of the same test suite.
    - **Goal:** Steady, high pass rates imply stable tests and framework reliability.
- **Resource utilization metrics:**
  - **CPU/memory utilization during test runs:**
    - **What it is:** Measures how efficiently the framework uses system resources during execution.
    - **Why it matters:** Inefficient tests can bottleneck infrastructure and inflate CI costs.
    - **How to measure:** Monitor using CI runner telemetry (e.g., CircleCI Insights, self-hosted GitLab Runner metrics).
  - **Infrastructure utilization efficiency:**
    - **What it is:** Ratio of available test runners/VMs/containers to how many are actually used during execution.
    - **Example:** If 10 agents are available but only 2 are used, parallelism may be under-optimized.
- **Scalability and throughput metrics:**
  - **Tests executed per hour (throughput):**
    - **What it is:** Total number of test cases completed per hour in CI pipelines.
    - **Why it matters:** Indicates the system's capacity to scale with increasing demand.
  - **Concurrency success rate:**
    - **What it is:** % of test jobs that complete successfully when executed in parallel.
    - **Why it matters:** Measures the framework's robustness under concurrent load.
- **Failure diagnostics and recovery metrics:**
  - **Mean Time to Diagnose (MTTD):**
    - **What it is:** Average time required to identify the root cause of a failed test.
  - **Mean Time to Recovery (MTTR):**
    - **What it is:** Time taken to fix the test or framework issue and get green builds back.
- **Time to add or modify a test:**
  - **Metric:** Average time (in hours) to add a new test or update an existing one.
  - **Why it matters:** A well-structured, maintainable framework should allow test cases to be added or changed with minimal setup or code duplication.
  - **How to measure:**
    - Track time spent on adding/modifying tests via JIRA or test management tools.
    - Compare metrics before and after framework updates.

- **Bug fix turnaround time:**
  - o **Metric:** Average time taken to investigate and fix bugs in test cases or framework code.
  - o **Why it matters:** Lower turnaround time indicates that test logic is well-organized and isolated, making it easier to debug.
  - o **How to measure:**
    - ▪ Use issue tracking tools (for example, Jira) to log test-related bugs and record time to resolution.

- **Test maintenance churn rate:**
  - o **Metric:** % of test code modified per sprint/release.
  - o **Why it matters:** Excessive changes may indicate fragile or brittle tests that are too tightly coupled to application logic.
  - o **How to measure:**
    - ▪ Use version control analytics to track changes in test directories.
    - ▪ Monitor files with frequent changes over time.

- **Onboarding time for new engineers:**
  - o **Metric:** Time it takes for a new engineer to write and run their first test independently.
  - o **Why it matters:** A maintainable framework should be easy to understand and adopt without extensive training.
  - o **How to measure:**
    - ▪ Gather feedback during onboarding.
    - ▪ Track onboarding milestones (for example, first test written vs. first test run in CI).

- **Code quality and duplication:**
  - o **Metric:** Number of duplicated code blocks or violations of test code standards.
  - o **Why it matters:** Maintainable frameworks should encourage reuse through abstraction and reduce redundancy.
  - o **How to measure:**
    - ▪ Use static analysis tools (for example, SonarQube, ESLint, PMD) to monitor test code quality and duplication.

- **Developer/tester satisfaction:**
  - o **Metric:** Survey-based feedback on maintainability (for example, ease of writing, debugging, and running tests).
  - o **Why it matters:** Subjective sentiment can highlight friction points not visible in code metrics.
  - o **How to measure:**
    - ▪ Quarterly surveys or retrospective discussions.
    - ▪ **Net Promoter Score (NPS)** for the framework internally.

- **Test failure root cause categorization:**
  - o **Metric:** % of test failures caused by framework issues vs. genuine defects.
  - o **Why it matters:** High maintainability should mean fewer false positives caused by brittle tests or outdated dependencies.

- o **How to measure:**
  - Label test failures by root cause (environmental, application change, test issue).
  - Track trends over time.

Refactoring versus rewriting

A significant decision that arises during the adaptation process is whether to refactor existing framework components or rewrite entire sections for long-term improvements. This decision involves careful consideration of several factors:

- **Refactoring:** Refactoring entails incremental improvements to existing code without changing external behavior. It is often seen as a less disruptive option, allowing teams to address immediate needs without overhauling the entire framework. Advantages of refactoring include reduced risk, quicker implementation, and preservation of existing functionality. This approach can be beneficial when the framework is still fundamentally sound but requires enhancements to meet new testing needs.

- **Rewriting:** Rewriting involves creating a new version of the framework from scratch. This option is typically considered when the existing framework is fundamentally flawed, outdated, or unable to effectively support future requirements. While rewriting can provide an opportunity to implement modern practices, technologies, and architectures, it carries higher risks, including potential project delays, loss of existing functionality, and the need for extensive testing and validation of the new framework.

Ultimately, the decision between refactoring and rewriting should be guided by a thorough analysis of the current framework's strengths and weaknesses, the urgency of the new testing needs, and the potential impact on long-term goals. Balancing short-term demands with a vision for the future will lead to more sustainable improvements in the test automation framework.

Example of adaptation

A notable example of adaptation in a test automation framework can be observed in a project that initially focused on functional and UI testing. The original framework was built using Selenium, which effectively automated web browser interactions and validated user interface components. However, as the project evolved, new requirements emerged that necessitated the integration of additional testing capabilities, such as:

- **Transition to API testing:** As the development team adopted a microservices architecture, validating the interactions between different services became imperative. To address this need, API testing was incorporated into the existing framework using Postman. This integration allowed testers to automate API calls, validate responses, and ensure services communicated effectively. By leveraging Postman's capabilities, the team could quickly create and execute tests for various endpoints, significantly enhancing the testing coverage and efficiency.

- **Incorporation of security testing**: Due to increasing security concerns, the project also required robust security testing measures. OWASP **Zed Attack Proxy** (**ZAP**) was integrated into the test automation framework to facilitate this. This tool enabled the team to perform automated security scans, identify vulnerabilities, and ensure that security best practices were followed throughout the development lifecycle. By incorporating security testing, the framework addressed functional and performance aspects and ensured that the application was resilient against potential threats.

Through these adaptations, the test automation framework evolved from its original focus on functional and UI testing to a comprehensive solution capable of handling API and security testing. This flexibility allowed the organization to maintain high-quality standards, respond to changing project needs, and align with modern development practices. The successful integration of these new testing capabilities demonstrates the importance of adaptability in maintaining a practical test automation framework in today's fast-paced software development landscape.

Balancing technical debt and architectural improvements

As organizations push to meet the demands of fast-paced development cycles, the introduction of workarounds and shortcuts is often necessary to maintain momentum. However, these quick fixes lead to the gradual accumulation of technical debt within the test automation framework. Over time, this debt becomes a burden, making the framework harder to maintain, less reliable, and more prone to failure. The challenge lies in balancing the need for rapid delivery with the long-term sustainability of the framework.

Types of debt

Several key types of technical debt can accumulate within a test automation framework:

- **Code smells:**

  o **Repeated test logic:** Repeating similar or identical test logic across multiple tests instead of encapsulating it in reusable functions or modules. This creates redundancy and makes maintenance more difficult, as updates to the logic must be propagated across many tests.

  o **Poor abstraction:** Test code lacking proper abstraction can lead to tests tightly coupled to specific implementations, making them brittle and harder to modify. For example, directly referencing UI elements in multiple places instead of using page object models results in more complex and error-prone tests.

  o **Overly complex test suites:** Test suites that grow without structure or proper modularity can become overly complex, making them harder to understand and debug. This complexity often arises from adding new tests without refactoring or simplifying the existing suite.

- **Tool dependencies:**

  o **Relying on outdated or non-scalable tools:** As technology evolves, some tools may no longer be the best fit for modern development practices. Continuing to rely on these outdated tools can introduce limitations, such as poor integration with new technologies or slow execution times, ultimately hindering scalability and flexibility.

  o **Vendor lock-in:** Relying heavily on a single vendor's tool or ecosystem can restrict the team's ability to adapt to newer, more effective tools. Over time, this dependency can create friction when trying to integrate additional testing capabilities or migrate to more modern testing practices.

- **Hard-coded data and configurations:**

  o **Test data tightly coupled to specific environments:** Tests that rely on hard-coded data or configurations specific to certain environments or components become difficult to scale and maintain. Such tests lack flexibility, making it challenging to execute them across different environments (for example, development, staging, production) without significant modifications.

  o **Lack of parameterization:** When test cases are not parameterized to handle different sets of data, each new scenario requires a new test case, leading to an unwieldy number of tests and increasing maintenance complexity.

The accumulation of technical debt in a test automation framework can significantly impact its performance, maintainability, and scalability. Identifying and addressing these types of debt, whether through refactoring, rewriting, or adopting more scalable tools and practices, is essential to ensure the framework remains adaptable to future needs. Regular evaluations and proactive debt management can lead to more efficient, reliable, and resilient test automation solutions.

Architectural improvements to reduce debt

Let us learn about the architectural improvements we can make to reduce debt:

- **Refactoring key components:** One of the most effective ways to address technical debt in a test automation framework is to refactor key components. As test automation frameworks evolve, what often begins as a monolithic codebase can become unwieldy, difficult to manage, and prone to errors. Refactoring these components into modular structures enhances maintainability, improves scalability, and allows for easier upgrades and enhancements in the future.

- **Modularizing monolithic test code:**

  o **Improved maintainability:** Breaking down large, monolithic test suites into smaller, modular components enables teams to isolate specific functions, making it easier to understand, maintain, and update individual parts of the framework. For example, separating UI tests from API tests and organizing them into distinct, well-defined modules allows changes in one area without affecting the others.

  o **Enhanced extensibility:** Modular code structures offer greater extensibility by allowing developers to introduce new features or testing types with minimal disruption to existing tests. This enables the team to adapt to new project requirements quickly and efficiently, such as incorporating load testing or integrating new testing tools.

- **Introducing abstractions:** Introducing abstraction into the test automation framework helps reduce the coupling between the framework and the tools it uses, allowing for greater flexibility when tools or technologies need to be upgraded. Design patterns like the Facade or Adapter pattern can be crucial in this effort.

  o **Facade pattern:** This pattern simplifies the interface of a complex system by providing a unified, higher-level interface. In a test automation framework, the Facade pattern can be used to hide the complexities of tool-specific APIs, providing a cleaner interface with which test scripts can interact. This abstraction allows the framework to swap out or upgrade testing tools without affecting the rest of the codebase.

  o **Adapter pattern:** The Adapter pattern helps integrate new testing tools or systems with interfaces different from existing tools. It allows the framework to adapt to new tools while maintaining the same test automation interface. For instance, if the team moves from one API testing tool to another, the Adapter pattern can help facilitate a smooth transition by adapting the new tool's API to match the existing framework's expectations.

By modularizing the code and introducing abstraction, test automation frameworks become more adaptable to future changes. This reduces the time and effort required for upgrades and makes long-term improvements more feasible. This ensures the framework remains robust and responsive to new testing requirements and emerging technologies.

Example of debt management

As the organization introduced new microservices into its architecture, the complexity of testing and maintaining the test automation framework grew. The existing framework, which was monolithic and tightly coupled, became increasingly difficult to manage. In response, the team embarked on a debt management initiative aimed at refactoring the framework to accommodate these changes better and reduce accumulated technical debt.

The key actions are:

- **Separation of test orchestration:** The team decoupled the orchestration logic from the test cases, making the orchestration independent of specific test implementations. This allowed for easier management of test execution flows across different environments, mainly when testing multiple microservices in parallel. The new, independent test orchestration module improved flexibility and enabled the team to introduce new orchestration patterns without rewriting core tests.

- **Modularizing test data management:** Managing test data across environments became increasingly difficult as the number of microservices expanded. To address this, the team created a separate test data management module. This module generated, loaded, and cleaned test data, enabling reusable and consistent data management practices across various tests. This change reduced the coupling between individual tests and their specific data sources, making them more adaptable.

- **Refactoring reporting:** The existing framework generated reports directly within test scripts, making it hard to upgrade reporting formats or change the reporting tool. By refactoring reporting into an independent module, the team introduced flexibility into how test results were collected and displayed. This allowed them to integrate new reporting tools and formats without touching the core testing logic, streamlining the process of generating consistent, customizable reports.

By separating these concerns, test orchestration, test data management, and reporting, into independent, reusable modules, the team successfully reduced technical debt while making the framework more maintainable, scalable, and future proof. This refactoring effort exemplifies how careful technical debt management can ensure that test automation frameworks remain agile and responsive to evolving project needs.

Strategies for continuous improvement

Let us now learn more about the strategies for continuous improvement.

Short-term versus long-term goals

When improving a test automation framework, it is important to balance immediate needs with the larger goal of long-term architectural improvements. In the short term, the focus should be on addressing critical pain points that are hindering the effectiveness of the framework, such as:

- **Critical test failures:** Immediate attention is needed for any test failures that impact the stability or reliability of the product. By prioritizing these failures, the framework can regain its ability to provide meaningful feedback to development teams.

- **Slow execution:** Speed is a key factor in the efficiency of automated testing, especially in CI/CD pipelines. Optimizing execution time in the short term, whether by parallelizing tests or identifying bottlenecks, can deliver quick wins that improve the overall testing process.

- **Flakiness:** Flaky tests, which pass or fail inconsistently, undermine trust in the automation suite. Tackling flakiness by isolating root causes (for example, timeouts, environment dependencies) is a crucial short-term goal to improve confidence in the framework's results.

While these issues are addressed, it is equally important to plan for long-term improvements. This could include revisiting the framework's architecture, modularizing the codebase, or improving integration with newer technologies. The goal is to build a robust, scalable framework that can evolve alongside the organization's testing needs.

Incremental updates

Adopting an agile approach allows teams to make incremental updates rather than attempting a large-scale overhaul of the test automation framework. This approach ensures continuous improvement without disrupting current operations. By iterating on small changes, the framework can evolve in a manageable, controlled manner. For example:

- **Small, focused improvements:** Each iteration could focus on a single area of improvement, such as refactoring a particular module, improving the reporting mechanism, or integrating a new testing tool. This keeps the process manageable and allows for quicker feedback on each change.

- **Agile deployment:** By following agile principles, the team can deploy updates regularly, enabling constant refinement of the framework. This strategy addresses short-term issues and builds toward long-term architectural goals.

- **Early wins:** Prioritizing incremental improvements also provides early wins for the team and stakeholders, demonstrating progress while laying the groundwork for more significant, impactful changes.

This agile, iterative approach to framework evolution ensures steady progress while minimizing disruption. It allows the team to balance short-term needs with the overarching vision for the framework's future.

Incorporating feedback loops

Let us now learn more about incorporating feedback loops.

Continuous feedback from teams

One of the most valuable strategies for evolving a test automation framework is to gather continuous feedback from the people who interact with it daily: developers, testers, and DevOps engineers. Their first-hand experience provides critical insights into inefficiencies, pain points, and areas of improvement within the framework. This regular feedback loop can help:

- **Identify bottlenecks:** Developers and testers can highlight which tests are slowing down the CI/CD pipeline or causing unnecessary delays.

- **Surface pain points:** Teams may encounter specific issues, such as tests that fail due to environmental conditions or test scripts that are overly complex or difficult to maintain.

- **Guide future improvements:** The feedback helps prioritize which areas of the framework need immediate attention and informs the roadmap for future updates or refactoring efforts.

Engaging with teams regularly ensures that the framework evolves to meet their changing needs and adapts to any new challenges they face.

Automated metrics and monitoring

Introducing automated monitoring tools into the test automation framework provides valuable, objective data that can supplement team feedback. The framework can offer real-time insights into its performance and effectiveness by tracking key metrics. Important metrics to monitor include:

- **Test execution time:** Monitoring how long tests take to run helps identify slow tests or performance bottlenecks, providing opportunities for optimization.

- **Test pass/fail rates:** Tracking the success rate of test executions over time highlights trends in test stability and reliability, helping teams address flaky or failing tests more effectively.

- **Code coverage:** Automated tools can measure the extent to which tests cover the codebase, providing insights into areas that may need additional testing focus.

By leveraging these metrics, teams can proactively identify performance issues and adjust the framework to improve efficiency and effectiveness.

Case example: Improving test execution time

After implementing automated monitoring tools, the team discovered that certain test suites were consistently slow and were becoming a bottleneck in the CI/CD pipeline. Detailed analysis revealed that these tests were sequentially executed, which contributed to prolonged execution times, especially as the test suite grew.

To address this, the team took the following steps:

1. **Parallelization:** They restructured the framework to run multiple tests in parallel, distributing the workload across different execution environments. By leveraging parallel execution, the test suite could handle more tests simultaneously, significantly reducing the overall runtime.

2. **Containerization:** The team introduced containerization techniques using Docker to further optimize the test infrastructure. This allowed tests to be executed in isolated, consistent environments, which helped eliminate environment-specific issues and increased test reliability.

As a result of these changes, the team was able to reduce test execution time by 50%. This improvement not only accelerated the CI/CD process but also freed up resources for additional testing and development efforts. This case demonstrates how careful monitoring and targeted optimization can significantly enhance the performance of a test automation framework.

Upgrading tooling and integrations

Let us now move on to tools and integrations.

Evaluating tools over time

As projects evolve and testing needs change, it is crucial to periodically assess the tools used within the test automation framework to ensure they remain the best fit for the organization's needs. This continuous evaluation ensures the framework stays adaptable and scalable over time. The key aspects of the evaluation process include:

- **Performance:** Assess whether the current tools are still performing efficiently under the growing demands of the project.

- **Feature set:** Determine if the tools still support all necessary features, such as the ability to handle new technologies like APIs, cloud services, or microservices.

- **Community and support:** Evaluate the level of support available for the tools, including active communities, documentation, and integration with other tools. This helps the team stay updated on best practices and emerging improvements.

By periodically reviewing the tools, the organization can make informed decisions about when to upgrade, replace, or keep existing tools in place to optimize the framework's efficiency.

Dealing with tool deprecation

Technology evolves rapidly, and tools that were once industry standards may become outdated or deprecated. When this happens, it is essential to have a proactive strategy in place to handle the transition to newer, more modern tools. This often involves:

- **Proactive upgrades:** Rather than waiting for a tool to reach the end of its life or become unsupported, teams should monitor the longevity of the tools they depend on. For example, as projects move toward more modern test frameworks, upgrading from Selenium to Cypress or moving from JUnit to TestNG may be necessary to keep pace with the latest features and community support.

- **Tool replacement:** In some cases, a complete replacement of the tool may be required. This could involve transitioning the entire test suite to a new platform, ensuring backward compatibility, and training the team on the new toolset.

By taking a proactive approach to upgrading or replacing tools, teams can avoid disruptions caused by outdated or unsupported technologies and ensure their test automation framework continues to meet the demands of modern software development.

Example of continuous improvement

In an effort to enhance the reliability and scalability of their test automation framework, the team decided to migrate their test execution environment to Docker. This transition was driven by the need for a more flexible and efficient testing infrastructure. Here is how this move contributed to continuous improvement:

- **Easier scaling:** By using Docker containers, the team could easily scale their test execution across different environments. This meant they could spin up multiple instances of the testing environment as needed, allowing for parallel execution of tests and reducing overall test execution time.

- **Consistent environments:** Docker ensured that tests were run in consistent environments, regardless of where they were executed. This eliminated environment-specific issues that often led to flaky tests and increased confidence in test results.

- **Improved test reliability:** The use of containerization reduced dependencies on specific hardware or operating system configurations, minimizing the risk of failures due to environmental discrepancies. This consistency in test execution resulted in a more stable and reliable testing process.

- **Streamlined CI/CD integration:** The Docker-based setup seamlessly integrated with the existing CI/CD pipeline, allowing for faster feedback loops and smoother deployments. As a result, the team could identify issues earlier in the development cycle, leading to quicker resolutions.

This example illustrates how adopting new technologies like Docker can drive continuous improvement in a test automation framework, enhancing both the reliability of tests and the efficiency of the testing process.

Key challenges and solutions

Let us now go over the key challenges and solutions.

Challenge 1: Balancing speed of delivery with framework stability

Problem: In fast-paced software development environments, there is often immense pressure to deliver new features quickly to meet market demands and customer expectations. This urgency can lead to the practice of adding more tests without adequately refining the underlying test automation framework. As a result, teams may experience an increase in flaky or slow tests, which can undermine the overall reliability of the testing process.

These flaky tests can cause false positives or negatives, making it difficult to trust the test results. Slow tests can also significantly impact the CI/CD pipeline, delaying deployments and feedback loops.

Solution

To address this challenge, it is essential to prioritize technical debt and test optimization as part of each sprint. This strategy involves several key actions such as:

- **Allocate time for refactoring:** Dedicate a portion of each sprint to refining and optimizing existing tests and the framework itself. This could include removing obsolete tests, improving test design, or enhancing the architecture to support more efficient testing.

- **Establish technical debt backlog:** Create a backlog specifically for technical debt related to the test automation framework. This backlog should be regularly reviewed and prioritized alongside new feature development, ensuring that architectural improvements are not overlooked.

- **Implement test optimization strategies:** Focus on optimizing test execution times and reliability. This may involve parallelizing tests, introducing smarter test selection algorithms, or leveraging techniques like mocking and stubbing to reduce dependencies.

- **Foster a culture of quality:** Encourage a mindset within the team that values quality alongside speed. This can be reinforced through team discussions, metrics tracking, and celebrating achievements related to improving framework stability.

By integrating technical debt management and test optimization into the regular development cycle, teams can ensure that the stability of their test automation framework keeps pace with the rapid delivery of new features. This balanced approach ultimately leads to a more reliable and efficient testing process, enhancing overall software quality.

Challenge 2: Managing framework complexity

Problem: As a test automation framework expands to accommodate an increasing number of tools and test types, such as UI, API, and security testing, its complexity can escalate significantly. This growing complexity can create several challenges, particularly for new team members who may struggle to understand the intricacies of the framework. As a result, onboarding becomes difficult, and productivity may suffer as team members spend more time navigating and comprehending the framework rather than contributing to the testing efforts.

Solution

To effectively manage this complexity, organizations should invest in clear documentation, modularization, and streamlined onboarding processes. Key strategies include:

- **Clear documentation:** Create comprehensive and accessible documentation that outlines the framework's architecture, key components, and usage guidelines. This should include clear examples, best practices, and troubleshooting tips to aid new users in understanding the framework quickly.

- **Modularization:** Break down the framework into smaller, manageable modules focusing on specific functionalities or testing types. This modular approach simplifies the framework and allows teams to work independently on different components, promoting better maintainability and easier upgrades in the future.

- **Structured onboarding processes:** Develop a structured onboarding process that includes guided training sessions, hands-on workshops, and mentorship programs for new team members. This will help newcomers gain practical experience and confidence in using the framework.

- **Regular review and updates:** Conduct regular reviews of the documentation and onboarding materials to ensure they remain up-to-date with the latest changes in the framework. Encourage feedback from new and existing team members to continuously improve these resources.

By implementing these strategies, organizations can significantly reduce the complexity of their test automation framework, making it more accessible for new team members and ensuring maintainability as the framework continues to evolve. This approach fosters a collaborative environment where all team members can contribute effectively, leading to improved testing outcomes.

Challenge 3: Resource constraints

Problem: One of the most significant challenges faced by teams working with test automation frameworks is allocating time and resources for continuous improvement while also managing day-to-day testing needs. The demands of ongoing testing, bug fixes, and feature releases often take precedence, leaving little room for teams to focus on enhancing the framework. This can lead to stagnation in the framework's evolution, resulting in technical debt accumulation and an inability to adapt to new requirements effectively.

Solution

To overcome these resource constraints, aligning framework improvements with business goals, such as faster releases and reduced bugs, is essential. Here are some effective strategies:

- **Establish clear business objectives:** Define specific business goals that can be directly linked to improvements in the test automation framework. For example, emphasizing the need for faster release cycles and lower defect rates can create a compelling case for dedicating resources to framework enhancements.

- **Demonstrate return on investment (ROI):** Use metrics to showcase the ROI of improving the framework. Highlight how enhancements can lead to shorter testing times, increased test coverage, and improved product quality. This data can help secure buy-in from stakeholders and justify resource allocation.

- **Integrate improvements into sprints:** Incorporate framework improvement tasks into regular sprint planning. By treating these improvements as part of the development process, teams can ensure they receive ongoing attention without derailing day-to-day testing activities.

- **Foster a culture of continuous improvement:** Encourage team members to view framework improvements as an integral part of their responsibilities. This mindset shift can lead to innovative ideas for optimizing the framework and a shared commitment to maintaining its health.

- **Leverage automation for efficiency:** Identify areas within the testing process where automation can free up resources. By automating repetitive tasks, teams can allocate more time to focus on framework enhancements.

By strategically aligning framework improvements with business objectives and demonstrating their value, organizations can effectively manage resource constraints while ensuring long-term health and adaptability of their test automation frameworks. This proactive approach enhances testing efficiency and contributes to overall organizational success.

Lessons from the framework evolution process

Let us now understand the lessons from the framework evolution process:

- **Agility in test automation:** In today's fast-paced software development landscape, agility in test automation is crucial. A flexible, modular framework is essential to accommodate changing project requirements and emerging technologies. This adaptability enables teams to quickly integrate new testing methodologies, tools, and technologies as they arise, ensuring the framework remains relevant and practical. A modular design allows for easy updates and enhancements, enabling teams to respond swiftly to project scope shifts, whether adding new types of tests (such as API or security tests) or integrating with different tools and environments. By prioritizing agility, organizations can ensure that their test automation framework supports ongoing development needs without becoming a bottleneck.

- **Managing debt while moving forward:** Maintaining a healthy test automation framework requires a continuous balancing act between short-term feature delivery and long-term architectural improvements. As teams work to deliver new features quickly, they often accumulate technical debt, which can undermine the framework's reliability and maintainability. To counteract this, organizations must prioritize technical debt management alongside feature development. This can be achieved by setting aside dedicated time for refactoring, adopting an incremental approach to improvements, and ensuring that architectural considerations are included in sprint planning. By proactively managing debt while meeting immediate project needs, teams can preserve the long-term health of their test automation framework, making it more robust and capable of evolving with the business.

- **Team collaboration:** Team collaboration is a vital component of effective test automation. Encouraging cross-functional collaboration between QA, developers, and architects leads to more informed decisions regarding the framework's design and implementation. When these stakeholders work together, they can share insights about testing requirements, identify potential challenges early on, and collaboratively develop solutions that enhance the framework's robustness. This collaboration fosters a shared understanding of testing goals and ensures that the framework aligns with overall project objectives.

By breaking down silos and promoting a culture of teamwork, organizations can build a more resilient test automation framework that adapts to changing needs while maintaining high quality and efficiency.

Conclusion

In the rapidly changing landscape of software development, continuous improvement is not just an option; it is a necessity. Just like software products themselves, test automation frameworks must evolve over time to remain relevant, scalable, and maintainable. As new technologies emerge and project requirements shift, frameworks that embrace flexibility, scalability, and modularity are better equipped to handle the challenges of modern development. By actively engaging in the continuous improvement of test automation frameworks, organizations can reduce technical debt, enhance test efficiency, and ensure that their testing efforts align with the evolving needs of their business.

To truly thrive in a dynamic environment, it is essential to future-proof the test automation framework. Building adaptability into the framework from the outset allows it to evolve alongside changing project, technology, and business needs. This proactive approach ensures that the framework remains flexible enough to integrate new tools, methodologies, and testing types as they arise. By prioritizing adaptability, teams can mitigate risks associated with obsolescence and position themselves for long-term success in an ever-evolving software landscape.

The journey toward an effective and resilient test automation framework is ongoing. By committing to continuous improvement and future-proofing their frameworks, organizations can maintain the integrity of their testing processes and deliver high-quality software that meets the demands of their users and stakeholders.

In the next chapter, we will look into the impact machine learning and artificial intelligence is having on the world of testing, automation and framework design.

Key takeaways

Maintaining a test automation framework ensures long-term reliability, scalability, and efficiency. Without regular updates, technical debt accumulates, thus making the framework harder to maintain, slower to execute, and less adaptable to new technologies. Continuous improvements, such as refactoring, upgrading tools, and incorporating feedback, keep the framework aligned with evolving business needs, enabling faster, more stable, and cost-effective testing. A well-maintained framework ultimately supports high-quality software delivery by reducing flakiness, improving test coverage, and seamlessly integrating with modern development pipelines.

The kay takeaways from this chapter are as follows:

- **Adapting to changing requirements and technologies:** A test automation framework must be flexible and modular to accommodate evolving business needs, emerging technologies, and new testing methodologies without requiring major rewrites.

- **Framework evolution cycle:** A structured evolution roadmap ensures the framework remains relevant, with periodic reviews, refactoring, and enhancements aligned to business and engineering priorities.

- **Balancing technical debt and architectural improvements:** Addressing technical debt incrementally while implementing new features prevents long-term maintenance challenges and ensures the sustainable growth of the automation framework.

- **Architectural improvements to reduce debt:** Refactoring legacy components, enforcing design patterns (for example, Page Object, Facade, or Adapter), and adopting layered architecture help minimize complexity and improve maintainability.

- **Continuous improvement:** A Kaizen approach to framework enhancements—incrementally optimizing test execution, maintainability, and scalability—ensures continuous efficiency gains.

- **Incorporating feedback loops:** Gathering feedback from testers, developers, and DevOps teams ensures that improvements align with real-world usage and pain points, fostering adoption and usability.

- **Upgrading tooling and integrations:** Regularly evaluating and integrating new testing tools, cloud environments, and CI/CD capabilities enhances the framework's efficiency, compatibility, and performance.

Exercises

1. How well does the current framework align with the organization's long-term testing and DevOps strategy?

2. How can the framework be improved to enhance engineering efficiency and developer experience?

3. Are there any new industry trends, tools, or methodologies that should be evaluated for integration?

4. How well does the framework handle scaling with growing test volumes and increasing complexity?

5. Is the framework modular and extensible enough to support new testing types (for example, AI, blockchain, IoT, AR/VR, API, performance, security)?

6. Are there opportunities to reduce maintenance overhead, such as automating test case management, versioning, and deprecating outdated scripts?

7. How easy is onboarding new team members to use and contribute to the framework?

8. How frequently should framework components be refactored or rewritten to avoid technical debt?

9. Is the framework compatible with new development platforms, architectures (for example, microservices, serverless), and emerging cloud technologies?

10. How well does the framework integrate with CI/CD, observability platforms, and defect-tracking systems?

11. How can test flakiness be further reduced, automatically detected, and mitigated?

12. Is test execution impacted by environment dependencies, infrastructure limitations, or CI/CD pipeline inefficiencies?

Join our Discord space

Join our Discord workspace for latest updates, offers, tech happenings around the world, new releases, and sessions with the authors:

https://discord.bpbonline.com

CHAPTER 15

Embracing AI and ML in Test Automation

Introduction

In today's rapidly evolving software development landscape, keeping up with the increasing complexity and pace has become a challenge for traditional test automation approaches. The integration of **artificial intelligence (AI)** and **machine learning (ML)** into test automation addresses this challenge by offering intelligent, data-driven strategies that enhance the overall efficiency and effectiveness of testing processes.

Structure

In this chapter, we will go over the following topics:

- Importance of AI and ML in test automation
- AI-driven test case generation
- AI-powered test case selection
- Intelligent test execution
- Predicting execution patterns
- ML algorithms for identifying flaky tests
- Continuous monitoring for adaptive learning
- Test optimization with AI
- Self-maintaining test suites
- Environment-aware testing
- Enhancing test insights with AI and ML
- Predictive analytics for test outcomes
- Automated bug triage and prioritization

- Smarter test refactoring suggestions

- Key challenges and considerations for AI and ML adoption in testing

- Key components of an autonomous testing ecosystem

- Vision of self-learning test automation

Objectives

By the end of this chapter, the reader will learn about the many new emerging AI trends and how they can benefit the test automation space. We will also dive deep into the different aspects of AI that already show benefits in the testing world, the challenges of adopting each, and how they can be overcome to best utilize them in your framework.

Importance of AI and ML in test automation

Many companies are looking to introduce new trends like AI and ML into their development and testing practices because they want to stay relevant and adopt the latest trends. However, AI and ML can offer incredible benefits to the software testing world if incorporated correctly and built on the foundation of good test design.

Managing complexity and speed

Modern software development cycles are faster and more complex than ever, driven by the adoption of agile methodologies, **continuous integration** (**CI**), and **continuous delivery** (**CD**). Traditional test automation frameworks, while effective for standard regression tests, often fall short when dealing with:

- Frequent changes in codebases that introduce new functionalities, requiring constant test case updates.

- Vast amounts of test data and configurations, which are difficult to manage and validate, without manual intervention.

- Increased demand for quality at speed, with shorter release cycles putting pressure on teams to ensure high-quality software without the time for exhaustive manual testing.

AI and ML introduce methods that can adapt to the dynamic nature of modern software development. ML models can analyze code changes, test results, and patterns in previous bugs to optimize which tests to execute, reducing the scope of manual intervention.

Intelligent, smarter testing approaches

AI-driven test automation moves beyond the repetitive, script-based nature of traditional automation and introduces smarter, adaptive testing strategies, such as:

- **Test case generation:** AI can automatically generate test cases by analyzing requirements, code changes, or user behavior patterns. This ensures broader test coverage without manually writing new tests for each code update.

- **Test optimization:** Machine learning algorithms can detect patterns in test executions to identify which tests are most likely to catch bugs or fail. By prioritizing these high-risk tests, AI ensures efficient use of testing resources, reducing test suite execution times while maintaining high quality.

- **Self-healing tests:** Traditional test scripts are fragile and break when there are UI changes or minor code modifications. AI can detect these changes and automatically update or heal the test scripts, significantly reducing maintenance overhead and preventing test failures due to minor changes.

Automating repetitive, tedious tasks

Many test automation tasks, such as managing test environments, running repetitive regression suites, and verifying results, require significant time and human involvement. AI excels at automating these repetitive, tedious tasks such as:

- **Environment setup:** AI-powered tools can automatically configure and optimize test environments based on each test's specific requirements. This includes setting up the appropriate data, dependencies, and infrastructure. Examples include:

  o **AWS Device farm:** Uses machine learning to suggest optimal device and environment configurations.

  o **Microsoft Azure DevTest labs:** Automates provisioning of test environments with policy controls and can integrate with AI for dynamic optimization.

  o **Testim (by Tricentis):** Uses AI to identify and configure necessary test environments, including smart locator technology.

  o **AutonomIQ (Sauce Labs):** Provides AI-driven test creation and environment provisioning based on test logic and dependencies.

  o **Katalon TestCloud:** Automatically provisions browsers and OS environments based on the test requirements.

- **Test execution:** By leveraging intelligent test orchestration, AI can autonomously decide when and where to run tests based on resource availability, priority, and test dependencies, allowing for smarter, more efficient execution. Examples include:

  o **Launchable:** Uses machine learning to select and prioritize the most relevant tests, reducing execution time and optimizing test coverage.

  o **Virtuoso:** Applies AI to orchestrate test execution based on application changes, resource availability, and historical results.

  o **Test.ai:** Automatically analyzes app behavior to determine the most effective test execution schedule.

  o **Tricentis Tosca AI center:** Predicts and schedules test execution by analyzing risk and change impact across systems.

  o **GitHub Actions with Copilot and ML workflows:** Enables intelligent test triggering based on file changes, commit history, or test patterns, using AI-assisted logic.

Decision-making and predictive insights

AI not only automates processes but also provides decision-making capabilities, enabling smarter, faster choices during the test automation lifecycle, such as:

- **Root cause analysis:** When tests fail, AI algorithms can quickly pinpoint the root cause of failures by analyzing test logs, error patterns, and past data, helping teams resolve issues faster.

- **Predictive defect identification:** Machine learning models can predict areas of the application that are more prone to failure, allowing teams to focus on testing efforts where it is most needed, thereby improving defect detection rates.

- **Performance prediction:** By analyzing historical data and performance metrics, AI can provide insights into how an application might perform under different conditions, helping to prevent performance issues before they impact production.

AI and ML bring intelligence and efficiency that traditional test automation methods cannot match. By automating repetitive tasks, optimizing test execution, and providing valuable insights through data analysis, these technologies are transforming how teams approach software testing, ensuring higher quality and faster time to market.

In this chapter, we explore how these new trends arising in the AI space have an impact on software testing and quality and try to provide some insight into how they work and can be leveraged to improve the outcome of software test automation and quality delivery in any organization or team.

AI-driven test case generation

Modern software applications often require frequent updates, and manually writing test cases for every code change becomes increasingly inefficient. AI helps companies overcome this challenge by automatically generating test cases based on code changes, user stories, or historical test data as follows:

- **How it works:** AI systems analyze the application's structure and past test results to generate test cases focusing on high-risk areas. This ensures comprehensive coverage and consistency while reducing the workload for testers.

- **Benefits:** The AI-driven approach speeds up the process of creating relevant tests, especially for large, complex systems. It also ensures test cases are consistently up to date, reducing the risk of manual oversights and gaps in coverage.

Here are some examples of tools doing this:

- **Diffblue Cover (for Java):**
  - Uses AI to automatically write unit tests by analyzing Java source code.
  - Identifies edge cases and complex logic paths that might introduce risk.
  - Continuously improves coverage as code changes.

- **Testim (by Tricentis):**
  - Learns from test history and DOM structure to automatically create and improve test scenarios.
  - Suggests additional tests for components with frequent defects or recent code churn.

- **Functionize:**
  - Uses NLP and ML to understand application flows and user interactions.
  - Generates test cases based on changes in application structure and prior test flakiness.
  - Focuses test generation on areas that are statistically likely to fail.

- **Mabl:**
  - Automatically identifies UI changes and regressions across builds.
  - Uses AI to prioritize tests for parts of the app most affected by recent changes or most critical to users.
  - Tracks test coverage vs. risk areas over time.

- **Launchable:**
  - Not a test case generator per se, but augments existing suites by ranking test cases by likelihood of failure based on recent changes.
  - Prioritizes execution of tests targeting risky areas, improving CI feedback loops.

- **Curiosity Software Test Modeller:**
  - Uses model-based testing driven by AI to map the application under test.
  - Identifies decision logic, high-impact paths, and generates tests focused on risk areas.

Let us go over some use case examples. Imagine a payments microservice that is changed frequently. An AI tool like Testim might:

- Notice that tests related to failed transaction edge cases are missing.

- Analyze production logs and code commits to identify patterns.

- Auto-generate test cases that simulate edge cases (for example, currency mismatch, fraud detection failure).

This reduces tester effort and boosts regression test accuracy.

ML-powered flaky test identification

Flaky tests, tests that fail unpredictably or intermittently due to factors other than actual defects in the software, have long been a significant issue in test automation. Companies are now employing ML algorithms to identify and reduce flaky tests:

- **How it works:** ML models can analyze historical test execution data to detect patterns in test flakiness. They track the consistency of test failures across different environments, configurations, or times of day, allowing teams to flag tests that are unreliable.

- **Benefits:** By identifying flaky tests, companies can fix or quarantine them, ensuring genuine failures get more attention. This reduces false positives, saving time and effort to investigate issues that are not defects.

Predictive analytics for test execution prioritization

As applications grow, the number of test cases increases exponentially, making running all tests for every build impractical. To optimize test execution, companies use predictive analytics to prioritize which tests to run based on real-time data and historical performance:

- **How it works:** ML algorithms analyze recent code changes, test history, and defect trends to predict which application parts will most likely have issues. Based on these predictions, tests more likely to catch defects are prioritized during execution.

- **Benefits:** This ensures that the most critical tests are run first, catching defects earlier and allowing teams to focus on the system's most important aspects. Additionally, it reduces the overall time spent on testing, improving time to market without compromising quality.

This case study demonstrates the transformative power of AI and ML in test automation. It offers companies smarter, more efficient ways to handle test case generation, flaky test identification, and test execution prioritization. These advances are helping organizations maintain higher-quality software with less manual effort, leading to faster release cycles and improved reliability.

Role of AI in test case generation, selection, and execution

One of the key advantages of incorporating AI in test automation is its ability to leverage pattern recognition techniques. By analyzing vast amounts of historical testing data, AI models can detect recurring trends and patterns in both the application's codebase and its test results. These insights allow AI to proactively identify potential risks, generate test cases, and ensure comprehensive testing coverage.

AI-driven pattern recognition for defect prediction

AI models can assess historical test data and track changes in the code to recognize patterns that are likely to introduce defects in future releases. This allows AI to automatically predict which areas of the code are more prone to bugs based on common patterns that have led to issues in the past. Refer to the following:

- **How it works:** AI algorithms scan the entire codebase and correlate it with historical bug reports and test outcomes. By doing so, they identify common patterns in code segments where bugs have appeared frequently. The AI model then uses these insights to predict high-risk areas in future code changes, allowing the system to generate test cases that focus specifically on those parts of the code.

- **Benefits:** This proactive approach ensures that critical areas of the code are thoroughly tested, reducing the likelihood of undetected defects making it into production. It also enables more efficient resource allocation by prioritizing testing efforts where they are most needed.

Some examples of tools and implementations that do this are:

- **Microsoft IntelliTest (part of Visual Studio Enterprise):**
  - o Analyzes .NET code to generate unit tests based on code paths and past failures.
  - o Uses historical test outcomes to suggest assertions and identify vulnerable branches of logic.

- **Launchable:**
  - o Uses ML trained on historical test run data and code change history to predict which tests are likely to fail for a given commit.
  - o Prioritizes test execution on risky code segments, optimizing CI runs and feedback loops.

- **Code Intelligence CI Fuzz:**
  - o Leverages past bug data and code structure to generate fuzz tests targeting historically error-prone areas.
  - o Continuously adapts test coverage as new vulnerabilities and patterns are discovered.

- **Seerene:**
  - o Combines code metrics, change frequency, and defect history to highlight hotspots in the codebase.
  - o While not generating tests directly, it enables engineering teams to focus testing on areas most likely to cause issues.

- **Facebook Infer (open-source static analyzer):**
  - o Analyzes code for patterns that have led to production issues in the past.
  - o While not generating test cases itself, it flags risky code based on internal bug history and machine-learned rules.

- **TestBrain (from Tricentis):**
  - o Monitors changes in the application and correlates them with historical test results and failures.
  - o Uses this data to predict where future test cases should focus, especially in SAP and enterprise app landscapes.

These tools use a combination of the following to focus quality efforts intelligently, maximizing coverage where it matters most while reducing manual triage work:

- Static code analysis
- Defect clustering
- Commit and change history
- ML from test outcomes

By applying pattern recognition techniques to test automation, AI can intelligently focus testing efforts on the areas most likely to introduce defects. This enhances the testing process by reducing human workload, increasing accuracy, and improving the overall quality of the software, making it a vital tool in modern test automation frameworks.

Filling test coverage gaps with AI in test automation

One of the most critical challenges in test automation is ensuring complete test coverage across an application. Traditional test automation often misses certain areas, either due to oversight or the limitations of manual test case creation. This is where AI steps in, offering advanced capabilities to identify and fill test coverage gaps. By analyzing the entire codebase and historical test results, AI helps ensure that no part of the application is left untested.

Identifying under-tested areas

AI models can analyze vast amounts of test data, code, and usage patterns to identify areas of the application with insufficient test coverage. These areas may include complex modules, edge cases, or sections that were not prioritized during manual test creation. Refer to the following:

- **How it works:** The AI system scans existing test cases and compares them to the codebase and usage data to detect under-tested areas. It identifies portions of the code that have undergone recent changes but have not been adequately tested, or where past defects indicate that more testing is needed.

- **Benefits:** By systematically highlighting areas with inadequate testing, AI ensures that all aspects of the application receive the necessary attention, leading to better overall quality and fewer untested scenarios in production.

Some examples of tools and implementations that do this are:

- **Diffblue Cover:**
  - o Uses AI to automatically write unit tests for Java code.
  - o Identifies code that lacks sufficient test coverage and focuses on recently changed code to ensure new logic paths are tested.

- **Launchable:**
  - o Analyzes code changes, usage patterns, and test history to determine which tests are most relevant.
  - o Surfaces under-tested areas in commits and helps optimize test selection for maximum impact in CI.

- **Tricentis Test Impact Analysis:**
  - o Assesses which parts of the application have changed and correlates them with test coverage.
  - o Highlights risky areas that are insufficiently tested and recommends relevant regression tests.

- **SeaLights Quality Intelligence Platform:**
  - o Tracks test coverage at the code and feature level.
  - o Detects which parts of the code are not being covered by automated or manual tests, even after recent deployments or releases.

- **GitHub CodeQL + CI Insights:**
  - o CodeQL helps analyze code for vulnerabilities, while integration with GitHub Actions allows tracking of which areas are tested.
  - o Teams can identify recently modified code that lacks associated tests and monitor test execution frequency.

- **Parasoft Development Testing Platform (DTP):**
  - o Aggregates data from multiple test activities (unit, API, UI) and code coverage tools.
  - o Identifies gaps in test coverage, especially in areas linked to recent defect patterns or recent code changes.

Automatically generating additional test cases

Once AI identifies areas that lack sufficient coverage, it can generate new test cases to ensure that those gaps are filled. These additional test cases target previously missed or under-tested sections of the code, providing more comprehensive coverage. Refer to the following:

- **How it works:** AI algorithms review the code structure, functional dependencies, and test history to generate test cases that address coverage gaps. These test cases are designed to test areas that have not been covered adequately, such as rare edge cases, complex business logic, or newly introduced code segments.
- **Benefits:** The AI-generated tests increase the thoroughness of test automation suites by automatically covering areas that human testers may not have considered. This leads to a more reliable and robust testing process, ensuring that potential defects are identified earlier in the development lifecycle.

Some examples of tools that support this approach are:

- **Diffblue Cover:**
  - o Uses AI to autonomously generate unit tests for untested or lightly tested Java code.
  - o Targets code paths and logic branches missed by developers, especially after new commits.
  - o Can help detect edge-case logic that is not explicitly covered by existing tests.
- **Functionize:**
  - o Leverages NLP and AI models to generate functional and regression test cases based on application behavior, past failures, and new UI/API changes.
  - o Helps fill gaps around complex user flows and under-tested integrations.
- **Testim (by Tricentis):**
  - o Uses AI to identify application changes and generate new test cases or update existing ones to keep coverage aligned.
  - o Can handle dynamic content and workflows, ensuring logic changes do not slip through untested.
- **Mabl:**
  - o AI-powered test generation for UI and API tests.
  - o Tracks application behavior, code changes, and user journeys, and recommends or auto-generates tests to ensure end-to-end coverage, especially in complex user scenarios.
- **Applitools Autonomous Testing (beta):**
  - o Uses visual AI and code analysis to autonomously create test scenarios that cover edge conditions and visually significant branches of an app.
  - o Especially useful for apps with complex visual logic or dynamic layouts.
- **Test.ai (now part of Keysight Eggplant):**
  - o Uses ML to understand the structure and behavior of applications and generate tests that cover rare paths or logic branches.
  - o Focuses on mimicking real user behavior while discovering uncommon or risky interactions.

- **Ponicode (merged with CircleCI):**

  o Previously focused on generating unit tests for corner cases and complex logic using AI models trained on code patterns.

  o Helped developers explore test gaps that are often missed in manual reviews.

AI-powered test case selection

Running a full suite of automated tests for every build can be time-consuming and inefficient in fast-paced software development environments. AI introduces risk-based test selection, which optimizes the test automation by intelligently choosing the most relevant tests based on various risk factors. This allows teams to focus their testing efforts on where defects are most likely to occur, reducing test execution time without compromising on quality.

Intelligent test selection using risk analysis

AI algorithms can assess various data sources, such as past test results, recent code changes, and user behavior patterns, to determine the most critical tests for a given build. This risk-based approach helps teams focus on areas more likely to contain bugs and avoids wasting resources on low-risk areas. Refer to the following:

- **How it works:** AI analyzes past test outcomes, identifying patterns where bugs have frequently appeared. It combines this data with information on recent code changes, focusing on the modified or vulnerable areas of the codebase. Additionally, AI can factor in user behavior, prioritizing features or workflows that are most frequently used or have the highest business impact.

- **Benefits:** This method significantly reduces the time and resources needed for test execution while ensuring that high-risk areas of the application are thoroughly tested. It also helps prevent missed defects by dynamically adjusting test priorities based on the evolving risk profile of the application.

Some examples of tools and approaches are as follows:

- **Launchable:** Uses ML to analyze historical test results and source code changes. It ranks and prioritizes test cases based on the likelihood of failure, enabling smart test selection that focuses on recently modified or risky code areas. It also integrates with CI pipelines to reduce feedback cycles.

- **SeaLights:** Provides Test Impact Analytics by correlating test results, code coverage, and change history to identify untested but changed code areas. It highlights risk and coverage gaps in your test suite to inform decisions.

- **Testim.io (by Tricentis):** Uses AI to continuously analyze application usage data and code change patterns to guide regression test creation and execution. It adapts tests dynamically as the application evolves.

- **Facebook's Sapienz (internal):** An AI-driven testing engine that leverages code changes and usage data to focus automated exploratory tests on parts of the app most likely to fail.

- **Approach:** Risk-based testing with AI: Some teams use custom implementations (for example, Python + TensorFlow + Git logs + Jira APIs) to:

  o Identify recently modified files (via Git).

  o Correlate defects to modules (via Jira).

  o Factor in telemetry or product analytics (via tools like Mixpanel, GA, or Amplitude) to weight test prioritization toward business-critical workflows.

Prioritization of high-risk areas

AI can prioritize testing in specific high-risk areas of the codebase based on its analysis of potential defects. These high-risk areas are identified using historical data on defect density, the frequency of code changes, and the complexity of the code. Refer to the following:

- **How it works:** AI assigns risk scores to different parts of the code based on historical data such as how often those parts have changed, how many bugs were found before, and their overall complexity. Features more prone to defects or have seen significant changes are flagged as high-risk, prompting AI to prioritize tests related to those features.

- **Benefits:** By focusing on high-risk areas, teams can catch defects early in the development process, improving software reliability. This approach also reduces the likelihood of releasing builds with undetected critical defects, as the most vulnerable sections of the code receive extra attention during testing.

Some examples of tools and approaches are:

- **Launchable:** Uses code change data and historical test failures to calculate test failure probability scores. This risk profiling allows you to run only the top percentage of tests likely to fail based on what changed in a commit or pull request.

- **CodeScene:** Performs change coupling and hotspot analysis by examining how frequently files change together and how complex they are. It gives each file a risk rating and recommends testing or refactoring areas with high scores.

- **SeaLights:** Leverages machine learning and code coverage telemetry to compute a Risk Index per component. It informs which tests should be prioritized when there are code changes in high-risk areas.

- **TestBrain (by Tricentis):** Evaluates risk distribution across code and tests using past execution data and test history. It helps QA teams know which test scenarios to execute first based on risk assessment.

- **Custom ML-based scoring models:** Teams with data science capabilities use tools like:

  o   Git logs (to measure code churn).

  o   Static analysis tools (to calculate code complexity).

  o   Jira/bug tracking data (to assess historical defect rates). These are combined into a weighted risk scoring model, which feeds into test orchestration logic (for example, in Jenkins, CircleCI, or GitHub Actions).

Developing teams can streamline their testing processes by implementing AI-driven risk-based test selection while maintaining robust defect detection. This approach not only reduces test execution time but also enhances the focus on the most vulnerable and high-risk areas of the codebase, ensuring that critical bugs are caught early. It is a powerful strategy for improving both the efficiency and effectiveness of test automation in modern, fast-paced software development environments.

Real-time test selection in CI/CD pipelines with AI

In modern software development, CI/CD pipelines are essential for delivering frequent and high-quality releases. However, as applications become complex, running a full suite of automated tests after every change can become inefficient and time-consuming. This is where AI-driven test selection comes into play. It allows development teams to run only the most critical tests, improving efficiency without sacrificing quality.

AI-driven test selection in CI/CD

By leveraging AI algorithms, CI/CD pipelines can dynamically select the most important tests to run in real-time based on recent code changes, past test results, and other risk factors. This ensures that critical tests are executed while unnecessary tests are skipped, significantly reducing the time required to get feedback from the pipeline. Refer to the following:

- **How it works:** AI algorithms analyze recent commits, code changes, and past test execution data to determine which areas of the codebase are most at risk of containing defects. It then selects the most relevant tests to run, based on that risk analysis, while deprioritizing or skipping tests that are less likely to yield defects in the current build.

- **Benefits:** This real-time test selection allows for faster feedback from the CI/CD pipeline, enabling developers to catch and fix defects sooner while reducing the computational overhead of running the full test suite. By optimizing which tests to run, development teams can iterate more quickly, leading to faster release cycles.

Some examples of tools and approaches are as follows:

- **Launchable:** Perhaps the most direct example—Launchable uses ML to:

  o Analyze Git commits, recent code changes, and test history.

  o Predict which tests are most likely to fail in the current code state.

  o Generate a Smart Subset of tests to run, reducing test cycle time significantly without sacrificing defect detection rates.

- **Facebook's Sapienz + TestArbiter:** Internally, Facebook has used AI models that evaluate code change metadata, bug history, and dependencies to:

  o Select test cases dynamically based on risk.

  o Skip tests unlikely to yield value, which helps them scale testing across frequent releases.

- **SeaLights test optimization:** Uses AI-driven coverage and change analysis to identify which tests are relevant based on recent code changes, enabling:

  o Test impact analysis.

  o Test skipping.

  o Risk-based prioritization in CI/CD pipelines.

- **Microsoft's Dynamic Test Selection in Azure DevOps:** Uses telemetry from prior test runs + commit diffs to:

  o Only run impacted tests during PR builds,

  o Minimizing regression cycles while keeping test relevance high.

- **Custom CI/CD integration with risk models:** Some engineering teams integrate their own:

  o Git commit analysis tools.

  o Code coverage tools (e.g., JaCoCo, Istanbul).

  o ML classifiers trained on defect data (via tools like TensorFlow, Scikit-learn) to flag high-risk modules and automatically determine the test selection set for each build.

Reducing feedback time

One of the most significant advantages of real-time AI-driven test selection is its ability to drastically reduce feedback time in the CI/CD pipeline. Instead of waiting hours for a full suite of tests to run, developers can receive feedback within minutes, focusing on the most relevant test results. Refer to the following:

- **How it works:** The AI system continuously monitors changes in the codebase and tracks test results to make real-time decisions on which tests to run based on risk analysis. If a critical area of the code is modified, the AI will prioritize running tests for that area, while skipping tests for sections of the code that have not been touched.

- **Benefits:** This targeted approach speeds up the testing process, allowing developers to catch issues early without being held back by long test execution times. Faster feedback improves developer productivity and helps maintain high delivery velocity in continuous integration environments.

Some examples of tools and approaches are as follows:

- **Launchable:**
  o Uses predictive test selection based on real-time Git commit analysis.
  o Continuously learns from prior test runs.
  o Prioritizes test execution based on code change risk and test failure likelihood.
  o Integrates with major CI tools like GitHub Actions, Jenkins, CircleCI, and so on.

- **SeaLights:**
  o Tracks which parts of the code were touched by commits.
  o Correlates that with test coverage and execution history.
  o Automatically selects only the impacted tests to run for every new build.

- **Tricentis LiveCompare (SAP-focused but illustrative):**
  o Analyzes transports, ABAP code changes, and business process models.
  o Uses this to determine exactly which tests are needed for impacted areas, reducing redundant testing significantly.

- **Microsoft Azure DevOps—Test Impact Analysis:**
  o Built into their CI/CD ecosystem.
  o Automatically reruns only the impacted tests based on code changes and past runs, reducing test cycles.

- **Atlassian's Intelligent Test Runner (Beta):**
  o In Jira/Bitbucket environments, this tool prioritizes which tests to run based on code churn and recent failures, in near real-time.

Optimizing resource utilization

Running a full suite of automated tests can be resource-intensive, especially for large applications. AI-driven test selection also helps optimize resource utilization in the CI/CD pipeline by intelligently selecting which tests to run in real time. Refer to the following:

- **How it works:** By running only the most critical tests, AI-driven selection reduces the load on CI/CD servers, freeing up resources for other tasks. This means that while important tests are being executed, unnecessary tests that provide little value for the current build are skipped.

- **Benefits:** This approach improves efficiency by cutting down on unnecessary resource consumption. It helps organizations save on computational costs while still ensuring that the most vital aspects of the application are properly tested. Additionally, optimized resource usage leads to faster test execution, enabling quicker release cycles.

Some examples of tools using this approach are:

- **Launchable:**
  - o Uses ML models to rank and select only the top x% most relevant tests per commit or pull request.
  - o Integrates with your existing test runners and CI tools.
  - o Enables smart test subsets (for example, run only the 20% of tests that catch 80% of bugs).

- **SeaLights:**
  - o Employs Test Optimization by tracking unused or redundant test executions.
  - o Flags tests that consistently pass and don't provide new insight.
  - o Skips low-value tests in CI runs to reduce test execution time significantly.

- **GitHub Actions + Launchable integration:**
  - o Developers can configure builds to only run tests with a minimum predicted failure probability, keeping pipelines fast and lean.

- **Test intelligence (Gradle Enterprise):**
  - o Selectively runs tests based on which source files were changed.
  - o Avoids rerunning tests unaffected by recent changes, saving CI/CD resources.

By integrating AI-driven real-time test selection into CI/CD pipelines, organizations ca drastically reduce feedback times, optimize resource usage, and maintain high test coverage in critical areas of the application. This allows teams to release faster and more frequently while minimizing the risk of defects slipping through the cracks, making AI a powerful tool for enhancing the efficiency of test automation in continuous delivery environments.

Intelligent test execution

Let us now understand more about intelligent test execution.

Self-healing tests with AI in test automation

In traditional test automation, test failures often occur due to minor changes in the application under test, such as updates to the **user interface** (**UI**), environment, or underlying systems. These failures typically require manual intervention to fix or update the tests, which can slow down the testing process and create maintenance overhead. AI-powered self-healing tests offer a solution by automatically detecting and correcting issues in tests without the need for human involvement, improving test resilience and reducing maintenance efforts.

Self-healing tests

Self-healing tests leverage AI and machine learning to detect changes in the application (such as modified locators, altered elements, or environmental changes) and automatically update the test scripts to accommodate these changes. This prevents tests from failing unnecessarily and ensures that the testing process continues smoothly without manual intervention. Refer to the following:

- **How it works:** AI monitors test execution and analyzes failures caused by minor application changes. For instance, if a UI element like a button is modified (for example, its identifier or position changes), the AI system can recognize this change and adjust the test script to point to the updated element. This dynamic adjustment prevents false failures, allowing the test to pass without requiring a human to update the script.

- **Benefits:** By implementing self-healing mechanisms, teams can reduce test maintenance significantly, especially in environments where applications are frequently updated. This leads to faster release cycles, fewer interruptions, and more reliable test execution.

Reducing manual test maintenance

The primary advantage of AI-powered self-healing tests is the reduction in manual intervention when tests fail due to minor application changes. Without self-healing, every small change, such as a renamed button or a slight alteration in the UI layout, can lead to failed tests, requiring testers to update the scripts manually. AI-driven self-healing eliminates this tedious task. Refer to the following:

- **How it works:** AI models can be trained to recognize UI elements based on a combination of attributes (such as XPath, CSS, element ID, and relative position). When a test fails due to a change in these attributes, the AI engine identifies alternative attributes or selectors to find the correct element, adjusts the test steps, and continues the execution without halting the process.

- **Benefits:** This dramatically reduces the maintenance burden on teams, especially for large, complex applications where the UI is regularly updated. It also ensures that test suites remain reliable and stable, even as the application evolves.

Improving test stability and resilience

One of the key challenges in test automation is maintaining test stability as applications evolve. Frequent changes in the codebase, UI elements, or test environments can lead to unstable tests, slowing development and delivery. Self-healing tests, powered by AI, make test suites more resilient to these changes. Refer to the following:

- **How it works:** AI-driven systems track changes in both the application and the environment. When tests fail due to modifications in either the AI engine dynamically adjusts locators, data, or environment configurations to keep the tests stable. For example, if a server URL changes or a database connection string is updated, the AI system can detect and update the affected tests automatically.

- **Benefits:** This leads to more stable and resilient test suites, reducing the number of test failures caused by non-critical changes. As a result, teams can maintain high test coverage without being bogged down by fragile or flaky tests.

By integrating AI-powered self-healing capabilities into test automation frameworks, teams can significantly reduce maintenance efforts, ensure test stability in dynamic environments, and increase the resilience of their test suites. This technology helps streamline testing processes, allowing developers and testers to focus on building new features and improving application quality rather than constantly updating test scripts.

Parallel execution with AI in test automation

As the demand for faster software releases grows, the ability to run tests in parallel has become a critical part of efficient test automation. Traditional test automation frameworks can perform parallel execution, but the process is often suboptimal, facing challenges such as inefficient resource allocation, load balancing, and poor prioritization. AI-driven parallel execution optimizes these processes by predicting the most efficient ways to distribute tests and resources, improving both speed and resource utilization.

AI-driven parallel execution

AI-driven parallel execution in test automation uses machine learning algorithms to manage and optimize the process of running tests concurrently. It considers factors such as the complexity of tests, system resources, historical test execution patterns, and potential bottlenecks to intelligently determine how tests should be distributed across multiple machines or environments. Refer to the following:

- **How it works:** AI analyzes the test suite, including the length of each test, the dependencies between tests, and the system resources available (for example, CPU, memory, bandwidth). Based on this analysis, the AI algorithm predicts the best execution strategy, determining which tests can be executed in parallel and allocating resources accordingly.

- **Benefits:** This approach ensures that tests are executed in the shortest time possible while utilizing the available resources optimally, leading to faster feedback, especially in large and complex test suites.

Intelligent test distribution

When running tests in parallel, it is crucial to ensure that system resources are not overburdened, and tests are properly distributed. Poor distribution can lead to tests being unnecessarily delayed or executed inefficiently. AI-driven algorithms can predict the ideal distribution of tests across available environments based on historical execution data and current resource availability. Refer to the following:

- **How it works:** The AI system tracks execution times, resource usage, and other performance indicators over time, building a dataset that enables it to predict which tests are likely to take longer or require more resources. It then allocates these tests across available machines to balance the load and prevent bottlenecks.

- **Benefits:** This leads to more efficient parallel execution, where no machine or environment is overloaded while others sit idle. It also ensures that longer tests do not delay the overall test suite.

Predicting execution patterns

One of the significant challenges in traditional parallel execution is the inability to predict execution patterns accurately. For instance, if certain tests tend to fail more frequently or take longer, they may introduce delays when scheduled inefficiently. AI can predict execution patterns, allowing for more intelligent scheduling of tests based on their expected behavior. Refer to the following:

- **How it works:** Using ML, AI algorithms can identify patterns from previous test runs, such as which tests tend to fail under certain conditions, which tests run slower on specific machines, or which environments encounter bottlenecks. Based on this data, the AI system can prioritize group tests so that the entire suite runs efficiently and tests with a higher likelihood of passing are executed earlier in the pipeline.

- **Benefits:** By predicting potential execution bottlenecks or failure points, the AI system can improve the test suite's overall performance and reduce the likelihood of delays during the testing process.

Real-time resource allocation and load balancing

One of the significant advantages of using AI for parallel test execution is real-time resource management. AI algorithms can monitor the resources available on each machine (for example, CPU, memory, disk space) in real-time and allocate tests accordingly. Refer to the following:

- **How it works:** If the AI system detects that a particular machine is approaching its resource limits, it can dynamically shift tests to another machine with available resources. This ensures that no machine is overloaded, preventing system crashes or performance degradation during test execution.

- **Benefits:** Real-time adjustments in resource allocation ensure that parallel execution continues smoothly, avoiding potential slowdowns caused by resource exhaustion. This also helps prevent scenarios where one machine becomes a bottleneck, while others remain underutilized.

Prioritizing high-impact tests

In some cases, it is not just about parallel execution but also about prioritizing critical tests to ensure that the most important ones are run first. AI can help identify high-impact tests based on factors such as recent code changes, the areas of the codebase that are most likely to introduce bugs, and the likelihood of critical failures. Refer to the following:

- **How it works:** The AI algorithm can analyze recent code commits and determine which parts of the codebase have the highest potential for introducing bugs. It then schedules tests related to these areas first, ensuring that any issues are identified as early as possible. This allows developers to get feedback on critical failures more quickly, even while the rest of the test suite is still running.

- **Benefits:** This approach ensures that high-risk areas of the code are tested first, providing faster feedback and allowing the team to address critical issues before they escalate. It also enables less-critical tests to be executed later in the pipeline, ensuring that overall testing efficiency is maintained.

By incorporating AI-driven parallel execution into test automation frameworks, teams can maximize their test efficiency, optimize resource allocation, and reduce execution times significantly. This allows for more effective use of parallelization strategies, especially in large-scale CI/CD pipelines, where rapid feedback is essential for maintaining high-quality software releases.

ML algorithms for identifying flaky tests

Flaky tests are a common challenge in test automation. They fail intermittently without consistent, reproducible reasons, making them unreliable. A test might pass in one execution and fail in the next, even though the underlying code being tested has not changed. This inconsistency complicates the test automation process, as developers and QA teams are left unsure if the failure indicates a genuine defect or if it is just a result of flakiness.

AI and ML in detecting flaky tests

AI and machine learning can assist in identifying flaky tests by analyzing historical test execution data to spot patterns of intermittent failure. AI models can:

- **Detect failure patterns:** By analyzing the frequency and conditions under which tests fail, AI models can determine whether a test is consistently unreliable and flag it as flaky.

- **Predict flaky tests:** ML algorithms can predict whether a new or modified test will likely be flaky based on historical data and changes to the codebase.

By leveraging AI-powered tools, teams can gain real-time insights into flaky test behavior, allowing them to address issues before they disrupt the testing process.

Flaky tests undermine the reliability and efficiency of test automation, but by understanding their causes, symptoms, and solutions, teams can reduce their occurrence. With modern techniques like AI-powered analysis, teams can also preemptively identify flaky tests and focus on building a more stable, trustworthy test automation suite.

Predictive models for test stability

As software development accelerates, maintaining the stability of test automation frameworks becomes crucial. Flaky tests, tests that produce inconsistent results, pose significant challenges, causing wasted time, confusion, and eroded trust in automated testing. To address this issue, leveraging ML models can be a game-changer. By analyzing historical test data, predictive models can forecast the likelihood of test flakiness before execution, allowing teams to manage unstable tests proactively.

Understanding flakiness

Flaky tests can arise from various factors, including:

- **Environmental issues:** Variations in hardware, operating systems, or configurations can lead to inconsistencies.

- **Timing problems:** Tests that rely on specific timing, such as asynchronous operations, may fail intermittently.

- **External dependencies:** Tests that interact with third-party services or databases can experience flakiness based on the availability or performance of these external components.

- **Test code quality:** Poorly written test cases or insufficiently isolated tests may exhibit flakiness due to their complexity or dependencies on other tests.

Role of machine learning

ML models can help identify patterns and characteristics associated with flaky tests. By analyzing historical test execution data, teams can train models to predict the likelihood of flakiness based on various features, such as:

- **Test metadata:** Information about test cases, including the author, complexity, and frequency of changes.

- **Execution environment:** Details about the environment in which tests are run, including OS, browser versions, and hardware specifications.

- **Test dependencies:** External components that tests rely on, such as APIs, databases, or services, along with their performance metrics.

- **Historical results:** Previous test outcomes, including pass/fail rates, execution times, and any contextual information regarding failures.

Building predictive models

Refer to the following:

- **Data collection:** Gather historical test data, including execution logs, metadata, and environmental information. This data should cover many test cases and their results over time.

- **Feature engineering:** Identify and extract relevant features that may correlate with test stability. This process involves cleaning the data, transforming it into a usable format, and potentially creating new features derived from existing ones.

- **Model selection:** Choose appropriate ML algorithms, such as logistic regression, decision trees, or ensemble methods like random forests. The choice of model depends on the data's nature and the desired prediction accuracy.

- **Training and validation:** Split the dataset into training and validation sets. Train the model on the training set and evaluate its performance on the validation set. Common metrics for evaluation include accuracy, precision, recall, and the F1 score.

- **Deployment:** Integrate the predictive model into the test execution pipeline. Before running tests, the system can analyze the likelihood of flakiness, allowing teams to prioritize or modify tests based on their predictions.

Benefits of predictive models

Refer to the following:

- **Proactive management:** By predicting flaky tests, teams can address potential issues before they disrupt the testing process, saving time and resources.

- **Informed decision-making:** With insights into which tests are likely to be unstable, teams can allocate resources more effectively, focusing on improving test quality or refining test cases.

- **Increased trust:** Reducing flakiness enhances the reliability of automated tests, fostering greater confidence among developers and stakeholders in the testing process.

Challenges and considerations

While predictive models offer substantial benefits, several challenges must be addressed:

- **Data quality:** The effectiveness of ML models relies on the quality and completeness of historical data. Ensuring accurate and comprehensive data collection is critical.

- **Model maintenance:** As software and testing environments evolve, models must be regularly updated and retrained to remain effective.

- **False positives/negatives:** Models may incorrectly predict flakiness, leading to unnecessary test modifications or overlooking genuine issues. Continuous monitoring and adjustment are essential.

Predictive models for test stability represent a powerful tool for improving the reliability of automated testing. By leveraging ML to identify characteristics associated with flaky tests, teams can take proactive measures to enhance test stability, optimize resource allocation, and ensure a more robust software delivery process. As organizations embrace automation, integrating predictive analytics into testing strategies will become increasingly vital for maintaining quality in fast-paced development environments.

Continuous monitoring for adaptive learning

Adaptive learning refers to the capability of ML models to update and refine their algorithms based on new information without requiring complete retraining from scratch. This continuous learning process enables the model to adjust to variations in test environments, dependencies, and other factors contributing to test flakiness.

Key components of adaptive learning

Rather than retraining the model on the entire dataset with each new batch of test execution data, incremental learning techniques update the existing model with new information. This approach is computationally efficient and allows for real-time adjustments to predictions. Refer to the following:

- **Feedback loops:** Incorporating feedback from test execution results helps the model learn from successful runs and failures. By analyzing the context of each execution, such as environmental conditions and dependencies, the model can identify patterns that contribute to flakiness.

- **Dynamic feature selection:** Adaptive learning can dynamically adjust which features are most relevant for predictions based on recent data. For example, if a particular environment configuration consistently leads to flaky tests, the model can prioritize that feature in its analysis.

- **Anomaly detection:** Using adaptive learning techniques, models can identify anomalies in test execution data that may indicate flakiness. This capability allows teams to address issues proactively before they become widespread.

Benefits of adaptive learning

The benefits are as follows:

- **Improved prediction accuracy:** As the model incorporates new data, its ability to predict flakiness becomes more precise. This leads to fewer false positives and negatives, allowing teams to focus on genuinely unstable tests.

- **Resilience to changes:** Software development environments are constantly evolving, with new features, dependencies, and configurations being introduced. Adaptive learning ensures that predictive models remain relevant and effective despite these changes.

- **Efficient resource allocation:** By continuously improving predictions, teams can allocate their testing and debugging resources more effectively, addressing issues where they are most likely to occur.

- **Enhanced CI/CD:** Integrating adaptive learning into CI/CD pipelines allows for real-time adjustments based on test execution data, fostering a more responsive development process.

Implementation of adaptive learning

Refer to the following:

- **Data pipeline integration:** Establish a robust data pipeline that collects test execution data in real time, ensuring that the model can access the latest information.

- **Model selection:** Choose ML algorithms that support incremental learning, such as online learning algorithms, ensemble methods, or neural networks designed for continuous training.

- **Monitoring and evaluation:** Continuously monitor the performance of the adaptive learning model, evaluating its accuracy and responsiveness to new data. Implement metrics to assess improvements in prediction accuracy over time.

- **Feedback mechanism:** Create a feedback loop where developers and testers can report on test stability issues, providing additional context for the model's learning process.

Challenges and considerations

While adaptive learning presents numerous advantages, several challenges should be considered, such as:

- **Data drift:** Over time, the characteristics of test execution data may change, leading to data drift. The model must recognize and adapt to these shifts to maintain accuracy.

- **Computational overhead:** Continuous learning can introduce computational overhead, mainly if the model requires frequent updates. It is crucial to balance the frequency of updates with resource availability.

- **Complexity in implementation:** Setting up an adaptive learning system requires careful planning, particularly in designing the data pipeline and feedback mechanisms. Teams must ensure that the system can efficiently handle new data without introducing significant delays.

Adaptive learning represents a powerful advancement in the field of predictive models for test stability. By enabling machine learning algorithms to learn continuously from new test execution data, organizations can enhance their ability to predict flakiness, improve the accuracy of their testing processes, and respond dynamically to changes in software development environments. As the demand for reliable automated testing grows, the integration of adaptive learning techniques will be essential for maintaining high-quality software delivery in an ever-evolving landscape.

Test optimization with AI

As software applications grow in complexity, maintaining an efficient and effective test suite becomes increasingly challenging. Test suites can become bloated over time with redundant or low-value tests, leading to longer execution times and reduced efficiency in the development process. AI presents a powerful solution for optimizing test suites by identifying and eliminating unnecessary tests, ultimately streamlining the testing process and improving overall software quality.

Need for test optimization

Test suites often expand in size as new features are added, bug fixes are implemented, and legacy tests are retained. This growth can lead to several issues, such as:

- **Longer test execution times:** Larger test suites require more time to execute, which can slow down the CI/CD pipeline and delay feedback for developers.

- **Diminished value:** Tests that no longer provide valuable insights or coverage can clutter test results, making it difficult for teams to identify critical failures.

- **Increased maintenance overhead:** Maintaining a large number of tests increases the burden on development and QA teams, requiring additional resources for updates and fixes.

Optimizing test suites with AI

AI-driven optimization approaches leverage data analysis and machine learning to identify tests that are redundant or provide minimal value. The optimization process typically involves the following steps:

1. **Data analysis:** AI systems analyze historical test execution data, including pass/fail rates, execution frequency, and test coverage. This analysis helps identify patterns and correlations between test performance and application changes.

2. **Test value assessment:** AI algorithms assess the value of individual tests by examining their impact on overall test results. This assessment may consider factors such as:

3. **Failure rates:** Tests that frequently fail may indicate redundancy if they do not provide significant value.

4. **Coverage gaps:** Identifying tests that do not cover unique scenarios can help determine which tests can be eliminated without compromising quality.

5. **Execution frequency:** Tests that are seldom executed or provide limited insights can be flagged for removal.

6. **Redundancy detection:** AI can identify tests that overlap in functionality or coverage. By clustering similar tests, teams can streamline their suite by retaining only the most effective tests.

7. **Recommendations for elimination:** Based on the analysis, AI systems can generate actionable recommendations for which tests to remove, ensuring that the test suite remains focused and efficient.

Benefits of AI-driven test optimization

Implementing AI for test optimization yields several significant benefits, such as:

- **Streamlined test suites:** By eliminating redundant tests, teams can reduce the size of their test suites, leading to faster execution times and more efficient CI/CD pipelines.

- **Improved test quality:** Focusing on high-value tests ensures that the remaining tests provide meaningful insights, enhancing the overall quality of the testing process.

- **Reduced maintenance overhead:** A smaller, more relevant test suite requires less maintenance, allowing QA and development teams to allocate resources to more strategic initiatives.

- **Faster feedback loops:** With optimized test suites, teams can receive quicker feedback on new features and changes, facilitating more agile development practices.

Challenges and considerations

While AI-driven test optimization offers many advantages, several challenges need to be addressed:

- **Data quality:** The effectiveness of AI algorithms relies heavily on the quality of the data used for analysis. Ensuring accurate and comprehensive historical data is critical for reliable recommendations.

- **Change management:** Removing tests can lead to resistance from team members concerned about losing coverage or valuable insights. It is essential to communicate the rationale behind optimization decisions effectively.

- **Continuous monitoring:** Test optimization is not a one-time process. Continuous monitoring of test performance and regular re-evaluation of the test suite are necessary to maintain optimal efficiency.

AI presents a transformative opportunity for optimizing test suites in software development. By leveraging data analysis and machine learning, teams can identify redundant or low-value tests, streamline their testing processes, and ultimately enhance software quality. As the complexity of software applications continues to rise, integrating AI-driven test optimization will become increasingly essential for maintaining efficient and effective testing practices.

Self-maintaining test suites

Maintaining a robust and effective test suite can be a daunting task, especially as applications undergo frequent changes. Traditional test maintenance often requires substantial manual effort to update test steps and assertions in response to minor changes in the codebase. However, advancements in AI have paved the way for self-maintaining test suites, which are systems that autonomously monitor test failures and dynamically update tests without requiring manual intervention. This approach not only streamlines the testing process but also enhances the overall efficiency of software delivery.

Challenge of test maintenance

As software evolves, changes such as code refactoring, UI updates, and feature additions can lead to test failures. Traditional test maintenance involves several challenges:

- **Manual intervention:** Test maintenance typically requires manual review and updates, which can be time-consuming and prone to human error.

- **Frequent changes:** In agile environments, software changes occur rapidly, constantly needing test updates to ensure alignment with the latest code.

- **Resource drain:** The time and effort spent on maintaining tests can divert resources from more critical tasks, such as developing new features or improving system performance.

Working of self-maintaining test suites

Self-maintaining test suites leverage AI models to monitor and respond to test failures dynamically. The process typically involves the following steps:

1. **Continuous monitoring:** AI models continuously observe test execution results, tracking failures caused by minor code changes or environmental factors.

2. **Failure analysis:** When a test fails, the AI analyzes the failure context, identifying patterns and common causes. This analysis helps determine whether the failure is due to a legitimate issue in the application or a minor change that necessitates an update to the test.

3. **Dynamic updates:** If the AI determines the failure is due to a minor change (for example, a UI element's position or a variable name), it can automatically adjust the test steps or assertions. This may involve:

   a. **Updating element selectors:** If a UI component's identifier changes, the AI can modify the test to reflect the new identifier.

   b. **Modifying assertions:** The AI can adjust assertions to accommodate changes in expected values or behaviors without requiring manual input.

4. **Feedback loop:** The system learns continuously from each test execution and update, enhancing its ability to make accurate adjustments in the future.

Benefits of self-maintaining test suites

The implementation of self-maintaining test suites offers numerous advantages:

- **Reduced manual maintenance:** By automating test updates, teams can significantly reduce the time and effort spent on manual maintenance tasks.

- **Increased test reliability:** Continuous monitoring and automatic adjustments help maintain test reliability, ensuring that tests accurately reflect the application's current state.

- **Faster feedback loops:** With reduced manual intervention, teams can receive quicker feedback on code changes, facilitating more agile development practices.

- **Higher test coverage:** Self-maintaining test suites can adapt to changes, ensuring that tests remain relevant and comprehensive as the application evolves.

Challenges and considerations

Despite the benefits, self-maintaining test suites also come with challenges:

- **Complexity of AI models:** Developing effective AI models that accurately analyze test failures and make appropriate adjustments requires significant expertise and resources.

- **False positives and negatives:** AI systems may occasionally misinterpret the cause of a test failure, leading to unnecessary adjustments or, conversely, failure to update tests when needed. Continuous refinement of the models is essential to mitigate this risk.

- **Integration with existing frameworks:** Implementing self-maintaining test suites may require adjustments to existing testing frameworks and processes, necessitating careful planning and execution.

Self-maintaining test suites represent a significant advancement in automated testing, enabling teams to adapt to changes swiftly and efficiently. By leveraging AI models to monitor and update tests dynamically, organizations can reduce manual maintenance efforts, enhance test reliability, and improve overall software quality. As the software development landscape continues to evolve, adopting self-maintaining test suites will be crucial for maintaining efficient and effective testing practices in increasingly complex environments.

Environment-aware testing

Environmental factors can significantly impact test reliability and outcomes. Issues such as slow network conditions, faulty databases, or resource contention can lead to consistent test failures that do not necessarily reflect problems in the application itself. Environment-aware testing leverages AI to recognize and mitigate these environmental issues, ensuring more reliable test results. By dynamically adjusting testing strategies and rerouting tests to more stable environments, teams can achieve better test outcomes and enhance the overall efficiency of their testing processes.

Challenge of environmental issues in testing

Testing applications in diverse environments is essential for uncovering issues that may only arise under specific conditions. However, environmental factors can introduce challenges:

- **Inconsistent test results:** Tests may pass or fail depending on the environment in which they run, leading to confusion and misinterpretation of results.

- **Time-consuming investigations:** Identifying whether a test failure is due to environmental issues or application defects often requires extensive troubleshooting, consuming valuable time and resources.

- **Reduced confidence in test suites:** Frequent environmental-related failures can undermine the confidence of development and QA teams in their testing efforts, making it difficult to gauge application stability.

Working of environment-aware testing

Environment-aware testing utilizes AI algorithms to monitor test execution environments and adjust testing strategies accordingly. The process typically includes the following steps:

1. **Monitoring environmental factors:** AI models continuously collect data on various environmental factors during test execution, such as network latency, database availability, CPU load, and memory usage.

2. **Identifying patterns:** The AI analyzes the data to identify patterns of test failures associated with specific environmental issues. For instance, if certain tests consistently fail under high network latency, the AI flags these tests for further action.

3. **Dynamic adjustments:** When environmental issues are detected, the AI can automatically adjust the testing strategy. This may include:

   a. **Rerouting tests:** The AI may redirect tests to more stable environments or instances with better resource availability, ensuring a more reliable execution.

   b. **Test prioritization:** The AI can prioritize tests that are less sensitive to environmental conditions, allowing for quicker feedback on critical functionalities.

4. **Adaptive learning:** The AI continuously learns from environmental data and test results, improving its ability to identify and respond to environmental issues over time.

Benefits of environment-aware testing

The implementation of environment-aware testing provides several key advantages, such as:

- **Improved test reliability:** By minimizing the impact of environmental issues on test outcomes, teams can achieve more reliable results and better understand application performance.

- **Reduced troubleshooting time:** Automated adjustments allow teams to spend less time investigating test failures, freeing up resources for other critical tasks.

- **Enhanced confidence in test suites:** With fewer environmental-related failures, teams can gain more confidence in the stability and reliability of their applications.

- **Faster feedback loops:** By optimizing test execution in real-time, teams can receive quicker feedback on changes, enabling more agile development practices.

Challenges and considerations

While environment-aware testing offers significant benefits, some challenges must be addressed, such as:

- **Complexity of implementation:** Setting up AI systems to monitor and analyze environmental factors can be complex and resource-intensive.

- **Reliability of environmental data:** Ensuring the accuracy and reliability of environmental data is crucial for the effectiveness of AI-driven adjustments.

- **Integration with existing frameworks:** Implementing environment-aware testing may require adjustments to existing testing frameworks and processes, necessitating careful planning and execution.

Environment-aware testing represents a significant advancement in automated testing practices, enabling teams to adapt to environmental factors that impact test outcomes. Organizations can improve test reliability, reduce troubleshooting time, and enhance overall software quality by leveraging AI to monitor and dynamically adjust testing strategies. As software applications evolve and operate in increasingly complex environments, adopting environment-aware testing will be essential for maintaining efficient and effective testing processes.

Enhancing test insights with AI and ML

Root cause analysis (RCA) is a critical process in software testing and quality assurance, aimed at identifying the fundamental reasons behind test failures or defects. Traditional RCA methods can be time-consuming and labor-intensive, often relying on manual review of logs, code changes, and historical test data. However, advancements in AI have revolutionized this process, enabling faster and more accurate identification of root causes. By automating data analysis and leveraging ML algorithms, AI can significantly enhance defect triaging, allowing teams to address issues more efficiently and effectively.

Challenge of identifying root causes

Identifying the root cause of test failures is essential for maintaining software quality and reliability. However, the traditional RCA process faces several challenges, such as:

- **Data overload:** The volume of data generated during test execution, including logs, metrics, and historical test results, can be overwhelming, making it difficult for teams to pinpoint the root cause of failures.

- **Complexity of interactions:** Modern software systems often involve intricate interactions between components, making it challenging to determine which specific change led to a failure.

- **Time-consuming investigations:** Manual investigation of failures can be labor-intensive and time-consuming, delaying the resolution of defects and impacting development timelines.

Working of AI-assisted root cause analysis

AI-assisted root cause analysis utilizes advanced algorithms and data analysis techniques to automate and streamline the RCA process. The typical workflow involves the following steps:

1. **Data aggregation:** AI systems collect and aggregate relevant data from various sources, including:
   a. **Test execution logs:** Detailed logs generated during test runs.
   b. **Code changes:** Version control data indicating changes made to the codebase.
   c. **Historical test data:** Information from past test executions and failure patterns.

2. **Pattern recognition:** ML algorithms analyze the aggregated data to identify patterns and correlations that may indicate the underlying causes of test failures. For example, the AI might detect failures frequently occurring after specific code changes or under particular conditions.

3. **Root cause identification:** Based on its analysis, the AI can suggest potential root causes for the observed failures. This may include:
   a. Specific code commits or changes that led to the issue.
   b. Environmental factors, such as resource availability or configuration changes.
   c. Dependences between components that may have been affected.

4. **Defect triaging:** The AI provides recommendations for triaging defects based on their severity and potential impact, enabling teams to prioritize their efforts effectively.

Benefits of AI-assisted root cause analysis

The integration of AI in root cause analyses offers numerous advantages:

- **Faster identification of issues:** AI can analyze vast amounts of data in a fraction of the time it would take a human, significantly speeding up the defect identification process.

- **Increased accuracy:** By leveraging ML algorithms, AI can identify subtle patterns and correlations that may be overlooked during manual analysis, leading to more accurate root cause identification.

- **Reduced manual effort:** Automating the data analysis process reduces the manual effort required for RCA, allowing teams to focus on implementing solutions rather than troubleshooting.
- **Improved decision-making:** By providing data-driven insights and recommendations, AI enhances the decision-making process for defect triaging, enabling teams to address the most critical issues first.

Challenges and considerations

Despite the benefits, AI-assisted root cause analysis also presents challenges such as:

- **Data quality and relevance:** The effectiveness of AI models depends on the quality and relevance of the data used for training and analysis. Poor-quality data can lead to inaccurate conclusions.
- **Complexity of implementation:** Integrating AI tools into existing testing frameworks and processes may require significant effort and expertise.
- **Continuous learning:** AI models must be continuously updated and trained on new data to maintain their accuracy and effectiveness over time.

AI-assisted root cause analysis represents a significant advancement in the field of software testing, enabling teams to identify and resolve defects more efficiently. By automating the analysis of logs, code changes, and historical test data, AI can speed up defect triaging and enhance overall software quality. As software systems become increasingly complex, adopting AI-driven RCA will be essential for organizations seeking to maintain a competitive edge and ensure reliable software delivery.

Predictive analytics for test outcomes

Traditional testing methods often react to failures after they occur, leading to delays and increased costs. Predictive analytics, powered by AI, offers a proactive approach by analyzing patterns from historical test executions to anticipate potential test failures or regressions. This capability allows development and testing teams to address issues before they impact the software's functionality, enhancing overall quality and efficiency.

Need for predictive analytics in testing

As software systems grow in complexity and size, identifying and resolving potential issues becomes increasingly challenging. Traditional testing methods often fall short due to several factors:

- **Reactive nature:** Most testing strategies focus on identifying defects after they occur, leading to a cycle of debugging and fixing that can slow down the development process.
- **Complex interdependencies:** Modern applications often have numerous dependencies, making predicting how changes in one area may affect others is difficult.
- **Resource constraints:** Testing teams may struggle to allocate sufficient resources to cover all potential scenarios, increasing the risk of undetected issues.

Working of predictive analytics

Predictive analytics utilizes AI and ML algorithms to analyze historical test execution data, identifying patterns and trends that can inform future outcomes. The process typically involves the following steps:

1. **Data collection:** AI systems gather and aggregate data from previous test executions, including:
   a. Test execution logs.
   b. Pass/fail results.
   c. Code changes and commit history.
   d. Environmental factors during testing.

2. **Pattern recognition:** ML algorithms analyze the collected data to identify patterns associated with test failures or regressions. This may include:

   a. Frequency of failures after specific code changes.

   b. Tests that fail under particular environmental conditions.

   c. Trends in test execution times or resource utilization.

3. **Risk assessment:** Based on the identified patterns, the AI can assess the likelihood of future test failures. It can generate risk scores for individual tests, indicating their susceptibility to regressions based on historical performance.

4. **Predictive insights:** The AI provides actionable insights, allowing teams to focus efforts on tests with a high likelihood of failure. This could include recommendations for additional test coverage, prioritization of regression tests, or re-evaluation of recent code changes.

Benefits of predictive analytics for test outcomes

The integration of predictive analytics into testing practices offers several significant advantages:

- **Proactive problem identification:** By predicting potential failures, teams can address issues before they impact users, reducing the cost and time associated with post-release defects.

- **Optimized testing resources:** Teams can prioritize their testing efforts based on predictive insights, focusing on high-risk areas and ensuring that critical functionalities are thoroughly tested.

- **Increased test efficiency:** By identifying redundant or low-value tests, teams can streamline their test suites, improving execution times and resource utilization.

- **Enhanced collaboration:** Predictive analytics fosters better communication between development and QA teams, as both can work together to understand and mitigate risks based on data-driven insights.

Challenges and considerations

While predictive analytics offers substantial benefits, organizations must also navigate several challenges:

- **Data quality:** The effectiveness of predictive models relies heavily on the quality and completeness of the data used for analysis. Inaccurate or sparse data can lead to misleading predictions.

- **Model training and maintenance:** AI models require continuous training and fine-tuning to remain effective. Organizations must invest the necessary infrastructure and expertise to support this ongoing effort.

- **Integration with existing processes:** Implementing predictive analytics may require changes to existing testing processes and tools, necessitating careful planning and coordination.

Predictive analytics for test outcomes mark a significant advancement in software testing, allowing teams to move from a reactive to a proactive testing approach. By analyzing patterns from historical test data, AI can help predict the likelihood of test failures or regressions, enabling teams to address issues before they occur. As software complexity rises, leveraging predictive analytics will be essential for maintaining high-quality software delivery and ensuring organizations remain competitive in the fast-paced digital landscape.

Automated bug triage and prioritization

In the fast-paced world of software development, timely bug identification and resolution are critical for maintaining product quality and user satisfaction. Traditional bug triaging methods often rely on manual processes, which can be time-consuming and subjective. Automated bug triage and prioritization, powered by AI, offers a transformative approach by systematically assessing and ranking defects based on their severity and impact on the overall system. This streamlines the bug management process and ensures that teams focus on the most critical issues first.

Importance of automated bug triage

Effective bug triage is essential for several reasons:

- **Resource allocation:** Development teams often have limited resources and time. Prioritizing bugs helps ensure that high-impact issues are addressed promptly, reducing the risk of user dissatisfaction.

- **Risk management:** Identifying and resolving severe defects quickly can prevent further complications, such as regressions or system failures.

- **Improved team morale:** By automating the triaging process, teams can minimize the frustration associated with manual bug management and focus more on development and innovation.

Working of automated bug triage

Automated bug triage systems leverage AI and ML algorithms to analyze and rank defects based on various criteria:

- **Data aggregation:** The AI system collects data from different sources, including:
  - Bug reports from issue tracking systems.
  - Test execution logs.
  - User feedback and customer support tickets.

- **Feature extraction:** Key features are extracted from the data, such as:
  - Severity level assigned by testers.
  - Frequency of occurrence.
  - Affected components or modules.
  - Historical resolution times.

- **Ranking algorithms:** ML models analyze the extracted features to rank bugs based on their potential impact on the system. Factors influencing the ranking may include:
  - **Severity:** The potential damage a bug could cause, categorized into levels (for example, critical, major, minor).
  - **Impact:** The extent to which a bug affects user experience or system functionality.
  - **Urgency:** How quickly a bug needs to be addressed based on business priorities or customer complaints.

- **Prioritization:** The system generates a ranked list of bugs, allowing teams to focus on high-priority issues first. Additionally, automated notifications can alert team members to critical bugs that require immediate attention.

Benefits of automated bug triage and prioritization

Implementing automated bug triage and prioritization offers several key advantages:

- **Enhanced efficiency:** Automation reduces the time spent on manual triaging, enabling teams to identify and address critical bugs quickly.

- **Objective decision-making:** AI-driven prioritization minimizes biases associated with human judgment, leading to more objective decisions about which bugs to tackle first.

- **Faster resolution times:** By prioritizing high-impact defects, teams can reduce overall resolution times and improve the software's stability and reliability.

- **Better resource management:** Teams can allocate their resources more effectively, focusing on critical issues while still keeping track of lower-priority bugs.

Challenges and considerations

While automated bug triage brings significant benefits, organizations should also consider the following challenges:

- **Data quality:** AI models' effectiveness depends on the input data's quality and comprehensiveness. Inaccurate or incomplete data can lead to suboptimal prioritization.

- **Model training:** Continuous training and adjustment of the AI model are necessary to maintain accuracy over time, especially as software systems evolve.

- **Integration with existing processes:** Organizations may need to adapt their existing workflows to incorporate automated triage effectively, which can require change management efforts.

Automated bug triage and prioritization significantly advance software testing and quality assurance practices. By leveraging AI to rank bugs based on severity and impact, organizations can streamline their defect management processes, enhance efficiency, and improve overall software quality. As software complexity continues to grow, embracing automated solutions will be crucial for teams seeking to deliver reliable, high-quality applications in a timely manner.

Smarter test refactoring suggestions

Frequent changes in the underlying codebase, combined with the potential for test cases to become brittle or outdated, can lead to increased flakiness and maintenance overhead. This is where smarter test refactoring suggestions powered by AI come into play. By analyzing patterns and trends in test executions, AI algorithms can provide valuable insights on when and how to refactor test cases, ensuring that the testing suite remains effective and efficient.

Need for test refactoring

Test refactoring is essential for several reasons:

- **Maintainability:** Test cases can become difficult to understand and manage over time, especially as the system architecture changes. Refactoring helps keep tests clean and maintainable.

- **Reliability:** Flaky tests, that fail intermittently without changes to the underlying code, can undermine confidence in the testing process. Regular refactoring can address issues that contribute to flakiness.

- **Alignment with code changes:** Tests must evolve accordingly as new features are added or existing ones are modified. Failing to update tests can lead to gaps in coverage and missed defects.

Working of smarter refactoring suggestions

AI-driven test refactoring suggestions involve several key components:

- **Data collection:** The AI system collects data from various sources, including:
    - Test execution results (pass/fail status).
    - Code change history from version control systems.
    - Metrics on test execution time and frequency of failures.

- **Pattern recognition:** ML algorithms analyze the collected data to identify patterns associated with test failures and code changes. This analysis may include:

  o **Frequent failures:** Identifying tests that fail repeatedly, indicating potential issues in the test logic or underlying application code.

  o **Code changes:** Monitoring changes in the codebase to determine which tests are affected and need updating.

- **Refactoring suggestions:** Based on the analysis, the AI system generates actionable suggestions for test refactoring. These may include:

  o **Removing redundant tests:** Identifying tests that are duplicative or provide little value, allowing teams to streamline the test suite.

  o **Updating assertions:** Recommending changes to assertions in tests that are failing due to minor changes in the application.

  o **Modularizing tests:** Suggesting the restructuring of complex tests into smaller, more focused units that are easier to understand and maintain.

Benefits of smarter test refactoring suggestions

Implementing AI-driven suggestions for test refactoring offers several key advantages:

- **Proactive maintenance:** Teams can address potential issues before they escalate, leading to a more stable and reliable test suite.

- **Improved test quality:** By continually refining tests based on real-time data, the overall quality and effectiveness of the test suite can be enhanced.

- **Time savings:** Automated suggestions save time for testing teams, allowing them to focus on strategic testing activities rather than manual test maintenance.

- **Enhanced collaboration:** The insights provided by AI can foster better communication between development and testing teams, ensuring that everyone is aligned on necessary changes.

Challenges and considerations

While smarter test refactoring suggestions bring significant benefits, organizations should also consider the following challenges:

- **Data dependency:** The effectiveness of AI-driven suggestions relies heavily on the quality and completeness of the data collected. Incomplete or inaccurate data can lead to misguided recommendations.

- **Model training:** Continuous training and validation of the AI model are required to ensure that it adapts to evolving testing practices and software architectures.

- **Change management:** Implementing AI-driven suggestions may require a cultural shift within the organization, necessitating buy-in from both development and testing teams.

Smarter test refactoring suggestions powered by AI represent a powerful tool for maintaining the effectiveness of test suites in complex software environments. By leveraging data-driven insights, organizations can proactively address issues in their testing processes, ensuring that tests remain reliable, maintainable, and aligned with the evolving codebase. As software systems continue to evolve, the integration of AI into testing practices will become increasingly essential for delivering high-quality applications efficiently.

Key challenges and considerations for AI and ML adoption in testing

In this next section, we will look at three common challenges facing many organizations looking to adopt AI into their testing processes and how they can overcome them.

Challenge 1: Data quality and volume

Problem: Dependence on high-quality historical test data

AI and ML are increasingly utilized in software testing to enhance test accuracy, predict failures, and optimize processes. However, the effectiveness of these technologies is heavily dependent on the quality and volume of historical test data available for analysis. Insufficient or poor-quality data can lead to several issues, such as:

- **Inaccurate predictions:** If the historical data is flawed or incomplete, AI models may generate inaccurate predictions about test outcomes, leading to misguided decisions.

- **Limited model training:** AI algorithms require diverse and representative data to learn effectively. A lack of variety can hinder the model's ability to generalize to new scenarios, diminishing its predictive capabilities.

- **Increased noise:** Low-quality data often contains noise, such as irrelevant information or errors, which can confuse AI models and result in poor performance.

Solution: Ensuring well-structured test suites

To mitigate the challenges associated with data quality and volume, organizations can implement the following strategies:

- **Structured test suites:** Organize test cases in a clear and structured manner. Categorizing tests based on functionality, criticality, and expected outcomes helps facilitate easier data retrieval and analysis.

- **Comprehensive monitoring:** Implement monitoring systems that track test execution, including pass/fail rates, execution times, and any anomalies observed during tests. This data should be logged meticulously to capture insights that can inform AI model training.

- **Detailed logging:** Ensure that test execution logs are comprehensive and include essential details, such as:

  o   Test case IDs and descriptions.

  o   Environment configurations.

  o   Input data used during test execution.

  o   Detailed error messages and stack traces for failed tests.

- **Regular data audits:** Conduct regular audits of the test data and logs to identify and rectify any issues. This includes checking for missing data, inconsistencies, or outdated information that could impact model accuracy.

- **Diverse test scenarios:** Encourage the creation of diverse test scenarios that cover a wide range of use cases and edge cases. This diversity enriches the dataset, enabling AI models to learn from a broader spectrum of data.

- **Integration of feedback loops:** Establish feedback mechanisms that allow the testing team to provide input on the data being generated. This collaboration can help refine data collection processes and improve overall data quality.

Data quality and volume are critical factors influencing the success of AI and ML in software testing. By ensuring well-structured test suites, comprehensive monitoring, and detailed logging, organizations can produce high-quality historical test data that supports effective AI model training. Addressing these challenges not only enhances the accuracy of AI predictions but also enables teams to make informed decisions, ultimately leading to more reliable and efficient software delivery.

Challenge 2: Building trust in AI-driven decisions

Problem: Hesitation to rely on AI-generated insights

As organizations increasingly adopt AI and ML to enhance testing processes, a significant challenge arises: building trust among test engineers and other stakeholders in AI-generated test cases and failure analyses. This hesitation often stems from several factors, such as:

- **Lack of transparency:** AI algorithms can be complex and operate as black boxes, making it difficult for users to understand how they arrive at specific recommendations or predictions. This opacity can lead to skepticism about the reliability of AI-driven decisions.

- **Limited understanding of algorithms:** Test engineers may not have a deep understanding of the underlying algorithms or the data used to train AI models. This gap in knowledge can create uncertainty about the accuracy and relevance of AI-generated outputs.

- **Fear of obsolescence:** Concerns may arise regarding the potential replacement of human roles in testing by automated systems, further contributing to resistance against adopting AI solutions.

Solution: Implementing explainable AI techniques

To overcome these challenges and build trust in AI-driven decisions, organizations can adopt the following strategies:

- **Explainable AI (XAI) techniques:** Implement XAI methods that enhance the interpretability of AI models. Organizations can provide insights into how AI models make decisions by using techniques such as feature importance, model-agnostic explanations, and decision trees.

- **Clear documentation:** Create comprehensive documentation that explains the AI models being used, including their purpose, underlying algorithms, and data sources. This information should be easily accessible to all stakeholders.

- **Regular training sessions:** Conduct training sessions and workshops to educate test engineers and QA teams about AI concepts, algorithms, and the specific models being employed. This initiative fosters a deeper understanding and encourages collaboration between teams.

- **Real-time feedback mechanisms:** Implement feedback loops where test engineers can review and assess AI-generated test cases or failure analyses. Providing a platform for input helps teams feel more involved in the decision-making process and encourages trust in the AI system.

- **Pilot programs:** Launch pilot programs that allow teams to test AI-driven solutions in controlled environments. This approach enables engineers to evaluate the accuracy and effectiveness of AI recommendations without fully committing to the technology, thus reducing resistance.

- **Success stories and case studies:** Share success stories and case studies that highlight the positive impacts of AI in testing processes. Demonstrating tangible benefits, such as improved efficiency and reduced defect rates, can help alleviate concerns.

Building trust in AI-driven decisions is essential for the successful adoption of AI and ML technologies in software testing. By implementing explainable AI techniques, providing clear documentation, and fostering a culture of collaboration and education, organizations can help test engineers feel confident in the insights generated by AI models. Establishing trust not only enhances the effectiveness of AI solutions but also paves the way for more seamless integration of AI into the testing process, ultimately leading to better software quality and performance.

Challenge 3: Integration into existing test automation frameworks

Problem: Challenges with legacy systems

The integration of AI tools into existing test automation frameworks presents a significant challenge for organizations, particularly those with legacy systems. The difficulties associated with this integration can include:

- **Complexity of legacy systems:** Many organizations rely on legacy test automation frameworks that may not be compatible with modern AI tools. The complexity and rigidity of these systems can make it challenging to incorporate new technologies without extensive modifications. AI tools typically rely on modern CI/CD pipelines, structured metadata, and machine-readable logs or APIs to function and only offer support for modern tools and approaches. Thus, legacy applications will likely need some refactoring to adapt to a modern framework approach.

- **Resistance to change:** Teams accustomed to established processes may resist adopting AI tools, fearing disruptions to their workflow or potential disruptions in the quality of testing.

- **Resource constraints:** Implementing AI tools often requires additional resources, including time, personnel, and financial investment. Organizations may struggle to allocate these resources while maintaining ongoing testing activities.

Solution: Developing a phased integration strategy

To effectively integrate AI tools into existing test automation frameworks, organizations can adopt a phased integration strategy that emphasizes gradual adoption. Here are the key steps in this approach:

1. **Assessment of current frameworks:** Begin by assessing the existing test automation frameworks to identify compatibility issues, strengths, and weaknesses. Understanding the current landscape will inform decisions on how to introduce AI tools best.

2. **Pilot programs:** Initiate pilot programs where AI tools are introduced in non-critical test suites. This allows teams to evaluate AI's benefits in a controlled environment without jeopardizing critical testing processes.

3. **Incremental implementation:** Gradually implement AI tools alongside existing frameworks, integrating them into specific areas that can most benefit from automation. These could include areas like test data management, reporting, or predictive analytics.

4. **Training and support:** Provide training and support for teams to ensure they understand how to use the new AI tools effectively. This can include workshops, documentation, and ongoing support from AI specialists.

5. **Feedback loops:** Establish feedback mechanisms to gather insights from users about their experiences with the new tools. This information can inform further adjustments and improvements to the integration process.

6. **Iterative refinement:** Use the feedback and results from pilot programs to iteratively refine the integration strategy. Based on what works well, scale up the adoption of AI tools across other test suites and processes.

7. **Communication of benefits:** Communicate the potential benefits of AI integration to all stakeholders. Highlight how AI tools can enhance testing efficiency, reduce manual effort, and improve overall software quality.

Integrating AI tools into existing test automation frameworks poses challenges, particularly for organizations with legacy systems. Organizations can successfully incorporate AI into their testing processes by developing a phased integration strategy that emphasizes gradual adoption, training, and feedback. This approach mitigates the risks associated with disruption and fosters a culture of innovation and continuous improvement, ultimately leading to enhanced software quality and testing efficiency.

AI-driven test automation ecosystem

As AI and ML technologies mature, they are set to revolutionize the test automation landscape. The future envisions a fully autonomous testing ecosystem with minimal human intervention for critical processes such as test design, execution, and maintenance. This transformation promises to streamline testing practices, enhance efficiency, and improve software quality.

Key components of an autonomous testing ecosystem

One of the key drivers AI offers the testing world is the idea of autonomous testing and having AI proactively driving the testing for the organization. However, for companies to investigate ways of making this a reality, they will need to explore specific aspects of their ecosystem and ensure these are in place before trying to leverage these emerging technologies to test for them. Some of these components are outlined as follows:

- **Automated test design:**

  o **AI-generated test cases:** Using historical data and AI algorithms, organizations can automatically generate test cases based on code changes, user stories, and system requirements. This approach not only accelerates the test design phase but also ensures comprehensive coverage.

  o **Adaptive test case creation:** As the application evolves, AI can adapt test cases in real time, modifying them based on code changes or user behavior, ensuring that tests remain relevant and effective.

- **Intelligent test execution:**

  o **Dynamic test prioritization:** AI can analyze past execution results to prioritize tests based on their likelihood of failure or importance to business objectives, allowing teams to focus on high-risk areas first.

  o **Environment-aware testing:** AI can identify and manage environmental factors that impact test execution, such as network conditions or system loads, dynamically adjusting test parameters to optimize performance and reliability.

- **Automated maintenance:**

  o **Self-healing tests:** AI-driven test suites can monitor test failures and automatically update test steps or assertions in response to minor changes in the application, significantly reducing the maintenance burden on QA teams.

  o **Continuous learning:** The system learns from previous test executions, continuously refining its strategies and approaches, leading to improved stability and reliability over time.

- **Comprehensive reporting and analysis:**

  o **Predictive analytics:** By leveraging historical data, AI can predict potential failures or regressions before they occur, helping teams proactively address issues and enhance the quality of releases.

  o **Root cause analysis:** AI can analyze logs and historical data to quickly identify the root cause of failures, facilitating faster defect triaging and resolution.

Benefits of an autonomous testing ecosystem

The benefits are as follows:

- **Reduced time and cost:** Organizations can significantly reduce the time and resources required for testing by automating repetitive tasks and streamlining processes.

- **Enhanced test coverage:** Autonomous systems can generate and execute a broader range of test cases than manual efforts, leading to improved coverage and detection of defects.

- **Improved software quality:** With fewer human errors and more efficient testing processes, the overall quality of software products is likely to improve, resulting in better user experiences.

The development of an AI-driven test automation ecosystem represents a paradigm shift in how software testing is approached. By harnessing the power of AI and ML technologies, organizations can move toward a fully autonomous testing environment that minimizes human intervention in test design, execution, and maintenance. This transformation enhances testing efficiency and empowers teams to focus on higher-level tasks, ultimately leading to more reliable and higher-quality software releases. As these technologies continue to evolve, they promise to make testing more agile, adaptive, and aligned with the fast-paced demands of modern software development.

Vision of self-learning test automation

As the landscape of software development evolves, the potential for AI to revolutionize test automation frameworks becomes increasingly apparent. The future may see the emergence of self-learning test automation frameworks that continuously adapt and improve based on real-time feedback from production environments. This evolution aims to bridge the gap between development, testing, and operations, fostering a more integrated and efficient approach to software delivery.

Key features of self-learning test automation frameworks

The following are the key features that form the foundation of a self-learning test automation framework:

- **Continuous learning from production feedback:**

  o **Real-time adaptation:** Self-learning frameworks can analyze feedback from production systems to identify patterns and insights that inform test case adjustments. For example, if a particular feature frequently encounters issues in production, the framework can automatically enhance its test coverage for that area.

  o **Dynamic test case generation:** By leveraging historical data and user interactions, these frameworks can create and refine test cases on the fly, ensuring that they remain aligned with current application behavior and user expectations.

- **Integration of development, testing, and operations:**

  o **DevOps synergy:** The self-learning framework facilitates better collaboration between development, testing, and operations teams. By aligning testing efforts with real-world usage, teams can ensure that tests accurately reflect the application's operational context.

  o **Feedback loops:** Continuous feedback loops enable real-time communication among teams, allowing for quicker resolution of issues and reducing the time between identifying a defect and deploying a fix.

- **Enhanced test maintenance:**

  o **Self-healing capabilities:** As production environments change, self-learning frameworks can autonomously adjust test cases to accommodate minor code changes or feature updates, significantly reducing the need for manual maintenance.

  o **Automated risk assessment:** The framework can evaluate the impact of code changes on existing tests, prioritizing those most likely to be affected and ensuring that critical areas are thoroughly tested.

- **Predictive analytics for proactive quality assurance:**
  - o **Anticipating issues:** By analyzing production data, these frameworks can predict potential failures or performance bottlenecks, allowing teams to address issues before they impact end users.
  - o **Continuous improvement:** Insights gained from production feedback can inform iterative improvements in testing strategies, leading to more robust and effective test automation processes.

Benefits of self-learning test automation frameworks

The benefits are as follows:

- **Reduced time-to-market:** By automating test case generation and maintenance based on real-time data, organizations can accelerate their release cycles, delivering higher-quality software to market faster.

- **Improved quality and reliability:** Continuous adaptation to production conditions ensures that tests remain relevant and practical, resulting in fewer defects and better user experiences.

- **Enhanced collaboration:** Breaking down silos between development, testing, and operations fosters a culture of collaboration, leading to more aligned objectives and shared accountability for software quality.

The evolution toward autonomous testing frameworks powered by AI promises to transform how software is developed, tested, and deployed. These frameworks can significantly reduce the gap between development, testing, and operations by enabling self-learning capabilities that continuously evolve based on feedback from production environments. Organizations embracing this future will benefit from improved testing efficiency, enhanced software quality, and more agile development processes. Ultimately, the integration of self-learning test automation frameworks represents a critical step toward achieving the goals of DevOps and continuous delivery in today's fast-paced software landscape.

Conclusion

Integrating AI and ML into test automation frameworks marks a transformative shift in how software testing is approached. These technologies empower teams to tackle persistent challenges such as flaky tests, inefficient test case generation, and burdensome maintenance tasks. By leveraging AI and ML, organizations can enhance test stability, streamline testing processes, and improve overall efficiency. The capabilities offered by these technologies, from predictive analytics to self-learning frameworks, enable teams to proactively identify potential issues and continuously adapt their testing strategies to meet the evolving demands of modern software development.

As we stand at the forefront of this AI-driven testing revolution, teams must embrace these emerging technologies and integrate them into their testing practices. The long-term benefits of intelligent testing extend far beyond immediate gains; they include reduced technical debt, increased test reliability, and more efficient CI/CD processes. By committing to this journey, organizations position themselves to deliver higher-quality software at a faster pace, ultimately enhancing user satisfaction and business success. Now is the time to harness the power of AI and ML in testing, paving the way for a future of smarter, more resilient software delivery.

In the next chapter, we will look at some additional emerging trends and technologies that are having an impact on the world of test automation.

Key takeaways

Here are some of the key benefits that AI offers the software testing world:

- **Significance of AI and ML in test automation**: AI/ML enhances test automation by reducing manual effort, improving accuracy, predicting failures, and optimizing test execution, leading to faster and more reliable testing cycles.

- **AI-driven test case generation**: AI can automatically analyze application changes, user behavior, and past defects to generate high-value test cases, improving test coverage while minimizing redundant tests.

- **AI-powered test case selection**: ML models prioritize critical test cases based on risk assessment, historical failures, and code changes, ensuring optimized and efficient test execution.

- **Intelligent test execution**: AI dynamically adjusts test execution by identifying high-risk areas, skipping unnecessary tests, and reordering execution for maximum efficiency.

- **ML algorithms for flaky test detection**: Machine learning identifies patterns in flaky tests by analyzing historical test failures, environment dependencies, and execution trends, helping teams address root causes proactively.

- **Continuous monitoring for flaky tests**: AI-driven monitoring tracks and detects flaky tests in real time, allowing teams to classify, quarantine, or resolve them before they impact development.

- **Reducing maintenance overhead**: AI-powered tools automatically update and heal tests when UI changes occur, reducing test failures due to minor application updates and lowering maintenance costs.

- **Handling environment-specific issues**: AI can detect environment-related failures by analyzing execution patterns across different environments, helping teams pinpoint and resolve environment-specific flakiness.

- **Advanced analytics and reporting**: AI-driven analytics provide real-time insights, failure trend analysis, and root cause detection, enabling data-driven decision-making for test automation strategies.

- **Improving code quality and stability**: AI enhances static code analysis, identifies risky code changes, and improves defect prediction, leading to higher code stability and better software quality.

Exercises

1. What challenges in your test automation process could AI/ML help address?
2. How can AI help you generate test cases based on user behavior or defect trends?
3. How can AI improve your test coverage without increasing test redundancy?
4. What data sources (logs, past defects, analytics) can you use to train AI for better test case generation?
5. How can AI help you select test cases based on risk, impact, and change history?
6. What KPIs can you track to measure the effectiveness of AI-powered test selection?
7. How can AI help us optimize test execution order for faster feedback?
8. How can you leverage AI to skip redundant or unnecessary tests dynamically?
9. How do we ensure AI-driven test execution aligns with our CI/CD pipeline?
10. What historical test execution data do you have that AI can analyze for flaky test patterns?
11. Do you have a system for tracking and categorizing flaky tests?
12. How can AI insights improve test reliability over time?
13. How much time is spent maintaining test scripts due to application changes?
14. How can AI help you with self-healing tests to reduce manual maintenance efforts?
15. How can AI help track test trends and predict failures before they occur?
16. What additional insights can AI-driven analytics provide beyond traditional test reports?
17. How can AI help detect code changes likely to introduce defects?
18. How do you measure the impact of AI-based code analysis on software stability?

## CHAPTER 16

Emerging Trends and Technologies

Introduction

In this chapter, we will explore many emerging technologies and some key strategies that can be applied to effectively test them. We will discuss some of the reasons why the pace of acceleration in the software realm is increasing—things we can do as software professionals to keep abreast with this pace of change, and then look at each technology in more detail, integrating a lot of the concepts already discussed into the process.

Structure

In this chapter, we will go over the following topics:

- Emerging trends in test automation
- Future tools and technologies shaping test automation
- Low-code and no-code animation tools
- Cloud-based test automation platforms
- Serverless architecture
- Containerized applications and Kubernetes
- Shift towards API-centric testing
- GraphQL and other API technologies
- Blockchain and decentralized applications
- Testing in DevOps and continuous delivery
- Shift-left and shift-right testing
- Key challenges in adopting emerging technologies
- Embracing new testing paradigms

Objectives

By the end of this chapter, the reader will learn about many of the recent and upcoming trends that are making a big impact on how we build and test software. We will then explore each of these areas in detail, unpack what testing challenges they bring, and, most importantly, how we potentially solve those problems through our frameworks.

Emerging trends in test automation

Let us understand the various emerging trends in test automation:

- **Accelerating pace of innovation in test automation:** The evolution of test automation is being propelled by a confluence of modern architectures, DevOps practices, and emerging technologies like **artificial intelligence (AI)**, **machine learning (ML)**, and cloud computing. This rapid transformation necessitates a proactive approach to ensure that test automation frameworks remain adaptable, relevant, and capable of meeting the evolving demands of development teams.

- **Shift towards microservices architectures:** Modern software architectures, such as microservices and serverless computing, introduce new complexities and challenges for testing. These architectures require shifting from traditional monolithic testing approaches to more flexible and modular testing strategies. Test automation frameworks must adapt to support **continuous integration and continuous delivery (CI/CD)** pipelines, enabling teams to run automated tests at various stages of the development lifecycle. The ability to execute tests in real time and various environments is critical to catching issues early and maintaining software quality.

- **Role of DevOps practices:** The adoption of DevOps practices emphasizes collaboration, integration, and automation across development and operations teams. Test automation is increasingly seen as a crucial component of this ecosystem, facilitating seamless feedback loops and ensuring that testing is integrated into the development process. As organizations strive for faster release cycles, test automation frameworks must evolve to provide quick, reliable feedback on code changes. This requires not only robust automation tools but also a cultural shift that prioritizes quality at every stage of development.

- **Harnessing AI and ML in test automation:** Emerging technologies, particularly AI and ML, are reshaping the landscape of test automation. These technologies offer the potential to enhance test effectiveness through predictive analytics and intelligent test case generation. By leveraging historical data, machine learning algorithms can identify patterns of test failures, predict potential issues, and suggest improvements to test coverage. This proactive approach to testing saves time and resources and improves the software's overall quality.

- **Impact of cloud computing:** Cloud computing is another transformative force in test automation. The cloud provides scalable resources that allow teams to run extensive test suites in parallel, significantly reducing execution times. Moreover, cloud-based testing environments enable organizations to simulate real-world scenarios more effectively, ensuring that applications perform well under varying loads and conditions. As organizations embrace cloud-native architectures, test automation frameworks must be designed to operate seamlessly within these environments, ensuring compatibility and efficiency.

- **Staying ahead of trends:** To remain competitive in this rapidly evolving landscape, organizations must prioritize continuous learning and adaptation in their test automation strategies. Staying abreast of industry trends, investing in new tools and technologies, and fostering a culture of innovation are essential to keeping test automation frameworks relevant. Organizations should also focus on creating modular, flexible architectures that allow for easy integration of new technologies as they emerge.

The accelerating pace of software development innovation presents challenges and opportunities for test automation. As modern architectures, DevOps practices, and emerging technologies reshape the landscape, it is crucial for organizations to adapt their test automation frameworks proactively. By embracing change and investing in the latest technologies, organizations can ensure that their test automation efforts remain effective, efficient, and aligned with the demands of the evolving software landscape. In doing so, they can enhance the quality of their software and accelerate their overall development processes, ensuring long-term success in an increasingly competitive market.

Overview of key trends in test automation

As the software development landscape continues to evolve, several key trends are emerging that will significantly shape the future of test automation. This chapter explores the innovative tools, methodologies, and practices that are driving these changes and emphasizes the need for test frameworks to evolve in response to the demands of next-generation software systems. Let us go over some of them now:

- **Shift to AI-driven testing:** As mentioned previously, AI and ML are revolutionizing test automation by enabling intelligent testing processes. AI-driven testing tools can analyze vast amounts of data to predict potential failure points, optimize test cases, and adjust testing strategies based on real-time feedback. This allows for more efficient test planning and execution, ultimately enhancing software quality and reducing time-to-market.

- **Increased emphasis on continuous testing:** Continuous testing has become essential for ensuring software quality throughout the development lifecycle with the rise of DevOps and agile methodologies. Test automation frameworks must evolve to facilitate CI/CD practices, allowing for automated tests to be executed at every stage of development. This shift emphasizes the need for frameworks that support rapid feedback loops and enable teams to identify and resolve issues quickly.

- **Integration of test automation with DevOps tools:** As organizations adopt DevOps practices, the integration of test automation with other DevOps tools becomes increasingly important. Test frameworks must seamlessly integrate with version control systems, build tools, and deploy pipelines. This integration enhances collaboration between development, testing, and operations teams, streamlining the software delivery process and improving overall quality.

- **Cloud-native testing solutions:** The adoption of cloud computing is transforming how applications are developed, deployed, and tested. Cloud-native testing solutions offer scalable, flexible testing environments across diverse platforms and configurations. Test automation frameworks must adapt to leverage cloud resources effectively, allowing for parallel test execution, better resource management, and the ability to simulate real-world scenarios.

- **Focus on test data management:** Effective test data management is critical for ensuring the reliability of automated tests. As applications become more complex, the need for accurate and representative test data grows. Organizations must implement strategies to create, manage, and protect test data while ensuring compliance with data regulations. Test frameworks should evolve to include robust data management capabilities, enabling teams to simulate various scenarios and validate application behavior under different conditions.

- **Shift towards BDD:** BDD promotes collaboration between technical and non-technical stakeholders by focusing on the software's desired behavior. Test automation frameworks must support BDD methodologies by allowing teams to write tests in natural language, making them accessible to all stakeholders. This shift enhances communication and ensures that automated tests align closely with business requirements.

- **Adoption of no-code and low-code testing tools:** As organizations seek to empower non-technical team members to contribute to testing efforts, no-code and low-code testing tools are gaining popularity. These tools enable users to create and execute automated tests without extensive programming knowledge, democratizing access to test automation. Test frameworks must incorporate user-friendly interfaces and functionalities to facilitate this trend while maintaining the robustness of automated testing.

- **Focus on security testing:** With the increasing prevalence of cyber threats, security testing has become a crucial component of software quality assurance. Test automation frameworks need to evolve to incorporate security testing practices, such as automated vulnerability scanning and penetration testing. Integrating security testing into the CI/CD pipeline ensures that security vulnerabilities are identified and addressed early in development.

The landscape of test automation is rapidly changing, driven by key trends such as AI-driven testing, continuous testing, and the integration of cloud-native solutions. As software systems become increasingly complex and the demands for speed and quality rise, test automation frameworks must evolve to meet these challenges. By embracing innovative tools and methodologies, organizations can ensure that their test automation efforts remain effective, efficient, and aligned with the future of software development. This evolution will enhance the quality of software products and empower teams to deliver value more rapidly in an ever-changing technological landscape.

Future tools and technologies shaping test automation

The integration of advanced AI and ML algorithms is revolutionizing testing. These technologies provide innovative solutions for enhancing test automation efficiency, accuracy, and adaptability. This section explores the capabilities of AI-driven tools that enable self-healing tests, predictive failure detection, and intelligent test case generation. Let us go over some advanced AI and ML algorithms-driven testing tools:

- **Self-healing tests:** One of the most significant advancements in AI-driven testing is the development of self-healing tests. These tools utilize AI algorithms to automatically detect changes in the application under test and adjust the corresponding test cases accordingly. Self-healing capabilities significantly reduce the maintenance overhead associated with test automation, especially in dynamic environments where applications undergo frequent changes. Refer to the following:

  o **Reduced maintenance effort:** By automatically updating test scripts in response to changes in the application, teams can focus on new feature development rather than constantly maintaining existing tests.

  o **Increased reliability:** Self-healing tests ensure that automated tests remain functional even as the UI or functionality evolves, leading to fewer false negatives and improved test reliability.

- **Predictive failure detection:** AI and ML algorithms are also being utilized for predictive failure detection, allowing teams to anticipate potential issues before they occur. By analyzing historical test execution data, these tools can identify patterns associated with test failures, enabling proactive measures to be taken. Refer to the following:

  o **Early identification of risks:** Predictive analytics can highlight test cases likely to fail, allowing teams to address potential issues before they impact production.

  o **Improved test coverage:** By focusing on areas with a higher likelihood of failure, teams can optimize their testing efforts and enhance overall test coverage.

- **Intelligent test case generation:** Another groundbreaking application of AI in test automation is intelligent test case generation. AI-driven tools can analyze application requirements, user behavior, and historical test data to automatically generate test cases that cover a wide range of scenarios.

  o **Enhanced test coverage:** Automated test case generation ensures that more scenarios are covered, including edge cases that might be overlooked in manual testing.

  o **Faster test development:** By automating the test creation process, teams can accelerate their testing efforts, enabling faster feedback loops and reducing time-to-market.

The integration of advanced AI and ML algorithms into test automation is transforming how teams approach testing. Organizations can significantly enhance their testing processes, reduce maintenance overhead, and improve software quality by leveraging capabilities like self-healing tests, predictive failure detection, and intelligent test case generation. As these technologies continue to evolve, they will play an increasingly crucial role in shaping the future of test automation, enabling teams to deliver reliable, high-quality software faster than ever before.

Low-code and no-code automation tools

The shift towards low-code and no-code platforms marks a significant trend in test automation, democratizing the testing process and enabling a broader range of stakeholders, including non-technical testers and business users, to participate in creating automated test cases. The need for faster development cycles, increased collaboration, and the growing demand for quality assurance across all levels of an organization drives this trend.

Challenge of traditional test automation

Traditional test automation frameworks often require a strong background in programming and testing methodologies, which can be a barrier for many potential users. Some of the challenges include:

- **Skill gaps:** Organizations may struggle to find enough skilled testers who can write and maintain automated tests, leading to delays in testing efforts.

- **Dependency on technical teams:** Non-technical stakeholders often have valuable insights into business requirements but lack the technical skills to translate those insights into automated tests.

- **Inefficiencies:** The reliance on technical teams for test creation can slow down the testing process, leading to bottlenecks and ultimately impacting time-to-market.

Rise of low-code/no-code platforms

Low-code and no-code platforms are designed to simplify the creation of automated test cases by providing intuitive interfaces and pre-built, easily configured components. These platforms empower non-technical users to participate in testing, fostering collaboration, and enhancing productivity. Key characteristics include:

- **User-friendly interfaces:** Low-code/no-code platforms typically feature drag-and-drop interfaces, visual workflows, and guided setups, making it easy for users to create tests without extensive coding knowledge.

- **Reusable components:** These platforms often provide libraries of pre-built test components and templates that users can leverage, allowing for quicker test case creation and reducing redundancy.

- **Collaboration tools:** Many low-code/no-code platforms include built-in collaboration features, enabling teams to work together in real time, share insights, and refine test cases based on collective feedback.

Benefits of accessibility in test automation

The trend towards accessibility in test automation offers several advantages for organizations:

- **Empowered teams:** By enabling non-technical testers and business users to create automated tests, organizations can harness the collective expertise of diverse team members, leading to more comprehensive testing coverage.

- **Faster test creation:** Low-code/no-code platforms accelerate the process of test case creation, allowing organizations to respond more swiftly to changing requirements and market demands.

- **Improved test quality:** When business users are involved in the testing process, tests are more likely to reflect actual user scenarios and requirements, resulting in higher-quality software.

- **Reduced bottlenecks:** With non-technical users able to create and maintain their tests, the dependency on technical teams is reduced, leading to a more streamlined and efficient testing process.

The trend towards accessibility in test automation through low-code and no-code platforms is reshaping how organizations approach testing. Organizations can enhance collaboration, improve test quality, and accelerate the testing process by empowering non-technical testers and business users to create automated test cases without complex coding requirements. As these platforms evolve, they will be crucial in democratizing testing efforts, enabling teams to deliver high-quality software more efficiently and effectively in an increasingly fast-paced development environment. Embracing this trend will not only streamline testing but also foster a culture of quality across the entire organization.

Benefits for speed and efficiency with low-code/no-code tools

The emergence of low-code and no-code tools in test automation is revolutionizing the way teams collaborate and execute testing processes. By providing a user-friendly platform that allows non-technical users to create automated test cases, these tools significantly enhance the speed and efficiency of testing efforts. This section outlines the following key benefits that low-code/no-code tools bring to the table, particularly in terms of collaboration, accessibility, and overall efficiency:

- **Enhanced collaboration among stakeholders:** Low-code and no-code tools facilitate improved collaboration between **quality assurance (QA)** teams, developers, and business stakeholders by providing a shared platform for test creation and execution. Key aspects include:

  o **Shared understanding:** These tools enable all stakeholders, regardless of technical expertise, to contribute to the testing process. This shared involvement fosters a common understanding of testing goals, requirements, and challenges.

  o **Real-time feedback:** With user-friendly interfaces, stakeholders can collaborate in real-time, making it easy to provide feedback and make adjustments to test cases as necessary. This immediate feedback loop helps catch potential issues early in the development cycle.

  o **Cross-functional teams:** Low-code/no-code platforms encourage the formation of cross-functional teams, where members from different disciplines work together, leveraging their unique insights to create more robust and relevant test cases.

- **Accelerated test automation processes:** The speed at which test cases can be created, executed, and maintained is significantly enhanced by using low-code/no-code tools. Key benefits include:

  o **Faster test creation:** Non-technical users can quickly design and implement automated tests using intuitive interfaces and pre-built components, reducing the time needed for test development.

  o **Streamlined maintenance:** With fewer technical barriers, test maintenance becomes more straightforward. Users can easily update or modify test cases in response to application changes without requiring extensive coding expertise, leading to faster iterations and less downtime.

  o **Quick adaptation to changes:** As business requirements evolve, teams can rapidly adjust their testing efforts. Low-code/no-code tools allow for swift modifications, enabling organizations to keep pace with changing needs without extensive delays.

- **Increased accessibility to automation:** By making automation tools accessible to a broader audience, low-code/no-code platforms enable organizations to overcome traditional barriers associated with test automation. Key points include:

  o **Empowerment of non-technical users:** Business stakeholders and non-technical testers can actively participate in the automation process, leading to greater diversity in test scenarios and enhanced test coverage.

  o **Reduced dependency on specialized skills:** With easier-to-use tools, organizations are less reliant on specialized technical skills, which can often be a bottleneck in the testing process. This allows teams to focus on strategic initiatives rather than getting bogged down by technical constraints.

o **Inclusive testing environment:** By democratizing access to test automation, organizations foster a culture where everyone feels empowered to contribute to quality assurance efforts, leading to improved morale and collaboration.

- **Improved efficiency in release cycles:** The cumulative benefits of enhanced collaboration, accelerated test automation processes, and increased accessibility improve overall efficiency in software release cycles. Key advantages include:

o **Faster time-to-market:** With more stakeholders involved in test automation and faster test creation and maintenance, organizations can release software updates and new features more quickly, staying ahead of competitors.

o **Higher quality software:** Improved collaboration and comprehensive test coverage result in fewer defects reaching production, leading to higher-quality software and enhanced user satisfaction.

o **Resource optimization:** By streamlining testing efforts and reducing the time spent on manual testing and maintenance, teams can reallocate resources to focus on more strategic activities, such as exploring new features or improving user experience.

The benefits of low-code and no-code tools in test automation extend far beyond ease of use. By enhancing collaboration among QA teams, developers, and business stakeholders, these tools significantly improve the speed and efficiency of the automation process. Organizations can leverage these platforms to create a more inclusive testing environment, accelerate release cycles, and ultimately deliver higher-quality software faster. As the demand for rapid development and deployment continues to grow, embracing low-code/no-code solutions will be crucial for organizations seeking to enhance their testing capabilities and maintain a competitive edge in the market.

Cloud-based test automation platforms

In today's fast-paced software development landscape, the ability to scale testing processes and maintain flexibility is crucial for organizations striving to deliver high-quality software efficiently. Cloud-based testing environments have emerged as a powerful solution, allowing teams to run tests at scale without the overhead of managing physical infrastructure. This section explores the key benefits of using cloud-based testing environments and their impact on scalability and flexibility in test automation, such as:

- **On-demand resource allocation:** Cloud-based testing environments offer the unique advantage of on-demand resource allocation, which is vital for accommodating varying testing needs:

o **Dynamic resource management:** Teams can quickly scale their testing infrastructure up or down based on project requirements. This dynamic allocation allows organizations to manage resources effectively, ensuring that they only pay for what they use.

o **Instant access to multiple environments:** Cloud platforms provide access to a wide array of testing environments, including different browsers, operating systems, and device configurations. This access enables teams to perform comprehensive testing across various platforms without the need for physical hardware.

- **Cost efficiency:** By leveraging cloud-based testing environments, organizations can significantly reduce costs associated with traditional testing infrastructure:

o **Elimination of infrastructure management:** Cloud testing eliminates the need for teams to invest in and maintain physical servers, reducing both capital expenditure and operational overhead.

o **Pay-as-you-go model:** Many cloud testing services operate on a pay-as-you-go basis, allowing organizations to manage their budgets more effectively and scale their testing efforts based on demand without incurring fixed costs.

- **Faster test execution and feedback:** Cloud-based environments facilitate faster test execution, enabling teams to obtain results quickly and iterate more effectively:

o **Parallel testing capabilities:** With access to multiple virtual machines, teams can run tests in parallel across various configurations. This capability drastically reduces testing time and accelerates feedback loops, allowing for quicker issue identification.

o **CI/CD support:** Cloud-based testing environments integrate seamlessly with CI/CD pipelines, allowing teams to execute tests automatically with each code change. This integration ensures that feedback is provided early and often, promoting a more agile development process.

- **Improved collaboration and remote accessibility:** The cloud-based nature of these testing environments enhances collaboration and accessibility for distributed teams:

  o **Collaboration across geographies:** Teams can collaborate in real-time, regardless of their physical location. Cloud testing platforms often provide shared access to test environments and results, fostering teamwork and communication.

  o **Remote access to testing tools:** As organizations increasingly adopt remote work policies, cloud-based testing environments allow testers and developers to access tools and resources from anywhere, ensuring continuity and productivity.

- **Enhanced testing capabilities:** Cloud-based environments expand the testing capabilities available to teams, allowing for more thorough and effective testing strategies:

  o **Access to latest tools and technologies:** Cloud platforms often offer the latest testing tools and technologies, enabling teams to stay current with industry trends and innovations. This access allows organizations to leverage advanced features, such as AI-driven testing, without requiring significant upfront investments.

  o **Scalability for performance testing:** For performance testing, cloud-based environments provide the ability to simulate a large number of users and transactions, offering insights into how applications perform under load. This scalability is crucial for ensuring that applications can handle real-world usage effectively.

Cloud-based testing environments play a pivotal role in enhancing the scalability and flexibility of test automation processes, as cloud providers like AWS, Axure or Google can all create ephemeral testing spaces that better replicate that of production. By providing on-demand access to various testing configurations and eliminating the need for infrastructure management, these environments empower teams to run tests at scale while optimizing costs and resources. The benefits of faster test execution, improved collaboration, and access to advanced tools make cloud-based testing essential to modern software development practices. As organizations continue to embrace digital transformation, leveraging cloud-based solutions will be vital for maintaining a competitive edge in the ever-evolving software landscape.

Integration with CI/CD pipelines

The integration of cloud-based testing environments with CI/CD pipelines is revolutionizing the **software development lifecycle** (**SDLC**). By streamlining testing processes and enabling rapid feedback, these integrations facilitate faster and more reliable software releases. This section discusses how cloud-based platforms support CI/CD practices, the benefits of such integrations, and their impact on overall software quality:

- **Seamless integration with CI/CD tools:** Cloud-based testing platforms are designed to integrate effortlessly with popular CI/CD tools, enhancing the efficiency of development workflows:

  o **Automated test execution:** Cloud testing environments can automatically trigger test execution whenever changes are pushed to the code repository. This automation ensures that tests are run continuously throughout the development process, providing immediate feedback to developers.

  o **Compatibility with various CI/CD tools:** Many cloud-based testing platforms support a wide range of CI/CD tools (for example, Jenkins, GitLab CI, CircleCI) and frameworks, allowing teams to incorporate testing seamlessly into their existing workflows.

- **Accelerated feedback cycles:** Integrating cloud-based testing with CI/CD pipelines enables teams to obtain faster feedback, leading to improved development agility:

  o **Rapid detection of issues:** With automated tests running continuously, developers receive immediate feedback on the impact of their changes. This rapid detection of issues allows teams to address defects early in the development cycle, minimizing the cost and effort of fixing bugs.

  o **Shortened release cycles:** Faster feedback cycles contribute to shorter release cycles, allowing organizations to quickly deliver features and fixes to users. This agility is crucial in today's competitive software landscape, with high user expectations.

- **Parallel test execution across multiple environments:** Cloud-based platforms facilitate parallel test execution across various environments, significantly enhancing testing efficiency:

  - **Simultaneous testing:** By leveraging the cloud's scalable infrastructure, teams can run tests in parallel on multiple configurations, such as different browsers, operating systems, and devices. This parallelism helps ensure comprehensive test coverage without extending the overall testing timeline.

  - **Performance testing:** For performance and load testing, cloud-based environments can simulate a large number of users across multiple instances, enabling teams to assess how applications perform under stress and ensuring reliability at scale.

- **Improved collaboration and transparency:** Integration with CI/CD pipelines enhances collaboration and transparency among team members, fostering a culture of quality:

  o **Shared visibility:** Cloud-based testing platforms often provide dashboards and reporting features that allow all team members to monitor test results and performance metrics in real time. This visibility promotes accountability and encourages proactive problem-solving.

  o **Cross-functional collaboration:** With integrated testing processes, developers, QA teams, and operations can work more closely together, ensuring that quality assurance is a shared responsibility throughout the development lifecycle.

- **Scalability and flexibility:** The scalability of cloud-based platforms complements the flexibility of CI/CD practices, making it easier for teams to adapt to changing project needs:

  o **Dynamic resource allocation:** As project demands fluctuate, cloud-based testing environments can scale resources up or down based on testing requirements. This dynamic capability ensures that teams can maintain testing efficiency without physical infrastructure limitations.

  o **Ease of integration for new tools:** As organizations evolve and adopt new technologies, cloud-based platforms make integrating additional testing tools and frameworks into CI/CD pipelines easier, supporting continuous innovation and improvement.

The integration of cloud-based testing environments with CI/CD pipelines is a game-changer for modern software development. By enabling seamless automated test execution, accelerating feedback cycles, and facilitating parallel execution across multiple environments, these integrations enhance testing processes' overall efficiency and effectiveness. As organizations strive for faster, higher-quality releases, leveraging cloud-based platforms for CI/CD integration will be essential for maintaining a competitive advantage and ensuring that software meets the demands of users and stakeholders alike.

Serverless architectures

The rise of serverless computing has transformed the way applications are developed, deployed, and maintained. By abstracting the underlying infrastructure, serverless architectures allow developers to focus on writing code without worrying about server management. However, this shift introduces unique challenges for testing frameworks, which must evolve to accommodate the stateless, event-driven nature of serverless applications. This section explores the implications of serverless computing on testing practices and outlines the necessary adaptations for testing frameworks.

In a serverless architecture, applications are composed of microservices that respond to events and run in stateless environments. This model provides several benefits, including automatic scaling, reduced operational overhead, and cost efficiency. However, it also necessitates rethinking testing strategies, as traditional testing methods may not align with serverless applications' event-driven and ephemeral nature.

Challenges in testing serverless applications

Testing serverless applications presents several challenges that must be addressed by modern testing frameworks, such as:

- **Statelessness:** Serverless functions do not maintain state between executions, making it essential to design tests that validate behavior without relying on persistent data.

- **Event-driven architecture:** Serverless applications often rely on events to trigger functions, requiring testing frameworks to simulate and validate these events effectively.

- **Limited execution context:** Serverless functions typically have a limited execution duration and memory allocation, necessitating lightweight testing approaches that align with these constraints.

- **Integration complexity:** Serverless applications often interact with multiple external services (for example, databases, APIs, cloud services), making it crucial to test these integrations thoroughly while managing dependencies.

Evolving testing frameworks for serverless applications

To effectively test serverless applications, testing frameworks must adapt in several key areas:

- **Event simulation and triggering:** Frameworks should provide capabilities to simulate event triggers that invoke serverless functions. This includes support for testing various event types (for example, HTTP requests, message queues, scheduled events) and validating the expected outcomes. Testing frameworks can leverage tools like AWS **Serverless Application Model (SAM)** or the Serverless Framework to create local environments that simulate cloud functions and events.

- **Stateless testing strategies:** Test designs must focus on validating the outputs of serverless functions given specific inputs without relying on retained state. This may involve mocking dependencies and ensuring that each test is self-contained. Using techniques like contract testing can help ensure that the interactions between serverless functions and external services adhere to defined contracts, enabling reliable integration testing.

- **Performance and load testing:** Testing frameworks should incorporate performance testing capabilities to assess how serverless functions behave under various loads. This includes simulating high-traffic scenarios and measuring response times to ensure that functions can scale effectively. Tools like Artillery or k6 can be integrated into testing frameworks to facilitate load testing of serverless applications.

- **Monitoring and observability:** Integrating monitoring and observability tools into testing frameworks is essential for understanding the behavior of serverless applications during testing. This includes capturing logs, metrics, and traces to diagnose issues effectively. Utilizing cloud-native monitoring solutions (for example, AWS CloudWatch, Azure Monitor) can help teams gain insights into function performance and troubleshoot problems in real-time.

Best practices for testing serverless applications

To maximize the effectiveness of testing in a serverless environment, teams should adopt the following best practices. These have been mentioned previously in other chapters, but will briefly just highlight them here as they are especially relevant to the serverless world:

- **Shift left testing:** Incorporate testing early in the development lifecycle to identify issues sooner. This includes unit testing serverless functions and using automated testing tools in CI/CD pipelines.

- **Use mocks and stubs:** Leverage mocking and stubbing to simulate external dependencies, allowing for focused testing of serverless functions in isolation.

- **Implement continuous testing:** Automate tests as part of the CI/CD process, ensuring that every code change is validated through automated tests that simulate serverless environments and event triggers.

As serverless computing continues to gain traction, testing frameworks must evolve to handle the unique challenges presented by this architecture effectively. By adapting to the stateless, event-driven nature of serverless applications and implementing best practices for testing, teams can ensure the reliability and performance of their serverless solutions. Embracing these changes will enable organizations to fully leverage the benefits of serverless computing while maintaining high-quality software delivery.

Key focus areas for testing in a serverless world

As serverless architectures become increasingly prevalent, it is essential to identify the key focus areas for testing these applications. Given their unique characteristics, particularly their statelessness and event-driven nature, testing methodologies must adapt to ensure reliability and performance. The following are the critical focus areas in testing serverless applications:

- **API testing:** APIs are central to serverless applications, facilitating communication between various microservices and external systems. Robust API testing ensures these interactions are functioning as intended and meet performance expectations. The key considerations are:

  o **Endpoint validation:** Test all API endpoints to ensure they return the expected responses for various inputs. This includes testing both successful and error scenarios.

  o **Security testing:** Validate authentication and authorization mechanisms to protect sensitive data, and only authorized users can access the API.

  o **Contract testing:** Implement contract testing to ensure that the API specifications are adhered to by all services consuming or providing the API. This helps avoid breaking changes that could impact integrations.

  o **Integration testing:** Test how the API interacts with other services and components to ensure seamless data flow and functionality.

- **Performance testing:** Performance is a critical aspect of serverless applications, particularly due to the nature of cold starts and varying workloads. Performance testing helps identify bottlenecks and ensures that the application can handle the expected load. The key considerations are:

  o **Latency testing:** Measure the response times of serverless functions under normal and peak load conditions. This includes testing for various user scenarios to ensure that performance remains consistent.

  o **Cold start analysis:** Cold starts occur when a serverless function is invoked after being idle. Testing should evaluate the impact of cold starts on response times and user experience. Understanding how different deployment configurations affect cold start times can guide optimizations.

  o **Load testing:** Simulate high traffic conditions to ensure the serverless application can scale effectively. This testing helps determine how many concurrent users the system can handle without performance degradation.

  o **Scalability testing:** Assess how the application scales in response to increased workloads. This includes evaluating the ability to manage increased requests and the effectiveness of auto-scaling mechanisms.

- **Validation of event triggers:** In a serverless architecture, functions are often triggered by events, such as HTTP requests, database changes, or messages from a queue. Validating these event triggers is crucial to ensure that the correct functions execute as intended in response to specific events. The key considerations are:

  o **Event simulation:** Create tests that simulate various events to ensure that functions trigger correctly and produce the expected outcomes. This can involve testing both successful events and edge cases that may lead to failures.

  o **Event data validation:** Verify that the data passed with events is accurate and complete. This includes checking for correct formatting and required fields.

  o **Error handling:** Test how functions respond to erroneous events or unexpected input. This helps ensure that functions can gracefully handle errors and provide meaningful feedback.

  o **Order of events:** In some cases, the order in which events are processed can impact functionality. Testing should include scenarios that validate the order of event processing.

Focusing on API testing, performance testing, and validation of event triggers is essential for ensuring the reliability and efficiency of serverless applications. By addressing these key areas, testing teams can effectively mitigate risks associated with serverless architectures, ensuring that applications perform optimally in production environments. As the landscape of software development continues to evolve, embracing these focus areas will be critical for organizations aiming to maximize the benefits of serverless computing.

Testing Lambda functions on AWS

AWS Lambda functions are a prime example of serverless computing, allowing developers to run code without provisioning or managing servers. As organizations adopt AWS Lambda for building event-driven applications, it becomes essential to implement robust testing orchestration that validates event invocations and ensures data integrity across distributed components. This section outlines key aspects of testing AWS Lambda functions, focusing on orchestration, event validation, and data integrity.

Testing orchestration for Lambda functions

Orchestration involves coordinating multiple Lambda functions and services to achieve specific workflows or business processes. Effective testing orchestration ensures that each component behaves as expected and interacts correctly with others. Let us understand more about it:

- **Workflow testing:** When multiple Lambda functions are chained together, it is crucial to test the entire workflow to ensure that each function triggers the next as intended. This involves:

  o **Sequential invocation:** Testing the flow of data and control between functions to verify that outputs from one function are valid inputs to the next.

  o **Error handling:** Ensuring that the workflow can gracefully handle errors or exceptions, such as retry logic for failed invocations or fallback mechanisms.

- **Testing event sources:** Lambda functions can be triggered by various AWS services, such as S3, DynamoDB, API Gateway, or SNS. Testing orchestration must validate that:

  o **Event triggers work:** Ensure that events from the source services trigger the Lambda functions as expected.

  o **Multiple event sources**: If multiple event sources trigger a Lambda function, test each scenario to ensure the function behaves correctly for all events.

Validating event invocations

Event validation is a critical component of testing Lambda functions. It ensures that functions are invoked correctly, and they can process incoming events as intended. Refer to the following:

- **Mocking events:** During testing, create mock event payloads that simulate real events from AWS services. This can include:

    o **S3 event notifications:** Testing Lambda functions triggered by file uploads to S3 by mocking the event structure that S3 sends.

    o **API gateway requests:** Simulating HTTP requests to test Lambda functions behind API Gateway, including headers, query parameters, and body content.

- **Unit testing:** Implement unit tests for each Lambda function to validate its logic independently. These tests should:

    o **Validate input handling:** Ensure the function can correctly handle various input scenarios, including valid, invalid, and edge case inputs.

    o **Assert outputs:** Check that the function returns the expected output based on the input, ensuring proper data transformation and processing.

Ensuring data integrity across distributed components

Maintaining data integrity across distributed components is essential in serverless architectures, especially when multiple Lambda functions interact with databases or external services. Refer to the following:

- **Data consistency checks:** Implement tests that verify data consistency after various operations. This includes:

    o **Transactional integrity:** Ensuring that updates to databases or external services reflect the expected state after Lambda function executions.

    o **Data validation:** After processing an event, check that the resulting data is correct and meets defined schema requirements.

- **Integration testing:** Conduct integration tests to assess how Lambda functions interact with other services, including:

    o **Database interactions:** Test the read and write operations on databases like DynamoDB or RDS to confirm that data is stored and retrieved accurately.

    o **External API calls:** Validate interactions with external APIs, ensuring that the Lambda function handles responses correctly and that any necessary error handling is in place.

Testing AWS Lambda functions requires a comprehensive approach encompassing testing orchestration, validating event invocations, and ensuring data integrity across distributed components. By focusing on these aspects, teams can build robust and reliable serverless applications that meet business requirements while maintaining high-quality standards. Implementing thorough testing strategies is vital to mitigating risks associated with event-driven architectures and maximizing the benefits of serverless computing.

Containerized applications and Kubernetes

The rapid adoption of containerization technologies, such as Docker, and orchestration tools like Kubernetes has transformed how applications are developed, deployed, and tested. Test automation frameworks must evolve to effectively support dynamic, ephemeral environments where components can scale rapidly. This section explores the significance of test automation in containerized environments and the key challenges that arise.

Importance of test automation in containerized environments

Containerization provides a lightweight and consistent way to deploy applications across various environments. Teams can ensure that code behaves consistently from development to production by encapsulating applications and their dependencies in containers. This consistency makes it crucial to implement test automation strategies that align with the containerized architecture. Let us now understand the importance of test automation in containerized environments:

- **Scalability:** Containerized applications often consist of numerous microservices that can scale independently. Automated testing helps verify that each component functions correctly under various load conditions. This includes testing the system's behavior when new instances of a service are instantiated and when instances are terminated.

- **Rapid feedback loops:** CI/CD pipelines benefit from automated tests that validate container images before they are deployed. This rapid feedback helps catch issues early in the development lifecycle, reducing time to market.

Key challenges in test automation for containerized environments

While the benefits of test automation in containerized environments are significant, several challenges must be addressed to ensure effective testing:

- **Managing test environments:**
  - o **Dynamic nature:** Containerized environments are highly dynamic, with containers being created, destroyed, and scaled based on demand. Managing these ephemeral environments can complicate the setup and teardown of test environments.
  - o **Environment parity:** Ensuring that testing environments closely mimic production environments is essential for accurate test results. However, variations in container configurations, service versions, and dependencies can lead to discrepancies.
  - o **Test data management:** Maintaining consistent and reliable test data across various containers and environments can be challenging. Strategies must be implemented to seed, reset, and manage test data effectively.

- **Handling network complexities:**
  - o **Microservices interactions:** Containerized applications typically consist of multiple microservices communicating over a network. Testing must account for the complexities of service-to-service communication, including potential network latency and failure scenarios.
  - o **Service discovery:** In dynamic environments, services may change locations frequently. Test frameworks need to handle service discovery to ensure tests can locate and interact with the appropriate service instances.
  - o **Fault tolerance testing:** Automated tests should simulate network failures and latency to validate how the application behaves under adverse conditions, ensuring it can gracefully handle issues like service unavailability or timeouts.

- **Orchestrating tests across microservices:**
  - o **Coordinating dependencies:** When testing microservices that depend on each other, it is crucial to ensure that tests are executed in the correct order and that all dependencies are satisfied. This orchestration can be complex in containerized environments where services can be scaled independently.
  - o **Parallel execution:** Automated tests should leverage the scalability of containerized environments to execute tests in parallel, reducing overall testing time. However, this requires careful management of shared resources to avoid contention and conflicts.
  - o **Observability and monitoring:** Implementing robust logging and monitoring solutions is vital for understanding test execution and diagnosing failures in containerized environments. This allows teams to gather insights into the health and performance of services during testing.

Test automation in containerized environments is essential for ensuring the reliability and performance of modern applications built with microservices architecture. While the adoption of containers and orchestration tools offers numerous benefits, it also introduces challenges related to managing dynamic environments, handling network complexities, and orchestrating tests across multiple services. By addressing these challenges with effective strategies and tools, teams can achieve successful test automation that supports the rapid development and deployment of containerized applications, ultimately enhancing software quality and accelerating time to market.

Integration with Kubernetes and CI/CD

The integration of testing frameworks with Kubernetes and CI/CD pipelines is crucial for modern software development. As organizations increasingly adopt containerized applications orchestrated by Kubernetes, testing frameworks must evolve to deploy and validate these applications in realistic, production-like environments. This section explores the significance of this integration and highlights key tools that facilitate seamless testing within containerized CI/CD workflows.

Importance of integration with Kubernetes

Kubernetes has become the de facto standard for container orchestration, providing a robust platform for deploying, scaling, and managing containerized applications. Integrating testing frameworks with Kubernetes offers several advantages:

- **Production-like environments:** Teams can replicate production conditions more accurately by deploying tests directly within Kubernetes clusters. This ensures that tests validate the application's behavior in environments resembling the final deployment scenario.

- **Dynamic resource management:** Kubernetes efficiently manages resources, allowing teams to scale their test environments up or down, based on demand. This capability enables automated tests to run in parallel, improving test execution speed and efficiency.

- **Isolation and independence:** Each test can run in its isolated environment, reducing the risk of interference between tests. This isolation is particularly beneficial in scenarios where tests need to interact with microservices or databases.

- **Easy rollback and recovery:** Kubernetes provides built-in mechanisms for rollbacks and recovery, which are invaluable during testing. If a test leads to issues, teams can quickly revert to previous versions of services or configurations.

Shift towards API-centric testing

As organizations increasingly adopt API-first approaches in their software development practices, the emphasis on API-centric testing has become crucial. This shift reflects the growing importance of APIs as foundational components of modern applications, enabling seamless interactions between various services and systems. Consequently, test automation frameworks must evolve to prioritize API testing, ensuring these critical interfaces' reliability, performance, and security.

Rise of API-first development

API-first development is a methodology that centers the design and development of applications around APIs from the outset. This approach promotes several benefits, such as:

- **Enhanced collaboration:** With an API-first focus, teams can work concurrently on different components (front-end, back-end, and integrations) without waiting for each other, fostering collaboration and speeding up the development process.

- **Improved user experience:** Well-defined APIs enable developers to create more responsive and dynamic user interfaces, leading to better overall user experiences.

- **Easier integration:** API-first design facilitates more straightforward integration with third-party services and applications, supporting a more interconnected ecosystem.

Importance of API testing

As the reliance on APIs grows, so does the need for robust testing strategies to ensure their functionality, security, and performance. Key reasons for emphasizing API testing include:

- **Reliability:** APIs often serve as the backbone of applications, and any failure can lead to significant disruptions. Testing ensures that APIs behave as expected under various conditions, including edge cases and error scenarios.

- **Performance:** APIs must handle varying loads efficiently. Performance testing helps identify bottlenecks and ensures that APIs can scale to meet user demands without degradation in response times.

- **Security:** APIs can be potential entry points for security vulnerabilities. Comprehensive security testing helps identify and mitigate unauthorized access, data leaks, and injection attacks.

Evolving test automation frameworks for API testing

To support the shift towards API-centric testing, test automation frameworks must incorporate several key features and methodologies, such as:

- **Comprehensive API test coverage:** Frameworks should enable users to create extensive test suites that cover various aspects of API functionality, including positive and negative test cases, response validation, and error handling.

- **Support for multiple protocols:** Modern applications often use multiple protocols (for example, REST, SOAP, GraphQL). Testing frameworks should support diverse protocols to ensure thorough validation of all APIs.

- **Integration with CI/CD pipelines:** To maintain agile development practices, API testing must be integrated into CI/CD pipelines, enabling automated tests to run with every code change. This ensures that all issues are identified early in the development cycle.

- **Collaboration and documentation:** API documentation is essential for developers and testers. Testing frameworks should facilitate collaboration by providing clear documentation and enabling the sharing of test cases among team members.

Tools for API testing

Several tools are available to support API-centric testing efforts, such as:

- **Postman:** A widely used tool for API development and testing, Postman allows users to create and execute API requests, organize tests into collections, and automate testing workflows. Its user-friendly interface makes it accessible to both technical and non-technical users.

- **SoapUI:** A comprehensive tool for testing SOAP and REST APIs, SoapUI offers advanced features for functional testing, performance testing, and security testing. It supports manual and automated testing, making it suitable for diverse testing scenarios.

- **Apache JMeter:** Primarily known for performance testing, JMeter can also be used for functional API testing. It allows users to create complex test scenarios and analyze API performance under different load conditions.

- **RestAssured:** A popular Java library for testing RESTful APIs, RestAssured provides a fluent API for writing tests in a straightforward manner. It simplifies the process of validating API responses and integrating tests into existing Java-based projects.

The shift towards API-centric testing is a vital aspect of modern software development, as organizations adopt API-first approaches. By emphasizing the importance of API reliability, performance, and security, test automation frameworks must evolve to address the unique challenges posed by APIs. Leveraging tools like Postman, SoapUI, JMeter, and RestAssured will empower teams to implement effective API testing strategies, ensuring the robustness and integrity of applications in an increasingly interconnected digital landscape.

GraphQL and other API technologies

The rapid evolution of APIs has introduced new paradigms, particularly with the adoption of GraphQL, which is fundamentally changing how data is queried and manipulated in applications. Unlike traditional REST APIs, which expose multiple endpoints for different resources, GraphQL provides a single endpoint that allows clients to specify exactly what data they need. This flexibility necessitates the development of specific testing strategies to ensure that these APIs function as intended and perform optimally.

Understanding GraphQL

GraphQL is a query language for APIs developed by Facebook in 2012 and released as an open-source project in 2015. It allows clients to request the data they need, reducing over-fetching and under-fetching of information. The key features of GraphQL include:

- **Single endpoint:** GraphQL operates on a single endpoint, simplifying client-server communication.

- **Flexible queries:** Clients can construct complex queries that fetch related resources in a single request, leading to more efficient data retrieval.

- **Strongly typed schema:** GraphQL uses a schema to define the structure of data, including types, queries, and mutations. This schema serves as a contract between the client and server.

Testing strategies for GraphQL APIs

The unique characteristics of GraphQL necessitate specific testing strategies that address its flexibility and complexity. Here are key areas to focus on when testing GraphQL APIs:

- **Schema validation:**
  - **Purpose:** Ensuring the GraphQL schema correctly defines and adheres to expected standards is crucial for maintaining data integrity and API usability.
  - **Testing strategies:**
    - **Schema introspection:** Use introspection queries to verify that the schema is as expected and contains the necessary types, queries, and mutations.
    - **Validation tests:** Implement tests to check that queries and mutations conform to the schema, ensuring clients can only request valid data.

- **Complex query testing:**
  - **Purpose:** Testing complex queries is vital to ensure they return the correct data and perform optimally under various conditions.
  - **Testing strategies:**
    - **Query depth limits:** Implement tests to verify that complex queries do not exceed predefined depth limits, preventing excessively nested queries that could lead to performance issues.

- **Variable inputs:** Test queries with different sets of variable inputs to validate response accuracy and error handling.

- **Performance testing:**

  o **Purpose:** Ensuring that GraphQL APIs can handle varying loads while maintaining performance is essential for user satisfaction and system reliability.

  o **Testing strategies:**

    - **Load testing:** Conduct load testing to evaluate how the API performs under traffic scenarios, including peak usage.

    - **Response time analysis:** Measure the response times of queries to identify potential bottlenecks or areas for optimization.

- **Error handling:**

  o **Purpose:** Verifying that the API correctly handles errors and returns appropriate error messages is crucial for the user experience.

  o **Testing strategies:**

    - **Error scenarios:** Create tests that deliberately trigger errors (for example, invalid queries, unauthorized access) to ensure the API responds with meaningful error messages and appropriate status codes.

Tools for testing GraphQL APIs

To effectively test GraphQL APIs, teams can leverage various tools specifically designed for this purpose, such as:

- **Apollo Engine:** A performance monitoring tool that provides insights into query performance, error tracking, and overall API health. It helps teams identify slow queries and optimize them accordingly.

- **GraphiQL:** An interactive in-browser tool for exploring GraphQL APIs. It allows developers to test queries in real time, making it easier to identify issues during development.

- **Postman:** While known for REST API testing, Postman also supports GraphQL queries, allowing users to construct, test, and automate GraphQL requests alongside traditional API tests.

- **GraphQL Voyager:** A visualization tool that helps developers explore GraphQL schemas interactively. It can be beneficial for understanding schema relationships and dependencies during testing.

As new API paradigms like GraphQL become more prevalent, testing strategies must evolve to accommodate their unique characteristics. Focused on schema validation, complex query testing, performance evaluation, and error handling, teams can ensure the robustness of their GraphQL APIs. Leveraging specialized tools further enhances the effectiveness of these testing strategies, helping organizations maintain high standards of quality and performance in their API offerings. As the API landscape continues to shift, staying adaptable and implementing targeted testing approaches will be crucial for success.

Challenges in testing new API paradigms

As organizations increasingly adopt new API paradigms like GraphQL, they face several challenges that can complicate the testing process. These challenges stem from modern APIs' flexibility and complexity, requiring teams to develop tailored strategies to ensure robust testing practices. Here are the key challenges associated with testing dynamic queries, ensuring proper data handling, and validating response performance in GraphQL and similar APIs:

- **Testing dynamic queries:**

  o **Challenge:** The ability to construct dynamic queries that can retrieve a wide variety of data presents a unique testing challenge. Unlike traditional APIs, where specific endpoints correspond to predetermined data structures, GraphQL allows clients to specify exactly what data they need, leading to highly variable queries.

  o **Implications:**

    ▪ **Query variability:** With numerous possible queries, generating comprehensive test cases can be difficult. The sheer number of permutations makes it challenging to ensure complete test coverage.

    ▪ **Error handling:** Dynamic queries can lead to unexpected errors or data formats, requiring robust error handling and validation strategies.

  o **Mitigation strategies:**

    ▪ **Query templates:** Develop a set of query templates that represent common use cases, allowing for systematic testing of different scenarios.

    ▪ **Automated testing tools:** Utilize tools that can generate and execute queries dynamically, helping to cover a broader range of possible inputs.

- **Ensuring proper data handling:**

  o **Challenge:** Properly handling data is crucial, especially given the flexibility that GraphQL provides. APIs often interact with various data sources, leading to potential issues with data consistency and integrity.

  o **Implications:**

    ▪ **Data relationships:** Ensuring that data relationships are correctly defined and maintained can be complex, particularly when multiple resources are fetched in a single query.

    ▪ **Data validation:** Testing must ensure that the data returned matches the expectations set by the schema, and that transformations applied to data are accurate.

  o **Mitigation strategies:**

    ▪ **Schema validation tests:** Regularly validate the API's responses against the defined schema to ensure compliance and accuracy.

    ▪ **Data integrity checks:** Implement checks that validate data consistency across related queries and ensure that modifications to one resource do not negatively impact others.

- **Validating response performance:**

  o **Challenge:** Performance validation becomes critical as APIs grow in complexity. Dynamic queries can lead to varying response times, and it is essential to ensure that the API can handle requests efficiently under load.

  o **Implications:**

    ▪ **Load management:** APIs must be tested under different load conditions to identify performance bottlenecks and ensure they can handle peak traffic without degradation.

    ▪ **Response time variability:** The dynamic nature of queries can result in unpredictable response times, making it essential to establish benchmarks and expectations for performance.

    o **Mitigation strategies:**

- **Load testing:** Utilize load testing tools to simulate various user interactions and assess how the API performs under stress. This can help identify slow queries and optimize them before deployment.

- **Performance monitoring tools:** Implement monitoring solutions to track response times in real-time, allowing teams to quickly identify and address performance issues as they arise.

The transition to new API paradigms such as GraphQL presents several challenges that require tailored testing strategies. Teams can effectively navigate these challenges by addressing the complexities of dynamic queries, ensuring proper data handling, and validating response performance. Implementing systematic testing approaches and utilizing specialized tools will not only enhance the reliability and performance of modern APIs but also contribute to a more seamless user experience. As organizations continue to embrace these evolving technologies, a proactive approach to testing will be essential for maintaining high standards of quality in API development.

Blockchain and decentralized applications

As blockchain technology continues gaining traction across various industries, testing frameworks must evolve to address the unique challenges distributed ledger technologies present. Unlike traditional software systems, blockchain operates in a decentralized manner, requiring specific approaches to ensure security, transaction validation, and integration with other decentralized systems. Here are the key challenges associated with testing blockchain applications:

- **Ensuring security:**

    o Security is paramount in blockchain systems, given their decentralized nature and the high value of the assets they often manage. Vulnerabilities in smart contracts or the underlying protocol can lead to significant financial losses or breaches of trust.

    o **Implications:**

- **Smart contract vulnerabilities:** Bugs or vulnerabilities in smart contracts can be exploited, resulting in unauthorized transactions or loss of funds.

- **Network attacks:** Blockchain networks can be targeted by various attacks (for example, 51% attacks, Sybil attacks), necessitating robust security testing.

    o **Mitigation strategies:**

- **Static analysis tools:** Use tools designed for static analysis of smart contracts, such as Mythril or Slither, to identify vulnerabilities before deployment.

- **Penetration testing:** Conduct thorough penetration testing to simulate attacks on the blockchain network, identifying potential security weaknesses in both the protocol and application layers.

- **Transaction validation:**

    o **Challenge:** Validating transactions in a blockchain involves ensuring that each transaction is legitimate and adheres to the rules set forth by the blockchain protocol. This process is critical to maintaining the integrity of the ledger.

    o **Implications:**

- **Complex validation logic:** Different blockchain platforms have distinct consensus mechanisms and rules for transaction validation, complicating the testing process.

- **State management:** Maintaining the correct state of the blockchain during testing can be challenging, especially when simulating real-world scenarios.

  o **Mitigation strategies:**

  ▪ **Testnets:** Utilize **test networks** (**testnets**) to simulate real-world conditions and validate transactions without risking actual assets.

  ▪ **Automated testing suites:** Develop automated testing frameworks that can verify the correctness of transaction validation logic under various scenarios, ensuring compliance with protocol rules.

- **Integration with other decentralized systems:**

  o **Challenge:** As blockchain applications often interact with other decentralized systems (for example, decentralized finance platforms, oracles), ensuring smooth integration and interoperability can be complex.

  o **Implications:**

  ▪ **Interoperability issues:** Different blockchain protocols may have unique standards and transaction formats, creating challenges for integration.

  ▪ **Dependency management:** Decentralized applications may depend on external services (for example, oracles for real-world data), necessitating thorough testing of these integrations.

  o **Mitigation strategies:**

  ▪ **Integration testing:** Implement comprehensive integration testing to ensure the blockchain application interacts correctly with other decentralized systems and services.

  ▪ **Standard protocols:** Advocate for the use of standardized protocols (such as ERC-20 for tokens) to facilitate easier integration and compatibility between different blockchain networks.

Testing blockchain applications presents unique challenges that require specialized frameworks and strategies. By focusing on security, transaction validation, and integration with other decentralized systems, teams can effectively navigate the complexities of blockchain technology. Employing automated testing tools, utilizing testnets, and conducting thorough security assessments will enhance the reliability and robustness of blockchain applications, ultimately contributing to the broader adoption of this transformative technology. As blockchain continues to evolve, so must the testing methodologies employed to ensure its integrity and security.

Testing in DevOps and continuous delivery

The integration of test automation frameworks into the DevOps cycle is essential for achieving a seamless and efficient software development process. As organizations strive for rapid delivery and high-quality releases, embedding continuous testing within DevOps pipelines ensures that software is rigorously validated at every stage, from code commits to production deployments.

Importance of integrating automation in DevOps

Here are some benefits that you will get from ensuring your test automation is built directly into your CI/CD process:

- **Continuous feedback loop:**

  o **Real-time insights:** By integrating test automation, teams can receive immediate feedback on code changes, allowing developers to identify and address issues promptly. This continuous feedback loop reduces the risk of defects accumulating over time and enhances overall software quality.

o **Shift-left testing:** Early testing in the development cycle encourages a shift-left approach, where testing is conducted alongside development rather than as a final phase. This proactive strategy helps catch issues before they escalate, reducing costs and time spent on fixes.

- **Faster release cycles:**

  o **Reduced time to market:** Automating tests within the DevOps pipeline enables faster execution and results in quick validation of new features. This speed allows organizations to release updates more frequently, enhancing competitiveness and responsiveness to market demands.

  o **Increased efficiency:** Automation eliminates the need for manual testing, reducing human error and freeing up QA resources to focus on more complex testing scenarios that require critical thinking and creativity.

- **Enhanced collaboration:**

  o **Cross-functional teams:** Integrating test automation fosters collaboration among development, QA, and operations teams. By working together in a shared environment, team members can communicate more effectively and ensure alignment on testing objectives and requirements.

  o **Shared responsibility:** With testing integrated into the DevOps cycle, all team members, including developers, are encouraged to take ownership of quality, creating a culture of accountability and shared responsibility for the final product.

Key strategies for effective integration

Here are some common strategies for integrating automation into your CI/CD practices:

- **Design a modular test automation framework:**

  o **Flexibility and scalability:** Having a modular test automation framework like we have been describing in this book allows for the easy addition or removal of test cases, making it adaptable to changes in the development process or project requirements. This flexibility is crucial in a fast-paced DevOps environment.

  o **Reusability:** Implementing reusable test components reduces duplication and maintenance overhead, enabling teams to scale their testing efforts efficiently.

- **Adopt a comprehensive testing strategy:**

  o **Test automation pyramid:** Implement a test automation pyramid strategy, prioritizing unit tests at the base, followed by integration tests, and end-to-end tests at the top. This approach optimizes testing efficiency and ensures that various testing levels are adequately covered.

  o **Include performance and security testing:** Incorporate performance and security tests into the pipeline to ensure that applications meet performance standards and are secure from vulnerabilities before deployment.

- **Implement monitoring and reporting tools:**

  o **Real-time monitoring:** Utilize monitoring tools to track the status of automated tests in real time. This visibility allows teams to respond swiftly to test failures and maintain a clear understanding of application health.

  o **Comprehensive reporting:** Generate detailed reports on test execution results and trends. This data can be invaluable for continuous improvement and identifying areas that require attention or enhancement.

Integrating test automation deeply into the DevOps cycle is vital for achieving continuous testing and ensuring high-quality software delivery. By leveraging automation frameworks within CI/CD pipelines, organizations can enhance collaboration, reduce release times, and maintain high software quality standards.

Implementing modular frameworks, utilizing CI/CD tools, and adopting comprehensive testing strategies are key to realizing the full potential of automation in DevOps. As organizations continue to embrace DevOps practices, a robust approach to test automation will be critical for sustaining competitive advantage in the fast-evolving software landscape.

IaC testing

As organizations increasingly adopt **infrastructure as code (IaC)** practices, the need for automated testing of IaC configurations has become paramount. IaC allows teams to manage and provision infrastructure through code, enabling greater efficiency, consistency, and scalability in deploying applications. However, the complexity of managing infrastructure through code also introduces potential risks. Automated testing plays a crucial role in ensuring that these deployments are safe, compliant, and correctly configured.

Importance of IaC testing

Here are some of the benefits that can be derived from adopting IaC testing practices and how they can be of value to any software development effort:

- **Risk mitigation:**
    - **Error prevention:** Automated testing helps identify errors and misconfigurations in IaC scripts before deployment. This proactive approach minimizes the risk of failures in production environments and reduces the likelihood of costly downtime.
    - **Security compliance:** Regular testing of IaC configurations can help detect vulnerabilities or non-compliance with security policies. This ensures that infrastructure is functional, secure, and aligned with industry standards and best practices.
- **Consistent deployments:**
    - **Standardization**: Automated tests can validate that IaC configurations adhere to predefined standards, promoting consistency across different environments. This standardization is essential for maintaining uniformity in production, staging, and development setups.
    - **Version control:** IaC testing integrates well with version control systems, enabling teams to track changes and ensure that the infrastructure remains compliant with the desired state over time.
- **Faster feedback loops:**
    - **Continuous validation:** Automating IaC tests within CI/CD pipelines allows for continuous validation of infrastructure configurations. This quick feedback enables teams to address issues early in the deployment process, enhancing the overall efficiency of the development lifecycle.

Key strategies for effective IaC testing

Let us now go over the key strategies for effective IaC testing:

- **Testing frameworks and tools:**
    - **Use established tools:** Leverage testing tools designed specifically for IaC, such as Terraform Compliance, InSpec, or Kitchen-Terraform. These tools facilitate testing configurations against specific compliance requirements and expected behaviors.
    - **Linting and static analysis:** Implement linting tools that analyze IaC code for potential errors or non-compliance issues before execution. Static analysis can help catch syntax errors, security vulnerabilities, and best practice violations early in the development process.
- **Automated unit and integration tests:**
    - **Unit testing:** Write unit tests for individual components of the IaC code to ensure that they behave as expected. This testing can verify the correctness of smaller infrastructure modules before they are integrated into larger systems.

o **Integration testing:** Conduct integration tests to validate the interactions between various components of the infrastructure. This testing ensures that changes in one part of the IaC code do not negatively impact other components or systems.

- **Environment validation:**

  o **Pre-deployment testing:** Implement automated tests to validate IaC configurations in a staging or testing environment before deploying them to production. This validation ensures the infrastructure is set up correctly and operates as intended.

  o **Post-deployment testing:** Conduct post-deployment tests to confirm that the infrastructure is functioning correctly after deployment. This testing can help identify any issues that may arise during the transition to production.

- **Monitoring and reporting:**

  o **Continuous monitoring:** Utilize monitoring tools to track the state of IaC deployments and ensure compliance with configuration standards. Continuous monitoring can help detect drift from the desired state, prompting corrective actions as needed.

  o **Detailed reporting:** Generate reports on the results of IaC tests, including any errors, compliance issues, or performance metrics. This data is essential for auditing and ensuring that infrastructure configurations remain secure and compliant over time.

Automated testing of IaC configurations is a critical component of modern software development practices. By ensuring that deployments are safe, compliant, and correctly configured, organizations can mitigate risks, promote consistency, and accelerate their development processes. Employing robust testing frameworks, conducting thorough unit and integration tests, and implementing continuous monitoring are key strategies for effective IaC testing. As IaC continues to gain traction in the industry, establishing a strong testing framework will be essential for maintaining the integrity and security of infrastructure deployments.

Shift-left and shift-right testing

This section phases on two key testing ideas that seem diametrically opposed but can actually be used well in unison when applied to the correct testing areas. It ensures that testing is brought earlier into the design phase, considers the complexities of production, and better allows teams to test a variety of things that may threaten a production environment and help to prepare and mitigate these.

Shift-left

The shift-left testing approach is a transformative methodology in software development, emphasizing the importance of integrating testing activities earlier in the SDLC. This proactive strategy helps teams identify and address defects sooner, ultimately leading to higher-quality software and reduced costs.

Key aspects of shift-left testing

The following are key aspects to ensure you have in place to shift-left your testing approach correctly. Some of the options we have covered in detail already in the book, but worth mentioning again to explain how they fit into this particular area:

- **Emphasis on early testing:** By shifting testing activities to the left, organizations encourage developers to conduct tests at the initial stages of development rather than waiting until later phases. This includes unit testing, integration testing, and performance testing conducted alongside coding efforts. Early testing allows teams to catch issues before progressing to later stages, reducing the complexity and cost of fixing defects.

- **Unit testing:** Unit tests are the cornerstone of the shift-left approach. These tests validate individual components or functions of the codebase, ensuring that each piece works as intended. Frameworks such as JUnit (for Java), NUnit (for .NET), and pytest (for Python) enable developers to write automated unit tests that run as part of the development process, providing immediate feedback on code changes.

- **Static code analysis:** Static code analysis tools analyze the source code for potential issues without executing it. These tools help identify code smells, security vulnerabilities, and adherence to coding standards. Integrating static code analysis into the development pipeline allows teams to catch errors early and enforce best practices consistently across the codebase.

- **Continuous integration and continuous feedback:** Shift-left testing is inherently linked to CI practices. By integrating automated testing into CI pipelines, teams can ensure that every code commit is validated against a suite of tests, providing immediate feedback on the quality of the code. This continuous feedback loop allows developers to address issues quickly and promotes a culture of collaboration between development and QA teams.

- **Collaboration between teams:** The shift-left approach encourages collaboration between developers, testers, and other stakeholders early in the development process. This collaborative environment helps to ensure that requirements are understood and testing objectives are aligned with business goals. Techniques like BDD facilitate this collaboration by allowing teams to define acceptance criteria in business language, ensuring everyone is on the same page.

Benefits of shift-left testing

The benefits of shift-left testing are:

- **Cost reduction:** Catching defects early significantly reduces the cost of fixing them. Studies show that fixing a bug during the design phase is considerably less expensive than addressing it during the testing or production phases.

- **Improved software quality:** By incorporating testing throughout the development process, teams enhance the overall quality of the software, resulting in fewer bugs and issues in production. This leads to increased customer satisfaction and trust.

- **Faster time to market:** Early testing and continuous feedback enable teams to quickly identify and resolve issues, accelerating the development process. As a result, organizations can deliver features and products to market faster, gaining a competitive edge.

- **Increased developer productivity:** Automated testing allows developers to focus on building new features rather than spending excessive time on debugging. This productivity boost translates into faster development cycles and more innovation.

The shift-left testing approach is a powerful strategy for modern software development, focusing on testing early and often to enhance software quality, reduce costs, and accelerate time to market. By emphasizing unit tests, static code analysis, continuous integration, and team collaboration, organizations can create a robust testing culture that fosters innovation and ensures the delivery of high-quality software. Embracing the shift-left mindset is essential for teams navigating the complexities of today's rapidly evolving software landscape.

Shift-right

Shift-right testing is an emerging practice that focuses on testing applications in the production environment. Although the idea of shifting right may seem in contravention of the above shifting-left principles, they can actually work well together when applied to the correct development area. As software development cycles shorten and the demand for rapid deployment increases, traditional testing methods alone are insufficient to ensure quality.

Shift-right practices, such as chaos engineering, canary testing, and A/B testing, enable teams to validate software performance, reliability, and user experience in real-world scenarios. This approach emphasizes continuous improvement and adaptation after deployment.

Key aspects of shift-right testing

Let us now understand the key aspects of shift-right testing.

Chaos engineering

Chaos engineering is a proactive approach to identifying weaknesses in a system by intentionally injecting faults and observing how the system behaves under stress. By simulating failures, teams can understand the resilience of their applications and improve their incident response strategies.

Tools like Gremlin and Chaos Monkey help orchestrate chaos experiments, allowing teams to validate how applications handle unexpected events, such as server failures, network outages, or sudden spikes in traffic.

Canary testing

Canary testing involves deploying a new version of an application to a small subset of users before rolling it out to the entire user base. This strategy allows teams to monitor the new version's performance and stability while minimizing the risk of widespread issues.

By using canary deployments, teams can gather real-time feedback on the new features, enabling them to make data-driven decisions about whether to proceed with a full rollout or revert to a previous version.

A/B testing

A/B testing, or split testing, is a technique for comparing two versions of a web application or feature to determine which performs better. By directing a portion of users to one version and the rest to another, teams can analyze user behavior and engagement metrics to make informed decisions.

A/B testing frameworks provide analytics and reporting capabilities to evaluate the performance of different versions, allowing teams to optimize user experience based on actual usage data.

Benefits of shift-right testing

The benefits of shift-right testing are as follows:

- **Real-world validation:** Shift-right testing allows organizations to validate their software in real-world conditions, providing insights that traditional testing environments cannot replicate. This approach helps uncover issues that may only surface under actual user interactions.

- **Faster issue resolution:** By testing in production, teams can quickly identify and address issues as they arise, reducing the **Mean Time to Recovery (MTTR)** for incidents. This leads to a more resilient application and improved user experience.

- **Enhanced user experience:** Continuous monitoring and feedback from shift-right testing practices enable teams to effectively refine features and address user pain points. By leveraging user data, organizations can make informed decisions that enhance customer satisfaction.

- **Cultural shift towards resilience:** Shift-right testing encourages a culture of resilience and experimentation within organizations. Teams become more adept at handling failures, leading to improved incident management and a better understanding of system dependencies.

Challenges of shift-right testing

The challenges of shift-right testing are as follows:

- **Complexity in test design:** Effective chaos experiments, canary tests, or A/B tests require careful planning and consideration of various factors, including user demographics, system architecture, and potential impacts on users.

- **Risk management:** While shift-right testing helps identify potential issues, it also involves risks, such as negatively affecting user experience or system performance. Organizations must develop strategies to mitigate these risks.

- **Tooling and integration:** Implementing shift-right practices often require specialized tools and integration with existing CI/CD pipelines. Organizations must ensure that their testing frameworks can effectively accommodate these practices.

Shift-right testing is essential in modern software development, allowing organizations to validate their applications in production environments. By leveraging chaos engineering, canary testing, and A/B testing, teams can gain valuable insights into application performance, user experience, and system resilience. Embracing shift-right testing enables organizations to adapt to changing user needs and continuously improve their software, ultimately enhancing quality and customer satisfaction in an increasingly competitive landscape.

Key challenges in adopting emerging technologies

Let us now work on some common challenges that many organizations face when trying to embrace modern technologies and tooling, and some things that can be done to prepare you and your team to overcome them.

Challenge 1: Skill gaps and learning curves

Problem: The rapid introduction of new tools and technologies in software development and testing, particularly with the shift towards serverless, containerized, and microservice architectures, poses significant challenges for teams. As organizations adopt these modern paradigms, the complexity of the development and testing processes increases. Many teams may find themselves grappling with:

- **Knowledge deficiencies:** With frequent updates and the emergence of novel tools, team members may lack the foundational knowledge or expertise required to utilize these technologies effectively.

- **Integration difficulties:** The integration of modern testing tools with existing workflows can be daunting, leading to resistance from teams unaccustomed to such changes.

- **Inconsistent practices:** Teams may struggle to establish consistent testing practices across various environments, resulting in variability in test coverage and quality.

- **Inefficiencies:** As teams attempt to navigate new technologies without sufficient training, they may encounter inefficiencies, slowdowns in development cycles, and increased error rates in testing.

Solution

To address these challenges, organizations must invest in continuous learning and upskilling for their teams. Here are several strategies to facilitate this transition:

- **Structured training programs:** Implement comprehensive training programs focusing on the latest tools and technologies in test automation. These programs can be tailored to different skill levels, ensuring that both beginners and advanced users receive relevant education. Consider partnering with training providers to offer courses or certifications in emerging technologies like serverless architecture, Kubernetes, or microservices.

- **Mentorship and knowledge sharing:** Establish a mentorship program where experienced team members can guide less experienced colleagues through practical challenges and share best practices. Foster a culture of knowledge sharing by organizing regular workshops, lunch-and-learn sessions, or tech talks where team members can present new tools or methodologies they have explored.

- **Hands-on learning:** Encourage hands-on experimentation with new tools through hackathons, coding challenges, or sandbox environments. Allow team members to explore these technologies in a low stakes setting to build confidence and familiarity. Implement pilot projects that allow teams to gradually adopt new technologies and practices, providing real-world experience while minimizing risk.

- **Incorporating continuous feedback:** Create a feedback loop to evaluate the effectiveness of training programs and ensure they meet team needs. Regularly solicit input from participants to identify areas for improvement and adapt the curriculum accordingly. Encourage team members to share their successes and challenges when using new tools, fostering a collaborative environment where learning from experience is prioritized.

- **Promoting a learning culture:** Advocate for a growth mindset within the organization, where learning is encouraged, and mistakes are viewed as opportunities for improvement. Allocate dedicated time for learning and development within work schedules, ensuring that team members can focus on skill enhancement without compromising their core responsibilities.

- **Utilizing online learning platforms:** Leverage online resources and platforms that provide courses, tutorials, and webinars on modern testing tools and practices. Platforms like Coursera, Udemy, and Pluralsight offer a wealth of information that can be accessed anytime. Encourage team members to pursue self-directed learning to cater to their individual needs and learning preferences.

Addressing the skill gaps and learning curves associated with the rapid evolution of testing tools and technologies is crucial for teams transitioning to modern architectures. By investing in continuous learning, fostering a culture of knowledge sharing, and providing hands-on opportunities, organizations can empower their teams to adopt and utilize new testing practices effectively. This proactive approach enhances team capabilities, improves overall software quality, and accelerates development cycles, ensuring organizations remain competitive in an ever-changing landscape.

Challenge 2: Tool overload and integration complexity

Problem: The proliferation of new tools for test automation and software development presents a significant challenge known as tool overload. As organizations strive to stay current with the latest innovations, they often adopt a multitude of tools to meet various testing needs. This can lead to several integration complexities, particularly in environments that include:

- **Legacy systems:** Older systems may lack compatibility with newer tools, creating friction in workflows and requiring significant effort to bridge the gap between modern and legacy technologies.

- **Large tech stacks:** With diverse tools and technologies in play, organizations may struggle to maintain a coherent testing strategy encompassing all tech stack components.

- **Redundancy and confusion:** Teams may use multiple tools for similar tasks, resulting in confusion over which tool to use for specific testing scenarios and potentially leading to inconsistent results.

- **Increased maintenance overhead:** Managing numerous tools can create significant overhead in terms of maintenance, updates, and training, diverting resources from more strategic initiatives.

Solution

To combat the challenges posed by tool overload and integration complexity, organizations should focus on selecting tool-agnostic, interoperable tools that can integrate seamlessly with existing systems and frameworks. Here are several strategies to effectively implement this solution:

- **Conduct a tool assessment:** Perform a comprehensive audit of existing tools and technologies to identify redundancies and gaps. This assessment should evaluate each tool's capabilities, integration potential, and alignment with organizational goals. Involve key stakeholders from development, QA, and operations to ensure all perspectives are considered in the assessment process.

- **Emphasize tool-agnostic solutions:** Prioritize the selection of tool-agnostic solutions that can work with various environments and technologies. This approach ensures that the chosen tools can adapt as the tech stack evolves and mitigates dependency on specific vendors. Look for tools that support industry-standard protocols and formats (for example, RESTful APIs, Selenium, JUnit) to maximize compatibility across different platforms.

- **Focus on integration capabilities:** Select tools that offer robust integration features, including APIs, plugins, and support for popular CI/CD platforms. This facilitates seamless communication between different systems and reduces the complexity of managing multiple tools. Evaluate the availability of pre-built integrations with other tools in the tech stack to streamline setup and configuration processes.

- **Implement a centralized tooling strategy:** Establish a centralized strategy for tool selection and integration to promote consistency across teams. This strategy should outline guidelines for evaluating new tools, ensuring they align with the organization's overall testing philosophy. Create a repository of approved tools and best practices to guide teams in their tool selection processes and foster collaboration.

- **Promote standardization and best practices:** Encourage standardization in testing practices and tool usage across teams to reduce confusion and streamline collaboration. Define clear guidelines for how and when to use specific tools within the organization. Share best practices for integrating tools into existing workflows to minimize disruption and maximize efficiency.

- **Invest in training and support:** Provide training sessions and resources to ensure that team members understand how to effectively use and integrate the chosen tools. This helps mitigate resistance to change and empowers teams to make the most of their toolset. Establish a support system or community of practice where team members can share insights and address challenges related to tool integration.

- **Monitor and iterate:** Continuously monitor the performance and effectiveness of the tools in use. Gather feedback from users to identify pain points and opportunities for improvement. Be open to iterating on the tooling strategy as technologies evolve and new needs arise, ensuring that the organization remains agile and adaptable.

Navigating tool overload and integration complexity requires a strategic approach centered on tool-agnostic, interoperable solutions. By conducting thorough assessments, emphasizing integration capabilities, and fostering standardization, organizations can reduce the friction associated with managing multiple tools. Investing in training and continuous improvement will ensure that teams are equipped to leverage their tools effectively, ultimately enhancing productivity and software quality. Embracing this strategy not only streamlines testing processes but also positions organizations for long-term success in an ever-evolving technological landscape.

Embracing new testing paradigms

In the rapidly evolving landscape of software development, adopting a future-ready approach to test automation is crucial for organizations looking to remain competitive and innovative. As modern architectures and practices shift, testing paradigms must also evolve to keep pace. Key components of this approach include:

- Organizations must be proactive in adopting emerging testing paradigms, such as shift-left and shift-right testing. This includes integrating testing earlier in the development lifecycle and extending testing practices into production environments to ensure ongoing reliability.

- Additionally, practices like chaos engineering and canary testing enable teams to assess the resilience and performance of systems in real-world conditions, providing valuable insights for continuous improvement.

- The adoption of AI-driven insights in testing can enhance decision-making and improve test effectiveness. Tools that leverage ML algorithms for predictive analytics can identify patterns in test failures, optimize test execution, and provide actionable recommendations for improvement.

- Embracing no-code and low-code platforms allows teams to empower non-technical users to participate in test automation. This democratization of testing can lead to greater collaboration and efficiency across teams.

- To future-proof test automation frameworks, organizations must focus on creating structures that are inherently flexible, modular, and adaptable:

- Designing frameworks with modular components allows for easy integration of new tools, technologies, and practices as they emerge. This reduces the risk of obsolescence and enhances the ability to pivot in response to changing needs.

- Modular frameworks also facilitate the separation of concerns, enabling teams to develop, test, and maintain components independently, ultimately leading to faster iteration cycles.

- Cloud-native architectures support scalability and flexibility, allowing organizations to run tests across various environments without the burden of managing physical infrastructure. This adaptability is essential for organizations that rely on dynamic, distributed systems.

- Incorporating microservices architecture into test automation frameworks enables teams to test individual components in isolation while also validating their interactions within the broader system.

Integrating emerging technologies

Staying ahead of emerging technologies such as blockchain, API-first development, and serverless computing requires frameworks to adapt to new challenges and complexities. This involves implementing strategies for effective testing of these technologies, such as service virtualization, contract testing, and event-driven validation.

Continuous learning and skill development for team members will ensure they are equipped to utilize new tools and methodologies effectively, fostering a culture of innovation and adaptability.

Looking forward

The next generation of test automation is poised to be defined by several transformative characteristics, such as:

- **AI-driven insights:** The incorporation of AI-driven insights will revolutionize the way teams approach testing. Predictive analytics will enable organizations to anticipate potential issues before they occur, streamline test execution, and optimize resource allocation. This proactive approach to testing will enhance overall quality and reduce time to market.

- **Increased accessibility:** The rise of no-code platforms will democratize test automation, allowing a broader range of stakeholders, including business analysts and product owners, to contribute to test case creation and execution. This shift will foster collaboration between technical and non-technical teams, leading to faster feedback loops and improved product quality.

- **Complexity management:** As software architectures become increasingly distributed and cloud-native, frameworks must handle the complexities associated with microservices, serverless computing, and API-centric development. This will require robust testing strategies that can validate interactions between disparate components, ensuring the integrity and performance of the entire system.

- **Adaptability to change:** The ability to adapt to new trends and technologies will be critical for the longevity of test automation frameworks. Organizations prioritizing flexibility and modularity will be better positioned to incorporate innovations, respond to evolving market demands, and maintain competitive advantages.

Adopting a future-ready approach to test automation involves embracing new paradigms, leveraging innovative tools, and fostering a culture of adaptability. By designing flexible and modular frameworks, organizations can ensure they are equipped to handle the complexities of modern software development. The next generation of test automation will be characterized by AI-driven insights, increased accessibility, and a focus on managing the challenges posed by distributed and cloud-native architectures. By proactively preparing for these trends, organizations can position themselves to sustain success in an ever-evolving technological landscape.

Conclusion

As software systems evolve, so must our approach to testing and automation. Emerging trends like AI, cloud computing, containerization, and decentralized technologies are reshaping how quality assurance is practiced. These are no longer optional enhancements but foundational to modern software delivery. To stay competitive, teams must develop a strategic mindset—balancing agility with stability—to evaluate, adopt, and integrate innovations without compromising reliability.

Success in test automation now depends not just on working harder, but smarter. Organizations that quickly adapt, invest in team skills, and foster a culture of continuous learning will be best positioned to deliver high-quality software at speed and scale. Testing must be viewed not as a fixed phase but as an evolving discipline that supports the entire software lifecycle.

Adopting new paradigms is not only about selecting tools, but it is about shifting mindsets. Teams must proactively assess how developments like shift-left testing, serverless architecture, and low-code platforms fit their unique context. Investing in test automation today is a strategic move that can accelerate delivery, reduce risk, and unlock innovation.

No single approach will remain optimal forever. Continuous reassessment of tools, frameworks, and practices is essential. The most successful teams will be those who embrace change, experiment with emerging technologies, and promote close collaboration across development, QA, and operations. By asking the right questions and refining strategies over time, teams can ensure their testing remains resilient, relevant, and ready for the future.

In the next chapter, we will look to conclude our book by wrapping up many of the points and how we can continue on a path to a sustainable test automation framework design.

Key takeaways

The rapid evolution of software architectures, development practices, and user expectations is reshaping how testing and automation are approached. Emerging trends and technologies are driving the need for more flexible, scalable, and intelligent testing strategies. Testers and developers must stay ahead by embracing these changes to ensure quality at speed and scale. Let us go over the following:

- **Low-code and no-code automation tools**: These tools empower non-technical users to contribute to test automation, accelerating test creation and reducing dependency on developers.

- **Cloud-based test automation platforms**: Cloud solutions offer scalability, parallel execution, and cost-efficiency, enabling teams to run tests across diverse environments seamlessly.

- **Serverless architecture**: Testing must adapt to ephemeral environments with event-driven execution, requiring new strategies for observability and validation.

- **Containerized applications and Kubernetes**: Testing in containerized environments demands automation tools that handle orchestration, isolation, and scalability of test environments.

- **Shift towards API-centric testing**: API testing is critical as more business logic moves to the backend, providing faster feedback and more stable tests compared to UI testing.

- **GraphQL and other API technologies**: Testing GraphQL requires the validation of dynamic queries, schema changes, and complex data relationships for robust API coverage.

- **Blockchain and decentralized applications**: Testing for blockchain involves verifying smart contracts, consensus mechanisms, and security, posing new challenges in automation.

- **Testing in DevOps and continuous delivery**: Continuous testing is integral to CI/CD pipelines, requiring automation at every stage to support rapid, reliable software delivery.

- **Shift-left and shift-right testing**: Shift-left emphasizes early testing (e.g., unit, integration), while shift-right focuses on production monitoring and resilience testing—both are essential for quality at speed.

- **Key challenges in adopting emerging technologies**: Challenges include tool integration, skill gaps, and maintaining test reliability amid rapid change, requiring strategic planning and training.

- **Embracing new testing paradigms**: Teams must evolve beyond traditional methods, adopting risk-based, exploratory, and AI-assisted testing to meet modern development demands.

Exercises

1. How are AI and ML influencing your current test strategy?

2. Are you leveraging any predictive analytics to identify potential defects before they occur?

3. What upcoming trends could disrupt our current approach to automation?

4. How do you evaluate and adopt new tools without introducing tool sprawl or integration issues?

5. Can you measure ROI for new testing technologies?

6. What governance is needed to ensure the maintainability of low-code test scripts?

7. How do we strike a balance between speed and control when adopting no-code solutions?

8. How do you effectively test ephemeral, event-driven functions?

9. Are you equipped to monitor and debug serverless applications in real-time?

10. What tools support serverless testing, and how do we integrate them?

11. How are you managing test environments using containers (for example, Docker)?

12. Are you testing microservices in isolation and as part of the whole system?

13. Are you prioritizing API testing in your automation strategy?

14. How do we handle dynamic data and schema validation in GraphQL tests?

15. What is your approach to security and performance testing in decentralized systems?

16. Are there test automation tools that you have that support blockchain-specific testing needs?

17. What skills do you need to upskill or hire for future-ready testing?

18. How do we manage resistance to change when introducing new testing approaches?

Join our Discord space

Join our Discord workspace for latest updates, offers, tech happenings around the world, new releases, and sessions with the authors:

https://discord.bpbonline.com

## CHAPTER 17

Conclusion: The Path to Sustainable Test Automation Frameworks

Introduction

We have covered a lot of ground in this book across a wide variety of different topics. In this chapter, we will summarize many of the key points we have covered and hopefully reiterate some of the key things that can be done to ensure your test automation approach is successful. From understanding the importance of software architecture in both the application and framework design, to the importance of developing around the tools and not for them, hopefully, you will be able to build a framework that can evolve with your organization.

Lastly, we will also summarize some of the best ways to develop and prepare teams for success in these endeavors. No approach can be successful without teams that can execute on them, and so, we need to ensure we allow for collaboration and an environment of learning to build teams that are capable of delivering with new test and automation approaches.

Structure

In this chapter, we will go over the following topics:

- Architecture as the foundation of test automation frameworks
- Need for flexibility
- Role of tool-agnostic frameworks in test automation
- Fostering continuous learning and adaptation in your framework
- Iterative improvement and refactoring in test automation frameworks
- Future of sustainable test automation

Objectives

By the end of this chapter, you will understand what it takes to build an automation framework that can be easily maintained and made adaptable to support changing demands and continuous improvement. We will take many of the principles already covered in the book and see how they can be combined to provide a framework that brings lasting value to an organization without needing to be changed and adapted frequently with tooling and technology changes.

Architecture as the foundation of test automation frameworks

In the realm of test automation, the significance of well-designed architecture cannot be overstated. Just as the architectural integrity of a building ensures its stability and longevity, a robust architectural foundation is crucial for developing scalable, maintainable, and adaptable test automation frameworks. Without such a foundation, these frameworks can quickly become fragile, making them difficult to maintain and evolve in line with the ever-changing software landscape.

Integration with modern technologies

A robust architectural foundation also ensures seamless integration with contemporary technologies. As organizations increasingly adopt microservices architectures, the need for flexible and efficient test automation frameworks becomes even more pronounced. Test frameworks must be able to interact with multiple services, each potentially written in different languages or technologies. An architecture emphasizing modularity and separation of concerns makes developing and maintaining tests for such diverse environments easier.

Moreover, with the growing reliance on cloud-based platforms, frameworks need to be adaptable to various environments and configurations. A well-architected framework can leverage cloud resources for test execution, allowing for parallel testing and quicker feedback cycles, which are essential for maintaining high development velocities.

The architecture of a test automation framework serves as its foundation, dictating its scalability, maintainability, and adaptability. By adhering to architectural principles like modularity, separation of concerns, and scalability, organizations can build frameworks that meet current testing needs and evolve gracefully as software landscapes change. A strong architectural foundation is not just beneficial; it is essential for the success of any test automation effort in today's dynamic and complex development environments.

Balancing flexibility and structure in test automation frameworks

Designing a practical test automation framework presents a unique challenge: achieving a balance between flexibility and structure. On one hand, a framework must be adaptable enough to incorporate new tools, technologies, and methodologies as they emerge. On the other hand, it requires a strong foundational structure to ensure stability, performance, and maintainability. Striking this balance is critical for the longevity of the framework, enabling it to evolve in alignment with the fast-paced nature of software development.

Need for flexibility

Let us understand the need for flexibility:

- **Adaptation to new tools and technologies:** The tech landscape is continuously evolving, with new testing tools and technologies emerging frequently. A flexible framework allows teams to incorporate these innovations without extensive rework. For example, if a new tool for test automation or reporting becomes popular, a well-architected framework should enable teams to integrate it seamlessly, adapting existing tests to leverage its features.

- **Support for diverse testing needs:** Different projects may require different testing strategies, be it unit testing, integration testing, or end-to-end testing. A flexible framework can accommodate these varying requirements, allowing teams to choose the most suitable approach for their specific contexts. This adaptability enhances collaboration and ensures the framework remains relevant across diverse domains.

Importance of structure

Let us understand the importance of structure:

- **Core stability:** While flexibility is vital, it must not come at the cost of stability. A structured framework provides a reliable core that ensures consistent performance across testing scenarios. By establishing guidelines, coding standards, and architectural patterns, teams can maintain a cohesive, organized framework that minimizes confusion and technical debt.

- **Performance optimization:** A strong structural foundation allows for the optimization of test execution performance. This includes organizing test suites efficiently, managing dependencies, and ensuring that tests are executed promptly. A framework that is too flexible may lead to chaotic test execution processes, resulting in increased execution times and unreliable results.

Abstracting tool dependencies

One of the most critical aspects of balancing flexibility and structure is the ability to abstract away tool dependencies. This means creating a framework that can operate independently of any specific testing tool, allowing for easier transitions between different tools as the need arises. Refer to the following:

- **Encapsulation of tool-specific logic:** By encapsulating tool-specific logic into separate components or modules, teams can insulate the core framework from changes in underlying tools. This encapsulation allows teams to replace or upgrade tools with minimal disruption to the overall framework, fostering adaptability while preserving stability.

- **Cross-domain functionality:** An abstracted approach enables the framework to remain functional across various domains. Whether testing web applications, mobile applications, or APIs, a well-structured framework should provide the necessary functionality without being tightly coupled to any specific technology. This versatility is essential for organizations that work across multiple platforms and technologies.

The challenge of designing test automation frameworks lies in balancing flexibility and structure. While adaptability to new tools and technologies is crucial for remaining relevant in a fast-paced development environment, a strong core structure is equally important for ensuring stability and performance. By abstracting tool dependencies and establishing clear guidelines and standards, organizations can create flexible and robust frameworks, enabling them to navigate the complexities of modern software development effectively. Achieving this balance is key to developing a test automation framework that meets current testing needs and stands the test of time as technologies evolve.

Role of tool-agnostic frameworks in test automation

Tool-agnostic frameworks are pivotal in enabling teams to pivot and embrace these changes without the need for a complete overhaul of their test strategies. By fostering reusability and compatibility, tool-agnostic frameworks ensure organizations can integrate diverse testing tools, cloud platforms, and testing paradigms while maintaining efficiency and minimizing technical debt.

Tool-agnostic frameworks play a crucial role in modern test automation by allowing teams to adapt to the evolving landscape of tools and technologies without overhauling their entire test strategy. These frameworks empower organizations to remain agile and efficient in their testing efforts by fostering flexibility, reusability, and seamless integration. Additionally, they help mitigate technical debt by reducing vendor lock-in and lowering maintenance costs, ensuring that teams can focus on delivering quality software at a sustainable pace. As the industry continues to evolve, the adoption of tool-agnostic frameworks will be instrumental in driving successful testing initiatives that align with organizational goals and technological advancements.

Fostering continuous learning and adaptation in your framework

Fostering a culture of continuous learning is essential to ensuring the longevity and effectiveness of any test automation framework. In an ever-evolving software development and testing landscape, teams must stay current with advancements in testing methodologies, emerging tools, and architectural patterns. By investing in upskilling and professional development, organizations can equip engineers with the knowledge and skills necessary to adapt their frameworks to new challenges and opportunities.

Importance of continuous learning

The following are some of the key benefits that you will gain from investing in continuous learning on the software testing and quality engineering side:

- **Staying current with advancements:** The field of test automation is dynamic, with new techniques and tools emerging regularly. Continuous learning enables teams to remain informed about the latest advancements, such as **behavior-driven development (BDD)**, **test-driven development (TDD)**, and other methodologies that can enhance testing efficiency. Staying up-to-date ensures that teams can incorporate best practices into their frameworks, improving overall effectiveness and quality.

- **Adapting to new challenges:** Testing frameworks must evolve accordingly as software systems grow in complexity and new technologies emerge. Lifelong learning equips teams with the ability to adapt their frameworks to meet these new challenges, whether they involve integrating with microservices, cloud environments, or addressing increased security requirements. A well-informed team is better positioned to make strategic decisions that enhance the framework's capabilities and resilience.

Investing in upskilling and professional development

Many things can be done to grow and develop technical testing skills in an organization. While many courses, books, and materials are available for this, the best methods of learning are actually hands-on programs and mentoring, where a person can learn with encouragement and be given the freedom to try new tools and improve their abilities in a safe space and free from criticism. Let us go over them:

- **Training programs and workshops:** Organizations should invest in training programs and workshops that focus on the latest tools, techniques, and architectural patterns. This investment not only improves individual skill sets but also fosters a collaborative environment where team members can share knowledge and experiences. Encouraging cross-functional training helps bridge gaps between development, testing, and operations, promoting a holistic understanding of the software lifecycle.

- **Mentorship and knowledge sharing:** Creating a mentorship program within the organization can facilitate knowledge sharing and promote lifelong learning. Experienced team members can guide less experienced colleagues through complex topics, share insights on effective testing strategies, and help them navigate the ever-changing technology landscape. Encouraging knowledge sharing through presentations, lunch-and-learn sessions, or internal blogs can further foster a culture of continuous improvement.

Encouraging experimentation with new trends

Another strong learning path is to allow for experimentation and innovation with new tools and approaches. This builds both confidence in new tools and approaches but also keeps skills up to date while broadening the skillset of a team as a result. Let us go over the following:

- **Exploration of emerging technologies:** Organizations should encourage teams to experiment with emerging trends, such as AI/ML-powered testing or new automation approaches and tools. These innovations can significantly enhance the capabilities of test automation frameworks, improving test coverage, efficiency, and accuracy. By allocating time for exploration and experimentation, teams can assess how these trends can be integrated into their frameworks and identify valuable use cases.

- **Evaluating new tools and methodologies:** Regularly evaluating new tools and methodologies allows teams to make informed decisions about which innovations to adopt. Setting up pilot projects or **proof of concept** (POC) initiatives can provide insights into the practical application of new technologies. This iterative approach mitigates risks associated with adopting unproven tools and empowers teams to refine their frameworks based on real-world experiences.

Embracing lifelong learning is vital for the sustainability and effectiveness of test automation frameworks. By fostering a culture of continuous learning, organizations empower their teams to stay current with advancements in the field and adapt to new challenges. Investing in upskilling and professional development enhances the capabilities of engineers, ensuring they can navigate the complexities of modern software development. Moreover, encouraging experimentation with emerging trends fosters innovation and helps keep frameworks future-proof. In a constantly changing landscape, a commitment to lifelong learning will be a cornerstone of success in test automation.

Iterative improvement and refactoring in test automation frameworks

Iterative improvement and refactoring are essential practices that enable frameworks to adapt to changing requirements, integrate feedback from real-world usage, and reduce technical debt. By establishing robust processes for regular reviews and optimizations, organizations can ensure their test automation frameworks remain relevant, effective, and sustainable in the face of new challenges.

Refactoring for technical debt reduction

Let us go over the following:

- **Continuous refactoring practices:** As software systems and frameworks grow, they can accumulate technical debt, resulting in increased complexity and decreased maintainability. Regular refactoring practices are essential for addressing this debt, as they allow teams to improve code quality, eliminate redundancy, and enhance overall framework performance. Refactoring should be viewed as an ongoing process rather than a one-time effort, ensuring the framework remains clean and efficient over time.

- **Adapting to new requirements:** A flexible framework can better accommodate new testing requirements arising from project scope or technology changes. As organizations adopt new testing paradigms (for example, security testing, performance testing, or chaos engineering), the framework should be structured to integrate these requirements without extensive modifications. By building flexibility from the outset, teams can enhance their frameworks incrementally, ensuring they remain capable of supporting diverse testing scenarios.

Building in flexibility for change

Let us go over the following:

- **Accommodating new test types:** Designing a test automation framework that supports a wide range of test types is crucial for its longevity. This includes functional testing, security, performance, and chaos testing. By establishing transparent abstraction layers and modular components, teams can more easily integrate new test types as the need arises. This adaptability helps maintain the framework's relevance as testing methodologies continue to evolve.

- **Supporting new architectures:** The rise of new architectures, such as serverless and containerized environments, presents challenges and opportunities for test automation frameworks. To sustain the framework over time, teams must design it to support these architectures from the beginning. This may involve incorporating features that allow for seamless integration with cloud services, container orchestration tools, and other modern technologies. By planning for flexibility and adaptability, organizations can ensure their frameworks can pivot to meet the demands of new architectural paradigms.

Iterative improvement and refactoring are critical components in the lifecycle of a test automation framework. Organizations can continuously enhance their frameworks to address new challenges and reduce technical debt by establishing processes for regular reviews and fostering feedback loops from real-world usage. Furthermore, building in flexibility for change, whether through the integration of new test types or support for emerging architectures, ensures that the framework remains relevant and sustainable over time. Embracing these practices will improve the framework's effectiveness and contribute to the overall quality and resilience of the software development process.

Encouraging collaboration across teams in test automation

Continuous improvement in test automation frameworks thrives on collaboration among various teams, including engineering, **quality assurance (QA)**, and DevOps. By fostering a culture of shared knowledge and mutual support, organizations can ensure their frameworks remain relevant, efficient, and effective for all stakeholders. Collaborative practices not only enhance the framework's quality but also encourage innovation and adaptability in the face of evolving challenges.

The following are some of the key benefits that teams can derive from involving multi-team collaboration in creating the best test automation framework for an organization:

- **Shared knowledge and expertise:** Collaborative efforts between engineering, QA, and DevOps teams enable the sharing of diverse perspectives and expertise. Each team brings unique insights that can significantly improve the testing process. For instance, engineers can provide valuable information on system architecture, while QA teams can share testing methodologies and user experience considerations. By working together, teams can identify pain points and collectively develop solutions that enhance the test automation framework.

- **Addressing pain points:** Open lines of communication across teams facilitate identifying and resolving common pain points. When team members collaborate, they can quickly highlight inefficiencies, bottlenecks, or recurring issues in the testing process. This collaborative problem-solving approach enables teams to implement targeted improvements in the test automation framework, ensuring it aligns with the needs and workflows of all stakeholders.

- **Ensuring framework relevance:** A test automation framework must remain relevant to support the entire organization effectively. Collaboration fosters an environment where feedback is regularly collected and integrated into the framework's evolution. By engaging in joint discussions about new requirements, testing strategies, and emerging tools, teams can ensure that the framework evolves in line with organizational goals and technological advancements.

- **Community-driven innovation:** Encouraging teams to engage in open-source contributions can catalyze innovation. By participating in open-source projects related to testing or automation, teams can gain exposure to new ideas, tools, and methodologies. This experience broadens their technical skills and fosters a spirit of collaboration and knowledge sharing that can be brought back to the organization.

- **Inspiration from the open-source community:** Leveraging community-driven innovations allows teams to explore best practices and emerging trends in test automation. By observing how others solve similar challenges, teams can find inspiration for enhancing their own frameworks. This exposure can lead to adopting new techniques, such as AI/ML-driven testing or implementing containerized testing environments, ultimately improving the framework's capabilities.

- **Regular cross-team meetings:** Establishing regular meetings that bring together engineering, QA, and DevOps teams can promote ongoing collaboration. These meetings can be forums for discussing progress, sharing insights, and brainstorming solutions to common challenges. Creating a space for open dialogue encourages a sense of ownership and responsibility among team members for the framework's evolution.

- **Cross-training opportunities:** Offering cross-training sessions can enhance collaboration by equipping team members with a broader understanding of each other's roles and responsibilities. When engineers understand QA practices and testers are familiar with the development process, teams can work more cohesively, leading to a more integrated approach to test automation.

- **Feedback mechanisms:** Implementing feedback mechanisms, such as surveys or suggestion boxes, allows team members to contribute their thoughts and ideas regarding the framework. This openness encourages participation and demonstrates that every team member's input is valued, fostering a culture of continuous improvement.

Encouraging collaboration across engineering, QA, and DevOps teams is essential for continuously improving test automation frameworks. By sharing knowledge, addressing pain points, and contributing to the framework's evolution, organizations can create a more relevant, efficient, and effective testing environment. Additionally, engaging in open-source contributions and leveraging community-driven innovation can inspire new ideas and approaches that further enhance the framework's capabilities. Ultimately, fostering a collaborative culture within and across teams will be a cornerstone of success in achieving long-term objectives in test automation.

Future of sustainable test automation

The journey toward creating a sustainable test automation framework is ongoing. Organizations that ground their frameworks in solid architectural principles, adopt tool-agnostic approaches, and foster a culture of continuous improvement will be well-positioned to maintain resilience, scalability, and adaptability in their test automation strategies. By focusing on future-proofing their frameworks, organizations can navigate the complexities and challenges that lie ahead in the fast-paced world of software development.

The following are some summaries of critical information we have covered in this book that are key for everyone to understand, to build test automation frameworks that will be ready to adapt to future software needs:

- **Importance of robust architecture:** A well-designed architecture is the bedrock of any sustainable test automation framework. By incorporating principles such as modularity, separation of concerns, and scalability, organizations can ensure that their frameworks can support long-term growth and handle increasing complexity. A strong architectural foundation allows teams to adapt to new technologies and integrate seamlessly with modern development practices like CI/CD, microservices, and cloud-based platforms.

- **Modularity and extensibility:** Designing frameworks with modularity and extensibility in mind enables teams to add or modify components as needed without overhauling the entire system. This flexibility ensures that the framework can evolve alongside changing requirements and technologies, allowing smoother transitions and minimizing disruption to testing processes.

- **Resilience against tool evolution:** Tool-agnostic frameworks empower teams to pivot and adopt new testing tools as the industry evolves, without redesigning their entire test strategy. This approach fosters reusability and compatibility, ensuring organizations integrate different testing tools, cloud platforms, and methodologies efficiently. By decoupling test automation from specific tools, teams can focus on maintaining a consistent testing approach that adapts to the best available resources.

- **Long-term strategy:** The tool-agnostic mindset encourages organizations to evaluate and select testing tools based on their specific needs, rather than becoming locked into a single vendor or technology.

This flexibility is vital for future-proofing the testing process, as it allows teams to take advantage of emerging technologies and methodologies without incurring unnecessary technical debt.

- **Embracing lifelong learning:** A culture of continuous improvement is essential for the longevity and effectiveness of any test automation framework. Teams must commit to staying informed about the latest advancements in testing methodologies, tools, and architectural patterns. By investing in professional development and encouraging experimentation with new trends, such as AI/ML-powered testing or low-code automation, organizations can adapt their frameworks to new challenges and opportunities.

- **Iterative evolution:** Sustainable test automation frameworks should evolve incrementally through feedback loops from real-world usage. Establishing processes for regular reviews, refactoring, and optimization helps organizations address technical debt and adapt to new requirements efficiently. Building in flexibility for change from the beginning, whether it is adding new test types or supporting new architectures, ensures the framework remains robust in the face of future challenges.

- **Anticipating future complexities:** The focus should always remain on building frameworks that can withstand the complexities and challenges of tomorrow. As software development trends shift towards more intricate architectures and higher expectations for testing quality, it is crucial to design frameworks that can scale and adapt. This proactive approach enables organizations to meet future demands while maintaining high standards of quality and efficiency.

- **Long-term vision:** Creating a sustainable test automation framework requires a long-term vision that aligns with the organization's broader goals and objectives. Stakeholders must prioritize investments in technology, processes, and talent development to ensure that the framework can evolve in tandem with changing business needs and technological advancements.

In conclusion, the path to creating a sustainable test automation framework is ongoing. It requires organizations to ground their efforts in solid architectural principles, adopt tool-agnostic approaches, and foster a culture of continuous improvement. By maintaining a forward-looking perspective and prioritizing adaptability, teams can ensure their test automation strategies remain resilient, scalable, and effective in the face of evolving challenges. The focus on building for the future will empower organizations to navigate the complexities of software development and ensure the longevity of their test automation efforts in a rapidly changing landscape.

Conclusion

In building a sustainable, tool-agnostic test automation framework, the key to long-term success lies in adaptability, maintainability, and scalability. By decoupling test logic from specific tools, teams can future-proof their automation efforts, reducing vendor lock-in and enabling seamless integration with evolving technologies. A modular design ensures that the framework remains extensible, allowing incremental improvements without costly rewrites. Moreover, a strong emphasis on cross-cutting concerns, such as reporting, test data management, and execution scalability, ensures that the framework remains robust and efficient. Ultimately, sustainability in test automation is not just about selecting the right architecture; it is about fostering a culture of continuous improvement, where feedback, innovation, and collaboration drive long-term value.

Key takeaways

Many organizations struggle to achieve a strong return on investment from their testing frameworks because they build them around specific tools, requiring frequent refactoring as technology evolves. Additionally, many framework architects prioritize rapid test scripting over foundational design principles, overlooking key elements that enhance maintainability. This short-sighted approach makes it harder for frameworks to adapt over time, reducing long-term value and sustainability.

By implementing the measures mentioned in this chapter and book, you will be able to overcome most of these challenges:

- **Architecture as the foundation of test automation frameworks:** A well-defined architecture provides structure, scalability, and maintainability, ensuring the framework can evolve with project and technology needs.

- **Need for flexibility:** A flexible framework can adapt to new tools, technologies, and testing requirements, reducing the risk of obsolescence and enabling seamless integration with CI/CD pipelines.

- **Role of tool-agnostic frameworks in test automation:** Tool-agnostic frameworks promote longevity by decoupling test logic from specific tools, preventing vendor lock-in, and allowing teams to switch technologies without extensive rework.

- **Fostering continuous learning and adaptation in your framework:** Encouraging a learning culture ensures that teams stay updated on best practices, new testing methodologies, and emerging technologies, leading to an evolving and resilient framework.

- **Iterative improvement and refactoring in test automation frameworks:** Continuous refinement through small, incremental changes helps address technical debt, optimize performance, and improve maintainability without requiring complete rewrites.

- **Future of sustainable test automation:** The future of test automation lies in intelligent frameworks that leverage AI, predictive analytics, and self-healing capabilities to enhance test stability and efficiency while maintaining adaptability.

Exercises

1. In your current framework, is the framework structured into independent, reusable modules, or is it tightly coupled?

2. Can test execution, reporting, and data management be modified independently?

3. Is the framework designed to work with multiple tools, or is it tightly bound to a specific tool or vendor?

4. Can new tools be integrated without requiring significant rework?

5. Are test scripts abstracted from the underlying automation tools?

6. Do test scripts and utilities follow reusable design patterns, or is there duplication across test cases?

7. Are standard functions (for example, authentication, data setup, API calls) centralized in reusable modules?

8. How much effort is required to update tests when application functionality changes?

9. Can the framework quickly scale to support more tests, environments, or parallel execution?

10. Can the framework be extended with new test types (for example, API, UI, performance testing) without significant restructuring?

11. How well does the framework integrate with CI/CD pipelines and cloud-based execution?

12. Is test data management modular and separate from test logic?

13. Can test data be parameterized and reused across different test cases?

14. Are configurations (for example, environment settings, credentials) externalized to allow easy modifications?

15. Is the framework well-documented, making it easy for new team members to onboard?

16. Are test scripts and utilities structured in a way that promotes collaboration across teams?

17. Does the framework enforce coding standards and best practices for maintainability?

Join our Discord space

Join our Discord workspace for latest updates, offers, tech happenings around the world, new releases, and sessions with the authors:

https://discord.bpbonline.com

Appendix

The following is the list of valuable materials on test automation frameworks and approaches.

Books

Here are some essential books on Test Automation that are worth reading, and where many of the concepts in this book are influenced:

- *Continuous Testing: With A Test Automation Framework*
- *The Art of Unit Testing: With Examples in .NET*
- *Test Automation Frameworks: An Expert Guide*
- *Automation Testing: The Complete Guide*
- *Java Unit Testing with JUnit 5: A Beginner's Guide*
- *Selenium Testing Tools Cookbook*
- *Test Automation Design Patterns in Ruby*
- *Building a Test Automation Framework: A Step-by-Step Guide*

Articles and research papers

- *A Study on the Effectiveness of Test Automation Frameworks*, Journal of Software Engineering Research and Development.
- *Evaluating Test Automation Frameworks*, Journal of Software Testing, Verification & Reliability

Online resources

- **Test Automation University:** testautomationu.com
- **Ministry of Testing:** ministryoftesting.com

Join our Discord space

Join our Discord workspace for latest updates, offers, tech happenings around the world, new releases, and sessions with the authors:

https://discord.bpbonline.com

Glossary of Terms

The following are some common testing and development terms that have been mentioned in the book. If you require a broader definition of these, then please feel free to look at them:

A

- **Acceptance testing:** A level of testing where the system is evaluated to determine whether it meets the acceptance criteria set by stakeholders. This can include **user acceptance testing (UAT)** and **operational acceptance testing (OAT)**.
- **Automated testing:** The use of software tools to automatically execute tests on a software application instead of manual testing to improve efficiency and coverage.

C

- **Continuous integration (CI):** A software development practice where code changes are automatically built, tested, and merged into a shared repository frequently, enhancing collaboration and reducing integration issues.
- **Continuous testing:** The practice of executing automated tests as part of the software delivery pipeline to provide immediate feedback on the quality of the code.

D

- **Data-driven testing:** A testing methodology in which test cases are executed based on data inputs, allowing for more extensive testing with less maintenance.

E

- **End-to-end testing:** This testing approach validates the complete flow of an application from start to finish, ensuring that all components work together as expected.

F

- **Flaky test:** A test that produces inconsistent results, passing or failing without any changes to the codebase. Flaky tests can undermine trust in the test suite.
- **Functional testing:** A type of testing that verifies that the software functions as expected and adheres to the specified requirements.

I

- **Integration testing:** The testing of combined parts of an application to determine if they work together as intended, focusing on the interactions between components.

L

- **Load testing:** A type of performance testing that simulates multiple users accessing the system simultaneously to evaluate how it handles increased load.

M

- **Mocking:** The practice of creating simulated objects or components that mimic the behavior of real ones for testing.

R

- **Regression testing:** A type of testing that ensures that new changes or enhancements do not adversely affect the existing functionality of the software.

S

- **Smoke testing:** A preliminary test to check the basic functionality of an application, ensuring that critical features work before more rigorous testing is performed.
- **Static testing:** The examination of software artifacts (for example, code, documentation) without executing the code. It includes techniques such as code reviews and static analysis.

T

- **Test automation framework:** A set of guidelines, best practices, and tools designed to streamline the process of creating, executing, and maintaining automated tests.
- **Test case:** A set of conditions or variables under which a tester determines whether a system or application is working correctly. A test case typically includes input, execution steps, and expected results.
- **Test coverage:** A measure of how much of the application's code is tested by automated tests, often expressed as a percentage.
- **Test suite:** A collection of test cases intended to be executed together to validate a specific aspect of the application.

U

- **User acceptance testing (UAT):** Testing conducted by end-users to determine if the software meets their needs and requirements before it goes live.

V

- **Version control:** A system that tracks changes to code or documents, allowing multiple contributors to collaborate and maintain different versions of files.

The aforementioned words are not exhaustive, but provide a good reference of the terminology we have used in this book to cover most aspects of software development and test automation.

Index

www.ingramcontent.com/pod-product-compliance
Lightning Source LLC
Chambersburg PA
CBHW061739210326
41599CB00034B/6733